D1575514

THE
Penguin History
of

AMERICAN
LIFE

MORE THAN FREEDOM

ALSO BY STEPHEN KANTROWITZ

Ben Tillman and the Reconstruction of White Supremacy

MORE THAN FREEDOM

Fighting for Black Citizenship
in a White Republic,
1829–1889

STEPHEN KANTROWITZ

THE PENGUIN PRESS

New York

2012

THE PENGUIN PRESS
Published by the Penguin Group
Penguin Group (USA) Inc., 375 Hudson Street, New York, New York 10014, U.S.A. • Penguin Group
(Canada), 90 Eglinton Avenue East, Suite 700, Toronto, Ontario, Canada M4P 2Y3 (a division of Pearson
Penguin Canada Inc.) • Penguin Books Ltd, 80 Strand, London WC2R 0RL, England • Penguin Ireland,
25 St. Stephen's Green, Dublin 2, Ireland (a division of Penguin Books Ltd) • Penguin Books Australia Ltd,
250 Camberwell Road, Camberwell, Victoria 3124, Australia (a division of Pearson Australia Group Pty Ltd) •
Penguin Books India Pvt Ltd, 11 Community Centre, Panchsheel Park, New Delhi—110 017, India •
Penguin Group (NZ), 67 Apollo Drive, Rosedale, Auckland 0632, New Zealand (a division of
Pearson New Zealand Ltd) • Penguin Books (South Africa) (Pty) Ltd, 24 Sturdee Avenue,
Rosebank, Johannesburg 2196, South Africa

Penguin Books Ltd, Registered Offices:
80 Strand, London WC2R 0RL, England

First published in 2012 by The Penguin Press,
a member of Penguin Group (USA) Inc.

Library of Congress Cataloging-in-Publication Data

Kantrowitz, Stephen David, 1965–
More than freedom : fighting for black citizenship in a white republic, 1829–1889 / Stephen Kantrowitz.
p.   cm.
Includes bibliographical references and index.
ISBN 978-1-59420-342-8
1. African Americans—Massachusetts—Boston Region—History—19th century.   2. African
Americans—Civil rights—Massachusetts—Boston Region—History—19th century.   3. Free African
Americans—Massachusetts—Boston Region—History—19th century.   4. Free African Americans—Civil
rights—Massachusetts—Boston Region—History—19th century.   5. Citizenship—United States—
History—19th century.   6. Boston Region (Mass.)—Race relations—History—19th century.
7. Boston Region (Mass.)—History—19th century. I. Title.
F73.9.N4K36 2012
323.1196′073074461—dc23
2011044724

Printed in the United States of America
1   3   5   7   9   10   8   6   4   2

Designed by Meighan Cavanaugh

Maps by Jeffrey L. Ward

For Pernille

Throw away your fears and prejudices then, and enlighten us and treat us like men, and we will like you more than we do now hate you, and tell us no more about colonization, for America is as much our country, as it is yours.—Treat us like men, and there is no danger but we will all live in peace and happiness together. For we are not like you, hard hearted, unmerciful, and unforgiving. What a happy country this will be, if the whites will listen.

—DAVID WALKER, *Appeal to the Coloured Citizens of the World*

I pondered all these things, and how men fight and lose the battle, and the thing that they fought for comes about in spite of their defeat, and when it comes turns out not to be what they meant, and other men have to fight for what they meant under another name.

—WILLIAM MORRIS, *A Dream of John Ball*

Contents

Part II

FIGHTING LIKE MEN

Part III

THE DISAPPOINTMENTS OF CITIZENSHIP

Introduction

As he prepared to watch the 54th Massachusetts Volunteer Infantry Regiment march through Boston in May 1863, the black activist and historian William Cooper Nell chose his place with care. The intersection of State Street and Devonshire, by the Old State House, was the perfect site from which to cheer the first Civil War regiment recruited from among the free blacks of the North. On that very ground, Nell reminded the readers of the New York *Weekly Anglo-African*, the former slave Crispus Attucks had become the first to fall in the cause of American independence, killed while confronting British soldiers in the Boston Massacre of 1770. But Nell also noted the less noble chapters of local history written on that same spot. In the 1850s, soldiers and policemen had marched fugitive slaves across the massacre site on their way from the Boston courthouse to the wharf, where ships waited to return them to slavery. The passage down State Street of the men of the 54th—many of them born enslaved, all of them until recently excluded not only from military service but from American citizenship itself—symbolized a renewal of the American Revolution's promise of liberty, and of African Americans' forceful claim to that heritage.[1]

The spectacle of black men as armed, disciplined citizens may have been something new under the sun to most of the day's white observers, but it represented the triumph of decades of political and ideological work by thousands of people. Since the 1820s, the nation's small and scattered free black communities had been mobilizing, developing institutions, debating issues, and searching out allies to help weave their yearnings into political victories and a place to belong.[2] Afro-America's revolutionary hopes for emancipation and citizenship, expressed in countless meetings, conventions, petitions, protests, and publications, revolts large and small, and innumerable small acts of courage and conscience had cast doubt on the common white perspective that free African Americans were a hindrance or a hazard to the nation's peace and prosperity. Moreover, that long campaign had helped bring the war in which these men's service was now required. The result was stirring: a crowd of black and white Bostonians together loudly cheering as black soldiers in U.S. uniforms marched off to win the nation's war and complete the work of emancipation. No wonder William Nell, his entire life devoted to this struggle, indulged in a moment of rapture, imagining "the free, the happy future, as within a seeming hailing distance."[3]

But the story of African Americans forging a new place for themselves in the nation cannot be compressed into this moment of triumph. Their road to that place of honor in the May sunshine had often seemed like little more than a succession of dead ends, washouts, and tollgates for which they had no coin. Most whites, North and South, regarded African Americans with scorn and suspicion, gleefully or sadly noting their failings and incapacities, and imagining a future for them as slaves, subordinates, or deportees. Fighting those ideas, and the laws and customs that perpetuated them, was an uphill battle for a small minority; along with organizations and debates came disagreements, some of them profound, that set black Americans against one another. Even in this moment of triumph, as the 54th paraded, Nell sadly noted that the unequal terms on which black soldiers fought—in separate units, under white officers—had sparked a campaign against enlistment.[4] Nell did not quite admit it, but that campaign had been remarkably effective: most of the men of the 54th were not from Boston, and most eligible Boston men were not in it. Such debates and divides were as consistent a feature of free black life as the desire to forge unity and to heal the wounds left by old disputes.

Those hard histories of white hostility and black division might have been intolerable without a vision of how African Americans could transcend them and become fully vested American citizens, equal not only before the law but also in the hearts and minds of their neighbors. Over decades of struggle, black activists developed a vision of belonging—of their place in the nation—that allowed them to imagine Nell's "free, happy future" even when the status of free black Northerners as Americans was at its most precarious. In 1857, to choose the most bitter example, the Supreme Court ruled in *Dred Scott v. Sandford* that African Americans had not been and could not be citizens of the nation. Within a few years Northern states and territories voted to exclude black migrants, and Southern legislatures debated reenslaving their free black residents. A resurgent emigration movement among African Americans depicted African and Caribbean destinations as more promising than the American republic. But even in these dark days, Nell's friend George Downing told a convention of the "Colored Citizens of New England" that the future held something very different: God intended the United States to provide a model for "a great principle, *the fraternal unity of man*." In preparation for that coming age of "universal brotherhood," African Americans must prepare themselves for "confident manly contact" in the wider world, nurturing a "consciousness of equality" and insisting that their white neighbors do the same. In the face of exclusion, segregation, and derision, embattled "colored citizens" like Nell and Downing envisioned a world in which white Americans not only recognized African Americans' equal rights but also embraced them as brothers and equals in every arena of life.[5]

Because they hoped for so much, black activists did not consider their battle won with the end of slavery in 1865, nor even with the revolutions of Reconstruction. Instead, they worked to shape and extend these victories. They threw themselves into the remaking of the postemancipation South, pressed for broader and more capacious laws of equal citizenship, and insisted that whites who continued to exclude them by law or custom stood in opposition to the victorious Union and the egalitarian "spirit of the age." The African American activists of the nineteenth-century North have long been dubbed "black abolitionists," but that term both understates the dimensions of their efforts prior to the war and neglects their decades of work after emancipation. "Abolition," essential but insufficient, was too small a box to contain their aspirations. Figures who spent the antebellum and war years building associations and demanding their rights hardly paused, even to celebrate, as they confronted the altered but still vexing challenges of the postwar world.[6]

In the postbellum decades Boston's black citizens demanded and won both civil rights legislation and seats in the state legislature, even before Reconstruction enabled black Southerners to do so. From a narrow foothold on Beacon Hill, they used numbers and moral force to establish themselves as a group to be reckoned with. They also came to grips with the frailty and the limits of what they had achieved, and in the decades after William Nell's reverie they constantly confronted the disappointments of citizenship. In Boston and throughout the United States, the people who called themselves "colored citizens" carried on with their fundamental project—the transformation of the American nation into a place where they finally, fully, belonged. That postwar part of the story—both its successes and its failures—is every bit as central to the meanings of emancipation, equality, and citizenship in American life as the struggles of the antebellum era and the victories of the 1860s. Black activists' experiences in the decades before the war explain a great deal about what they thought and did in the period that followed; the often grim realities of the postwar era help us understand both the dazzling scope of their hopes and triumphs, and the powerful constraints within which they were imagined and enacted. Neither the prewar nor the postwar story can be well understood without the other. This work explores both.[7]

This is the story of a vision of a republic in which African Americans could fully belong, a vision Northern free blacks developed and promoted during the six decades when the expansion, destruction, and aftermath of slavery preoccupied the nation. It begins in the era of David Walker, whose 1829 pamphlet *Appeal to the Coloured Citizens of the World* represented the anger, yearning, and solidarity of free black Northerners; it ends sixty years later, as the inheritors of Walker's legacy passed from the scene. During this era, no group focused more sharply on shaping events than those blacks who were free before the war. Through persistent efforts, they sought to write themselves into the national narratives of democracy and fraternity. They wielded the weapons of petition, protest, and insurgency; forged associations to amplify their scattered voices; denounced white Americans for betraying their own stated principles; and banded together to take part in the rituals and celebrations of political and associational life. Throughout a critical phase of the nation's history they waged an unceasing political campaign to establish African Americans as citizens, and to give that word a fullness of meaning. Their campaign began long before reliable white allies were anywhere in evidence, and it lasted long after the guns of the Civil War had fallen silent.

To call oneself a "colored citizen," as David Walker's admirers began to do during the 1830s, was to claim a role in at least two simultaneous efforts. On the one hand, African American activists created networks and institutions to bind their scattered communities together, investing themselves in projects as various as newspapers, Protestant denominations, and Masonic lodges.[8] Excluded from public life in many of its forms, they created what some scholars have dubbed a "black counter-public," in which they looked to one another for support and affirmation.[9] They practiced citizenship as a matter of survival. But although what they built was for many purposes a world apart, it did not represent a full-scale or principled withdrawal from the wider world. Even if they had wished to forge such an enclave, they could not create walls that slavery and prejudice were bound to respect.

Rather, most of the leading voices in that black world of speech and action sought a rapprochement of hearts and minds with white Americans. They understood that a future in the United States required them to establish their place among their white countrymen. "Citizenship" meant being legally and politically vested, but it also meant something more: bonds of trust and even love across the color line. It meant knowing and being known; it meant a warm welcome to the full duties, rights, privileges, and pleasures of American life, whether understood in George Downing's grand language of "universal brotherhood" or in William Nell's disarmingly candid vision of "the free, the happy future." It meant a citizenship of the heart.[10]

That they sought a sense of belonging in no way meant that they relied on moral and emotional appeals. Far from it. As inheritors of the ideological legacy of the American Revolution, they believed that freedom belonged only to those willing to seize it. Even as they described themselves as law abiding and "respectable," they issued strident and even violent challenges to proslavery and inegalitarian laws. They were a people militant, and often armed, long before the United States government authorized them to march in its ranks. Citizenship, they understood, was something one demonstrated to oneself and to others. It had to be asserted. It had to be won.[11]

This book explores that expansive vision of citizenship through the struggles of Boston's black leadership to give that vision life. It focuses in particular on a group of men and women who came of age in the generation before the Civil War, and who, over careers lasting as much as fifty years, worked for inclusion, equality, recognition, and the end of the

American system of racial caste. They were freeborn sons and daughters of Massachusetts, and freeborn Southerners who migrated north. They were ex-slaves who had gained their freedom, as well as fugitive slaves who had snatched it from slave owners and whose claim to it remained precarious. Some knew one another intimately, others by acquaintance or simply by reputation. On most questions they did not speak with one voice. But they shared the common experience of working together to end slavery and create a world in which "colored citizen" was not a contradiction in terms.

Greater Boston is not the only place about which such a story could be told, but it played an important and often singular role during the era.[12] Massachusetts's egalitarian revolutionary constitution, which began with the words "All men are born free and equal," encouraged some of the state's enslaved people to sue for their freedom during the early 1780s; state court rulings soon made it plain that slaveholders had no legal recourse, and slavery collapsed as people asserted their freedom.[13] By the nineteenth century African American residents of Massachusetts faced comparatively few formal disabilities, and black men could vote on the same basis as white. Though their community was small compared to those of New York or Philadelphia, Boston's African Americans were intimately involved in, and often at the forefront of, regional and national movements. They spearheaded the first substantial alliances with antislavery whites, and undertook the first sustained engagement in antislavery party politics. They helped shape the terms under which black men served in the Union army, and they became the first postbellum black elected officials. Finally, a substantial fragment of what they wrote made its way into archives: enmeshed in the city's world of politicized intellectuals and historical self-consciousness, Boston's black activists left unusually rich records of their thoughts, activities, and relationships with one another. The community was certainly not "representative" or "typical," because no community was, but it was highly significant and sometimes clearly pivotal in shaping broader events.

Not all the men and women who shaped these struggles in Greater Boston are represented here. The surviving record does not allow us to get close enough to many of the participants to understand their hopes and fears, and many people who played important roles elude the historian's pursuit, remaining little more than names on a petition, if not entirely anonymous. Libraries and archival collections favor some kinds of actors over others: the fully literate over those less so; professionals over laborers; longtime residents over sojourners. As the frequent references to "brotherhood" and "fraternity" suggest, that record also reveals more about men's words and actions than it does about women's. But the body of letters, newspapers, pamphlets, diaries, proceedings, and reminiscences on which this book is built, subjective and incomplete though it is, nevertheless casts rich light onto the lives and thought of many of the leading members of Greater Boston's black community.

Like the people it studies, this book ranges into other communities. Blacks made up only about 2 percent of Boston's population during most of this period, and most understood, often from personal experience, that their little world was just one island in an archipelago scattered across North America. The book therefore includes both long-term residents and sojourners; it follows people into Boston and out of it again and traces the development of the networks and alliances they made. Its cast of characters includes black activists from other cities and towns as well as a changing constellation of whites—abolitionists, antislavery politicians, Republican officials, and others—whose plans, purposes, and sometimes hearts impelled them toward their black neighbors. But those black activists who made their homes in and around Boston remain at the center of the book.

This book traces the antebellum emergence, the Civil War–era struggles and triumphs, and the postwar legacies and defeats of these activists and their vision of the United States. It argues that the "colored citizens" failed to remake the nation in the way they had hoped, but that they nonetheless left it forever changed. Without them, white abolitionists would have remained abstracted idealists or cautious gradualists, and fugitives would have had no safe resting place south of the Canadian border. Without them, and their resistance to the assaults of slaveholders and the federal government on their liberties, the mass of white Northerners might never have come to see the "Slave Power" as subversive of white Northern liberty, or been willing to go to war against the slaveholders. Without them, the vast army of free and just-freed black men who fought under the American flag might not have been able to make their insistence on equality heard and felt across the North. Without them, the architects of Reconstruction might have been satisfied with the bare liberal freedoms envisioned by Abraham Lincoln—security of life, liberty, and property—and retired soon after the war was won, their task accomplished. Without them, in other words, the Civil War might not have come, freedom could not have meant what it did, and Reconstruction's unfinished revolution would scarcely have begun. And even as the transformations they championed redefined American citizenship, their quest for belonging infused the word "citizen" with meaning beyond a common set of rights and obligations—with a vision of solidarity, regard, and even love that continued to reverberate for generations to come.

Part I

CONFRONTING SLAVERY AND FREEDOM

1.

A Place for "Colored Citizens"

efore William Nell could stand on a Boston street and imagine "the free, the happy future"—before there could be a regiment of black soldiers in Union uniforms, or a friendly newspaper to report its progress—there had to be a transformation in free African American life that made such things not just possible, but imaginable. During the first three decades of the nineteenth century, the free African Americans of Nell's parents' generation began to build institutions, networks, ideas, and alliances. This work helped knit them together and create a common sense of purpose and destiny. It also shaped their confrontation with the forces that hemmed them in and assaulted their dignity: the persistence of Southern slavery, the limits of Northern freedom, and the conviction, shared by most whites, that there could never be an equal place for them in the American republic. By the beginning of the 1830s, they were ready to declare themselves "colored citizens," as a statement of their resolve and of their hopes.[1]

FREE BLACKS IN A
SLAVEHOLDING NATION

Slavery bounded free black life. Until the Thirteenth Amendment in 1865, nearly 90 percent of African Americans lived in slavery, and blackness was intimately intertwined with lifetime hereditary bondage. These realities were not at first matters of North versus South: in the era of the American Revolution slavery was a national institution, and enslaved people lived and labored nearly everywhere. That only gradually changed, as some parts of the new nation grew more dependent on slave labor and others less.

During the early nineteenth century, slavery grew and thrived in the states south and west of Maryland, as the profits from cotton and sugarcane wore away the revolutionary generation's ambivalence about slavery. That profitability protected the institution against most challenges as U.S. settlers seized Indian lands as far away as Missouri, Louisiana, and Florida and created a slaveholding republic out of the Mexican province of Texas. Over the first four decades of the century, that expansion propelled hundreds of thousands of the enslaved, through slave markets and forced migrations, to new homes across this vast arc of settlement. Some died on the way; most were separated forever from friends, families, or communities they had known in the East. By the end of the 1830s the nation's enslaved population reached two and a half million, overwhelmingly concentrated in fertile areas of the South from Virginia to Missouri and South Carolina to Louisiana; about one of every seven inhabitants of the United States was enslaved and lived in states where people of known African descent were legally presumed to be slaves unless they could provide proof to the contrary.[2]

Even as slavery expanded across these new domains, the institution was dead or dying in the states north and west of Maryland. The early Congress largely barred slavery from the Northwest territories—today's Midwest, more or less—and although people did keep and work slaves in that re-

U.S. SLAVERY IN 1840

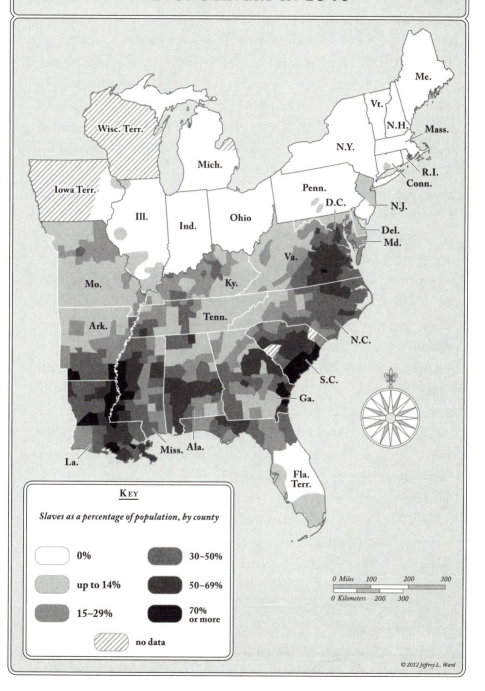

KEY

Slaves as a percentage of population, by county

- 0%
- up to 14%
- 15–29%
- 30–50%
- 50–69%
- 70% or more
- no data

0 Miles 100 200 300
0 Kilometers 200 300

© 2012 Jeffrey L. Ward

gion, the institution never gained a firm legal foothold. To the east, from Pennsylvania northward, courts or voters set the clock ticking on slavery's demise. Sometimes this took place early and dramatically: in Massachusetts, slaves' suits for freedom in the 1780s led courts to declare slavery illegal under the state's new constitution. By contrast, slavery flourished in New York until the last days of the eighteenth century, and the state's "emancipation" at the turn of the nineteenth was a painfully gradual process: children born to slaves after a certain date became technically free but subject to lengthy and involuntary "apprenticeships," while their parents remained enslaved for decades more. This gave slave owners ample time to extract profit from bondspeople and their children, sometimes by illegally selling them southward. As a result, slaves remained in the "free" states in considerable numbers into the 1820s and persisted in some corners of the North for decades after that. New York's final emancipation in July 1827 left people formally enslaved next door in New Jersey until 1846, while Delaware remained legal home to thousands of slaves until the ratification of the Thirteenth Amendment in December 1865.

Emancipation did not bring equality. Since the seventeenth century, American racial practice had treated any visible African descent as a stain, one that clung to its inheritors and implied a host of legal, moral, and intellectual incapacities. Although by 1840 half the nation's free black people, or about two hundred thousand men, women, and children, lived in states where slavery was over or nearly so, the institution hung over them as a constant rebuke. The legal codes of the emancipated states included numerous "black laws"—sometimes unenforced, but always available—that restricted free black rights of suffrage and testimony, required free black residents to post bonds guaranteeing their good behavior and ability to be self-supporting, or even barred them from taking up residency. Free blacks were treated as burdens, threats, or subordinate members of their communities.[3]

In the early decades of the nineteenth century, life in some parts of the South offered opportunities to certain free black people that were difficult to reproduce elsewhere. William Nell's father, William Guion Nell, was born free in the late-eighteenth-century free black community of Charleston, South Carolina. In Charleston, as in New Orleans and a few other Southern cities, free people of color constituted an intermediate third caste between free whites and enslaved blacks. They gained skills and built institutions; some even became slaveholders in their own right.[4] William Guion Nell spent seven years as an apprentice to Jehu Jones, a prosperous black tailor and hotelier. During the War of 1812, however, Nell left Charleston as a steward on a U.S. vessel; he ended up in Boston, and in 1816 married Louisa Marshall, a free black resident of the neighboring town of Brookline, about whose early life little is known. Nine months later their first child, whom they named William Cooper, was born.[5]

By the time William Cooper Nell reached school age in Boston, the position of Southern free people of color was coming under siege. After the 1822 discovery and violent suppression of a slave insurrection conspiracy led by free black Charlestonian Denmark Vesey, the doors formerly open to free black residents began to close. By 1850 the governor of South Carolina warned his legislature that those free people of color who did not own real estate or slave property were "essentially corrupt and corrupting." They were "spies in our camp," ready "to disseminate through the entire body of our slave population the poison of insubordination, prepared in the great northern laboratory of fanaticism."[6] Even wealth and attainment did not protect Jehu Jones or his neighbors from the growing suspicion and hostility of the Southern white leadership. Boston proved to be a more welcoming home for free black aspirations, if only by comparison.

The black Boston of the 1820s and 1830s was a cultural crossroads. The city's black population of about two thousand, just over 2 percent of the city's total, was distributed across several neighborhoods and did not make up anything like a majority in any of them. More than half, though, lived in the modest and closely set buildings on the northern slope of Beacon Hill and the adjacent blocks of the city's West End. That proportion would continue to grow for many decades to come.[7]

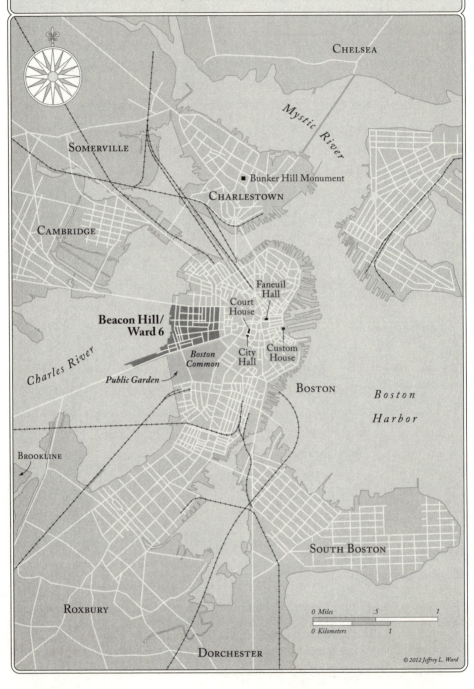

BOSTON AND ADJACENT CITIES IN THE 1850s

CHELSEA

Mystic River

SOMERVILLE

■ Bunker Hill Monument

CHARLESTOWN

CAMBRIDGE

Faneuil
Hall

Court
House

**Beacon Hill/
Ward 6**

Charles River

*Boston
Common*

City
Hall

Custom
House

Public Garden

BOSTON

*Boston

Harbor*

BROOKLINE

SOUTH BOSTON

ROXBURY

| 0 Miles | .5 | 1 |
| 0 Kilometers | | 1 |

© 2012 Jeffrey L. Ward

DORCHESTER

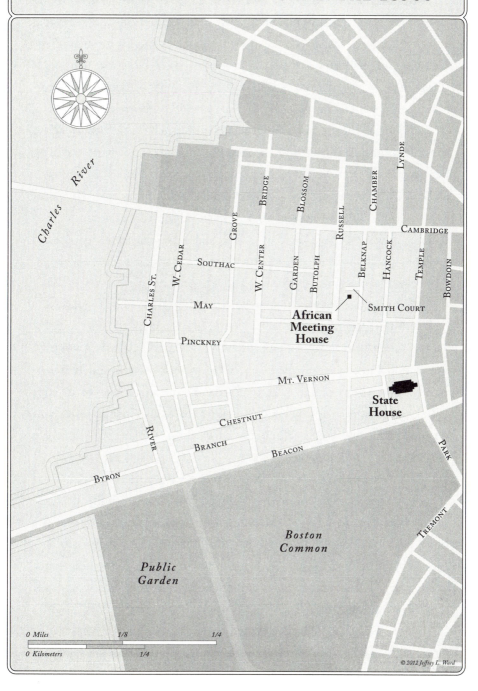

BEACON HILL AND WARD SIX IN THE 1850s

Charles River

GROVE
BRIDGE
BLOSSOM
CHAMBER
LYNDE

W. CEDAR
SOUTHAC
W. CENTER
GARDEN
BUTOLPH
RUSSELL
BELKNAP
HANCOCK
TEMPLE
BOWDOIN

CHARLES ST.

MAY

CAMBRIDGE

African
Meeting
House

SMITH COURT

PINCKNEY

MT. VERNON

State
House

CHESTNUT

RIVER

BRANCH

BEACON

PARK

BYRON

TREMONT

Boston
Common

Public
Garden

0 Miles   1/8   1/4
0 Kilometers   1/4

© 2012 Jeffrey L. Ward

In this neighborhood, a few hundred yards and a world away from the Beacon Street epicenter of New England's wealth and power, the collective adjective "colored" covered a host of backgrounds and experiences. People's clothing, patterns of speech, and many-shaded faces revealed a rich diversity of origins. More than half of the black people living in Boston at midcentury had, like the elder William Nell, been born outside Massachusetts; these included both migrants from other Northern states and a substantial population of Southerners. Some of the latter were freeborn people, mainly from Virginia, many of them light-skinned, who migrated to Boston in the face of the South's diminished opportunities and legal restrictions. Others were fugitive slaves whose fundamental aim was remaining at liberty.[8] Regardless of their origins, the great majority of these men and women worked at the bottom of the city's wage scale, as laborers, porters, seamen, domestic servants, and laundresses.[9] Yet there was also a tiny stratum of proprietors, mainly barbers, tailors, and shopkeepers.

In Boston, William Guion Nell found an openness to black organizations—even antislavery organizations—that stood in marked contrast to the ever harsher strictures in his home state. The new and reinvigorated organizations of the 1820s helped many thousands learn to constitute themselves as formal bodies, hold debates and celebrations, and negotiate differences and difficulties. In the face of widespread poverty and hardship, early-nineteenth-century black Bostonians formed Baptist and Methodist congregations, created mutual aid societies, established schools to serve their children and literary societies to cultivate their minds, and gave new life to the oldest institution of them all, the city's black Masonic lodge. These organizations became the training grounds for a generation of black leaders. By the second quarter of the nineteenth century, activists became ready to undertake broader and more ambitious feats of organization.

Independent black churches emerged and developed in response to white supremacy. As in other cities, Boston's white Christians relegated black parishioners to balconies and forbade them to purchase or rent pews. At the beginning of the century, a group of Boston's black Baptists broke away from a mainly white congregation, and with the combined aid of black and white residents soon built a redbrick home of their own on a small court off Belknap Street. The African Baptist Church, led by the newly ordained Reverend Thomas Paul, was not a perfect refuge: at its 1806 opening celebration, the first floor of the church was reserved for white guests, while others—including the church's own members—were asked to remain in the galleries.[10] But the church became an important spiritual home for many and grew to a hundred members. Other congregations sprang up, including Reverend Samuel Snowden's Methodist congregation a few blocks away.

A church was seldom only a place of worship, for black Boston's religious and community life were mutually entangled. The African Baptist Church, also widely known as the African Meeting House, became the site of countless meetings, schools, and organizations for almost a century to come.[11] Even if congregations themselves did not undertake explicitly antislavery work, congregants certainly did: Reverend Thomas Paul's wife, Catherine, and the couple's children, Susan and Thomas, pursued both educational and antislavery activities, for instance.[12] Theology and politics easily converged, as when Thomas Paul's parishioner John T. Hilton told an 1828 gathering that "if thy religion teaches you that slavery is right and just, proclaim it not, unless you wish to bring it into contempt and ridicule."[13] But if a church could be more than a house of God, it could also feel like less than one. By the late 1820s, the African Baptist congregation was riven by dissension so serious that members ostracized one another, nailed pew doors shut, and took one another to court. The particular causes of these ruptures remain difficult to trace, but a sympathetic observer in the 1830s rued the "unhappy bickerings" that repeatedly tore these Christians asunder.[14]

Black activists, most of them church members, also looked to other forms of organization to build bonds among themselves and with black communities elsewhere. What one historian calls "an irrepressible enthusiasm for combination" swept the ranks of community leaders in the late 1820s, and Boston was at the forefront.[15] In 1826, leading men of the community organized the Massachusetts General Colored Association (MGCA), a group dedicated to fighting slavery and elevating free blacks. One described the purpose of the institution as "to unite the colored people, so far, through the United States of America, as may be practicable and expedient; forming societies, opening, extending, and keeping up correspondences, and not withholding anything which may have the least tendency to meliorate our miserable condition."[16]

A similarly ambitious vision of unity and improvement led free blacks to embrace Freemasonry. In 1775, members of the occupying British army initiated black men led by the former slave Prince Hall into the brotherhood. They later obtained a charter from the Grand Lodge of England that allowed them to work as Masons and initiate other men, and they helped plant further black Masonic lodges in Providence and Philadelphia.[17] From a distance, Freemasonry, whether among white men or black, might appear to be little more than the play of elaborate rituals and arcane architectural symbology; alternatively, its secrecy could seem to shelter conspiratorial, even subversive designs. But Freemasonry's play and politics were each far more supple and important than these caricatures would suggest.

Freemasons were meant to be comrades. The order aspired to be "the Means of conciliating true Friendship among Persons that must else have remain'd at a perpetual Distance," and Masonic intellectuals envisioned the lodge as a place of "innocent mirth" as well as high drama. But Anglo-American Freemasonry's appeal reached beyond sociability. It fused an ecumenical Christianity with values of universalism, brotherhood, and mutual support. It challenged brethren to see themselves as the inheritors of a millennia-old legacy of universal truths, destined to help perfect the world. This vision reached across barriers of origin and experience: although the lodges and networks black Bostonians built were composed entirely of black men, Freemasonry declared itself a cosmopolitan project that welcomed men "of all nations, tongues, kindreds, and languages."[18]

Freemasonry's appeal was also connected to politics. It provided an institutional framework, separate from state authority, where men forged political subjectivities, developed organizational expertise, fostered leadership at the community, state, and national levels, repaired schisms, and reconciled rivalries.[19] Its symbolism and stories encouraged men to see themselves as political actors in a broad and idealistic sense. The Constitution and the churches might have left them out in the cold, but Freemasonry's universalism offered another possible avenue for reconciliation with whites on terms of "brotherly love, relief, and truth." These principles meshed perfectly with the needs of a people facing enslavement and subordination, and appealed particularly to those who imagined themselves showing others the way. Meanwhile, Freemasonry's forms familiarized these men with the human dimensions of politics: the rules governing debate, the pleasures of election, the challenges of officeholding, and the pride of self-constitution. The combination of spiritual sustenance and practical experience proved irresistible to many of the men who led Boston's black activist community, notably the young Boston barber and MGCA leader John T. Hilton, his pastor Thomas Paul, his friend James G. Barbadoes, his sometime employer Peter Howard, and a migrant from North Carolina named David Walker.[20]

By the end of the 1820s organized black activist communities in cities across the North began reaching out to one another. Black New Yorkers were the first to seize hold of the new, cheaper printing technology that was revolutionizing the world of newspaper publication. In 1827 Boston activists thrilled to the arrival of the first weekly produced by African Americans, New York's *Freedom's Journal*, which allowed men and women from distant cities to learn more systematically about others' ideas and projects. Hilton's Masonic brother and activist colleague David Walker became the paper's local agent.[21] Soon, many free black activists began imagining a national meeting where the conversation could take place face-to-face. After an initial meeting in 1830, five successive "Annual Conventions" of "the People of Colour" met to discuss projects of improvement and education.[22] They faced daunting challenges—white hostility, a scarcity of capital, and mutual suspicions and jealousies born of their circumstances. *Freedom's Journal* lasted just two years, and few of its successors would last much longer. Still, it was a beginning. Although black political unity was a project, not a given, a scattered "people" were coming to see their fates and interests in more than local terms.[23] The churches, associations, and newspapers that served as arenas for fellowship and debate at the same time allowed them to imagine themselves as a national community with common interests, and to begin making that community real.

THE RISE OF THE WHITE REPUBLIC

While free African Americans organized and debated during the early decades of the nineteenth century, solidarity among white men was altering the terms of American political life. As lands taken from native peoples opened up possibilities for whites of all stations, long-standing hierarchies distinguishing between politically worthy and unworthy white men lost their force. Yet the dissolution of old barriers among whites did not improve the status of free blacks. What emerged, rather, was a white man's republic. In the revolutionary era, status and wealth played key roles in determining who stood among the political citizenry; relatively few adults could vote, but their numbers included those African American men and white women who possessed sufficient property. In the early nineteenth century, however, voting rights more and more became the common entitlement of white men alone. Racialized democratization unfolded alongside other social and intellectual currents that sharpened racial hierarchy and reinforced its power.[24] In particular, by the 1820s, eighteenth-century notions of racial difference as produced by environmental factors lost ground to more rigid notions of race as irreducible biological essence. Whites understood slavery to be the natural status of people of African descent and—even in states where slavery was fading—regarded free blacks as low-status, ill-educated laborers, much more likely to be subjects of police control than wielders of state authority.[25]

Free African Americans therefore found their status growing ever more precarious. Across the nation, the borders of their freedom shrank in both law and custom. Most states where some free black men had once voted now limited those rights, as New York did in 1821, or revoked them entirely, as Pennsylvania, North Carolina, and Tennessee did in the 1830s. Many states enacted new "black laws" or enforced old ones. Although free black men could vote and testify in Massachusetts, the state was no shining beacon of liberty: as late as 1821, the legislature considered barring free blacks from migrating into the state on the grounds that they were likely to wind up in the jails or on the poor rolls.[26] In 1829 Cincinnati's city fathers decided to insist on the surety bonds required by law of free blacks, and turned a blind eye to white mob action against black residents; as a consequence, a thousand men, women, and children—half the city's black population—fled the state.[27] Mobs pursued a variety of victims through nineteenth-century America's streets, but no group was as acutely vulnerable or as persistently persecuted as men and women of African descent.

Southern and Northern repression of black aspirations differed in scope and in murderousness. By the time William Guion Nell, John T. Hilton, and David Walker assembled in the MGCA in 1826, any such organization, let alone one openly demanding the abolition of slavery, would have been flatly forbidden in the slave states. In Boston, by comparison, these men could meet, organize, petition, and protest. They could even undertake frankly antislavery activity without wondering if they would share the fate of Vesey and his colleagues—their heads cut off, affixed to pikes, and arrayed along the roads and rivers as a warning to others.[28] Yet across the North, blacks faced constant indignities, and official hostility encouraged whites to drive black residents off city streets and public parks, and

to attack antislavery gatherings. In the years after the legal end of the Atlantic slave trade in 1808, Boston's blacks held celebratory marches on the
Boston Common each July 14, followed by banquets and toasts. But as
white abolitionist Lydia Maria Child recalled, "it became a frolic with the
boys to deride them" as they marched.[29] On at least one occasion during
Child's early life, whites rioted against the black marchers and chased them
up Beacon Hill, clubs and brickbats flying. This was no mean-spirited
child's play, but a serious confrontation that almost ended in bloodshed as
her neighbor George Middleton, a black man who had served in the Revolution, joined the fray with his rifle.[30]

These violent outbursts took place against a backdrop of persistent derision. "Patience, I say," counseled Boston black community leader Prince
Hall in 1797, "for were we not possessed of a great measure of it, we could
not bear up under the daily insults we meet with in the streets of Boston."[31]
Whites gave the annual freedom celebration the scornful nickname "Bobalition" and made it the basis for a whole genre of racial mockery—
printed broadsides featuring caricatures of pompous black men on the
march, with dialect dialogues that mocked black men's civic understanding and command of English. Black leaders complained that these "[c]uts
and placards descriptive of the negroe's deformity" were everywhere.[32]

With white hostility so naked and so prevalent everywhere black Bostonians turned, there was little as demoralizing as their shabby treatment
at the hands of whites who proclaimed themselves "friends." The state of
the community's school was a powerful case in point. Black community
leaders had established a school for black children in the late eighteenth
century, and were heartened in 1815 when the urging of onetime teacher
Prince Saunders led a wealthy businessman, Abiel Smith, to leave a substantial endowment in his will. Only once this bequest became known did
the Boston school board take belated notice of the school; among its first
acts was the firing of its black teacher. The Smith School quickly became
an inferior ward of the white school board, with poorer facilities, larger

classes, and lower salaries than its white peers. A white teacher appointed in the 1820s was accused of "improper familiarities" with four girls at the school, but the board retained him, casting aspersion instead on the girls' characters.[33]

Still more dispiriting for free blacks were those self-proclaimed "friends" who supported the wholesale emigration of blacks out of the United States. The largest and most respectable "antislavery" organization of the day, the American Colonization Society (ACS), proceeded from the premise that people of African descent could not prosper in the United States. Colonizationists, who included some of the nation's leading politicians and public figures, envisioned a reversal of the mighty human flow of the slave trade. They sought the gradual and voluntary emancipation of American slaves by their owners, but only in tandem with freedpeople's permanent emigration to settlements in Africa, where they would build American-style governments and spread Christianity. Colonizationists imagined that this benevolent repatriation would transform the United States into a white republic untroubled by the sons and daughters of Africa. In 1830, a letter to the *Boston Courier* lamented the sorry state of racial prejudice and black deprivation, but could not imagine how America could be anything but a despotism to people of African descent, or that their continued presence could serve the common good. The obvious solution was "the removal of our whole colored population."[34] By the 1820s, a growing majority of black activists understood colonization as an arrow aimed not at slavery, but at their own aspirations to belong in America's national life. Free blacks envisioned freedom in rather different terms and hoped for allies who would do more than lament the conditions that made their collective expulsion seem necessary.

THE EMERGENCE OF THE "COLORED CITIZENS"

In sorrow, in anger, and in hope, free black Northerners began to demand a place in the American nation, and to insist that it honor its own revolutionary heritage of "liberty."[35] In 1829 these aspirations saw print in a pamphlet by David Walker. The four-part *Appeal* spoke *"to the Colored Citizens of the World, but in Particular, and Very Expressly, to those of the United States of America."* It gave those subordinated Americans a common name, announced their collective determination, and rattled the slave-holding nation.

Walker gave voice to the rage that both slaves and free blacks felt at their subordination. The *Appeal* condemned white people's hypocritical Christianity and exclusionary legislation. In numerous prophetic passages, Walker foresaw a day of reckoning for the evils of slavery, imagining God punishing at least some of "the Americans" for their part in slavery. "The Americans have got so fat on our blood and groans, that they have almost forgotten the God of armies," he wrote. "But let them go on."[36] Walker did not quite propose to launch such an army himself; despite his anger at whites' hypocritical Christianity and republicanism, and their abuse of his people, he "would not wish to see them destroyed." Still, "[t]he will of God must however, in spite of us, *be done.*"[37] That will would surely manifest itself, somehow, as violent, retributive justice. But the *Appeal*'s fury at slaveholders and colonizationists was matched by its frustration with African Americans themselves for complicity in their own subordination: for refusing to rise in revolt, betraying revolts in the bud when they did emerge, and failing to make the most of the opportunities freedom gave them.

Perhaps because it spoke so eloquently to both the anger and the aspirations of free blacks, the *Appeal* moved the nation as no previous work by an African American ever had. Its message first rang loudly among free black Northerners, and within a year the work went through three editions. But Walker aspired to a wider audience. He mailed the pamphlet south, and employed sympathetic sailors to carry it to black preachers and others in Southern ports. Yet Walker's prophecies of God's vengeance meant something quite different to white Southerners than it did to African Americans. Discovered by officials in Georgia, Virginia, Louisiana, and the Carolinas, the work provoked a panic about slave insurrection.[38] Such fears were common to white Southern life, and in 1830 the memory of the Denmark Vesey insurrection conspiracy was still fresh.[39] The mayor of Savannah asked his counterpart in Boston to investigate Walker. When a revolt led by the prophetic slave Nat Turner swept across southern Virginia in 1831, leaving dozens of whites dead, the governor of that state pronounced the *Appeal* partly to blame.[40]

But Walker was a revolutionary of a different and arguably more terrifying kind than the one who generally haunted the imaginations of Southern state officials. Rather than seeking to overthrow the American republic, Walker sought to claim a place in it. His pamphlet rebuked white Americans for their hypocrisy in claiming the right of revolution and establishing a republic based on natural rights, but then denying all of that to black Americans. Near his conclusion, Walker reprinted in their entirety the opening lines of the Declaration of Independence, with its invocation of "life, liberty, and the pursuit of happiness" and its assertion that "all men are created equal."[41] "Do you understand your own language?" he demanded of white Americans.[42] At the same time, Walker imagined the path to the future not in terms of armed revolution so much as through education and self-improvement. In this, he represented a dominant tradition in nineteenth-century black thinking—a vision of collective uplift that would make blacks' "respectability" so self-evident that whites would no longer be able to ignore it. His predictions of violence against slaveholders were scarcely more upsetting to the racial order of slavery than his calls for free people's social, educational, and economic advancement.

Although Walker mocked the pretensions of "American" liberty, he and his comrades nevertheless claimed the American Revolution as their birthright and the American nation as their home.[43] Walker's rejection of colonization, in particular, was rooted in this conviction. "Will any of us leave our homes and go to Africa?" he asked. "I hope not."[44] The pioneering female orator Maria Stewart, a great admirer of Walker, similarly lambasted white Americans for their oppression of blacks, vowing that "[t]he blood of her murdered ones cries to heaven for vengeance against thee."[45] Yet she too declared America "the land of freedom" and promised that "before she would be driven to a strange land, 'the bayonet shall pierce me through.'"[46] American liberty was steeped in hypocrisy and contradiction, but only because whites so eagerly subordinated the nation's essential values to the preservation of slavery and racial caste.[47]

Boston's black activists even performed a striking, repeated feat of legerdemain, extending the promise of liberty and equality past what either the Declaration or the Constitution actually stated. The Declaration of Independence's claim that "all men are created equal" came achingly close to matching their own state's constitutional promise that "all men are born free and equal"—so close, in fact, that sometimes they simply asserted that the two were one. For decades, black residents of Massachusetts wishfully or intentionally misattributed to the national founding documents variants of the so-welcome phrase "all men are born free and equal."[48] Even as state after state moved to redefine suffrage as the sole province of white men, black activists in Boston continued to suggest that the nation's founding documents promised them equality.

As they sought to establish new, broader networks of affiliation, black activists claimed the Declaration in other ways as well. In 1830 the official proceedings of the first national meeting of "people of colour" described the Declaration as "inestimable and invaluable"; the next year's convention called its truths "incontrovertible."[49] The example of the Declaration's unilateral assertion of rights and independence also proved valuable. In 1827 John T. Hilton announced, on behalf of the African Grand Lodge, a "Declaration of Independence" from white American Freemasonry, which refused to acknowledge him and his fellow black Masons as brethren of the order. Now African American Freemasonry would stand on its own, not requiring the sanction of American or British Masonic authorities to issue charters to other black Masonic lodges. Black Freemasonry, and the rest of the emerging black organizational world, would develop without white oversight.

If the language of the Declaration of Independence and of the Massachusetts constitution provided one hopeful avenue for people such as Hilton, Walker, and Stewart, Boston's tradition of self-celebration as the cradle of revolutionary liberty provided another. Black activists' assembly, petition, and protest all took place in a city that sometimes appeared to be a vast, living memorial to its own revolutionary past. Just above the African Meeting House, on the crest of Beacon Hill, stood the statehouse; beneath it, many knew, lay the grave of John Hancock, the patriot leader and first governor of the state. A short walk across the bridge into neighboring Charlestown brought one to the foot of a newly erected two-hundred-foot granite obelisk commemorating the revolutionary Battle of Bunker Hill. Around the corner from the statehouse, just off the Boston Common, Paul Revere's grave lay in the old burial ground. From there it was only a few blocks to the site of the Boston Massacre. Faneuil Hall, where so much of the public business of the Revolution had been done, had become a city-owned forum for public discussion and debate: you petitioned the city council for its use, then took your place at the podium where Sam Adams and George Washington had once spoken.

Some of the city's black activists proudly noted that they were direct descendants of black men who had served in the Patriot army. James G. Barbadoes, whose own father had served on the American side in the Revolution, drew on this part of the revolutionary heritage to protest his exclusion from a ferry's cabin on a miserable passage to Philadelphia. Whites should remember, he warned, "that in the revolutionary struggle with Great Britain, our fathers were called upon to fight for *liberty*; and promptly did they obey the summons—gallantly contending, shoulder to shoulder, with those who then made no distinction as to the color of a man's skin, that they might secure to themselves and their children the rights and privileges of freemen."[50] Barbadoes was fascinated to learn, later in the 1830s, that "a colored man by the name of Airtiks" had shed the first blood in the cause of American independence.[51] It would fall to the next generation to bring Crispus Attucks into clearer focus, both for black Bostonians and for the white descendants of the Revolution whom they hoped to persuade and convert.

Walker and his comrades understood slavery and their own subordination to be entangled with one another, for whites as well as blacks. A "Great Mass Meeting of Colored Citizens of Boston" declared that "the degradation of the colored population at the North, arises, in a measure, from our being identified with the slave population of the South"; it was therefore "an important part of our duty to labor incessantly for the overthrow of slavery, as a preparatory work to our entire enfranchisement."[52] That "entire enfranchisement" would mean being able to move through the world without constantly being reminded that they belonged to a suspect class; sharing the experience of daily life without wondering when they would next be rebuked, mocked, excluded, or set upon; joining in the rituals and customs of public life without apology or apprehension. These final steps would require a change in white people's hearts. David Walker put it this way in the *Appeal*: "Throw away your fears and prejudices then, and enlighten us and treat us like men, and we will like you more than we do now hate you . . . Treat us like men, and there is no danger but we will all live in peace and happiness together . . . What a happy country this will be if the whites will listen."[53]

But getting whites to listen was, if anything, harder than it first appeared. Even a comparatively sympathetic white reviewer of Walker's *Appeal* could not help noting that while he would be pleased to walk arm in arm down Boston's Washington Street with a black man who was a gentleman, he did not believe that such a man yet existed.[54] People such as this writer, black activists understood, must be persuaded otherwise. Even as they labored, debated, and confronted state power, black activists often suspected that victory would require white allies who truly accepted their claims to belong in America, and who wanted to help them achieve it. The pursuit of whites' hearts and minds was sometimes a spiritually inspired project, but it also reflected raw social reality: black activists lacked the numbers, wealth, and political influence, they well knew, to assert and defend their rights in the many forums, professions, and institutions where they had no foothold. They needed friends.

The "colored citizens," that is to say, approached the question of citizenship as a matter not only of law but of love. The "happiness" Walker imagined consisted of more than the peaceful enjoyment of their property; while African American activists sought education, prosperity, comfort, and security, they were not simply the rational, individual subjects favored by Adam Smith or John Stuart Mill. They sought a more encompassing welcome into realms of shared experience beyond the courthouse or the polling place. They had many names for the millennium they sought: not just "entire enfranchisement" but also "the fraternal unity of man," "universal brotherhood," and William Nell's "the free, the happy future." Whatever its name, the belonging they sought had to include communities of shared experience: political citizens assembling to debate, to vote, to celebrate; citizen-soldiers drilling and feasting at a militia muster; followers of Christ assembled to honor God and love one another; cosmopolitan men of the world recognizing one another and sharing Freemasonry's ancient wisdom of "brotherly love, relief, and truth." "Citizenship" construed in this expansive way was more than a question of "rights." It was a way of describing people's enmeshment in a common world of human joy and struggle.[55]

WHAT WAS A "COLORED CITIZEN"?

Even after Walker's death, his *Appeal* lingered in memory. In 1835 John T. Hilton issued "An Appeal to the Free Colored Citizens of the United States."[56] During that decade, and for years to come, "colored citizens"

became a common way for self-constituting groups of African Americans
to describe themselves and to assert their right to be heard. But what, after
all, did it mean to be a "colored citizen"?

Claiming the status of "citizen" was partly a matter of rhetorical performance. In the years after the French Revolution, the word gained currency
in Europe and beyond as a way of announcing people's liberation from
what Immanuel Wallerstein calls "the dead weight of received hierarchies."
But the word's content remained vague, ambiguous, and often contradictory.[57] This was true even in the *Appeal*: after the title page Walker used
"citizen" only a handful of times, and never in a clarifying way. Instead,
Walker and a generation of African Americans to come drew on the word's
connotations of equality, inclusion, and participation to underline the propriety and legitimacy of their activities. They were neither slaves nor subjects, residents nor denizens; they were fully vested members of a political
community.

By qualifying the term "citizen" with the adjective "colored," Walker
and his successors were acknowledging the possibility of refusal, confronting head-on the power of racial hierarchy to negate republican equality.
Indeed, the phrase "colored citizens" forced two ideas into juxtaposition
in a way that no doubt struck many whites as a contradiction in terms. In
that way, in the 1830s and for decades thereafter, the phrase "colored citizens" articulated a powerful critique of American liberty and equality. It
implicitly called for a nonexclusive definition of citizenship.

Despite its acknowledgment of difference, the use of "colored" marked
a shift away from older differentiations and toward a more intrinsic relationship to the nation. In the late eighteenth century the preferred term for
people of discernible African descent was "African"; thus black Bostonians
accepted the British authorities' designation of their "African Lodge" and
proudly announced their own "African Baptist Church." But in the 1830s
this usage fell from favor, frequently replaced by "people of color," "Negro"
(with or without capitalization), and "colored Americans."[58] The pastor of
the newly renamed First Independent Baptist Church of the People of

Color—still at home in its brick building off Belknap Street—explained it this way in 1838: "[T]he term African is ill applied to a church composed of American citizens."[59] Those who offered alternative coinages proceeded from the same assumption: a man proposing "Africamerican" argued that its blending of the two words "asserts that most important truth, that the colored citizen is as truly a citizen of the United States as the white."[60]

Taking the name "colored citizen" was a bold assertion and remained one for decades to come. As late as the Civil War, black Cincinnati activist Peter Clark described the much more common contrary assumption—the "ellipsis universal in American writing or speaking" by which white Americans spoke in grand universalisms but meant "white men."[61] Sometimes Clark's colleagues across the North expressed their frustration about the uncertainty of their status in still bleaker terms. Especially after the Fugitive Slave Law of 1850, which rendered all African Americans vulnerable to arrest and enslavement with little recourse, they adopted self-descriptions like "the nominally free."[62] One newspaper aimed at free blacks called itself *The Aliened American*. Its title, the editors announced, reflected the ways whites made blacks into "aliens—through their Law, their Public Opinion and their Community-Regulations."[63] Attendees at the same convention at which George Downing imagined "the fraternal unity of man" also described America as their "own loved but guilty land."[64]

Rhetoric aside, citizenship remained a complex and at times maddeningly elusive concept. Twenty-first-century Americans sometimes think of citizenship as a category with clear, fixed boundaries: one either is or is not a citizen of a nation, and that citizenship carries with it a well-defined bundle of rights and obligations in relation to that nation. The reality is, and was, far more ambiguous.[65] Questions of who is and is not a citizen, for what purposes, and with what concomitant rights and obligations were the subject of political and ideological struggle along many axes, but antebellum American citizenship (especially for African Americans) was particularly inchoate and ill-defined.[66]

Americans of African descent experienced federal citizenship as a set of ambiguities and exclusions, not rights and assurances. To begin with, the U.S. Constitution did not clearly or consistently define what distinguished citizens from simple inhabitants, nor what rights or privileges followed from that citizenship. But even where the obligations of the national government were explicit, as in the protection of citizens overseas, black Americans experienced great variation and unpredictability: sometimes secretaries of state provided black citizens traveling abroad with passports; sometimes they did not.[67] The Constitution made no direct reference to race, and even its references to slaves were squeamish allusions to "other persons" to be enumerated and taxed at three-fifths of their actual number. But the first Congresses dropped strong hints that people of African descent, slave or free, belonged in a separate category than whites. The new nation's lawmakers seemed determined to limit the growth of their numbers and to limit the privileges of national citizenship to "white persons," and the 1790 federal Naturalization Act limited the acquisition of citizenship to immigrants defined as "white."[68] Although that law had no clear bearing on the status of native-born black Americans, Congress soon followed up with the federal Militia Act of 1792, which limited service to white men. Most ominous was the federal Fugitive Slave Law of 1793, which provided for the return across state lines of people "held to service or labor."

The primary context in which politicians debated the status of free blacks was in debates over the extension of slavery into new territories. In the debates over the admission of Missouri to the Union in 1821, which centered on the question of whether slavery would be permitted in the new state, members of the United States Senate disagreed as to whether there could be such a thing as a "colored citizen" of the nation. Senator James Burrill of Rhode Island noted matter-of-factly that some states recognized such citizens as indistinguishable from others, while constitutional framer C. C. Pinckney of South Carolina declared flatly that when the document was ratified "there did not then exist such a thing in the Union as a black or colored citizen, nor could I then have conceived it possible such a thing could ever have existed in it; nor, notwithstanding all that is said on the subject, do I now believe one does exist in it."[69] Their dispute was shelved, not resolved, by the subsequent Missouri Compromise, which drew a line of demarcation between territories open and closed to slavery across the Louisiana Purchase, and frightened farsighted observers including Thomas Jefferson.[70] The conflict articulated in the exchange over "colored citizens" played an important role in the sectional crises to come.

Confronted with a federal policy that wavered between hostility and incoherence, as well as with the stigma of their association with slavery, "colored citizens" took advantage of the diffusion of citizenship between federal and state governments. In some states, and especially in Massachusetts, black men and women could make strong claims to be citizens, not just residents or inhabitants. States could offer much, or withhold it: rights of suffrage, testimony, and jury service, among others. Yet state citizenship was also ambiguous and offered only weak and compromised guarantees, especially where the rights of free blacks were concerned. In states with large slave populations black people were in general legally presumed to be slaves unless they proved otherwise.

The status of free blacks in any given state could have implications for free blacks everywhere. "The citizens of each state shall be entitled to all privileges and immunities of citizens in the several states," reads Article IV, Section 2 of the United States Constitution, but in almost the very next clause it goes on to stipulate that persons held to service or labor must be returned to those to whom they owed that labor. In the lives of black Americans, this crucial modifier undid the first clause's guarantee of citizenship. From the first federal Fugitive Slave Law in 1793 through a host of enactments and rulings, the U.S. Congress, legislatures, and courts made it ever easier for real or presumed slaveholders or their paid agents to claim black individuals as their property, while denying the people so claimed an opportunity to defend their freedom in court.[71] Even in states without slavery, therefore, black citizens were vulnerable to seizure upon the accusation that they were in fact fugitives from slavery elsewhere. Under the federal Constitution, the laws of Virginia, South Carolina, and other slaveholding states had dire implications for free black people wherever they lived or traveled.[72]

Yet the difference between being a nominal citizen in one state and presumptively enslaved in another was real and meaningful, and over time the tension between the rights of some states' free blacks and other states' slaveholders grew into a significant constitutional problem. If citizens of a given state were entitled to the "privileges and immunities" afforded citizens in other states, how could free black citizens of Massachusetts be presumed slaves when they entered Georgia? What about when free blacks traveled to the District of Columbia, one of the rights plainly guaranteed to U.S. citizens by the Constitution? The latter question provoked an outcry in 1826 when Washington, D.C., police arrested a visiting New Yorker named Gilbert Horton for being unable to prove his freedom. When Horton was unable to pay his own jail costs, authorities threatened him with sale as a slave. He was freed only after appeals by the New York Manumission Society brought intervention by President John Quincy Adams himself.[73] This difference in status between the state of one's residence and the state one visited made a profound impression on black Bostonians, particularly since it involved the nation's capital. John T. Hilton, recounting the Horton story to his fellow Masons in 1828, contrasted "the Capitol of the nation, the nursery of freedom," with the vulnerability of visiting citizens to enslavement. "Americans," Hilton intoned, "implore the aid of your God to assist in removing this foul blot from thy fair country's name."[74]

Whatever its shortcomings, "liberty" did mean something in Massachusetts. Free black people there were not simply "slaves of the community," at least not in all respects. John T. Hilton recognized this when he described his colleagues as "partially enjoying the fruits of liberty."[75] David Walker certainly experienced it following the discovery of the *Appeal* in Georgia, as evidenced by the response of Boston's mayor to an urgent inquiry from his counterpart in Savannah about Walker's pamphlet. "I perused it carefully," wrote Mayor Harrison Gray Otis, "in order to ascertain whether the writer had made himself amenable to our laws; but notwithstanding the extremely bad and inflammatory tendency of the publication, he does not seem to have violated any of these laws." Absent any such violation, and no matter Otis's personal abhorrence for the pamphlet's contents, he informed the Georgian, "[W]e have no power to control the purpose of the author."[76] It is true that Walker died soon after, in August 1830, and that many, then and since, believed his death to have resulted from a slaveholders' conspiracy. Surely slaveholders wanted Walker dead and would have hanged him if they could, but it appears that tuberculosis found him first, killing both him and his daughter that same season.[77] In any case, neither the outrage at Walker's words nor his sudden death dissuaded his colleagues from continuing the work of "colored citizenship."

Black residents of Boston played central roles in that project, taking full advantage of the local presumption of liberty. To call Massachusetts the "most free" state would be to slight the overhanging threat of the Fugitive Slave Law, and the insults and disabilities pervading African American life. But it is fair to say that nowhere else in the United States in the early 1830s was the authority of slaveholders under such concerted attack, nor people of African descent so openly and centrally involved in that assault.

The gap between Georgia's outrage at Walker's *Appeal* and Massachusetts's grudging toleration of it mirrored wider conflicts over free blacks' status, conflicts that set state legislatures against one another. In the wake of the *Appeal* and Nat Turner's 1831 revolt, several Southern states passed laws designed to deter free blacks from entering. Georgia levied a high tax on free blacks entering the state. South Carolina and other states passed "negro seaman" laws forbidding free black sailors from coming ashore or requiring their imprisonment while their ships were in port. These states, in other words, claimed the right to subject free black sojourners, even though citizens of other states or countries, to discriminatory laws and punishments. These acts provoked petitions of protest to the Massachusetts legislature. Legislators finally conducted a hearing at which a free black sailor, George Tolliver, testified to having been imprisoned seven times in Southern ports along with other "northern colored citizens." Although the legislative committee voted narrowly not to pursue the matter, a few legislators loudly proclaimed their commitment to defend the "persons, liberties, and lives" of all the state's citizens.[78]

The struggle among the states about the question of free black citizenship—a struggle the "colored citizens" provoked—would play a critical role in causing the Civil War. As they pursued their interrelated goals of abolishing slavery, achieving formal equality, and re-creating the nation in the image of "fraternal unity," they could not help inflaming the wound slavery left in the American constitutional order. Whether they crossed state lines to organize churches, distribute pamphlets, or incite revolts, they troubled the nation. Even those who remained in the North could vex slaveholders from afar, either by successfully fleeing their claims of ownership or, like Walker, by warning them that God would not suffer their crimes forever. The "colored citizens" were already a troublesome presence by 1830. Once they found white allies to work beside them, lending practical political aid and the possibility of genuine fellow feeling, they would become a still more potent force, and a far graver threat to the white republic.

2.

Fighting Jim Crow in the Cradle of Liberty

Every year the city of Boston honored the best students from each of its public schools with a celebratory dinner at Faneuil Hall and a medal stamped with the likeness of Benjamin Franklin. All its public schools, that is, except one: the Abiel Smith School, the city's segregated facility for African Americans. In 1829, the mayor and a school official visited the Smith School to examine its students and found three especially worthy, but no medals or dinner invitations were forthcoming. Instead the mayor presented each with a voucher good for one copy of Benjamin Franklin's *Autobiography*.

For one of those students, the twelve-year-old William Cooper Nell, this experience of exclusion was searing, formative, and radicalizing. He redeemed the voucher and kept the book for decades, but as a child of the city's black activist leadership he also felt compelled to protest. He found out which black men had been hired as waiters for the awards dinner—the pool of potential candidates was not large, and Nell's family was well connected—and persuaded one of the men to let him serve in his place. As Nell hoped, the official from the examination recognized him. The man tried to sympathize with Nell's situation, telling him, "You ought to be here with the other boys." Nell was not appeased. "Of course, the same idea had more than once been mine," Nell wrote later, "but his remark, while witnessing the honors awarded to white scholars, only augmented my sensitiveness all the more, by the intuitive inquiry, which I eagerly desired to express—'If you think so, why have you not taken steps to bring it about?'"[1]

Nell's 1829 confrontation with the rituals of exclusion was tentative and exploratory, but in two respects it foretold much of his life's future course. First, he drew upon the resources and knowledge available within the black community: Nell experienced an injustice and, with the collaboration of his fellow black Bostonians, determined how best to confront it. Second, he boldly admonished whites, forcing them to consider their complicity in such injustices. Nell's very presence that night was itself a protest, and he was readying himself to ask the question provoked by the school committeeman's empty sympathy: how could whites square their avowed principles with their collective treatment of their black neighbors?

Nell's analysis truly marked him as one of David Walker's "colored citizens." This was no surprise, for he grew up at the center of that world. His parents were prominent members of the city's black activist leadership. He would later be present at the earliest moments of the alliance with white abolitionists, and become a lifelong devotee of William Lloyd Garrison. As a young man he chaired countless meetings, created organizations, and led the campaign to desegregate the city's public schools. He also became one of the first published African American historians, re-narrating the history of the United States from the Revolution to the present to include the struggles, sacrifices, and achievements of his fellow "colored patriots." But in the world of William Nell's birth, these abilities and aspirations were no defense against derision, exclusion, or even en-slavement. He discovered early on that self-ownership, literacy, and hard work were by themselves insufficient—even in the freest precincts of the antebellum United States—to establish him as a full and equal participant.

Little more than a decade after that painful night at the banquet, both Nell and the community to which he belonged would be better organized, more ready, and earnestly engaging with whites, some of them ready to take a step past sympathy. A growing sense of common cause among black Bostonians was matched by a growing number of allies. Through both of these developments, David Walker's *Appeal* lived on in the increasingly confident and even militant activities of Boston's "colored citizens."

The 1830s and early 1840s began a new era in African American life. Black activisits, standing upon the scaffolding of their hard-won institu-tional achievements, began to seek alliances with antislavery whites. As these alliances bore fruit, the "colored citizens" began to imagine concrete victories in the battles against Southern slavery and for Northern liberty. At the same time, whites' experiences working with blacks began to pull white "antislavery" away from paternalism and abstraction and toward a more personal experience of equality and brotherhood. Black activists reveled in these relationships, fraught though they were, and held them out as symbols of how they might prevail in the confrontation with slavery and white supremacy. William Nell's participation in this world of interracial collaboration demonstrates how the "colored citizens" reshaped white abolitionism, leveraging those moral energies in the service of African Americans' own evolving vision of a more expansive citizenship. Even as they did, though, for most whites "colored citizen" remained an unimagi-nable contradiction in terms.

JIM CROW IN THE CRADLE OF LIBERTY

To an outsider who knew Massachusetts only as the Northern seat of the Revolution and the place with the fewest restrictions on black liberty, William Nell's childhood experience of exclusion might have come as a surprise. Black men there could vote on the same basis as white men. In practice the state excluded people of color only from juries, as well as the militia, as dictated by federal law. Yet in most realms of life, being a "citizen" of Massachusetts offered no guarantees or protections whatsoever. Churches, charitable societies, fire companies, medical societies, cities and towns, banks, corporations—all of these had extensive powers of self-regulation, and all had direct, daily impacts on people's lives far surpassing those of the national or state governments. In the absence of a general rule, this array of associations and corporations determined who was counted in or out far more than what legal historian William Novak calls "the abstract and underdeveloped constitutional category" of citizenship.[2]

The city of Boston's practice of segregating its public schools violated no state law, and other associations, corporations, and private bodies acted similarly. The state bar and medical associations were under no obligation to credential trained black applicants. Harvard's medical school accepted a few black students one year, only to expel them after protests from white students. On some streets a black Bostonian could buy or rent whatever home he or she could afford, on others not at all; more than half of Boston's black population resided on a few streets on Beacon Hill and in the adjacent West End. The owners or operators of restaurants, hotels, and other accommodations excluded or segregated black men and women. Unlike the segregation imposed by some states in the later nineteenth century, these exclusions and insults were not official policies. Neither were they illegal. In the absence of "rights" that followed from a clearly defined "citizenship," black people found their public worlds governed by white people's preferences.

In a region where black people were a tiny and economically inconsequential minority, white preferences developed out of two forces: casual encounters with blacks as laborers and domestics, and a popular culture saturated with depictions of African Americans as jesters, knaves, and fools, people best off in slavery.[3] The most popular entertainment of the day was the minstrel stage, which drew large audiences from the 1820s through the mid-twentieth century. White men dressed in comical clothing, blacked their faces and hands with burnt cork, painted on exaggerated lips and eyes, and mocked blacks in song and speech. The rural buffoon "Jim Crow" and the urban dandy "Zip Coon" offered paeans to a mythical South in which slavery provided a safe home for an improvident, incapable people, and presented black "respectability" as nothing more than grotesque mimicry. A black newspaper editor denounced minstrel players as "the filthy scum of white society," who "pander to the corrupt taste of their white fellow citizens."[4]

White hostility and derision, the Northern counterpoint to Southern enslavement, shocked even fugitives from slavery such as the Maryland-born Frederick Douglass. In his early twenties, Douglass borrowed clothes and free papers from a black sailor and fled slavery for the freedom of Massachusetts. Though he would one day be the most famous and celebrated black man in America, he found his early welcome in the North cold indeed. In the early 1840s, he described his experience in Massachusetts and the other "free states" as a constant, oppressive awareness of being perceived as an inferior. "Prejudice against color is stronger north than south," declared Douglass; "it hangs around my neck like a heavy weight . . . I have met it at every step the three years I have been out of southern slavery."[5] The orator William Wells Brown drove the point home in terms the people of Massachusetts could not misunderstand. "[T]he term Cradle of Liberty, as applied to Boston, was a mockery," he declared.

"If it ever was the cradle of liberty, the child had been rocked to death."[6] Their friend William J. Watkins, the voluble and tempestuous son of a prominent free black Baltimore family, "found this prejudice at the North, much more virulent than at the South."[7]

The practical power of prejudice struck black orators and organizers like Watkins, Douglass, and Nell whenever they ventured aboard a train to attend a convention or give a lecture. Since the state asserted no role in determining whether or on what terms corporations must accommodate particular citizens, individual railroad lines could exile black patrons to separate cars, which quickly came to be named after the caricatured figure of the minstrel stage—"Jim Crow." It was in William Nell's Massachusetts that racially segregated railroad cars first gained that nickname.[8]

In the Jim Crow North, Douglass and other black patrons sometimes argued with train conductors, asserting their right to remain in the seat they had chosen. While traveling from his new home in New Bedford, Douglass sometimes resisted moving to the Jim Crow car. On a few occasions he clung to his seat and refused to be dislodged, until the conductor and his assistants ripped him and his seat from the railroad car and threw them out together.[9] Gender was no barrier to such resistance, or such retaliation: after Mary Newhall Green, holding her infant child, refused to move to the Jim Crow car on another Massachusetts train, white men hit her, dragged her and her baby from the train, and threw them to the ground.[10]

At other times, black travelers encountered a less violent but equally painful hostility. "[W]herever they go," a white observer noted in 1846, "a sneer is passed upon them, as if this sportive inhumanity were an act of merit."[11] Derision of African Americans sometimes masqueraded as play. A Boston traveler declared himself repulsed to find a black woman traveling in his train car, and asserted that his fellow white passengers felt the same way. "Out of compliment to the sex of the intruder," he reported, the response of the other white passengers was limited to sneezing, the curling of lips, and the tune his traveling companion began to whistle: a popular minstrel song whose chorus ran, "Go 'way, nigger gal, don't come nigh with me."[12]

Jim Crow was a maddeningly unpredictable tyrant. Black activists challenged their exclusion by insisting that the state dignify their "citizenship" with equal treatment, but the failure of early campaigns to bar segregation on state railroads left the question in the hands of corporations or individuals.[13] The Massachusetts-born black orator Charles Lenox Remond, a prosperous resident of the North Shore town of Salem, frequently traveled between Boston and his home on the Eastern Railroad.[14] Hearing reports that the railroad had abandoned the "colored car," he arrived at the Salem station for a journey to an antislavery convention, only to be directed once again to the "Jimmy." He refused and so was left sitting in the station house, "disappointed in my feelings, and frustrated in my business engagements," scribbling his report of the affair on a piece of paper propped on

Charles Lenox Remond
Courtesy of the Massachusetts Historical Society

his leg. Indignity and injustice—emotional and legal insult—were of a piece.[15] For the rest of that century and for much of the next, African American travelers would share his fate, never entirely sure when or where they could proceed in safety and dignity.

Beyond the railroads, injury and insult could go hand in hand, as Charles Remond learned when Jim Crow joined him at Faneuil Hall. In 1842, Remond took the podium to address thousands of white and black Bostonians gathered for an antislavery meeting. He would have been the first African American to do so, had he been able. The white men who spoke before him had drawn some hissing from the proslavery folk salted heavily throughout the audience, but when Remond tried to take the stage there erupted what one hostile newspaper described as "one general, tumultuous burst of indignation." Remond pressed on vainly in the face of "riot and confusion, mingled with hisses, groans, and the most unearthly sounds, such as 'down with the nigger! turn the darkey over! tip him into the pit!,'" and "sell the nigger." As Remond persisted, the tumult swelled so that "not a word could be heard . . . Rings were formed upon the floor, and the popular dances of 'Jim along Jo,' 'Take your time, Miss Lucy,' and 'Clare de Kitchen' were broken down in the most approved style."[16]

The minstrel show armed white crowds with the ammunition of ridicule. In "Take Your Time, Miss Lucy," a lover concludes that if his beloved proves to be a scold, he'll simply "tote her down to Georgia / And trade her off for corn."[17] It was a peculiarly Northern form of white supremacy. Southern slaveholders shied away from acknowledging the centrality of the slave market and its forcible separation of black families, preferring the self-serving fantasy of paternalism. But Northern white supremacy gleefully established the line between white and black by taunting African Americans with the fact that their most intimate ties were at the mercy of the market.[18]

The Northern proslavery vision did not depict black Americans as lesser citizens but as anticitizens, people who were intrinsically incapable of acting properly, and whose efforts to participate threatened the social and political order. Their presence on the stage in Faneuil Hall was a mockery, to which the only appropriate response was an equally mocking rejoinder. So while some men danced (and presumably sang, or shouted) "Miss Lucy" to drown out Remond's remarks, others assaulted figures they found equally troubling. In the meeting, "two colored ladies had their bonnets and shawls torn off them."[19] Even a more genteel opponent made the same point: only bad could come of "thrusting upon a Faneuil-Hall audience" speakers like Remond and Douglass, for black men "could not be expected to discuss with ability and force the great questions before the meeting."[20] In the white man's republic of the 1830s and 1840s, people of color were excluded by definition from the rites, and rights, of citizenship; if they refused to submit to that exclusion, the assaults they experienced were the well-deserved results of their own bad judgment. This was true in Faneuil Hall, but even more so in any workplace or form of employment claimed by white workers. Even the poorest European immigrants, the Irish refugees who arrived in growing numbers during the late 1840s, were often able to press black workers out of many forms of low-paid employment.[21]

While public assaults left black Bostonians injured and angry, they were chilled by reminders that whites simply preferred their absence— on the streets, and on the continent.[22] When President William Henry Harrison died suddenly in 1841, William Cooper Nell and his friends debated whether or not to attend the funeral procession in a body, unsure "whether they will be treated as citizens should be treated."[23] The state's governing Whigs did in fact bar them from the procession, and months later Nell was still "smarting under the recollection of their expulsion."[24] The possibility of a more existential expulsion continued to hang over their heads: the deportation program called "colonization," which remained the most popular "antislavery" position in the 1830s and 1840s. As late as 1862 Abraham Lincoln advised a visiting delegation of African Americans that he thought black and white would both live more happily if the blacks departed for other shores.[25]

Most whites, like the sympathetic reviewer of David Walker's *Appeal*, remained unable to imagine a black man with whom one would want to "walk arm in arm . . . through Washington-street."[26] Blackness and whiteness seemed so radically distinct and so hierarchically ordered that a member of the Massachusetts legislature asked rhetorically, "Who had ever heard of such a thing, in social life, as a mixed *party*?" No one answered. He went on to articulate his own vision of such a party, imagining integrated dining rooms in public hotels as chessboards, with a stern and mechanical law of equality "placing a black man and a white alternately from end to end of the table."[27]

No state law barring segregation or removing particular racial proscriptions would have prevented the moments of insult or the apparently genuine disbelief that whites would ever voluntarily associate with blacks. Nor would the end to formal segregation—whether state mandated or as a matter of company policy—be a panacea. No law could restrain the spirit of white supremacy that cast a black man's public speaking as an outrageous affront, that allowed the convention of a man's "compliment" to a woman to take the form of a vicious insult, that could not envision black and white companions walking together. The challenge before the activists of William Nell's generation was not simply to change the laws and to invest "citizenship" with civil guarantees and protections; it was also to move beyond the realm of law and government in pursuit of a fuller belonging in their communities, and in the nation.

THE GROWTH OF
INTERRACIAL ANTISLAVERY

The emergence of the radical antislavery movement known as abolitionism forever changed the landscape of possibility for the "colored citizens." There had been abolition societies before, but the movement of the 1830s immeasurably cheered the "colored citizens" while deeply alarming those committed to slavery's future. For the first time, a significant group of whites began to imagine the end of slavery not as a gradual and conditional event, likely requiring "colonization" and certainly not implying equality, but as immediate and absolute. "Immediatism" was an antislavery around which free black people could rally, both because it acknowledged the sinfulness and horror of slavery, and because it seemed to promise a battle not just with the slaveholders, but also with the forces that made freedom so unequal and infuriating.[28]

The search for white allies who would heed David Walker's plea to "listen" soon yielded the radical Christian and egalitarian editor William Lloyd Garrison. Born to a poor family in Newburyport, Massachusetts, Garrison as a young man went to work on a Baltimore antislavery newspaper, *The Genius of Universal Emancipation.* Playful, passionate, and unable to stop himself from pursuing a moral cause, he served a sentence for libel

William Lloyd Garrison
Courtesy of the Massachusetts Historical Society

in a Maryland jail after accusing a local merchant of trading in slaves. In 1829 Garrison reported sympathetically on Boston black community affairs for the *Genius*; unlike his Baltimore employer, though, Garrison soon came to reject colonization outright. In speeches and a pamphlet, he described his own passage from the false antislavery of colonization to the forthright defense of the rights of black people, slave and free.[29] "This is their native soil," he wrote.[30]

Garrison's lacerating indictment of the colonizationists' inhumanity, un-Christianity, and hypocrisy occasionally echoed the cadences of David Walker. This was not a great surprise, for Garrison read the *Appeal* in Baltimore after the storm caused by its arrival farther south. He wrote that "it breathes the most impassioned and determined spirit," and wondered at "the bravery and intelligence of its author."[31] Still, its tone worried him, and he deprecated its "general spirit" of anger and vengeance. Upon his arrival in Boston, though, a few months before Walker's death, he realized how powerfully Walker's *Appeal* summed up the feelings and thoughts of the city's free blacks. When he initiated his own abolitionist newspaper, *The Liberator*, in January 1831, he announced his intention to create the "revolution in public sentiment" that black activists sought.[32] His words in opposition to slavery, colonization, and prejudice were searing and uncompromising, and he quickly gained the attention of many black Northerners. In the *Liberator*'s inaugural issue in 1831, Garrison promised "our free colored brethren" that "moral and intellectual elevation, the advancement of your rights, and the defence of your character, will be a leading object of our paper."[33] Although Walker died shortly after the third edition of his pamphlet appeared in August 1830, and the two men may never have met, Walker's impact on Garrison was unmistakable.[34]

Garrison was perhaps the first white person in living memory to approach the city's black community not just with good intentions, but with genuine outrage about both slavery and the unequal status of free blacks. The *Liberator* quickly became an important weekly source of information, news, and commentary for free blacks in Boston and far beyond. By the third issue Garrison's paper was already proving its practical value, publishing James Barbadoes's warning to be on the lookout for efforts to capture fugitives and return them to slavery, as had been recently occurring.[35] In hard times Garrison called on his "free colored brethren" to patronize the paper, and they did.[36] Throughout the paper's early years, African Americans made up the bulk of its subscribers and kept the paper afloat.

Garrison's paper served as an organizational nexus for a small but growing band of white men and women who embraced the unqualified, immediate abolition of slavery—"immediatism"—as their life's work. They not only took their project seriously; they took it to their black neighbors. At the beginning of 1832 Garrison and eleven other white men gathered in the vestry of the African Meeting House, the hub of black organizational life, to sign their names to the constitution of a new body.[37] But from the beginning these white allies were not of one mind.

Garrison wanted to call the group the Philo-African Society—a neologism meaning "love of Africans"—and an article in the *Liberator* explained his vision for it.[38] "A Dream" presents an elaborate fantasy in which a white gentleman awakens into a future world fully rid of both slavery and the badge of racial caste. He learns that over many decades a society of white "philo-Africans" helped blacks of education and attainment make their way into white society. There, their "talents, learning, and energy" enabled them to flourish and paved the way for the rest of the race. The white allies, a black man informs the dreamer, "would not rest satisfied with a scanty measure of justice, but continued to urge our full and free admission to all political and social privileges." The final result was a world of equality and harmony, in which black and white together sang, courted, and politicked.[39]

Perhaps the more cautious among Garrison's white allies could not bring themselves to accept this radical vision; in any case, they rejected the "Philo-African" name. Although the editor was famous for his refusal to compromise, he capitulated in this instance, accepting a moniker that betokened a narrower but still incendiary mandate. Thus the New England

Anti-Slavery Society, or NEAS, was born.[40] The name change signified the divisions already evident among white allies. Garrison saw racial caste and white distaste for free black people as evidence of a "spirit of slavery," part of the same larger evil he sought to combat.[41] America might not have a class of hereditary nobility, as a fugitive slave later explained in the columns of the *Liberator*, but it still had one "based on the color of a man's skin." This "republican negro hate" clung to white Americans, and must be got rid of if they were to honor their own claims to "justice" and "humanity."[42] Not all of Garrison's white comrades saw it this way, and "love of the African" gave way to the cooler and narrower "anti-slavery."[43]

The free black leaders of the 1830s no doubt preferred Garrison's original formulation, but they did not quibble. White men declaring friendship had come to their house to pledge their aid, asking nothing in return. A teenage William Nell peered through a window as his father and the other men of the Massachusetts General Colored Association assembled for a momentous ceremony: the white founders of the New England Anti-Slavery Society signing their own constitution, a document that declared slavery contrary to Christianity and American liberty, insisted on the right of citizens to protest against it, and described New England's "unrighteously oppressed" black citizens as standing "in need of our sympathy and benevolent co-operation." That cooperation would serve both to improve the black population's "character and condition" and to "obtain for them equal civil and political rights and privileges with the whites."[44] In form and in spirit, it was as if a handful of whites really had begun to hear the words of David Walker and consider their black neighbors worthy of fellowship.

From its organizational roots in Garrison's *Liberator* and the New England Anti-Slavery Society, an abolitionist network grew up across the North, merging with existing local groups, spawning state societies, and finally establishing a national organization, the American Anti-Slavery Society (AAS). Under these auspices, abolitionists assembled in annual conventions, chartered and circulated a host of new newspapers, and sponsored tours by lecturers, including freeborn blacks and fugitive slaves. They also mounted petition campaigns, calling on states to reform their laws and on the U.S. Congress to abolish slavery in the District of Columbia. Abolition became a mass movement: in a twelve-month period during 1837 and 1838, local activists working through the AAS sent 415,000 petitions to Washington.[45]

The movement's formal leadership was primarily white, but in other respects its interracialism, however imperfect, was striking. By 1833, Nell's father and the other members of the MGCA formally asked to become an auxiliary of the organization. Both Frederick Douglass and Charles Remond became regular participants on the AAS's antislavery lecture circuit, explaining to audiences—sometimes even integrated ones—the evils of slavery and prejudice. Interracial assemblies grew common within the abolition movement, as abolitionists across the North responded to their exclusion from public forums by creating their own meeting halls, such as Boston's Marlboro Hotel and Chapel.[46] When Garrison returned from an antislavery tour of Great Britain in 1840, two thousand people, white and black, filled that chapel to welcome the editor and his companions back to Boston. The *Liberator* claimed that this meeting, on August 20, was the "first instance of a mixed assembly thus brought together in Boston."[47] Garrison, surveying the audience, lauded "this temple of Liberty!"[48] His black colleague Charles Remond, who remained in England for the time being, read of the event and exulted that "[s]uch a meeting, ten years ago, . . . would have moved the foundations of the Old Bay State." Now, what was most striking was the meeting's mixed composition: "above all," Remond noted, "colored ladies and gentlemen sitting promiscuously with this body."[49]

The presence of the "ladies" was unusual in other respects as well. Women did much of the organizational work of antislavery and provided most of the signatures on petitions, unusual developments made all the more surprising by the cooperation of black and white women.[50] Louisa Nell, William Nell's mother, was among the founders of the interracial

Boston Female Anti-Slavery Society (BFAS).[51] The BFAS sponsored the Antislavery Bazaar, a market selling imported goods between Christmas and New Year's each year. The funds raised there helped sustain the publications and lecturers of the AAS. Similar associations soon formed all over the Northern states, leading to an Anti-Slavery Convention of American Women that met three times in the late 1830s.[52] By then, white abolitionist women such as Abby Kelley and the sisters Sarah and Angelina Grimké were beginning to venture where Maria Stewart had gone before. Despite encountering "all manner of censure, scorn, contempt, reproach, and still severer prosecution," they delivered public speeches and published articles on both abolition and women's rights.[53]

Garrison's own public commitment to a wider array of radical causes, not limited to women's rights, worried some antislavery blacks and whites. His attacks on the established churches for welcoming slaveholders into fellowship incensed a number of white abolitionists, and this—together with his advocacy of women's rights and his disavowal of party politics—finally caused detractors to bolt the AAS and form their own antislavery society by 1840. Black activists were generally less concerned with doctrinal purity than their white colleagues, and they were on the whole more open to women's rights. But they were concerned by Garrison's espousal of nonresistance, a broad philosophical pacifism that declared all forms of coercion to be sinful. Nonresistance appeared to preclude violence undertaken in defense of one's life or one's freedom, a stance few black activists could support. They began to challenge and question the editor. Faced with a potential wedge cutting to the heart of their burgeoning alliance, Garrison's black allies repeatedly called community meetings—often with Garrison himself present—to allow the editor to air his true positions. Garrison helped matters by proving surprisingly tolerant of dissent from his positions, and by engaging his black critics directly and respectfully, in their own meeting houses.[54] Despite his ferocious prose and his reputation for doctrinal rigidity, in person the young editor was in fact both warm and playful; his colleague Thomas Wentworth Higginson never forgot his first encounter with Garrison's sense of humor—the "little puns which were essential to his conversation, and which at first appeared to the stranger as inappropriate as if one should track a lion to his lair, and find him refreshing himself with peppermints."[55] Even those black activists who disagreed with the editor's positions remained admirers and colleagues.

Black and white abolitionists were further united by their common enemy. Abolitionism's radical challenge to the prevailing hierarchies of race and gender provoked passionate and well-organized responses, from the halls of Congress to the streets of Northern cities. Antislavery petitions to Congress became the subject of a special "gag rule," which required them to be tabled without being read. Southern politicians began to articulate an emphatically proslavery vision, celebrating the superiority of the region's hierarchical social relations to the cutthroat capitalism of Northern wage labor. Most ominously, merchants and politicians eager to protect their crucial business ties to Southern merchants and planters fomented riots against abolitionists. These riots swept the country in the mid-1830s, with most of the organized violence taking place in Northern cities.[56]

Boston's "Garrison mob" made its assault on October 21, 1835.[57] The Boston Female Anti-Slavery Society had invited the British abolitionist George Thompson to speak, which provided antiabolitionist editors and merchants with sufficient xenophobic cause to rally a crowd against the meeting. Thompson was not in fact present, but the mayor brought constables to the meeting and told the women present that he could guarantee their safety only if they would disperse immediately. The mob briefly seized Garrison himself, then tied and roughed him up, before police rescued the editor and hustled him off to the city hall, where the mayor "protected" Garrison by jailing him overnight—the only action taken by city officials in response to the riot.[58] This was not a spontaneous upwelling of antiabolitionist fervor but a coordinated assault on abolition by those who feared its impact: the "Garrison mob" was one of four antiabolition riots that took place in various Northern cities on that single day.[59]

This violent opposition to abolitionist speech and action helped cement

the relationship between white abolitionists and "colored citizens." The
realization that a white man was willing to endure danger and humiliation
for the cause of antislavery moved black activists not just to read and un-
derwrite the *Liberator*, but to band together in secret to protect Garrison
and his home against assault. The editor was a passionate believer in nonviolence, but John T. Hilton later confessed that "a few of our number
used to guard the dwelling of Mr. Garrison" on the dark nights of mob
rule.[60] Garrison was too important to lose.

INTERRACIAL SOCIABILITY AND
THE MEANING OF CLASS

For black activists, Garrison represented the entering wedge in the great
struggle to come: the conquest of white hearts and minds. They had to
persuade individuals, then groups, to think and feel their way past the
idea that to associate with blacks on equal terms was repulsive or absurd.
Garrison was a priceless example of the possible. The founder of the
American Anti-Slavery Society, the editor of the *Liberator*, and a constant
presence at antislavery gatherings, Garrison was the most prominent white
face of antislavery. More, he remained a "philo-African" in a broader sense
as well. He was the leading white articulator of free black people's plight,
one of the rare white Americans to acknowledge what black activists had
been saying for decades: their "freedom" lacked both equality and dignity.
Under his editorship the *Liberator* cataloged the indignities endured by his
black neighbors: "to be forbidden to eat with fellow citizens; to be assigned
to a particular gallery in his church; to be excluded from college, from municipal office, from professions, from scientific and literary associations."
Black Northerners were "excluded from every department of society, but
its humiliations and its drudgery." All of these, Garrison understood, were
badges of inferiority and guarantees of its perpetuity. Garrison adopted,
too, his black comrades' skeptical view of self-congratulatory American

nationalism. Black citizens were "stripped of all the best benefits of society," Garrison sneered, "by fellow-citizens who, once a year, solemnly lay their hands on their hearts, and declare that all men are born free and equal, and that rulers derive their just powers from the consent of the governed."[61]

Black activists appreciated words of sympathy and understanding, but they cherished acts of solidarity. The growth of abolition societies in the 1830s and the mixed audiences their conventions attracted meant that white and black abolitionists traveled together more and more frequently, and new contexts created new possibilities. On those occasions when the young Frederick Douglass chose not to fight his "colonization" to the separate railcar, he urged his white companions to leave him and travel in comfort. Secretly, though, he hoped for more, and "while I was entirely honest in urging them to go, and saw no principle that should bind them to stay and suffer with me, I always felt a little nearer to those"—including the upper-class intellectual and agitator Wendell Phillips—"who did not take my advice and persisted in sharing my hardships with me."[62]

William Cooper Nell felt the same way. Once in the early 1840s, as Nell journeyed by train with Garrison, the conductor ordered Nell into the Jim Crow car. Garrison joined him, remarking with a smile that he had become so tanned on his recent passage home from England that he "might perhaps be taken for a color'd man." Nell and Garrison both loved to joke, but here Nell responded earnestly, telling Garrison that while he might not literally be a colored man, "he always knew how to feel as one."[63] Nell recounted this story in a letter to his patron and sometime employer Wendell Phillips, who soon followed Garrison's example.[64] White abolitionists had not always made such choices. Charles Remond—the only black delegate from the United States to the World Anti-Slavery Convention in London in 1840—was Jim Crowed on the vessel crossing the Atlantic, restricted to a two-man berth in steerage that was only two feet wide, and even Garrison did not join him there.[65]

For Garrison and Nell, interracial fellowship was the key to dissolving racial antipathies, and in the antislavery movement they saw it beginning to take hold: "Already have people of color crossed the thresholds of many whites, as guests, not as drudges or beggars."[66] Yet this measure of equality was a bold step even white abolitionists could not always bring themselves to take: white abolitionists traveling to Philadelphia in 1837 sat with their black companion on the train, defying convention, but then balked at sharing a dinner table.[67] Garrison was gesturing hopefully at events that remained rare and exceptional.

Class mattered. Prominent white abolitionist leaders—from Lewis Tappan, New York's merchant prince, to Phillips, Harvard-educated scion of one of Boston's first families—occupied a social stratum no blacks and indeed very few whites ever entered. Key figures such as Francis Jackson and Edmund Quincy shared Phillips's genteel origins, as did Maria Weston Chapman and her six sisters. The Chapman parlor in Boston's South End formed the center of what friends and foes alike called the "Boston Clique," the group of white Bostonians who, as funders and organizers, exerted great influence over the *Liberator* and the antislavery societies.[68] For men like Quincy, who keenly felt the loss of polite society that had followed his conversion to abolitionism, the Chapmans' was a blessed island of gentility and grace. By contrast, the rank and file of Boston's black community were among the city's poorest residents. In the 1830s and early 1840s only a few black activists could claim a skilled trade such as barbering; the very first black doctors and lawyers would not emerge until later in the 1840s. The black activist leadership, though drawn mainly from the upper end of the highly compressed black social structure, shared much more with their poorer peers than they did with most whites.

Farther down the white social scale, even white abolitionists of comparatively modest means were mainly accustomed—as Garrison acknowledged—to encountering African Americans in menial capacities. For those whites near the bottom of the economic order, race mattered because it had the power to move them at least one step up the ladder;

insisting on distinctions of race became a way of asserting that they themselves were respectable and worthy in ways their black neighbors were not. And most white wageworkers, like the great majority of whites of all stations, were simply not abolitionists.

Neither the white abolitionist leadership nor the rank and file, that is to say, had much feeling for the lives, work, or experiences of the black members of their alliance, any more than they would have for comparably impoverished or ill-educated white Bostonians. There were few or no black guests in the Chapman-Weston orbit. Quincy was prone to openly racist utterances when irritated with his black compatriots. And along with exclusion and occasional contempt came guilt, soon accompanied by resentment. The genteel white abolitionist Lydia Maria Child, doing paid work for the Boston Female Anti-Slavery Society, felt humiliated in 1841 when two African American members of the executive committee openly discussed cutting her salary. After hearing the two say that "they earned their money too hard to spend it so lavishly," she spent the next day "crying," in her own words, "like a fool."[69] It was hard to be rebuked by the objects of one's benevolence.[70]

William Nell respected, admired, and relied on Wendell Phillips, but their relationship suggests how class and race limited the intimacy between most black and white activists. Nell wrote frequent letters to Phillips and consulted him on matters great and small. He prized the older man's advice, as well as the access to his library. Indeed, Nell's admiration for Phillips, Garrison, and the other white leading lights of the abolition movement verged on the reverent. "[T]hese be my Gods," he once wrote.[71] "Were mine the eloquence of a Phillips," he told one audience, "did I possess the talent of a Garrison, united with the concentration of influence attributed to them, all should be employed in this one noble service, of stimulating our brethren to action and progress in literary attainments."[72] Nell's deep respect for Phillips was as obvious to outsiders as the inequality between them: Nell's good friend the fugitive and author William Wells Brown wrote that Nell was Phillips's "ardent admirer" and—offering one of the references to English letters demanded by Brown's Anglophilia—"seems as much attached to that distinguished orator as Boswell was to Johnson."[73]

Yet the distance between Phillips's elegant childhood home at the fashionable summit of Beacon Street and Nell's modest rooms down the northern slope was much greater than the number of steps between their doors. Phillips was wealthy and Harvard educated. Nell was literate, ambitious, and a dogged organizer, but he constantly felt both the financial strain of looking after his unmarried sisters and the nagging awareness that his lack of formal education held him back. One was patron, the other client. Theirs was an economic relationship, that is, as much as or more than a social one. Nell did all manner of errands for Phillips: picking up packages from his tailor; guarding the family home from burglars while the couple went out of town; delivering a shawl to an old Phillips family servant in neighboring Charlestown.[74] His willingness to perform such tasks granted him access to a world of famous and accomplished white men and women who had cast their lot with abolition. Through Phillips he met antislavery moneyman Francis Jackson, became the patient of the European-trained physician Henry Bowditch, "had a shake of the hand from Charles Sumner," did copying for the antislavery feminist Lucy Stone, and became Sunday superintendent at abolitionist minister Theodore Parker's church.[75] Yet however warm the relations between himself and Phillips, Parker, or Stone, Nell was at bottom their employee. He was proud to hold the keys to the downtown office of the Anti-Slavery society and to Parker's church and Phillips's house—but these small jobs also constituted the piecework by which he supported himself.[76] Nell wrestled with the gap between his dreams of joining their world of accomplishment and acclaim, and the reality of his poverty and subordination.

He worried, for example, about his errand to Miss Manning, the old Phillips family servant. Nell had traveled to Charlestown to present her with the older man's gift, and then enjoyed a cup of tea with her and her family. On his departure, though, the social call abruptly lost its egalitarian tone when Miss Manning pressed fifty cents upon him as thanks, or payment, for bringing her the gift. He had at first refused it—"of course," he told Phillips—but she had urged it upon him so insistently that he relented. Had he done right to accept the gratuity, he asked, or would it have been better to hold firm?

Nell's discomfort with white paternalist largesse came wrapped in layers of race, class, and aspiration: he wanted to see himself as a gentleman, a dignified professional, but he was a black man in a city where virtually all black men and women were servants or laborers of one kind or another. Moreover, his present situation—scribe, watchman, doorkeeper, errand boy—belied his self-conception as a rising man of color, a citizen among equals. Had he been doing Phillips a favor, performing a gentleman's act of noblesse by proxy? Or was he in fact just one of Phillips's servants on a minor errand involving another? Miss Manning's half-dollar offered an unwelcome third possibility. It transformed their tea together into a white person's act of polite condescension to a well-mannered black man. Such dilemmas were part and parcel of a black man's place in the world of the white antislavery leadership.[77]

Within the Boston antislavery movement contacts across the color line mostly remained tentative, self-conscious, and symbolic. Organizations or "mixed meetings" that were formally racially integrated often consisted of white assemblies with a scattering of black members, or predominantly black assemblies with a small proportion of white attendees. Although both the New England society and its successor, the Massachusetts Anti-Slavery Society, included black men among their officers, white leaders and white speakers dominated these organizations. Black and white women worked together in the Boston Female Anti-Slavery Society, but as few as twenty-seven black women could be counted among the six hundred who belonged to the group at one time or another.[78] More tellingly, white members of the BFAS insisted that their black sisters sit separately at their

meetings.[79] As weak as this commitment to interracialism was, it constituted an improvement over the situation elsewhere: between the revolutionary founding of Pennsylvania's abolition society and the eve of the
Civil War, the group admitted only one black member.[80] In other words,
Garrison's open advocacy of interracial sociability as a means of improv-
ing society was rare even among committed white abolitionists.

Ironically, the sense of social distance between white and black was so
profound that it permitted one legal liberalization to move forward: the
repeal of the state law barring the marriage of persons of different races.
An antislavery newspaper described this action as a "staggering blow . . .
to the monster prejudice," but it signaled neither a momentous transformation nor a daring act of legislative radicalism.[81] Few thought the law would
amount to much. Later in the nineteenth century, white supremacist campaigns asserting that black men harbored sexual ambitions toward white
women made such topics prohibitively dangerous for reformers: whites
courted a loss of public respectability for suggesting such unions were
anything other than horrific or coercive, and black men and women faced
much worse. But in 1843 the supporters of repeal presented their position
as one of principle, not personal interest, and opposition was apparently
limited to "vulgar ribaldry."[82] The primarily white Boston Female Anti-
Slavery Society endorsed the repeal of the marriage law, and even legislators who were openly hostile to desegregating the railroads could not
muster quite the same antagonism for the repeal of an intermarriage law
they regarded as superfluous. Interracial wedlock in the abstract might
provoke revulsion or anxiety, but it was not yet the bright line for white
supremacy that it would become.[83] Yet Garrison himself took care to explain that "[o]ur object has been not to promote 'amalgamation,'"—the
era's term for interracial sex and reproduction—"but to establish justice,
and vindicate the equality of the human race."[84] Equality in the abstract
was far more comfortable ground, even for the radical editor.[85]

FUGITIVES AND THE RISE OF MILITANT ABOLITIONISM

Despite its limitations, the alliance between black activists and white abolitionists bore fruit in the movement to defend fugitives and other free blacks from capture and enslavement. Those threats to black liberty, rooted in the Constitution's promise that fugitive slaves must be returned to their owners, played out in complicated ways. States followed a variety of courses in determining, first, whether people were to be presumed enslaved or free; second, what protections were available to persons held as fugitives; and third, what responsibility the state bore for carrying out the law. A related set of issues involved slaveholders' rights to carry their human property with them into states where slavery had been abolished. Here, Massachusetts's high court stood at one end of the national spectrum of positions in these matters: a unanimous ruling in 1836 held that "slavery was contrary to natural right" and that any slave brought to Massachusetts became free. Over the next decade courts and legislatures in several other Northern states incorporated this same principle into their laws. Petitions from antislavery forces led to new laws in Massachusetts and elsewhere providing jury trials and other safeguards against the kidnapping of free citizens.[86]

On August 1, 1836, black Bostonians began a new chapter in their opposition to slavery after the agent of a Baltimore slaveholder seized as slaves two black women just arrived in Boston Harbor. Whether the women were indeed fugitives or not remained unclear, but when the case came to the Supreme Judicial Court on August 1, the black and white abolitionists crowded the courtroom, including a delegation from the BFAS. The women's abolitionist lawyer, Samuel Sewall, one of the signers of the charter in the African Meeting House, made a rousing speech about human freedom and liberty, but the judge ruled in his favor on simpler grounds: the terms of the Fugitive Slave Law of 1793 had not been met, and so the women were discharged. But this did not end the matter. The slaveholder's agent continued to make threats, and a constable locked the door leading out to the street. Spectators feared the worst and quickly sprang into action. Men and women rushed to the bench and, over the judge's protests, picked up the two women, carried them through the judge's entrance, out into the street, and away.[87]

The forceful confrontation with slavery clarified the limits of the interracial alliance, but also the ways that events could reshape it. Garrison called the action "unjustifiable"; there remained a great distance in philosophy between him and nearly all black activists. But the rescue demonstrated to reluctant whites that slaveholders had little regard for anyone's liberties, even theirs. And it showed black citizens that some whites would risk their own safety for black freedom. At the end of August a relative of the Baltimore slaveholder, a U.S. naval officer, entered Samuel Sewall's office and struck him with "the butt end of a horsewhip." As other whites felt the sting of coercion, they too learned to think a bit differently about what might or might not be justifiable to prevent a person from being enslaved.[88]

The Boston slave rescue of 1836 was part of an emerging pattern of action across the nonslave states. At least three dozen times between the 1830s and the 1850s crowds headed by black men and women took similar action, rescuing slaves or those at risk of enslavement.[89] Boston's 1836 tumult was nothing compared to events in Buffalo, New York, that year. A Nashville slaveholder arrived in the city in pursuit of a fugitive couple and their child; learning that they were now across the border in Canada, he hired kidnappers to return them forcibly to Tennessee. Buffalo's antislavery forces quickly mobilized, and a mainly black posse of about fifty men including William Wells Brown, himself a recent escapee from Missouri slavery, rescued the fugitives from their captors. A larger sheriff's posse then confronted the rescuers and, though one of the latter was killed and forty arrested, the fugitives made it safely back to Canada.[90] Black activists' defense of fugitives was beginning to make an impression on white authorities, to outrage slaveholders, and to force deadly confrontations.

Both black activists and white authorities paid close attention to the even more dramatic rebellions of enslaved people themselves. The 1839 revolt aboard the slave ship *Amistad*, led by the African Joseph Cinque, turned the eyes of the nation to the rebels' subsequent imprisonment and trial. Black and white antislavery activists celebrated when the U.S. Supreme Court finally declared them free in 1841. That same year, enslaved Americans being shipped to New Orleans on board the *Creole*, led by a Virginian bearing the startlingly perfect name of Madison Washington, seized control of the ship and steered it to the British territory of the Bahamas, where slavery had been abolished a few years before. The two successful shipboard revolts resonated powerfully for black activists, confirming their sense that force could sometimes achieve what peaceful means could not. William Wells Brown named his daughter "Cinque." Frederick Douglass wrote a short novel about Madison Washington entitled *The Heroic Slave*.[91]

In the more closely monitored waters of Boston Harbor, individual fugitives had no opportunity to become Cinques and Washingtons, and their friends on the shore could do little to help. In June 1841 John Torrence, a fugitive from North Carolina, was discovered on a Boston-bound ship, but to the dismay of the city's black and white antislavery folk could not be rescued from the chains and guards surrounding him in the harbor.[92] The best they could do was to have the ship's mate, who was foolish enough to stay behind when the ship left port, charged with kidnapping.[93]

Boston's antislavery folk needed a new strategy for responding to the seizure of fugitives who reached the city, particularly by water. In the wake of Torrence's return to slavery, an interracial antislavery meeting organized a vigilance committee, probably influenced by the earlier example of New York City's Committee of Vigilance, organized by *Liberator* agent David Ruggles and others in 1835, and the similar body created by American Anti-Slavery Society stalwart Robert Purvis and other Philadelphians in 1837.[94] The new Boston body would seek "to protect the liberties of persons alleged to be slaves, and to rescue from bondage persons of color who are entitled to be free."[95] The constitution they forged imagined a network of societies, on the "great lines of northern travel" and in the seaports, which would quickly spread word of fugitives' or kidnappers' arrivals. The organizers asked for contributions totaling a thousand dollars to get things going—an ambitious figure, given that a large public meeting three weeks later was able to raise less than twenty dollars. As if to underline the importance of organization, the very day that the Boston Vigilance Committee formed, slave catchers discovered another fugitive aboard a vessel in the harbor and quietly shipped him back to South Carolina before word could circulate.[96]

Black activists did not always trust that their white allies would do whatever was necessary to free the enslaved and defend the free. A few weeks later, another fugitive stowaway appeared in the harbor on a ship from Mobile. The owners of the vessel, eager to remain in the good graces of their Southern trading partners, immediately charged the penniless fugitive seventy dollars for the passage from Mobile to Boston; when he could not pay, they had him arrested and jailed, preliminary to his return to slavery. Black Bostonians did not wait until concerted action could be arranged; once they got wind of the affair, they cobbled together the funds to bail the man out. White abolitionist Samuel Sewall obtained a writ granting the man a hearing, but by the time it was served the Alabama fugitive had already skipped his bail and was on his way to Canada.[97] They may have been wise not to wait: the Vigilance Committee's constitution of 1841 vowed in its first article to "employ every legal, peaceful and christian method, and none other."[98] The explosions of antiblack violence racking black Northern communities suggested the shortcomings of this position. On August 1, 1842, for example, Robert Purvis sat waiting with pistols as a white mob howled outside his Philadelphia door after his comrades' celebration of West Indian emancipation day outraged white residents and inspired them to attack.[99]

White abolitionists clung to the law, but antislavery blacks embraced both legal and extralegal means. During the spring and summer of 1842, the U.S. Supreme Court's ruling in *Prigg v. Pennsylvania* seemed to make enforcement of the Fugitive Slave Law entirely a federal responsibility, and to hold open the possibility that a state could forbid its officials from taking part in such renditions of fugitives.[100] A twenty-five-year-old William Nell and his new friend Robert Morris took notes at a "Meeting of the Colored Citizens of Boston," which resolved to petition the next legislature for an act forbidding rendition by state authorities.[101] "Personal liberty laws" sought to establish rudimentary rights for persons seized as fugitives. The 1842 meeting asked the legislature "to prohibit their officers and citizens from interfering to aid slaveholders in seizing and returning fugitive slaves."[102] They also asked the U.S. Congress to repeal the Fugitive Slave Law of 1793 and guarantee trial by jury for persons claimed as fugitives.[103] They had little reason to believe they would win the day— not as long as the rights of slaveholders trumped those of everyone else; not as long as Massachusetts could become "a slave state" whenever a slaveholder journeyed there to claim a fugitive; and not as long as black sailors, citizens of Massachusetts, could still be summarily imprisoned in Charleston.

The "colored citizens" therefore rejected a purely legal strategy, and the 1842 meeting's resolutions sounded a very different note from the Vigilance Committee's constitution. "[I]n obedience to a higher power, and in conformity to the principles of liberty inherent in the breast of every member of the human family," they resolved, "we will not permit ourselves nor [our] brethren to be transferred to the southern prison-house."[104] That summer they formed the New England Freedom Association, to "hide the outcast, and deliver him . . . out of the hands of the oppressor."[105] Militant sentiment grew common across the black North, and Boston's black leaders readied themselves, though they did not yet know precisely for what.

THE LATIMER WAR

The answer came that autumn, in a campaign that marked a turning point in black Bostonians' interracial alliances. In early October 1842, George Latimer and his pregnant wife, Rebecca, fled their Norfolk, Virginia, owners. George Latimer had set off northward once before without success, but this time he was better prepared. His light skin and long years working in and around the businesses of Norfolk enabled him to pass as a white man and book a cabin on the sailing ship from Norfolk to Boston; his wife traveled as his servant. Within a week they were in Boston, where George had the singularly bad luck to be identified almost immediately by a former employee of his owner, James Gray. George Latimer held Gray in very low regard, and not simply because he was a slaveholder; having worked under a dozen masters during his young life, Latimer viewed Gray as among the worst—a "passionate" man who beat him severely with fists, sticks, and straps for minor infractions.[106]

This time the Vigilance Committee was ready. On October 19, 1842, when agents of James Gray seized George Latimer on a Boston street, word of the arrest spread quickly among the city's black citizens. By the time the slave catchers hauled their prisoner before a judge that evening, Rebecca Latimer was safely ensconced at the home of antislavery folks, and nearly three hundred residents of the Yankee metropolis, most of them black men, crowded outside the door of the courthouse.[107] As many as half the black men in the city had come to protest and bear witness.[108] It was the beginning of a struggle that would involve several more such crowds, and an unprecedented mobilization of antislavery resources.

Everywhere in the ensuing events could be seen the earnest figure of William Nell, chairing meetings and hurrying through the streets. Men and women who were children in the days of David Walker now stepped forward more openly than any of their forebears, and Nell was becoming one of their leaders. Neatly dressed, with a beard like the one Abra-

William Cooper Nell
Courtesy of the Massachusetts
Historical Society

ham Lincoln would later grow, and thick, wavy hair brushed back from
his forehead, Nell had the sad eyes of a lovelorn poet. But he was in fact
an indefatigable organizer as well as a budding historian. For the next
thirty years he would remain an irrepressible presence among the "colored
citizens."

The activists seeking to free George Latimer combined high-flown
rhetoric and hard-nosed street politics. During the first week after Latimer's arrest, they met over several nights to chart a strategy. They depicted
their struggle as part of an American battle of liberty against tyranny. Resolutions accused the authorities of conduct "unworthy of free Americans,"
a point they underlined by decrying Latimer's seizure "within sight of Bunker Hill, and on the soil that drank the *first* blood that was shed in the
revolution that secured the independence of these United States"—a refer-

ence to the Boston Massacre of 1770, and Crispus Attucks.[109] They flattered their white neighbors as the inheritors of that legacy.

Even as they recruited white allies, black activists did not assume that white sympathy would trump white supremacy, or override the law of slavery. They relied instead on careful organization, and on unruly crowds. Precisely how hundreds of black residents knew to make their way to the courthouse is not clear, but their numbers and mood suggest a campaign to bring them out in force. The crowd at the courthouse the night of Latimer's arrest seethed "in a very feverish state of anxiety," reported the *Liberator*.[110] When antislavery lawyers obtained a writ of habeas corpus, Latimer was moved to the jail "amid much tumult and confusion."[111] The next day, as the examination before the judge began, the mainly African American crowd was again in the streets, "giv[ing] vent to their feelings, in no measured language." As Latimer was returned to jail, a few of the black men tried to interfere with the constable escorting the prisoner; the authorities arrested and indicted them for riot, and three were later convicted of interfering with the constable.[112]

Although the crowd did not seize Latimer, they unnerved his captors. When abolitionist lawyers obtained a continuance of several weeks, the judge placed Latimer in the custody of James Gray, stipulating that he stay in Boston while the case proceeded. This apparent victory unnerved the Virginian. He understood that the crowds in the streets were determined to free Latimer, and he could see only one practical option. As Gray's lawyer put it, "To attempt to keep Latimer in the city in any other place than the jail, was to raise at once a signal for riot, if not bloodshed," as his supporters would surely break down the door of any less secure facility.[113] So Gray persuaded the city jailor, Nathaniel Coolidge, to continue holding Latimer for him.

The use of a public facility as a private slave jail brought still more people to Latimer's defense. White antislavery activists helped circulate petitions calling on the sheriff to dismiss Coolidge for improperly holding Latimer in the city lockup. These efforts drew the support of suddenly

indignant white citizens, including many not previously prominent as abolitionists.[114] Three young men of upper-class families started a newspaper
to draw attention to the controversy, the *Latimer Journal and North Star*.[115]
Pressures now converged on the jailor and on his elected superior, the
Suffolk County sheriff, that went far beyond the shouts and petitions of a
suspect minority.

The mobs compelled the court to station police officers in the jail yard
for every hearing. Latimer's lawyer, who also served as counsel to those accused of interfering with the constable, then announced his plan to call
Latimer as a witness in their trials as well. This meant that Latimer's captors would have to repeatedly haul the fugitive back and forth between
his cell and the courthouse, each time running a gauntlet of outraged and
potentially violent protestors. On November 18 jailor Coolidge, now no
doubt under considerable pressure from his superiors, capitulated. He
declared that after the next time Latimer left the jail he could not be
brought back. Gray's heart must have sunk: he knew that without walls
and bars it would be impossible to keep the determined black citizens of
Boston from freeing George Latimer. He promptly offered to free Latimer for what must have seemed the bargain price of eight hundred dollars.
This concession further emboldened Latimer's defenders, who began to
press harder, suggesting that they would pay less, or nothing at all. Cutting
his losses in this most inhospitable slave market, Gray quickly accepted
a payment of four hundred dollars collected by an abolitionist minister.
George Latimer was free.[116]

In the wake of Latimer's release, the victors followed up on their earlier demands by initiating a "Latimer and Great Massachusetts Petition"
for a new state personal liberty law.[117] Here the alliance with antislavery
whites made an enormous difference. The "Latimer Committee" that had
produced the *Latimer Journal and North Star* recruited white citizens to
circulate what became a "monster petition," ultimately bearing more than
sixty-five thousand signatures of Massachusetts men and women.[118] The
petitions, pasted end to end and rolled together, resembled a small barrel;

their presentation to the legislature by representative Charles Francis Adams caused a sensation. The state representative's father, former president John Quincy Adams, introduced a petition of comparable girth to the U.S. Congress, calling for the repeal of the federal Fugitive Slave Law of 1793.

The Fugitive Slave Law was too important to the national compromise over slavery to be repealed, but the Massachusetts legislature was not hog-tied by sectional considerations. On March 24, 1843, an "act further to protect personal liberty"—known popularly as the Latimer Law— prohibited Massachusetts judges from hearing cases under the Fugitive Slave Law, forbade law officers from taking part in the arrest of persons claimed as fugitives or from lodging them in public buildings, and established penalties for violations, including removal from office.[119] The state would not lend its aid to the hunters of the runaway slave. Over the next two decades the Latimer Law would become the model for similar efforts elsewhere.[120]

Even before the Latimer Law, William Nell and his allies had loudly reminded the state legislature of black seamen's rights under Article IV of the U.S. Constitution.[121] The following year Massachusetts sent two agents south to determine how many such men were being held, and to bring suits for their freedom.[122] That was still in the future; already, though, their victory in what became known as the "Latimer War" revealed how far "colored citizens" had developed their resources of organization, protest, and alliance since David Walker's untimely death. Through their independent mobilization and their interracial alliances, black activists made antislavery a means as well as an end: a way to free fugitives, to win laws securing their own liberties, and to demonstrate that although they were few in number and humble in station, they could play important roles in struggles whites were accustomed to thinking of as their own.

THE EDUCATION OF HENRY BOWDITCH

The relationship between black activists and the growing array of white antislavery allies remained complex. Garrison and a few other white abolitionists might insist that their purpose was full and equal citizenship without regard to race, but in practice they focused most of their efforts on abolishing slavery. For most other white abolitionists, equal citizenship was hardly thinkable. Even in the midst of the Latimer War, therefore, a gulf yawned between black and white activists' explanations of what was at stake. The fate of a fugitive hit black Bostonians literally where they lived; they issued a "Declaration of Sentiments" that lingered over the particular injuries George Latimer had endured during his arrest and imprisonment. They made the man himself a central figure in their debates, and adjourned their meeting "subject to the call of Latimer."[123] White Bostonians, meanwhile, moved George Latimer to the edge of the stage, focusing instead on the things that mattered to them: their nation, their city, or themselves. Sometimes they explicitly forswore any particular concern for their black neighbors. "*We* do not exist therefore out of compassion for Latimer, but out of compassion for this community," wrote one of the *Latimer Journal*'s editors.[124] They struck blows for liberty, not for Latimer or his people.

The *Latimer Journal* chased even empathy down a different road than black activists might have wished. That Latimer was a "very light mulatto" mattered as the newspaper warned of the literal and figurative enslavement of white Northerners.[125] Slavery, in the form of James Gray and his agents, had invaded Massachusetts and "seized on one of our inhabitants, ay, WHITE [in] color, and dragged him without warrant to [pri]son."[126] The paper warned that the same principle allowing Latimer to be captured for another individual's profit would allow a white woman to be captured for "lust"; one article imagined an unscrupulous white Virginian who "fixes his eye on any darkly colored woman whose poverty has rendered her obscure and friendless" and "swears she is his slave." What power would Massachusetts have, under current law, to prevent him from taking her to Virginia? What prevented any slave-state visitor from turning free but friendless people into "The White Slaves of the North"?[127] The Latimer case exposed "the insecurity of the liberty of all of us" and "the fate of several hundred of the colored population of this city and State, who are fugitives seeking a shelter, and perhaps of thousands more who were born and bred here," as well as "the fate of man[y] a stranger of *white* complexion, who has no *free papers* with him, and who may feed the malice, cupidity, or lust of some kidnapper."[128]

This focus on what slavery and slaveholders might do to white people and their liberties echoed over the next decades. For many white abolitionists, too, a preoccupation with black people's suffering, degradation, emancipation, and uplift fit into broader ideas about the nature and perfectibility of society in general, often in ways that had little to do with the needs of actual African Americans.[129] The problem of slavery as a human institution remained abstract, especially compared to what they saw as the slaveholders' corrupting effect on white Northern society and government. Pushing actual slaves to the side, they worried about the erosion of their own liberties and the secret plottings of slaveholders and proslavery politicians—a sinister force they dubbed the "Slave Power."[130]

In the days before Latimer's ransom, when it seemed likely that the fugitive would be returned to slavery in Virginia, the *Latimer Journal* satirically proposed a parade to celebrate the occasion. The city marshal and the police would march "in the livery of their master," slavery. Next would come the city government officials "with ropes around their necks," the clergy who would not read the Latimer petition to their congregations, and the morally bankrupt merchants and shipowners of the city, "their eyes bandaged with cotton, and their mouths stopped with sugar and tobacco." Finally came Latimer himself, in irons, with an honor guard of all the city's past Fourth of July orators. Through the middle of the procession would move "His Majesty," James Gray, whose property rights as a slaveholder had trumped all else in Boston. At the conclusion of the parade, at the dock, the mayor would prostrate himself and present his neck to the "king's" foot, the American flag would be raised on the ship's mast, and Latimer would be sailed off to slavery to the sound of cheers and a salute from Bunker Hill.[131] The city's wealth, history, piety, and liberty would be perverted, self-government and revolutionary freedom curdled to obeisance and servility. Latimer's liberation, by contrast, was a vindication of the city, and of the morally courageous residents who rescued it from the shame of such a spectacle.[132]

Henry Ingersoll Bowditch, one of the editors of the *Latimer Journal*, represented the army of benevolent-minded white Americans who stood beyond Garrison and the close circle of committed white abolitionists. These were young white men and women whose spiritual and social yearnings led them to commit themselves to uplifting the less fortunate—the "benevolent empire," some called them. Bowditch, the son of a renowned mathematician, spent several years in Paris training as a physician before returning to Boston in the mid-1830s. He quickly immersed himself in charitable activities, tending patients in the city hospital's charity ward and teaching a Sunday school class for poor children at the Warren Street Chapel. He seemed destined for a life of distinction, refinement, and good works, the sort of person for whom the phrase "noblesse oblige" entered the American lexicon.

Few of the people in Bowditch's orbit would have called themselves abolitionists, but the emergence of an interracial abolition movement in the 1830s and 1840s brought some of them into their first sustained contact with African Americans in any relationship other than that of employer and employee. Teaching Sunday school, caring for the sick and aged, promoting temperance, these white men and women took their first hesitant steps into homes that appalled them, sometimes in the neighborhood some of them no doubt knew as "Nigger Hill."[133] Benevolent activities, taken by themselves, did not force whites to step outside a familiar conversation in which free blacks were wards of a white community that had no choice but to look after them. They saw themselves as blacks' defenders and benefactors, not their peers. But antislavery sometimes forced them into situations of proximity and even intimacy with black citizens. The Latimer War and the crisis over slavery's expansion during the following decades drew many more whites into meaningful contact with the city's black activists.

The Garrison mob of 1835 recruited Henry Bowditch to abolitionism. Like many of his peers, he had grown up idealizing Massachusetts as the cradle of American liberty; he was shocked to discover that it often excluded not only blacks, but also abolitionist whites. During the attack on Garrison, Bowditch approached a city official and volunteered to help put down the mob, only to discover that the man had no plans to protect the abolitionists' free speech and indeed sympathized with the mob. Bowditch "left him with utter loathing," vowing, "'I am an Abolitionist from this very moment, and to-morrow I will subscribe for Garrison's 'Liberator.'"[134]

Henry Ingersoll Bowditch
Courtesy of the Massachusetts Historical Society

Over the next few years, Bowditch came to grips with the pervasive exclusion of black Bostonians, and with antislavery ideas. He threatened to quit his hospital when it tried to exclude black patients, successfully forcing a reversal of the policy. He resigned from the Warren Street Chapel because it allowed Sunday school teachers to segregate their classes and because its directors, offended by a speech in which he had denounced national Whig leader and slaveholder Henry Clay, denied him permission to host antislavery lectures.[135]

This principled combat among upper-class white men did not press Bowditch to feel more than outrage, defiance, and satisfaction. The Latimer War, however, cast him into collaboration with black Bostonians whom, in principle, he accepted as colleagues and equals. Bowditch's practical reckoning with his abstract commitment to equality came with shocking abruptness.

At the height of the Latimer War, Bowditch attended a public meeting featuring Frederick Douglass, then emerging as a leading antislavery orator. Meeting Douglass for the first time shortly afterward, Bowditch impulsively invited the fugitive to dinner in his rooms, and together the two men set off down the street. This was something rare under the Boston sun: a moment in the interracial antislavery alliance when invocations of equal political citizenship and defenses of an embattled people seemed to blossom into a spirit of fellowship.

For Douglass, as for African Americans throughout the free states, an invitation such as Bowditch's was rare indeed. To be approached by a wealthy and accomplished young physician who had enlisted in the cause, to be invited back to dine in his rooms, to walk together with him—perhaps arm in arm, and definitely down Washington Street—all of this was as unexpected as it was delightful. Four decades later Douglass still held the day dear, reminiscing publicly that "[t]he home of Dr. Bowditch . . . gave me the first shelter I received in this city."[136] What Douglass remembered was his reception as a guest in Bowditch's home: a warm, intimate association that moved beyond formal equality. The two men's separate descriptions of the day show that they shared a series of moments as respectable, even leisured men, entitled to make and accept social appointments, walk together down a city street, and be served together in the privacy of a gentleman's quarters. It mattered to Douglass. An African American reporter who witnessed Douglass's 1886 recollection of the moment described the reunion between Bowditch and Douglass that night as "affectionate in the extreme."[137]

But what Bowditch remembered about the day was his terror. Without fully considering the implications, he had invited a black man to dine with him. Before he knew it they were walking side by side down a public street where anyone might see them. This was deep water for the white doctor, and cold. Bowditch was normally an energetic, gregarious man, apt to stop in the street to tell a friend a story, then bound off to his next engagement. But not on this day.[138] The promenade instead became a harrowing rite of passage. "It is useless to deny that I did not like the thought of walking with him in open midday up Washington Street," Bowditch later wrote. "I *hoped* I would not meet any of my acquaintances." As soon as they turned onto that thoroughfare, though, they met a woman Bowditch knew, and, moreover, one who had previously signaled her disapproval of the doctor's abolitionist leanings. What could Bowditch do? He bowed graciously, "as if I were 'all right,'" but received a look in return that told him "she thought me 'all wrong.'"

If Douglass noticed Bowditch's discomfort, he made no mention of it, though he did later note that "[t]he time was, when I walked through the streets of Boston, I was liable to insult, if in company with a white person."[139] But perhaps his consciousness of the woman's dismay was overpowered by his awareness of how bravely Bowditch responded. Disregarding that glare of disapproval somehow released the young doctor. It was "somewhat like a cold sponge bath,—that Washington Street walk by the side of a black man,—rather terrible at the outset, but wonderfully warming and refreshing afterwards!" The warmth came from the conquest of fear—the pride that, as Bowditch put it, "*I did not skulk.*" For this, he thanked God for "giving me a love of freedom, and something like a conscience." The warmth also came from the knowledge, gained only later, of his companion's gratitude: "Beautiful to me seems now the act, inasmuch as it helped to raise a poor down-trodden soul into a proper self-appreciation."[140] Douglass certainly did not need Bowditch's invitation to properly appreciate his own gifts; he would soon chafe under the "guidance" of Garrison and other white abolitionists. But Bowditch must have shared his table more freely than his condescension, for Douglass remembered the event only as a happy one.[141]

Bowditch's initial move toward the warmer sense of belonging sought by the "colored citizens" captures both the power and the limits of that project. The "terrible" quality of the initial immersion passed. Bowditch went on to a lengthy career in the service of antislavery and racial equality. He spoke to William Nell's young men's literary society, joined the Boston School Committee as a foe of segregation, and mounted hopeless campaigns for office under antislavery banners. He was never again afraid to walk with Douglass. In 1844 the two men marched literally arm in arm when the doctor served as marshal of an August 1 celebration at Hingham. These anniversaries of British West Indian emancipation drew increasingly large and integrated audiences.[142] In places with particularly strong traditions of independent black self-organization, such as New Bedford, August 1 was primarily a black community celebration.[143] But there were also signs of mutual recognition: sometimes whites organized August 1 celebrations only to call them off so as not to interfere with already scheduled black-organized festivities.[144] And sometimes these festivals brought the whole array of abolitionist-minded Bay Staters together, at least for a day. Garrison's *Liberator* trumpeted the 1844 procession's egalitarian democracy: "[Y]oung and old, rich and poor, male and female, mingled with harmony and pleasure."[145]

Now emancipated from his uneasiness with Douglass, Bowditch enjoyed the occasion, but he continued to find it unsettling to be part of a "mixed party." Indeed, the honored ceremonial guest was strikingly attentive to the event's juxtaposition of the respectable—a category which for Bowditch now emphatically included Douglass—with the obscure, absurd, and discomforting. As the doctor and the now famous fugitive led the Suffolk County delegation, Bowditch reported to his wife, they were immediately followed by "four fat black women."[146] Considering that as many as six thousand people were present at Hingham that day, this gratuitous observation stood in dramatic contrast to the social niceties Bowditch elsewhere cherished.

The rest of the day forced a more extended combat between Bowditch's earnestness and his discomfort and revealed the social geography of this fragile interracialism. On the way back from Hingham, the ferry carrying the party ran aground. The captain told the many hundreds of passengers, most without a berth or even a seat, that they would be stranded there until the next morning's high tide. As night fell, the usual codes of transportation etiquette gave way to the intimacy of lodging, and to contrasts that Bowditch described simply as "ludicrous." He reported elegantly dressed white women sitting next to others "of every hue and color"— though the latter, he noted seriously, "behaved much better than their whiter companions."

Bowditch seemed not quite sure how to respond to this "heterogeneous mass of human beings." At moments he simply stood outside it all, a detached observer. As the night went on, though, he threw himself into the complicated social world of the boat, finding comfort in his role as a cultured gentleman. He acted his part just as convincingly as he had on his first walk with Douglass: he spent the night making jokes for the benefit of fellow passengers, then improvising chairs for female passengers, then finally restraining an overly "antic spirit of merriment" that came over some of the male passengers. At one point some of the rowdies somehow went so far past the bounds of gentlemanly propriety that Bowditch "rushed into the crowd and caught hold of two or three of the most conspicuous and told them I was ashamed of them as men and abolitionists."

Elsewhere on the boat men made speeches, and Frederick Douglass debated the church with the independent minister James Freeman Clarke.

Bowditch was not alone in being peculiarly moved by the unexpected moment of interracial community: when breakfast time came, the giddy party fell into a round of puns in which they discussed the meal as if it were the subject of a formal meeting. Garrison "laughed till he cried," and even Douglass was so caught up in the spirit of the moment that he "rose to a *pint* of order."[147] At other times and places, black and white stood at a distance forged by history and reinforced by prejudice. Here, forced together by circumstance, they found a way to belong to the same community. Even dead metaphors can sometimes draw breath: for a few accidental hours, they were all in the same boat.

3.

Our Unfinished Church

For one former slave, Lewis Hayden, the encounter with interracial antislavery proved both transcendent and life changing. He was not present that August night in 1844 when the ferry ran aground, for he was still in slavery in Kentucky with his wife, Harriet, and their son, Jo. It was a year later, as a fugitive slave on his first visit to Boston, that Hayden felt the power of black and white souls together committing themselves to human freedom. A large antislavery convention was already well under way when a minister announced that the fugitive Lewis Hayden, a featured speaker, could not be found, and that his former owner had been seen in the city.[1] Outraged determination welled up from the large crowd, and the presiding officer told the assembly that a slave catcher with "any design of interfering with the personal liberty of Mr. Hayden" ought to take out a life insurance policy. Finally, someone located Hayden and brought him up on the stage to reassure the audience that he had not been captured.[2] What the fugitive saw and heard from that vantage point— "thousands of men and women assembled to see what could be done" for his enslaved comrades, and their "expressions of sympathy and encouragement" for him in this moment of peril—moved him deeply. Perhaps only someone who knew the sting and ache of a life of rejection and subordination could appreciate the moment as Hayden did. Looking out over the zealous crowd now mobilized in defense of his freedom, he felt "for a time that I was in Paradise."[3]

For Hayden, as for all people unlearning the habits and expectations of enslaved life, few things mattered more than the sense of being acknowledged, accepted, respected, and included. Slavery violently sundered the ties of family and shadowed even sacred institutions with oppression and fear. It denied the enslaved the right to read, to share their thoughts without fear of retaliation, or to enter in any direct way into public affairs. Every meaningful form of belonging was clandestine, illegal, or dangerous. Hayden experienced all of this intimately during the years before his escape, and it shaped his life in freedom. It deepened the joy he took in his individual freedom, but also in the ties of family and spiritual community, and the sense of engagement in a project of transformation that was more transcendent than personal.

Hayden's passage from slavery to freedom was followed by a life spent struggling to make that freedom live up to the promise of his early tastes of "paradise"—a world of common struggle against slavery in which racial hierarchy seemed to dissolve into human unity and affection. At moments he and other "colored citizens" succeeded. The accidental, transient world of the Hingham ferry was not the only place where black and white men and women could find moments of common purpose, even joy. Particularly for people born and raised in bondage, such moments could be both breathtaking and inspiring. They invigorated the campaigns of the "colored citizens," reminding them that "entire enfranchisement" was more than a matter of law and offering them a hint of what David Walker's "happy country" might look like.

Yet the conditions of black freedom—the economic hardship, the insults of Northern Jim Crow, and the condescension of white "friends"—

taught Hayden to temper his yearning for a community with a more pragmatic spirit. Black activists, whatever the circumstances of their birth and upbringing, sooner or later came to understand that most of the opportunities for spiritual and emotional communion that appeared would be imperfect. Not every victory needed to provide transcendence; while Hayden and his comrades spoke in the language of millennial transformations, they lived in a world of human agency, one where progress was possible but not preordained. Neither God nor Garrison would rescue them.

The journey of the Hayden family out of slavery sheds light on how black activists negotiated the evolving face of white people's antislavery. Antislavery whites engaged in bitter struggles over doctrine and strategy, pitting Garrison and the other early allies of the AAS against a variety of opponents, some of whom saw electoral politics as the best battleground against slavery. Various factions in these conflicts sought to enlist the moral authority of black activists, but as time went on "colored citizens" resisted signing any exclusive ideological contracts. It was not an accident that few people in the mid-nineteenth century meant the term "abolitionist" to include black activists; while African Americans played critical roles in all kinds of antislavery organizations, they were neither confined within nor defined by the ideological struggles that racked white-led antislavery debates and organizations. They cherished both the utopian aspirations and the pragmatic politics of the antislavery project and could not imagine doing without either one. Lewis Hayden rejected demands, mainly from white abolitionists, that he choose between principle and pragmatism. This pragmatic position would become almost universal among black activists in the years to come, for their project of citizenship was too large to honor orthodoxy. Hayden's first years in freedom therefore help explain how the "colored citizens" found their way into white-dominated party politics without abandoning the alliances they had made in the 1830s.

The Haydens' passage also provides a rare window into the more personal dimensions of becoming a "colored citizen." Just below the surface of black activists' many steadfast declarations of their purpose and commitment lay doubts and fears, rooted in their comparative poverty and lack of education. Hayden's dramatic rise from slave to citizen, and later to statesman, was often a bumpy road. Along with intimations of "paradise" came moments of anger, frustration, and despair. Some of these were born of his own limitations; others stemmed from the harshness of the free-labor world, and the sometimes pitiless calculations of his own white allies. The civic education of Lewis Hayden in his first years in freedom exemplifies not only the possibilities but also the pitfalls and compromises awaiting a would-be "colored citizen."

"TORE FROM ME MY WIFE AND CHILD"

Slavery taught Lewis Hayden that the most intimate ties could be severed in an instant. He was born in Lexington, Kentucky, in 1816, to an enslaved woman named Millie, whom he described as "very handsome . . . of mixed blood—white and Indian," with "long straight black hair." Her husband, Lewis's father, belonged to a different owner, who had broken up that marriage by moving himself and his enslaved property away. Millie and Lewis's owner, a Presbyterian minister named Adam Rankin, expressed no greater interest in slaves' bonds of family and affection; it was said that he had preached "that there was no more harm in separating a family of slaves than a litter of pigs."[4]

Indeed, Rankin soon sold Millie, with disastrous consequences. The man who bought her did not value her skills as a milkwoman; he had first approached her with "proposals of a base nature." When she refused his overtures, he simply bought her. But despite the law of slavery, which made the rape of an enslaved woman by her owner no crime at all, he could not have his way. With the "high spirit" Hayden attributed to her Indian heritage, she refused "to live with this man, as he wished." She had no legal right to refuse, and so like any unwilling or insubordinate slave she was jailed, flogged, and subjected to various punishments "so that at last," as

Hayden recalled, "she began to have crazy turns." Hayden did not say directly that his mother was raped, but his explicit comparison of her to the figure of Cassy, the enslaved woman in Harriet Beecher Stowe's novel *Uncle Tom's Cabin* who is sexually pursued and raped by white men, strongly suggests this was his meaning. Following his mother's brutal treatment, he explained, she tried to take her own life at least twice, with a knife and with a noose.

While jailed for her disobedience, Hayden's mother talked incessantly of Lewis and her other children. The jailer suggested to her former and current owners that a visit to those children might calm her, and so Millie came briefly back to her old home. Hayden remembered coming home to Rankin's property, unaware that his mother was there, and his surprise at finding her in one of the slave cabins. The sight of her son did not calm Millie at all. "She sprung and caught my arms, and seemed going to break them, and then said, 'I'll fix *you* so they'll never get you!' I screamed, for I thought she was going to kill me; they came in and took me away. They tied her, and carried her off." Hayden was no more than eight years old.

This was not the last time Hayden saw his mother, and it may not have been the worst. Later, "[s]ometimes, when she was in her right mind, she used to tell me what things they had done to her." But she survived her ordeal. She was soon sold "for a small sum," and she married again and raised more children. Then her new husband "either died or was sold"— Hayden could not remember which, and since in terms of human relationships they often amounted to the same thing, it hardly mattered. Sold once again herself, Millie by sheer chance wound up near her first husband, Lewis's father. That man too had formed a second family, but he and Millie "came together again, and finished their lives together." Their good fortune was likely someone else's tragedy, but it was nearly enough to save her. "My mother almost recovered her mind in her last days," Hayden recalled.

Within a few years, Hayden lost the rest of his family. Rankin, deciding to follow the Lord's call to Jerusalem, sold off most of his slaves including all of Hayden's brothers and sisters. Watching them on the block, being auctioned off one by one, each to different owners, young Lewis imagined for a moment that his owner might spare him, and even take him to a place where he could obtain his freedom. Instead, his master traded him for a pair of carriage horses. "How I looked at those horses, and walked around them, and thought for *them* I was sold!"[5]

All of this took place in and around the small but comparatively cosmopolitan entrepôt of Lexington. Like many urban slaves, Lewis and the people he knew did not mainly work in the fields; instead, they played important roles in the mercantile and manufacturing world of the upper South. His mother had been a milkwoman in a dairy; his father worked in a bagging factory.[6] After being sold by Rankin, Hayden traveled the state in the service of his new master, a peddler of clocks. As his owner greased his sales pitch with engaging conversation, and as the pair passed through inns and taverns, the young man listened and learned. At some point, he even taught himself to read from newspapers and the Bible. While William Nell considered the injustices of the Boston school board and watched his father and the others observe the signing of the antislavery charter, Lewis Hayden was gaining a very different education.

Slavery was a normal part of Hayden's world, but he, like many enslaved people, developed an antislavery consciousness that matured into a critique of the system as a whole. Peering through slaveholders' scrim of paternalist self-justification and self-congratulation, he began to understand that no master, no matter how kind or indulgent, could protect enslaved people's families and communities from the ravages of the market. "Intelligent colored people in my circle of acquaintance," he explained, "*felt no security whatever for their family ties.*" Those belonging to wealthy men might imagine themselves safe, but "those of us who looked deeper" understood that appearances were deceiving and wealth evanescent. A market crash or a marriage, a death or simply a whim, and a slaveholding family's human assets might be scattered to the four winds. "The trader was all around," Hayden realized, "the slave-pens at hand, and we did not know what time any of us might be in it." Some masters pretended it was otherwise, while others held out the prospect of sale to the rice swamps or cotton fields as a threat. And then there were those like Rankin, who professed not to care a whit what their slaves thought.[7]

Hayden deduced the nature of slavery not just from observation, but from repeated, searing experience. When he grew to manhood, Lewis married Esther Harvey, the property of a Lexington merchant, and they had a child. Slave marriages, though, carried no legal weight. Before long Harvey's master sold the mother and child to the Kentucky political giant Henry Clay, a former secretary of state, U.S. senator, and speaker of the House of Representatives. Hayden was able to maintain contact with Esther, for soon she was pregnant again with another of their children. This infant died soon after its birth, about which tragedy Hayden (in typical nineteenth-century form) said very little. This was but a prelude to the greater loss to come. Just three weeks later Clay sold Esther Harvey and the couple's surviving son to a trader "to go down the river"—down the Ohio and Mississippi Rivers, that is, to the vast acres of cotton land opening up in 1830s Mississippi and Alabama.[8] Esther came to Lewis as he worked, bringing him the news that "tore from me my wife and child."[9] "I have not seen or heard from either since," Hayden wrote.[10] The memory was almost too painful to touch. "I have one child who is buried in Kentucky," he reflected in 1853; "that grave"—and the sweet hereafter to which the newborn babe had gone—"is pleasant to think of." But the other child was a different matter. "I've got another that is sold nobody knows where," Hayden managed, "and that I never can bear to think of."[11] Years later, he still ached for that first, lost family, "the wife of my youth, and my first born child," whom he imagined "dragging out a life on some tyrant's plantation . . . driven all day, under the lash, and then at night to be at the will of any demon or deacon that has a white face."[12]

Fortune did smile on Hayden from time to time. He was the kind of attentive and insightful servant who could make a gentleman's day go well, and in the hotels of the horse racing town this was a valuable talent. Like many skilled urban slaves, Hayden could produce the easiest profits for his owners by making his own labor arrangements and bringing his owners a fixed sum at regular intervals. This brought him an unusual degree of autonomy among enslaved people. It also brought him to his final place of work, at Lexington's Phoenix Hotel, which was where he met Harriet Bell. A housekeeper and child nurse in the household of Patterson Bain, Harriet was remembered as a trusted family favorite.[13] She and Hayden married about 1842. Unless they had known each other for many years before this, Harriet's son Joseph, born about 1839, was Hayden's stepson.[14]

Hayden's roles as a self-hiring worker, husband, and father shaped his bid for freedom. As for many slaves before him, including Frederick Douglass, the experience of earning and receiving a wage, only to hand most or all of it to another man, filled Hayden with a sense of grave injustice. And, like Douglass, he framed this understanding in the language of manly independence. He wanted to "crack his own whip," he later explained. First, he persuaded his owners to allow him to purchase his own freedom, saving the surplus he earned until he had enough. Soon, though, he began discussing the possibility of escape. To be free in the way he wanted, Hayden realized, he would have to have his family with him; a "freedom" that meant the agony of another separation would be no freedom at all. But this posed serious obstacles. The great majority of fugitives from slavery were men traveling without women and children: it was easier for one adult to evade detection than a pair or especially a group including children; too, enslaved black men were much more commonly dispatched on tasks and errands than women, making a male fugitive's presence on the road easier to explain. But Hayden apparently refused to consider any escape plan that did not involve his family.

Opportunity came in the form of two incognito abolitionists, the Ohio Methodist minister Calvin Fairbank, late of the interracial college at Oberlin, and the Vermont schoolmistress Delia Webster; both of them had come to Kentucky with the secret purpose of rescuing slaves. Fairbank undertook this work, he later said, at the urging of his black students.[15] It was the late summer of 1844, and Lewis Hayden hired out by the month at the hotel.[16] Fairbank had come to rescue a different fugitive, one who supposedly had money enough for Fairbank to hire a carriage and make the other arrangements for flight. That plan fell through, and Fairbank, his resources exhausted, was preparing to leave Kentucky without accomplishing a rescue. But Fairbank got wind of Hayden's interest in freedom and found an opportunity to interrogate him. "To my question: 'Why do you want your freedom?' he replied: 'Because I'm a man.'" This was all Fairbank needed to hear. "I was deeply interested in him, and at once began to plan a way for his escape."[17] Fairbank must have similarly inspired Hayden's trust, since Hayden supported him during September, at least, on the money he had saved toward the purchase of his and his family's freedom.[18]

The night they chose for the escape was propitious in many ways: in the chaotic last days of the September racing season, it was the final night of Hayden's hire at the hotel, making his departure expected. As if to please a Victorian novelist, it was also a stormy night. At Bain's place, Harriet passed Jo (as they called Joseph) to Lewis through a window. They also left with at least some property; Harriet had two trunks, a witness recalled, and these disappeared with her. She was sick with anxiety: another of Bain's slaves had "learned something" of their plans, and she worried that they would be betrayed.[19] But they pressed on. As arranged, the Haydens met Fairbank, Webster, and an enslaved driver named Israel on the outskirts of town. With Jo hidden beneath the carriage and Lewis and Harriet's faces bleached with flour—a crude expedient that would deceive a person only glancing briefly into a passing coach—they set off for the Ohio River. Once across the river in Ohio they headed rapidly north, finally reaching the safety of British Canada. Fairbank and Webster returned to Kentucky to throw off suspicion, but in the meantime their abolitionist identities had been ferreted out. For their role in the Haydens' escape they were arrested, tried, and convicted; although Webster was able to get free, Fairbank was sentenced to fifteen years.[20]

"OUR UNFINISHED CHURCH"

From the safety of British Canada, Lewis Hayden reflected on what a life in freedom might mean. Following the course of a number of other fugitives, he expressed these in a letter to Lewis Baxter, his last owner. Hayden could read, but he could write barely if at all at this early point in his freedom, so he dictated a letter indicting the "robbing & crushing slavery" that had denied him a proper education, leaving him a schoolboy at twenty-eight and requiring him to articulate his thoughts through an amanuensis. His son, he promised, would not suffer this lack: he too was already at

Lewis Hayden as his own master
Courtesy of the Ohio Historical Society

school, where he would gain the ability to "weild his own pen at the instance & impulse of his own swelling soul." This was part of the grand
project he had begun, "to be my own master & manage my own matters &
crack my own whip."[21] There were many forms of mastery to achieve.

Lewis and Jo Hayden attended school over the next few years, but Harriet Hayden apparently did not; indeed, she did not learn to write until
twenty years later. The reason her literacy seemed less important to the
family, like the reason she is so much harder to trace throughout most of
her life, lies in Hayden's response to Fairbank's question—"Because I'm a
man"—and in the way that answer instantly caused Fairbank to recognize
a person worth helping.

By "man" Hayden did not mean simply "human being." To be a
"man" in mid-nineteenth-century America was to be self-owning and self-
directing. It implied the capacity and the determination to protect one's
autonomy and one's dependents. Asked the same question by Fairbank,
Harriet Hayden could have responded, "Because I'm a woman," but this
would not have carried the same set of connotations; to most listeners, such
a statement would have meant not that she was willing to fight and die for
her freedom, but that she sought Fairbank's help to protect her children,
or her virtue. Women were beginning to challenge these assumptions, carving out roles for themselves as public speakers and confronting the laws
and customs that made them economically and politically subordinate to
husbands and fathers. In assemblies of "colored citizens," women spoke
and sometimes even voted.[22] But this was not yet the norm. For the time
being, freedom was men's to seize.[23]

Hayden's attack on slavery, in his letter to Lewis Baxter and in the
years to come, was about matters beyond the denial of self-ownership.
Nineteenth-century intellectuals imagined liberal freedoms as belonging to self-owning individuals, almost always implicitly or explicitly men.
These individuals entered society in order to safeguard their lives, property, and dependents, and they relied on the contract—an agreement between formally equal parties—as the essential instrument of negotiation

Harriet Hayden
Courtesy of the Ohio
Historical Society

and exchange.[24] Hayden certainly understood "freedom" to include some version of this security and equality, but he did not see it as only a matter of individual rights. Freedom for him meant acknowledgment of one's ties of family, friendship, and faith—of one's enmeshment in a social world that was about more than exchanges and profits.

As much as or more than for the feel of the whip handle, Hayden yearned for the hand of fellowship with other Christians. This, too, he accused Baxter and his other masters of denying him. The Reverend Rankin first taught Hayden to see white people's Christianity as essentially hypocritical and self-serving. A later master, another minister, acted "so very full of grace and Methodism" yet forbade Hayden to go to religious meetings himself and threatened to beat him if he did. "I thought if that was religion I would be off," Hayden mused.[25] Indeed, he found more warmth among the gamblers at the hotel, who "were very kind to me."[26] No wonder he later imagined the white fiend who might even now be abusing his lost first wife as "demon or deacon."

Hayden's freedom, and perhaps the example of a white Christian who was willing to sacrifice himself for it, finally allowed the fugitive to accept the Christian faith. In Canada, and then back on the U.S. side of the border in Detroit, the Haydens found communities where black and white women and men worshipped together.[27] Among their new friends in Detroit's growing black community was John Mifflin Brown, one of the former Oberlin students who had persuaded Fairbank to make his fateful trip to Kentucky.[28] Brown had founded a Sunday school among the congregants of a new African Methodist Episcopal (AME) church; now he was appointed pastor and set about organizing a congregation and raising funds for a church building.[29] Something about the spirit in Brown's endeavor kindled the fugitive's hopes, and Hayden plunged headlong into the project. In a letter seeking funds from potential benefactors, he described their work in rapturous terms: "All classes, Rich, poor, all Colors assemble together in our unfinished church. Prejudice vanishes. The true gospell gains ground Light breaking upon us. I yesterday met a Gentle[man] of wealth of the highest rank, who confessed his views were altered & his heart was drawn by the truth." To hear Hayden tell it, the church had worked near-miraculous changes in the social fabric of Detroit: "One would scarcely know the place by reason of the change from oppression to Liberty."[30]

Hayden's reference to "all Colors" assembled together in the Detroit church suggests the presence of a few white radicals searching for places of worship untainted by slavery. Garrisonians insisted that a true antislavery commitment required one to withdraw from fellowship with slaveholders—and this included membership in churches that welcomed slaveholders as members. People holding such beliefs attacked the established churches fiercely and vituperatively, and many sought the consolation and community of fellowship with like-minded souls. Some, like Hayden's "Gentle-[man] of wealth," sought fellowship with black congregants.[31]

Other white radicals founded new churches of their own, sometimes known as "free churches." Free churches were "free" both in the sense that they did not demand rent for pews, and in the sense that they were open to all comers without discrimination. Hayden described his Detroit AME church in similar terms, but most self-described free churches were mainly or entirely white in membership. Boston had several such congregations, led by renegade or dissident Unitarians, where rich and poor worshipped together, and where slavery and prejudice were at least formally forsworn.[32] Theodore Parker led a congregation of seven thousand men and women that included many leading Boston radicals. The minister who had paid four hundred dollars to free George Latimer, Reverend Nathaniel Colver, the next year founded the Tremont Temple, where a contemporary reported that "men of all ranks, conditions, and complexions, are on an equality."[33] Across town, Reverend James Freeman Clarke, who had debated religion with Frederick Douglass on the Hingham ferry, ran the antislavery Unitarian Church of the Disciples.[34]

Hoping to raise funds from this network of predominantly white antislavery churches, Lewis Hayden and John Mifflin Brown traveled to Boston in 1845. Despite early troubles that cast some doubt on their honor and credibility, the pair apparently succeeded and earned the gratitude of the Detroit congregants.[35] In seeking aid, Hayden also encountered some of the luminaries of Boston's white antislavery community. James Freeman Clarke gave Hayden a platform at his church and introduced the fugitive to important allies.[36] "When I was in slavery," Hayden told Clarke's congregation, "I used to say in the morning when I arose, 'I have a wife and child this morning, but they may not be mine tonight.'" He continued "until the audience was moved to tears."[37] Hayden's own "swelling soul" was reaching others in the mingled precincts of Christianity and abolition. No wonder the rousing defense of his liberty, offered by another group of whites on that Boston trip, moved him so.

Hayden found another kind of communion as well in those early years, one that put him in fellowship with many of the North's leading free black men. As he traveled the states from Detroit to Boston, he learned about Prince Hall and the brotherhood of Freemasonry. Like several generations of men before him, he was no doubt drawn to the promise of intimate association with other ambitious and energetic black men. We do not know precisely when Hayden was initiated into Freemasonry. During the years between 1845 and 1848 he and Harriet considered several homes, including Detroit, New Bedford, New York, and finally Boston. If one record is to be believed, in March 1845 he was already a Freemason in New York, taking part in the formation of a new statewide body.[38] In any case, no later than 1847—before his final relocation to Boston—he was a Master Mason, a fully vested member of the fraternity, and was playing a role in the order's most ambitious projects.

Hayden understood both Christianity and Freemasonry as sacred undertakings, and as institutions through which human agency did the work of higher powers. He once explained to a traveling slaveholder, who argued that God would free the slaves in his own time, that "he will most probably do this through the free agency of his children who have been blessed with a free gospel."[39] Although Hayden was a lifelong Christian who spoke feelingly of God's will, he put his spiritual energies to practical use mainly in the lodge, a project that spoke divine truths but sought paradise in this world rather than the next. For him, Freemasonry offered "the strongest possible ties known among men." The obligations Freemasons took to one another—to treat one another with brotherly love, to bring relief to one another's widows and orphans, and to deal honestly with one another—he considered "sacred" and "holy."[40] In other words, he saw God's work being accomplished in Freemasonry's growth and development.

Yet Freemasonry, like the Christian church, also bore witness to the power of white supremacy. Prince Hall's descendants were not recognized as Masons by the white brethren of Massachusetts or any other state. On rare occasions during the first half of the nineteenth century, white Masons raised a black man into Masonry, visited black lodges, or even accepted a black member, but over time these contacts all but ceased.[41] Instead, white Masons betrayed the ostensibly "cosmopolitan" order's precepts, denying the legitimacy of black Masonry in toto. Hayden, looking back into his own past, reported seeing traces of this degraded white Masonry shaping his own early life: the man who bought and so cruelly abused his mother was, he reported, "a member of the Masonic lodge" behind the college in Lexington.[42] Slavery and racial caste corrupted the most sacred institutions.[43]

THE WAR IN PARADISE

Hayden must have seemed one of the likeliest African American adherents to the Garrisonian faith. On his first trip to Boston, in 1845, Hayden met the white editor, who described him privately as "a rare young man" who "won the esteem and friendship of all with whom he has become acquainted." Garrison hoped the Hayden family would relocate to Massachusetts, for Lewis Hayden could be "made very serviceable to our cause."[44] Although the men and women of the Boston Clique epitomized the literary skill and training of which slavery had "robbed" him, Hayden seems to have found a way to engage them.[45] In a letter reporting on the good work Boston's aid had done for his church, he addressed even the formidable Maria Weston Chapman with earnest directness: "I am your brother," he wrote.[46] Eighteen months later he would be employed by their AAS as a paid lecturer.

Yet Garrison, Chapman, and the AAS would not be Hayden's only contacts among Boston's antislavery whites. Hayden also drew on a second stream of interracial fellowship and camaraderie—the very one that led him to the Boston stage in 1845. That audience was not composed of radicals from the Garrisonian abolitionist orbit. Instead, it was a meeting affiliated with a comparatively new political force on the national scene, the Liberty Party. Emerging at the end of the 1830s, the Liberty Party sought the end of slavery by electoral means. In 1840, it ran a national ticket headed by a repentant ex-slaveholder from Alabama, James G. Birney, as well as state and local candidates in many Northern districts.

The Liberty Party became a philosophical and tactical rival to the AAS, whose leaders took an absolutist position with regard to political or religious fellowship. Garrison and his allies argued that it was a sin to take part in any institution tainted by slaveholding or reliant on force. This meant disassociating themselves from churches that accepted slaveholders as members. It required them to support for office only candidates who would not swear loyalty to what they considered the proslavery Constitution of the United States—candidates, that is, who would rarely if ever be elected and could not serve at the federal level even if they were. By 1844 orthodox Garrisonians went further, declaring, "No Union with Slaveholders!" This became the virtual motto of the AAS, and its adherents meant it literally: the Constitution had been written as a proslavery document and remained so; until slavery was abolished, these "disunionists" vowed that the "Spirit of Truth" required withdrawing from that document's obligations. If that led to the destruction of the Union, so be it. So while the Liberty Party's call for abolishing slavery by legislation might strike many other Americans as radical, to Garrisonians the new party was from the outset compromised and indeed corrupt.

Liberty Party supporters, for their part, found seeds of antislavery in the same Constitution the Garrisonians reviled, and insisted that its tendency was toward liberty. The men who framed the document had barred slavery from the Northwest; its Fifth Amendment guaranteed "life, liberty, and property." Liberty men promised to end the federal protection of slavery in the capital and the territories—to accomplish the "divorce" of the federal government from the protection of slavery. More, in language that went to the heart of the project of the "colored citizens," they described the denial of rights and privileges to free blacks as "remnants and effects of the slave system." Their 1843 platform began with the resolution "That human brotherhood is a cardinal principle of true democracy."[47]

The Liberty Party's emergence was part of the anti-Garrisonian ferment that split the antislavery movement in two, leaving "old organization" Garrisonians in charge of the AAS and sending "new organization" folk to the newly formed American and Foreign Anti-Slavery Society, as well as to the Liberty Party.[48] By the early 1840s, "new" and "old" partisans were at war, each side enforcing its orthodoxies and rebuking apostates. After Henry Bowditch ignored Garrisonian strictures by making a donation to "new organization" minister Nathaniel Colver for the ransom of George Latimer, Edmund Quincy lectured him that he must choose sides: "[O]ne must be right & the other wrong, one must be a friend & the other an enemy of the slave—one is of Christ & the other of Belial. No man can serve them both."[49] "New organization" men returned the favor, accusing Garrison of identifying himself "with every infidel fanaticism which floats," often meaning women's rights, which they feared would discredit the entire antislavery cause.[50] Pragmatic yet idealistic activists such as Bowditch found the rigidity on both sides more than a little infuriating. When one Latimer War meeting began to dissolve in recrimination between adherents of the "new" and "old" organizations, Bowditch leapt to the platform to chastise the adversaries: "He had expected to meet a noble band of united hearts," he lectured them. "Now he was bowed down with shame."[51]

THE APPEAL OF ELECTORAL POLITICS

Lewis Hayden was among the many free African American activists who refused to become partisans in these internecine struggles. Hayden sought aid from Garrisonians and, as we have seen, caught Garrison's interest, but he also spoke at the Liberty Party meeting. Many of Hayden's sustained contacts in Boston were among the Garrisonians' rivals.[52] The possibility of wielding actual political power was too enticing for black activists to cast it aside in favor of the philosophical purity of nonresistance. Here, as in so many other ways, African Americans stood in a different relationship to American citizenship than their white allies. It was one thing to withdraw from a polity out of principle, as white Garrisonians chose to, but quite another to feel that one stood forever on the threshold of political citizenship. Not surprisingly, black activists sought to break down the barriers that kept them at the margins of electoral politics.

Interest in the Liberty Party flowed from a long and uninterrupted history of black men's electoral participation in Massachusetts. The fathers of several prominent Boston activists had campaigned for the Federalists in their communities. The Federalists' successors in the Whig Party sometimes openly appealed to the small black community to turn out for its candidates; in 1834 they held a Beacon Hill meeting for black voters at which both white politicians and influential black figures spoke.[53] Yet whatever Whig sympathies Nell and his friends might once have felt had been erased in 1841, when officials of that party barred them from President Harrison's funeral procession. In the ensuing election, some black men may even have cast protest votes for the Democrats, usually considered the more aggressively antiblack party.[54]

The arrival of a third-party alternative would have mattered little but for an oddity of Massachusetts electoral law in the 1840s, under which a successful candidate had to poll an absolute majority of the voters, not just a plurality. If no candidate won an outright majority, the election was repeated until someone did. This gave small blocs of voters and third parties unusual power, since by turning out in closely contested districts they could repeatedly deny election to either of the major parties, until one or the other decided to compromise with them. A comparative handful of voters, even black voters, might be able to exert some political power, and third parties could be small without being marginal.[55]

The Liberty Party drew in many black activists who were personally loyal to Garrison. In 1841 William Nell's good friend J. B. Sanderson mulled over the question of voting for the Liberty Party and worried, like a good Garrisonian, that it would hide the "moral beauty" of abolitionism "beneath the rubbish of corrupt political Party influences."[56] William Nell believed that politics corrupted the cause, but his views would soon shift, and in any case his purist position was far from universally shared. Many black leaders believed it to be "the duty of every lover of liberty to vote for the Liberty ticket," and some did.[57] Strong Liberty Party turnout in 1841 from the well-organized black community of New Bedford helped prevent either the Whig or the Democratic candidate for a local seat from achieving a majority.[58]

In the years just before Hayden arrived in Boston, the city's Liberty Party and Garrisonian partisans each sought to sway black activists. In the early 1840s white Liberty men such as editor Elizur Wright tried to re-create their New Bedford success on Beacon Hill, and black orators such as New York's Henry Highland Garnet addressed local meetings on the party's behalf.[59] The 1841 Boston city elections did not go well for the Liberty Party, but it achieved its best result in Ward Six, which mapped the north slope of Beacon Hill.[60] Nonetheless, the Liberty Party did not receive the support its leaders felt it deserved from black voters. Like the Garrisonians, Liberty Party organizers branded their opponents as hypo-crites and fools—in one case angrily charging Garrisonian orators Doug-lass and Remond with being Whig stooges, since their opposition to voting helped that party retain power.[61]

Nervous Garrisonians took the Liberty Party's bid for black support seriously. In the midst of one of the antislavery society's periodic financial crises, Maria Weston Chapman reluctantly urged her colleagues at the Anti-Slavery Society to keep William Nell—their sole black employee—on salary. Word that he had been given notice caused grumbling among black Bostonians, she wrote, and "Elizur Wright made a great handle of it, we heard, in getting votes for the Liberty Party in Belknap St.," the home of the Baptist church.[62] Even though the Garrisonians did not seek black votes, the allegiance of black activists ratified their antislavery as the genu-ine article. They could not bear to see this organizational energy and sym-bolic value directed toward the corrupt world of party politics.

Fond neither of slavery nor of the political compromises that sustained it, Lewis Hayden nevertheless claimed to have found antislavery politics compelling since childhood. Lexington, a gambling town close to the state capital at Frankfort, attracted more than its share of Kentucky politicians,

and Hayden, a valet to those men, paid close attention. He lay under a
buffalo robe, pretending to be asleep, while men read aloud an antislavery
speech by Congressman William Slade of Vermont; this, he told Liberty
Party gatherings, "opened a new world to his view." If there were places
where men who held such views were in power, then Hayden wanted to
be there as well—"to be where he could be somebody, and to put his wife
and child where they could be somebody."[63]

By the time he reached his twenties, Hayden was offering interpreta-
tions of the political world that belied his status as a slave. His quick mind
caught the attention of the brilliant and theatrical Kentucky Whig orator
Tom Marshall, who regularly employed him as a servant when he stayed in
Lexington.[64] But it did not do for a slave to understand too much. One day
Marshall, no doubt playing to a crowd, asked Hayden about his politics.
The politician may have considered the question absurd in itself, and designed it to provoke an unintentionally amusing answer from Hayden. Or
perhaps he hoped to engage Hayden in praise for the Whigs, ratifying
Marshall's view of himself and his party as benevolent. The Whigs were in
no sense an antislavery party—no party and no politician hoping to com-
pete in the South could be—but party leader Henry Clay was a leading
colonizationist; among white Southerners this was considered a more
flexible and humanitarian position, since it at least contemplated emancipation. Perhaps Marshall meant Hayden to say that he foresaw a free future for himself in Liberia, thanks to the farsighted policies of Henry Clay.

Hayden instead responded that he was a Democrat, an answer that
surprised Marshall. In the late 1830s and early 1840s, the period during
which this event must have taken place, the Democrats were well established as the party unequivocally committed to white citizenship and black
slavery. But when Marshall pressed for elaboration, no doubt still smiling,
what Hayden said must have chilled him. President Andrew Jackson,
Hayden explained, "put an end to the Bank of the United States." This
was true: Jackson vetoed the renewal of the bank's charter, effectively killing the institution. Hayden, though, was aiming at another point. When

the U.S. government withdrew its deposits from the bank, it helped set off a chain of events that led in 1837 to a broad financial panic, and a painful national depression, one that set men of commerce and industry back on their heels, and that put an end to the boom times in Alabama and Mississippi. By killing the bank, Hayden concluded, Jackson inadvertently "broke up the slave trade" that took so many black Kentuckians, including most of the people Hayden once called family, down the river. This answer revealed Hayden's powerful understanding of the forces that shaped his world, and beneath it all a profoundly antislavery consciousness. The joke was over, and with it Marshall's good mood. "Do you know what I'd do with you if I owned you?" the politician responded, the smile long gone. "I would send you down South and sell you."[65]

Hayden's knowledge of national politics and political economy was far from exceptional among enslaved men and women, particularly those who were literate or who lived in cities. Slaves listened carefully to their free owners and neighbors, and they passed political news on to one another, especially when it seemed to portend the coming of freedom. Their information was not always accurate. In 1800, for example, the slave rebel Gabriel based his plans on the theories that the merchants of Richmond, Virginia, would side with him against the rural slaveholding elite, and that French forces were poised to support his cause. But slaves' profound stake in events taking place in the wider political world sometimes made them surprisingly good analysts, as Marshall discovered to his dismay. Sometimes even their misunderstandings were prescient, as when slaves assembled secretly to discuss the likelihood of their emancipation if 1856 Republican presidential candidate John C. Fremont was elected, years before that man's party moved to do more than stop the expansion of slavery.[66]

A few years later, as Hayden savored his first months of freedom, he began to imagine a more immediate relationship to party politics. In the early letter to his former master, Hayden mapped his journey from Lexington slavery to Detroit freedom as a partisan passage into the Liberty ranks. Michigan was hardly an egalitarian commonwealth, but it was the adoptive home of Liberty leader James G. Birney. Hayden described his relocation from Clay's Kentucky to Birney's Michigan as a lightning bolt that transformed his political polarity. Previously, he claimed, he had electioneered for "the honorable Mr. Clay," but now that he was in "a Birney state" his Whig days were behind him. "The battery was so heavy charged and my exit so sudden as to shake all Whigism out of me," he wrote.[67] Perhaps Hayden was likening himself to another traveler, hit by a bolt of lighting on the road to Damascus and turned into a servant of God. In any case, Hayden already knew that there were whites who actually sought to use politics to make him free.[68]

His advocacy of the Liberty Party persisted past that first burst of enthusiasm for Birney. When he first rose to speak at Clarke's church that day in Boston, he met a young antislavery lawyer named John A. Andrew, a Liberty man and later the state's Republican governor, who became Hayden's closest white political ally.[69] In the years to come he addressed a Vermont Liberty convention, among many other explicitly political gatherings.[70] He told the editor of the Liberty Party's Boston newspaper that he hoped the friends of the slave would "be encouraged to persevere in talking, praying and voting for the slave . . ."[71] Perhaps most of all, he never forgot that the audience that sent him to "paradise" was a Liberty Party convention.

As the Haydens considered whether to move to Massachusetts, the question of voting may have loomed large. In fact, Lewis Hayden had already taken steps to secure himself the franchise elsewhere. In upstate New York, the eccentric antislavery philanthropist Gerrit Smith—another Liberty Party man—had begun distributing tracts of land to black New Yorkers. His hope was both to help lift them out of urban poverty and to provide them with the substantial taxable property requirement that New York state required of black voters. Hayden approached Smith about participating in this experiment in 1846. Smith initially turned him down, explaining that his offer was for New Yorkers only. The following year, though, the Haydens did apparently consider themselves New Yorkers; Lewis Hayden even represented the black Masons of New York at an important gathering in Boston.[72] Soon, Hayden came into the possession of his own "Smith lands," although there is no record that the Haydens ever settled on or even visited them.[73]

Far from choosing sides in the war among white antislavery folk, Hayden tried to sidestep the organizational schism by becoming ally and protégé of both factions. This refusal to choose flowed naturally from the broad change he imagined, in which both utopian hopes and pragmatic politics would play a role. Like so many others, he had looked into the eyes of William Lloyd Garrison—and the columns of his *Liberator*—and seen something rare: a whole-souled commitment to the full equality of the "colored citizens." So Hayden equivocated. In June 1847 he spoke before the Liberty Party's grand breakfast in Faneuil Hall; two months later he was lecturing in tandem with an orthodox AAS man.[74] His vision of himself as a free person and "colored citizen" allowed and perhaps even demanded both kinds of work.

From the outside, this refusal to commit to one side or the other could appear to be ignorance or faulty analysis. Garrison's private assessment of Hayden was that "[h]e needs to be more with us, fully to understand the position we occupy, in regard to Church and State." By this Garrison meant not the separation of those two entities, but the necessity of withdrawal both from churches that allowed slaveholders into their fellowship and from a constitutional order that protected the rights of slaveholders.[75] On one occasion, after delivering an AAS-sponsored lecture, Hayden told a white Garrisonian in attendance "that he felt himself unable to make such an exposition of the relationship of the Constitution and the Government of our country to that institution, as would be satisfactory to himself."[76] A white observer took this to mean that Hayden was intellectually or doctrinally out of his depth, but it seems likely that the fugitive spoke literally—he was genuinely conflicted about the question, and unwilling to make a definitive choice. Hayden had entered a thrilling new world in

which there were many ways to be part of something transcendently meaningful. He was as yet unwilling to give any of them up.

ALLIES AGAINST THE SLAVE POWER

Hayden imagined confronting slavery in yet another way. From his first
refuge in Canada in 1844, he pondered the neat piles of cannonballs the
British had stockpiled near the American border, probably a legacy of the
military conflict between Americans and Britons during the Canadian
Revolt of 1837. The British, Hayden well knew, had abolished slavery in
their West Indian possessions in 1838; the Crown also opposed the impending U.S. annexation of the slaveholding Republic of Texas. And so,
in Hayden's letter to his former master, the material evidence of imperial
preparedness for war prompted a sudden, militant fantasy. Recalling Lewis
Postlethwait, the slaveholder who had professed religion but forbade
Hayden to attend a prayer meeting, Hayden imagined this American joining a proslavery Texan army—and imagined himself enlisting in an antislavery British army that would fight in Mexico against them. If that were
to come to pass, "then I should perhaps meet with Capt Postlethwait"
again. Hayden relished the prospect. "I think such [a] one better prepared
to fight than pray," he informed his former master, "& so am I."[77]

He did get to fight, but not in the way he had imagined. The terrain on
which free blacks and Texans did battle that decade was not Mexico, but
American politics, whose landscape was radically altered by proslavery
expansionism. The annexation of Texas (1845) and the subsequent war
with Mexico (1846–1848) made it quite conceivable that American slavery
would soon extend into vast new territories. This caused a growing number of white Northerners to believe that the U.S. government was under
the control of the "Slave Power," a conspiracy devoted to slaveholders'
political, economic, and territorial ambitions at the expense of all else.[78]
The fear of slaveholder domination of the Union brought more Northern

whites into the antislavery fold than the call to sympathy with actual slaves
ever had.

Annexation and war in the interests of slaveholders caused some Northern Whigs and Democrats to rebel against the expansion of slavery, and
the major parties began to splinter over that question. Most dramatically,
in 1846 Pennsylvania Democrat David Wilmot inflamed the controversy
over the Mexican War by offering an amendment that would prohibit the
extension of slavery into any territory gained from the war.[79] To the shock
and dismay of slaveholders, the Wilmot Proviso gained overwhelming support among representatives in the states where slavery had faded or disappeared; it even passed the U.S. House before finally failing by a narrow
margin in the Senate. Fear of the Slave Power provided a rhetorical and
ideological bridge over old political divides. Over the next few years antiextension Whigs, Democrats, and Liberty men fumbled toward a political
embrace that would culminate in the rise of the Free Soil Party.

The rapid change in white Northern opinion braced black activists
as much as it alarmed proslavery forces. As recently as 1843, the Latimer
Law's minor adjustments to state law seemed a great triumph against slaveholding; by 1847, the Massachusetts legislature eagerly passed a resolution
calling the war with Mexico "wanton, unjust, and unconstitutional," a war
against liberty with the ultimate goal "of obtaining the control of the Free
States, under the constitution of the United States."[80]

Anti-Texas and antiwar activism in Boston drew black activists into
political coalition with whites who were neither Garrisonian purists nor
Liberty Party activists.[81] John A. Andrew and other antislavery figures such
as Charles Sumner, a young lawyer who could sometimes be found in political conversation with black Bostonians, finally abandoned their political homes in the Whig Party for a new "anti-extension" alliance.[82] These
new arrangements permitted mainstream white political figures to share
a Faneuil Hall stage with black activists; William Nell and Charles Remond
both took part in predominantly white meetings against the war with
Mexico.[83]

As hostility to the Slave Power grew, so did the circumstances that might bring black activists before largely white audiences. White antislavery groups of all kinds increasingly sought out former slaves and free blacks as symbols of their collective commitment. The abolitionists of the AAS had been pursuing this strategy since the late 1830s, when they began employing free black men such as Charles Remond as speakers. In the 1840s, predominantly white political meetings, such as the anti-Mexico gatherings in Faneuil Hall, brought a sprinkling of black activists to the platform as a way of expressing their opposition to the Slave Power and its ambitions, and in order to signal to more abolitionist whites that they might comfortably join this movement. More and more whites identified the fate of their own liberties with those of their black neighbors, and the millions of slaves they represented.

The AAS and other antislavery organizations saw ex-slave speakers as particularly important ambassadors, for they could represent the true, lived experience of slavery in ways that white audiences found persuasive. They employed a growing list of freeborn and ex-slave lecturers, including Douglass, Hayden, Henry Bibb, William Wells Brown, and many more. Listening to these black speakers and purchasing narratives of slavery allowed whites to signal their political and moral convictions. As these markets grew during the 1840s, so did the opportunities for black activists to make themselves heard and understood. Abolitionists and those sympathetic to the cause purchased fugitives' autobiographies such as Frederick Douglass's *Narrative*, published in 1845, and created a market for many more depictions of slavery. A few years later, *Uncle Tom's Cabin* became the bestselling American novel of the century.

But it was a complicated business, representing one's own experience while also meeting the demands of one's sponsors for a portrait of slavery both "authentic" and acceptable. Black speakers who impressed their audiences were scorned as impostors, since obviously no slave could speak so well.[84] White abolitionists even warned Frederick Douglass to keep "a little of the plantation" in his speech so that he not "seem too learned" to have actually been a slave. "Give us the facts," one admonished him. "We will take care of the philosophy."[85] If they did offer "philosophy," fugitives and free blacks speaking from AAS platforms were supposed to toe the disunionist Garrisonian line on the Constitution, as Lewis Hayden well understood.

What was more, a predominantly white movement, overseen by upper-class men and women and run largely on unpaid labor, seemed to regard these black speakers as auxiliaries to the work. When the AAS and other societies sent out lecturers, they generally paired a black speaker with a white one and paid the white lecturer more. Displays of autonomy or requests for more pay by black speakers could bring chilly refusals and sharp rebukes. Edmund Quincy's talent for invective against his factional opponents included epithets more ordinarily associated with abolition's enemies, as when he referred to black abolitionists he perceived to have overstepped their proper bounds as "unconscionable niggers."[86]

Many black lecturers chafed within these limits, but it was Frederick Douglass who got the first real opportunity to do something about it. In 1847, Douglass returned from a lecture tour in the British Isles with the resources to begin a newspaper of his own. Garrison and others, reluctant to see their most impressive fugitive writer and orator leave the fold, discouraged him from launching the *North Star*. For a time they believed they had succeeded. When Douglass finally announced his removal to Rochester, New York, to publish the weekly antislavery newspaper, they reacted as if betrayed. It was the beginning of a decade of bitter recriminations between Douglass and the white Boston leadership, a struggle that would ultimately pit black Bostonians against one another as well.

At the outset, though, the newspaper drew leading activists together. When Douglass founded the *North Star* as a national paper for black Americans, William Nell joined him in Rochester as the paper's publisher. The move offered Nell an opportunity to rise in the professions as some of his friends had begun to do. It may have seemed to promise the more comfortable living that had so far eluded him in Boston. Martin Delany, the fiery editor from Pittsburgh, also joined Douglass and Nell; Delany's dispatches from his travels across the North kept up a drumbeat of encouragement, criticism, and celebration of black achievements.[87]

Like Douglass, Delany, and Nell, Lewis Hayden sought to make a place for himself in the world of abolition. But Hayden's own rough beginnings on the antislavery circuit suggest the obstacles a fugitive could face in the white-dominated abolitionist world that the North Star implicitly challenged. As he feared, others discerned his educational limitations. When he first arrived in Boston in 1845, in company with another black man, James Freeman Clarke "chose the one he thought would make the best speech"—not Hayden, though Clarke quickly amended his initial evaluation after Hayden's appeal so moved his congregation.[88] Something about him in these early months and years bespoke hesitancy, or simply lack of education. The following year Garrison described Hayden as "an apt scholar, [who] has made very good progress in a short time"; sometimes, he gently added, Hayden struggled "to find language to express the facts of his history."[89] Still, the distance he had traveled since he crossed the river out of Kentucky in Reverend Fairbank's carriage could hardly be measured. In 1846 he followed Ralph Waldo Emerson on the platform at an August 1 celebration in Henry David Thoreau's grove at Concord, "stammering out touchingly," as the Liberator's correspondent put it, "that which none has power fully to utter, what a glorious thing liberty is."[90] Hayden must have kept company with such men with a mixture of elation and anxiety; since his first days in freedom, he had wondered whether he would ever catch up with freeborn people.[91]

But Hayden rapidly improved. At the 1847 New England Anti-Slavery convention he "made out very well," even emboldening a fellow fugitive, who had earlier faltered before the large assembly, to rise and try again.[92] Hayden must have been ecstatic to be selected as a lecturer by the American Anti-Slavery Society that fall. Paired with Erasmus Hudson, a white physician and fierce antislavery activist, he crisscrossed eastern and central New York.[93] The experienced white lecturer was to receive twelve dollars each week, Hayden twenty-five dollars per month.[94] From the standpoint of his white AAS employers and colleagues, Hayden was very much the junior partner. He was "a good fellow, improves, does good, helps some," read Hudson's cautious appraisal.[95]

Hayden and Hudson found themselves in the middle of an emerging struggle between rival antislavery bodies. The appearance of the *North Star* caused grave concern among the Boston managers of the AAS. Their newspapers survived only through contributions, and they worried that Douglass's new venture might absorb what abolitionist money was available.[96] So as Hayden and Hudson spoke to antislavery audiences across rural New York in the winter of 1847–1848, part of their job was to keep them loyal to Garrison, Boston, and the *Liberator*, and to prevent them from switching their allegiance to Douglass, Rochester, and the *North Star*. It was not yet an open war; too many close relationships and overlapping loyalties

Wendell Phillips
Courtesy of the Library of Congress

linked Douglass, Nell, and Delany in Rochester with Garrison, Chapman, and Quincy back in Boston. But tension enshrouded the rival camps. "I don't wish to do anything to alienate, or widen the breach if there is one," Hudson wrote to Wendell Phillips back in Boston.[97] Still, he proposed to take the contest to Douglass by lecturing with Hayden in the western counties of New York near Rochester: subscriptions to the AAS's *National Anti-Slavery Standard* were expiring in that region, and Douglass's crew might take the opportunity to redirect local subscription moneys to the *North Star*. Should he and Hayden go?[98]

Instead, Wendell Phillips informed the partnership that their agency had been terminated. They would not be sent to western New York; indeed, they would no longer be paid after the first of March. Given the precarious finances of the antislavery societies, the effort of mounting dueling teams of lecturers had exhausted everyone's treasuries. The AAS leadership reduced expenses by cutting short the subsidy to Hudson and Hayden; Charles Lenox Remond was similarly cut off sometime later in 1848—an event his employers in the western New York society described as a "painful necessity."[99] When Hudson read Phillips's letter dismissing Hayden, he protested on his own and Hayden's behalf—"He can't get home now, the lakes froze up, & he would be dropt a stranger & helpless"[100]—and begged the committee back in Boston to reconsider. But they held firm.

Lewis Hayden found himself suddenly without employment, five hundred miles from his family in Detroit, in the dead of a Northern winter. He had spent the equivalent of two months' wages setting up his family and equipping himself for the lecture season, and now the white abolitionists who held the purse strings pulled them tight. He lacked even the money to get home. He protested in his own labored hand, in waves of unpunctuated despair, recrimination, and defiance. When Phillips and the other AAS directors had recruited him, he wrote, they "did not know then what I was . . . did not know but what I was a second yourself." But how could he have been? Hayden angrily wondered. "[Y]ou all know it is not so you know it is me jest three years from slavery." He would try to make up the gap, for "if I am not Wendell Phillips now, it ought not appear what I shall be. . . . I shall do all I can," he promised, "to make myself a man."[101] In his early letter to his former master Hayden declared his resolve "to try how it will seem to walk about like a gentleman."[102] Now his home, and that vision of confident self-possession, both seemed suddenly far away.

Lewis Hayden's letter to Wendell Phillips, February 21, 1848
Ms Am 1953 [673], Houghton Library, Harvard University

PARADISE RECONSIDERED

Lewis Hayden's life in slavery was filled with heartbreak, but freedom offered challenges of its own. After 1845, the experience of "cracking his own whip" proved less rhapsodic than it had amid his Detroit congregation or the Boston Liberty convention. Yet somehow, even as he matured into a skilled and pragmatic political activist, he managed to retain a spiritual vision of human brotherhood and to insist that the institutions he cherished live up to it. Many people would have been left embittered by the abrupt dismissal that had marooned Hayden, penniless and alone, in an upstate New York winter. But Hayden drew upon resources not immediately evident in his devastated letter to Wendell Phillips. We do not know what route he took home from western New York to Detroit, nor what hardships he endured on the way. We do know that he was able to move past his disappointment and self-doubt and to assert himself as a self-confident citizen among equals. Slavery had taught him to expect trials and rebukes, and they did not break him.

Being fired by the AAS may have hurt most because he did not expect it. More predictable insults seemed rather to impel him to assert himself, no matter whom he had to confront. In 1847, he and Harriet were ejected from the first-class car of a New York–bound train. Although Hayden protested to the railroad agents, the couple were eager to make their Vermont engagement, and so they at first let the insult pass. But the condition of the second-class car, which Hayden described as "crammed to overflowing with the lower grade of emigrants," convinced him that they should instead return to Boston. Hayden then paid a call on the superintendent of the railroad, protesting his unequal treatment. Not only did the man refund his money, but he gave the Haydens free tickets and a personal letter to the railroad authorities in Rhode Island, where they had been Jim Crowed. The Rhode Islanders complied with the letter, if not with its spirit, by adding an additional car to the train for the Haydens' exclusive use.

When they reached the next leg of the trip to Vermont, an overnight voyage up the Hudson by steamer, the struggle began again. Hayden preemptively located the captain of the boat and showed him the superintendent's letter, hoping to make sure that the inevitable officious clerk would not declare "that it was an utter impossibility for a negro to find lodging on the boat." But soon they were Jim Crowed from the breakfast table; the steward incredulously asked Harriet Hayden if she expected "to eat with *white* people?" Denied equal accommodations, the couple refused to eat. Their witness shamed or embarrassed the captain, who visited Lewis Hayden in their quarters, pressing him to come and eat at an extra table set especially for him. But Hayden declined the offer. "I thanked him, adding that I was not so aristocratic as to require a table to myself."[103] He no more wanted a table to himself than he had wanted a private railroad car; the point was to be accepted as one among equal, respectable citizens.

At about the same time, late 1847, Lewis Hayden finally had a chance to engage the architect of one of his greatest misfortunes, Henry Clay. The Kentucky Whig's supporters were preparing the way for his next campaign for the presidency. Part of their job was to persuade Northern Whigs that the slaveholding Clay was no proslavery ideologue, but in fact a moderate and humane man—even a friend of emancipation. It was a tough sell, and it relied in large part on Clay's long-standing commitment to colonization. In the fall of 1847 a Kentucky writer to the leading national Whig paper, Horace Greeley's New York *Tribune*, warmly described Clay as unsurpassed in his "ardent and efficient advocacy of emancipation."[104] Lewis Hayden felt compelled to respond. The *National Anti-Slavery Standard* published his letter to Greeley, in which he asked whether the editor would have published such a letter "if Mr. Clay had sold his wife and child, as he has mine?" They were "sold by that friend of the coloured race, Henry Clay! . . . May God save us all from such a friend." He detailed further cruelties of Clay's, including the story of an enslaved man whom Clay tied up and had his overseer flog so mercilessly that the man took his own life.[105]

Clay could not let this stand. Just the year before, a former slave of his named Lewis Richardson publicly charged Clay with great cruelty as a master. The politician formally ignored this, but his overseer and others flooded newspapers with rebuttals, describing Richardson as a drunkard and gambler.[106] Clay seems initially to have believed the new charges were from the same Lewis, and he replied angrily.[107] The details he provided alerted Hayden that the former senator was thinking of a different man, and the editor, Sidney Howard Gay, told Clay of his error. Clay probably regretted having responded in the first place. In reply, however, he doubled down, flatly denying that he had ever owned the people in question or ever sold "any woman and child to go down the river or to go South." These were unpersuasive claims: Hayden had not given the names of his first wife and child, and a slaveholder might easily sell a slave, at auction or to a trader, without knowing where they would be taken. Clay had no way to be sure his claims were true. More important, Clay was bothered enough to write not one but two letters. The etiquette of slaveholding society demanded that a slaveholder, confronted with insolence from an inferior, either ignore the affront or respond with violence. Under the circumstances, Clay could do neither. Despite his protestation that "I cannot consent, by the publication of my letters to be brought into contact with Lewis Hayden," that contact had clearly occurred.[108]

Not every fugitive so successfully got under the skin of a three-time candidate for president. The story suggests, however, how the divided nation's comparatively tiny population of free black people could wield influence far beyond their numbers, and not only before audiences of white abolitionists. Fugitive slaves and freeborn African Americans who lived in places of comparative freedom inserted themselves into debates, disrupting the assumption that public life was for whites only. They did so in the Latimer War and other, even more assertive slave rescues. Symbolically important in antislavery and antiextension politics, vocal fugitives muddied the claim that slavery, if not a good in itself, was the most comfortable home people of African descent would find in the United States. Lewis

Hayden, though barred from nearly every ballot box and witness stand in the nation, had successfully inserted himself into national political life.

Even so, national politics pushed the Haydens out of Michigan for good in 1848. Detroit had its church and its vigilance committees, but it also had Kentucky slaveholders on the prowl for their fugitive property. In the summer of 1848 the U.S. circuit court in Detroit unexpectedly granted slaveholders the right to sue vigilance committee members for damages when their actions prevented the return of fugitive property.[109] It was a serious blow: all a visiting slaveholder now had to do was swear that a person was his property and the machinery of the law would side with him against anyone who interfered with his efforts to force that person into slavery. The Haydens responded quickly; Martin Delany, visiting Detroit for the *North Star*, reported that they "became alarmed and left for Boston."[110] Their flight eastward took them through the newspaper's home office in Rochester, where they paused long enough for Lewis Hayden to meet Douglass and sign up as a subscription agent.[111] The reasons for their final destination were many: Boston offered many friends, churches, and societies; it was home to the oldest lodge of black Freemasons in the world; and in that city Lewis Hayden would be a voter.

An important task remained: the repayment of a great debt. While the three Haydens were exploring the meanings of freedom, Calvin Fairbank was paying the price in a Kentucky prison. Abolitionists circulated petitions calling for his release, but the turning point came when Lewis and Harriet's former owners agreed to join the petition if they were paid six hundred fifty dollars in compensation for their losses at Fairbank's hands. Lewis Hayden began to raise funds to meet the men's demands. Whatever limitations or hesitations had marred his earlier performances on the lecture platform, this effort was a great success. He began in April 1849 and within sixty days had raised the entire amount. The abolitionist lawyer Ellis Gray Loring, one of Garrison's first recruits, remitted the money to Kentucky. Soon Hayden had freed the man who had once freed him.[112]

Hayden may have raised additional capital as well, for within a month of the end of this effort he was able to establish his first business, a clothing store.[113] When a correspondent of the *North Star* encountered "my old Friend Louis Hayden" in Boston in the fall of 1849, he was impressed with the fugitive's upward course: "Five years ag[o] he left Michigan, depressed in mind, and poverty knawing at his pockets. Now I find him in Boston pushing up into the ranks of her Merchant Princes."[114] This might have been an overstatement, but the Haydens' businesses, which soon expanded to include a boardinghouse, provided the family with a modest livelihood. They also served as centers of antislavery activity, helping to clothe and shelter fugitives such as the Haydens had been only five years earlier. Now, by the standards of this world, the Haydens were as respectable as any of their wealthier neighbors. William Lloyd Garrison and Frederick Douglass no longer agreed on much, but they shared the same assessment of the Hayden family. The *Liberator* declared his new enterprise "worthy of patronage" by "the friends of humanity," wishing the "exemplary" self-emancipated proprietor "all possible success."[115]

Hayden took those wishes to heart. At the annual meeting of the Massachusetts Anti-Slavery Society in 1849, when Wendell Phillips offered a cautious, disappointed resolution on an antislavery political movement, Lewis Hayden rose to support it.[116] Barely a year had passed since the Brahmin's shocking letter of dismissal, and as Hayden rose to speak he had to feel both humbled and proud. Although cracking his own whip the past five years had proven complicated, the former slave had just paid his former owners six hundred fifty dollars, representing months of work and rescuing his former liberator. His pride must have been tempered by the awareness that he was owed far more than that for his years of labor—and that those dollars might well be used to purchase another slave.

The Haydens confronted slavery and won, but in the years following that moment on the Boston stage Lewis Hayden also came to understand that freedom could be chilly, and even in its own way brutal. He had been humbled by the harshness of a free-labor economy and an antislavery movement that could cut a man loose from employment in the middle of a frozen wasteland. Yet here he was, walking like a gentleman into an antislavery meeting and offering confident words in response to the man who had fired him. In this realm, where wealth, education, and race mattered less than egalitarian commitments backed up by determined action, he and Phillips were in some sense equally gentlemen and citizens. In this slaveholders' republic, it was a start—but only that. Hayden and the rest of the "colored citizens" were already looking well past the white abolitionist world as they attempted to work out their relationships with one another, with their white neighbors, and with the United States. At home in Boston, and across the continent, they were already engaged in earnest debate and sometimes bitter struggle over the best route to what Nell would soon call "the free, the happy future"—and what Hayden probably still sometimes thought of as "paradise."

4.

The Means of Elevation

Unlike his friend William Nell, the young lawyer Robert Morris had not grown up attending Boston's black community meetings. Nonetheless, he had quickly made a place for himself. The rhythm of exhortation, discussion, and planning suited him well. He enjoyed speaking before crowds, and he was particularly eager to perform one Monday evening in early September 1849. Earlier that day, as part of the ongoing campaign against racially segregated education in Boston, he and his colleagues had mounted a boycott and blockade of the Smith School, just next door. The boycott was part of a larger strategy in which he had an important role. Working side by side with a much more seasoned lawyer, Charles Sumner, Morris was challenging the principle of school segregation in the Massachusetts courts. If the Smith School stood empty, thoroughly rejected by black Bostonians, the two men's arguments for the abolition of racially segregated education would carry much greater weight.

Perhaps when the first stone crashed into the wall of the meetinghouse Morris did not know what to think, but he no doubt quickly realized what was happening. The day's blockade would not have been necessary if the city's black residents were united, but they were not. Now the morning's act of coercion had provoked an even more violent response this late-summer night—not from a mob of young Yankee or Irish toughs, but from enraged "colored citizens" who supported an all-black Smith School. In a hail of rocks, they gave voice to their resentment of Morris and his colleagues for blocking its doors. Nor was this the end: before the struggle over the school reached a conclusion, men would assault one another in the streets, and one would even be tarred and feathered.[1] When Lewis Hayden reflected in later years on the "jealousies and bickerings" that oppression inspired among its victims, he was thinking not only of the people held in slavery but also of his neighbors.

The struggle over the Smith School sheds light on crucial dimensions of the "colored citizens'" efforts to band together, demonstrate their abilities, and transform themselves from pariahs into brethren. It also reveals the tensions within those efforts. During the 1840s and 1850s, black activists worked to build institutions and networks to promote their "elevation." Segregation and exclusion taught them that they could not rely on white-controlled institutions to help them rise in the world. At the same time, most saw the dissolution of racial hierarchy as a key goal. How could they square the encouragement of "exclusive institutions"—however essential to the challenges of the moment—with their universalist aspirations? Disputes rooted in this conundrum vexed, divided, and sometimes even destroyed the very schools, lodges, conventions, and churches that were supposed to prepare "colored citizens" for lives of exemplary achievement.

There were very few dogmatists in these struggles. Activists who in one context seemed defiantly "separatist" at other times took clearly "integrationist" positions, based on their assessment of the particular institutions under debate. Observers a century later, when chants of "freedom now" gave way to "Black Power," might have been tempted to characterize the participants in such struggles as either "integrationist" or "separatist," "assimilationist" or "nationalist." But these categories are best understood as dynamics or impulses, not character traits or rigid ideologies.[2] With few exceptions, black activists in this era took part in an almost entirely African American world of speech, debate, and action. At the same time, virtually all black activists worked to break down the barriers between themselves as a people and the rest of the nation and world. In almost every sphere of black collective struggle, they sooner or later turned to the wider world and sought rapprochement with their white neighbors.

To understand black political consciousness and practice in the era of abolition, Civil War, and emancipation requires us to see the impulses of separation and integration not as distinct and warring camps, but as an ongoing dialogue among hard-pressed people. Burdened by white supremacy and the ordinary run of human difficulties, men and women chafed with petty jealousies and righteous indignation; they remembered old grievances and manufactured new ones. As debates simmered and sometimes exploded, friendships could curdle into rivalries and tactical differences fester into doctrinal schisms. But the "colored citizens" also understood the dangers of permanent division. They formed tight bonds and lasting affections, and worked hard to heal and forgive the difficulties that periodically estranged them from one another. The only ones who did not have to make ongoing choices between community cohesion and the battle for acceptance were those few who gave up completely on the idea of American belonging.[3] For everyone else, the heated, fraught, but essential debate continued.

EDUCATION, "ELEVATION," AND EQUALITY

The fierceness of the fight over the Smith School reflected the common view that education was the essential means of "elevation," and therefore the pathway to equality and respect. At an 1853 meeting in Boston, Frederick Douglass spoke passionately of the need to overcome "the spirit of

Caste" that excluded blacks from most avenues to advancement, by teaching children to do the most useful and important work in society: "to make boots, as well as black them, to construct bridges, as well as walk over them."[4] Through education and self-discipline, African Americans would become so respectable and prosperous that caste itself would dissolve. Nell explained that "the victim of American colorphobia can rise superior to the present prejudices, and compel justice, only by making himself an object of regard by his character, and of respect by his attainments; thus forcing the white man to concede the right so long withheld. . . . I shall begin to take hope of the colored Americans," he averred, "when they begin to *educate* themselves, and to lay up their money."[5] Historians have noted that these values meshed extremely well with the ideology of the market society in which free African Americans struggled.[6] Yet "elevation" was not as cautious, conservative, or simply bourgeois a project as it might superficially appear, for its goal was never acquisition for its own sake. For Douglass, the cultivation of "[i]ndustry, sobriety, honesty, combined with intelligence and a due self-respect" would transform blacks' reputation, for "[i]n their presence, prejudice is abashed, confused, and mortified," and its arguments become "powerless and unavailing."[7] But the consensual ideology of "elevation" did not dictate how education, its essential means, should unfold.

During the 1840s, the shabby treatment of the Smith School and its children by white school authorities produced a renewed effort to abolish the school and integrate black students into the rest of the city's schools.[8] Boycotts began in the mid-1840s, spurred by reports that the school's white master was mistreating his pupils, and spearheaded by young men like Nell and Morris as well as seasoned activists such as John T. Hilton.[9] Dubbing themselves the School Abolishing Party, they pulled the growing repertoire of black protest strategies into play, reaching out not only to white abolitionists but also to radical antislavery politicians such as Henry Wilson, who together with Henry Bowditch made up part of the pro-integration minority on the Boston School Committee.[10]

The "School Abolishers" saw the Smith School as both a symbol and a perpetuator of racial caste. The existence of the separate school, asserted an 1849 meeting, "strengthens a feeling of prejudice between white and colored children"; its abolition "will foster a regard for each other."[11] A segregated school confirmed the poor opinion of whites, and kept black students from avenues to success. Black students, feeling the sting of exclusion, learned to "undervalue themselves," and to "look upon white children as their oppressors. . . . From this source may be traced hatreds, combats, insults, and numerous other vices, which serve to keep up a perpetual enmity between the white and black members of the community."[12] The "spirit of Caste" had ramifications past individual acts of exclusion, for it encouraged others to indulge that prejudice as well. As a result, blacks were excluded preemptively. "Even abolitionists," Douglass charged, "will not take us into their stores, their counting houses, as clerks, book keepers &c., because, say they, it will hurt our business. They will not take our children into their work shops for their hands will not allow it."[13]

Winning the fight would constitute more than a victory over discriminatory principle and practice. The experience of common schooling would help white students overcome old habits of "colorphobia," and would put black students in a position to rise into other professions, trades, and places currently closed to them, since white employers would no longer fear the effect of the black presence on their white customers or workers. Victories such as this would resonate throughout society, for the power of moral example could not be overestimated. When white abolitionists joined William Nell in "the indignities of a Jim Crow car," they did more than vindicate their own claims to virtue; they also "had the best effect upon lookers on."[14] Magnify that by the presence, day after day, of black and white children studying together on terms of equality, and the potential for social change could hardly be measured. It might, in fact, lead to the day when white people learned, as the *North Star* put it, "to take the spirit of slavery out of their own hearts, and learn to acknowledge really— not in words only, but in deed and in practice, that the colored man is a man. All the silly ba[ld]erdash that can be strung together about man's equality, is just so much idle wind, until they accomplish this."[15]

William Nell, as close to an integrationist ideologue as Boston's black community produced, played an integral role in this struggle. His early experience of discrimination as a schoolboy caused him to declare publicly against all forms of racial separatism. As the alliance between black community leaders and Garrisonian abolitionists evolved, he energetically opposed all racially "exclusive" institutions, from the black convention movement to the whites-only public schools. He generally extended this past the color line to include exclusions based on sex. It pleased him that even the mainly black literary society he founded on Beacon Hill, the Adelphic Union, drew a "number of white young men," and it was no surprise that one of the Adelphic's meetings featured a debate on the question "Do separate churches and schools for colored people tend to foster prejudice?"[16] Nell's own experience of interracial friendship during his years in Rochester confirmed his sense that such things were possible. While an editor on Douglass's *North Star* he shared many hours of joyful conversation and spiritualist experimentation with the white abolitionists Amy and Isaac Post; when he fell ill, a "motherly" Amy Post applied wet bandages to his head.[17] But he returned to Boston and to the ranks of the School Abolishers in time for the climax of the struggle.

The "colored citizens" pursued a variety of strategies to integrate the Boston schools. Robert Morris took on Nell's cause as his own, appearing before the school committee to argue for integration. In letters to the press, he demanded to know why Smith School students did not share in the prizes and dinners awarded their white peers.[18] A number of black parents voted with their feet, moving their families to neighboring cities whose schools were not segregated by race. John T. Hilton moved his family across the river to Cambridge; his daughter, who had performed poorly under the inferior and abusive teacher of the Smith School, now "carried away the school honors." Others followed him, among them John J. Smith, a freeborn Virginian who ran a Boston barbershop. Morris himself headed north rather than west, taking his household over the channel to Chelsea.[19] Finally, the black activist and printer Benjamin Roberts sued the city, seeking the admission of his daughter Sarah to her local school. Roberts's case headed for the state's highest court.[20] There was reason for hope: campaigns of protest, including boycotts, had already brought integrated schools in Douglass's Rochester, in Buffalo, and in the Massachusetts communities of Salem, Nantucket, New Bedford, and Lowell.[21]

But the School Abolishers faced potent foes from within their own community. The "School Supporters," who emerged as an organized force in the late 1840s, advocated keeping the Smith School open under African American leadership. Many black Bostonians feared the results of school integration and preferred to build strong black institutions. Not surprisingly, many African Americans worried that in white-dominated settings their children would be "shunned by their school fellows, and often neglected by the master," and that they would become "subjects of contempt and ridicule."[22] Black students in mainly white settings, argued convention delegates in 1847, found themselves underprepared, underfunded, and "thrown in the midst of hundreds" who demonstrated "repugnance to colored men."[23] At a minimum, classrooms that included white children would almost certainly be instructed by white teachers, which meant fewer opportunities for black teachers. Beyond this, one of the leading School Supporters intimately understood the depth of white opposition to school integration. Thomas Paul, son and namesake of Boston's famous minister, had been a student at New Hampshire's integrated Noyes Academy when local white residents literally broke up the school by dragging the building into a swamp.[24] His experience was far from unique. In some parts of the North, even segregated education for blacks provoked whites to violence.[25]

School Supporters had no doubt that a segregated institution could produce extraordinary results. The African Free Schools of New York City, founded by the New York Manumission Society, educated hundreds of students each year; many went on to become important community leaders and pioneering professionals. These schools prepared James McCune

Smith for a medical degree, Isaiah DeGrasse for the ministry, and school-mates Henry Highland Garnet and George T. Downing for lives as black political activists. What was more, protest had brought black New Yorkers a significant degree of community control over these institutions.[26] An 1847 black national convention endorsed this vision, calling for a "collegiate institution, on the manual labor plan," to help educate generations of young black people.[27] These examples no doubt inspired Thomas Paul and his cousin Thomas Paul Smith to champion a similar model for Boston as "extremely politic, expedient, and useful."[28] Paul himself was ready to take on the leadership of the school, having taught in all-black schools in Albany and Providence.[29]

But Smith and Paul's campaign enraged the School Abolishers. To begin with, the School Supporters' very existence gave comfort to white supremacy. In response to Nell's early school desegregation efforts, the ironically named Boston *Olive Branch* decried any move toward the "unnatural amalgamation of two races, *whom God intended should ever be distinct.*" The antagonistic editors argued that white Boston should "[g]ive the negro his liberty, but KEEP HIM IN HIS PLACE."[30] With the emergence of a pro–Smith School campaign, whites who opposed school integration could now point to evidence of support for the school from within the black community itself. Beyond this, Smith appears to have committed fraud during his petition campaign in support of the school: when asking for signatures, he offered a petition calling only for Thomas Paul's installation as the Smith School's teacher, should the school remain open; he then replaced the petition's text with language praising the segregated school itself. Thus even Benjamin Roberts, the initiator of the desegregation lawsuit, found his name on a petition lauding the segregated school.[31] Angry words followed, at community meetings and in protests filed with the school committee.[32]

As the opening of the 1849 school year approached, Nell and his fellow School Abolishers organized a boycott of the school, seeking to show the community's resistance to the stigma of segregation by keeping the school empty of students. But their efforts met strong opposition from the outset, and community meetings dissolved into furious acrimony. School Supporters charged that their opponents rammed resolutions through meetings without sufficient discussion.[33] At one meeting, Thomas Paul Smith described himself and the other School Supporters present as a beleaguered minority; John T. Hilton responded that this could not be so, "for John C. Calhoun, Henry Clay, the American Colonization Society, and the entire pro-slavery community, were with him." To Hilton and Nell, people like Smith and Paul were the pawns of hostile whites, receiving the "bribe" of a school appointment in exchange for taking part in a "crusade against our legal rights and fondest hopes." The conspirators were "white wire-pullers and the colored wire-pulled." Smith was "a degenerate son of the free North," a poor contrast to Southern-born newcomers such as Lewis Hayden and William J. Watkins.

Although Paul and Smith faced opposition from most of the black Boston leadership, they appear to have had somewhat more support among the city's black population generally. The evidence was unmistakable: the continued presence of some black students in the Smith School, despite the call for a community-wide boycott. This was why the School Abolishers supplemented their boycott with a physical blockade on the first day of school in September. Blocking the door in the morning provoked the shower of rocks in the evening, as angry black residents protested a meeting from which they felt excluded and with whose tactics they strongly disagreed.[34]

In the short term, the fate of the Smith School was decided by white Bostonians, not black. At the end of 1849, the state's Supreme Judicial Court heard Benjamin Roberts's suit demanding his daughter's admission to her local all-white school. The School Abolishers' case was presented by Charles Sumner, the white abolitionist, orator, and lawyer who, despite his deep roots in Boston's white upper class, allied himself with the black Beacon Hill community. That mixed heritage shaped Sumner's argument in the case that became *Roberts v. Boston*.[35] On the one hand, Sumner drew on a translation of revolutionary French principles to assert Americans' "equality before the law" in order to press the case that American institutions were inherently egalitarian. But Sumner, like a small but growing number of white allies, also offered a critique of racial inequality that spoke to its human and social costs as much as its legal or moral incongruity.

Black protest thought presented equality as a universal benefit and inequality as debilitating to people on both sides of the color line. Slavery and caste were simply wrong, not because they injured African Americans but because they created an unjust society. This argument distinguished David Walker's vision of the "happy country this will be, if the whites will listen," from the thinking of most early white abolitionists, who depicted black slavery as wrong in the abstract but dangerous in practice because it threatened white people's liberty. Black protest thought, by contrast, held that freedom must be universal in order to be meaningful. A committee of the 1847 National Convention of Colored People referred hopefully to "our steadily approaching triumph—or rather the triumph of the glorious truth 'Human Equality,' whose servants and soldiers we are."[36] Nell's friend Jeremiah B. Sanderson told the American Anti-Slavery Society's 1845 meeting that "I come not here as a colored man—I know that slavery strikes at the root of the whole liberty tree." He meant that a truly encompassing understanding of liberty required forswearing all the privileges of color—the momentary moral superiority that could accrue to a black man speaking before white abolitionists, as well as the much broader set of advantages that whites of all descriptions enjoyed.[37] The stigma of slavery, which so limited the opportunities open to free blacks, also crippled whites' moral and political imaginations.

Charles Sumner's argument before the Massachusetts court embraced this egalitarian vision and stood as a testament to the powerful impact of black activist thinking on white radicalism. The enforcement of legal inequality, Sumner explained, did not simply injure black and white citizens in the abstract; it diminished their fitness for democratic self-government, and permanently cramped their hearts. The common school was "the little world where the child is trained for the larger world of life," and it "must cherish and develop the virtues and the sympathies needed in the larger world." Boston's schools, instead of honoring the state's formal commitment to equality, reinforced invidious distinctions of color. Blacks, he explained, lived as a "despised class, blasted by prejudice." Segregation "deprives them of those healthful, animating influences which would come from participation in the studies of their white brethren . . . , widens their separation from the community, and postpones that great day of reconciliation which is yet to come." The law injured whites as well, teaching them "to deny that grand revelation of Christianity, the Brotherhood of Man." This malign early lesson left whites "debased" and "less fit for the duties of citizenship . . . Hearts, while yet tender with childhood, are hardened," Sumner declared. Having learned "the sentiments of Caste," white children became "unable to erase it from their natures." The solution was obvious. Integrating the city's schools would "remove antipathies, promote mutual adaptation and conciliation, and establish relations of reciprocal regard."[38]

The Supreme Judicial Court rejected Sumner's vision of "equality before the law" and "reciprocal regard." The ruling nominally accepted the principle of equality, but it also held that that principle did not require that all be "subject to the same treatment." Men and women, adults and children, might be "equal," but this did not mean they were "clothed with the same civil and political powers." It fell to the overseers of a particular law or institution—in this case, the prosegregation majority of the Boston School Committee—to determine how the general principle of "equality" was to be administered. Chief Justice Lemuel Shaw, speaking for a unanimous court, ruled that separate, equal accommodations met that standard.[39]

Black Bostonians sought to heal the breach that the fight had opened among them. In the midst of the struggle, people on each side made gracious overtures to their opponents. When one of Nell's friends proposed to limit the right of School Supporters to speak in a meeting, his own allies insisted that the customary "latitude of speech" familiar to these meetings must be preserved.[40] Even Thomas P. Smith struck a note of reconciliation. Despite "gross misrepresentations of my language, my purposes, and my motives," he wrote, "I freely forgive." He called one opponent a "young man of genius and promise" and wished him "nothing but future honor and success."[41]

Yet such rapprochements did not survive the legal defeat of 1849. Two years later, after Smith again testified in favor of separate schools, a small band of School Abolishers including Benjamin Roberts and William Watkins ambushed Smith near his home. They roughed him up, then attempted to establish who was on the right side of history by coating Smith with tar and feathers, the revolutionary mark of shame. Smith's brother retaliated the next day, chasing down one of the assailants, but Smith was again attacked late that same evening. At his trial for assault, Benjamin Roberts was unrepentant. Though he did not quite admit having taken part, he admitted knowledge of the violence and explained that its purpose was to "frighten" the man whose statements in favor of continued segregation made him "extremely obnoxious to every respectable colored man, woman, and child in this city."[42] Unity among the colored citizens remained a project, not a given, and in hard times it could come calamitously undone.

THE "COLORED ELITE OF BOSTON"

Boston's debates and struggles took place in a dense, complex social world in which people distinguished themselves less by wealth or descent than by accomplishment and bearing. Whatever consciousness of color or lineage existed among people of African descent, it did not lead to rigid social segmentation. The freeborn Howards, a leading family from the early years of the nineteenth century, prospered as hairdressers and musicians while also employing younger people, including John T. Hilton, who lacked their formal education. The same was true in other cities. In New York,

Thomas Downing's oyster bar made him a wealthy man, but he remained an activist figure in the city's black community; his son George Downing followed in his antislavery and organizational footsteps, later becoming an important figure in Massachusetts and Rhode Island. Such comparatively wealthy people did, of course, seek out one another's company, and the family trees of the wealthiest men and women of color intertwined. Soon after his arrival in Boston in the 1850s, the European-educated physician John V. DeGrasse, son of a prominent free black family of New York, wooed and wed Cordelia Howard.[43] Such ties were common: back in New York, John DeGrasse's sister Serena married George Downing; later, the couple's son married another of the Boston Howards.[44]

But webs of intermarriage among men and women of property and attainment coexisted with assertions of a broad identity of interest with the "people of color" generally. This sense of solidarity, born of proximity, economic interdependence, and common oppression, meant that even the most accomplished and prosperous black Bostonians usually kept at least one hand on the plow of common purpose. The skilled workers and tradespeople who led the churches, called the meetings, and described themselves as "colored citizens" constituted a small and comparatively privileged fraction of the city's complex social world, but many of them believed that this distinctiveness brought responsibilities. Rather than keeping the laboring majority at arm's length, they often built and supported institutions of uplift, education, and solidarity. John DeGrasse, for example, lived and worked among people without his education or wealth. His developing medical practice brought him into contact not only with the wealthy Howards, but also with the households of fugitives and other working people.[45] Other businessmen and professionals remained similarly invested in the survival and prosperity of those around them. The freeborn Joshua B. Smith, sometimes dubbed the "prince of the caterers" and much sought after by wealthy white customers, labored in antislavery vigilance organizations and urged fugitives to arm themselves against recapture. Mark De Mortie, a transplant from Norfolk, Virginia, busied himself with both a shoe store and fugitive defense.[46] Self-interest formed an additional bond: beacons of black entrepreneurship such as Christiana Carteaux Bannister's chain of beauty shops and De Mortie's shoe store relied on patronage from less wealthy black residents; so did the more modest used-clothing stores run by African Americans up and down Cambridge Street, the commercial artery that defined the border between Beacon Hill and the neighboring West End.[47] These entrepreneurs and activists asserted an identity of interest among all people of African descent—an interest born of common oppression at the hands of white Americans. "We are as a people, chained together," a national convention would assert a decade later. Free and enslaved, Northern and Southern, light-skinned and dark, "[a]s one rises, all must rise, and as one falls all must fall."[48]

Yet neither self-interest nor rhetorical assertion created true unity among black Bostonians beyond the common fight against slavery. The MGCA, the African Lodge, and the churches' advocacy of encouraged temperance and self-improvement were met with indifference or even hostility.[49] Dissenters from the ideology of moral improvement and uplift through formal education challenged both the plans and the authority of the self-appointed betters who edited newspapers, chaired meetings, and headed associations.[50] Beyond the common opposition to slavery, unity was more asserted than felt or enacted.

The national conversation among black activists, always concerned with seeing black people rising out of the lowest-paid trades, periodically erupted into bitter debate over such employment. While all agreed that the emergence of black tradespeople, proprietors, and professionals was a good thing, and a necessary step toward both economic equality and the respect of others, there was less consensus about the place of "menial labor." In *The Self Elevator*, editor Benjamin Roberts underlined the importance of practical education: he insisted that the road to black people's "General Improvement" lay through mastery of the skilled trades, "whereby they might command respect of all good citizens." At the same time, though, Roberts lavished praise on William Nell for his semiformal work as an employment agent serving those "[c]olored persons wishing employment at occupations commonly pursued by them."[51] The outspoken Martin Delany once told a black national convention that he would rather his wife and children die than do menial work for white employers.[52] But this position was not tenable among the coresidents of a city such as Boston, not even by the most ardent proponents of self-improvement. The fiction that women could be "respectable" only if they shunned paid employment or remained within a protective domestic sphere had little purchase in the black North.[53] Men and women plied different trades and labored under different expectations, but they all worked.

For those without densely interlocking ties of family and inherited wealth—for almost everyone, that is—prosperity was difficult to achieve and easy to lose. This was true even among the lucky, propertied minority. Louisa Marshall Nell died in 1834, and William Guion Nell followed in 1845. This left William Cooper Nell the de facto head of a household that included very little capital and three younger siblings. It was a burden he found difficult to shoulder, especially since, even after years of work as a clerk, author, and jack-of-all-trades, he remained financially unable to marry and start a household of his own.[54] Six years after his father's death he was still burdened by obligations to his two as yet unmarried younger sisters, seeking lodging for one and a "situation" with a Vermont family for the other.[55] Although he pursued these tasks determinedly, he found it difficult to imagine ever getting out from under them. Visiting his sister Louisa at her rooming house, he listened to a favorite child recite lessons ("he improves—and I am delighted . . ."), but prematurely grieved that he would never prosper sufficiently to become a father and husband ("too late—too late").[56]

In this world, attainment was measured less in dollars than in respectability and self-improvement. William Nell, though frequently penniless, could move comfortably in all quarters of this world. He visited the Howards often, staying late to make spiritualist experiments in their Poplar Street home, and on one dark day helping to oversee the funeral of the patriarch, Peter Howard.[57] He loved the late-summer weeks when the people he dubbed "the Colored Elite of Boston" met their acquaintances from other cities at the seaside resort of Newport, Rhode Island. And if he lacked the means to spend as much time at play as some of that set did, he could at least arrange antislavery meetings in the handsome resort town and that way spend a few days in the company of his wealthier friends.[58] When newcomers joined the activist leadership, Nell welcomed them and was welcomed in turn into their circles. He did not let his envy at their professional attainments prevent him from enjoying their company—or from drawing them into local activism.

From the top to the bottom of the black economic ladder, all understood that exclusions and assaults rooted in prejudice would sooner or later come their way. Unless they were willing and able to pass as white, or until they decided to abandon the United States for another home, they would face a common destiny as a suspect and subordinated people, even where the law seemed to bring them within a hair's breadth of formal equality. Divided by birth, class, education, and descent, their common and apparently inescapable predicament bound them together. These were the conditions of freedom for black Bostonians.

Robert Morris began learning these lessons long before the fight over the Smith School. The grandson of an enslaved African, and the son of a waiter named York and his wife, Mercy, Morris was born in Salem in 1823. Before he turned thirteen he was, like his father, waiting on the tables of the town's upper crust. Soon he was called to serve a party that included the Boston lawyer and abolitionist Ellis Gray Loring. Morris struck Loring as just the sort of boy he wanted to do chores in the family's home. Arrangements were quickly made for Morris to accompany the Lorings back to Boston the next day.

Loring was no ordinary employer. He was among the first white abolitionists in Garrison's orbit, but he did not cut quite the same uncompromising figure as the society's founder. Indeed, Loring was among the small group of founders of the New England Anti-Slavery Society who hesitated to endorse the organization's constitution as it was hammered out over the winter of 1831–1832. Immediate emancipation struck him as unproductively radical; so did the "philo-African" label Garrison initially sought for their work. He was not, therefore, among the group that assembled in the vestry of the African Meeting House that blustery night in January 1832. Not until more than a year later did the lawyer finally return to take a place of responsibility in the society.[59] In the context of Garrisonian radicalism, he remained a cautious, compromising figure. When the Lorings, departing Salem for Boston, discovered that the young black boy would not be permitted inside the stagecoach, they set off regardless through the chill November air, with Robert Morris silently freezing up on the box beside the driver. Morris entered the world of Boston's white abolitionists a shivering outsider.

Morris's rise, like Loring's egalitarianism, came gradually. He worked as a servant for several years in the Loring household before opportunity struck. A young white man employed to do copying and other business in Loring's office neglected his duties, and Loring sent Morris to the office in his place. Morris's work and manner impressed Loring enough that he finally offered to help Morris gain a skilled trade. Morris chose Loring's profession, the law, and after the custom of the day he studied law in Loring's office in preparation for the bar examination.

Only one black man had ever been admitted to the bar of Massachusetts: a Maine-trained lawyer named Macon Allen, who attained that honor in 1845. Morris became the second, in 1847. Apparently, however, he was the first to try a case before a jury. When he announced himself to his first opposing counsel, the white man threatened Morris and shook his fist in his face. The man's fury left Morris so dejected that years later the memory made him struggle to maintain his composure. At the time, even that was beyond him. "I sat down, and I cried," he told a friend. But he also resolved to "prove myself a man and a gentleman, and succeed in the practice of law," or die trying.[60] At his first trial, "[t]he court room was filled with colored people," eager to see an attorney of their race at

Robert Morris
Courtesy of the Social Law Library, Boston

work.[61] He won the case, becoming a minor celebrity in the abolitionist world and a symbol of how much "elevation" was possible, at least in Massachusetts.

THE LIMITS OF "EXCLUSIVE INSTITUTIONS"

Although most of black Boston's leading activists opposed segregation in law and principle, nearly all took part in racially separate institutions. These organizations spanned a wide range of human activity and experience, and few people dogmatically applied the same criteria to all of them. But at the bottom of every debate over each "separate" or "exclusive" institution lay a fundamental question: under the prevailing order of racial caste and inequality, did the utility of a separate space for black association outweigh its violation of the principle of universal brotherhood? Could such "exclusive" associations advance that egalitarian principle along the highways of protest and elevation? Or did they constitute a self-imposed obstacle on the road to belonging? Black churches and black conventions raised these issues in ways sometimes as troubling as separate schools.

The existence of independent black churches never sparked violence among activists, but it provoked many of the same questions and concerns as the debate over separate schools. There were unmistakable differences between the cases: churches were private bodies, not state run; they attracted members and were governed through communities of feeling and affinity, not law. They might function as training grounds for citizenship, but everyone knew that was not their primary purpose: they existed to bring Christian souls together. Even so, some of Nell's colleagues in Boston and Rochester saw the persistence of all-black congregations as self-destructive. They were "fetters of our own forging," charged William J. Watkins in the *Liberator*. It was a curse, not a blessing, that two thousand black Bostonians had "*five* colored churches," for this allowed whites to feel that blacks acquiesced in the principle of proscription.[62]

Frederick Douglass shared Nell's distaste for separate institutions, but he also reflected that "[s]ome of these institutions we have deemed necessary, in our present circumstances, excluded as we are from the like institutions among the whites." Still, he asserted that "we have ever looked forward to the time when it would be our duty to abandon all complexional institutions, and go for equal and universal brotherhood, and demand admission to all institutions enjoyed by other men." At his most impatient, he proclaimed that the time for such a demand had long since come. "We would to God," he exploded in 1848, "that on the very next Sabbath, every colored church could be abandoned, and their members make their way to the white churches from which they came out, and demand admission on equal terms with white persons," saying, "Come, brethren, let us be men, equal men—Christians and equal Christians; let us show that we know our rights, and mean to assert them."[63]

But black churches, as places of spiritual communion, solace, and joy, were too important to abandon so precipitously. Black Christian worship took many forms, including the high-church formality of some East Coast congregations and the enthusiastic, emotionally intense worship of many former slaves in some Baptist and Methodist churches. Afro-Christianity was in general an egalitarian gospel, emphasizing the admonition in Acts that "God has made of one blood all the nations of men."[64] But too many black Christians experienced the condescension of Northern congrega-

Leonard Grimes
Carl J. Cruz Collection, New Bedford
Historical Society

tions or the humiliation of slaveholders' theology to want to leave their hard-won communities of faith and consolation for another interracial battleground.[65]

Yet as the life of Reverend Leonard Grimes makes clear, a life of pastoral devotion might also be one of passionate, political, interracial activism. Born free in Leesburg, Virginia, in 1815, Grimes early on became heartsick at the violence inflicted on rural slaves. In adulthood, he moved to Washington and turned his trade as a hackman to the wealthy into a cover for ferrying Virginia fugitives to freedom. Arrested and convicted for the rescue of a mother and her seven children, Grimes was sentenced to two years at hard labor in Richmond. Confinement cost him his business and left him deeply depressed, but just as he had helped save enslaved people, one now returned the gift. A "godly slave" imprisoned alongside him helped Grimes reach a profound religious awakening—"that great spiritual change which makes all things new for the soul."[66]

At the end of his imprisonment Grimes returned to Washington, where he obtained a license as a Baptist preacher and began to work. In 1846 he and his wife, Octavia, moved to New Bedford, Massachusetts. Two years later Grimes answered the call of a small congregation of Boston fugitives who worshipped together in a third-floor hall but had no regular minister.[67] Grimes took charge of the tiny congregation and helped it flourish and grow. Soon they began raising a new building on Southac Street— the Twelfth Baptist Church—that could seat as many as six hundred persons.[68] Grimes impressed people with his genteel, sunny disposition. "No man in the city has fewer enemies or more friends," wrote William Wells Brown.[69] But the minister was as determined in his aid to fugitives as he was a preacher of the gospel, and the "Southac Street Church" joined its denominational cousin just up the hill on Belknap as a common forum for community meetings and celebrations.[70]

By the time Grimes reached Boston, the black denominations were joined by a resurgent black convention movement that, like those churches, consisted entirely of African Americans. Beginning in the 1830s, the quest for a stronger collective voice found expression in mass meetings, state conventions, and a succession of national conventions. The first phase of this movement generated a short-lived national association, the American Moral Reform Society, which created a few local auxiliaries and met annually but collapsed by 1841.[71] But freestanding black national conventions recommenced in 1843, with subsequent meetings in 1847 and 1848.

National conventions sought to foster understanding, trust, and collective action among the nation's free black communities. Like the black newspapers they endorsed and relied upon, they encouraged a national conversation and national strategies. Here Ohioans and Pennsylvanians, representing large black communities that struggled against pervasive discrimination and state black laws, debated strategy with representatives of the much smaller but less restricted populations in New England. New Yorkers, with their robust institutional life but racially restrictive suffrage laws, took seats beside their neighbors from New Jersey, where slavery itself persisted until well into the 1840s. Convention delegates and observers formally considered the means of abolition and the limits of "free state" life; when the meeting adjourned, they could establish more personal bonds of common purpose and common feeling.

Even William Nell, devout opponent of "exclusive institutions," could not resist the pull of the black national conventions. Although he confided to Wendell Phillips that he hoped for a "veto put upon all 'Colored Conventions'" and that "the best way is to have nothing to do with them," Nell was drawn into the conversation.[72] He joined Hilton, Sanderson, Remond, Douglass, and others in representing Boston at the 1843 National Convention of Colored Citizens.[73] He returned four years later, despite his insistence that "the most feasible plan for eradicating the foul spirit of caste" involved the common efforts of all those "prompted by a common feeling against Slavery and prejudice."[74] It helped that the 1847 meeting was officially dubbed a "Convention of Colored People, and their friends."

These conventions endorsed the creation of national institutions for free blacks, including newspapers, banks, and especially colleges. They asserted the practical necessity of such plans to the work of "elevation." Divisions of opinion concerned practical rather than doctrinal questions. The 1847 convention's committee on the press, for example, praised the work of the existing black newspapers, but noted that none of these economically marginal enterprises was secure, let alone able "to support one literary man of color and an office of colored compositors." A national body, able to draw subscribers and supporters from the entire free population of color, would solve this problem.[75] Hayden, Nell, and Douglass all opposed the creation of a national press, but not because they objected to the notion of an all-black editorial staff. Rather, they wanted the convention to support existing papers, such as Nell and Douglass's just-born *North Star*, and feared a new paper would be dominated by a clique of New Yorkers, as they perceived that year's convention to have been.[76] The following year's convention gratified them by formally endorsing the *North Star*.[77]

"INTENDED FOR THE BETTER GOVERNMENT OF MAN"

The *North Star* editors and Hayden voted together many times at these conventions, but on another key aspect of black associational life they were in strenuous disagreement: Freemasonry. By 1847 Hayden was already a leading member of this order, while Nell and Douglass both decried it as exclusive, superficial, and self-indulgent. In the pages of the *North Star* Nell denounced free black people's growing fondness for such associations as a distraction from the fight against discrimination and slavery. He suggested, in fact, that white people generally ignored the activities of black fraternal organizations precisely because they posed no challenge to the spirit of proslavery caste.[78] When African American Odd Fellows held an 1847 celebration in Faneuil Hall, Nell wondered whether they would have received permission "if the Hall had been applied for by the Colored people for an object of universal Humanity," such as antislavery meeting.[79]

Douglass similarly chastised his fellow black citizens for showing more devotion to these orders than to struggles against slavery and caste. "If we put forth a call for a National Convention, for the purpose of considering our wrongs, and asserting our rights . . . we shall bring together about fifty," he complained, "but if we call a grand celebration of odd-fellowship, or free-masonry," four or five thousand would flock. Freemasonry and Odd Fellowship were "swallowing up the best energies of many of our best men, contenting them with the glittering follies of artificial display, and indisposing them to seek for solid and important realities."[80]

Yet those "glittering follies" appealed to an ever expanding circle of leading black men. During the 1840s and 1850s black Freemasonry grew and spread well beyond its Northern coastal origins, reaching free black men in Pennsylvania, Ohio, and communities along the Ohio and Mississippi valleys all the way to New Orleans. It established beachheads from the Eastern slave-state cities of Baltimore, Washington D.C., and Alexandria, to the far-flung outposts of Canada West (today's Ontario) and California.[81] During this era it attracted a new generation of able and ambitious men, such as Ohio's John M. Langston, Illinois's John Jones, Pennsylvania's Martin Delany, and a great proportion of the men who had risen to prominence in New York and Massachusetts, including Hayden, Robert Morris, and John V. DeGrasse, among many others.[82]

Masonic intellectuals such as Martin Delany idealized the fraternity as a world-historical project that taught men to understand, emulate, and transmit the essential wisdom of the ages. Freemasonry was "originally intended for the better government of man," Delany explained, and its doctrines of "rectitude of conduct and purpose of heart" were "the only surety for the successful government of man, and the regulations of society around him." Each era's Masons conveyed the order's "mysteries" to their successors through elaborately scripted rites of passage that taught them mythic stories and bound them to secrecy and confraternity.[83] These symbols and myths saturated the ordinary politics of organizational life with a sense of sacred duty, encouraging its members to think of these as temporal means of achieving transcendent ends.[84] Some went further than Delany. John T. Hilton once contrasted the "ambition" and "ungovernable passions" of politicians and even the "Christian denominations," where "pride, contention, &c." were often evident, with the Masonic Hall, where "you will find all is peace and unity."[85]

Yet the politics of the lodge inevitably mirrored the realities of the wider world. Personal rivalries and alliances formed in the lodge as easily as anywhere else. Elections, especially for the master of the lodge, could become heated contests. Perhaps this was why, while hand voting sufficed for routine lodge business, the election of officers—in midcentury Boston, at least—was by secret ballot.[86] Even this did not prevent political conflict among the brethren as men vied for election and as lodges clashed over questions of authority and payment.[87] By the 1840s such fractures became so serious that in several states rival Masonic bodies competed with and denounced one another.

To resolve this crisis in the fraternity, leading black Freemasons in New York, Philadelphia, and Boston put their heads together. In June 1847, a small group—including then New York resident Lewis Hayden—met in Boston to unite black Masons under a single national authority, what came to be known as the National Compact or National Grand Lodge (NGL).[88] Its constitution, ratified by some state grand lodges in 1848, established a triennial assembly composed of representatives from each of the existing grand lodges, along with a slate of elected officers including a national grand master. The NGL did not replace the state bodies, but it did take on executive, legislative, and judicial functions, setting policies to promote the order and resolve disputes among the grand lodges. Its regularization of Masonic practice also required the Massachusetts brethren to reorganize, giving them an opportunity to drop the now disfavored "African" appellation and, in honor of their founder, become the Prince Hall Grand Lodge. John T. Hilton was named the first national grand master, and Hayden remained one of its leaders after his move to Boston.[89] With the formation of the National Grand Lodge, wrote Delany a few years later, "the differences and wounds which long existed were all settled and healed, [and] a complete union formed."[90] Despite the quick secession of a number of grand lodges from the new body, Freemasonry's rapid spread during the 1850s took place mostly under the aegis of the NGL.[91]

Even as it grew, Freemasonry remained highly "exclusive." Only men were eligible for membership, and any man could be excluded from lodge membership by a single negative vote. An order proclaiming universal truths thus allowed individuals the power of exclusion, a paradox John T. Hilton explained this way: "When the knowledge of Masonry shall have become universal, and her noble principles diffused and practically enforced, then will commence a new era in the moral world; . . . it will be a time of universal peace; virtue and Religion will shield the human race. Man will sheath his sword, and learn war no more."[92] Like the Smith School supporters, Hilton imagined a future era in which there would be no need for exclusiveness, but he held that that time had not yet come. His brethren apparently agreed. By the time of the Civil War, black Freemasons could be numbered only in the thousands.

In some of the other secret ritual associations that emerged during this era, women as well as men were eligible for membership and for office, and Freemasonry faced calls to follow suit.[93] Historian Martha Jones has identified one pre–Civil War moment of public protest by women against their exclusion from Freemasonry, and there were doubtless others.[94] Yet the order's masculine character was widely understood to be essential and immutable.[95] Limiting the order to men did keep black American Freemasonry in harmony with the traditions honored in the rest of the Anglo-American Masonic world, but beyond this lay Masons' self-conception as a training ground for leadership. In some respects, black Freemasons welcomed women's entry into public life. Black Masons such as Lewis Hayden were vocal supporters of women's rights, and a growing number of black activists accepted the possibility of women as orators, voters, and independent economic actors. Women also remained integral to the political, social, and cultural life of black Freemasonry; wives and daughters of Masons threw festivals and banquets, and Masonic temples, like churches, frequently opened themselves for concerts, orations, and other activities.[96] A women's auxiliary order, the Heroines of Jericho, emerged in some cities.[97] But few Masons were yet ready to imagine women in the roles of political leadership aspired to by black Masonic leaders.

Black Freemasons championed a notion of "brotherhood" extending beyond the borders of nations, religions, and languages.[98] They hewed to a Masonic watchword that their white brethren honored only in the breach: cosmopolitanism. "[W]e are . . . of all nations, tongues, kindreds, and languages," read the codifying document of modern Anglo-American Masonry, James Anderson's *Constitutions of the Free-Masons.*[99] John Jones, Chicago's leading black defender of fugitives and advocate of equal rights, expressed Masonic universalism more dynamically: "[B]y secret and inviolable signs, carefully preserved among the fraternity throughout the world, masonry becomes a universal language . . . The distant Chinese, the wild Arab, the African in his native home, and the American savage, will embrace a brother Briton, French or German, and will know that, besides the common ties of humanity, there is still a stronger obligation to induce him to kind and friendly offices."[100] The "Declaration of Sentiments" issued by the National Grand Lodge at its founding declared "all genuine Masons, of all nations and shades of complexion, to be our brethren."[101] That final word expressed their commitment to regarding others as equals and themselves as men of the world.[102]

The appeal of this Masonic cosmopolitanism to people accustomed to derisive and exclusionary treatment is not hard to imagine. Such claims had been made before—by religions, and even by the white Enlightenment figures who framed the evanescent promises of liberty and equality. But while Christian churches and American institutions had betrayed those ideals, Freemasonry's timeless and universal principles offered another way of imagining full citizenship in an ancient community of worthy souls. Freemasonry's language of universal love and brotherhood echoed the liberatory egalitarianism of both Afro-Christianity and the Declaration of

Independence, but it abjured the sectarian disputes and exclusionary practices of white churches. It also stood outside the national political framework, corrupted by slavery, which had eroded the idealism of the American
Revolution.

Black Masons insisted that white Masons live up to their professed
universalism, and they made repeated overtures to white Masonic bodies
for formal recognition. The NGL's Declaration of Sentiments professed
puzzlement at "the separate organizations of white and colored Masons in
the United States of America": "We do not know of any good reason why
there should be" such division, they wrote, "and we have made several
attempts without success to have but one." In 1846, Lewis Hayden was
among a group of black men who petitioned the white Grand Lodge of
Massachusetts for Masonic recognition. A committee of white Masons met
with them and approvingly noted their sincerity and propriety—but the
grand lodge's minutes concluded that the white Masons had found "insuperable objections to granting the petition which it is not necessary to
mention."[103] Although the exclusion of black men was not complete, it
was the general rule throughout the eighteenth, nineteenth, and twentieth
centuries.[104]

Nineteenth-century white Masonic bodies derided black Masons as
"counterfeit" or "clandestine," "irregular" and "fraudulent"; they aggressively swatted down those white Masons who dissented, and based their
continued exclusion of black men on the *Constitutions'* restriction of membership to "freeborn" men.[105] This, they explained, extended to those who
were born slaves but became free, "on the principle that birth, in a servile
condition, is accompanied by a degradation of mind and abasement of
spirit, which no subsequent disenthralment can so completely efface as to
render the party qualified to perform his duties, as a Mason."[106] Their
unwillingness to imagine that their petitioners might never have been
slaves indicated how fully blackness and slavery were wedded in their
imaginations.

Although neither the National Grand Lodge nor the Massachusetts

Grand Lodge named the white Masons' "objections" to Hayden and his fellows in 1846, everyone understood racial proscription to be white Masonry's increasingly dogmatic rule. The following year the white Grand Lodge of Ohio forbade its members to recognize black lodges, a pattern followed by white Masonic bodies throughout the land. In 1848, when the city of Boston held a public celebration of its new aqueduct, the black Masonic lodge unsuccessfully sought to enter the procession alongside white Masons. After being rejected, they were finally invited to join ranks with the Order of United Americans, an anti-immigrant political association.[107] If black Freemasonry was a separate project, it was not for lack of trying to walk side by side with white Freemasons. But that effort would continue. The universal brotherhood posited by Freemasonry was too compelling, and too intimately related to the project of equal citizenship, to abandon. And while blacks worked for the "new era in the moral world," black Freemasonry provided a place to hone the skills and vision they needed for the fight.

THE CRISIS OF COUNCIL AND COLLEGE

Perhaps the Masons' forging of a national body, or their profound appeal to men he admired, inspired Frederick Douglass in ways he did not let on. In 1853 he called for a national convention of black Americans—the first since 1848—to assemble at Rochester. The delegates arrived to find an ambitious agenda prepared for them, including the establishment of the National Council of the Colored People, a representative body intended to bind black citizens to one another and promote their elevation in every sphere of life in the free states. Its federal structure, under which local assemblies elected state bodies, which in turn elected national delegates, resembled that of the United States. It also mirrored that of the new national Masonic organization. This council was ambitious, but not unprecedented: the now defunct American Moral Reform Society had originally been envisioned as such a national body, and the 1848 Colored National Convention had resolved vaguely to form a national association "the better to unite and concentrate our efforts as a people."[108] The 1853 convention also voted to establish a freestanding training school for young black people that would help them advance in the trades and mechanical arts, the first national institution of its kind created by and for African Americans.

The troubled course of this council sheds light on the way ideological and personal tensions shaped plans for "elevation" and practices of citizenship. The council did partly succeed in creating the national network it envisioned; for the next several years, local meetings in several states did elect delegates to state councils, which in turn elected members of the National Council, to meet in annual session. But the meetings of the Massachusetts state council, in particular, devolved into a proxy war, in which William Nell and a few allies grimly defended the motives and programs of the AAS against the majority of black activists, who sided with Frederick Douglass. Questions of autonomy, independence, and servility became intensely personal, a roiling brew of ideological, tactical, and personal differences.

By the 1850s, the troubled relationship between Douglass and the white AAS leadership captured the essence of black activists' frustration with their white allies. Douglass was heartily sick of the condescending cant of Garrison, Phillips, and other AAS leaders. Annoyed at his former associates' rigidity about political action and the U.S. Constitution, in 1853 he charged that several particularly radical anticlerical abolitionists had absented themselves from a recent AAS meeting in order to protect the society from the charges of "infidelity" that had plagued it over the past few years. Garrisonians believed Douglass was charging the movement with hypocrisy as well as infidelity. The white editor denounced his black colleague's "libellous conjecture" and "blindness of mind," and implied that Douglass's tactical flexibility had left him both intellectually and morally bankrupt.[109]

This rupture with the AAS leadership complicated an already difficult situation for the society's chief black spokesman in Boston, William Nell. His personal relations with Douglass had been difficult since he left Rochester. Like many others in the movement, Nell was deeply troubled by the appearance of a romantic liaison between the married black editor and the white Englishwoman Julia Griffiths, who worked on Douglass's paper. He hoped Douglass could shake off such "evil" influences but had "very little affinity with or confidence in him now."[110] Douglass's attacks on white abolitionists and his espousal of "exclusive" organizations confirmed Nell's already considerable worries about Douglass's moral condition.

The dam burst in the summer of 1853. Douglass attended an August 1 celebration in New Bedford, at which he and Nell remained on friendly terms. The next day Douglass made the long trip north and west, through the rain, to another celebration in the city of Framingham. Wet and exhausted, Douglass took the seat friends offered him in a pew down front, only to find the featured speaker, Wendell Phillips, mounting an attack upon him.[111] Phillips remained an impressive figure for many in the movement, Nell and Douglass among them: "[H]e is esteemed as a gentleman, as well as an abolitionist, and has the reputation of being a just, as well as a generous man," Douglass explained; "his words, therefore, have the power to curse, as well as to bless." And curse Phillips did, in the only way he knew. He fixed his "fiery glance and supercilious scowl" upon Douglass, asked him how he dared sit there after making the charges he had against the three abolitionists and the AAS in general, and demanded that he immediately account for his actions. Douglass declined to enter into an impromptu debate and resented the suggestion that he was not entitled to criticize the conduct of white abolitionists. The measured tone of his response did not convey the depth of injury he felt.[112] Nell's second-hand report was that a "scene occurred between Wendell Phillips and Fred[eric]k Douglass."[113] From Douglass's perspective, it was much more than a "scene"—it was the crowning injury in a succession of slights and attacks that had been accumulating since his move to Rochester almost six years before.

The conflict, now quite public, quickly extended to relationships among black leaders. A series of black community meetings in Boston over the next weeks brought a violent rupture between Douglass and Nell over the council's plans and Douglass's break with the AAS leadership. To begin with, Douglass's proposal for a "colored training school" at the 1853 convention generated a predictable furor over the question of "exclusive" institutions. As soon as the proposed manual training school was described as an institution for young black people, Nell and several other delegates began to object, offering resolutions forswearing any proscription of white teachers or scholars. A frustrated Douglass beat back charges that he sought to create the very racial proscription he abjured in whites. The council and school did not seek to "build up a Nation within a Nation," he fumed. "The charge is absurd." On the contrary, he pointed out, the convention "asserted boldly that we are American citizens." Ideally, of course, "there would be no necessity of separate action," and that ideal world must be brought into being. The question was how. Working with white abolitionists was all well and good, but those whites had never worked to "promote mechanical trades," which in Douglass's view of elevation—the common view, in fact—was essential for black people to rise in wealth and reputation. "We are simply doing for ourselves, what no others have proposed to do for us," the editor concluded. "We have a right to associate with each other to promote our interest."[114]

Douglass was infuriated by the way the convention and its work had been represented to black Bostonians. "[M]uch of my work" in the city, he explained to his readers, "has been to defend the late Colored National Convention from the ill-natured and treacherous misrepresentations" of three black activists in the Garrisonian orbit: Charles Remond, Pennsylvania's Robert Purvis, and—most shockingly—William Cooper Nell. They had, Douglass asserted, been busy propagandizing against the convention, the school, and the council, and they continued their attacks during his visit. Indeed, at the end of one of Douglass's meetings, his friends claimed, William Nell rose to dissuade the audience members from subscribing to

Frederick Douglass' Paper, since its editor had treated William Lloyd Garrison so ungratefully.[115]

Douglass angrily described Nell's actions as those of a "contemptible tool" and "pitiful fool."[116] Nell was a hypocrite: he went "grumbling about in private" over being passed over for promotion at the *Liberator* in favor of white men, Douglass claimed, but then "whiningly arraigned me before the colored people of Boston, as having been unkind, ungenerous, and ungrateful to his Boston Anti-Slavery friends."[117] The charge stung, for Douglass was not alone in portraying Nell as the token black man in the Anti-Slavery Office. Some black Bostonians shared the view that Nell huddled too closely under the wing of the Garrisonian leadership. One black critic attacked Nell and his white employers as "a little clique, who, in defiance of truth and honor, rule and riot at 21 Cornhill."[118] In the antislavery world that orbited Douglass rather than Garrison, the suggestion was common that Nell's allegiance to interracial organizing had been ill repaid. In these accounts, Nell was "invariably . . . thrust aside" while whites filled the "lucrative and important offices."[119]

Many seemed to choose sides with Douglass, most painfully including Robert Morris. Nell and Morris were capable of public recrimination and private reconciliation; a decade before, after a meeting, a mutual friend suggested that Nell had been "rather severe as if personal" in challenging one of Morris's positions. Nell immediately wrote to reassure Morris of his personal friendship and regard, but also to clarify the reason for his hard words. Morris had been defending a mutual colleague, a man who in Nell's judgment had "greatly offended." Nell defended his harshness as stemming from a defense of principle, not personal animosity: as he reminded Morris, it was his "oft repeated saying: that I deal not in Personalities in Society meetings."[120] The rift was apparently healed. But in 1853, as Douglass sparred with his former friends, Morris took Douglass's part in a violent denunciation of Nell.

Morris and Nell's break was not an ideological split over "exclusive institutions." During the meetings in Boston that August week, Morris himself decried Douglass's espousal of a "Manual Labor College in which white children were to be excluded" as ill-conceived, considering that the Smith School remained a "relic of oppression" and "a foul blot upon the city of Boston." But his admiration for the editor was great, and a few nights later, after Nell rose to rebut Douglass and discourage black Bostonians from supporting his paper, Morris struck. In what a friend of both men publicly described as an "ungenerous and ungentlemanly attack upon Mr. Nell," the lawyer "descend[ed] to personalities of the grossest character." His remarks were "wholly gratuitous," William Watkins declared—so much so that he would not repeat them in print.[121]

To Nell, it must have seemed that much of Boston's black activist world had turned against him. Watkins professed to be angry with Morris for his treatment of Nell, but he nonetheless returned to Rochester to take a position on Douglass's paper. He promised to keep Garrisonian content in Douglass's paper, but Nell was not comforted: "Between F.D. and J[ulia] G[riffiths] I tremble for his integrity," he wrote.[122] Douglass cultivated close ties with Grimes and Hayden.[123] Although the two men claimed neutrality, Nell was skeptical; when Douglass was in town he could always be found with one of them.[124]

Nell was being shut out of the movement's informal councils, which perhaps explains why he overcame his own dislike for "exclusive" organizations and sought election to the Massachusetts state council. The council was fast building in late 1853; elections went forward in several states, and a convention of black residents of Canada petitioned to be admitted. It seemed possible the council might become what the convention movement never had: an ongoing political forum, even a shadow legislature for the interests of black Americans.[125] Nell may have felt he had no choice but to take part. It was great irony that only in this venue, restricted to people of color, could he continue to stand for passionately held positions: opposition to separate institutions, and justice to the race's white friends.

Those friends now included not just Garrison and other AAS leaders, but the novelist Harriet Beecher Stowe. As the 1853 convention met,

Stowe's novel *Uncle Tom's Cabin* was already a sensation in the United States and England. The Christlike martyrdom of its title character, the dramatic escape of the light-skinned slave woman Eliza across the icy Ohio river, babe in arms, and a host of other melodramatic characters and situations brought the human dimension of slavery home to white audiences through well-grooved pathways of sentimental literary convention. Abolitionists, black and white, took umbrage at the minstrel-like depiction of some of its darker-skinned enslaved characters and bridled at the epilogue, which appeared to endorse Liberian colonization. But for many in the struggle, black and white, the white sympathies won by the novel far outweighed its ideological shortcomings.

Stowe even shaped the fate of the National Council, revealing the unavoidable impact of interracial alliances on all aspects of black activism. Douglass had spoken to Stowe about his plans for a manual labor school, and he believed she had promised to contribute fifteen thousand dollars toward its creation. His disappointment and anger were great, then, when he saw Stowe retreating from this commitment, under what appeared to be pressure from white Garrisonians, steadfast opponents of "exclusive" projects. In early 1854, at the first meeting of the Massachusetts state council, this matter took center stage. Lewis Hayden offered a series of resolutions squarely representing Frederick Douglass's position: thanking Harriet Beecher Stowe for her promise of aid to the school; expressing regret and mortification that she had withdrawn her offer, having been "acted upon by other influences than the dictates of her own good heart"; and defiantly promising to build the institution in any case, "believing that we are fully capable of accomplishing all for ourselves that we need, or that others might do for us." Opposition by Nell and a number of others failed to prevent these from entering the record.[126]

Douglass blamed Nell and others like him for the council's subsequent collapse, but it was not their opposition that doomed the project.[127] Like the national assemblies that preceded it, the council failed to attract the concerted attention and support of the people it strove to represent. New York's James McCune Smith, one of the leading spirits behind the council, declared that "the almost isolated labors of less than a hundred colored men" had achieved "cheering and grand results. . . . What may we not do if we secure the hearty, earnest, and steady cooperation of ten thousand men?" The real and imagined numbers told the whole story.[128] By 1855 Douglass acknowledged that his school would also remain theoretical. "The fiat," Nell reported him saying, "had gone forth from the central organ at Boston"—by which Douglass meant the *Liberator*—"that all efforts to elevate the free colored people, while slavery existed in America, are useless. He expected to see the school voted down, and should say no more."[129] Short on enthusiasm, money, and unity of purpose, the movement to build the school collapsed by the end of that year. The National Council itself soon met the same fate.[130]

Nell and Douglass did not reconcile for some time.[131] At the New England Anti-Slavery Convention in 1854 they passed each other without a word. Both men attended the sadly diminished National Council meeting in mid-1855, where their icy antagonism continued.[132] "I cannot easily imagine the circumstances that would result in my speaking to him," Nell privately told his white abolitionist friend Amy Post.[133] But relations among the Boston men, however much strained by this conflict, remained strong, and even in hard times Hayden and other Douglass allies offered gestures of reconciliation.[134] Finally, Nell and Douglass both decided it was time to move on. After a year without any contact at all, they encountered each other as the editor was leaving Hayden's shop on Cambridge Street. The two exchanged civil greetings.[135] Hard feelings and second thoughts followed: when Nell learned that William Wells Brown had, under similar circumstances, refused to respond to Douglass, he became uncertain whether or not he had done the right thing.[136] But that was William Nell in a nutshell, his courage and his self-doubt all too subtly intertwined.

BLACK PARTISANS

Since the second half of the 1840s, electoral politics increasingly preoccupied Boston's black activists, no matter what side they took in struggles
over the school or the council. The movements against the annexation of
Texas and against the Mexican War rallied increasing numbers of white
Northerners against the expansion of the slaveholders' domain. This sentiment crystallized powerfully, if unsuccessfully, in the Wilmot Proviso. By
1848, opponents of the extension of slavery within both the Democratic
and Whig parties broke with their old loyalties and founded the Free Soil
Party, a broad new Northern coalition against the expansion of slavery.
Although there were good reasons to question the motives and beliefs of
white antislavery politicians, and although black men could still vote in
only a handful of Northeastern states, electoral politics engaged the energies of countless African Americans across the North.[137] The notion that
electoral politics might begin to turn the United States away from its proslavery policies was compelling enough in itself, but the possibility that
black voters and political organizers might play a role in forcing that turn
made partisan engagement irresistible.

Although the Free Soil coalition took in many Liberty Party voters, it
was not abolitionist: most antiextension voters favored neither immediate emancipation nor equal rights. The party's platform was limited to
preventing the extension of slavery into new territories. Its supporters
often sounded their call in explicitly white supremacist language, echoing
David Wilmot's unapologetic call to safeguard the Western territories "for
the sons of toil of my race and color."[138] But the antiextensionists did see
slaveholders as political enemies, not potential allies, and this by itself
marked a sharp break from the Northern status quo. Antislavery could
coexist with explicit expressions of racial hierarchy and exclusion. This of
course limited what "colored citizens" might expect from Free Soil in the
way of the fuller embrace they sought from their countrymen, a vexing

reality that was always close to the surface of the black conversation about the movement.

The political debate among black Bostonians evolved rapidly during 1848. Early in the year Benjamin Roberts and Thomas Paul Smith, already emerging as opponents in the school fight, together helped lead several meetings in the Belknap Street Church to form a "colored auxiliary" to the Liberty Party. They were routed by John T. Hilton and Robert Morris, who argued that the time was not ripe to endorse an antislavery political party. Morris would soon serve as Roberts's lawyer, but he was not yet persuaded that even the Liberty Party's egalitarian platform held anything for his people: black activists entering white party politics would inevitably be deceived and disappointed, sacrificing along the way their position of moral purity.[139] Ironically, the much less radical platform of the Free Soil Party, with its potential to attract large numbers of white voters, soon persuaded Morris to alter his position. By midsummer, he did an about-face, accepting an invitation to serve as marshal for a carload of delegates to the Free Soil forces' "People's Convention," which would elect delegates to the national Free Soil meeting that summer.[140]

Appointing Morris to this honorary position served the nascent party in several ways. First, it might help rally the state's black voters; although they were few, every vote counted. Second, and probably more important, appointing Morris was a relatively painless way to signal to white radicals that the Free Soil coalition, although brimming with prominent ex-Democrats with antiabolitionist pasts, was not simply white men's business as usual. Morris was therefore offered up as a symbol of the new party's openness to a forceful antislavery agenda—at least for the time being, in Massachusetts. But it was a sign of things to come: the party's national convention at Buffalo followed suit, with black men serving as delegates and making speeches.[141]

Morris likely understood the symbolic dimensions of his role, but he experienced it as real and meaningful. The young lawyer undertook this first foray into partisan political activity with a clear sense of the limits of his endorsement, as became evident at that summer's August 1 celebration, where he was called to account before the stern judges of white Garrisonianism. Morris fearlessly endorsed the antislavery coalition that had helped produce the Free Soil Party in Massachusetts. "Political machinery and political movements" were necessary, he declared, and "we must be content to have them as good as we can get them, if we cannot get them as good as we desire." It was a bold statement of political pragmatism to make before such an audience. Yet Morris stopped short of endorsing the movement's fall ticket before its head had been chosen: if the ex-Democrat and former president Martin Van Buren was its nominee for president—as indeed he soon would be—Morris said he would not vote for him.[142]

The real debate over partisan political action was no longer between black and white activists, but among black activists themselves. Throughout the fall of 1848 the pages of Douglass, Nell, and Delany's *North Star* were filled with the heated back-and-forth of a national political debate conducted mainly by, for, and among black activists. As Morris foresaw, Van Buren's nomination stood at the center of their concerns. Could black voters in good conscience support the New Yorker, who stood on a platform opposing the extension of slavery but who also supported his home state's restrictions on black men's suffrage, reaffirmed just two years earlier?[143] The conversation continued at the 1848 Colored National Convention. Some wanted to endorse the Free Soil Party; others pointed to that movement's manifest inadequacy on bedrock questions of equality. A compromise resolution "heartily" recommended the new party while insisting on "the higher standard and more liberal views which have heretofore characterized us." Principle and pragmatism led to different conclusions, individually compelling and mutually incompatible.[144] In any case, to a close observer of partisan politics, the notion that black institutional efforts heralded a separate "Nation within a Nation" must have seemed wildly off base.

In the end, few black Boston activists could resist an antislavery political party that appeared to have so much momentum. Boston witnessed unprecedented partisan activity among African Americans; a Free Soil club flung a banner from a headquarters on Cambridge Street, the commercial heart of the black community at the foot of Beacon Hill.[145] Some connections were emotionally resonant: the party's vice presidential candidate was Charles Francis Adams, who as a Massachusetts legislator had presented the great Latimer petition just five years before. But at the bottom of it all was the thrill of achieving an unprecedented degree of inclusion in a party whose platform stood foursquare against the plans of slaveholding expansionists.

Sensing that they were at a turning point in their alliances, Boston's black activists seemed sometimes to want to square the circle—to express their devotion to the editor who stood with them, but not at the cost of squandering their newfound ability to participate in national political events. At the AAS's 1849 convention in New York City, Thomas Paul Smith pledged the continued support of Boston's black population to the antislavery movement and exhorted black New Yorkers to "stand true and steadfast to principle." At the same time, though, Smith acknowledged that "he, with most of the colored voters of Boston, went with the Free Soil party in the last election," and he described the new party, notwithstanding the "defects and errors" of its standard-bearer Van Buren, as the "child of the Anti-Slavery Society." It was an incoherent argument that bespoke an irresolvable conflict. Garrison's response bespoke a similar collision of personal loyalty and ideological commitment: he had known Smith since childhood, he said, and although he appreciated Smith's earnest candor, he disagreed with his analysis. The editor left it to other speakers to point out more directly that one could not logically espouse both Garrisonian principles and Free Soil voting, as Smith had just done.[146]

Smith was not the only one feeling torn, for Free Soil both thrilled and disappointed. The party did not gain the presidency in 1848—Zachary Taylor took that prize for the Whigs—but it did win an astonishing 14 percent of the popular vote in the nonslave states and elected a dozen members of the new Congress. Out in Rochester, Frederick Douglass pondered the implications. Antislavery, he agreed, would always "be followed at a greater or lesser distance by a political party of some sort." The question was what such a party could accomplish. He had supported the Free Soil Party, and it had gained a substantial number of votes, but now that the election was over, it lay dormant. Worse, the party had absorbed the energies once devoted to more thoroughgoing antislavery newspapers, first diluting their once powerful message, then leaving them for dead as soon as election season was done.[147] Douglass for the moment concluded that party politics was a bad bargain, but it was a close call, and one he would soon revisit.[148]

Even William Nell broke with the antiparty orthodoxy of his AAS patrons. After returning from Rochester to Boston in 1849, he did not just pick up the banner of the school fight: the very next year he joined the Free Soil Party's slate of candidates for Boston's numerous seats in the state legislature. In doing so he likely became the commonwealth's first black nominee for elected office. It was a symbolic honor, for the Free Soil slate was virtually certain to lose. But Nell shared the satisfactions of having his righteous candidacy fail alongside those of ticket-mates he had come to know as allies: Henry Bowditch, who now was also his personal physician, and Elizur Wright, who (although neither man knew it) had saved Nell's job earlier that decade through his Liberty Party organizing among black Bostonians.[149]

Once again, tactics and personal judgments mattered far more than any particular orthodoxy. Even as Nell stridently defended some of the principles held dear by the AAS leadership, he was violating others quite boldly. Douglass's attack on him as a "contemptible tool" was, from this perspective, most unfair: Nell knew his own mind, and pursued his own course. When he stood with Garrison he did so out of principles that were firmly his own. He could struggle with people in one realm and simultaneously cooperate in another; in 1853, even as Nell and Hayden fell out so dramatically over the council, school, and Stowe, the two men's names appeared together on the Free Soil slate for state representative from Boston.[150]

In political life, as in antislavery agitation, principle and pragmatism coexisted. While black activists always insisted on the "entire emancipation" of both the enslaved and the free, they knew these changes would not come suddenly or cataclysmically, through some miraculous turn in the hearts of whites. They would come through what Lewis Hayden called the "free agency" of people "blessed with a free gospel."[151] Already there were hints that the Free Soil alliance could take them where they wanted to go: the Free Soil faction in Ohio's legislature, where no party held a majority, used its leverage to begin repealing Ohio's black laws, including the ban on black testimony.[152] Victories need not be complete to be consequential, and ethereal ideals needed to find earthly expression.

Black activists' allies in the Free Soil ranks quickly rose to power in Massachusetts. The state's Free Soil movement pulled in many antislavery Whigs and Democrats; by 1850, playing on a host of dissatisfactions with the long-governing Whigs, the Free Soil and Democratic forces came together and took power as a coalition government. Suddenly, a party that was part of a governing majority both took notice of black men's claims and included them on its slates. Equally important, black voters for the first time seemed to be playing a significant role in the outcome of elections. Although the black voters of Ward Six composed only about a seventh of the ward's electorate, their willingness to turn out allowed them to decide close races. In a special election for the city council in 1853, the Free Soil candidate triumphed by seventeen votes after organizers "rallied the colored population."[153] The power of this small minority was no longer entirely symbolic.

The Free Soil–Democratic coalition collapsed in 1853, but antiextension forces regrouped in 1854 in response to a profound challenge: Democrats in Congress and the White House opened the huge Western domain known as Kansas and Nebraska to settlement. In the process, they repealed the Missouri Compromise, which since 1821 had barred slavery from those northern parts of the Louisiana Purchase. Across the North, the possibility that new slave states would be carved out of the Western plains brought a swift, strong backlash that dwarfed earlier antiextension movements. "Anti-Nebraska" and "Republican" parties quickly coalesced, pulling in even more disaffected Northern Whigs and Democrats than their Free Soil predecessors. In the process, they pushed the tottering Whig Party a long step closer to total collapse. In the summer of 1854, a hundred fifty delegates representing Boston's new "Republicans" met to select delegates to a state convention.

The Republicans brought with them Free Soil's comparative egalitarianism. Lewis Hayden was among those who spoke at the Boston meeting.[154] The new state Republican Party promised to prohibit slavery from the territories and, "disregarding the aristocratic, hereditary distinctions of birth and color," to "maintain the right of all men to freedom and equality before the law."[155] That fall, the Republican slate for representatives from Boston included Hayden and Nell.[156]

Of course, by the fall of 1854 it hardly mattered who was on the Republican ticket, for state politics had been radically redirected by the sudden emergence of political nativism. Waves of immigration from Europe to Boston and other Atlantic seaports were capped in the late 1840s and 1850s by a vast influx of starving refugees from Ireland. Most of them brought little in the way of capital or locally useful skills, and their Catholicism instantly made them suspect in largely Protestant polities. No place absorbed as many of these exiles, per capita, as Greater Boston. In 1830 New England's white population was overwhelmingly Protestant and native born; by 1855 nearly a quarter were of foreign birth, mainly Irish Catholics.[157] The arrival of a large group of desperate, low-skilled workers of a despised nationality and a suspect religion had consequences that were not hard to predict.

Massachusetts—like other states—had already seen anti-immigrant political movements in the 1840s; the Order of United Americans, which had invited the black Freemasons to march with them in 1848, remained strong in the early 1850s. Now, with the apparent threat growing by the month, anti-immigrant writers poured vitriol on Catholicism and on the Irish, calling for restrictions on their immigration and naturalization. Catholic tyranny menaced American democracy, nativist writers urged, because "Bishops and Archbishops held absolute control over the minds of their spiritual subjects," directing their votes toward "the advancement of their Church." To put it more bluntly, "republicanism and Romanism are antagonistic in their elements and tendencies, and cannot co-exist in the same place in harmony."[158]

That anti-immigrant sentiment soon found partisan expression. While the Democratic Party welcomed immigrants, courting their votes and facilitating their acquisition of citizenship, neither the Whig Party nor the Free Soil Party responded by moving toward full-throated nativism. It therefore found other channels. The result was a secret fraternal order, a nativist political movement organized much like the Freemasons. In 1854 it suddenly appeared as the "American" party, always better known by the epithet "Know-Nothing," part of the unfortunately chosen phrase—"I know nothing"—that members were supposed to utter when asked about the secret group. The Know-Nothings capitalized on the weakness and disarray of their opponents in the existing parties, and on the widespread feeling among native-born Protestants that they were in danger of losing control of their society. In the Massachusetts state election of 1854, Know-Nothing candidates won the governorship and virtually every other important office in the commonwealth, including all but three members of the state legislature and every one of its U.S. congressmen.[159] The nativist legislature dismissed Irish-born state workers, disbanded Irish militia units, banned the teaching of foreign languages in the public schools, and called for daily reading from the King James Bible—anathema to Catholics—in the public schools. It called on the federal government to extend the period of naturalization for citizenship (and voting) to twenty-one years, and to limit public office to native-born citizens.[160]

The new party appeared to have come out of nowhere, but many of these "Know-Nothing" officeholders were actually former Free Soil and now Republican politicians who sensed the wind and jumped on board the nativist ship just as it left port that fall. John Andrew, Henry Wilson, and *Commonwealth* editor Charles W. Slack were just a few of the anti-slavery men who made the move.[161] By December 1854, as the Know-Nothings took control of government throughout the state, those with previous political experience had a significant advantage. The former Free Soil men quickly rose to the top ranks of the Know-Nothing-dominated legislature and controlled the Boston city council. For many of these politicians the election marked not a sudden lurch into nativism so much as a cold-eyed assessment of where events were heading, and how best to take advantage of them.[162] For others, antislavery Know-Nothingism seemed a natural convergence of antipathies; as Republican nativist Anson Burlingame put it, "Slavery and Priestcraft . . . have a common purpose . . . one denies the right of a man to his body, and the other the right of a man to his soul."[163]

Whether or not black activists shared this view, nativist politics proved a godsend to them, and they seized the moment. Hayden, Grimes, and a few other leading figures, in a quiet collaboration with the Free Soil and Republican men, helped turn out the black community's votes for the Know-Nothings.[164] No more than four hundred voters in the entire city supported the Republican ticket, from its gubernatorial nominee down to its at-large candidates for state representative, and in Ward Six only forty-five did. In other words, most black voters seem to have voted for the Know-Nothing Henry Gardner for governor and also to have abandoned the black candidates lower on the ticket; it seems plausible that Hayden, who by election day was working with his newly minted Know-Nothing allies, did not even vote for himself.[165] As a result, even though the Republican Party dissolved around them, the topsy-turvy political season of 1854 left Boston's black activists in a better political situation than they could ever have dreamed.

This was pragmatic politics, and it was also the perhaps inevitable by-product of the "colored citizens'" persistent identification of themselves as "American citizens." As white political activists moved toward a frankly anti-immigrant politics, black activists sensed the potential for common ground as "Americans" in opposition to an even more despised class of foreigners. This could have been tactical, as when the black Freemasons accepted the nativist invitation to parade with them in 1848, but in some instances it seems also to have been deeply felt. Lewis Hayden, remember, stood his ground after one Jim Crowing only because he could not stand to be packed in with a horde of "the lower grade of emigrants"; he found "the stench rising from whiskey, ship-diseases, &c. &c. was almost insupportable."[166] As two despised peoples mostly living and working at the bottom of the occupational ladder, Irish immigrants and African Americans would have been likely to clash in any case; the alliance of Irish American voters with the antiblack Northern Democratic Party sealed this antagonism. But the commonplace nativism of Hayden and others, and the alliance between Republicans and Know-Nothings, played their part as well. In seeking to exchange the exclusions of racial hierarchy for the unity of American belonging, black activists could hardly remain immune to nationalism's own exclusions.

THE "TRIUMPH OF EQUAL SCHOOL RIGHTS"

Yet this ugly seed yielded welcome fruit, as the new interracial political coalition finally resolved the fight over the Smith School. In early 1855, the Know-Nothing executive committee appointed three abolitionist members of the legislature "to wait upon" the city's black leadership. The men, editor Charles Slack among them, asked a group consisting of Hayden,

Grimes, and several others what they wanted, presumably in exchange for continued electoral support from black voters. The answer was simple: "mixed schools."[167] Abolishing the Smith School would bring a long-sought victory, and closure to a painful phase of black community life. Just as important, it was within the gift of the new governing party.

The white politicians quickly kept their end of the bargain. Slack, from his seat on the legislature's Joint Committee on Education, prepared a report calling for desegregation of the Boston schools; his colleague John Andrew introduced the legislation on the assembly floor. Debate began in April 1855, and by the end of the month the legislature had approved the measure and the Know-Nothing governor signed it into law.[168] One of the black leadership celebrated the impending triumph in *Frederick Douglass' Paper*: "Never before have we had so many faithful anti-slavery men in our Senate and House," he wrote, "and never before has our Legislature committed itself so strongly on the side of Freedom."[169] The triumph seemed equally remarkable from less friendly quarters of the North. The *New York Herald* articulated the view from the heart of the white republic: "Now the niggers are really just as good as white folks. The North is to be Africanized. Amalgamation has commenced . . . God save the Commonwealth of Massachusetts."[170]

For once, antislavery Boston held a meeting and William Nell was not the secretary but the guest of honor. At the end of 1855 the Twelfth Baptist Church hosted a meeting to celebrate the desegregation of the Boston public schools, and especially the part Nell had played. A child presented him with a gold watch inscribed to him on behalf of "the colored citizens of Boston," and men and women lauded his steadfast advocacy of their cause—"you, who were never weary or disheartened." Nell pronounced it "the proudest moment of my life." Words could not express what he felt, he told the audience, but that was all right: those before him felt just as deeply about what this victory meant. "Your own hearts can best interpret mine," he said. Then he turned the celebration back to the audience, itemizing the contributions of his black and white allies in the struggle. He particularly lauded "the *mothers* (God bless them!) of these little bright-eyed boys and girls, who, through every step of our progress, were executive and vigilant," accompanying him throughout his campaign, all the way through to the prior September 3, when they went school by school to ensure that the new law was being carried out.[171]

The breach that had opened so painfully in 1853 was finally healed, as the victory restored longtime colleagues to public and private amity. The 1855 celebration meeting took place in Grimes's church, with the grand old man John T. Hilton presiding and more than a dozen ceremonial officers in attendance—including Lewis Hayden and Robert Morris.[172] Nell took special care to note the efforts of his "zealous friend Lewis Hayden" in collecting signatures, and to make appreciative puns on the names of the abolitionist Know-Nothings in the legislature who made good on their promises. His list went on, through Henry Bowditch and John Andrew, to his old employer and idol Wendell Phillips. Bursts of applause followed each name; there was a place for everyone in this victory. Indeed, the victors were really celebrating one another, with Nell playing the part of master of ceremonies.[173] He confessed privately that he had found it "a difficult part to perform" and was, typically, unsure how well he had done.[174]

In a certain sense, the coalition between black activists and white allies seemed to have triumphed. When Wendell Phillips took his turn at the rostrum, he described it this way: "The moment a colored man and an Abolitionist sign a petition, it is fated—it will be granted in the end."[175] But it was nearer to the truth to say that black political activity had impelled white antislavery politicians to finish a task that Garrisonian abolitionists could not. The American Anti-Slavery Society was no longer the center of gravity for the interracial alliance on Beacon Hill, and an uncharacteristic joke by Phillips, at Nell's expense, signaled the Brahmin's awareness of an altered relationship. He declared himself glad to have the struggle won because "[h]e was tired of having Mr. Nell coming to him with his petitions. He could never be met without them." Phillips "was glad he had got rid of him, and was quite willing to take free schools instead." Nell may have gamely laughed along, but the terms of the two men's relationship had forever changed. Nell and his comrades, having stepped decisively into the world of partisan combat and political compromise, would never again simply be "black abolitionists," and white abolitionists had taken note. In that moment, too, Nell may have suddenly gained a new understanding of what Douglass so angrily noted and Lewis Hayden likely never forgot—Phillips's ability to punish with a word.[176]

What Phillips thought still mattered, but not nearly so much as in years past, for political victory brought many kinds of liberation. With the rise of a state government hostile to slavery and racial caste, a new insouciance animated black resistance to exclusion in Massachusetts. In 1855 the manager of one of Boston's two segregated theaters found himself the victim of a retaliatory reverse Jim Crowing by a black barber, who would agree to shave him only in a small storeroom at the back of his shop.[177] A visiting slaveholder, holding forth on the essential benevolence of slavery before a Massachusetts legislative committee, was shocked to find himself eloquently and satirically rebutted by their next witness, Lewis Hayden.

Robert Morris, whose first, freezing journey to the city had taken place in segregated exile on the roof of a stagecoach, finally had the last laugh.[178] The summer after the school integration law passed, Morris climbed into a Boston omnibus, one of whose passengers was a white Southern visitor to the city. The man found Morris's presence irritating enough, but when the well-known lawyer was allowed to join in the group's conversation, that irritation turned to fury. The Southerner demanded to be let out—into the rain—to finish his journey on foot. Later in the day, with the weather even wetter, Morris entered another omnibus for his return journey only to find the same visitor complaining to a carload of white Bostonians about the outrage that had befallen him that morning. At Morris's entrance, the other passengers began to laugh; the Southerner, not ready for another soaking, shut his mouth, and Morris quietly made his way back to the comforts of his suburban home.[179]

Yet in the wider world, the mid-1850s were clearly not a moment of triumph. The rise of the Republicans meant that growing numbers of white Northerners now shared a common enemy with their black neighbors. But the Slave Power showed no sign of retreating. The overthrow of the Missouri Compromise, abetted by a Democratic senator from Illinois and his Northern allies, proved that the slaveholders' control of national politics remained strong. Proslavery armies of U.S. citizens had fought or were fighting in Cuba, Mexico, and Nicaragua, seeking to bring these territories within the ambit of American slaveholders; when such "filibusters" were prosecuted in the Southern states, juries invariably acquitted them. In other words, the terrain on which "colored citizens" might have to confront proslavery armies grew and grew. Indeed, proslavery interests had even enacted a new fugitive slave law, one so powerful that it threatened to extend the territory of slavery deep into the American North itself. All the struggles of the early 1850s had taken place in the shadow of this new law, its existential threat to free black life, and the increasingly militant black and white resistance to its enforcement—subjects to which we must now turn.

Even against this backdrop, Robert Morris's quiet victory on the Chelsea omnibus might be seen as grounds for hope. There were not many Robert Morrises in the country yet, and perhaps even fewer buses full of well-disposed whites. But the assumptions of racial solidarity and hierarchy the white Southerner brought with him—assumptions that only a decade or two before would have met with nearly unanimous white Northern agreement—no longer seemed to work so well in Boston. Proslavery visions of a white republic still held sway over the national government, yet an alternative to their hegemony was now on view: Boston's black and white citizens now voted, traveled, and conversed together; thanks in part to Morris's own efforts, their children even learned together. "Colored citizen," once a defiant or ironic posture, seemed to be gaining practical meaning and moral force. Robert Morris might even have believed that his happy passage home signaled a white republic in peril.

Part II

FIGHTING LIKE MEN

5.

The Heirs of Crispus Attucks

I n early October 1850, less than two weeks after the new fugitive slave bill became law, black Bostonians held an emergency meeting to consider their options. Federal officials and slave catchers might now seize, shackle, and send any of them off to slavery after nothing more than a cursory hearing. It was a moment of crisis, an emergency that threatened not only free black Northerners' grander visions of equal citizenship, but also their literal freedom. So when a large and anxious crowd of black Bostonians assembled in the Belknap Street Church that October 5, William Nell offered the crowd the words of inspiration he believed they most needed to hear: a history lesson.

Nell was neither a pedant nor a fool. The history he sketched reminded his listeners of Boston's revolutionary heritage of liberty and the militant struggle to win it, including the Boston Tea Party and the Boston Massacre. He reflected on the state's revolutionary bill of rights, which declared that all men were "born free and equal." And he lingered over the story of the former slave Crispus Attucks, whose actions in the Boston Massacre of

1770 both set the American Revolution in motion and made him its "first martyr."[1] Since those days, Nell continued, the United States had been a beacon to those around the world who struggled for freedom, and Boston had been the symbol of clear-eyed devotion to that struggle. But although black Americans had been present and engaged since the very start, they were denied liberty's blessings. Indeed, with the passage of the new law black men, women, and children, both "bond and nominally free," were "hunted like partridges on the mountain."[2]

During the first half of the 1850s, Boston's black activists found themselves thrown into a life-or-death struggle over the fate of fugitive slaves that was in large measure the result of their own success. Compared to the American slave population, which now numbered well over three million, a thousand or so successful escapes each year might have seemed to be insignificant blows against a vast and thriving institution. But the escape of people such as the Latimers and Haydens, the aid and shelter they found in Northern black communities, and personal liberty laws such as the 1843 Latimer Law, enraged Southern slaveholders. By 1850, the issue of fugitive slaves, combined with the struggle over the fate of slavery in the territories taken in the Mexican War, threatened to split the Union in two. A Southern regional convention considered secession from the United States, and South Carolina—ahead of the pack, as always—was even preparing to vote on it.[3] As the U.S. Congress debated compromise measures to defuse the crisis, South Carolina's John C. Calhoun warned his Senate colleagues that Northerners could resolve this crisis only by exhibiting good faith on two scores: ensuring that slaveholders received an equal stake in the territories taken in the war with Mexico, and faithfully adhering to their constitutional responsibility to return fugitives from slavery.[4]

Free blacks, in alliance with abolitionist whites, made the issue of fugitive recapture so important to slaveholders that the congressional "Compromise of 1850," designed mainly to resolve the territorial question, included a new, stronger fugitive slave law to replace the weaker law of 1793. The new law gave the Constitution's fugitive slave clause a formidable new set of teeth, making it easier than ever to return fugitive men and women to slavery. It guaranteed slaveholders the right to a speedy hearing of their claim, unencumbered by vexing writs of habeas corpus or the testimony of defendants. It removed almost every legal recourse available to a person seized as a fugitive, including most features of the personal liberty laws enacted since *Prigg.* And it allowed federal authorities to call any citizen into service to aid in the law's enforcement. Had the Fugitive Slave Law of 1850 been in place in 1842, George Latimer would likely have found himself in irons, under federal guard, and on a Virginia-bound ship, all within a day of his arrest. With the passage of this law, in other words, the federal government shifted its great weight decisively toward enforcing the rights of slaveholders at the expense of free and fugitive African Americans.

This existential threat provoked a militant response. Nell and his fellow colored citizens saw themselves as the proud inheritors of a revolutionary heritage of freedom, entitled to participate fully in the life and government of their country. But when that country's government declared war on them and their liberties, that same heritage required them to go to war against the Revolution's false heirs: the Constitution that protected slavery, the craven lawmakers who did the slaveholders' bidding, and the people of Boston or any other place who stood ready to enforce the Fugitive Slave Law. On that October evening, the "colored citizens of Boston" promised the slave catchers a sustained, disciplined fight. Nell's resolutions called for active and uncompromising resistance to the law—not by individuals alone, but by a League of Freedom, "composed of all those who are ready to resist this law, rescue and protect the slave, at every hazard," even at the risk of life and limb.[5]

Free blacks openly promised defiance in part because they understood a critical dimension of American conceptions of liberty: it was earned in struggle. Their resolutions sought to rally the Boston black community around the defense of the city's many fugitives, but they also appealed to whites, in the hope that they would recognize the tenor and resolve of a

Broadside announcing black activists'
determination to thwart the
Fugitive Slave Law, 1850
Boston Athenæum

genuine revolutionary struggle for freedom. The contemporary struggles
of Hungarian, Italian, and other European patriotic movements moved
white Americans, who easily identified with other people's struggles to cast
off the chains of political tyranny. But the "slavery" against which these
patriots fought was metaphorical. American slavery was real. Black activists knew that most white Americans doubted whether blacks genuinely
deserved freedom or could even appreciate its blessings.

The notion that God had distributed human capacity according to a
hierarchy of race, with whites at the top and blacks on the bottom, had
deep roots even among those whites who owned no slaves. The failure of
American slaves to cast off their shackles seemed, to many whites, to affirm
the ideology of white supremacy. A great many whites saw no contradiction

in "liberty's chosen home" also being a home to slaves. If those slaves deserved freedom, they would seize it as the revolutionaries of 1776 had.[6]
Some black activists, such as Frederick Douglass, even put forward varia-
tions on this theme; in 1855 the fugitive orator concluded an account of
his life-changing act of resisting a beating with a paraphrase of Lord Byron:
"Hereditary bondmen, know ye not / Who would be free, themselves
must strike the blow?"[7] The struggles over the Fugitive Slave Law in the
early 1850s set the stage for a renewed conversation about slaves and their
capacity for revolution, one that would flower in complicated ways later in
the decade. Yet all understood that with the coming of the new law, whatever American slaves did or did not do, free blacks must actively and
publicly resist enslavement or reenslavement, or their claims to citizenship
would lack both credibility and force.

After 1850, therefore, black Bostonians added a potent new dimension
to their assertion of citizenship: concerted physical resistance. In secret
meetings, paramilitary mobilization, and street warfare, they openly re-
belled against the federal government and its laws. They physically resisted
the enforcement of the Fugitive Slave Law, in raids that defied city, state,
and federal authorities. They even took the life of one of the law's enforc-
ers. Yet at the same time they insisted that this was not disloyalty to American ideals or American history, but rather a defiant assertion of those
national values in the face of the craven surrender of white people and
political parties to the Slave Power.

Despite the violence of their rhetoric and actions, these activists mainly
depicted themselves as American patriots, not revolutionaries seeking to
overthrow the social order. Balancing self-assertion and self-restraint, they
insisted on being both bold insurgents and dignified, respectable citizens.
Indeed, even in the midst of the fugitive defense riots of the early 1850s,
the heirs of Crispus Attucks simultaneously began to demand a place for
black men in the state militia. When the state rejected their numerous
petitions, they formed and equipped their own companies, drilled, and

paraded through the city. They insisted, against all evidence and despite persistent discouragement, that they be allowed to continue the tradition of African American military service to state and nation.

The militant mobilization of free black Northerners during the 1850s, and their explicit claim to the American revolutionary tradition, transformed the "colored citizens" into important actors on the national stage. The violent defense of fugitives and the militant assertion of national belonging persuaded some white allies to take their claims more seriously and drew black and white activists into scenes of shared struggle that resembled war as much as politics. This terrified slaveholding elites, who recognized in these scenes fundamental challenges—to the property rights of slaveholders, to a national politics premised on white solidarity and supremacy, and to the federal government's commitment to both. Black activists' forcible efforts to free fugitives from federal custody, their threats against slave catchers, and their well-organized networks of fugitive aid did not make the Civil War inevitable, but they were critical factors in the growing regional polarization about the meaning of slavery and the nature of slaveholders' power. Outmatched in every conceivable way, they nonetheless fought the federal government to a draw, along the way persuading many white Northerners that the time had come to oppose the slaveholders' will, and perhaps even to see their black neighbors as leading figures in that contest. They wanted only, as William Nell put it, to serve in "Freedom's army." In time, they would do just that, with decisive results. In a sense, their final battle against American slavery began in the Belknap Street Church, where William Nell reminded them of the legacy of Crispus Attucks and urged them to defend their liberty by any means necessary.

DEFENDING THE FUGITIVE

William Nell and the other leaders of the October 5, 1850, meeting urgently demanded that the black population of the city resist rather than run. Their audience did not need persuading that slave catching was wrong, but they did need some encouragement to risk remaining in Boston.[8] Already, a New York fugitive was on his way back to slavery, only hours after having been seized.[9] More were sure to follow. "In many towns in the West," Frederick Douglass warned a Faneuil Hall audience that month, "nearly the entire colored population, freemen and fugitives, are so alarmed that they are disposing of their property, and making their way to the British shores" of Canada.[10] So the organizers of the Belknap Street meeting aimed their arguments squarely at men and women whose names rarely appeared in newspapers or minutes of conventions: the laboring men and women, both free- and slave-born, who made up the great majority of the city's black population. This was a time for solidarity. One speaker approvingly noted the presence among those assembled of many "men of over-alls—men of the wharf—those who could do heavy work in the hour of difficulty." He did not have to specify the kind of work; at least some of those men had been at the courthouse back in 1842, and stories of George Latimer would have been common coin on the wharf, especially since the passage of the new and hated law. The speaker did not forget the other half of the city's black workers: in the next breath, he urged the working-women, whose washing and other labors often took them through the city's hotels and boardinghouses, to keep watch for slave hunters. This open appeal to women "was greeted with lively demonstrations," Nell noted.[11] So was Nell's reference to the 1836 fugitive rescue, which he presented as having been the work of the city's black women.[12]

Black political thinkers insisted that they would not be chased away. The British Empire might have abolished slavery, but speaker after speaker insisted that fugitives should remain in the United States, fighting to claim the soil of their birth, dying rather than submitting. Even as the new law moved toward passage earlier that year, black activists resolved "to live in Boston; live *freemen* in Boston, and die *freemen* in Boston."[13] Their insistence in part reflected the fact that thousands of fugitives already populated Canadian settlements. By the end of the 1850s the black population of Canada West—probably exceeded twenty thousand, many of them fugitives. This was more than twice Massachusetts's black population, and among the free states only New York and Pennsylvania's communities were dramatically larger.[14] A national identity other than American seemed to be a reasonable choice for many fugitives. Many black Northerners found this prospect both understandable and deeply troubling.[15] While they helped fugitives flee north, they loudly proclaimed that the best choice was to stand and fight.

They contemplated dying rather than returning to slavery, but they also discussed killing. At the early October meeting, the freeborn Joshua B. Smith, although rapidly gaining a thoroughly respectable fame as a caterer, urged fugitives to arm themselves.[16] Charles Remond told the crowd that Massachusetts "should be our Canada"—our safe haven from slavery, in other words—and that he would fight if he had to. He promised to resist "unto death" rather than leave Massachusetts. "If to avow this was treason," he explained to much cheering, "he gloried in it."[17] In New York City, George Downing declared himself willing "to die, or to teach the individual who undertakes to carry out the provisions of this bill, that his life is in danger . . . if any man—any found in human shape—dare to cross the threshold of my castle, I'll send him to h—l before he shall accomplish his mission."[18] Although a native New Yorker, the defiant Downing soon made himself at home among the black radicals of Boston. Lewis Hayden, presiding over the Boston meeting, said nothing, but no one who knew him doubted that he would fight rather than flee.

Another Belknap Street meeting nine days later spawned a revitalized Boston Vigilance Committee (BVC), which included a small number of black men and took nominal charge of defending the city's fugitives. It sought to mobilize antislavery whites and to drum up moral, political, and financial support for the project of fugitive defense. A widely published appeal reminded white readers that fugitives "sought a refuge in Boston, perhaps having heard that our fathers took some interest in the freedom of mankind, and thinking a few sparks of manhood might burn in our hearts."[19] It succeeded. This third incarnation of the Boston Vigilance Committee defied precedent by remaining a vital organization for almost a decade to come.

The BVC's official records suggested a primarily white-run organization with a sprinkling of black managers, but this belied the actual division of labor. While white members dominated most of its committees, the relief committee, which did most of the practical work, included Nell, Hayden, and Joshua Smith. Nell was later appointed general agent.[20] Of the three, only Smith had substantial economic resources of his own; the other two organized relief on the ground and were reimbursed for their efforts by the committee. During the 1850s the relief committee assisted more than four hundred fugitives, a quarter of whom (the rhetoric of October 1850 notwithstanding) it helped send on to Canada or other safe havens.[21] This took an immense amount of day-to-day work, and the records of the committee's expenses represent every phase of this activity: twenty-seven dollars to Lewis Hayden for hiring a carriage to take fugitives out of the city; nearly fifty dollars for an appeal to be circulated to thousands of churches across the state; hundreds to reimburse Nell and others; down to three dollars paid one Peter Kelly for posting three hundred handbills "describing the personal appearance of Slave Hunters."[22]

It is tempting to imagine this network of money and effort as a well-oiled machine, one that could instantly perform the alchemy of turning fugitives into free people. In later years, the ivy of myth curled fondly around these obscure labors, and eager authors polished them into a gleaming "Underground Railroad" of clearly marked stations and numerous conductors. But if this was a machine, it was a crude and unreliable device, not the steam-driven marvel of popular legend. The people running it did not manage a seamless and efficient network of safe houses; indeed, they could not always tell a fugitive from an impostor. Even a slave hunter whose name and description had been widely circulated could move freely in a crowd of black citizens by the simple expedient of changing his hat.[23] A creative, improvisational, and imperfect network of friends and conspirators, this "railroad" ran on good faith and good luck and could be undone by a shortage of either one.

The story of fugitive defense in Boston during the first half of the 1850s is not one of antislavery activists growing ever more skillful and staunch. In fact, the stories from that era that became the subjects of public conversation chart a quite different progression: the steadily growing ability of city, state, and federal authorities to thwart the plans of fugitives' defenders. It became harder, not easier, to interfere with the Fugitive Slave Law once its own railroad picked up steam. The story of efforts to rescue fugitives also traces the growing rage, despair, and even recklessness of black Bostonians and their allies as they realized that they were unable to prevent fugitives from being returned to slavery. Their victory over the Fugitive Slave Law, such as it was, came not from superior strength, but because their resistance grew so militant that it provoked their enemies to overreach politically—to respond with such overwhelming force that even antiabolitionists began to wonder whether the federal government had put the rights of slaveholders ahead of all other considerations, including white liberty. Their real victory against the law took form not in captives liberated—there were few of those—but in the political backlash against federal enforcement by whites who once thought they had little at stake in this fight.

Fugitive defense in the wake of the Fugitive Slave Law began with a pair of success stories that seemed to bode well: the protection of William and Ellen Craft, and the rescue of Shadrach Minkins. The Crafts, husband and wife, had escaped slavery in Macon, Georgia, by a brilliant feat of transracial cross-dressing. Ellen, who was very light-skinned, disguised herself as the sickly young scion of a white planter family, who was traveling north for medical treatment; William played the young "man's" enslaved valet. They arrived in Boston in the late 1840s, and their improbable story and its happy conclusion quickly made them antislavery celebrities. By 1850 William had his own carpenter's shop, a few doors down from Lewis

Hayden's clothing store, while Ellen worked as a seamstress. The couple boarded at the Haydens' house on Southac, a lodging common to many fugitives as well as to long-term residents of the city.[24]

Their fame embarrassed and enraged their former owner. Following the passage of the Fugitive Slave Law, he sent slave hunters to Boston with orders to obtain a warrant, bring the Crafts before a federal commissioner, and return them to slavery.[25] The Boston Vigilance Committee quickly identified his agents, Hughes and Knight, when they reached Boston; the committee nailed up handbills all over the city describing the Georgia men and warning black residents of their presence. At a Vigilance Committee meeting, Lewis Hayden insisted passionately that the Crafts should stay and defy the law. They agreed.[26]

Vigilance men moved from hard talk to armed defiance. While Henry Bowditch drove Ellen Craft to a safe house in neighboring Brookline, William Craft barricaded himself in his shop on Cambridge Street.[27] Theodore Parker arrived at the shop to find the Georgia fugitive cool, determined, and extremely well armed, with several pistols and two knives.[28] When Bowditch later offered to drive Craft out to see his wife, the fugitive handed him a pistol and agreed to go only if Bowditch was prepared to use it. After a moment of shock at the thought of killing a man, the doctor reflected "that if I were Craft I should glory in slaying any one who attempted to make me or my wife a slave." Bowditch took the pistol and the plunge, experiencing yet another moment of icy but exhilarating immersion in the company of a fugitive slave.[29]

The Crafts were protected by far more than a white man's courage: fugitive and freeborn African Americans mobilized on their behalf. "No man could approach within a hundred yards of Craft's shop," a reporter claimed, "without being seen by a hundred eyes, and a signal would call a powerful body at a moment's notice."[30] Craft soon moved from his barricaded shop to even safer quarters at the Haydens'. Many years later, he reported that Lewis Hayden had readied kegs of gunpowder in the basement, in case the slave hunters forced their way inside. If the choice became one of slavery or death, he explained, Hayden was prepared to set the powder alight and destroy them all. The story became a favorite, told and retold in ever more elaborate versions, until finally it took the form of Hayden standing before the slave hunters and above the gunpowder, lit match in hand, forcing the Southerners to retreat. If this most dramatic version of the tale rested on flimsy foundations, at its core remained the unassailable truth that these people had prepared the means to kill or die rather than return to slavery.[31]

While the Crafts went to ground, the Vigilance Committee and large numbers of black Bostonians harassed the slave hunters in the courts and in the streets. Abolitionist lawyers had the Georgians charged with attempted kidnapping and other crimes, while great numbers of black Bostonians, some of them threatening violence, pursued the two men wherever they went. The astonished slave hunters asserted that fifteen hundred black men, women, and children had attended their arraignment for attempted kidnapping, a figure equal to three-quarters of Boston's black population.[32] Surprise and unease probably inflated the estimate, but not the black population's determination. Soon another crowd of black Bostonians chased the slave hunters down Cambridge Street and clear across the bridge, causing them to run the tolls, for which infraction Vigilance Committee lawyers promptly had them arrested.[33] Had Latimer's onetime owner James Gray returned to Boston in 1851, he might have concluded that he had had it comparatively easy.

As in 1842, the tactics of legal and extralegal harassment functioned together. Theodore Parker made this point all but explicit when he, Bowditch, and other white Vigilance Committee members called on Hughes and Knight at their hotel.[34] Parker warned them, Hughes recalled, "that he had kept the mob off of me for two days, and was afraid he could not do it any longer."[35] It was the same game that white and black defenders of George Latimer played on his captors, executed this time with larger numbers, better coordination, and more physical confrontation. The slave hunters understood perfectly what Parker was telling them. Within days they left the city, and the Crafts were on their way to safety and fame in England.

Even as the street battles tested the limits of proper behavior in response to the Fugitive Slave Law, men and women—even those who professed a strong commitment to women's equality—also drew clear distinctions between their proper roles. Consider the Crafts. Before they left for England, Theodore Parker officiated at their wedding, held at the Haydens' house. In solemnizing the union, Parker told William Craft that in addition to the duties marriage always imposed, the present situation required something more of him as a husband. As an outlaw, he had no legal right or means to protect himself and his wife, only a right under natural law. "So I charged him," Parker wrote, "if the worst came to the worst, to defend the life & the liberty of his wife against any slave-hunter at all hazards, though in doing so he dug his own grave & the grave of a thousand men." He picked up a Bible and—from the armory still strewn about the Haydens' parlor— a bowie knife, and put one in each of William Craft's hands: "one for the body, one for his soul."[36]

Parker's bit of theater, with its elevated rhetoric of chivalric protection, did not tell the whole story, for fugitive defense was a practical as well as a principled undertaking. Had the combined activities of the Vigilance Committee and the vigilant community failed to drive Hughes and Knight from the city, preparations were under way to have William Craft arrested for various offenses—for example, for assault with a dangerous weapon. Antislavery lawyers hoped in this way, if all else failed, to have Craft prosecuted in a state or local court and thereby force the question of whether the Fugitive Slave Law could override a state criminal process. Abolitionist lawyers contemplated an even more hard-nosed strategy, one that turned Parker's piety on its head. Slave marriages had no legal force, South or North, yet the Crafts were living in Massachusetts as man and wife even before Parker's ceremony. William Craft might therefore have been arrested for the criminal offense of fornication, placing him in state custody and at least potentially out of reach of the Fugitive Slave Law. According to one antislavery paper, William Craft had been willing to go along with this strategy if it became necessary. It did not mention whether Ellen Craft was consulted.[37]

The apparent silence of women during such militant adventures was only apparent. The crowds that chased Hughes and Knight likely included both men and women, for women had been taking part in fugitive rescues since at least the 1830s. In 1847, for example, a slave hunter reached Beacon Hill and actually entered a home in search of his quarry before he was discovered. It was the middle of the day, when few men were about. The women and children of Smith Court, led by the intrepid world traveler Mrs. Nancy Prince, physically dragged the slave hunter back outside and sent him running, shouts and stones following him down the street. But this story did not come to light until the 1890s, for the physical work of fugitive defense in the 1850s was generally presented as the work of men.[38]

Yet women's activism and public activity flowered during the 1850s. Extraordinary figures such as Sojourner Truth and Harriet Tubman came to be revered for their physical strength and courage, while white and black women emerged as lecturers and even newspaper editors.[39] Black male activists, perhaps even more than their white counterparts, welcomed the rise of these women and the movement for woman suffrage. Suffragists remembered Douglass warmly for his support for women's right to vote at the Seneca Falls women's rights convention in 1848.[40] He was not the only one. After William Watkins moved to Rochester to join *Frederick Douglass' Paper*, he became a "friend" of the Rochester Ladies' Anti-Slavery Society and served alongside Susan B. Anthony as secretary for a women's rights convention.[41] William Nell and the rest of the speakers at a meeting of black Free Soil men publicly regretted that women "were yet denied their right to vote," though Nell added that "their means of appeal to husbands, father and brothers, intelligently directed, were various and powerful."[42] This was not a universal position among black activists—a meeting of leading Illinois men split over the question of women's voting rights, and it took strenuous debate before Mary Ann Shadd could be admitted as the lone female delegate to a meeting of Douglass's National Council.[43] Women's rights as a cause, however, was clearly gaining strength.

Within the fugitive defense movement itself, though, women's work often took place behind the scenes or in ways that are difficult to discern in the historical record. Most of the payments made by the Vigilance Committee account books went to men, but this fact takes on richer meaning when one considers that most adult women were subject to coverture, the legal subordination of wives and children to husbands and fathers in economic matters. The numerous payments made by the Vigilance Committee to Lewis Hayden, for example, almost certainly do not reflect the division of labor within the Hayden household, which in the early 1850s included a boardinghouse and a used-clothing store.[44] It may well have been Lewis Hayden himself who provided fugitives with clothing and hired carriages to take them out of the city. But while he moved about the city, who took charge of the residence up the hill on Southac Street, and its many boarders? Almost certainly the day-to-day management of the boardinghouse was Harriet Hayden's responsibility, and even that was too much work for one person: a British-born domestic servant lived with the Haydens that year, and at least one servant lived with them when they relocated down the street a few years later.[45] Only one name entered the records of the city's lawyers and bookkeepers, but the couple's labors were complementary and mutually necessary.

Lewis Hayden soon entered the public record in a much more dramatic way, as the war over Boston's fugitives escalated that winter. In Washington, both President Millard Fillmore and Secretary of State Daniel Webster, the Massachusetts Whig luminary who had staked his reputation and political future on the compromise legislation of 1850, sought to reassure their Southern partners that the compromise would hold. The Craft fiasco notwithstanding, they promised, slave property would indeed be sacrosanct, even in Massachusetts. Elsewhere around the North, slave catchers seized dozens of black people. As foes of the law had feared and expected, the great majority were deemed to be fugitives and returned to slavery. But as autumn ebbed into winter, the handful of efforts by slaveholders to re-capture fugitives in Boston came to nothing.[46]

The high point of Bostonians' successful defiance of the Fugitive Slave Law came in February 1851, following the arrest of Shadrach Minkins, a fugitive from Norfolk. Minkins's owner, learning that the fugitive was in Boston, hired a hardfisted constable named John Caphart to bring him back. Caphart obtained a warrant, and on the rainy morning of Saturday, February 15, deputy U.S. marshals seized Minkins as he worked in a Court Square coffee shop, hustling him quickly across the street into the U.S. courthouse.[47]

As fast as the deputy marshals could secure the courtroom and hurry the proceedings along, the Vigilance Committee and less well-known black activists mobilized. Several hundred people, more than half of them black, converged on the courtroom. So did half a dozen lawyers seeking grounds for Minkins's release. The captive's prospects seemed bleak: Caphart had brought evidence of Minkins's identity and status with him, and that was all the Fugitive Slave Law required. Further, the federal commissioner hearing the case was a loyalist of the procompromise Whig leader Daniel Webster, and therefore presumably committed to the law's speedy enforce-ment. The antislavery lawyers, Robert Morris among them, failed to obtain a writ of habeas corpus, which would have brought the case before a state judge. They did, however, obtain a three-day delay in the proceedings. Once the delay was announced, federal marshals began to clear the court-room, herding the spectators to the doors. One black clergyman, Leonard Grimes, was allowed to remain inside with Minkins. Had the marshals known of the minister's prior record of helping fugitives escape, they might have reconsidered this decision.[48]

Here an old victory may have made all the difference, for the Latimer Law of 1843 impeded the marshals' work clearing the courtroom. Accord-ing to that law, state officials faced fines or dismissal if they participated in the rendering of a fugitive; constables and other court officers, worried about putting their jobs in jeopardy, therefore refrained from aiding the marshals. Likewise, the law forbade the use of state facilities in returning fugitives, so the authorities confined Minkins in the federal courtroom itself, and not in the more secure state-run jail. Outside the courtroom, an increasingly restive crowd swelled as the news spread across the city, and the federal officials now faced this throng with insufficient help, in a courtroom that had not been designed to serve as a citadel. The grubby and unglamorous work of collecting signatures for the monster Latimer petition back in 1843 was now proving its worth.

A small opening was all the militants needed. As marshals shooed the last few spectators out through the courtroom's vestibule, the guard attempted to pull the outer door shut after them. Here the protestors in the hallway made their move, grabbing the door and holding it open. For a moment the marshals within held on, but soon they were overwhelmed; more than a dozen black men wrenched the door open and rushed into the vestibule. The outnumbered marshals tried to hold the inner door shut, but soon they too gave way. A large group of black men rushed into the courtroom, lifted Minkins into the air, and carried him downstairs and out into the square. They then set off toward Cambridge Street and the foot of Beacon Hill, a jubilant crowd following. The rescuers put Minkins in a cab, but the crowd surrounded it so closely that it could not move, a scene that might have been comical but for the danger to the fugitive's freedom. They took him out again and hustled him down Cambridge Street, then up the hill on Garden Street, heading toward Southac.

Somewhere along the way—probably as a key figure in the courtroom struggle itself, but the record is unclear and contradictory—Lewis Hayden joined the rescue party.[49] Morris was already among them, and the two men must have conferred quickly. They dared not hide Minkins at the Haydens' house, where the authorities would know to look. Instead, they took refuge at the nearby home of a widow known to be friendly to the cause.[50] Soon a hired carriage stopped at the corner, and Hayden and Minkins got in. Hayden directed the driver down the hill and across the Charles River bridge to Cambridge. From there, John J. Smith, a Cambridge resident since the school boycott, helped carry the fugitive west to Concord. In a matter of days, Shadrach Minkins was safe in Canada.[51]

The rescue infuriated the Fillmore administration and "deeply mortified" the city's leading men of business and respectable party politics. The fugitive slave commissioner in Boston described the rescuers as "levying war" on the United States. Henry Clay took to the Senate floor to vent his anger at this "outrage," the work of "African descendants . . . people who possess no part, as I contend, in our political system." If Clay came to realize, as the government began its prosecution of those arrested for the rescue, that the Lewis Hayden named in those charges was the man who had troubled his sleep before, he said nothing. Hayden, for his part, certainly must have taken satisfaction in having provoked Clay's outburst. The former fugitive was levying war on the white republic in the name of the American Revolution, and winning, it seemed just then.[52]

"A holy day in my calendar," Henry Bowditch called the Minkins rescue, but black celebrants had little time for joyful reflection.[53] Many of the leaders of Boston's black abolitionist community, including Grimes, Morris, and Hayden, now stood in legal jeopardy. Nell, who had been recovering from an illness at the Remond home in Salem during the arrest and trial, keenly regretted missing all the excitement. Had he been in Boston, "in all probability I should have been present . . . and stood a chance to share the glory now monopolized by a few of my friends stigmatised as Rioters—but let us work on."[54] Nell's lamented glory was of dubious value. Constables found Hayden at the Anti-Slavery Office and placed him under arrest. Witnesses identified him as a ringleader in the escape and the court held him for trial. The authorities charged Morris, too, along with other neighborhood conspirators including Thomas Paul Smith, Morris's opponent in the ongoing school fight. Elizur Wright and another white abolitionist were also arrested. By the beginning of March, federal authorities had indicted ten men, most of them black, for taking part in the rescue.[55]

While black Bostonians applauded the rescue of Shadrach Minkins, they did not draw from it unanimous conclusions. The Vigilance Committee, now meeting nightly, went on a war footing, appointing a committee of ten "minute men, who might be called upon for services in any emergency."[56] But for others, the lesson of the affair was not that rescues might succeed, but that Boston's fugitives could be seized. Minkins's near-rendition experience persuaded many black Bostonians that they were indeed in jeopardy. Hundreds followed him to Canada over the next few months.

None of the real or alleged conspirators could be convicted. Hayden went on trial in April, but the jury hung, voting nine to three for conviction; many men later claimed to have hidden their abolitionist convictions in order to serve on the jury and protect Hayden.[57] The community followed the case closely. At a meeting to bid farewell to British antislavery ally George Thompson, the news of the jury's final deadlock in Hayden's case "brought down the house," reported the *Liberator*.[58] Although zealous authorities continued mounting cases into 1852, they failed to win convictions: on jury after jury, minorities of antislavery white men refused to vote to convict, forcing the release of Morris and the other accused participants.[59]

The Minkins rescue, though, mobilized more powerful opposition than mere local officials. The U.S. secretary of state himself kept tabs on the prosecution; Daniel Webster's carefully negotiated sectional compromise over slavery, and a long-planned presidential campaign based on that achievement, hung in the balance. Federal pressure on local authorities to prevent any further rescues was therefore intense. They would not be caught flat-footed again, no matter what the Latimer Law said.

The forces of slavery's law and order got a chance to demonstrate their determination just two months later, in April 1851, when Boston slave catchers seized a fugitive named Thomas Sims.[60] Though the Vigilance Committee immediately rallied its forces on Sims's behalf, the antislavery forces seemed less prepared and less determined than before Minkins's escape. "[T]here is neither organization, resolution, plan nor popular sentiment," fumed the radical minister Thomas Wentworth Higginson; "the negroes are cowed & the abolitionists irresolute & hopeless, with nothing better to do on Saturday than to send off circulars to clergymen!"[61] The Vigilance Committee's meetings were no more than "a disorderly convention, each having his own plan or theory."[62] Garrisonian nonresistants disclaimed any resort to force. Free Soil men sought to stay within the law. Of all the antislavery workers in the city, only Hayden and Grimes— Higginson's dig at "the negroes" notwithstanding—seemed eager to concoct a plot to free Sims.[63]

Higginson, despite his skepticism about African Americans' capacity to safeguard their own liberties, would play an ever larger role in their militant campaign for citizenship. A gifted writer, a self-styled rebel, and a man supremely confident in his own judgment, Higginson would go on to lead black troops in battle against the Confederacy, to shepherd the poems of

Thomas Wentworth Higginson
Courtesy of the Massachusetts
Historical Society

Emily Dickinson to their first publication, and to fill the pages of leading journals such as the *Atlantic* with his own writing. At this early moment, he was simply a Harvard-trained minister of abolitionist inclinations working somewhat unhappily in the conservative North Shore town of Newburyport. Within a year he would abandon this Whig-dominated home for an antislavery congregation among the industrial workers of Worcester. He was already known as a friend of fugitives, of the Free Soil movement, and of white radicals like Garrison and Parker. No matter what city he called home, he kept one foot, and sometimes both, in the roiling waters of Boston's movement for fugitive defense.[64]

In the case of Sims, the city, state, and federal governments took no chances. The aldermen refused to open Faneuil Hall for a protest meeting; they had already committed it as the garrison for a militia company called in by the governor to prevent a rescue attempt. Policemen drilled in Court Square with drawn swords. In a measure as remarkable for its symbolism as for its effect, city officials draped a chain around the courthouse and closed it to the public except by written permission of the U.S. marshal. Judges on their way to the bench stooped to pass beneath its links, presenting an image of justice bowing before the Slave Power that no abolitionist commentator could resist.[65]

"[T]he display of physical force goes beyond the sublime & takes the step into the ridiculous," Higginson wrote to a newspaper, but privately he found officials' precautions anything but absurd. The best plan he, Hayden, and Grimes could devise was a desperate one: it called for Sims to jump from the ungrated window of his third-floor cell onto mattresses laid on the street below. The conspirators secured the bedding in the nearby law office of Henry Bowditch's brother William. Grimes, visiting Sims as a member of the clergy, apprised him of the plan. As the hour approached, however, the authorities, one step ahead of them, began installing bars on Sims's window. Without this precaution—anything but "ridiculous," under the circumstances—the government might have lost another fugitive.[66]

Black men had demonstrated their willingness to challenge the government, and now the government pushed back. Suspecting that an armed assault on the courthouse was planned, constables stopped black men walking nearby and searched them for weapons. One unarmed victim of such a search swore out a complaint and had the offending officer himself arrested. But police continued the practice, stopping and searching William Nell's good friend Isaac Snowden, who was walking with his brother near the courthouse at one in the morning; something about the men's "free and independent" demeanor, the arresting officer explained, had alarmed him. Found to be carrying a pistol, Snowden was bound over at six hundred dollars' bail.[67]

White allies fulminated loudly but kept their protest within the bounds of nonviolence.[68] Some, like Henry Bowditch, feared that violence would bring bloodshed without freeing the captive. The doctor went to bed dispirited on Friday, April 11, only to be awakened at three by a close comrade in the Vigilance Committee who told him that officials were preparing to move the fugitive to a waiting ship. Bowditch immediately "feared that a small band of ardent but rash men were about to attempt a rescue." What he saw when he hurried to Court Square initially terrified him: a hundred policemen staring grimly at as many furious antislavery activists. But no mass confrontation materialized. The Vigilance Committee leaders realized the presence of so many heavily armed opponents gave them no hope of freeing Sims by force, at least not in the city itself. They remained on the scene only in order to bear animated witness to the fugitive's rendition. Learning this, Bowditch rushed home to rouse his oldest son, Nat, and bring him back to take part.[69]

Sims's return to slavery in those early morning hours lingered in witnesses' imagination as evidence of a revolution betrayed. Shortly before dawn, the nightmare spectacle Bowditch and his comrades had conjured in the *Latimer Journal and North Star* a decade before came creaking to life. With the mayor and chief U.S. marshal in attendance, the police and city watch formed a hollow square and placed Sims within it, marching him away from the courthouse and down State Street toward the wharf, where the brig *Acorn* waited. Bowditch, no longer the author of this drama, was but a helpless witness and bitter commentator. He, his son, Nat, and their comrades kept pace with the military procession, heckling the soldiers and officials with a call-and-response of condemnation: "'Where is Liberty?' says one. 'She is dead!' cried another." They arrived finally at the wharf, where more police waited. Other antislavery men tried to board the vessel next to the *Acorn*, perhaps as part of a plot to intercept the vessel carrying Sims, but were driven back at sword point. The ship sailed for Virginia, and the defeated protesters walked back up State Street, pausing for a prayer at the site of the Boston Massacre. On the way down the street, Bowditch and his comrades had pointed out "to those minions of slavery the holy spot over which they were treading," a generic reminder of the revolutionary heritage and its despoliation. But on the return journey there was a new note in the song: the Massacre site was an appropriate place for prayer because it was "where Attucks fell" in 1770. In the aftermath of Sims's reenslavement, a martyred black revolutionary had renewed appeal.[70]

Sims's rendition was not the end of their defiance, for fugitives and their allies across the North confronted slave hunters and officials with increasing militancy. After 1850, both the fierceness of such defenses and the makeup of the defenders underwent changes. In Christiana, Pennsylvania, in 1851, armed fugitives fired upon their pursuers, killing one slaveholder's son. Gradually, radicalized whites began to play larger parts. In Syracuse, New York, shortly after Sims's rendition, a band of armed black and white men broke a fugitive known as Jerry McHenry out of his jail. Though many of the rescuers openly avowed their participation, no one was successfully prosecuted.[71]

Boston soon developed a band of semiprofessional fugitive rescuers—a crew of black and white men, operating in Boston Harbor under the command of the white abolitionist sailor and Vigilance Committee agent Austin Bearse. Once a crewman on slaving ships, Bearse now commanded yachts—the *Flirt*, and later the *Moby-Dick*—to rescue fugitives from the vessels that had carried them to Boston. His sturdy physical presence also made him an ideal doorkeeper for the private meetings of the Vigilance Committee. The committee underwrote his activities, and some white men, among them Henry Kemp and William Bowditch, joined him in his raids. Sometimes black men on the docks alerted him to a sudden emergency. At other times, Wendell Phillips arrived at his door with word that had come through private channels.[72]

Another figure played a key role in these events: Lewis Hayden. Unlike Bearse and other figures, he never published an autobiographical account detailing his exploits, but in the margins of others' accounts one can glimpse him at work: hurriedly leaving a church service to see to "a slave mother and child just arrived in a vessel from Virginia," or reaching out his arms to lift a fugitive girl, Arianna Sparrow, from Bearse's boat to the wharf, never setting her down, she recalled, "until we landed in his doorway."[73] Sparrow's story was a common one: once fugitives made it ashore they often ended up at the Hayden house. By the mid-1850s the building probably lacked much value in terms of secrecy. Authorities and slave hunters had known about it for several years, and Harriet Beecher Stowe probably ended whatever mystery remained when Bearse brought the newly famous author there to visit a dozen fugitives in 1853.[74] Still, as late as the autumn of 1854 fugitives found lodging at the Haydens'; the arsenal within and vigilant neighbors without must have provided security after secrecy no longer could.[75]

"COLORED PATRIOTS"

Alongside this open, revolutionary defiance of the law, black Bostonians continued to imagine themselves as people the polity could call on for defense rather than as people it should fear. Even black activists who provided minds and muscle for illegal activities such as the rescue of Shadrach

Minkins fought simultaneously for a quite different goal: the right to serve as citizen-soldiers in the state militia. In practice, militia duty was hardly a martial profession. It consisted mainly of annual musters, parades in fancy dress, and cotillions and levees hosted by admiring female relations. But for these reasons as well, exclusion was hard to stomach. Black men parading in state uniforms would stake a claim to the city's streets that only the boldest rowdies could dispute. Elegant ceremonial evenings honoring these men would draw respectful press notice and affirm black men and women's dignity and propriety as equal citizens.[76] Militia activists hoped that the incorporation of well-ordered black companies marching in state militias would undercut the stereotype of black men as a danger to good order while also establishing their capacity for discipline and bravery. No more would they stand merely with the slave rebels against whom white solidarity was forged, and with whom the nation's enemies sought alliance.

Black activists could not take part in militia drills and festivals, which were restricted to white men only. That bar did not originate in a state policy but in the explicit terms of the federal militia law of 1792, which restricted militia service to adult white men. Though black men had served in every army the United States had fielded, the facts were no match for a constitutional order set on protecting slaveholding. While several private military companies had existed as early as the 1820s, these were not formal parts of the state militia system.[77] The white republic could not formally acknowledge "colored citizens" as soldiers and still retain its character.

At the same time, local circumstances provided an inspiring alternative, for just to the south Rhode Island sanctioned a black company in its state militia. After black men helped the state's governing party suppress the Dorr, they were well rewarded. An 1842 convention enfranchised all adult males, rejecting a proposal to duplicate New York's racially discriminatory property qualification. From then on, as well, the state authorized a black militia unit. The lesson was clear: military service to the state could establish men's worthiness and bring them closer to formal equality.[78]

Aware of these contradictions between history and law, and between state and nation, members of Boston's black activist leadership launched a campaign of petitions, protests, and organization against their exclusion from the militia. Throughout the 1850s they asked statewide assemblies to remove the word "white" from the state's militia law, and for the official sanction and stand of arms that would make them legitimate citizen-soldiers. When that failed, they created militia companies of their own. Black Bostonians were not alone: a New York company had formed by 1848, and militia fever soon seemed to take hold of black communities throughout the North.[79]

The leader in the Boston effort was Robert Morris, whose activism over the past few years had landed him in the courtroom as both a lawyer and a defendant. In 1852 and 1853, Morris organized petitions to the state legislature—then controlled by the Free Soil–Democratic "coalition," some of whose members were friendly to African American claims—and was called to testify before its Joint Committee on the Militia. Each time, he asked that the legislature strike the word "white" from the state's militia laws, or for permission to form a military company. Morris described the racial proscription as an anachronism and a contradiction: it violated the general trend of the state's laws, he argued, and the state's erasure of racial distinction in every governmental realm but (at that point) the common schools. The exclusion also ignored the fact that black men had participated in every one of the country's military undertakings, from the Revolution and War of 1812 to the suppression of the Dorr Rebellion.[80]

Morris and his colleague William J. Watkins had these facts at their fingertips thanks to William Nell. In the early 1840s, with the aid of Wendell Phillips's substantial library, Nell began recovering the history of Attucks and other black veterans of the Revolution.[81] By the early 1850s he had published two editions of a pamphlet, *Services of Colored Americans in the Wars of 1776 and 1812*, which chronicled and documented black men's service to the republic while studiously ignoring the thorny truth that in each struggle at least as many took up arms for the nation's foes.

Nell was not the only one who believed past glories could lend encouragement to present struggles. On March 5, 1851—the anniversary of the Boston Massacre, and just weeks after Minkins's dramatic rescue—Remond, Hayden, and several other black men joined William Nell in petitioning the state legislature for a monument to Attucks's memory.[82]

Nell's documentation of black military service and his promotion of Attucks as a black revolutionary hero were tactical moves in the war against caste. In Nell's view, "colored citizens" needed to demonstrate their active connection and commitment to the American revolutionary legacy in order to take their rightful place in its rituals, memory, and government. He hoped, too, to shame and provoke his white neighbors and allies into defending black Americans' common stake in the Revolution and the republic. Most of all, he and his colleagues sought to inspire their friends and allies to resist the Fugitive Slave Law as fiercely and bravely as Attucks had resisted the tyranny of the Crown. Nell hoped to use Attucks and his heirs as the entering wedge for a much broader demonstration of black worthiness for full citizenship.[83]

While he hoped to persuade whites, Nell's primary purpose as a scholar was to provide ammunition for his black colleagues around the nation in their war against exclusion and hostility. It was a job that needed doing. The Cleveland *Aliened American*, edited by William H. Day, one of the best-educated black men of the era, frankly acknowledged that "[t]he facts in Mr. Nell's work are not generally known."[84] With the pamphlet's publication, those facts could quickly reach the people who could best put it to use: the orators and activists making the case for black people's integral part in the American revolutionary heritage and military tradition.

Nell's historical work provided his friends in the militia movement with both encouragement and ammunition as they approached the legislature in the early 1850s. They had reason to be hopeful, for these were the years when their Free Soil allies, in coalition with Democrats, dominated the state legislature. Both Watkins and Morris had campaigned for the

Free Soil party, and Morris corresponded with antislavery U.S. senator Charles Sumner, whom the coalition legislature had sent to Washington. Morris stumped for Free Soil among black Bostonians, telling an 1852 meeting stories of the Shadrach Minkins rescue. Watkins, for his part, "eloquently enforced the duty of every colored voter to sustain the Free Soil party." They were not alone: the Free Soil banner had the support of other leading men such as William Nell and Lewis Hayden. "Stirring times here" among the "Colored Free Soilers," Nell reported in late 1852.[85]

Watkins quickly joined Morris as a prime mover in the militia campaign, and the two appeared before an 1853 legislative committee armed with arguments. Watkins's remarks, later published as "Our Rights as Men," described the petitioners as "men, proud of, and conscious of the inherent dignity of manhood," but "dignity" emphatically did not mean turning the other cheek. Watkins derided the title character of *Uncle Tom's Cabin* for a "Christian meekness and becoming resignation" ill suited to the present moment.[86] Instead, Watkins emphasized the twin critical components of revolutionary citizenship: on the one hand, propriety, respectability, and dignity; on the other, men's uncompromising insistence on their rights.

Watkins himself sought to embody both militancy and propriety. He had already been a ringleader in the tarring and feathering of Thomas Paul Smith. Soon he treated the readers of *Frederick Douglass' Paper* to a reverie on the qualities of "the bold and dashing Reformer," who "lives in the tempest" and "comes with his flaming sword" to cut through the ignorance of an oppressed and blinkered people. The "Reformer" faced this opposition with "strong nerve, and potent arm, determined will, moral courage, strong powers of analysis, depth and breadth of comprehension, indomitable perseverance, correct judgment, and a world-wide heart, full of hope and love."[87] The fact that this figure was in fact a writer, "whose pen should manufacture words of fire," made it clear Watkins was talking about himself. Yet in the law-bound confines of a hearing room, Watkins understood that legislators, like judges, sought the comfort of precedent. He therefore brought Nell's pamphlet on black military service with him, and spent about a quarter of his time before the committee reading directly from it—a testament to Nell's impact on black martial consciousness, if not to Watkins's rhetorical acumen.[88]

Although they both embraced the militia and Free Soil causes, the rapid rise of an anti-immigrant movement in the state, largely directed against Irish Catholic refugees, exposed a divide between Watkins and Morris. In keeping with his criticism of meekness, Watkins dove into state politics with a becoming ruthlessness: the petitioners, he continued, were "law-abiding, tax-paying, liberty-loving, NATIVE-BORN, AMERICAN CITIZENS." Morris did not echo Watkins's nativist emphasis on black men's status as native-born Americans. In fact, he had many Irish American clients in his law practice and employed an Irish office boy, Patrick Collins, who later became the mayor of Boston.[89] Instead, he told the legislative committee that he admired the pluck of Irish immigrants who had formed a militia company despite the opposition of native-born Protestants.[90] They had acted as men should.

But neither the nativism of Watkins nor the eloquence of Morris kept the 1853 legislative committee from turning down the militiamen's petition, a blow to both men's sense that they were becoming part of the political mainstream. Morris had expected that the lone Free Soil member on the committee would support his petition, but the man had not even offered a minority report on their behalf.[91] They then turned their attention to an 1853 state constitutional convention, petitioning to remove the word "white" from the qualifications for military service and testifying before the convention's committee on the militia.[92] The convention's delegates included some men they had reason to think they could count on, particularly Henry Wilson of Natick, whose language in favor of their petition must have heartened Nell. "The first victim of the Boston Massacre, on the 5th of March, 1770, which made the fires of resistance burn more intensely, was a colored man," Wilson told his colleagues. "They feel the exclusion as an indignity to their race." But many delegates continued to believe federal law explicitly limited enrollment to white men.[93]

Their chief nemesis in the convention, Benjamin F. Hallett, explained that the federal government would never accept the enrollment of black militiamen; further, enrolling black men in the militia was as unconstitutional (and as incongruous) as enrolling women. "You may just as lawfully raise a battalion of 'Amazons,'" he mocked. He understood, and just as clearly rejected, Watkins's pursuit of "Our Rights as Men." The state attorney general concurred, in language that made the whiteness of citizenship still more apparent: "Why call them to the parade, unfurl the national banner over their heads, bid them march to the music and mimic the pride, pomp and circumstance of glorious war," he asked, "when the discriminations and disabilities of color must, under the law, cleave to them even there."[94] The committee rejected the black men's appeal, and, in a desultory end to a frustrating process, the convention finally refused even to enter the petitioners' anguished protest in its official journal.[95]

The failure to win any acknowledgment at all caused a momentary crisis of faith in party politics. Given the Free Soil success, militia activists had entered 1853 with high hopes of a civic transformation stirred by the ballot. But after the militia movement's rejection by both the 1853 legislature and the subsequent constitutional convention, Watkins excoriated the weakness of the white Free Soil men in terms Nell described as "caustic."[96] At an August 1 speech in New Bedford later that year, Watkins lit into the Free Soil delegates at the constitutional convention. Their speeches had been "admirable specimens of rhetoric," he fumed, but when the majority moved to reject their claims, these "eloquent *talkers* in the cause of liberty" folded.[97] Black men could be the victims of state power, but they could not yet be its agents.

CONFRONTING THE "GREAT SLAVE REPUBLIC"

In his usual spirit of bravado, Watkins declared at the end of 1853 that "no more fugitives will be carried out of Boston."[98] Despite the lingering memories of Thomas Sims and the long chain of federal power around the courthouse, many activists agreed. The quiet success of Bearse and his crew in rescuing fugitives from ships in Boston Harbor and the absence of any further renditions probably led many to believe that the danger had passed. After June 2, 1854, they would have no such illusions.

The fugitive this time was Anthony Burns, who had fled from Virginia only to be seized by slave catchers and locked in the Boston Courthouse at the end of May 1854. The timing could not have been worse, or better, depending on one's standpoint. Burns's arrest came just as Illinois Democrat Stephen Douglas pushed through his legislation establishing the Kansas and Nebraska Territories and repealing the Missouri Compromise. The Kansas-Nebraska Act suddenly reopened the long-settled question of slavery in the Louisiana Purchase territories and submitted it to the "popular sovereignty" of the Americans who settled there. The slave catchers took Burns at the very moment that proslavery Democrats in Boston and elsewhere toasted the passage of Douglas's incendiary law.[99] Together, the Kansas-Nebraska Act and the arrest of Anthony Burns proved to many that the Slave Power was on the march, seeking domination in the halls of Congress, on the Western plains, and now on the streets of Boston as well.

The Vigilance Committee's members pursued multiple strategies to win Burns's freedom. Abolitionist and Free Soil lawyers sought to tie up the case in court. Vigilance men set a watch on the courthouse. They called a Faneuil Hall protest meeting for the following night, and considered an armed rescue attempt.[100] Some, including Wendell Phillips, vaguely hoped that a fiery Faneuil Hall meeting would rouse the city's people to such indignation that Burns would be rescued from the courtroom as Shadrach Minkins had been.[101]

Lewis Hayden did not feel the need to decide between strategies. First, aided by another Vigilance man, lawyer Seth Webb, he swore out a complaint against Burns's claimants, charging them with conspiracy to kidnap. The slave catchers were arrested but quickly made bail. Hayden then joined Higginson in a plot to rescue Burns from the courthouse jail. They planned to begin a rescue attempt during the Faneuil Hall meeting, then stage a dramatic announcement in the meeting to bring the crowd to their aid. Although this part of the plan misfired owing to misunderstandings among the conspirators, the assault on the courthouse quickly took shape. Hayden pledged ten black allies. Higginson bought a box of hand axes. Others stashed a large timber in an alley near the courthouse. All that remained was to bring enough people to batter down the door, overpower the guards, and spirit Burns to freedom.[102]

Many of the Vigilance men at Faneuil Hall did not know what was happening down the street when a voice called out from the hall's main entrance: "Mr. Chairman, I am just informed that a mob of negroes is in Court Square attempting to rescue Burns."[103] Indeed, the assault was beginning, though "negroes" made up only part of the force. In the square, a dozen men wielded the wooden beam as a battering ram against the courthouse's central door. Near the front of the ram stood Higginson, across from an unnamed black man whose valor the minister would never forget. Lewis Hayden and Seth Webb, their legal efforts suspended, also helped swing the timber, as did several of Hayden's close associates on black Beacon Hill—among them the Freemasons, political organizers, and fugitive defenders Mark De Mortie and George Downing. Hundreds of people now filled Court Square, and some militants began peppering the courthouse with cobblestones and occasional gunfire; the guards inside responded in kind. As the stout wooden panels of the door began to give way, the besieging party dropped the beam and broke out their hand axes.[104]

The door finally opened just enough for Higginson and his unnamed black companion to enter, but inside the balance of forces was suddenly reversed. Deputy U.S. marshals stood ready with clubs, and they began to beat Higginson and the other man about the head. As the two would-be rescuers defended themselves, at least one of the antislavery men at the threshold raised a gun and fired into the courthouse foyer. Deputy U.S. Marshal James Batchelder fell, mortally wounded.

Just who killed Batchelder remained a mystery, and no one was successfully prosecuted in his death. But Lewis Hayden believed that he had fired the fatal shot. He carried two pistols that day, one of them loaded with a slug. When he reached the broken door of the courthouse, he saw Higginson trapped in a corner with deputy marshals clubbing him about the head. "They would have killed him," he later explained. "Then I fired & they fell back."[105] In the confusion after the shot, Higginson and his anonymous black comrade made their escape, and constables forced the door shut after them. The courthouse was secured, and the crowd dispersed; only a few were arrested. By the next day a vast force of soldiers held Court Square, and the disheartened Vigilance men concluded there was nothing to be done. Higginson, who had been wounded on the chin and would therefore be easily recognized, fled to the comparative safety of Worcester.

To black leaders across the North, Hayden's action would have come as no surprise. In 1853, Martin Delany offered Hayden as a glorious counterpoint to the unbecoming meekness he perceived in another fugitive, Henry Bibb. At one point in Bibb's narrative of slavery, he described helplessly pleading, hoe in hand, as his master stripped the clothes from his wife and whipped her bloody. Delany was not shy about judgmental comparison. "[H]ad this been Hayden," Delany opined, "he would have buried the hoe deep in the master's skull, laying him lifeless at his feet."[106] Frederick Douglass offered a similar assessment. Months before Burns's arrest, Douglass made a none too oblique reference to the widespread belief that Hayden had been responsible for Minkins's rescue. Hayden, he wrote, "would be among the last to look with composure, or to stand idly by, when a brother man guilty of no crime, was about to be robbed of his liberty. It would be just like him, warm hearted, fearless man, to sing out, stand back, gentlemen, I must have a hand in this. Here is a matter which concerns me."[107]

Many found the violence perfectly justified. It fell to William J. Watkins, now working as Douglass's assistant editor in Rochester, to summon up the inevitable revolutionary analogy. He declared that the man who had killed Batchelder would not be considered a murderer if the subject of the rescue had been a white man. "If he be a murderer," Watkins wrote, "then was Gen. Washington. . . . We should certainly kill the man who would dare lay his hand on us, or on our brother, or sister, to enslave us."[108] Indeed, upon further reflection, Watkins declared he "would rather behold every U.S. Marshal in the country weltering in his own blood, than to see one *man* re-enslaved."[109] But none of this rhetoric could obscure the fact that the raid had failed.

Following the unsuccessful effort to rescue Burns, Hayden also made his escape from Boston, after an official warned him that he faced imminent arrest. The man, a white deputy U.S. marshal named Asa Butman, was no friend of abolition or even of Hayden; indeed, it was Butman whose arrest of Burns had set these events in motion. But the marshal was, like Hayden, a Freemason, and according to Hayden felt obligated by their mutual bond.[110] This rare moment of interracial Masonic recognition must have been particularly welcome under the circumstances. Hayden turned for help to Vigilance man and onetime *Latimer Journal* editor William F. Channing, who took him to confer with Theodore Parker. They agreed that William Bowditch should take Hayden to Brookline until things cooled off.[111] Henry Bowditch visited his brother that night and found Hayden conferring with some of his compatriots; the doctor joined the men to read them a letter he had just received from John Greenleaf Whittier, in which the Quaker poet and abolitionist had declared his resolve that Burns "*must* not be sent out of Boston as a slave. Anything but that!"[112] Even Friends, it seemed, were catching the militant spirit.

In the face of violent interracial resistance to the Fugitive Slave Law, all of the remaining orthodoxies of nonviolence teetered on the verge of collapse. Antislavery men of all stripes imagined themselves capable of killing the U.S. marshal who held poor Anthony Burns. Joshua B. Smith, who had spoken so plainly in 1850 of the need for fugitives to arm themselves, stopped in at the Anti-Slavery Office on Cornhill sometime that Friday morning. The office was all but silent—William Nell, like most of the regulars, was "up and doing"—but Smith found Maria Weston Chapman's sister Anne Weston there alone, struggling with her conscience.[113] The Burns affair had left her nonresistant principles, she reported, "terribly in abeyance." Perhaps Smith intuited this, for he quickly told Weston that "[i]f any one will guarantee my wife and child $10,000 I will be the man to settle the marshal if I find myself in Heaven next minute." Weston held

Joshua Smith
*Courtesy of the Massachusetts
Historical Society*

her tongue, but thought that, if she had agreed, Smith would have kept his end of the bargain. "I wish you could have seen how he looked," she wrote.[114]

All legal stratagems and efforts to purchase Burns's freedom soon failed. On June 2, the federal commissioner ruled that Burns's identity and the slaveholder's title to him had been proved: he was a fugitive slave and must be returned immediately to Virginia. Marshals cleared the courtroom, and this time neither Reverend Grimes nor anyone else was allowed to accompany the prisoner or even to speak privately with him. Outside, Court Square and the streets leading into it were filled with militiamen, police, and U.S. troops, all under military command. The rendition of Anthony Burns played out in a familiar theater of overwhelming federal force: the mayor ceded authority to the chief of police and a federal officer; U.S. soldiers waited with their swords drawn, a loaded cannon at the ready; and police and U.S. Marines formed a hollow square around the prisoner. Inside that phalanx, Burns was trundled down State Street.[115]

The scene on State Street portended larger battles. The sectional politics of slavery had changed dramatically in a dozen years, and even more in the last three. This time, more than a pack of enraged activists mourned the rendered fugitive's passage. As troops marched Burns down State Street, law and newspaper offices draped their fronts in black crepe or flew the U.S. flag upside down. An improvised coffin hanging over the street bore the label "Liberty."[116] The Woman's Rights Convention, meeting in the Meionaon, adjourned to take part in the protests.[117] Police seized the large banner reading "Freedom" carried by a band of Worcester men, but George Downing, fresh from the battle of the courthouse, waded into the crowd and tore it from their hands; somehow it wound up in Robert Morris's office.[118] No one present that day forgot the sight of the procession moving slowly down State Street. Bowditch again brought his son, Nat, to witness the march of the Slave Power; watching from an abolitionist friend's building, they hissed the state militia and U.S. Marines as they once again "trampled over the place where Attucks fell."[119]

Hayden did not witness the terrible moment. From his refuge in Brookline, just a few miles from the reach of the Boston police, he continued west to Worcester, where Higginson was pledged to keep him abreast of any impending prosecution.[120] It must have been a frustrating stay. Although Hayden believed that his shot had saved Higginson's life, Higginson had no idea how his assailant had fallen and grew irritated at the former slave when he explained his presence in Worcester by saying, "rather mysteriously as if I sh[ou]ld understand it," that he had thought it safer to be out of town. This struck Higginson as "a bit of a brag on his part." Not until twenty years later did Channing finally persuade Higginson that Hayden had fired the shot.[121] Until that moment, Higginson must have thought Hayden a bit self-important. Perhaps he was thinking of Hayden when he later wrote of the "upstart conceit" he found so "offensive among free negroes at the North," what he mocked as "the dandy-barber strut."[122] More likely he was simply annoyed by Hayden's hints at heroism. In any case, Hayden appeared to be in no immediate danger of arrest and quickly returned to the city.[123]

Their crushing defeat by the federal juggernaut unexpectedly metamorphosed into victory. This was not immediately apparent outside the city: "The brave people of Boston have permitted Burns to be carried back before their eyes," wrote a black Canadian exile. "These are the people who prate so much about liberty, justice, and bravery . . . they talk flippantly enough about what 'our fathers' did, &c . . . Henceforth let them keep silence."[124] But the reality was far more complex and heartening. The unsuccessful attempt of a handful of black militants and white allies to repeat their rescue of Minkins provoked a massive federal response, and the vast contingent of soldiers and policemen who for a moment had made Massachusetts into slave territory left white Bostonians awed and angered. Many in Massachusetts now saw the Slave Power in precisely the way that Canadian commentator would have wished. The loss of Burns brought clarity that was itself an abolitionist victory.

Less than a week after federal troops marched Burns through the city in chains, the change in white opinion across the state outstripped what anyone could have expected. "You cannot conceive of the change, even in Boston," wrote Higginson. No jury, he thought, would now convict him or any other person for the death of the constable.[125] One of Higginson's relatives thought the crowds on State Street "more moved" by Burns's rendition than anything he had seen before. He did not mean just radical- ized working people and antislavery regulars: "The conservative & influ- ential classes appear at length to be fairly touched, their pride & humanity both stung to the quick."[126] The Whig industrialist Amos Lawrence exag- gerated only a little when he declared, "We went to bed one night old fashioned, conservative, Compromise Union Whigs, and waked up stark mad abolitionists."[127] Bowditch told Senator Sumner that "[m]en who have heretofore scoffed at me—now greet me with the right hand of fel- lowship," and that men with no reputation for violence now seriously proposed that the fugitive slave commissioner be tarred and feathered.[128]

Dr. Bowditch sensed an imminent crisis, a moment at which the com- promises would collapse and Massachusetts prove truly free soil. "The hope of such a time even [if] it be preceded by oceans of blood, alone sustains me." The only alternative was subservience within "a great Slave Republic."[129] He set about with great earnestness organizing a secret soci- ety, the Boston Anti-Man-Hunting League, to prevent any future fugitive from being successfully captured. Bowditch and his comrades quickly stitched together a statewide network of similar clubs. Their determination and the astonishing shift in public opinion made Anthony Burns the last fugitive to be publicly returned from Boston.[130]

The federal government had overreached, and no one knew what might happen if another such rendition occurred. James Freeman Clarke noted that during the march to the wharf officers ordered their men "to aim at the citizens" who pressed close upon them near the Boston Massacre site. "If they had fired, the results no man can tell."[131] Boston's revulsion at the return of Burns to slavery might easily have ended in violence, leaving many dead and Burns perhaps freed. Far from helping restore the sectional compromise over slavery, such an event would have enraged white North-erners, further dividing them from their party-mates and trading partners in the South. Such an outcome was too much to risk. From the middle of 1854, fugitives who reached the streets of Boston were effectively safe from return.[132] Nell told the story of one man who had made two unsuccessful bids for freedom before finally reaching Boston. While walking down State Street, "over the spot where Attucks fell, and over which Sims and Burns were dragged back to slavery he exhibited a pistol loaded and capped, declaring that he had resolved to die rather [than] be again any man's slave." The city was, for the moment at least, free soil.[133]

In the aftermath, the state legislature overrode the Know-Nothing gov-ernor's veto to enact a new personal liberty law, retooling the Latimer Law to meet the challenge of the Fugitive Slave Law. The new law explicitly guaranteed extensive rights of due process, going so far as to say that "upon every question of fact . . . the burden of proof shall be on the claim-ant." It aimed not only at officeholders and state employees, declaring their positions forfeit if they took part in the judicial processes of rendi-tion, but forever barred even slaveholders' lawyers from employment and office in Massachusetts. Heavy fines and significant jail terms deterred everyone from judges to jailers to militiamen from participating in another Burns affair.[134]

Massachusetts was not the only such place where efforts to return fugi-tives to slavery generated a political backlash. Across the upper North, the Fugitive Slave and Kansas-Nebraska Acts were together accomplishing the same unintended result, encouraging whites to see the Slave Power in-fringing on their liberties and making their communities into slave terri-tory. Just a few months before the rendition of Burns, a mostly white crowd in Milwaukee, Wisconsin, stormed the city jail and freed the Missouri fugi-tive Joshua Glover, sending him on to Canada West. The state's supreme court not only allowed the rescuers to go free, but declared the Fugitive Slave Law itself unconstitutional. The brand-new Republican Party claimed the state's lower house in 1854.[135]

The Fugitive Slave Law and the Kansas-Nebraska legislation, taken together, called into question whether any American territory was truly "free." Black Northerners had forced a conflict over the Fugitive Slave Law that ended by making it unenforceable in parts of the North. The battle then shifted to the other territory whose status was now uncertain, the formerly "free" precincts of the Louisiana Purchase. The Kansas-Nebraska law opened these to slaveholding settlement, preliminary to the adoption of a state constitution by the new settlers that would decide the question of slavery in the territories. Most white Northerners lived far from that frontier, but after 1854 they had a much more immediate understanding of what the Slave Power intended: it would have its way, though Northern liberties fell before it. Free Soil colonists began organizing to settle the Kansas Territory, and their proslavery counterparts did the same. Soon there would be war among the whites over the question of slavery. Black Americans, as William Nell could have predicted, would be sure to find a way to make the battle their own.

BLACK MEN ON THE MARCH

For some black activists, antislavery insurgency was essential but still insufficient. They continued to seek an official welcome into the ranks of the citizen-soldiery. The rise of the Know-Nothing Party in Massachusetts, with the state's Republican leadership quietly massing in its upper echelons, gave them hope. In 1855 Robert Morris and his colleagues renewed their campaign to be admitted to the state militia. In other cities, similar black militia companies now received state arms. Special charters artfully circumvented the federal prohibition. In 1856, William Nell watched a black military company named the Attucks Blues parade in the streets of Cincinnati.[136] He heard of another such company in Pittsburgh.[137] Morris and his allies, now including Dr. John V. DeGrasse, entered into correspondence with black militia leaders in Providence and elsewhere.[138]

By mid-1855 Morris became convinced that the best course was to follow his own advice from the 1853 hearings: proceed despite opposition. He laid public plans for the formation of a company called the Massasoit Guards, after the Indian tribe from whom the state drew its name. A Beacon Hill meeting chose John P. Coburn for captain, Morris himself as lieutenant, and DeGrasse as surgeon.[139] The Boston correspondent of *Frederick Douglass' Paper* described the prospective company as "picked men active and intelligent," and surmised that "in case of a war for liberty, I believe they would 'fight like tigers.'"[140] William Nell wondered why they had chosen the name "Massasoit" over "Attucks," but he accepted the explanation that a New York company had already claimed the name.[141] By the next spring they had purchased arms and devised uniforms, and again petitioned the legislature for permission to form an "independent military company."[142]

But the Massasoit Guards never did march, done in both by the legislature's continuing resistance and by Morris's own scruples. Morris proclaimed that the guards would "make a peaceable public parade, whenever we deem it proper to do so."[143] But that moment never came. Morris presented himself as an armed man of action, a vigorous fighter in the war against racial caste. No one could deny that this was true. But he was also an officer of the court, and aspired to be accepted as a gentleman.

Morris's sense of himself as a gentleman included what some saw as a troubling responsiveness to white opinion. At least once in the 1850s he faced accusations that he was too law abiding to help a fugitive. After his acquittal in the Shadrach Minkins case, some whispered that Morris insisted on his actual innocence and accused those who still thought him complicit in the escape of holding him "up to public odium." If Morris had indeed made such statements, the *Liberator* opined, it suggested that the rescue of a fugitive was cause for shame.[144] Others believed it was an utter fabrication. "[T]raitors," Douglass thundered, had tried "to excite prejudice against" Morris, "by circulating the absurd story that he had said he would send a fugitive slave back to his master, under the Fugitive Slave

Bill." Morris rejected the charges emphatically.[145] Yet Morris was keenly attuned to the opinions of his white neighbors and colleagues. In the white suburb of Chelsea, where his family had moved during the school fight, that sometimes meant deferring to the prejudice that surrounded him. Morris would not leave an omnibus because a stranger resented his presence, but he hesitated to occupy a home he had purchased in a high-toned new development once it became clear that some of the locals did not want him—"threatened," in fact, "if I bought the house and lived there, to sell out, or go somewhere else to live, and let out their houses to Irish tenants." The land company's officers feared a cascading collapse in their project's value and appealed to Morris, as a gentleman, not to "push myself into the vicinity or neighborhood of persons who did not wish to have me as a neighbor." Morris complained that he could not pick up stakes at the whim of every person so prejudiced, but then, unaccountably, abandoned his plan and withdrew from the contract.[146]

In the case of the Massasoit Guards, Morris seemed paralyzed between mutually contradictory imperatives of defiance and respectability, unable to take the final step for which his men prepared. Many members, never able to don their handsome uniforms, shoulder their weapons, and march, resigned from the company.[147] At least one observer held Morris responsible for the collapse of these dreams: it was he "who started the Massasoit Guards in Boston, and failed to keep the company together."[148]

Other black men, less conflicted than Morris, dared to do what he did not. By 1857 another military organization, dubbed the Liberty Guard, formed in Boston. The Liberty Guard was not the unit Morris had equipped: their uniforms were entirely black, unlike the Massasoit men's dark blue with light-colored trim. The Liberty Guard's leader, Lewis Gaul, was not a lawyer, doctor, or proprietor, but a coachman. Were his men dissidents from the Massasoit Guard? Or were they other men—"men of the wharf, men of over-alls," far removed from the high-toned leadership of the older unit? It is impossible to say whether the rank-and-file membership of the two groups overlapped, but Morris's snobby distaste for them was unmistakable. At an 1858 August First celebration in New Bedford, Morris publicly condemned the Liberty Guards for parading, pointedly noting that "the respectable and intelligent young colored men of Boston were not represented here to-day by a military company. It was high time they left off playing and went down into seriousness. They were dressed up to-day in soldier's uniform, without commission or legal right. When the State gave the colored man this right, they would form military companies and fine ones too."[149] Another reporter heard him articulate this critique even more definitively: "The colored men of Boston would not recognize any such military organization until they had it by right."[150] And the sneeringly racist reporter for the *New York Herald* argued that Morris's hostility reflected a conflict between the black "aristocracy and their 'low niggers.'" In this reading, Morris represented the former and the Liberty Guard the latter—"an ignorant set, not possessed of that refinement and moral culture which their own standard requires . . . made up mostly of waiters, boot blacks, and carpet cleaners, while their gallant commander is a barber."[151] Considering that Lewis Gaul was in fact a coachman, the entire analysis may have been a malicious fantasy. But Morris's distinction between the Liberty Guard and Boston's "respectable and intelligent young colored men" left the black militia open for this ridicule.

Morris lived and moved amid these contradictions. On the very stage from which he dismissed the black company for having paraded without authorization, he urged the audience to "trample" upon the Fugitive Slave Law. "Let us be bold," he declared, "and if any man flies from slavery, and comes among us. When he's reached us, we'll say, he's gone far enough." Morris suggested a mutual defense pact to the people of New Bedford. "If any man comes here to New Bedford, and they try to take him away, you telegraph to us in Boston, and we'll come down three hundred strong, and stay with you; and we won't go until he's safe. If he goes back to the South, we'll go with him. And if any man runs away, and comes to Boston, we'll send to you, if necessary, and you may come up to us three hundred strong, if you can—come men, and women too."[152] It was, perhaps, his answer to the irritating blare of the marching bands of the Liberty Guards and their colleagues the New Bedford Blues, the noise of whose street parades interrupted the convention's proceedings that morning. But it was also Morris's fate to walk a tightrope, balancing his role as a gentleman who understood his civic responsibilities with his claim to be the proud heir to a revolutionary tradition of liberty.

Morris may have been particularly peeved that men without his scruples became the first to parade through Boston, as the Liberty Guard did in November 1857. They seemed to know there would be trouble. "For prudential reasons," a friendly newspaper explained, "the company did not wear their uniform, but came out in citizens' dress."[153] Perhaps Gaul did not want to press his luck, or perhaps he had struck a deal with city authorities. In any case, at their armory at the corner of Joy Street and Cambridge their leaders lectured them on proper public deportment and the importance of not responding to provocations. Then they set off for a two-hour march through the major streets of the city, escorted by police. The police scattered a few North End brick throwers, but there was little other trouble before they reached State Street in the midafternoon. With Captain Gaul leading the way, they paraded through dense crowds of onlookers, facing nothing worse than the mocking calls and epithets to which black Bostonians were well accustomed.

Midway, Gaul told the police escort that they could safely withdraw, but he spoke too soon. The guard was trailed by a crowd of about fifty black supporters and an equally large mob of white detractors, and it was among these less disciplined forces that the trouble began. The whites began peppering the black spectators with small rocks. They also hurled paper bags filled with flour, intending an insult not hard to discern. Fighting broke out among the spectators, and the Liberty Guard's supporters at first got the best of it. Then the whites regrouped, armed themselves, and the black crowd ran, putting the Liberty Guard itself between them and their foes. The company had crossed the common now, and was marching up Charles Street at the western edge of Beacon Hill, not far from their muster room on Cambridge Street. The white mob closed upon them, flinging bricks. This was, as one nonabolitionist paper reported, "too much for negro-manity to bear." Breaking ranks, members of the guard ignored their orders, fixed bayonets, and charged the white attackers. This sent the assailants flying, and ended the engagement.[154]

After this battle with white supremacy, the Liberty Guard finally achieved every militia unit's cherished ambition: a banquet at which admiring women celebrated the citizen-soldiers. A crowd assembled in Faneuil Hall that rainy November night to eat from Joshua Smith's catering table, escort the ladies in from their carriages for a grand promenade, and accept from a committee of three women an "ancient banner which was carried by a colored military company in the revolutionary war."[155] The company's second lieutenant proudly accepted the flag.[156] Whatever Morris thought, the Liberty Guard had achieved a good measure of legitimacy.

The women's role was more than ceremonial, for they too understood what had been at stake in the march. Miss Sarah Hill told the men of the Liberty Guard as she presented them with the banner: "[You have] proved that you can exist without a charter. . . . You and your Officers have been placed in a position today which required the exercise of great self-control, and you have behaved like gentlemen, and true, brave, soldiers." Confirmed in both courage and dignity, they celebrated until the early hours of the morning.[157] It remained to be seen what combination of gentlemanly restraint and manly defiance would persuade some of their white allies to see them as real, whole citizens of the republic.

RECKONING WITH THE "MODERN CRISPUS ATTUCKS"

William Nell continued to believe that the answer to that last question lay in history. By 1858, his commemoration of Crispus Attucks came close to proving him right. As Anthony Burns returned to slavery, Nell resolved to turn his pamphlet into a book whose broad coverage of "*Colored* antislavery" as well as military service would offer something to each of the "various parties among colored people." He recruited prominent figures in other states—William Howard Day in New York, John Mercer Langston in Ohio—to encourage its circulation throughout the North. Nell struggled to scrape together the capital for publication, but obtained Wendell Phillips's help in securing the last hundred or so dollars required. He was even ready to sell his Gerrit Smith lands—a legacy of the time he had spent working with Douglass in New York—if that was what it took. History was too potent a weapon to let the cost stand in his way.[158]

Finally published in 1855, *The Colored Patriots of the American Revolution* bore the subtitle "with sketches of several distinguished colored persons: to which is added a brief survey of the condition and prospects of colored Americans." But even this list did not capture the work's panoramic ambition. Nell began his story, naturally, with the story of Crispus Attucks.[159] He continued with a state-by-state account of black military service in the years since, with long detours to mark milestones in other areas: the emergence of black college professors, doctors, lawyers, and dentists; slave revolts; black national conventions; and—not incidentally—an account of the fugitives who had violently resisted recapture at Christiana, Pennsylvania, in 1851.

The purpose of this account was to establish African Americans as an inextricable and militant element in the history of American freedom. In his conclusion, Nell appealed to his readers to follow the example of Attucks and his other protagonists by taking part in what Nell called "our battle for equality," as "valiant and consistent soldiers in Freedom's army." Nell made it plain that this would be an army without "a colored section," for people "of every complexion, sect, sex and condition" would together bring a second, regenerative revolution and an era of "Universal Brotherhood."[160] Unlike Lewis Hayden who earlier invoked a harmonious and egalitarian congregation, though, Nell evoked the martial image of an army. His work depicted African Americans who gave themselves to this struggle as worthy of a full and unshadowed place in the nation they helped build and defend.[161]

By the late 1850s, Nell's rehabilitation of Crispus Attucks, the reinvigoration of the tradition of black soldiery, and the rescue and defense of fugitive slaves worked a profound change in the relationship between black activists and their white allies. The experiences of fugitive defense and fugitive rescue provided some whites with models of black militancy that they could not ignore; the story of Crispus Attucks gave them a way to link that militancy to an American Revolution that they cherished but had begun to doubt.[162] The change could be noted even in Wendell Phillips. At Nell's public commemoration of Attucks in Faneuil Hall in 1858, Phillips could not resist urging the young black men of Boston, "[G]o you to-morrow and show your valor in the field, valor in life, valor in education, valor in making money, valor in making your mark in the world, and instantly the papers will begin to say—O yes! they have always been a brave, gallant people. Was there not ATTUCKS in '70?" He had always been more interested in lecturing black Bostonians than in paying attention to what they were actually doing. But Nell's work of historical recovery, side by side with the militant new stride of his friends and colleagues, seemed to have moved Phillips toward a richer understanding of the place of "colored citizens" in his glorious city's embattled past and present. Phillips also told the 1858 crowd that he was proud that the fathers of the Revolution had honored Attucks in Faneuil Hall, in which they were now assembled. Here Phillips sought to rescue the hall from the proslavery white mobs who had sometimes ruled its stage in the preceding decades.

As Phillips went on, his sense of having been personally liberated by the "Colored Patriots of the American Revolution" became even more apparent. Thinking of John Hancock's banner, received by the Liberty Guards and now hanging in Faneuil Hall as part of Nell's great exhibition, Phillips recalled that Hancock had originally presented it "from his own balcony in Beacon Street." The wealthy avenue that was Phillips's childhood home now stood for the compromising, prounion, proslavery spirit

that had marched Burns to the Virginia-bound boat. But the banner reminded him of Hancock's "good deed," he told the Attucks commemoration, and "shall perfume Beacon Street and make it worthier. (Cheers). I
always thought that I had a pride in having been born in it; now I know
the reason." William Nell, the recipient of his money, books, and condescension, had hewn for Phillips the battering ram of a usable past.[163]

More important, for perhaps the first time in white imaginations, black
people could be more than victims of the present political and social order.
Nell's account, together with recent events, gave them hope that the republic had not been entirely corrupt from its inception, revising the history
of the American Revolution in a way that allowed men like Phillips to re-
claim their own heritage. A letter from Thomas Wentworth Higginson,
read from the podium that 1858 day, made a move that would have been
unthinkable even to the most radical white abolitionists just a few years
before: it placed militant black men at the vanguard of the current struggle.
Once Higginson thought all the "negroes cowed" and irresolute. Now,
thinking back to the storming of the courthouse in 1854, the minister
lauded the black comrade who had stood by his side wielding history's
heavy beam, and who had been the first to force his way inside. White men,
Higginson declared, could learn much from this "modern Crispus Attucks" standing "at the Court-House door . . . When he stands there
again," the minister concluded, "may there be more of us to follow him."[164]
Such an acknowledgment had been a long time coming. If Higginson's
belated recognition of black bravery and leadership caused Lewis Hayden
to bite his tongue, he did not let on.

6.

Outlaws

The militancy of the 1850s, together with the growing respect shown the "colored citizens" by white allies, the rise of a powerful antiextension political movement, and the victory in the school fight, kindled flames of hope in antislavery Boston. On March 6, 1857, Chief Justice Roger Taney did his best to smother them. That day he announced the decision of the U.S. Supreme Court in *Dred Scott v. Sandford*, the case of an enslaved man who claimed that long residences in free states and territories entitled him to his freedom. The court ruled against Scott by a vote of seven to two, offering a cascade of rejections that went to the core of African Americans' standing in the United States. Congress, the court held, had acted unconstitutionally in barring slavery from the Northwest territories in the 1780s. Scott had no standing to sue for his freedom. As a black man, he was not and could not be an American citizen: the Constitution's use of that word did not extend to African Americans, and never had. People of African descent, Taney himself wrote, had from the nation's beginning been considered "so far inferior, that they had no rights which the white man is bound to respect."[1] The ruling, and especially Taney's own opinion, made "colored citizens" an oxymoron. It cast blacks as permanent outsiders, excluded by constitutional definition and innate incapacity from American self-government. It could not have escaped William Nell's notice that the chief justice gravely declared America once and evermore a white man's republic on the anniversary after the day that Crispus Attucks fell.

"The colored people in the free States," William Wells Brown told the New England Colored Citizens' Convention in 1859, "are in a distracted and unsettled condition." The *Dred Scott* decision, with what William Nell called its "wanton perversion of the Constitution of the United States in regard to the rights of American citizens," left many wondering whether they could ever truly belong in and to the United States.[2] The decision was so unmeasured and encompassing that it emboldened their worst adversaries; they were, Nell and Hayden asserted, "daily taunted, by precept and example, by word and deed," with its fatal dismissal of black claims to American citizenship.[3]

The court's ruling, though it left black and white activists scrambling to recover some semblance of hope, did not extinguish those claims. Instead, it sent a new wave of desperate energy surging through the political world of black Northern activists, reigniting long-standing debates that went to the core of their relationship to the American nation. In Republican politics, they sought a reversal of the decision by making their voices heard and votes felt, although they well understood the ambivalence or outright hostility with which many in that party regarded them. But they did not limit themselves to party politics. People who had spent decades imagining themselves into American citizenship through petition, protest, and the disciplined rebellion of revolutionary patriots now contemplated a different kind of revolution—a slave revolt that would upend that institution and the political system now bowing before it. Far more than in earlier decades, most were willing to contemplate bloody, violent upheaval, even if they wondered whether it made any practical sense.

Republican politics and slave rebellion might seem to have been contradictory strategies, but to black activists on the ground in the late 1850s the important debates concerned what would work to free the slaves, and make "free state" and "colored citizen" meaningful terms. Their campaigns all aimed at the same goal: rejecting the logic of *Dred Scott* and establishing the permanent, unstigmatized place of free and equal "colored citizens" in the United States. The remaining alternative—one they had hitherto generally rejected—also returned in the late 1850s: departing the United States for a home on another shore. Emigration, unlike the painful compromises of electoral politics or the calamitous violence of slave revolt, was beyond the pale for most of Boston's black activists, and they devoted considerable energy in the post–*Dred Scott* era to combating its advocates. In moments of grave despair, though, even some of the boldest contemplated abandoning the project of national belonging.

REPUBLICANS IN HARD TIMES

Dred Scott left would-be black Republicans searching for hope. They had counted on the new party to contain slavery within the existing slave states and to weaken the Slave Power's hold on the national government. But if Congress lacked the power to restrict the spread of slavery into new territories, as the court now held, all hope of that lay very far off. In the short run at least, Republicans would be powerless to overturn *Dred Scott.* Almost from its birth, therefore, the party seemed both so hemmed in by the court's ruling and so cool to black aspirations as to be a very unlikely vessel to carry the "colored citizens" across.

Yet the Republican Party was with astonishing speed becoming the dominant party in Northern politics, its growth tracking the outrage among white Northerners about the fate of liberty in the Kansas Territory. In the wake of the Kansas-Nebraska Act in 1854, proslavery Missourians and other Southerners began moving westward, bringing slaves into the once free provinces of the Louisiana Purchase, while antislavery forces sponsored companies of antislavery emigrants to the territories. A battle for political supremacy in the Western lands quickly turned nastily violent, with kidnappings, beatings, murders, and paramilitary raids. The guerrilla war known as "Bleeding Kansas" had begun. White abolitionists with a taste for conflict headed west into the maelstrom, among them Higginson, who published his letters from the territory as a small, proud book, and a Scottish newcomer named James Redpath, who worked simultaneously as a journalist and slave rescuer. John Brown, head of the lone white household among the black New Yorkers holding Smith lands, headed west to join his sons in the fight.[4]

Massachusetts antislavery folk played key roles in Bleeding Kansas, and in its sequel in the halls of Congress. The state Republican Party boasted some of the sternest white critics of slavery, among them Robert Morris's former colleague U.S. Senator Charles Sumner. In May 1856 Sumner offered a blistering attack on proslavery Kansas and on his Senate colleague Andrew Pickens Butler of South Carolina, mocking his love for the "harlot, slavery." In response, U.S. Congressman Preston Brooks, Andrew Butler's younger relative, entered the Senate chamber and attacked Sumner at his desk, beating the corpulent older man senseless with a heavy cane. When Congress expelled Brooks for his action, South Carolina voters immediately chose him again. It would be years before Sumner recovered from the attack, and the outrage of "Bleeding Sumner" provided Massachusetts's voters with yet another materialization of the Slave Power's arrogance and violence, expressed as a literal assault on the liberty of white Northerners.

The Republicans appealed successfully to the growing majority of Northerners who hated and feared the Slave Power. But like its Free Soil parent, the Republican Party did not require those supporters to take a stand for black citizenship. Many Republicans imagined liberation from the Slave Power primarily as a blow for white liberty, and they feared being identified as the "black man's party." The Free Soil Kansans whose fate so preoccupied Boston's antislavery activists crafted a "free state" constitution that barred black immigration.[5] Neither the Democratic nor the Republican Party "aims to be entirely just and humane to the black man," an angry Frederick Douglass despaired in 1859. "The first would admit the black man into Kansas as a slave," he charged, "and the other would seem to wish to exclude him as a *freeman*."[6] Republicans in Minnesota Territory similarly crafted a constitution that limited suffrage to white men; their explanation, according to the *Liberator*, was that the Democrats had "raised this cry of *Nigger!* NIGGER! **NIGGER**! and we must take the wind out of their sails."[7] Republican defensiveness could be heard too in the Illinois senatorial election debates of 1858. There, Democratic candidate Stephen Douglas sneered at the "black Republicans"—to which Republican Abraham Lincoln's supporters shouted back their preferred adjective: "white! white!"[8] Perhaps this explained why, as Theodore Parker noted, "[c]olored waiters at public festivals say, 'the Democrats treat us better than the Republicans'": Democrats did not have to worry about establishing their white supremacist bona fides.[9]

However insightful, Parker's reflection did not tell the whole story. In 1856, the Republicans of Massachusetts began to emerge from the Know-Nothing shadow, and Boston's black political leadership for the first time found a home in a ruling party. Indeed, Boston's white Republicans actively courted black voters, knowing that their hundreds of potential votes could make the difference in close elections. This first became clear during the tumultuous 1856 campaign season, as various coalitions of the Know-Nothings, Whigs, Democrats, and Republicans all vied for control of state offices and the congressional delegation. Republicans, hoping to maximize black turnout for their ticket, recruited a larger number of black precinct captains than ever before, including Nell, Hayden, and a newcomer, John S. Rock.[10] These men were particularly hungry to exert some political force, for the insults to their citizenship continued during Know-Nothing rule: when Rock and twenty-six other black men petitioned the mayor and aldermen of Boston to remove references to color from the city's voting and tax lists, their petition went unanswered.[11] They needed a victorious party behind them to give force to their threats that "we should not forget those men at the polls" come the December city elections.[12]

Although he had been in the city only since 1853, John S. Rock played a central role in the negotiations with Republicans, and in much else, during the 1850s. A broadly accomplished man of color, he was already a seasoned political activist when he arrived in Boston.[13] Born free in New Jersey in 1826, he began educating himself while employed in a white lawyer's office, and he never stopped. He became a licensed schoolteacher at sixteen, a dentist at twenty-four, and a physician two years later. By his twenties Rock also became one of New Jersey's leading black activists, organizing conventions to demand the right to vote and giving antislavery speeches in Philadelphia. In 1853, just after receiving his medical degree,

John S. Rock
Courtesy of the Library of Congress

he and his wife, Catherine, moved to Boston, where they initially boarded at the Haydens' house on Southac. Rock set up a medical practice on Cambridge Street and transferred his Masonic membership to a Boston lodge. In addition to his other callings, he quickly became a well-regarded and sought-after public lecturer; his final profession, the law, would come later in the decade, after chronic illness kept him from his other callings.

For activists such as Hayden and Rock, who had weathered the passage from Free Soil to Republican to Know-Nothing and back again, the election of 1856 offered an opportunity. Although Republican presidential candidate John Fremont was certain to win the state, first-term Republican congressman Anson Burlingame seemed poised for defeat. Burlingame's hatred for domineering slaveholders was nearly legendary; when South Carolina sent Preston Brooks back to Congress after his attack on Sumner, Burlingame denounced him so heatedly that Brooks challenged him to a duel.[14] For Beacon Hill's black voters, Burlingame's fight for reelection was an opportunity to show what they could do. Rock and his colleague Mark De Mortie, two of the men first approached by the Know-Nothing delegation in 1855, canvassed the ward for the Republican ticket during the six weeks before the election.[15] Burlingame himself took the unusual step of addressing a meeting of black voters at Reverend Grimes's church, where he heard "enthusiastic cheers for Fremont, and . . . reiterated expressions of determination to rally the entire colored vote" for his own reelection.[16] The votes they brought out seemed to have made the difference for the incumbent. Late on a tense election night Burlingame prevailed by just seventy votes, aided by an unusually high turnout in Ward Six.[17] As Burlingame's star rose in later years, this triumph would not be forgotten; indeed, black politicos would repeatedly claim it as evidence of their influence and their importance. In 1858 Robert Morris used this anecdote to remind audiences of the power and pleasure of political victory: "He claimed that the black voters of his district secured the election of Anson Burlingame. He rehearsed with much glee the scenes of triumph on election night, in which the colored men participated."[18] More than a dozen years later Lewis Hayden was still reminding Beacon Hill voters of that glorious night.[19]

The tradition of black Beacon Hill Republicanism quickly flourished. In late 1857, as Massachusetts Republicans made their ultimately successful bid to shed the Know-Nothing label and govern the state on their own, Ward Six witnessed a "spirited demonstration" for gubernatorial candidate Nathaniel P. Banks "by colored voters and others."[20] The conservative Republican was no abolitionist, but his negotiations with antislavery Know-Nothings finally brought the Republican Party out of the nativist shadow.[21] Meanwhile other Republicans deftly appealed to the ward's black voters by asking John S. Rock to repeat a recent public lecture on "Ancient and Modern Tribes and Nations in Africa." The leading white men who made this rare and gracious invitation, like the ward-heeling lecturer who accepted it, did not pick a date at random when they scheduled the talk for the Thursday evening just prior to the state elections.[22]

But how far could they trust the Republicans to stand with them? Even before *Dred Scott*, black activists regarded the party with both hope and skepticism. Frederick Douglass aptly described the party as caught between the Scylla of antiblack prejudice and the Charybdis of antislavery votes; sail too far in either direction and the ship would founder.[23] Even as "colored citizens" such as John S. Rock endorsed the 1856 nomination of John Fremont and the Republican state and national tickets, his colleague George L. Ruffin gave voice to what must have been a widespread view: that they would go no "further with the Republicans than the Republicans will go with us."[24] After *Dred Scott*, Ruffin decided to go no further at all, at least for the present; he and his Boston-born wife, Josephine St. Pierre, decamped for England.[25]

Some white Republicans responded to *Dred Scott* with loud, and no doubt often heartfelt, anger. The Massachusetts legislature resolved that "all citizens of Massachusetts are citizens of the United States; that all negroes, not aliens, domiciled within her limits, are citizens of Massachusetts, and are entitled to all the rights, privileges and immunities of citizen-ship, in the courts of the US and elsewhere."[26] Republicans gave their black allies a voice in legislative hearings, drawing appreciative responses.[27] Their petitions were taken up in the legislature's Committee on Federal Relations, which invited Nell, Morris, and Hayden to address its members.[28]

But there were strict limits to what black activists could expect. During the late 1850s and early 1860s Republicans welcomed or excluded their black members as the currents of state and national politics demanded. Powerful state and national Republican figures addressed meetings of "colored voters" in Ward Six, and one black Republican was among the ward delegates who selected the party's nominee for state senate in 1859.[29] But many other convention delegations and ward meetings were entirely composed of white men.[30] And despite Republican dominance in Massachusetts politics, much that black activists held dear remained out of reach. A strengthened personal liberty bill, supported by a petition of sixteen thousand citizens of the state, failed by a slim majority in the 1859 legislature.[31] Even if it had not, Governor Banks would almost certainly have vetoed it: the bill called for long terms of imprisonment for anyone aiding in the rendition of a purported fugitive—three to twenty years if they acted under the terms of the federal Fugitive Slave Law, ten years to life if they did not. "We shrink from an act," legislative opponents of the bill explained, "which in our opinion, is a virtual declaration of disunion and of civil war."[32] That same session, a legislative committee refused to act on a petition from William Nell and others that would have included the "name of every adult citizen" in the pool for jury service.[33]

Despite these evident limitations, Republican participation offered both hope and excitement. Robert Morris declared himself "a republican," and therefore "always bound to stump his district"—the nearly all-white suburb of Chelsea. More than that, Morris relished the thought of taking the next logical step, into elected office. At an 1858 convention he argued that politics was a promising avenue to acceptance and progress: "He believed in voting," a journalist reported Morris saying. "He should stump his district, and thought he might be elected to the Legislature. He advised the colored people to stand together and vote together."[34] "Perhaps, in the course of time," he continued to much applause, "he would be rewarded like others by a seat in the legislature." He urged his colleagues in New Bedford, where the black community was clustered more densely than in Boston, to "put their best young man upon the representative ticket and run him in."[35] Two years later, New Bedford's black voters did almost exactly that when they elected former slave Thomas Bayne to the city council, making him the first black elected official in the state.[36]

While the prosperous Morris fantasized about elective office, others were struggling with economic as well as political hard times. The Haydens' clothing store, which had moved up and down Cambridge Street several times in the early 1850s, failed in 1856, leaving Lewis Hayden bankrupt and burdened with nine thousand dollars of mostly unpayable debt. Over an ensuing year of legal proceedings, most of the store's many creditors accepted settlements of a little more than five cents on the dollar, with John V. DeGrasse trading his unpaid medical bills for some of the store's stock.[37] Many of Hayden's friends found themselves in this position. His Masonic brother Jonas W. Clark held a mortgage of fifteen hundred dollars on the remaining stock, more than three-quarters of its assessed value. Wendell Phillips got back the two hundred dollars in principal that he had earlier loaned Hayden, but none of the interest.[38] Bankruptcy proceedings dissolved Hayden's business on July 2, by which time Clark had already assumed control of the store at 99 Cambridge Street.[39] Without a store, Hayden was cast economically adrift.

Nell, nearly a decade after his nomination on the Free Soil ticket, faced similarly bleak prospects. His hopes that *Colored Patriots of the American Revolution* would bring him financial solvency proved forlorn.[40] Two years after its publication, the book had not yet earned enough even to allow Nell to retrieve the remaining four hundred copies from the printer. At the age of forty he remained a debt-ridden bachelor of marginal employment, residing in a boardinghouse.[41] As Theodore Parker noted about Nell's efforts, "Negroes get few honors."[42] Emotionally as well as financially, Nell could almost feel the frayed ends of his own rope. If he could not find "profitable employment" in Boston, he confided to Phillips, he would have to leave the city the following spring. "I don't want to say I am discouraged," he wrote, "but I must try something else, somewhere else. . . . I want to accomplish something. If I find I cannot do it after so long wishing to be like other men I have no way to render me at all agreeable to myself—but to bid adieu to what perpetually annoys me, viz seeing others flourish while I am a failure."[43] What made this imagined farewell particularly upsetting was that he had already tried it once, when he had moved to Rochester to work with Douglass. Now, almost ten years later, he found himself facing the same painful dead end.

But Nell continued to work. His colleague and friend the fugitive William Wells Brown argued that the *Dred Scott* decision "proved that we needed a more genuine anti-slavery in the land—that they needed to go into the school-houses and small meeting-houses, as they did fifteen or twenty years ago, and preach the gospel of anti-slavery."[44] Nell followed this course. In 1858 he traveled to Michigan on an antislavery tour with poet and lecturer Frances Ellen Watkins, cousin of his good friend William Watkins.[45] Most ambitiously, he arranged the 1858 Faneuil Hall celebration of Crispus Attucks. But still there was no money, and by 1860 Nell took a new position working for the proprietor of a gymnasium, one that for the first time in many years took him outside the Anti-Slavery Office.[46]

Politics eased Lewis Hayden's hard times in a new and unexpected way. In January 1858 Nathaniel Banks and his Republican administration took power, and Berkshire antislavery man Oliver Warner became secretary of state. Like the rest of the state's executive officers, Warner had the right to appoint his own small staff, and sometime in late 1858 or early 1859 he appointed Hayden his "Messenger," a position the fugitive would hold for the rest of his life.[47] Warner may have made his own independent judgment, or the farmer from the state's westernmost county may have relied on local advice in choosing an employee. In either case it could not have hurt that another of the rising Republicans of this era, John A. Andrew, had been Hayden's patron, ally, and friend for more than a decade. Andrew lived in Ward Six and frequently addressed its political meetings. He had made a comfortable home for himself in the Know-Nothing legislature and by the end of the decade had come to represent the Republicans' radical wing, the so-called Bird Club.[48] He probably already had his sights on the governorship, which he would win in 1860.

Hayden's appointment served several purposes. With the statehouse sitting just a few blocks from the center of his political and social community, whatever duties he was nominally assigned did not seriously interfere with his life as an organizer. Indeed, during the three decades of his employment as messenger, Hayden would spend significant periods elsewhere than the secretary's office: he traveled west to attend conventions, do Masonic business, and recruit black soldiers; later he would head south to investigate the war and Reconstruction; as an older man he would periodically be bedridden with kidney disease; and for a brief time he even served in the state legislature itself. But he never gave up the sinecure and could always return to it, even after Warner left the secretary's office in 1876.[49] Hayden became both a symbol of Republican goodwill and the conduit between the governing party and the black and white activists of the neighborhood and beyond. "Send me if you please some of your speeches, in pamphlet form," Hayden wrote to the now recovered Charles Sumner in June of 1860, from the office of the secretary of state; "as I pass through the streets people are calling upon me for them."[50] Massachusetts now paid him to do part of his life's work.

THE QUESTION OF SLAVE REVOLT

Just beside the story of local patronage and political engagement flowed another powerful stream of thought and action, one that foresaw no electoral solution to slaveholders' grip on national power. The end of slavery might require concerted physical force—in short, a slave revolt. While the notion struck most whites and even many abolitionists as horrific, a cataclysm rather than a liberation, African Americans expressed deeply ambivalent feelings about large-scale revolutionary violence. The impulse that drove David Walker to prophesy God's wrath descending on the slaveholders, and that caused Martin Delany to imagine Lewis Hayden burying a hoe in an overseer's head, led many to wish that the enslaved people of the South would rise up. The painful knowledge that centuries of American revolts had brought reprisals and executions, not liberation, did not prevent free people from hoping for a different result.

Most free black observers understood that for a revolt to unfold successfully, slaves and free blacks would have to exploit divisions among the white majority. They were well aware of the eighteenth-century revolution in the French colony of St. Domingue, in which slaves and free blacks overthrew colonial rule, ended slavery, and at the dawn of the nineteenth century established Haiti as the first black republic. But they knew that their own North American circumstance was different in essential respects. In the Caribbean enslaved people made up large majorities of the population, while the United States had a substantial white majority. There were places—South Carolina and Mississippi, especially—where the enslaved outnumbered the free, but even there whites were free to arm and train themselves, communicate, and call for aid from their fellows elsewhere. Enslaved people had none of these freedoms, and their independent plans of insurrection were either betrayed before they unfolded or brutally put down by soldiers, militiamen, and vigilantes. They would require help. In the United States, that was to say, a successful slave revolt would require some sort of alliance with whites.

Throughout the nation's history, wartime alliances were how black people had extracted many of their rights and freedoms. In the Revolutionary War and the War of 1812, African Americans had served one army or another in exchange for the promise of freedom.[51] In the 1830s, fugitive slaves and the Seminole Indians among whom they lived had done battle with U.S. troops on the Florida frontier, and black refugees from U.S. slavery had fought with the British against American troops during the Canadian Revolt of 1837. Siding with the governing party in Rhode Island against the white populist insurgency of the Dorr Rebellion in the early 1840s, black residents were rewarded both with voting rights and a militia company. In the midst of the Latimer War, a largely black audience in Boston must have listened attentively to the lectures William Nell had booked for them—one on the Dorr War, and another on "the character of Toussaint L'Ouverture," the free black general of the Haitian revolution.[52]

Many white allies understood the principle of fighting for liberty but hesitated to apply it literally to the war against slavery and racial caste. While Garrisonian nonresistants renounced all forms of force, even the less orthodox white abolitionists of the 1841 Vigilance Committee swore to "employ every legal, peaceful and christian method, and none other."[53] Free black activists sometimes took principled or pragmatic stands against violence; in 1837, editor Samuel Cornish of the *Colored American* condemned the "disgraceful riot" made by black New Yorkers in an attempt to rescue a fugitive, in particular chastising black women for taking on so grossly inappropriate a role.[54] But black debates more often concerned the efficacy, not the morality, of particular tactics. If the only path to freedom lay through violent struggle, most black Americans were willing to consider it. If slavery was robbery, rape, and murder, as free blacks knew it to be, then why was violence—revolution, in fact—not the proper response?

Some, like the young New York orator Henry Highland Garnet, argued that justice and self-respect simply demanded a violent and collective response to slavery. In 1843, when leading free black men from across the North gathered in Buffalo for a national convention, the greatest energy at the meeting flowed in response to Garnet's fiery "Address to the Slaves."[55] He called on the enslaved to revolt, and on his colleagues to make this call their official position. Standing in opposition to Garnet was another rising star, Frederick Douglass. The Maryland fugitive navigated carefully among the rocks. At that time he firmly believed, following his Boston mentors, that the Constitution was a proslavery document; this ruled out voting as a means to end slavery.[56] But Douglass also knew from his own experience as a slave that the kind of revolt Garnet imagined stood no real chance of success. All that was left was "moral suasion," the force of example and witness to turn white people's hearts against slavery. Douglass knew this was weak tea, and he did not offer it as an eternal principle. Instead, he urged his fellow delegates to refrain from calling for violence "a little longer." Douglass's position beat Garnet's among the delegates by a single vote.[57] Many of those present, including William Wells Brown, never forgot Garnet's lesson; in 1847 Brown told another convention that if the United States asked for black men to serve in its army in Mexico, they should "fight against the United States."[58]

As frustration with the *Dred Scott* decision boiled over during the late 1850s, many black activists lost patience with party politics and reconsidered Garnet's position. A growing number of black activists across the North shared the determination of Cincinnati's Peter Clark "never to petition for a right again," but to "seize" them.[59] Some went further. Charles Remond had always doubted the promises of party politics, and at the 1858 Convention of the Colored Citizens of Massachusetts he disparaged his colleagues for their caution. The time for talk had passed, he said; "[i]t makes no difference what Mr. Hayden and Mr. Morris think of the [*Dred Scott*] decision."[60] What was at issue was "the slave's right to shed blood and take life, to obtain his liberty."[61] The proper model for slaves to pursue, he held, was that of the "Revolution of the past," a legacy first embodied by Attucks and Washington, and more recently by the Christiana fugitives, who "opened the Revolution of the present, when they shot down Gorsuch and his son."[62] Remond declared himself a "traitor" to the United States, and wished for a divine thunderbolt "to bring destruction upon this nation." He proposed inciting a slave revolt in South Carolina. He wanted the convention to move beyond resolutions and produce insurrectionary propaganda that would "encourage their brethren at the South to rise with bowie-knife and revolver and musket."[63]

But Remond's 1858 call for an immediate, spontaneous rebellion by American slaves was as extreme a position as his wholesale rejection of electoral politics. Many Southern- and slave-born activists present at the convention understood the daunting odds facing slave rebels. They responded that Remond's call for revolt revealed either ignorance of those facts, or a pigheaded unwillingness to acknowledge them. "When I fight," explained the former slave Josiah Henson, now a leader among Canadian blacks, "I want to whip somebody."[64]

Remond's proposal reflected the frustrations of the late 1850s and the desire for a radical break with the unhappy present. He cast the question of revolt as an indicator of manly determination and he suggested that a man like Henson—an emigrant who chose Canadian safety over American struggle—was "not willing to do his duty." He supposed "there would be cowards, and time-servers, and apologists among colored men as among whites, and he felt contempt for them." Then Remond jabbed harder. By 1858 Josiah Henson was already firmly (though falsely) identified in the public mind as the inspiration for Harriet Beecher Stowe's character Uncle Tom, the devout Christian who forswore violence and sacrificed himself for others.[65] Remond declared that he "did not go so far as Uncle Tom, and kiss the hand that smote him. He didn't believe in such a Christianity." Henson in turn cast doubts on Remond's courage and sincerity. "He believed that if the shooting time came, Remond would be found out of the question." Having foolishly called for an impossible revolt, he would bolt: "Remond might talk, and then run away, but what would become of the poor fellows that must stand?" Three or four thousand would be hanged, he imagined, to no purpose.[66]

Yet this yearning for revolution against the United States remained more ambivalent than it sometimes appeared. William Wells Brown found the American Revolution and its slaveholding hero, George Washington, far inferior to Haiti and Toussaint L'Ouverture. His lecture "St. Domingo: Its Revolutions and Its Patriots" sought to make the slaveholders "tremble" with the knowledge that "the slave in his chains, in the rice swamps of Carolina and the cotton fields of Mississippi, burns for revenge." He predicted "that the slave would rise and vindicate his right to freedom by physical force."[67] Yet Brown, as much as his friend Nell, sought to reconcile his prediction of revolt with his hope that American citizenship could mean what it promised. Should American slaves unchain themselves, he concluded his lecture, "the revolution that was commenced in 1776 would then be finished, and the glorious sentiments of the Declaration of Independence . . . realized." The American Revolution might have produced a morally bankrupt slaveholding nation, but its ideals continued to inspire the "colored citizens."[68]

THE QUESTION OF REVOLUTIONARY CAPACITY

Haiti appealed to these activists in part because its very existence squarely addressed the question of whether blacks as a race possessed the capacity for revolution. It was a question they could scarcely bear to keep answering, but one they could not avoid, for many white abolitionists nurtured the suspicion that black men, as men, lacked the revolutionary spirit deemed essential for republican citizenship. This skepticism struck at the heart of their claim to American citizenship and hung over African American discussions of revolution and violence. The stakes were enormously high: that African Americans suffered in bondage made them objects of sympathy and pity, but it also raised the question of why they had not, like the American patriots of the 1770s, rejected their "slavery" and seized freedom. While African Americans debated the tactics that would bring freedom and equality, then, they did so in the shadow of a much harsher conversation, one that called into question their overall fitness for citizenship.

Some speculated about the damage slavery inflicted upon black manhood. James Redpath, a radical white abolitionist, explained that while "slavery eats out the manhood of the slave," prejudice made free black men "jealous, suspicious, envious, doubtful of every human being; distrustful of all friends; an unbeliever in disinterested action."[69] Theodore Parker consoled a white abolitionist colleague who felt deceived by a black Bostonian; the fellow had come with William Nell's recommendation, but Nell was, after all, only "the most '*respectable*' colored man in Boston." Bracketed and italicized respectability was clearly not the genuine article.[70]

Others suspected that the problem lay with African Americans themselves. Millions of blacks endured slavery without revolting because, as a race, they lacked the capacity for revolution. Parker argued that "Africans fail to perform the natural duty of securing freedom by killing their oppressors" because they lacked the instinctual vengeance and ferocity of "the Caucasian . . . The stroke of an axe would have settled the matter long ago," Parker concluded, "[b]ut the black man would not strike."[71] James Redpath well understood the forces preventing slaves from assembling and arming for revolt, but he argued that "[i]f the Southern negroes had any chance of successfully asserting their rights by arms, I would not feel a single throb of sympathy for them." Should circumstances change, they would have to prove their worthiness by rising in revolt.[72]

No one refuted these challenges more forcefully than John S. Rock. He ridiculed the incoherence of contemporary notions of racial classification and hierarchy, and he directly challenged Theodore Parker's claim of racial incapacity. "I have heard white men say, that we will not fight," Rock replied, but the evidence in fact showed that "we have both physical and moral courage." Did not hundreds flee each year, despite having the entire republic "arrayed against them"? Had not black men fought courageously in history's battles, from the Caribbean to the American Revolution? And what did it say about the alleged superiority of Parker's race that it took tens of millions of them to keep a much smaller population in chains?[73]

Yet Rock was in some ways caught in the same double bind that restrained Morris from bringing the Massasoit Guard out to march. On the one hand, he had to demonstrate that he and his people were capable of violent revolution. On the other, he had to demonstrate his gentility and respectability by leading an exemplary public and private life. The difficulty inherent in squaring this circle became clear on many occasions during this superheated period—including the day, sometime in 1860, when James Redpath hit John S. Rock in the face.

Redpath put it a bit more elliptically: in order to "chastise" Rock, he had brought his hand "in contact with his face, violently." Rock, in his view, earned the blow by writing Redpath a slanderous and threatening letter, simply "because I prevented him from cheating a colored woman who was friendless."[74] But nothing here was very simple. The two men, in fact, played out in dramatic form the abolitionist debate about race and manhood—about whether black men could save ostensibly helpless women and children from their fates, or whether white men had to take charge.

The nominal cause of their conflict was the honor of Mrs. Malinda Noll, a former slave both Rock and Redpath knew well. Noll had become free in 1857 and spent the next years earning money to purchase her sons' freedom. She succeeded in freeing one in 1858, but another remained in slavery in Missouri. She contacted Wendell Phillips, and he sent her to Redpath, whom he knew to have both experience helping slaves escape and knowledge of the Missouri-Kansas border country. Redpath claimed that despite being near the top of the proslavery Missourians' most-wanted list, he "made unusual efforts to run off the boy . . . at the eminent hazard of my own life & safety."[75]

Noll later visited Boston on several fund-raising trips, and on one of those visits she stayed at Dr. Rock's home.[76] Rock apparently borrowed twenty-five dollars from her, which, in Redpath's account, he "dodged payment of." In Rock's version of the story, Noll's loan to him was offset by other transactions. But Redpath became convinced of Rock's perfidy and advised Noll to put a bill collector onto him. Rock expressed umbrage in a letter to Redpath, and Redpath replied by charging that Rock was laying claim to "sacred" money that Noll needed to free her son. This seems

to have enraged Rock. He replied with what Redpath called a "very inso-
lent" and "sneering" note in which he referred to "the moral relations"
existing between Redpath and Noll—a phrase Redpath interpreted as an
insinuation of an improper sexual relationship—and made what Redpath
considered a veiled threat of violence. Redpath, whose office was adjacent
to the Anti-Slavery Office, stormed over and showed Rock's threatening
letter to Garrison, Phillips, and Nell; he told them "that I w[oul]d chastise
Rock whenever I met him." He then proceeded to the bill collector's office
to tell him to press the claim immediately, and began reading the collector
Rock's offending letter.

At this point, Rock himself arrived. Redpath, feeling inspired to violence, began to leave. He had "determined to wait below," he explained,
"till Dr. Rock came down." But Rock acted first. "[H]e had the coolness,"
Redpath fumed, "to say I misunderstood him." Redpath responded by
angrily reading Rock's own letter back to him and asking him directly what
his words meant. He finished by striking Rock across the face. "That is the
whole story," Redpath concluded. But not quite. Rather than respond in
kind, Rock swore out a warrant for Redpath's arrest. This was never served
because Redpath sailed for Haiti, as planned, just two days later. Rock's
outrage followed him, though, in the form of letters to their mutual associates on the island (and perhaps elsewhere) describing Redpath as "an
enemy of our race, in the guise of a friend."[77]

The encounter tells us a great deal about the world in which these men
operated. Even viewed through a single lens—Redpath's defensive account
of the exchange to William Watkins, who understandably wanted to know
why his white employer had assaulted the most accomplished black man
in Boston—it reveals that black and white men could approach the vindication of manhood in very different ways. Each had something to prove,
to himself, to the other, and to those who had witnessed or might hear of
the encounter. Redpath admitted that losing his temper had been foolish,
but he tried to reframe his outburst as a backhanded blow in defense of
Rock's equality as a man. "Under the circumstances I w[oul]d have as-

saulted *a white man*," he explained; "had I dispised [*sic*] colored men, as such, I w[oul]d *not* have assaulted Dr. Rock." By striking Rock, "I taught that I regarded a colored man as having rights which I was bound to respect—among them the right to be chastised for slandering a fellow being without cause."[78] By striking Rock, in other words, he was treating Rock as an equal, defying Justice Taney, and standing up for the rights and dignity of black men generally. More than this, Redpath claimed to be modeling the principled resistance to injustice that so many white abolitionists believed was lacking in "the negro." "When I believed in fight[ing]," Redpath explained, "I did fight, & was not ashamed of it."[79] Rock, by contrast, did what was required of a law-abiding gentleman. When Redpath struck him, Rock did not strike back, but swore out a complaint against him and informed mutual acquaintances of Redpath's bad behavior. White radicals might be able to reinvent themselves as dashing figures who disdained convention, but Rock aspired to something quite different. His own lecture "Voyage of an American Outlaw" was not an account of frontier heroics such as Redpath's, but a discussion of being treated as a gentleman while in Paris for medical treatment, a trip he took despite the fact that the post–*Dred Scott* federal government had denied him a passport.[80]

Indeed, while Redpath bragged of his ferocity, Rock claimed to have achieved heights of gentlemanly dignity that allowed him to pass unmolested even where other men of color endured insults. "I have never been insulted" in Boston, he declared flatly in 1860; "no one ever says a pert thing to me. Even drunken loafers pass me by without unpleasant remarks made in my hearing. I have no friends ashamed to meet me anywhere, or to invite me to their houses, or to visit me in return." Charles Remond professed astonishment at this claim, but Rock would not retreat.[81] "When the avenues to wealth are opened to us," he argued, "we will then become educated and wealthy, and then . . . black will be a very pretty color . . . flattery will then take the place of slander, and you will find no prejudice in the Yankee whatever."[82] He claimed that he had already made that transformation real. Perhaps Rock had offered these thoughts before Redpath struck him. Perhaps he agreed that Redpath had been motivated by something other than racial prejudice. In any case, Rock claimed he had found a way to embody a black manhood both powerful enough to cow the bullies and dignified enough to engender respect.

"THIS ROUTINE OF BUSINESS FOR A FEMALE LOOKS MASCULINE"

Somehow, amid all the talk of "leading men" and the silent compression of "slaves" into the figure of a rebellious or submissive male slave, Malinda Noll herself almost disappeared. Noll, though, was not the helpless, put-upon figure that Redpath implied in his narrative of chivalric protection. While Redpath was figuring himself as her knight, Malinda Noll was successfully recruiting allies and funds. In December 1860 she announced in the *Liberator* that she had raised enough money to ransom her second son and would now free her mother as well "by the profit of anti-slavery books which she proposes to sell."[83] Her activist career was not defined by Rock and Redpath's manly jousting.

Noll's efforts suggest how black women were pressing into a variety of new roles, despite facing their own double bind of self-assertion versus respectability. Although the range of professions open to black women was of course even smaller than that open to black men, some did carve out professional identities that could yield income, recognition, or other satisfactions.[84] Yet black women working in public faced the challenge Mary Ann Shadd knew all too well from her stint as an editor: that "this routine of business for a female looks masculine."[85] The public stage required them to carefully manage their appearance and comportment, remaining within the bounds of mid-nineteenth-century "respectability" in dress and speech, and insisting on one's womanly honor. To do this while pressing for radical social change was a tall order. It provided an easy target for those who equally rejected black women's and black men's public roles as unwarranted presumption. Frances Ellen Watkins strove diligently to present herself as an eminently respectable lady of color, but when she lectured she heard remarks such as "She is a man."[86]

Black women set conventions of "womanly" behavior aside in far more extreme ways when they took part in the operation of the Underground Railroad. In general such women remained anonymous, but Harriet Tubman famously did not; after making her own escape from slavery, she repeatedly returned to Maryland to lead other fugitives to freedom and emerged as a leader in fugitive rescue and defense.[87] There were precedents for such trespass of the bounds of gender, including a tradition of women disguising themselves as soldiers and sailors—a tradition that inspired fascination, titillation, and sometimes admiring acknowledgment of their work and daring.[88] William Nell had even celebrated such a woman for her exploits as a soldier in the Revolutionary War.[89] Tubman may not literally have cross-dressed, but she fulfilled all the other aspects of this role.

Yet Tubman also found that white male abolitionists, lauding her courage and ability, could not refrain from figuring her as a man. "If you do not know her already," read Wendell Phillips's note of introduction for her to the Reverend James Freeman Clarke, "let this introduce to you '*Moses*' or *Genl Tubman* . . . to whom *150* human beings owe their freedom. Let her tell you her plans story & wishes."[90] The Kansas antislavery guerrilla John Brown also called her "General Tubman," but he went much further than Phillips, referring to Tubman as "he," and describing her as "the most of a man, naturally; that I ever met with."[91] He meant it as a high compliment. Brown's turn of phrase reflected a deeper sense, shared among his sympathizers and colleagues, black and white: aggressive revolutionary leadership was male—even when performed by women.[92]

Stories of powerful, daring women such as Tubman had been circulating among Boston's friends of the fugitive for decades, at least since 1836, but in the late 1850s they returned in more complicated form. In 1858, when Robert Morris urged the people of New Bedford and Boston to make a pact for mutual defense, he added, "[C]ome men, and women too." But he finished with a final note: "[A]nd protect the fugitive with the ample folds of her garments," which apparently provoked "great laughter."[93] Morris then offered a new and unlikely version of the rescue of Shadrach Minkins, in which a "big woman . . . stood on the stairs of the Court room with arms akimbo, and her 'noble feet' spread over the stairs, so that nobody could pass her, and when she got a chance she took the runaway by the hair and lifting him up said, 'God bless ye, honey! have they got ye?' and carried him down the stairs till he could take to his heels, and was next heard of in Canada."[94]

Perhaps this was Morris's vision of Harriet Tubman. But if so, the story contained dissonant notes. Why did Morris conclude by saying that women could protect fugitives in "the ample folds of her garments"—and why was this exhortation met with "great laughter" from the mainly black crowd?[95] It may simply have been the risqué or absurd image of a male fugitive sheltering in a woman's skirts. But perhaps it had something to do, as well, with the image of a woman large enough to spread her feet wide and block a staircase, and to hide a grown man beneath her. It may be that many in the audience, Morris included, wanted to create some distance between themselves and a woman who looked, talked, and acted like the one in his story. Perhaps, in other words, a particular vision of black womanhood—physical and imposing—threatened the aspirations of other black women and men, just as it had discomfited Samuel Cornish in the 1830s or Henry Bowditch in the 1840s.

Morris might have been misquoted or been speaking for comic effect, but two years later the role of his nameless woman was undertaken—with deadly seriousness—by Tubman herself. As a fugitive was about to be rendered into slavery from a courtroom in Troy, New York, Tubman seized him, hauled him down a flight of stairs, and passed him to rescuers, all the while being beaten by policemen. When the fugitive was quickly recaptured and locked in the judge's chambers, Tubman led a charge that broke down the door and accomplished, finally, the fugitive's escape to Canada.[96] Life imitated art, and this time it was no laughing matter. Black women were bursting onto stages, into public conversations, and even into judge's chambers. They were, carefully or recklessly, laying claim to all the rights demanded by their fellow "colored citizens."

JOHN BROWN AND THE RAID ON HARPERS FERRY

Tubman and Hayden soon got an opportunity to go beyond defending individual fugitives or debating the merits of a hypothetical slave revolt. To mount a successful rebellion—to transform the rude, rumbling machinery of the Underground Railroad into something grander and more terrible—took a visionary and a zealot, one with the time and freedom to nurture plans and alliances. In the 1850s such a visionary emerged in the person of John Brown. A religious idealist and unsuccessful wool merchant, Brown had long affiliated himself with white antislavery radicals. In 1849 he purchased land from Gerrit Smith with the purpose of aiding the black settlers Smith had drawn to his lands in upstate New York. More than most white radicals, he actively sought to live in a racially egalitarian world, and he devoted his life to the end of slavery.[97]

In Kansas, Brown styled himself "Captain of the Liberty Guards" and led free-state volunteers against proslavery forces in a war without mercy.[98] Most infamously, in 1856 Brown oversaw the brutal slaying of five proslavery militants whom his men dragged from their cabin at Pottawatomie Creek. Despite the controversy surrounding this event, and in part because of it, Brown became a celebrated figure in Eastern antislavery circles. He sent reports to Frederick Douglass, who printed them in his paper. Brown was well known among the black activists of the free states as one of the few white people who put his own life at risk in the name of freedom.

By 1857, Brown began planning something more ambitious: the invasion and occupation of the Southern highlands by an abolitionist army. Brown's plan was to begin with the seizure of the federal arsenal at Harpers Ferry in western Virginia, a dramatic event that would at one stroke arm the conspirators and rally the slaves of the surrounding area. From there they would retreat into the mountains, carving out a free republic within the territory of the Slave Power itself. This would spark escalating revolts among the slaves of Virginia and states to the south, drawing fugitives like a magnet to an ever growing network of mountain bastions, and eating away at slavery in its own heartland. Brown's plan also had a Northern component: while he and his rebels hid in the mountains, one commentator alleged, "his New England partisans would in the meantime call a Northern Convention, restore tranquility and overthrow the pro-slavery administration."[99] It was hard to say which element of the plan was more fanciful.

Brown's plot required elaborate planning and financial support, but for credibility and for recruitment it relied above all on the cooperation of the continent's leading black activists. Brown took Frederick Douglass up on an invitation to visit him in Rochester, staying three weeks in a spare room and writing a "Provisional Constitution" for the mountain republic. He corresponded with black leaders across the North, including John Jones in Chicago, George T. Downing in Providence, and Martin Delany in Canada.[100] He also solicited the aid of prominent white radicals such as Higginson and Parker, asking for their help raising funds from abolitionist men and women.[101] One of the white men Brown approached, Concord's Franklin Sanborn, conferred with Higginson over the request, concluding that should Brown succeed, "[t]reason will not be treason much longer, but patriotism."[102] Sanborn, Higginson, and other prominent Massachusetts residents including Samuel Gridley Howe and Julia Ward Howe would later become infamous as most of the "secret six" who funded Brown's raid.

These six may have provided Brown with money, but the guerrilla persistently sought the endorsement and the military aid of prominent and bold black leaders. In the spring of 1858 he traveled to Canada to meet with two of the boldest, Harriet Tubman and Martin Delany. Later he held a convention in Chatham, at the heart of black Canada, where nearly fifteen hundred blacks now resided.[103] Giving the impression that they were meeting to form a Masonic lodge, black and white men assembled to hear Brown's plans. After discussion, they voted to adopt Brown's constitution and offered support, as well as some skepticism. Plans were delayed as recruiting and finances lagged, but in the interim Brown's work continued: in December 1858 he mounted a raid on Missouri slaveholders, leading eleven slaves on a successful thousand-mile flight to Canada, aided by black and white allies all along the way.[104] Near the end of the line, Brown met again with black leaders in Detroit, including Douglass and Detroit Vigilance Committee leader George DeBaptiste.

Finally, fearful that his plans for revolt were about to be betrayed, Brown set the machinery in rapid motion. He called on his sympathizers in and around Boston to recruit raiders, turning to a man who knew the fugitive defense network inside out: Lewis Hayden. First, Hayden established contact with Harriet Tubman, probably seeking her help as a recruiter.[105] She traveled to Boston in the late spring of 1859, residing at a Cambridge Street boardinghouse just down the hill from the Haydens.[106] But as Brown's timetable for the raid accelerated, Tubman took sick; she was apparently laid up in New Bedford and unable to help as the last recruits were raised.[107] In the weeks leading up to the raid, Hayden was "in consultation" with Brown's close associate George L. Stearns about sending recruits on to Brown.[108] Hayden "entered warmly into the work" and enlisted six men, making use of money he had solicited from an erratic young white gentleman, Francis Merriam. Of the six, though, apparently only one reached Harpers Ferry.[109]

On October 16, 1859, Brown led his band of black and white men to the federal arsenal from a nearby farm, but nothing went right. No slaves flocked to their side, and they were soon besieged by units of the United States military. A few of the raiders managed to flee, but others were killed or, like their leader, captured and put on trial for treason by the Commonwealth of Virginia.

A villain to Virginia authorities and sober-minded nationalists, Brown quickly became a hero to black radicals and their white allies. They rejected depictions of him as unbalanced or insane, focusing instead on his unapologetic opposition to slavery. From his Virginia cell, Brown added to his following in the weeks before his execution. His demeanor brought him the admiration even of his captors, as did his refusal to plead insanity. The Virginia jury reached a verdict of guilty in forty-five minutes, but Brown's impending execution spurred a rush of celebration among growing numbers of Northerners: Emerson described him as "the new saint awaiting his martyrdom," which would "make the gallows glorious like the cross."[110] By the second half of November, Brown began to represent the highest idealism the North had to offer. His letters from prison, humble and resigned, supported this view.

In Boston and throughout the black North, December 2, 1859, was a day of mourning. Black residents wore crepe armbands, black-owned businesses shut down, and hundreds joined with white allies at the Tremont Temple for a mass meeting to mark Virginia's execution of John Brown.[111] Thousands filled the hall and thronged the streets outside as black minister J. Sella Martin likened Brown to the heroes of the Revolution. Just over the hill at Reverend Grimes's Twelfth Baptist Church on Southac, a prayer meeting for Brown had been in continuous session since the previous evening, addressed by Grimes, Remond, Nell, and others.[112] The New York *Weekly Anglo-African*, the closest thing to a national newspaper for black Americans, draped the white space between its columns with bars of mourning black.

Meanwhile, federal authorities were moving quickly to determine who, beyond Brown and his raiders, had been involved. They discovered documents implicating a circle of Northerners, many of them in Massachusetts, as well as Frederick Douglass. Some fled, while others—Higginson, notably—dared Virginia or the federal government to come after them.

Douglass, more vulnerable than his white colleagues, might well have been arrested by authorities in Philadelphia if a sympathetic telegraph operator had not warned him. Given a head start, he escaped to Rochester, then abroad. Governor Henry Wise of Virginia made his outrage at Douglass's flight well known, and still hoped to capture him. Douglass wrote home to deny that he was or could be a "traitor" to the United States: the government he was accused of rebelling against was not his own, for "allegiance and protection are said to go together, and depend upon each other. When one is withdrawn"—as *Dred Scott* had withdrawn protection from Douglass and his peers—"the other ceases."[113] He and others seemed on the verge of reconsidering their relationship to the nation that so reviled and rejected them.

Soon a U.S. Senate committee, under the leadership of Virginia's James Mason—author of the Fugitive Slave Law—set about exploring the conspiracy. In January 1860 the committee issued summonses for a number of men thought to be Brown's coconspirators, among them Gerrit Smith, Frank Sanborn, James Redpath, Samuel Gridley Howe, and two black men named in the evidence before them: Detroit's George DeBaptiste, and Boston's Lewis Hayden.[114] The risks of extradition for trial were greatest for Hayden and DeBaptiste: if brought to Virginia, they would not even have been legally permitted to testify in court and might have been convicted—and executed—without being allowed to utter a word.

But the complex symbolic politics of slave insurrection led the Mason committee to proceed with caution. John Brown's raid had not inspired Virginia's slaves to rebel, and this failure allowed defenders of slavery to assert that Brown's fundamental premise was mistaken: Southern slaves did not, they claimed, seethe with impending revolt against a tyrannical system. Brown's murderous and treasonous error should, in this sense, comfort the friends of slavery and good order. To interrogate two black men and present them as important coconspirators would undermine this narrative, raising awkward questions about free black and fugitive involvement in the raid. The investigators found it politically more expedient to use the hearings to expose Brown's raid as a conspiracy of white Northern radicals than to explore the central role played by African Americans. Members of the Mason committee did at several points try to elicit more information about Lewis Hayden's activities from their witnesses, but they learned nothing.[115] On May 24, 1860, the committee formally reported that the summonses for these two men had not been served, offering as explanation only that the parties in question had turned out to be "negroes."[116]

About Hayden's movements and concerns during this period we know almost as little as the Mason committee. He appears to have been lowering his profile. He probably consulted with Harriet Tubman, who reportedly stayed on Southac Street in late 1859 before heading to Canada, and he may have remained in communication with Redpath.[117] As late as the end of October 1859, the Boston Vigilance Committee's treasurer recorded Hayden busily at work, but after that a silence falls over the historical record; his name is nowhere to be found in the entries for 1860 and 1861. Instead, a new figure, one "Lewis Howard," began to receive reimbursement for boarding fugitives.[118] When Harriet Tubman appeared publicly during these years, her name was sometimes recorded as "Harriet Garrison" to avoid attracting unwanted legal or vigilante attention.[119] Perhaps her colleague and unindicted coconspirator had taken the same precaution.

The one known reference in print to Hayden during the months following the raid suggests both caution and resolve. At the end of December 1859 a correspondent in Peterboro, New York, wrote to the *Liberator*, urging armed resistance as the only means of securing freedom for fugitives. The letter explained that the Crafts had been safe at Hayden's home in 1851 because the U.S. marshal feared to serve the warrant Hughes and Knight had obtained. "He knew that the road to hell lay over Lewis Hayden's threshold; and the cost to him would be rather more than the Slave Power would be ready to make up to him."[120] This may simply have been an anecdote. But it is also possible that someone in Gerrit Smith's hometown was offering an oblique warning that the former fugitive from Kentucky remained armed and dangerous.

Brown's daring but disastrous raid left black activists trembling with rage and excitement. For years they had imagined and debated such an effort, and now it had actually occurred. Leaping ahead, far past the grim realities, some began to talk as though Brown had succeeded, or soon would. John Rock, throwing caution to the wind, told a Boston audience that "I believe in insurrections." His hyperbole knew no bounds: "In case of a contest with our enemies, fifty negroes would take the State of Virginia without the loss of a man . . . One thousand negroes would sweep the slave States from the Potomac to the Rio Grande, and the time and places that know the slaveholders now would shortly know them no more forever."[121] A year later Douglass too imagined Brown's raid into a success, dreaming that with a mere thousand rebels in Brown's mountain stronghold, "slavery is dead." In the short term, "[s]laveholders sleep more uneasily than they used to," Douglass averred, and that meant they were more likely to make mistakes.[122] Failure or not, Brown had forced slaveholders and others to ponder realities that had slumbered since Nat Turner swung from the gallows nearly three decades before.

OTHER SHORES

Such giddy hopes leavened but could not lift the post–*Dred Scott* despair. As the 1850s gave way to the 1860s a growing number of black activists began to conclude that they might never achieve equality and inclusion under the American flag. Once again, the question of emigration arose.[123] Much was at stake in the ensuing debate: the related questions of whether or not colored citizens could find full belonging in America, and whether the establishment of a separate and competing home might encourage white Americans to treat them with more respect. Even John Rock, no emigrationist, brought the point home in language guaranteed to shiver Bostonian certainties, and cut to the heart of his colleague William Nell's cherished project: "I am not yet ready to idolize the actions of Crispus Attucks," he declared, for the government Attucks's sacrifice helped create "has used every means in its power to outrage and degrade his race and posterity."[124] As Rock and his comrades debated whether to leave the United States, and for what destination, black spokespeople mixed politics, theology, and history to debate the nature of God's plan for the sons and daughters of Africa on the American shore. Reconsidering the relationship between "emigration" and the long-despised plan of "colonization," some black activists even summoned up the startling vision of African Americans destroying the slaveholding economy by establishing cotton-growing colonies of their own.

The most accessible and well-understood destination was British Canada. Canada was no paradise, but slavery had been abolished there and local governors generally refused to extradite fugitives to the United States.[125] Black men residing there fought against American intervention in 1837 and thereafter served in provincial militias. Their votes mattered to local officials: in 1843, as Charles Remond was smarting from the minstrel mockery he had endured in Faneuil Hall, the mayor of Toronto barred a circus from entering his city unless it promised not to perform minstrel songs, "'to save the feelings of the gentlemen of colour' who so strongly supported his administration."[126] After visiting Canada West in 1858, William Nell reluctantly conceded that if blacks must leave the United States, this was the best destination—though he was quick to add that he did not suggest "the idea of a general emigration of colored Americans."[127] The fugitive slave and Illinois orator H. Ford Douglas reflected that while the United States denied blacks "all participation in the government," both liberties and rights could be secured nearby: "[E]scaping from the beak of the American eagle, we can nestle in the shaggy mane of the British lion."[128] By the 1850s the black settlements of Canada West had swelled to tens of thousands, made up in large part of fugitives from the United States and their children.[129]

Others understood the relationship between Canadian and American freedom in different terms. Some black migrants to Canada saw their destination as final, but for many others, as for the Haydens fifteen years before, Canada remained a way station in which to wait out American slavery—or perhaps even stand ready to destroy it.[130] A black Canadian convention took on David Walker's tone, declaring that black imperial subjects would "hang as a threatening *black* cloud over the American Union, waiting and praying for the Lord's day of vengeance, when we may be the humble instruments in his hands, and do the terrible work, of his settling, for centuries of oppression, wrong and blasphemy."[131] For still others, Canada's black communities were a safe and logical place to recruit emigrants for a more distant black homeland in which colored citizens could work out their destinies not as subjects or members of a tolerated minority, but—as Nell's onetime editorial colleague Martin Delany put it—a "distinct nationality."[132]

By the 1850s the range of real and potential destinations beyond North America swelled to include various African and Central American locales, and Delany emerged as the nation's leading spokesman for black emigration. As a traveling journalist he had been mobbed in Ohio, harassed on the new National Road, and—like so many leading colored citizens— denied entrance to the professions. In 1851 he and two other black men briefly enrolled at Harvard Medical School, but white students had objected so strenuously that the head of the school quickly dismissed Delany and the others. It was a bitter blow, and perhaps a turning point. By 1853, Delany had concluded that the best hope for black citizenship lay not in the United States, but elsewhere, where no government enforced inequality and where black citizens could forge their own institutions and networks free from the constraints of prejudice and discrimination.[133]

Delany's loss of faith in the American project preceded the *Dred Scott* decision, which indeed he very nearly predicted. Black Americans, he argued in an 1854 address, should not be addressed as "citizens"—"a term desired and ever cherished by us—because such you have never been."

They were not part of the nation's "ruling element," and therefore would never inhabit it in safety.[134] It did not matter whether Massachusetts passed a fine-sounding personal liberty law, for "[i]t is useless to talk about our rights in individual States: we can have no rights there as citizens, not recognised in our common country. . . . We are in the hands of the General Government," he concluded, "and no State can rescue us."[135] The occupation of Boston during the Burns rendition demonstrated the truth of his argument: "[I]f the United States may, with impunity, garrison with troops the Court house of the freest city in America; blockade the streets; station armed ruffians of dragoons, and spiked artillery in hostile awe of the people; if free, white, high-born and bred gentlemen of Boston and New York, are smitten down to earth, refused an entrance on professional business, into the Court Houses, until inspected by a slave hunter and his counsel; all to put down the liberty of the black man; then, indeed, is there no hope for us in this country!"[136]

Delany assembled a Cleveland convention to focus black activists' attention on emigration, but he quickly drew sharp opposition, amplified through the pages of Douglass's newspaper. From Illinois, John Jones asserted that his brethren would have nothing to do with emigration.[137] Out in San Francisco, Nell's friend J. B. Sanderson took part in a countermeeting to Delany's.[138] William Watkins accused Delany and other emigrationists of accepting the colonizationist line that black people's destiny lay outside the United States.[139] Blacks in Boston, he added, did not support the movement.[140] He went further, seeking to refute Delany's argument about citizenship: black voters, at least in Massachusetts, were a part of the "ruling element," and therefore part of "the people." "We look forward to the day when our rights as citizens, shall be acknowledged," he concluded, "and shall suffer no movement based upon despondency and despair, to alienate us from the cause of our elevation here."[141]

Dred Scott dealt a stunning blow to Watkins's brand of optimism, and by the late 1850s emigration had gained both a new following and new destinations. Delany and others, including Henry Highland Garnet, shifted their eyes to African destinations: the former ACS colony of Liberia, the Niger valley, or other sub-Saharan locales in which African Americans could build nations beyond the reach of slavery and caste. Anticipating the inevitable objection that they were doing the work of colonizationists, they presented their efforts as aimed at simultaneously elevating free black American migrants and the Africans among whom they would settle. Garnet, the mastermind behind the 1858 establishment of the "African Civilization Society," described its purpose as the creation of "a grand centre of negro nationality, from which shall flow the streams of commercial, intellectual, and political power which shall make colored people respected everywhere," including, he hoped, in the United States.[142] Africans would be Christianized and civilized along (perfected and casteless) American lines, and free blacks would demonstrate to white Americans and the world the full range of their capacities.[143]

Some black activists even argued that African colonies would unshackle the slaves by means of the market. The African Civilization Society called for the production of cotton in Africa, supervised by black emigrants. Garnet imagined this industry as an engine that would transform the continent, building it into a commercial and political power that would destroy the slave trade, first by drying up the supply of new slaves and ultimately by producing free-labor cotton more cheaply than slaveholders could.[144] Martin Delany plunged into his own similar African venture with both feet, traveling to Liberia, then up into the Yoruba regions of what is now Nigeria, where he signed a treaty with a local ruler establishing an area for settlement and cotton cultivation.[145]

In the years after 1857 such plans gained adherents even in Massachusetts. Black residents of Cambridge—"Afric American Voters," as they pointedly described themselves—assembled to announce their intention to emigrate to Liberia. Unable to obtain "the full and entire benefits" of other Northern freemen, they resolved "the time has come that Africa should become a Nation among Nations, and, like the Pilgrim Fathers," build a new Christian city on a hill on the African littoral. The president of the meeting, Enoch Lewis, had spent forty years as superintendent of the residence halls at Harvard University.[146]

In 1859, Boston gained a powerful proponent of emigration with the emergence of Reverend J. Sella Martin. Born into slavery, Martin escaped to Chicago in 1856. Three years later, only twenty-seven years old, he was already a well-known and well-traveled orator and an ordained Baptist minister. Martin lectured on "the destiny of the negro race," and his view of his own destiny was bold. "Born on the day [Nat] Turner was hanged," writes his biographer, "Martin saw himself as a providential replacement of the great slave martyr."[147] After serving as a visiting minister in several Boston area churches earlier in 1859, he was called to the pulpit of the Joy Street Baptist Church, the congregation occupying the old African

Reverend J. Sella Martin
Courtesy of the Massachusetts
Historical Society

Meeting House. It was there, fittingly enough, that he welcomed Henry Highland Garnet and provided a local home for the African Civilization Society.

Emigration activists infused their campaigns with arguments about God's will. Martin spoke of the society and its potential results in prophetic, providential terms: "[T]he cloud of revolution is ascending, and the great spirit of Liberty enthroned upon it is hurling his thunderbolts thick and hot against the garrisons of slavery and of wrong; and if that society is wrong it will not escape, and if it is right God will do with it what we cannot do without it—make it a mighty instrument of the overthrow of slavery."[148] Like many others, he compared modern emigration with the biblical exodus—the Israelites' escape from bondage. Since at least the eighteenth century, the story of a people's divinely protected escape from slavery in Egypt had played a central role in the cultural, religious, and political lives of African Americans, north and south. God's deliverance of his people from pharaoh to freedom in the land of Canaan offered hope that the hard hand of oppression would be lifted, and that blacks as a people would find physical and spiritual freedom.[149] For some midcentury free people of color, this story remained figurative—a parable whose lesson was the importance of remaining hopeful, aware, and active in the cause of freedom. For others, such as Martin, the story had more literal implications.

The conflict over emigration also revealed deep wells of mistrust among black activists in this era of crisis. Antiemigrationists asserted that the movement represented a flight from reality. Dr. J. B. Smith of New Bedford suggested that black men, "religious in the wrong sense," had become "submissive" and "taught to look forward to the new Jerusalem, as an asylum from all his woes . . . He wanted a part of that new Jerusalem here."[150] Emigrationists fired back. Garnet mocked Nell for embracing black conventions as an opportunity to attack the African Civilization Society. He further asserted that his own African plans did not contradict his American identity. African colonization was a means toward the elevation and liberation of African Americans, not an end in itself. When those larger goals were accomplished, Garnet said, "we should lay aside all distinctive labors, and come together as men and women, members of the great American family."[151] As it was, he keenly resented the effort to strangle his movement and blamed it on the tyrannical impulses of certain men of his own race. There were blacks in Boston, he complained "who, if they became plantation masters, 'would make the blood fly from their slaves.'"[152]

Garnet's greatest antagonist in this moment of crisis was his old classmate from New York's African Free School, George T. Downing. Downing's accomplishments extended far beyond his militant part in the Burns crisis. He was a rare black son of privilege, having grown up in the household of Thomas Downing, proprietor of New York City's most famous oyster house.[153] After a formal education, he established a catering business of his own in New York, and soon also in Newport, Rhode Island, where he served elite clients during their summer vacations.[154] But even as he prospered, he remained an ardent fighter against slavery and caste. He took part in fugitive aid and defense, joining the Committee of Thirteen—a New York equivalent of the revitalized Boston Vigilance Committee—in the wake of the Fugitive Slave Law.[155] He refused to be Jim Crowed on streetcars, once even sharing Frederick Douglass's fate of being ejected forcibly rather than comply with the order to leave.[156] By the 1850s, Downing had established a foothold in Boston's activist community, close by his brother-in-law John DeGrasse.

Downing had once shared Garnet's skepticism about American nationalism. As schoolboys, he and Garnet agreed that black Americans should not celebrate the Fourth of July because slavery and inequality made the Declaration of Independence "a perfect mockery."[157] Notes of that position remained in the 1850s: even as he campaigned for the desegregation of Rhode Island's public schools in the wake of Boston's triumph, he seemed uncertain whether the Jim Crow North was any more virtuous than the slaveholding South.[158]

But by the 1850s Downing hewed to a different providential vision than

Garnet. Downing not only believed that African Americans belonged in the "great American family" of Garnet's imagination, but also that the nation could not be perfected without them. He insisted that the Negro had "an inseparable, providential identity with this country," and especially with its founding ideal, "universal brotherhood." America, Downing explained, existed in order to "work out in perfection the realization of a great principle, *the fraternal unity of man*," and black Americans were essential to that process. Their stigmatized presence, whether as oppressed slaves or "nominally free," forced the question of how deeply Americans were committed to their founding ideals: "All of the great principles of the land are brought out and discussed in connection with the Negro." Emigrationism would thwart God's plans for the race, and for the nation. Should they depart, "[t]he great ethical school of the times, would be closed for the want of a subject." By providing that subject, that human test of the nation's avowed principles, black Americans constituted "the life of the nation's existence." In the grammar of American liberty, Downing declared, "[w]e are the alphabet; upon us, all are constructed."[159] A role this important must not be abdicated.

For the "fraternal unity of man" to become a reality, black Americans would have to "see through and endure"; they would have to reject the call of weaker souls to give up and emigrate. Downing was unequivocal on this point. "We will not be driven off; we will rear and educate our children here, in this our native land, around our sacred altars; altars which our children's children will gaze upon here."[160] William Nell echoed Downing. Closing a letter to a friend, Nell avowed his conviction that he was "[w]orking and hoping for that civilization in the United States which will annihilate slavery and melt the distinctions between man and his brother the wide world over."[161] Others did not choose such transcendent language, but—like Douglass—"simply and briefly repl[ied], 'we prefer to remain in America.'"[162]

For the moment, these arguments sufficed. The African Civilization Society did not make measurable progress toward its goals, and as the

1860s began, it remained marginal in most communities. Yet the questions it raised remained unanswered, and it would not be long before others emerged to ask them again. In the world *Dred Scott* had made, black activists' insistence on American belonging was increasingly provisional and marked by intense ambivalence. Rock, Nell, Downing, Hayden, and the rest rejected emigration, but even the most vehement often seemed to be trying to persuade themselves. Rock's own conclusion was that no other country offered better prospects. "This being our country, we have made up our minds to remain in it, and to try to make it worth living in," he said, noting simply that "we have ties here, and friends that we are unwilling to leave to their fate."[163]

But what reasons were there for hope? Slavery, Rock also argued, "is making every intelligent colored man hate his country, and swear vengeance against it. I doubt very much whether any considerable number of colored men would, in case of war with any foreign country, take up arms to defend a government which has never ceased to oppress them." Brown's raid had not rekindled the spirit of liberty, but was instead followed by renewed Republican promises not to interfere with slavery where it already existed and conversations—even among Republicans—that suggested black people might not have a future in the nation. "[W]e are sleeping," Rock warned, "on the crater of a slumbering volcano."[164] Sick to death both of proslavery zealots and compromising Republicans, Rock did not foresee that it would be the struggle between those two forces that would finally bring the volcano to life.

7.

The Fall and Rise of the United States

As the sectional crisis bubbled over into war in the 1860s, the black activists of the North and the proslavery leaders of the South found agreement only in their mutual enmity, and in their common question: Was the United States a good idea?[1] Black activists posed that question repeatedly in the years between *Dred Scott* and the end of American slavery. They asked it as Southern secessionists finally achieved success after the North elected Republican Abraham Lincoln president in 1860. They asked it as Northern politicians sought to forestall disunion with a host of concessions, including a constitutional end to African American voting rights and a renewed colonization effort. They asked it as policemen shut down black efforts to volunteer in the wake of the firing on Fort Sumter, declaring, "We want you d—d niggers to keep out of this; this is a white man's war."[2] And they asked it during the early years of the Civil War, as the U.S. government and military, seeking to reassure nervous whites in the border states and elsewhere that this was not a war of emancipation, returned fugitives to slavery and refused black Northerners' repeated requests to serve as soldiers. During these critical years, as during their militant resistance to the Fugitive Slave Law, black Northerners generated much greater anxiety and outrage among the slaveholders than seemed warranted by their small numbers, formal power, or material challenge to the institution of slavery. Their provocations helped lead the nation to war.

Once war began, black activists continued to shape Union policy, most crucially by their threat to withhold military service except on terms of equality. At first the Union emphatically rejected both their service and emancipation as an aim of the war. This only hardened their resolve—so much so that many remained defiant even once the Union forces began to recruit black men. Activists who spent much of the 1850s insisting on equal militia rights as part of an encompassing citizenship were not satisfied with payment as military laborers and service in white-officered regiments, the terms finally offered by the War Department. Some became active recruiters, but many others wavered. A few remained steadfast opponents of black military service on these terms.

In the end, black activists' conflicted relationship to the recruitment of black troops proved politically productive. Those who recruited helped bring a vast army of black men to bolster the Union, even as white citizens' morale flagged. Those who resisted helped ensure that these soldiers would eventually be paid and treated just as white soldiers were. Both efforts bore fruit. Black military service, bringing together the principled assertion of equality and the disciplined exercise of armed force, at last forged a claim to equal national citizenship that many whites could not ignore. When the troops returned home, whether to parades or to funerals, they did so as saviors of the nation. Together, pragmatists and idealists at last created a black soldiery that white Americans could recognize as having a legitimate claim to the legacy of revolutionary freedom.

The history of black military service did not have to unfold in this way, and for much of the war Boston's black activists had little faith that it would. During the early years of the war they provided relief to refugees from slavery, badgered their white allies to take up their cause in the state and the nation, and wondered whether the time had finally come to abandon the United States entirely. In other words, black activists participating in the events of the early 1860s remained profoundly uncertain whether it made sense to entrust their long-cherished hopes to a Union government that seemed too eager to compromise away their rights and rudely rejected their demands to take part in the war effort on terms of equality and respect. They were right to wonder. As Abraham Lincoln took the oath of office, the future of free black America hung in the balance.

THE WINTER OF THEIR DISCONTENT

Things did not look quite so bleak in the fall of 1860. Boston's black leadership entered into the Republican campaign that year with high energy, and achieved new degrees of inclusion in party affairs. Black Republicans took part in the formation of party clubs, though they were excluded, as usual, from the ward steering committees.[3] Under the leadership of Lewis Hayden and Mark De Mortie, they formed one of the city's "Wide-Awake" clubs—a marching company whose men promoted the candidates in public parades and worked to get out the vote on election day. In October a hundred or more uniformed and torch-bearing "West Boston Colored Wide-Awakes" paraded across the channel and on to Chelsea, in company with several white Wide-Awake companies. The *Boston Courier*, a Democratic paper, reported "some wincing among the less advanced Republicans, until reminded by Mr. Slack that the four hundred colored votes, which were good for Mr. Burlingame, might be periled by any symptoms of mutiny in the white and colored Wide-Awake army."[4] It may have been the first time in living memory that black and white companies marched under the same banner, recognizing one another as equal participants.

But what about the ticket for which they were marching? Ward Six's Republican voters could easily support the reelection of U.S. Congressman

Anson Burlingame; he himself came to thank and to rouse his constituents in Ward Six on election eve.[5] Lewis Hayden, at least, must have emphasized the good qualities of his employer, Secretary of State Oliver Warner, whose name stood a few rungs higher on the ticket. Higher still was John Andrew, who in fifteen years had ascended from abolitionist lawyer to Republican candidate for governor. But at the top of the ticket, his beardless face crudely rendered amid flags and lanterns, was a less familiar and less welcome name: Abraham Lincoln.[6]

Neither the friends of the slave nor the advocates of equal citizenship found Lincoln wholly appealing. The Illinoisan did insist that all people, including free blacks, deserved the right to be secure in their persons and their property—a position that separated him from some Republicans and from virtually all other politicians. But Lincoln asserted unambiguously that black people were inferior to whites. Worse, in keeping with the Republicans' limited antiextensionist platform, he promised to uphold the Fugitive Slave Law, prompting Wendell Phillips to dub him "the slavehound of Illinois." H. Ford Douglas, one of the leading black activists in Lincoln's home state, noted that in 1849, amid the efforts to find a compromise for the territorial crisis, Lincoln had introduced a fugitive slave bill for Washington D.C. The political calculation suggested by this disgusted Douglas. He interpreted Lincoln's "talk about the inferiority of the negro race" as similarly bankrupt political truckling, typical of Republicans who "think it is absolutely necessary, for the success of their party, to cater to the dark spirit of slavery."[7] Against such arguments, white Republican radicals such as U.S. senator Henry Wilson could offer only bare-knuckled political pragmatism. According to Wilson, nothing short of a Republican sweep could change the nation's laws, and the composition of its Supreme Court. Then, and only then, would slavery crumble, and with it the spirit of caste.[8]

The 1860 election in Boston was quiet—the Democratic *Herald* noted mockingly that in Ward Six "the Republican and his colored brother walk arm-in-arm to the polls unmolested."[9] But the peaceful day masked what was in national terms a political hurricane. Lincoln, though facing three opponents and denied a place on the ballot in ten slave states, nonetheless won a majority in the Electoral College and was elected president. Republicans, including John Andrew and most of the Massachusetts Republican ticket, swept to power across the North. Embarrassingly for black activists, Anson Burlingame was defeated, but when the *Herald* congratulated Burlingame's opponents "on the selection of a man who would remember the interests of white men," black activists could only have felt more sure that their Republican votes had been well cast.[10]

During the months following Lincoln's election the rambunctiousness of national political life turned to frenzy. Federal officials in the South began to resign; secessionists called for the prompt election of delegates to state conventions; governors exchanged secret letters. Leading Southern politicians warned crowds that if they failed to separate themselves from a Republican-governed Union they would face an apocalyptic choice—"*slay the Negro, or ourselves be slain.*"[11] Compromise-minded Northerners, hoping to alert their neighbors to the seriousness of the crisis, invited secessionists to come north to present their views.

When secession began, just before Christmas 1860, the South Carolina politicians who accomplished it explained themselves publicly in a "Declaration of Immediate Causes." Their theme was the insecurity of slave property. Although the document's first paragraph spoke of the "encroachments" on the rights of states by the federal government, this was a red herring: the declaration was in fact a moral and constitutional indictment of the legal and extralegal impediments Northern states and individuals had placed in the way of slaveholders who sought to recover their fugitive property. By tolerating abolitionism and enacting personal liberty laws, Northern states had "encouraged and assisted thousands of our slaves to leave their homes" and incited the rest to revolt. By abrogating their responsibilities to federal law and to the laws of other states, Northerners had subverted the Constitution. These actions (and the federal government's inadequate response) paled in comparison to what slaveholders

should expect, now that a regional political party dedicated to the "ultimate extinction" of slavery was set to take power. Slaveholders had no
choice but to withdraw from the national compact.

Free black Northerners had done their work so well that they seemed
almost to have caused the crisis. Anyone who knew the history of abolitionism, fugitive defense, or incitement to flight or rebellion—the chief features
of the secessionist indictment—also knew that Northern black activists
played crucial roles in all of these inflammatory developments. Secessionists did not explicitly acknowledge this, but they did offer, as proof of the
"great political error" that now governed white Northern society, Republicans' willingness to court the votes of free blacks—"persons who, by the
supreme law of the land, are incapable of becoming citizens," but whose
"votes have been used to inaugurate" Republican rule. Both as lawless
rebels and as Republican voters, free blacks represented the Northern corruption of American citizenship.[12]

The leaders of the new Southern Confederacy tacitly acknowledged the
power of the "colored citizens" by loudly asserting, in the moment of their
nation's founding, the "great truth" that blacks were inherently unfit for
citizenship. Confederate vice president Alexander Stephens explained that
the "cornerstone" on which his new government rested was the axiom
"that the negro is not equal to the white man; that slavery is his natural and
moral condition." President Jefferson Davis similarly described slavery as
"a form of civil government for a class of people not fit to govern themselves." In the secessionists' campaigns, the "racially exclusive character of
citizenship" was both an article of faith and a strident rejoinder to the alleged egalitarianism of Northern Republicans.[13]

Procompromise Northerners, eager to maintain the profitable trade that
a war would disrupt, likewise understood the symbolic importance of
black political activity. So when a coalition of black activists and Harpers
Ferry conspirators held a memorial meeting for John Brown in Tremont
Temple in December 1860, on the anniversary of his execution, the Union-
minded white men of Boston sprang to action. Having packed the front

rows of the meeting and salted themselves throughout the audience, the conservatives seized the day. Before the meeting could get under way, well-dressed gentlemen took the floor and refused to let Redpath and Reverend J. Sella Martin organize the meeting. Boston businessman Richard Fay, claiming to represent "the reasoning men of the North and the South," offered prepared resolutions condemning John Brown and insisted that "irresponsible persons and political demagogues" not be allowed "to disturb the public peace and misrepresent us abroad."[14]

The challenge produced the collision the businessmen sought, allowing them to demonstrate a renewed white Northern resolve against blacks and abolitionists. James Redpath tried to throw Fay out of the hall, while Frederick Douglass declared, "I know your masters . . . I have served the same master that you are serving." That charge brought shouts, then a rush of men to the platform "to sweep it clear of the negroes." The policemen present offered only desultory resistance, and Douglass quickly found himself in the middle of a fierce brawl. "Mr. Douglass fought like a trained pugilist," one observer noted, but he was finally dragged away by police and thrown down a staircase. It seemed to be "a gentlemen's mob," Douglass explained, "well dressed, well conditioned, well looking." Its members "doubtless, on occasion, pass very well for gentlemen." But its language was not at all gentlemanly: calls echoed to "[p]ut all the niggers out! All out! Blow them up!" When the police finally cleared the hall, they were forced to physically remove many of the original antislavery attendees, dragging women from their seats.[15]

The determination of their adversaries seemed only to embolden black activists and their allies. Against the protests of his trustees, Reverend J. Sella Martin announced that the meeting would resume that evening at his Joy Street Church. Women and men flooded into the church and into the narrow streets surrounding it to hear Douglass, Phillips, and John Brown Jr.[16] A sympathetic German visitor noted the "interest and enthusiasm manifested by the colored women,—quietly, it seemed to us."[17] The spirit, though, was militant: Douglass, his blood still up, spoke of his joy at the thought of insurrections, declaring, "The only way to make the Fugitive Slave Law a dead letter is to make a few dead slave-catchers."[18] This moment of shared commitment and danger made old enmities seem less important: Douglass, who had already fully reconciled with Nell at one of George Downing's parties, publicly mended fences with Phillips as well.[19]

But now antiabolitionist mobs returned to Boston's streets. When the Joy Street meeting ended, "the street mob took to hunting negroes as they came forth. Some were knocked down and trampled upon and a few more seriously injured." Many windows were smashed, amid occasional gunfire; the only person arrested was a black man who emerged from his besieged home with a hatchet and injured one of his assailants. White men searched streetcars for "colored victims."[20] A week later, Wendell Phillips left his own speech at the Music Hall—his topic, pointedly, was "Mobs and Democracy"—to find thousands massed against him. This was not 1835, though, and antislavery voices could also call on militant defenders and even state authority. When Boston's mayor refused to send uniformed police to guard Phillips at a subsequent speech, Higginson called a meeting, organized sixty volunteers—"German & English," not black—into companies, and stationed them around the hall. In the end, after newly elected governor John Andrew leaned on the mayor, a hundred policemen joined the black and white stalwarts who escorted the orator home.[21] The mob did not in the end prevent black activists from celebrating the heroes of Harpers Ferry. On New Year's Day 1861, Twelfth Baptist hosted a surprise guest: Osborne Anderson, a black man who had been with Brown on the raid and was even now a fugitive from justice.[22]

Faced with the prospect of secession, many Northern leaders and legislatures, including those who had recently championed both John Brown and resistance to the Fugitive Slave Law, scrambled to appease the slaveholders. The seceding states' declarations of "immediate causes" made it easy for peace-and-union men to know where to begin. Slaveholders' access to the territories would have to be guaranteed for all time, certainly, but their grievances required redress in the East as well as the West. Outgoing president James Buchanan told Congress that, unless Northern states repealed their personal liberty laws, Southern states "would be justified in revolutionary resistance to the Government of the Union."[23] Northern state legislatures began voting to comply.[24] The Fugitive Slave Law, so routinely challenged by black activists, would have to be rigidly enforced.[25] Even the legislature of Wisconsin, whose personal liberty law echoed Massachusetts's in its efforts to interfere with the activities of fugitive slave commissioners, seriously debated repeal.[26] In Massachusetts, some politicians seemed nearly as eager to appease. Two weeks after South Carolina left the Union, Boston's Common Council called it "the highest civil duty of every patriot, christian & man" to ease sectional tensions. The time had come "to cancel every error which we have made or are supposed to have made," including "certain acts upon our statute books" that have caused complaint "by the people of other states"—the personal liberty law.[27] Leading politicians, including outgoing governor Nathaniel P. Banks, suggested that if the state's personal liberty law was in conflict with the federal Constitution, it should be repealed.[28] The status of the "colored citizens" had never seemed more important, nor more imperiled.

But as foretold by Martin Delany and confirmed by *Dred Scott*, the most important challenges to black citizenship came from the federal government. With a lame duck in the White House and the president-elect maintaining a deliberate silence, the congressional leadership tried to halt the rapid dissolution of the Union.[29] A Senate committee debated the compromise package crafted by Kentucky Whig John J. Crittenden. The "Crittenden Compromise" promised the repeal of personal liberty laws and offered federal compensation for the owners of runaways; it also called for the permanent security of slave property in all current or future American territory lying south of the old Missouri Compromise line. In January, as Georgia joined South Carolina in secession, compromisers bolstered the Crittenden proposals with two new articles aimed squarely at Northern free blacks. One would strip all persons of African descent of the right to vote or hold office at any level of government, a breathtaking extension of

Dred Scott v. Sandford that cut to the heart of whatever political citizenship black Northerners hoped to claim. The other startling proposal, already put forward by Frank Blair, a leading Republican ally of the president-elect, would provide federal funds to allow states to deport their free black and "mulatto" inhabitants to Africa or South America.[30] Finally, as Lincoln took the oath of office in March 1861, Congress passed a constitutional amendment that would permanently secure slavery where it currently existed. In his inaugural address the new president referred approvingly to the proposed proslavery thirteenth amendment. It had already been sent on to the states for ratification.[31]

Black activists in Boston and elsewhere responded in mixed tones of hope and horror. William Nell took heart when Henry Wilson opposed the Crittenden measures, rebuking his Senate colleagues for their "monstrous proposition," reminding them that "the ancestors of the men you would now . . . trample beneath your feet, freely gave their blood for the liberties and independence of America."[32] But others seemed to despair. In a Beacon Hill meeting John T. Hilton and John J. Smith thought that "everything looked dark," for "[t]he North had always obeyed the Slave Power" and would capitulate.[33] More than fifteen hundred of the state's black residents signed petitions to the legislature calling for the rights of "colored citizens" to be respected.[34] George Downing published an "Appeal to the White Citizens of the State," suggesting that the proposed disenfranchisement of black citizens was not directed at the small number of black voters, but was instead an attempt to "humiliate the New England States" for their commitment to the principle of "government by consent of the governed." He couched his appeal as a reminder of the common humanity and shared values of black and white citizens: "We have appealed with the feelings of men—through the relationship of social beings—through the patriotism of the citizen—. . . in the name of the Christian religion."[35] But these hopeful phrases did not tell the whole story. Downing, who had so proudly identified black Americans with the nation's divine project just a few years before, now pleaded with his countrymen not to abandon that common destiny: "Drive us not to an inhospitable land, either soon to die of fever or deteriorate in intellect, under the influence of a superstitious religion."[36] He now seemed to speak from fear and despair more than conviction. He confessed to having "no doubt that the North would sacrifice the whole race of colored people to save the Union."[37]

No surprise, then, that at the hour of secession the question of emigration returned with a vengeance, suddenly appealing even to people at the pinnacle of the black Northern leadership. The new proposed destination was Haiti. Unlike Liberia or other potential destinations, Haiti represented black freedom and self-government achieved by force of arms, close by in the Caribbean. Its unlikely American apostle was none other than James Redpath. He had traveled to Haiti several times in 1859 and 1860, and soon became the paid American agent of its government, charged with encouraging African American emigration and securing diplomatic recognition.[38]

Redpath's grasp of the emotional and spiritual predicament of black Northerners was as keen as it was opportunistic. In his *Guide to Hayti*, which mingled facts about the republic with appeals to potential emigrants, Redpath voiced the well-justified skepticism many black Americans now felt about their future in the United States. "The schools of New England and other States are open to your children, and they can now receive the advantages of a liberal education. And then? Rendered sensitive by this culture, what prospect is opened to them? A long, petty war with mean men, a fruitless assault on the citadel of place, political and social." He likened such a struggle to the attempt to "drive back an ocean, which, by its mere physical superiority, will throw up the bodies of your children, after a generation or two, pale and unrecognizable, on its Saxon shores!" Haiti offered something different: the freedom for the "colored race" to "develop itself in freedom . . . exhibit its capacity and genius . . . She offers you a home, a nationality, a future."[39] Redpath's agents, including onetime antiemigrationists William Watkins and William Wells Brown, urged blacks to see emigration as a means of proving the race's capacity for self-government while remaining near enough to render aid should the slaves finally rise up in revolt.[40] Under the suddenly dire circumstances of the secession winter, the long-standing antiemigrationist consensus seemed to crack.[41]

In the midst of the North's apparent capitulation to the secessionists, even the staunch antiemigrationist Frederick Douglass gave the project a second look. "If we go any where, let us go to Hayti," Douglass wrote in January 1861, and that conditional "if" quickly moved toward personal interest.[42] In the early spring of 1861 Douglass announced that he was about to depart for a tour of the country, hoping to do justice to her people but also to investigate the island as a possible home. He acknowledged what many of his readers across the North were thinking: "During the last few years the minds of the free colored people in all the States have been deeply exercised in relation to what may be their future in the United States. . . . At the North there are, alas! too many proofs that the margin of life and liberty is becoming more narrow every year. . . . The apprehension is general, that proscription, persecution and hardships are to wax more and more rigorous and more grievous with every year; and for this reason they are now, as never before, looking out into the world for a place of retreat, an asylum from the apprehended storm which is about to beat pitilessly upon them."[43] Pleas, remonstrances, elections, and revolts—all had failed to turn the hearts of white Americans. Perhaps, finally, the time had come to look elsewhere.

THE WHITE MAN'S WAR AND THE ROAD TO EMANCIPATION

The outbreak of war in April 1861 turned Douglass's boat in the water but otherwise did little to change the bleak outlook. Few Northerners desired a war, and still fewer imagined fighting one over abolition or equal citizenship. Secessionist leaders, it is true, understood their movement as a preemptive strike against a Republican federal government and the threat its platform posed to the long-term survival of slavery within the United States. But their rants against putatively abolitionist "black Republicans" reflected the need to solidify their Southern base, not an accurate analysis of the party now in power. Lincoln and his government did not go to war to free the slaves; they called out the federal militia because secessionists shelled Fort Sumter, the federal outpost in Charleston Harbor. Lincoln's purpose was to put down the secessionist challenge to federal authority— a challenge his proclamation of April 15 described as "combinations too powerful to be suppressed by the ordinary course of judicial proceedings, or by the powers vested in the Marshals by law." The secessionist leadership went to war to protect the institution of slavery, but the Union government and most Union citizens rejected secession for reasons having little or nothing to do with African Americans.

The transforming rush of patriotism and anti-Southern hostility following the attack on Fort Sumter quickly sent hundreds of thousands of men into federal service, many more than called for by Lincoln's proclamation. But this was a movement to restore the status quo and put down a rebellion against the nation, and it did not immediately alter the reactionary "compromise" direction of Northern politics during the winter of 1860–1861. The mobilization was for white men only. In April, many border slave states had not yet decided whether to secede, and farsighted observers understood how important it was to keep as many of them as possible— their manpower, resources, and territory—within the Union. "I hope to have God on my side," Lincoln is said to have quipped, "but I must have Kentucky." No surprise, therefore, that black volunteers were neither permitted to form nor to join regiments sent to defend Washington. Northern movements to repeal personal liberty laws persisted. The United States was still a slaveholding union, officially hostile to African American claims to full citizenship.

While many black Northerners rushed to offer their services to the wartime nation, a strong current of skepticism and resistance marked even the first florid moments. At a Beacon Hill meeting soon after the fall of

Fort Sumter, one reporter observed "that the division of sentiment was large on the subject of volunteering." Robert Morris offered a set of "very modestly written" resolutions that "expressed the patriotic feelings of the colored men towards the States and the Union declaring themselves ready to defend the flag of the common country against the common foe." Morris even deferred to the administration's rhetoric about the rebellion and refrained from using the word "slavery." But after ten years of frustrated efforts to be accepted into the state militia, the lawyer appended a critical qualification: black men would volunteer "when the removal of disabilities allowed them to do so on terms of equality." That plainly meant the removal of the word "white" from the state's militia law. The resolutions he offered were not universally popular, but at least some of the resistance came from people who took an even more militant position. William Wells Brown, for example, "thought that self respect demanded that the people should not beg for the removal of disabilities." This early determination to withhold the offer of service "except it be on equality with all other men" was shared by the captain of a Philadelphia military company, attendees at a New York meeting, and no doubt many others across the black North. Black men should not have to ask for what the nation should already have given.[44]

They did ask, however, for all the good it did. In May, petitions from Robert Morris, John T. Hilton, and other "colored citizens of Massachusetts" asked the legislature to take up again the question of the word "white" in the militia law.[45] George Downing sought an interview with Governor Andrew, hoping to win his support.[46] Despite the efforts of several friends in the statehouse, including Charles W. Slack, who somehow obtained the Liberty Guard's prized revolutionary ensign and displayed it to his legislative colleagues, they were refused.[47]

If they could not enter the army or the militia, perhaps they could play another role. Two weeks after Fort Sumter fell, a meeting of "colored citizens" assembled on Cambridge Street "to form a drill company" of black men to defend the commonwealth in the present emergency. With John

S. Rock presiding, and with speeches by Hayden, Morris, Downing, De Mortie, and others, the meeting was a smashing success: one hundred twenty-five men enrolled in this "Home Guard." The captain of the Liberty Guards, apparently a vital organization four years after their tumultuous debut, gave the men their first lesson in military drills. Similar preparations and offers of service came from black assemblies in Providence, Philadelphia, New York, Cleveland, Detroit, Washington, and Canada West, but white authorities universally rejected them. The Boston assembly's offer to form "military companies" ("with permission to elect their own officers") were referred to legislative committees, where they died, as did renewed petitions to remove the word "white" from the state's militia law. Republicans declared their "willingness to remove every vestige of disability from the colored citizens," but "[t]his was not the time." To do so now would "cast a firebrand among the ranks of the united North and West and the Border States" and "initiate a calamity." Patience, they said. Unlike their white male allies, who could choose whether or not to enlist, Boston's black men saw the door close in their faces. Northern politicians, determined to fight a white man's war for the Union, rejected them and their comrades across the region.[48]

Life for black Bostonians continued in its rhythms of accomplishment and frustration. When John Rock reflected on the state of things in summer 1862, he reached conclusions remarkably similar to those of his archrival Redpath. Massachusetts was a land of "many rights . . . but few privileges," a place where young men could gain an education only to run up against "the embittered prejudices of the whites"—"you can hardly imagine the humiliation and contempt a colored lad must feel in graduating the first in his class," he wrote, "and then being rejected everywhere else because of his color." Meanwhile the state's "liberal anti-slavery politicians dine at the Revere House, sup at the Parker House, and take their cream and jellies at Copeland's"—all places that refused to serve blacks.[49] The war so far seemed to have changed almost nothing.

Yet a profound transformation was already under way, one led by fugi-

tive slaves acting in concert with the unlikely figure of Massachusetts Democrat Benjamin Butler. Few men's careers predicted the transformations of
the 1860s better than Butler's. In the years just prior to the war, his Democratic race-baiting made him a symbol of all the social forces threatening
the Republicans' rise and limiting free black citizenship. When the war
came, Butler, a leader in the state militia, was appointed a general of Massachusetts troops. Among the first on the ground in Maryland and Virginia,
he initially outraged Boston Republicans by offering to use his troops to
put down any threatened slave insurrection. The war, after all, was intended to suppress the rebellion, not free the slaves. Butler claimed to be
motivated by fears of "the horror of San Domingo a million times magni-
fied" among the Southern citizenry. "Could we justify ourselves to ourselves," he asked, "in letting loose four millions of worse than savages upon
the homes and hearths of the South"?[50]

Benjamin Butler
Courtesy of the Library of Congress

Butler quickly came to understand that Southern slaves interpreted the arrival of Union troops not as an opportunity to exact vengeance but as a chance to seize freedom. Further, he began to see how both he and the Union war effort might profit. When fugitives arrived at the gates of Virginia's Fort Monroe, Butler quickly colluded with them, accepting their stories of having been put to work on behalf of the rebel war effort, then craftily redefining these erstwhile articles of property as "contraband of war"—resources that, if returned to the enemy, as the Fugitive Slave Law would still seem to demand, might be used as a weapon against Union troops.[51] Those who understood the military potential waiting among the Confederacy's enslaved millions heralded Butler's innovation for what it was: a "master-stroke," as William Nell put it, "destined, under God, to materially weaken the rebel power."[52]

The old antiabolitionist Butler's sleight of hand succeeded where overtly abolitionist tactics failed, and soon "contraband" replaced "fugitive" in the Northern vernacular. News spread rapidly among enslaved people that, if they had the right story to tell, the Union might welcome them. They began to arrive, in ever growing numbers, at Union forts and camps. Once they did, the Union military began putting them to work, easing the lives and labors of white officers and enlisted men, and denying valuable military and agricultural labor to the Confederacy. Slaveholders still loyal to the Union protested, and Union policy vacillated, but Nell's assessment proved correct. By early 1862 the Northern public was well on its way to seeing the subversion of slaveholders' property rights—once understood as the great threat to national unity—as a means to weaken the rebellion.

Although federal officials often seemed intent on holding back the emancipatory potential of the war, critical turning points came with stunning speed. The slaveholders' departure left the Republicans firmly in control of Congress, and the "contraband" policy provided the necessary opening for antislavery legislation as a matter of war policy. In a series of acts during 1861 and 1862 Congress made it ever easier to confiscate slave owners' property, including their slaves; in the spring of 1862 Congress abolished slavery in the District of Columbia, then in the territories. Prompted by Secretary of State William Seward, an old abolitionist, the attorney general of the United States formally concluded in 1862 that free blacks were indeed citizens of the United States. In July of that year Congress formalized the employment of "contrabands" as laborers with the Militia Act, which authorized the recruitment and payment of black men as military laborers.

By that time, Abraham Lincoln had reached a similar conclusion. In September 1862 he announced that unless the rebels ceased their struggle, the slaves in areas still under Confederate control would be legally freed on January 1, 1863. This preliminary proclamation was not abolition: it exempted slaves in the slave states that remained loyal to the Union, as well as those in areas of the Confederacy already under Union control; as many people noted, the proclamation declared free only those slaves whom Lincoln had no actual power to free. But it marked a dramatic step away from the "white man's war" and toward a war for emancipation.

The period between the preliminary proclamation in September and the January 1 deadline left many people worrying and wondering. The *Liberator* sternly warned that a man like Lincoln, "so manifestly without moral vision, so unsettled in his policy, so incompetent to lead, so destitute of hearty abhorrence of slavery, cannot be safely relied upon." It took comfort only in the fact that slaves were already aware of the proclamation and would seize freedom regardless of what the president did or did not do.[53] There were real reasons to question whether Lincoln was serious— whether the promised emancipation would take place, and what it would mean if it did. Even as Lincoln announced his plans for the proclamation he was pursuing colonization schemes.[54] Congress appropriated a small sum to subsidize a colony in Central America or the Caribbean, and in August Lincoln urged a delegation of Washington's black leaders to put aside "selfish" concerns for their own comfort and instead consider the future of their race as a whole. "I think your race suffer very greatly, many of them[,] by living among us, while ours suffer from your presence," he proclaimed. "But for your race among us," after all, "there could not be a war, though many men engaged on either side do not care for you one way or the other." Equality within the United States was not a possibility, in Lincoln's view. "Go where you are treated the best, and the ban is still upon you." The full embrace of their white compatriots remained out of reach, Lincoln acknowledged. Of this fact he said, "I cannot alter it if I would."[55]

Despite its evident limitations, the Emancipation Proclamation moved the Union measurably closer to an outright policy of abolition. The proclamation established the line of Union control as the threshold of freedom, encouraging more slaves to flee their rebel masters. It marked the end of Lincoln's flirtation with colonization. And, crucially, the final proclamation took a radical new step, authorizing the recruitment of black men into Union military service. This offered a means for slaves not just to flee the Confederacy but also to fight for the freedom of those they left behind. It sealed the fate of slavery within the Union as well, as black Kentuckians and other Union slaves flocked to military camps in astounding numbers.[56]

With great hope and no little anxiety, William Nell took charge of the celebration of the Emancipation Proclamation in Tremont Temple that January 1. He described emancipation as the "policy of John C. Fremont and Charles Sumner . . . accepted and proclaimed by Abraham Lincoln." As Boston crowds anxiously awaited word that the president had indeed issued the proclamation, speakers held forth in Tremont Temple. When the announcement finally came over the telegraph wires and runners reached the hall, Frederick Douglass described the effect as "startling beyond description," "wild and grand." People shouted and sobbed, and "joy and gladness" instantly replaced anxiety.[57] In the dizzy aftermath speakers described emancipation as a vindication of the early abolitionists. John Rock honored the absent Garrison—he and Phillips, out of their distrust of the president, had refused to attend—by paraphrasing the credo that had sustained the *Liberator*: "[T]hey would not equivocate; they did not retract a single inch; and they would be heard. . . . I know," he declared, "the colored man has true friends among the white race." But honor also belonged to those who had not labored in abolition's school. Lincoln had exceeded Rock's expectations, "and if he is not anti-slavery, he is, I believe, the man destined by Providence to unite the friends of free government, and to redeem our country from its degradation and its shame."[58]

BLACK SOLDIERS IN BLUE

By the time Lincoln signed the final Emancipation Proclamation, the War Department had already taken a few hesitant steps toward enlisting former slaves. Most notable for black Bostonians was the 1st Regiment, South Carolina Volunteers, composed of former slaves and commanded by Colonel Thomas Wentworth Higginson. The minister had been preparing himself for this moment. After Harpers Ferry he threw himself into a series of essays on slave rebels, and once the war began he imagined publishing these under the title "The Negro as Soldier." When Governor Andrew did not receive early permission to enlist a black regiment, Higginson took a position as an officer in a white Massachusetts regiment. In November 1862, however, he was offered the colonelcy of the ex-slave regiment and soon shipped out for Port Royal, South Carolina.[59]

Once the Lincoln administration authorized broad recruitment of African Americans in 1863, it began by mobilizing black Northerners in the place where officials expected support to be the greatest: Massachusetts. The War Department tapped John Andrew to assemble a regiment. Andrew in turn called together a committee of leading white men, foremost among them the John Brown coconspirator and industrialist George Stearns, to get recruiting under way for what would become the 54th and 55th Massachusetts infantry regiments.

But it rapidly became clear that the terms of black military service would fall short of the full equality long demanded by black activists. Morris and several colleagues visited the governor in early February 1863.[60]

What exactly they said to him is not clear, but a few days later Andrew telegraphed Senator Charles Sumner: "Get me leave to commission colored chaplains, assistant surgeons and [a] few second lieutenants." Perhaps John V. DeGrasse accompanied Morris on the visit to Andrew, for the governor continued with descriptions that sounded like the two men: "[A]n interdict [on black commissioned officers] including member Mass. Med. Soc. speaking four languages, and member Suffolk bar, is prejudicial."[61] Andrew obtained the secretary of war's promise that the men recruited would earn the same pay as white soldiers, but despite his pleas for permission to offer officers' commissions to black men, the secretary refused.[62]

Without black officers, there was going to be grumbling at the very least, for the black regiments would not stand on the equal footing that had been the rallying cry of their advocates. William Nell, chronicler of black military exploits, now reported the disillusionment of his colleagues with the wartime Union's continuing rejection of black military equality. "[N]o one," Nell agreed, "can successfully controvert the argument" that blacks were invited to participate only as inferiors. But Nell hoped that "the three fold motives of patriotism, magnanimity, and hope" would win the battle against prejudice and pessimism.[63]

African American activists confronted this dilemma, and split. Notable black leaders appeared to boycott a mid-February meeting in the Joy Street Church to promote the black regiment. Robert Morris, disappointed by Andrew's inability to appoint black officers, declared that the time had not yet come to enlist: "He thought it the colored man's duty to 'go right.'" Not only should the word "white" be struck from the state's laws, but "[l]et black regiments be officered by men of their own color and a great blow would be struck. He for one would go when he could go as he should."[64] "Equality first," William Wells Brown agreed; "guns afterwards."[65]

White abolitionists blanched. It was one thing to stand on principle, but another to ignore the overwhelming political promise of black military achievement. Antislavery men as politically various as Elizur Wright and Wendell Phillips agreed that it was unfortunate that the call for soldiers did not come with perfect equality. This "higgling about the color of the officers and other conditions," however, was not sufficient reason to refuse to enlist.[66] Given the urgencies of the moment, many habitual mavericks began to regard principled resistance as a bit self-indulgent. James Redpath reflected in 1862 that "[o]f course we abolitionists delight in embarrassing administrations, but national safety sometimes demands that we should forego the pleasure of performing *such* duties."[67] Even the famously obstinate Phillips, who as recently as 1861 cheerfully contemplated the dissolution of the United States, believed the time had come to support the government. In a public meeting in February 1863, he openly disagreed with Robert Morris and encouraged Boston's black men to enlist. "True, all that could be desired was not yet granted," he admitted, "but nevertheless the time was near at hand when colored men would enjoy their full rights."[68] Phillips alluded directly to one of Morris's main objections: "I hear there is some reluctance because you are not to have officers of your own color. This may be wrong . . . But if you cannot have a whole loaf, will you not take a slice?"[69]

How big a slice was sufficient? Did service have to come on terms of perfect equality, or was the overture itself too important to pass up? For Phillips to make the latter argument smacked of hypocrisy, for he himself seemed almost congenitally unwilling to make the kind of compromise that he now urged upon his black allies. John S. Rock threw the orator's words back at him, resenting the call to defer indefinitely in the hope that all would be "right in the end." "This living entirely for posterity sounds well from the rostrum," he argued, "but a loaf of bread to-day is worth a barrel of flour next year."[70] Others made more canny appeals rooted in black militants' own experiences. Elizur Wright recalled standing in the courtroom twelve years before during the rescue of Shadrach Minkins and, in language that was doubtless aimed directly at Robert Morris, argued that the time had come again for black men to seize the day. Wright recalled noticing "that the brave and patriotic colored men who vindicated their manhood and the constitution" as they liberated Minkins "did not wait until the court room door was pried open, but squeezed in as soon as ever they could." Their decisive action in a moment of crisis could become a metaphor for present possibilities: "There will be no excluding you from the full and just share in the however-bounded republic which is due to your mind and manhood, forever and forever more, the moment you begin to pour into its armies with fixed bayonets."[71]

Some men heeded the call. During the winter and spring of 1863 a slow but steady stream of recruits arrived at the training camp in Readville, about eight miles from downtown Boston, from points west and south. George Stearns moved across upper New York State and Canada, while Frederick Douglass threw himself into the work of recruiting from his home in Rochester, sending two sons and many young admirers into the ranks of the 54th Massachusetts.[72] By the 1863 anniversary of the Boston Massacre, there were a hundred fifty in camp, and a week later a hundred more.[73] Men continued to arrive from New York, Pennsylvania, and Ohio, and these three states ultimately provided nearly half the troops who served in Massachusetts's two black infantry regiments.

Yet during the first year of recruitment of black Northerners, recruitment among Boston's militarily eligible black population lagged well behind expectations. In the main, the black population with the closest political relationship to the Republican state administration refused to enlist. Colonel Robert Gould Shaw, the white commander of the 54th Massachusetts, reported some early success, noting that by the time the regiment's camp opened during the last week of February, he had already sent twenty-seven men "from Philadelphia and Boston."[74] But early optimism soon curdled into something a good deal more sour, at least where Boston was concerned. The regiments were always meant to draw from the entire black North, not just Massachusetts. But the overall figures present a stark portrait of recruiting failure on Beacon Hill: fewer than forty of the unit's members listed Boston as their place of residence.[75] This was a very poor turnout compared to the one hundred twenty-five volunteers who had instantly stepped forward for the Home Guard in 1861, or to the ninety-odd men who had signed one or more militia petitions during the mid-1850s. Indeed, of all those militia enthusiasts, only two enlisted in the Massachusetts regiments.[76] This laggard recruiting in Boston was particularly striking when viewed in the context of the broad general mobilization of black Northern men that had taken place by 1865.

Where were the black men of Boston in this black Massachusetts regiment? Some recruits may possibly have been put off by violence aimed at them by what a captain in the regiment called a "rougher element" opposed to black enlistment (although he did not clarify whether this "element" was white or black).[77] But knowledgeable people complained frankly about black Bostonians' role in discouraging enlistment. William Nell publicly lamented that "[o]wing to a combination wholly unexpected and never to be too much regretted, numbers of young men were induced to refrain from enlisting in the 54th, and thus lost the golden privilege of having their names enrolled in the first colored regiment from the North." He noted a countercampaign, in which "the young ladies of Boston organized themselves" to persuade their reluctant peers.[78] Even this note of optimism, though, confirmed that it was not self-evident to the black men of Boston that the time had come to enlist. The commander of the 54th, Colonel Robert Gould Shaw, eschewed Nell's careful circumlocutions, complaining in April 1863 that "the influential colored men of Boston . . . have done us more harm th[an good]."[79] Years of rejection, coupled with formally unequal terms of service, chilled black Bostonians' enthusiasm for serving the nation.

Yet for others the invitation, however hedged, was enough. Lewis Hayden supported the recruitment effort from its beginnings; later reports even credited him with giving Andrew the idea to form a black regiment, though this was too widespread a notion to belong to any one man.[80] From the beginning, the Haydens wholeheartedly promoted the Massachusetts black regiments. In the spring of 1863, as the men of the 54th moved through their drills with increasing confidence and a steady stream of visitors came to see and meet them, Lewis Hayden shared trips to Readville with the governor and other black recruiters. In May, as the unit prepared to embark, visitors flocked in. Douglass and a good many others traveled to Boston, stopping for breakfast with the Haydens before hiring a carriage to visit the camp.[81]

Some of Hayden's friends shared his enthusiasm for the recruitment of black troops. Leonard Grimes thought men "should not hesitate a moment," and declared his own willingness to go, carrying either Bible or musket.[82] William Nell heralded the formation of the 54th as "a most auspicious sign of the times; for, although some colored citizens have manifested anxiety as to whether their status as equals under the law would be advanced thereby, my conviction has been from the first . . . that by accepting the opportunity of becoming soldiers in this our nation's trial hour, the result cannot be otherwise than a full acknowledgment of every right." The 54th's success would conquer both Southern rebels and "Northern prejudice," Nell predicted. His prescient wish was that "on their return from victory, they may march up State street over the spot consecrated by the martyrdom of Crispus Attucks, amid the plaudits of admiring citizens."[83] William Wells Brown's "Equality first, guns afterward" quickly thawed into warm support; before the end of February the committee overseeing recruitment for the 54th employed him to help with enlistments in New York City.[84] Men and women from farther afield, including Martin Delany, Mary Ann Shadd, and John Jones threw themselves into the work.[85]

John S. Rock took a more measured view. He found it unsurprising that "[a]fter pressing their claims for two years . . . many should have become discouraged and disheartened." Given the wording of the state's militia law, the absence of black commissioned officers, and the vulnerability of black troops to enslavement if captured, "you ought not to be surprised why we have hesitated, and not rushed pell-mell into the service, and urged others to follow us." Yet he urged those who could "conscientiously" do so to enlist, and lauded the "proficiency of drill and manly bearing" of the

54th Massachusetts on its march through Boston, foreseeing great fruits from this undertaking. "We have not been treated right," he explained, but he had "not one word to say against colored men enlisting now."[86] Although neither a young man nor healthy enough to serve himself, Rock would ultimately become an earnest recruiter for the black regiments.

Recruiting across the North moved rapidly forward, and by May 1863 the 54th was ready for deployment. Two more black regiments would be raised in Massachusetts. The 55th Volunteer Infantry, which was already enlisting men, sailed for North Carolina in late July 1863.[87] The 5th Cavalry, authorized later, saw service in 1864.[88] As the 54th mobilized, Nell declared that the "colored young men" of Boston were "fast augmenting" the ranks of the 55th.[89] This claim, like Nell's others, was a bit too sunny. When the 55th left a few months later, its ranks included only about forty new recruits who had listed Boston as their home, in addition to a small group of men who transferred over from the 54th.[90]

The ongoing local struggle notwithstanding, the march of the 54th through Boston on May 28 recapitulated the victories of the past decade. The regiment passed by Wendell Phillips's home, where William Lloyd Garrison stood on a balcony with his hand resting on a bust of John Brown. Later in the day they marched down State Street, and as they approached the spot where Attucks fell, the band took up the "John Brown song," which proclaimed that the martyr's soul "goes marching on."[91] The historian Nell had positioned himself there, imagining Attucks's martyrdom and remembering the passages of Thomas Sims and Anthony Burns over that same spot as they were returned to slavery. But now the scene had changed. Sims himself, now redeemed from slavery, stood in the crowd. Nell imagined hopefully that the former slave could see among the thousands of faces gathered for the event "some of the—perhaps repentant—participants in those disgraceful offerings to the South."[92] On the cusp of a new era, this regiment of "Freedom's army" set sail for the South to help usher in that better day when mere admittance would become warm acceptance.

FIGHTING WITH THE UNION

This triumphal moment not withstanding, the war with the Union was far from over. As Nell joyfully turned from military history to military journalism, he presented both the heroic and the painful dimensions of the black wartime struggle. He filled columns of the *Liberator* and other newspapers with stories of military valor, side by side with complaints about the continuing refusal to commission black men, and the indignities of serving under white officers "who read the Boston *Courier*, and talk about 'Niggers.'"[93] He understood that neither the battle with the Confederacy nor that with the Union was yet won. Indeed, the worst of the latter struggle was still to come.

Although the 54th gained fame for its role in the heroic but doomed assault on Fort Wagner in Charleston Harbor, Union politicians and officials failed to honor the secretary of war's promise to John Andrew that black units would receive equal pay and treatment. In June 1863, the Bureau of Colored Troops announced that the only legal basis for the payment of such troops was the Militia Act of 1862, which authorized the employment of black men as military laborers in Union service. The terms of such employment were ten dollars a month, with up to three dollars deducted for wear and tear on clothing. In practice, this meant that black soldiers would receive little more than half the thirteen dollars a month received by white Union privates.

But the men who did enlist turned out to share the egalitarian determination and political sensibilities of their resistant colleagues. As rumors of the pay disparity reached the camp of the 54th in South Carolina, its soldiers acted as though they had their governor's ear, and his sympathies. Sergeant Frederic Johnson sent Andrew a letter about the pay crisis, in care of his minister, Leonard Grimes. The minister was out of town, but his wife, Octavia, investigated the question. Even though a member of Congress told her that the soldier must be mistaken, she sent the letter on to

Andrew.[94] Johnson told the governor that "the men seem to feel as though they have been duped," but that he and others were working to persuade them otherwise. Still, he seemed deflated. "[R]ather than take the proffered sum, or for the state of Massachusetts to make up the balance," he asked, "we will beg of you to call us Home and use us for the Defence of the Old Bay State or Honorably discharge us."[95] There seemed to be broad agreement on this point in the regiment: even the 54th's sutler—the contractor who would travel with the regiment and supply its men with goods, relying on their paychecks for his profit—Mark De Mortie, was urging them to refuse the ten dollars.[96]

Perhaps Governor Andrew understood how serious this was. Johnson was one of those young men whom established leaders noticed: he confidently directed Andrew to confer with Grimes, Hayden, and Nell; he was already a noncommissioned officer, which was as high as black men could then rise in the ranks. Mrs. Grimes referred to him as "a respectable young man [and] a christian." If such a person lost faith in the project, maintaining morale and discipline among the others could become an impossible task. No wonder Andrew fired back a letter to this young soldier promising to work ceaselessly for their rights and asking him to "assure" the men on his behalf.[97]

Andrew had considerable credibility with black activists, and Johnson's sharing of this letter with his men had some effect. Another sergeant in the 54th described it as "the most important letter Gov. Andrew, has addressed to our regiment."[98] But there was little question that the men would refuse to accept inferior pay, especially as in the months after Fort Wagner they found themselves relegated to exhausting fatigue duty. The sergeant, along with Johnson himself, sought a way out—perhaps as drill sergeants for another unit—for all of this "made us lose heart with the 54th."[99]

Andrew was in a tight spot. He pleaded with the secretary of war, to no avail. The governor then tried to devise his own version of Butler's "con-

traband" gambit: he told De Mortie to have the men make use of the
language of the Militia Act—which referred to the employment of persons
of "African descent"—and claim that they were the children of American
parents. "Col'd Americans are as much of American descent as white
Americans," Andrew asserted, and the paymasters were not competent to
prove otherwise.[100] This ploy failed. When the paymasters offered only ten
dollars at the end of the month, the men refused it. Another black man
who had Andrew's confidence, the 54th's future chaplain Samuel Harrison,
reported that when he tried to persuade them to take the money for the
sake of their families, "[t]hey were indignant and I desisted."[101] Harrison
soon found that although he was a commissioned officer—among the very
few authorized by the end of 1863—the paymaster refused to offer him
more than the seven to ten dollars awaiting other "military laborers." Suddenly Harrison too saw this as "an urgent matter," and "an intolerable
insult to my manhood."[102]

When Andrew tried another improvisation, having the Massachusetts
legislature make up the difference in pay, he learned the depth of the insistence on unstinting, unmeasured equal citizenship. Andrew's offer, complained one member of the 54th, "advertises us to the world as holding out
for *money* and not from *principle.*"[103] In December, when Andrew sent a
high-ranking white officer to persuade the men of the 55th to accept the
state's offer, Sergeant Major James Monroe Trotter explained the men's
case so eloquently that the officer reversed himself, disregarded his assign-
ment, and came out in agreement with the black soldiers. "He says that
he came down here with an entire misconception of the whole subject,"
reported one of Henry Bowditch's nephews, a captain in the regiment.[104]

The pay crisis caused previously ambivalent recruiters to reverse themselves, and several now joined Morris in openly opposing enlistment. William Wells Brown had urged black men to go to war, he told an August
1863 meeting, "to convince this God-forsaken nation that black men are
as valiant as other men. But our people have been so cheated, robbed,

deceived, and outraged everywhere, that I cannot urge them to go." John
S. Rock, though a friend of Governor Andrew's, now agreed. "If we are not
to be treated as men now when in this hour of peril we have come forward
and forgiven two centuries of outrage and oppression what reason have we
to expect anything, how do we know that it may not be wrested from us?
Is this nation any better at heart now than it was four years ago?" William
Nell's suggestion that black women picked up the slack in recruiting fervor
must be balanced against the words of Mrs. Christiana Carteaux Bannister,
who rose in an August 1863 meeting to urge support for the soldiers who
were already in the field, but also to declare that "she did not want any
more to go to aid a government that had treated them so cruelly. She would
rather beg from door to door than that her husband should go to war."[105]

Robert Morris remained entirely defiant. "We told you this is the way
they would treat us," he glowered. "I want you to understand I am not
going to the war; God forbid, that I should ask any man to go . . . But if
any one chooses to make a fool of himself he can do so. We have rights as
well as the white people, and it looks to me as though they intend to use
us and do not mean to do anything for us. If we are not careful they will
give us what they gave our fathers in the Revolution."[106] Morris was clearly
still thinking about other revolutionary legacies: in a speech before the
Prince Hall Grand Lodge shortly after the preliminary Emancipation Proclamation, Morris named his own honor roll of freedom: the slave revolutionaries "Denmark Veazie [sic] and Nat Turner, whose very names were
a terror to oppressors; who, conceiving the sublime idea of freedom for
themselves and their race, animated by a love of liberty of which they had
been ruthlessly deprived, made an attempt to sever their bonds."[107] This
defiant spirit held him, almost until the end of the war, unreconciled to the
nation. Twenty years later, a eulogy by his protégé Edwin G. Walker celebrated Morris's stand and suggested that it had brought the lawyer to the
verge of being locked up as a foe of conscription.[108]

The conscription controversy and the pay strike reflected the lessons learned by the "colored citizens" over the past decades: they must demonstrate both their courage and their understanding of the principles of equality. By continuing to serve but refusing to take unequal pay, some believed, they were doing both. Others on occasion claimed that the Massachusetts men's protests were out of proportion to the moment's importance. "[T]hose few colored regiments from Massachusetts make more fuss, and complain more than all the rest of the colored troops in the nation," wrote a black soldier in 1864. "I sincerely hope they will stop such nonsense, and learn to take things as soldiers should."[109] If the historic power of black military service in the war that ended slavery must not be shortchanged, however, it is also true that the pay fight was a crucial battle in the black soldiers' second war, their struggle with the United States.[110]

By the end of 1863, with conservatives in Washington continuing to block equalization of pay, the grumbling and defiance within the black regiments turned to outright rebellion. Sergeant William Walker of the 3rd South Carolina regiment told his men to stack their arms; in February 1864 a court-martial found him guilty of mutiny, and a squad of Union soldiers shot him. Even so, the rebellion spread. That spring a soldier in the 55th Massachusetts assaulted his lieutenant, and officers in the 54th shot several of their men for refusing orders. As Andrew's agents among the regiments sounded increasingly frantic notes, the governor penned an open letter to the secretary of war, seeking to shame the federal government to action and to improve morale by letting the men in his regiments know that Massachusetts stood with them.[111]

During the long pay struggle Andrew's ability to rely on Lewis Hayden may have made a considerable difference.[112] When Andrew sought to reassure the men of the 55th Massachusetts, then encamped in South Carolina, that he was doing everything in his power to make sure they received equal pay, he did not simply have the colonel of the regiment convey his sentiments. Instead, he sent along a packet of his letters to various federal officials, with a covering letter from Lewis Hayden urging the commanders of the 54th and 55th to "communicate this information to the men of your regiment[s]."[113] The covering letter was in the handwriting of the governor's military secretary, but it bore Hayden's unmistakable signature; his was the name that mattered.[114]

Andrew also sought to firm up support for his efforts from key black political figures, in part by pressing their names forward for plum appointments. He eagerly sought George Downing's aid as a recruiter, and endorsed him as quartermaster for the new regiments forming in North Carolina.[115] He relied on Leonard Grimes to keep the black citizens of Boston informed about his efforts on behalf of the black troops.[116] When it came time for the commander of the 54th to choose a sutler Colonel Robert Gould Shaw received two applications: one from a leading black man in Buffalo, the other from Boston's Mark De Mortie. Shaw preferred the Buffalo man, as the regiment "has been half filled up from there," thanks to George Stearns's heroic recruiting efforts. De Mortie, on the other hand, represented the "influential colored men of Boston," whom Shaw had already disparaged.[117] Andrew strongly favored De Mortie, though, and Shaw assented.[118]

The crisis finally abated in June 1864 when Congress granted equal pay to the black regiments, retroactive to the beginning of the year. It took another nine months, however, for every black regiment, including those recruited before the Emancipation Proclamation and in the slave states, to receive equal pay.[119] George Ruffin's brother James, now a sergeant in the 55th, wrote home that "[t]he boys are in great glee," celebrating the arrival of the pay for which they had held out so long.[120] The critical battle in the war with the Union had been won.

THE HAYDENS' WAR

Lewis Hayden recruited men across the North for an army whose victory would remake the nation. Black soldiers were going to be part of this fight, he understood, and their actions, regardless of the particular circumstances, would significantly affect the claims black people would be able to make following a Union victory. As Governor Andrew put it in a letter to Hayden, if the Union triumphed without black assistance, African Americans would be left "a poor, despised, subordinated body of human beings, neither strangers not citizens, but 'contrabands,' who had lost their masters but not found a country." On the other hand, "[n]o one can ever deny the rights of citizenship in a country to those who have helped create or to *save it.*"[121] Frederick Douglass made the point best in a recruiting speech earlier that year. While acknowledging the rightness of insisting on "equal and exact justice" to black enlistees, he saw immediate military service as "the speediest and best possible way open to us to manhood, equal rights and elevation. . . . Once let the black man get upon his person the brass letters U.S.," Douglass asserted, "let him get an eagle on his button, and musket on his shoulder, and bullets in his pocket, and there is no power on the earth or under the earth which can deny that he has earned the right of citizenship in the United States."[122]

Once Massachusetts began to recruit, leading black men across the North turned to Hayden, the governor's friend, whose networks from New Haven to Chicago provided a natural conduit for their questions and requests. John Jones, seeking Andrew's permission to recruit cavalrymen out in Chicago, dropped Hayden's name.[123] From Pittsburgh came a note from John Peck reminding Hayden of Rufus Sibb Jones, a young man he had met at Peck's barbershop. Would Hayden arrange for Andrew to authorize Jones to enlist a company? Hayden forwarded the letter to Andrew, and although this particular overture didn't bear fruit, the recommendation seems to have been a good one: young Jones enlisted in the 8th U.S. Colored Infantry, where he rose to the rank of sergeant.[124]

Hayden needed all the help he could get because, by the time the 5th Massachusetts Cavalry Regiment began recruiting, the Union was seething with dissent over the newly imposed federal draft. In the summer of 1863, white reaction against federal conscription exploded in July's terrible New

York City draft riots, in which antiwar New Yorkers attacked and murdered black New Yorkers, burned draft offices, and forced a military
response and occupation of the city. Antidraft violence burned elsewhere
across the North; even in Boston, a crowd laid siege to an armory in the
North End and was repulsed with cannon.[125] But New York's violence, directed so mercilessly at African Americans, showed the most malevolent
face of the white republic and bespoke how deeply many white Northerners remained committed to its future.

In the context of the riots, anything that eased the pressure on the home
front was welcome, including the enlistment of black troops who could
be credited to a state or locality's quota of enlistments, thereby reducing
the number of white men who must be recruited or drafted. White Northerners who had once insisted that the Civil War was a white man's fight
now became quite happy to enlist as many black men as possible, bolster-
ing the army's ranks while undercutting opposition among whites to the
draft.

Lewis Hayden was among the recruiters who ventured throughout the
Union in pursuit of black men who would be credited to their states. Representing Massachusetts carried certain advantages: as the first state to recruit black troops and the home of the 54th, now famous for its sacrifice
at Fort Wagner, Massachusetts had cachet. Hayden may have been utterly
in earnest when he told Andrew of the hope he had entertained when he
"left the State House on this mission . . . of awakening in the minds of our
leading Colored men, an active, energetic, and enthusiastic devotion to the
Old Bay State. So far, I have the pleasant satisfaction to believe I have succeeded."[126] But recruitment proved a difficult, often cutthroat business.
Rival recruiters whispered that Massachusetts, not the federal government,
was responsible for the inferior pay received by the men of the 54th. Only
the fact that Andrew's name carried weight across the black North, Hayden
flatteringly reported, made it possible for him to recruit any men at all.[127]

For Harriet Hayden and other black women, the war opened channels for many kinds of work, some of it quite familiar: the task of supplying "contrabands" with relief, employment, and education in many respects resembled that of prewar aid to fugitive slaves. "Contrabands" in the occupied Confederacy lived in a perilous limbo, subjected variously to military law, individual caprice, and Confederate raids. While some forged their own structures of governance and association, others found white and black allies. Some black Northerners, such as the Remonds' young charge Charlotte Forten and Mark De Mortie's relative John Oliver, left Boston during the war to help organize and educate the freedpeople.[128] Others urged refugees from slavery to seek work and safety in the North. Building on the existing networks of free and fugitive migration, they helped draw thousands of former slaves to cities and towns across the North, from the Minnesota territory to the urban centers of Massachusetts.[129] During and immediately after the Civil War, recently liberated black Southerners gained employment in Boston and other Northern locales, their rocky paths smoothed a little by networks of black and white activists. Octavia Grimes served as a labor agent, placing slave-born black workers with Boston employers for a five-dollar fee; her husband met the Virginia ships as they docked in Boston and conducted these new migrants through what was now a thoroughly aboveground "railroad."[130]

During the war, even more than in the previous decade, women's roles in public life came to seem routine and unexceptional. Boston's Colored Ladies Sanitary Commission raised funds and gathered supplies for freedpeople's communities in the South; after the pay strike began in the summer of 1863, the group secured relief for the families of black soldiers.[131] This work culminated in the Boston Colored Soldiers' Fair of October 1864, headed by a committee of notable women including Christiana Carteaux Bannister and Octavia Grimes.[132] This wartime labor would play a key role in authorizing women's independent organization and activity in the years to come.[133] These experiences would lead women such as George Ruffin's wife, Boston native Josephine St. Pierre Ruffin, to join or found

a range of suffrage and aid organizations in subsequent decades. In the
1890s, after her husband's death, Josephine Ruffin would become a guid-
ing force in the emerging black women's club and convention movement.[134]

For Harriet Hayden, the war offered an opportunity to gain literacy.
Benevolent-minded white Bostonians offered the new migrants many
kinds of aid; one of them, Mrs. Apphia Howard, began a small class in her
home to teach people born in slavery to read and write. Most of her students were recent arrivals to the city, but in 1862 they were joined by Harriet Hayden. It may have taken a great leap of faith for her to seek openly
what her husband had gained two decades before, but she took hold of
"this glorious blessing." On Christmas Eve she and her fellow pupils presented their teacher—"a true friend"—with a likeness drawn by a rising
young black artist, William Simpson, accompanied by a presentation address composed by Hayden herself. Some things did not change quite so
quickly: the address was read to Mrs. Howard by Lewis Hayden, who accompanied his wife that evening.[135]

Lewis Hayden's travels continued into late 1864, when he made the
dangerous trip to Union-occupied New Orleans. This was probably not a
recruiting trip but an effort to see his son Joseph, then serving in the U.S.
Navy in the Gulf. The navy had not barred black men outright from service, and several thousand Northern black men enlisted as Union sailors
during 1861, including some four hundred from Massachusetts.[136] Hayden
enlisted with the rank of landsman at Portsmouth, New Hampshire, in
November 1861. He reenlisted at Portsmouth in 1863 and then again later
at Fort Gaines in Mobile Bay, where he was stationed after the Union's
victory there in August 1864.[137]

A visit to this theater of war required Lewis Hayden to think about his
status as a free American. Although slavery was effectively defunct in the
Union-controlled parts of the South, the Union occupation government in
Louisiana had replaced it with a system of contract labor that set stringent
limits on the mobility and autonomy of black workers. Provost marshals
enforced a de facto slave code in nominally "liberated" Louisiana. Hayden

was lucky to have a friend in the local military government, his longtime ally John L. Swift, who was serving in the adjutant general's office. Before he left Boston, he asked for Swift's help in staying clear of these limits on his freedom, and Swift obliged with a letter to the provost marshal of New Orleans in which he vouched for Hayden's "citizenship" and sought passes to enable father and son to travel unmolested.[138]

Neither his reputation nor his friends could help Lewis Hayden bring his son back to Boston. In June 1865, age twenty-six and childless, Joseph Hayden died of disease in camp at Mobile Bay. The family name ended with him. About this tragedy Lewis and Harriet Hayden maintained public silence, as would have been appropriate in their Boston world. But Jo was never far from their thoughts: for the rest of their lives, a portrait of the young man hung above their mantel. Lewis Hayden expressed his feelings on the point only obliquely, many years later, in a letter to Reverend James Freeman Clarke. At a social occasion at Clarke's home, Hayden had once met two children—"angels they were to me"—but he had "ever since missed their beautiful & lovely faces." Hayden knew as well as any the realities of child mortality; it appears that he and Harriet had lost a young daughter during the 1850s.[139] But it was not his place, he wrote feelingly to Clarke, "to inquire after them, not knowing what the answer might be." "[T]he will of God be done," he concluded.[140] It was as close to an epitaph as he publicly offered for his son.

"IF SLAVES WILL MAKE GOOD SOLDIERS . . ."

Robert Morris finally won his war with the Union, but others got the spoils. In late 1863, when the Massachusetts legislature reorganized the state militia, it accepted Lewis Gaul's petition to form a black company. On September 21, he was named captain of the new unit.[141] The following winter, the Massachusetts legislature finally struck the word "white" from the state's militia laws.[142] The door Elizur Wright had invoked during the struggle over recruitment was at last fully open. By early 1864, Gaul was reporting his men's names on the roster of the 14th Unattached Company of Militia. Dubbed the "Shaw Guards," in honor of the fallen white colonel of the 54th Massachusetts, Gaul's company quickly became regular participants in Boston's civic affairs.[143]

By late 1864 black men in arms ceased to seem a threat to the American state and instead became one of its lines of defense. Black activists took note. In October 1864 John S. Rock took a step past the profound ambivalence that so often characterized black abolitionist views of the United States. He began in familiar terms: "Many of our grandfathers fought in the Revolution, and they thought they were fighting for liberty; but they made a sad mistake, and we are now obliged to fight those battles over again, and I hope, this time, to a better purpose." Now he also celebrated the new laws and concluded, "There are but two parties in the country today. The one headed by Lincoln is for Freedom and the Republic; and the other, by McClellan, is for Despotism and Slavery. . . . The friends and the enemies of the country are defined."[144] His people were at last counted among the friends. These triumphs did not persuade everyone in the North—not even in the Union military, where the contributions of the two hundred thousand black combatants were most evident. Black soldiers were still disproportionately assigned to fatigue duty, digging latrines and doing other work shunned by white soldiers. And blacks in the officer corps—the positions so prized by Morris and his comrades—confronted white fellow officers who rejected their authority, doubted their competence, and did them lasting harm.

The wartime humiliations of the Haydens' neighbor John V. DeGrasse suggested that the battle for the hearts and minds of white Americans would not be as easily won as the struggle over equal pay. DeGrasse, a member of the Massasoit Guard almost since his arrival in Boston, actively sought an officer's commission, and Andrew clearly had him in mind for an appointment once federal authorities allowed such a step.[145] In April

1863 he was commissioned assistant surgeon to the 35th Infantry, one of the three regiments of the U.S. Colored Troops recruited largely from among the former slaves of North Carolina, and under the command of the tempestuous Brookline abolitionist Edward Wild.[146] The physical conditions of camp life were doubtless unfamiliar and difficult for the genteel urbanite, but the greatest challenges he faced came from white Union officers. These men generally shunned black officers, not only giving them "the *cold shoulder*," but—as an infuriated Lieutenant James Monroe Trotter reported in April 1864—refusing to share tents with them.[147] For comradeship DeGrasse could rely only on the tiny group of other black men who shared his degree of authority—surgeons, chaplains, and recruiters.

John V. and Cordelia DeGrasse
The Museum of African American History, Boston and Nantucket, Massachusetts

It was in the company of one such man—the spy and recruiter Abraham Galloway—that DeGrasse confronted Union white supremacy at its most raw. On a recruiting trip to the coastal town of Plymouth, the men were accosted on the street by several drunken naval officers who took exception to the black surgeon's officer's straps. "Who the hell gave you the right to recruit niggers?" asked one. "I'll let you know that we did not come here to fight for niggers." He then made an effort to punch DeGrasse in the face, but the doctor's quick reaction and the man's own inebriation deprived the blow of its force. As DeGrasse felt for the service revolver in his pocket, Galloway came to his aid, asking, "Why don't you shoot him, doctor?" Instead, like Rock with Redpath, DeGrasse and his colleague took their complaint to their commander, who had the men brought up on charges.[148]

Here DeGrasse was unambiguously the injured party, and his frankly abolitionist white commander ensured that the assaults on his dignity did not pass unredressed. The same was not the case a year later, when De-Grasse himself faced a court-martial on charges of drunkenness on duty and conduct unbecoming an officer. A white physician and a hospital steward each testified that DeGrasse had been derelict in February 1864, refusing to get out of bed to dress soldiers' wounds because he was intoxicated. More than this, some asserted, when under the influence of liquor his normally "quiet and gentlemanly" demeanor gave way to something much coarser: two white officers testified that in June 1864, on the steamer *Mary Benton*, he had made crude and explicit sexual advances to "a colored woman" in the ship's saloon. The jury accepted these charges and by November 1864, a year and a half after he had entered the service, De-Grasse was cashiered.

Were the charges against DeGrasse accurate? Scattered hints suggest that the doctor inspired an unusual degree of hostility for someone so prominent in the black activist world. At the end of 1864 Boston's Prince Hall leadership election became "very stormey" and even "unmasonic" as members fought to prevent the election of Robert Morris as grand master, apparently because it was known Morris had intended to appoint De-Grasse as his deputy.[149] It is possible, as his military detractors alleged, that alcohol played a role in DeGrasse's troubles; an African American resident of Beacon Hill interviewed three decades later remembered about Dr. De-Grasse only that at his untimely passing in 1868 he "died drunk."[150] But all of this is hearsay and speculation.

More clear is that the campaign to drum DeGrasse out of the service fit a broader pattern of concerted hostility to black officers, and perhaps particularly surgeons, by their white comrades. Elsewhere in the black regiments white officers expressed outright resistance to commissioning black medical staff.[151] One black physician who was commissioned surgeon at the rank of major was removed from his Maryland camp and placed on detached service after frankly racist complaints by lower-ranking white assistant surgeons.[152] The drunken sailors in Plymouth were certainly not the only ones who resented DeGrasse, but they may have aimed crudely at ends others pursued more deviously. The court-martial could well have been a racially motivated campaign to cut a leading black man down to size. Indeed, there was plenty of evidence to contradict the jury's findings: the lone woman aboard the *Mary Benton*, known in the record only as Patty, denied having been insulted by DeGrasse; other officers likewise denied that the doctor had been intoxicated on the dates mentioned; and DeGrasse himself clearly believed that his immediate superior, Surgeon Marcy, was behind a malicious prosecution.[153]

It was not terribly hard to bring down the first black member of the Massachusetts Medical Association, and the motives of at least some of his detractors would have been familiar to any "colored citizen." As the sailor grumbled after his assault on DeGrasse, "These goddamned niggers walking around here with shoulder straps are making them too damn'd common."[154] It remained to be seen whether the victorious Union would know what to do with this angry insistence on maintaining the privileges of whiteness, or with the determined black citizens now clearly emerging from its shadow.

Yet there was reason for hope. Black military service helped win the war, defeating the Confederacy and assuring the final end of slavery in the United States. Before the war was over, nearly two hundred thousand African American men served in the army and navy; at war's end their numbers in arms exceeded the total number of white Confederates still fighting.[155] Their service provided an unexpected answer to slaveholders who argued, like Confederate officer and politician Howell Cobb, that "if slaves will make good soldiers, then our whole theory of slavery is wrong." More important, it finally resolved the skepticism of those Northern white allies who had previously doubted the physical and moral courage of slaves and free blacks. The stigma of cowardice and incapacity removed, once-skeptical whites came to celebrate "the modern Crispus Attucks" just as Higginson had in the years before the war. No one now questioned whether blacks possessed the will and determination for liberty.

With military service therefore came a renewed claim to full civil and political enfranchisement, one recognized as legitimate even by many moderates and skeptics. The black role in the Union victory helped John Jones persuade the Illinois legislature to repeal laws barring black immigration and testimony in that state.[156] Philadelphia's black activists, continuing a long struggle against streetcar segregation, were now able to draw on the moral claims of soldiers' wives and families, who sought to visit their wounded relatives in nearby hospitals but refused to ride on the open platform. With Republican officials and prominent citizens joining their fight, victory neared on that front as well.[157]

Even Abraham Lincoln began to reconsider his dictum that black and white could never happily coexist, and to ponder what this meant for the future. The president's ongoing encounter with black people's capacities and determination, from the White House to the battlefield, had changed him. He had in no way set out to create an interracial republic, but the words and deeds of African Americans during the war had unexpectedly made such a thing imaginable to him. In a letter to the new Union governor of Louisiana in early 1864, he offered a private suggestion: voting rights for "some of the colored people . . . for instance, the very intelligent, and especially those who have fought gallantly in our ranks. They would probably help, in some trying time to come, to keep the jewel of liberty within the family of freedom." When even "the slave-hound of Illinois" was prepared to include African Americans in "the family of freedom," could the day of "fraternal unity" be far off?

Part III

THE
DISAPPOINTMENTS
OF CITIZENSHIP

8.

Radical Reconstruction
on Beacon Hill

A s Union troops moved through ever larger swaths of the Confederacy in 1864, Massachusetts men among them sent their abolitionist war governor mementos of slavery's destruction. One forwarded John Andrew a boat made of straw, fashioned by a fugitive who used it to float past rebel pickets and reach Union lines. Another man sent a gavel carved from the whipping post outside a Virginia courthouse. These two pieces of handiwork told stories of freedom seized and tyranny transformed, and captured for Andrew this moment of great, even millennial change.[1]

Andrew, just elected to a fifth one-year term, was too good a politician to let these potent artifacts languish in a statehouse storeroom. Instead, he converted the gifts into a different kind of political currency. Addressing himself to Lewis Hayden, he presented the twin "memorials of the barbarous institution" to "the association of free colored citizens, over which you preside"—the Prince Hall Grand Lodge, of which Hayden was grand master. "I know of no place more fitting for the preservation of these memorials," wrote the governor.[2]

For Hayden, Governor Andrew's recognition portended a new relationship between those "free colored citizens" and the nation. The gifts, he told his Masonic brethren, represented the materials "colored citizens," north and south, would need as they completed the era's great work. The gavel, once used "to subdue the corporeal man to a tyrant's will," would bring ennobling law and justice. The boat bore witness to the fugitive's faith in the fruits of God's creation to carry him to freedom. Together with institutions of democratic government overseen by men such as Andrew, these wartime transformations would help create a "new fabric" for American life. Acts of recognition and respect such as Andrew's "would be used as cement in the future to bind the black and white in this country into one common mass, to which service in the future they will be devoted." Beyond this, Hayden was supremely gratified that Andrew publicly recognized the North's leading black citizens and acknowledged their aspirations. The Prince Hall Grand Lodge itself represented another essential ingredient for the transformation of the United States from a white republic into a home for all its people: it embodied the skills, institutions, and solidarities black Northerners had developed and now hoped to deploy as their campaign for a full place in American life reached its culmination. Robert Morris called for three cheers for the governor, which were given.[3] American slavery was drawing its last breaths. Caste would surely follow.

Northern free blacks' ascent toward recognition, acceptance, and belonging seemed unstoppable during the second half of the 1860s. They sought new state civil rights laws to establish broad parameters of equal access and equal treatment. They pressed federal officeholders for laws and amendments to replace the rotted proslavery pillars in the edifice of government. With their white Republican allies in ascendancy, they garnered a few patronage positions previously reserved for whites; more important, they regularly won election as Republican officeholders and even found defensive Democrats willing to put black men forward as candidates. By the early 1870s, they seemed to have achieved nearly full integration into the political life of Massachusetts. Having served as soldiers, they now insisted on being recognized as citizens, not "other persons." They loudly claimed the Union victory as their own, only occasionally reminding one another that their insistence on equality sometimes had set them at odds with the Union.

Given the scope of the transformations that took place from 1862 to 1865, it is not surprising that longtime black activists imagined the reconstruction of the South would be theirs to shape. In the remaking of the nation that followed Confederate defeat and slave emancipation, they planted themselves in the former slave states, building churches, lodges, and schools, hoping by effort and example to guide freedpeople and the region toward the happy future that now seemed so near. At home in Boston, and across the free states, they sought to "bind the black and white in this country into one common mass" by consolidating and extending the gains of past decades. They sought to replace black laws with equal citizenship, to extend the suffrage to all, and to encourage acts of warm recognition such as the governor's gifts.

Full-hearted acknowledgment, not formal citizenship, proved the most elusive. The resistance of former Confederates as well as many white Northerners shaped the formal victories of Reconstruction. It quickly became clear that the extension of rights and privileges to African Americans would hinge at least as much on expediency as on principle. And black activists, while of one mind about broad principles of equal justice and equal suffrage, were less certain about the precise legal and institutional forms these must take. They also remained unsure how to move past these principles of law toward the "new fabric" Hayden contemplated. For the first time, though, there were hints that a wider and warmer belonging of "Freedom's army," in the bosom of "fraternal unity," might be within their reach.[4]

Most accounts of the careers of black activists end with, or shortly after, the monumental achievements of the mid-1860s. There are several reasons for this abrupt ending. The history of the era that follows, unlike that of earlier decades, does not seem to point like an arrow at climactic dramas such as the Civil War and the fall of slavery. Nor is the longer view easily summarized as a tale of triumph. The story of the "colored citizens" from the late 1860s through the 1880s includes many agonizing compromises, harsh disappointments, and painful realizations. But it also complicates the narrative depicting these men and women as "black abolitionists," because it clearly reveals that they in no sense considered their work accomplished in 1865, nor even with the Thirteenth, Fourteenth, and Fifteenth Amendments, which ended slavery, established national citizenship, and prohibited civic discrimination based on race. The "colored citizens" who helped topple slavery believed, with good reason, that no one could speak to the particular needs of free black Americans, now numbering more than four million, as well as they could. Their efforts to take up that role are essential to understanding how post–Civil War "freedom" took on the meanings it did, for better and for worse.

BRINGING THE VICTORY HOME

The transformative events of 1865 offered powerful reason for hope. In January 1865, Congress passed the Thirteenth Amendment, the first formal step toward the constitutional abolition of "slavery or involuntary servitude." The Massachusetts legislature moved swiftly, ratifying it a week later, and other Union states followed.[5] That spring, the Union armies besieging the bastions of Virginia finally broke through, putting the Confederate leadership to flight and bringing the final surrender of Robert E. Lee's Army of Northern Virginia at Appomattox Court House. By the beginning of summer the last rebel armies laid down their arms. Black men in Union blue marched through the streets of Richmond, Charleston, and Montgomery. Edmund Ruffin, the proslavery intellectual who delightedly fired the first shot on Fort Sumter, put a bullet through his brain. In De-

cember, after a final wave of ratifications by former slave states, the abolitionists' long-cherished goal of human freedom became the Thirteenth
Amendment to the U.S. Constitution. The fate of slavery was sealed.

Chief Justice Roger Taney had died on the day in 1864 that his home
state of Maryland abolished slavery, but the Union's triumph over the Confederacy did not by itself wholly dispense with *Dred Scott*'s dicta about
black people's rights. It remained unclear what "freedom" meant, besides
not literally being the property of another. The framers of the amendment
did not assume that freedom guaranteed citizenship. Nor did they share a
clear, common conception of what rights citizenship need respect. Most,
though, did not mean the expansive, embracing conception held and
hoped for by many "colored citizens."[6] Black laws remained in force
throughout much of the North—not just the restriction or outright denial
of manhood suffrage, but also laws banning black people's right to testify
in certain states or even to enter them, such as those John Jones worked so
hard to dismantle in Illinois. The end of slavery did nothing to change this.
Nor, more pressingly, did it address the situations of black Southerners,
whether they lived under the enforced-labor regimes of military rule, the
whites-only governance of Union provisional governments, or the tottering
edifice of the slaveholders' Confederacy.

The question of political rights for the freedpeople loomed large in
black activists' imaginations, for despite Abraham Lincoln's hesitant con-
templation of voting rights for some black men, freedom in the main arrived without suffrage. Frederick Douglass was unequivocal about the
central importance of the vote: "Slavery is not abolished," he declared in
May 1865, "until the black man has the ballot."[7] Disenfranchisement left
"colored citizens" vulnerable to all manner of discrimination. Douglass
noted that three Midwestern states had only recently prohibited black men
from testifying against whites. When the wartime provisional government
of Louisiana established a constitution that did not include "white" as a
precondition for voting, the *Liberator* remarked that this made it "a better
Constitution for the colored citizen than that of Connecticut, New York,

New Jersey, Pennsylvania, or any Western state."[8] As was true a decade before, only five New England states allowed black men to vote without restriction.

But emancipation did begin to make these exclusions seem less natural. Prodded by their leading black citizens, some Northern states moved to formally prohibit discrimination in public accommodations. Less than a month after Appomattox, Massachusetts took up a bill to prohibit discrimination in theaters and "public amusements," eventually expanding it to take in transportation, hotels, and meeting places. This legislation "forbidding unjust discrimination" passed by an overwhelming margin but offered only the modest penalty of a fine not to exceed fifty dollars.[9] Over the next year black Bostonians, William Nell among them, struggled to mobilize public opinion against the numerous theaters and other places of amusement that continued to bar or segregate black customers.[10] Colleagues in other cities pursued similar strategies, and Philadelphia's Equal Rights League successfully moved its allies among radical Republican officeholders to prohibit discrimination on the city's streetcars.[11] Soon the U.S. Congress also challenged some of these local laws and customs, seeking to guarantee the right to travel unimpeded and without fear of segregation or exclusion. Massachusetts's Senator Henry Wilson introduced sweeping legislation that would guarantee "colored passengers" the same treatment as others, regardless of state or municipal rulings to the contrary—a guarantee enforceable in federal court against both corporations and individuals, backed up by a fine of not less than five hundred dollars or not less than six months' imprisonment.[12]

A petition of "Colored citizens," headed by Benjamin Roberts, soon demanded that Boston cease marking its tax and voting records with the indicator "Col." Ten years before, the city council had rejected John Rock's similar petition. This time the committee hearing their petition, headed by Charles Slack, agreed that the "spirit of the time," combined with "that republicanism which recognizes all citizens as standing upon the same equality before the law," required the city council to grant the request. The "well known and orderly" petitioners asked simply to pay taxes, serve on juries, perform military service, put down riots and insurrections—"in short, whatever the good citizen is expected to do, they want to do, having no particular noise made about it."[13] Equality of citizenship was the new status quo.

This "spirit of the time" defined the context in which black Republicans finally emerged as a force in Massachusetts politics. Although more potent in symbolism than in numbers, they nonetheless found ways to become important figures in city, state, and national politics. Part of this importance lay in the popular identification of black progress, and even equality, as fruits of the Union victory. But black activists were also able to insert themselves into the Republican Party's councils, help determine the outcome of elections, and even achieve office themselves.

The stars of apportionment, population density, and partisan division aligned to create a surprisingly congenial political climate for Boston's black Republicans immediately after the war. The densely populated blocks of Ward Six included the elite neighborhood near the statehouse as well as the humbler north slope of Beacon Hill and the adjacent West End. Home to about fourteen hundred black Bostonians in the 1860s, this small area held nearly two-thirds of the city's black population; the approximately four hundred twenty-five adult men in this population—the potential black electorate—made up about 14 percent of the ward's nominal voters.[14] Although the ward leaned heavily Republican, those four hundred or so votes were significant in the wider world of city and state politics. The capital city was not as reliably Republican as its state, so in order to elect Republicans to the mayor's office, the state senate, or Congress, party leaders had to rally their most loyal voters.

As Anson Burlingame well understood, a few hundred votes could make a big difference. In fact, black ballots in the Beacon Hill ward sometimes exceeded the margin of victory in the local state senate race. When highly motivated, the ward's black voters could turn out in extraordinary numbers—in the 1868 presidential voting, a friendly newspaper claimed, only two short of their total registration.[15] The clustering of black voters and their high rates of turnout converged to create a tiny patch of New England in which an interracial alliance could ensure Republican success, even before significant numbers of black voters affected Southern elections. Black voters found that through thorough organizing and partisan solidarity, they could demand some say in party affairs. Over the next two decades similar dynamics would give black voters measurable influence in pockets of Philadelphia, Chicago, Cleveland, and Cincinnati. More famously, and to much greater effect, interracial Republican parties would govern most of the former Confederate states for longer or shorter periods between 1868 and the mid-1870s. But Boston's Ward Six was the first place where an interracial Republican coalition marched, campaigned, nominated, and elected both black and white men to office.[16]

The black partisan organization begun in earnest during the Know-Nothing years became a systematic enterprise during Lincoln's reelection campaign in 1864. Its foot soldiers included the old stalwarts, but also younger men, in particular the ambitious Virginian George L. Ruffin. The black Republicans' immediate project was to ensure an overwhelming reelection victory for Lincoln and the party ticket in their home ward.[17] Organizing the city's black voters began with the establishment of clubs and marching companies. The Sixth Ward's Lincoln and Johnson Club hosted several hundred people at an October rally in its headquarters, the vestry of Grimes's Twelfth Baptist Church. It featured a band, a "thoroughly Union" speech by Rock, and the presentation of a flag by George Ruffin.[18] Behind the spectacle and ceremony young Ruffin and the old regulars cobbled together a working list of the city and ward's black voting population, made sure they were registered, confirmed their addresses, and got them out to vote.[19]

George Ruffin's labors suggest how thoroughly these black Republican ward heelers did their work. His notebook entitled "Colored Voters Boston 1864"—dated October 17, the day of the rally at Twelfth Baptist— sought to list every black voter in the city and noted whether the man had

George L. Ruffin, painting by Melvin Robbins
Courtesy of Historical & Special Collections,
Harvard Law School Library

paid the tax that entitled him to vote. The surviving pages of the book contain the names of well over three hundred men; a full alphabetical list would have numbered close to four hundred.[20] On the eve of the election Ruffin and his colleagues were joined by the white allies who relied on their aid, including U.S. Senator Henry Wilson.[21] Amid high turnout in the ward—better than 70 percent—the Republicans won an easy victory in the city, state, and nation that November.[22]

The next step was elected office. In late 1865, with Appomattox behind them and the ratification of the Thirteenth Amendment a foregone conclusion, black Republicans for the first time put forward a serious candidate for the state legislature. William Nell, Lewis Hayden, and others had sought this office during the early 1850s, when Boston's legislative delegation was still elected at large and the parties to which they belonged had little chance of winning. Since then, a shift from at-large to ward-based

voting for the legislature, combined with the Republican ascendancy, created a very different political calculus. Black Republicans' first effort fell
just short: in the Republican caucus to select nominees for Ward Six's two
seats in the legislature, longtime activist John J. Smith placed third. But the
next year, following the state's decennial reapportionment, Ward Six
gained an additional legislative seat. This lowered the threshold for success
just enough to make the difference.

Victory in largely white Ward Six required both that black ward heelers
organize black voters and that they alert white power brokers to the stakes.
With three seats available in 1866, there was a great deal of interest, and
men crowded the wardroom at the end of October for the selection of the
ward's three nominees. The room was so full that the counting grew slow
and confused. When the beleaguered clerk calculated the results, he mis-
takenly announced the victory of four men, the last of whom was a veteran
of the 55th Massachusetts, Lieutenant Charles L. Mitchell. Impressively,
the officer's total fell just behind that of prosperous white lawyer and longtime state representative Harvey Jewell.

A tense standoff ensued. When the error became obvious and Jewell
claimed the third spot, Mitchell's disappointed partisans moved that he
instead be named the third candidate. This led to a "confused and disorderly" proceeding in which Mitchell indeed was declared the third member of the ward ticket. But this left a significant number of white voters so
disgruntled that the next day the officers of the meeting reversed themselves, making Jewell the third nominee. This could have been the beginning of a serious rupture pitting elite whites against black voters, the most
reliable supporters of the Republican ticket. Someone no doubt urged a
pause for reconsideration. Soon the top vote getter, insurance executive
Benjamin F. Stevens, stepped aside, leaving Mitchell the third man on the
ticket. Whether this was an act of magnanimity or pragmatism, it worked.
One white Republican operative breathed a sigh of relief that "the disaffection among a large number of Republican voters at the proceedings of
the nomination convention . . . has ceased."[23] Had a split followed, at least

one writer worried, it could have cost the Republicans in the general election in the ward and beyond. As matters stood, "[w]e have a right to expect the re-election" of the Republican incumbent to Congress "by a very
large majority, if faith is kept with the colored voters of the district."[24] If a
black Republican entered the legislature, in other words, it would be because a well-organized bloc of black voters insisted on it, and because there
were white allies who were willing to bend to that insistence rather than
risk a damaging split. This is just what took place.

On election day itself, Mitchell and his two ticket-mates won easily; in
fact, Mitchell outpolled the other two Republicans by more than forty
votes, perhaps a sign that not every black voter was mollified enough to
vote for the entire ticket. The celebration was electric. "The colored men
of Ward Six were exceedingly joyous over the election of Lieut. Mitchell
to the House of Representatives," reported a Republican newspaper.
"They formed in procession and marched around the streets of the ward,
singing and hurrahing as they marched. They serenaded Lieut. Mitchell at
the house of his friend, Mr. De Mortie, on Anderson street, and received
his hospitalities."[25]

Similar celebrations echoed from across the channel in Charlestown,
where Republican voters had selected black lawyer Edwin Garrison Walker
to join Mitchell in the legislature.[26] The son of David Walker and the namesake of the *Liberator*'s editor, Walker had been a successful leatherworker
and antislavery activist before turning to the law; he became Robert Morris's protégé and passed the bar in 1861.[27] Like Morris, he lived in an
overwhelmingly white world. If the inheritor of these radical legacies could
win election with scarcely a black vote, perhaps anything was possible. In
any case, Massachusetts had elected two black state representatives to its
1867 session—the first time such a thing had occurred in the nation's history.[28] While Walker's Charlestown victory ultimately proved singular,
Ward Six's black Republicans gained more or less secure footing in the
Massachusetts assembly. In 1867 John J. Smith was nominated and elected
to the legislature. He was reelected in 1868, and succeeded by George

Ruffin, while Hayden, De Mortie, and others took part in party councils and served as election officers.

A strange sequel followed that was, in its own way, even more encouraging. In the immediate postwar era, Democrats in some Republican strongholds cast about for ways to diminish the party's reputation as a nest of disloyal "copperheads." The Boston area Democrats' gambit was to try to outdo Republicans and, not incidentally, split the black vote by nominating black candidates themselves. Never mind that this violated the party's fundamental self-definition as the party of white men; there were black candidates available. After Richard S. Brown failed to win the Republican nomination for city council in his ward, he promptly accepted the Democratic nomination. He lost in a runoff, even though the ward's small number of black voters turned out for him, voting along the way for a Democratic mayoral candidate who "never professed the least friendship for the colored men."[29] Strange bedfellows indeed, and not comfortable ones: within a few years Brown was again seeking the Republican nomination.[30]

Odder still was the mayoral contest in Chelsea, the tiny city north of Boston where Robert Morris made his home. Democrats seeking an opening in a tough race came within a few votes of making Morris himself the nominee of an anti-Republican "Citizens'" ticket, though Morris made no public comment on their efforts.[31] Republicans could not resist taking a poke at their Democratic colleagues, archly noting the "beautiful spectacle of true fraternity and entire freedom from bias" shown by the erstwhile party of slavery and white supremacy.[32]

RECONSTRUCTING CITIZENSHIP

Yet developments in Massachusetts did not quite reflect a nation transformed. Even as the commonwealth's Republicans and Democrats appeared to be achieving consensus on the inclusion of black voters and officeholders, the status of Southern freedpeople seemed to be collapsing toward something very like slavery. First under Lincoln and then, after his assassination, under President Andrew Johnson, whites-only electorates in former Confederate states elected new governments. In late 1865 these governments began passing "black codes" that seemed to reimpose slavery under other names. Laws prohibited African Americans from owning urban property, from being self-employed, or from moving freely; the penalties for violating these laws included involuntary agricultural labor. Beyond this, the black codes earned their name by openly discriminating by race—for example, permitting the whipping of black but not white offenders of certain crimes. Even as Boston's black activists celebrated the third anniversary of emancipation in January 1866, they understood that the struggle with slavery had not yet ended. Lewis Hayden headed a petition to the state's federal delegation, demanding that Congress bar the ex-Confederate states from reentering the nation's councils until they pledged their "solemn recognition of the equality of all men before the law."[33]

The former Confederates returned to power in part because President Andrew Johnson allowed it. Convinced that the South must be reconstructed on the basis of white electorates, the Tennessee Democrat quickly betrayed the hopes Republicans had placed in him. He claimed to distrust the slaveholding interests who had initiated secession. He himself had taken the brave stand of being the lone senator from a seceding state to remain in Washington when the war began. But when forced to choose between democracy and white supremacy, President Johnson showed no hesitation. He granted countless pardons restoring political privileges to former Confederates, spoke explicitly against enfranchising black men, and seemed to be setting the stage for a national reunion in which the freedpeople would play no political part.[34]

Incensed by Johnson's cozying up to former Confederates, outraged at the black codes' relegation of freedpeople to a status far from equal citizenship, and fearful now of losing the peace, congressional Republicans seized control of Reconstruction policy. First they refused to seat the congressional delegates from states readmitted under Johnson's terms. They then overrode President Johnson's veto of the federal Civil Rights Act of 1866, which went some way to establishing the equality Hayden demanded as a principle of national law. It guaranteed inhabitants of the United States the same rights to enter into contracts, sue, testify, purchase, and sell, and it insisted on equal treatment under the law. It also moved enforcement of these rights into the federal courts. Stunningly, building on the precedent of the Fugitive Slave Law, it empowered federal officials to call on any citizen for aid in arresting local officials who violated its provisions.[35]

All of this would come to nothing unless Congress moved to ensure that the freedmen could vote. Until then, Southern states would continue to limit the rights of black citizens in reality, if not in law. Worse still, Southern states with large black populations but a whites-only franchise would eventually return to Congress in even larger proportions than they once had under the Three-Fifths Compromise; there were no more "other persons," so a state's entire black population would count for purposes of apportionment, even though it could not cast a single ballot. To address this fearsome possibility, Republicans proposed a Fourteenth Amendment, building on and extending the terms of the new Civil Rights Act.

Viewed from some angles, this amendment marked the triumph of the "colored citizens." It included a host of powerful new articulations of phrases already found in the Constitution, especially "equal protection" and "due process." It also established these as rights guaranteed by the nation and not to be abridged by states. Most essentially, the Fourteenth Amendment declared that all persons born or naturalized in the United States were citizens of the United States, and of their state. Citizenship would now be national.

But viewed from other angles, the amendment was a grievously missed opportunity to establish political equality. In its original form, devised by the newly appointed Joint Committee on Reconstruction in 1866, the amendment would have given Congress "power to make all laws necessary and proper to secure to all citizens of the United States, in every State, the same political rights and privileges," in addition to the basic protections

of all people's "life, liberty, and property."[36] The final version passed by
Congress made no such explicit promise of federally guaranteed political
equality, substituting instead the vague phrase "privileges and immunities."[37] The Fourteenth Amendment fell far short of guaranteeing black
men the right to vote. Instead, it created a negative incentive: states would
lose representation in Congress to the degree that they did not enfranchise
their otherwise eligible adult male population. The amendment's failure to
specify equality of political rights would haunt the next century of American history.

Far from establishing the robust national citizenship envisioned by the
"colored citizens," the Fourteenth Amendment closely tracked antebellum
white Republican visions. A decade earlier, in his dissent from the Supreme
Court's ruling in *Dred Scott*, Associate Justice Benjamin Curtis distinguished
between "mere naked citizenship," which was established by nativity or
naturalization, and the more extensive "privileges and immunities" citizens
might or might not possess, among them suffrage.[38] This "citizenship"
closely resembled what Abraham Lincoln had in mind in 1858, when he
abjured "social and political equality" for blacks but argued that it did not
follow from this that "the negro should be denied everything."[39] Many
Republicans of the late 1860s, like Curtis and Lincoln a decade before,
believed that national citizenship should protect life, liberty, property, and
the right to sue in federal court, but that these rights were separate and
distinct from the broad range of "privileges and immunities," including
jury and militia service, the right to testify, laws pertaining to marriage
and education, and—crucially—the vote. Which groups of citizens were
entitled to part or all of this extended list of rights was not to be determined by the federal government, but by states, cities, and other kinds of
associations—what historian Michael Vorenberg dubs "the more intimate
community rather than the general one."[40] Such antebellum distinctions
powerfully shaped the postbellum constitutional settlement.

Many black activists and white allies, understanding these limitations
from the outset, deemed the proposed amendment insufficient. Under

these terms, they argued, a state such as South Carolina, despite its substantial black majority, could remain a whites-only polity by accepting a greatly reduced congressional delegation.[41] Charles Sumner spent two days on the floor lecturing his U.S. Senate colleagues on the necessity of black manhood suffrage.[42] Wendell Phillips declared that the amendment's suffrage provisions "concede that this is a white man's Government."[43] But the amendment passed Congress and was sent to the states. Tennessee quickly ratified it and was readmitted to the Union and to Congress, establishing what radicals considered an alarming precedent: reconstruction without black voting rights.[44]

As Charles Mitchell and Edwin G. Walker took their seats in the Massachusetts legislature in 1867, therefore, the proposed Fourteenth Amendment was coming under heavy fire as inadequate to secure a meaningful citizenship for the Southern freedpeople. The fate both of the amendment and of ten as yet unreadmitted Southern states remained unclear. When Massachusetts held its own debate on ratification that winter, opponents of the amendment were well organized.[45] Mitchell presented a petition from Leonard Grimes and others, against the amendment, early in the session.[46] A narrow majority of the legislature's Committee on Federal Relations agreed that the state legislature should not affirm a constitutional change that violated its members' principles.[47]

Then, probably for the first time in American history, a state legislature heard one of its own members articulate the circumstances and desires of the "colored citizens." The floor fight over ratification brought David Walker's son to his feet to argue that the amendment not only violated the spirit of equal citizenship, but in fact ratified racial caste. Permitting disenfranchisement on racial grounds, he argued, even with the amendment's penalties, would establish "a system of serfdom" and "place the men whom the people of the country had called upon, and had used . . . at the mercy of their enemies." It said to the former Confederates, in essence, "'[W]e used the blacks; we know you hate them; we know they helped us greatly; but their interests are not great; we recommend, gentlemen, that you use them respectfully, give them the right to vote, cease to abuse them; we leave the matter with you to settle; do as you please; we leave a place in the constitution large enough, and wide enough, for you to say that the black man shall take no part in legislation.'"[48] Walker's point was one his father might have made—that the Fourteenth Amendment left the Constitution what it had been from the outset: a bargain among white men. Construed in this way, national citizenship was a shattering disappointment.

Events, though, were overtaking Walker's bitter objections. Congressional Republicans, outraged by the black codes and by brutal 1866 riots against the black populations of Memphis and New Orleans, took a step beyond legal guarantees. With the first of the Reconstruction Acts in March 1867, they placed ten of the eleven ex-Confederate states, all but Tennessee, under military rule, with instructions to hold elections for state conventions that would draft new constitutions. Crucially, the elections for constitutional convention delegates would be open to men without regard to race.

While this enfranchisement fell well short of guaranteeing universal suffrage, it did take some of the steam out of Walker's arguments. His legislative colleague, onetime fugitive defender Richard Henry Dana, offered the new legislation to rebut Walker's arguments against ratification, arguing that "the passage of the reconstruction act" by Congress "had essentially changed the aspect of the whole matter."[49] Conventions elected on the basis of adult manhood suffrage would assuredly write constitutions that established nonracial suffrage. Most white radicals agreed, and reluctantly went along with the Fourteenth Amendment as written. A radical Republican newspaper, bowing to the realities, wished the state's legislators would make explicit their preference "that the settlement should be placed upon the simple broad principles of universal suffrage and universal education, embodied in the national constitution."[50] Under the circumstances, though, it concluded that there was nothing to do but "make the best of a bad bungle."[51] In the end, Representatives Mitchell and Walker were part of tiny minorities that voted to reject the Fourteenth Amendment and to replace the ratifying resolve with one asking Congress for an amendment "prohibiting the disfranchisement of any citizen on account of color."[52]

The momentous importance of this "bad bungle" was clear to Walker, but too many obstacles stood in the way of the universal, affirmative claim he would have preferred. Like other "colored citizens," Walker insisted on the removal of the explicit and implicit "white" that almost everywhere bracketed the rights, privileges, and obligations of citizenship. As a practical matter, though, given the resistance to such a position in Congress and even in the Massachusetts legislature, he framed the demand for suffrage as a quid pro quo—as something earned through military service. The argument that those desiring freedom must themselves "strike the first blow" had a noble pedigree, but it also cast the "privilege" of the franchise as something that African Americans had earned, not something to which they were entitled by the simple fact of national citizenship.

Following the election of 1868, Republicans began to discuss what black activists and their allies had been demanding: an additional constitutional amendment that would directly and affirmatively establish black voting rights. Charles Sumner reminded nervous Republicans that this would not only aid the party in the slave states but perhaps provide winning margins in the closely fought and heretofore whites-only electorates of many Northern states. The three thousand adult black men in Connecticut or the fifteen thousand in Pennsylvania might not match the multitudes of South Carolina's freedpeople, but those voters might mean just as much to the party's strength in Congress or the Electoral College.[53] Republicans also noted uneasily what others pointed to as rank hypocrisy: while the Reconstruction Acts effectively required the ex-Confederate states to accept black male suffrage, Congress made no such demand on the rest of the states.[54]

Yet the final constitutional victory of Reconstruction, the amendment guaranteeing voting rights sought by Mitchell, Walker, and so many others, also fell far short of what most black activists and some white radicals envisioned. The Fifteenth Amendment was debated in several forms,

among them Senator Henry Wilson's version, which would have prohibited denying the suffrage not only on the basis of race and color but also
"nativity, property, education or creed," leaving only such bases of discrimination as age, residence, and gender to the discretion of the states.[55]
But Republicans representing a host of more restrictive visions—including
those who opposed black suffrage, those who feared enfranchising Chinese
immigrants, or those who insisted on the continued right to restrict suffrage according to education or property—demanded a far narrower framing. The amendment as finally reported out of committee and presented
to Congress in 1869 guaranteed neither adult male suffrage nor the right
to hold office. Instead, it established that states could not limit suffrage
rights on the basis of "race, color, or previous condition of servitude."[56]
This short list left the door open for disenfranchisement according to many
other criteria.

For all its shortcomings, the Fifteenth Amendment represented a great
improvement on the Fourteenth Amendment, and some saw its ratifica-
tion in March 1870 as enough.[57] "The great battle is over," Joshua B.
Smith marveled to his friend Charles Sumner.[58] Now black activists—the
men, at least—could participate in all of the nation's councils and debates.
It was a time for celebration, and for a parade through Boston. With
Charles Mitchell in command, the procession moved down State Street to
Faneuil Hall.

First in line were the Shaw Guards.[59] Over the past six years they had
become a fixture in Boston's civic culture. During the war, they served as
honor guards for the coffins of the fallen from the black regiments, paraded on the common, and stood ready in November 1864 in case of a
Democratic-inspired election riot.[60] In June 1865, they took part in the
national memorial observance for Lincoln.[61] That September, they received
the 54th Massachusetts on its triumphal return to the city for mustering
out.[62] Shortly after that, the Shaw Guards brought Robert Morris's dream
of black officers to a new height of fulfillment. In 1866, the heretofore
"unattached company" was joined with another company, likely the former

members of the New Bedford Blues, to become the 2nd Battalion of the active militia. A battalion required a major to command it, and Lewis Gaul was promoted to that rank. So in 1870 a black major led his troops through the city to celebrate the great civic victory of voting rights, closely followed, in "the place of honor," by Lewis Hayden, William Nell, and Leonard Grimes. The state's highest elected officials marched along behind.[63]

HEARTS AND MINDS

Even beyond the realms of the government and militia, where laws and elections governed, Boston's free blacks seemed to be moving inexorably from "nominally free" toward formal equality, as barrier after barrier seemed to crumble before the leveling spirit of the age. With the stigma of slavery erased, and with at least a narrowly defined national citizenship confirmed, it was hard to see what respectable bases could remain for exclusion of African Americans from the many "more intimate communities" that together composed the world of human association.[64]

For the leaders of Boston's "colored citizens," nothing more powerfully symbolized this transformation than the breaching of Harvard University's ramparts. The alma mater of white allies such as Phillips and Higginson stood at the apex of American higher education and of local white upper-class prestige. Until the late 1860s, however, African Americans entered within its walls only to cook, clean, and serve. Rare exceptions such as the brief and troubled enrollment of Martin Delany only demonstrated the general rule. In the post–Civil War moment of possibility, however, abolitionist alumni saw another opportunity.

They chose Richard T. Greener, whose boyhood in Boston and Cambridge included both the educational patronage of antislavery elites and deep immersion in the black activist world of the Haydens and De Morties.[65] At sixteen he had stood with the antislavery radicals at the 1860

John Brown meeting in Tremont Temple, later borrowing a pistol from one of the Brown family to help guard Wendell Phillips. During the Civil War, financial assistance from abolitionist elites had enabled him to take college preparatory courses first at Oberlin, where he befriended John M. Langston, and then at Phillips Academy back in Massachusetts. Another patron now persuaded the officers of Harvard to admit an African American student, and Greener enrolled in the fall of 1865. Though he had to retake his first year, he soon flourished, and graduated in 1870.[66]

The second act of Harvard's post–Civil War opening was, if possible, both more impressive and more cheering in its implications for the interracial future. George Ruffin followed right on Greener's heels, entering Harvard Law School in 1866 and three years later becoming its first African American graduate.[67] His experience as an organizer and orator served him well when it turned out that the university's elegant lawns and impressive buildings still nurtured overt prejudice. In 1868 conservative students attempted to exclude Ruffin from the law student assembly on explicitly racial grounds. Rebuked by a majority of their white classmates, the disgruntled minority then turned to Ruffin, asking him whether he insisted on remaining among them despite the objections of "a respectable minority." Such arguments had dissuaded Robert Morris from occupying a home in Chelsea ten years before, but a different man and a different moment produced a different answer. "[H]e was not responsible for the prejudices of the minority, however respectable it might be," Ruffin explained to them. "He was there, a member, entitled to all the privileges and immunities of all other members," and "if their prejudices were so strong that they could not stand him he knew of no better way than *for them* to leave." The startled and dismayed conservatives gave up.[68] Ruffin may even have been surprised at his success: to assert that the "spirit of the age" was inclusive rather than exclusive was a familiar tactic of the "colored citizens," but its success often consisted of moral witness. This time, bolstered by the language of the Fourteenth Amendment and the broad sense that the era of racial exclusion was passing, Ruffin's self-assertion as an equal member of the student body won the day.

Could the same matrix of moral and political claims win the day behind the walls of an equally exclusive fraternity, the Masonic lodge? No form of acceptance outside the realm of state power was more keenly sought by black activist men. Indeed, Lewis Hayden was one of many who imagined the postwar Masonic fraternity as the most likely vehicle for bonds of true affection and understanding to emerge between white and black men. The war had made equality "the spirit of the age." If white Masons now dismissed black Masons simply because they had not been born free, they were working against the "new birth of freedom" that Lincoln had invoked at Gettysburg and that Congress continued to extend. To continue the exclusion based on race, it seemed to Hayden, was "to lead the Masonic fraternity against the government of the United States."[69] So Hayden and other black Masonic leaders reached out to "our friends among the white Masons, for there are such," urging his white neighbors to be his brothers—to accept not only his right to a seat in a first-class railway car or a common school, but his welcome to a position of equality in the fraternal sphere of lodge meetings; to go beyond the formal inclusion represented by nondiscriminatory state policies and include black men in the supposedly universal brotherhood of the Craft. This would be a victory within men's hearts and among them, and would match "the advancing civilization of this enlightened Christian age."[70] Hayden's fellows joined the chorus. "We petition you with seven thousand voices," John Jones urged white Masons in 1865, to "make us heirs at law" to the common Masonic heritage.[71]

Hayden and Jones presented Masonic brotherhood, Christian fellowship, and equal justice under Reconstruction as complementary and mutually reinforcing. "Equal law," Hayden argued, was not just a feature of Reconstruction but a transcendent truth of human law: both pagan and Christian philosophers "attributed to their gods as commanding equal justice to all." The Golden Rule articulated by Jesus was the same "principle of equity" written into America's Reconstruction legislation. The English codifiers of modern Freemasonry took as their founding principle "the unification of the human race." "Now," Hayden argued before his Masonic brothers as a civil rights bill reached the floor of Congress, "this is Heaven's Civil Rights Bill," representing not only "the 'great light in Masonry,' but the laws of our country as well, which to-day know no man on account of color or race."[72]

Black Freemasons took moral and spiritual encouragement from European Masons, who seemed increasingly willing to accept black American Masons as their brethren.[73] One black Masonic leader, a friend of Hayden's, wrote to the United Grand Lodge of England to express his hopes for "the auspicious era when the genius of universal Masonry shall trample in the dust the foul incubus of caste" and "br[ing] our oppressors to the true Knowledge of its *cosmopolitan* and *humanitarian* ideas, which embrace *all* without regard to color or race in a common union, by the still stronger and more indissoluble ties of a common interest and a common brotherhood."[74] By the mid-1870s this seemed to be coming to pass. A flurry of European overtures of friendship culminated in 1875 with the grand lodges at Hamburg, Germany, and Bern, Switzerland, officially recognizing the black grand lodges of Massachusetts and Ohio.[75] Richard Greener lauded these "white brethren who believe in justice and right," asserting that "[t]he unmasonic fabrics of caste are tottering under the strong blows, which these sturdy Liberals of Europe and the true masons of America are striking."[76]

Hayden sought a similar transformation in the hearts of white American Masons, particularly the white Masons of Massachusetts. Although he admitted in 1865 that "the Masons of Massachusetts, the white Masons I mean, have not yet caught the spirit of the age; they are still exclusive, intolerant, and proscriptive," he claimed to find "ground for hope."[77] Black Masons asked their white brethren to recognize "*virtue* and not *caste* as the true standard of man's fitness for the benefits of our Order." The white Masons of the Grand Lodge of Massachusetts—the first white grand lodge in the nation—had not yet officially spoken on the question of black Masonic recognition. They might yet honor the spirit of their state, their governor, and the age. "We await your answer with hopeful hearts," he told his white brethren.[78]

Perhaps change would begin with one man. In October 1867, as the Reconstruction Acts brought hundreds of thousands of black men to the polls across the former slave states, Boston's St. Andrew's Lodge—one of the city's oldest and most prestigious white Masonic bodies—unanimously voted to initiate a man of African descent: Joshua B. Smith, the famous and popular caterer, antislavery militant, and longtime associate of Charles Sumner and others.[79] Charles Slack, one of the very few abolitionists or radical Republicans among the white Masons of Boston, hailed this as "the dawn of a new era in fraternal association," the "first step towards bringing the African Lodges of this State into harmonious relations with the Massachusetts Grand Lodge."[80] Lewis Hayden took heart. In 1868, he and other black Masons from lodges across the state organized a great petition to the Grand Lodge of Massachusetts, seeking recognition and signed by nearly two hundred fifty men working under the Prince Hall Grand Lodge.[81] Claiming inspiration from both the egalitarian "spirit of the age" and the "'cosmopolitan' character of our fraternity," the petitioners left up to the white Masons the means by which they were to be acknowledged in their "equal Masonic manhood."[82] For the first time, such a petition was not immediately tabled but instead was referred to a committee of eminent white Masons. Over the next year, the committee appeared to take its work seriously, even visiting black Masons to examine the charter Prince Hall had received from England in the 1780s.[83]

Hayden seems to have been working behind the scenes to arrange the rapprochement, seeking a formula for recognition that would pass muster both with the suspicious white Masonic leadership and with his own black brethren. When he broke the news of a tentative agreement to his fellows in late 1868, the master of a Springfield lodge responded with surprise and only partly modulated delight at "the early fruits of your sowing, for little did I expect to turn the hearts of modern Pharoah's [*sic*] so soon."[84] But Hayden's friend also carefully outlined the preconditions for any union to come. White Masons must meet black "on equal grounds, as men, and Masons, and not as supplicants or beggars, for we wish no favors, only rights, we will go through no healing process, or anything humiliating, thereby acknowledging ourselves clandestine, and our past existence a lie."[85] Equal association of equal citizens would have to recognize one another unreservedly, in the intimate terms of brotherhood.

No less than a past grand master of Massachusetts's white grand lodge seemed to support these efforts. Winslow Lewis praised Hayden's pamphlets on the legitimacy of black Freemasonry. "[I]f the door of our order was open to all irrespective of color," he wrote, "it would make it, as it should be, truly cosmopolitan," signing himself "your friend and brother according to *my feelings.*"[86] This frank statement offered just what Hayden and the others sought—their welcome as equal participants not just in the realms of law and justice, but also in the worlds of emotional and spiritual life. The first was essential, for without it neither life nor property could be safe. But the first without the second was cold and hollow, a grudging admission that could easily coexist with the constant harassment, disparagement, and mockery by the white North. Both forms of belonging were necessary, and either without the other was ultimately unsatisfactory. Hayden worked and waited for the new day of universal brotherhood to dawn.

Emancipation and victory seemed to be creating openings beyond the gender-specific confines of male colleges and lodges. The late antebellum and Civil War development of women's organizations and public activity reached new heights in the postbellum era, as growing numbers of women became teachers, speakers, and professionals.[87] Black women's names and voices entered the historical record as delegates to conventions, officers of organizations, authors of books, and makers of speeches. More important, this visibility signaled that women were moving into positions that would mark them as self-determining and self-respecting participants in society's work—the criteria that most people of the era thought necessary for formal citizenship.

While black men worked to dismantle the barriers of caste that barred them from white associations, black women claimed roles that challenged the inequality of sex in a wide range of associations. The women of both the African Methodist Episcopal and AME Zion churches demanded the right to preach and hold formal offices in church societies, and by the 1870s they were winning, aided by longtime male champions of women's rights.[88] Many of the same women simultaneously claimed new formal roles in what had once been "fraternal" life: during and after the Civil War gender-integrated associations flourished, such as the Brothers and Sisters of Love and Charity, in which John S. Rock played a leading role. Meanwhile, orders restricted to men established female auxiliaries.[89] The scattered women's auxiliaries of the Heroines of Jericho gave way in the 1870s to a national women's Masonic auxiliary, the Order of the Eastern Star, which was already flourishing in white Freemasonry.[90]

It was in this context, nearly forty years after she entered the campaigns against slavery and for equal rights, that Harriet Hayden at last became visible as a public figure in her own right. In 1875 she was the founding president of Boston's Prince Hall Auxiliary Association, composed of the female family members of leading Prince Hall Masons.[91] The association raised funds for a new Masonic hall, and for black Bostonians' observance of the national centennial the following year. Association member Eliza Gardner, an antislavery veteran and a leader in the movement to expand women's rights in the AME Zion church, explained that "although ignored to a certain extent . . . yet we are American citizens . . . Our fathers, and *mothers, too*, fought to secure that glorious boon of liberty."[92] At their centennial celebration in 1876, the women heard Lewis Hayden praise their efforts—from serving the nation to raising funds for a new Masonic hall—and declare that although the men of Massachusetts had not yet "recognized your rights," none should rest "until every human being is made equal before the law."[93] In 1884 Harriet Hayden led a fund-raising meeting of the group at an AME Zion church, this time at last addressing the audience herself with "a few appropriate remarks."[94] She was also active in a women's temperance club that had left the Order of Good Samaritans because of its white members' resistance to integration, joining the more welcoming Good Templars.[95]

Habits of propriety and laws of coverture no longer masked Harriet Hayden's contributions, or her character, from broader public view. In the 1880s a visiting journalist lauded her neat and decorous appearance and the "kindness and openhandedness" with which she greeted visitors, before turning to less anodyne and conventional assessments. He noted her heretofore unpublicized "trenchant wit," and an unexpected ferocity. The memory of slavery, he wrote, could still evoke a powerful reaction in her; as she recalled the days before her escape, "a strange, hard look came into her eyes and the resolute lines about the mouth became more pronounced."[96] This was no superficial posture. After Lewis Hayden's death, Harriet would wrangle publicly with old associates, including George Downing and Mark De Mortie, whom she perceived to have slighted her husband's provisions for his own burial.[97] The apparent distance between this figure and the "happy and industrious wife" praised in Douglass's newspaper in 1853 raises the question of what roles she might have silently assumed in earlier days, before such things could comfortably be noted publicly about a "respectable" woman.[98] During the height of fugitive defense in the early 1850s, when the Haydens' parlor served as an arsenal, was she among those who carried the weapons and readied them for use?

THE RACIAL POLITICS OF EMPLOYMENT

While a few men achieved elected office or obtained degrees, more obtained federal patronage positions within the gift of local Republican leaders. The possibility that abolitionists might be appointed to federal positions had been a nightmare of the Southern slaveholders, and one of their rationales for secession. Once those slaveholders had left Congress in 1861, Republicans indulged their practical and symbolic wishes, appointing not just white radicals but soon also black men to a host of state and federal positions. Mark De Mortie, appointed messenger by Boston's federal collector of customs in June 1861, thus became the second black ward heeler on Beacon Hill, after Lewis Hayden, to obtain a Republican patronage position.[99] With his subsequent appointment as sutler to the 54th Massachusetts, he undoubtedly became the first to hold two such positions.

Real access to the patronage meant more than a few token offices. The more numerous positions in the federal bureaucracy, particularly the post office, remained closed until 1864, when Charles Sumner succeeded in opening them. This proved a godsend to several up-and-coming men, including Lieutenant James Trotter of the 55th Massachusetts, the man who had persuaded John Andrew's emissary, and the somewhat older but perhaps even more grateful William Nell.

Proud to have become the first black postal clerk, Nell was even happier when that position finally enabled him to marry. In April 1869, at the age of fifty-two, he wed a young New Hampshire woman, Frances Ames. Ten months later she gave birth to their first child, whom they named William. Soon the Nells moved into lodgings of their own.[100] About this late but apparently happy marriage Nell publicly said almost nothing, but it is possible, between the lines, to speculate that he found husbandly contentment: "I seldom go out evenings," the formerly irrepressible organizer told William Lloyd Garrison in 1873.[101]

Yet the employment of Nell, his nephew, Ira Nell Gray, and a dozen other African Americans in the Boston post office still left the great majority of the city's black population stuck at the bottom of the wage scale. Racial discrimination continued to exclude them from many workplaces and most labor unions. In the middle of the war, white caulkers at the Boston Navy Yard walked off the job rather than tolerate a single black caulker in their midst. It was June 1863, and the military officer in charge simply dismissed the men.[102] But this was a distinctly new phenomenon; much more often in the antebellum and war years, private employers either preferred to run whites-only shops or acceded to their employees' demands that they do so. White hostility to black workers, usually simmering, could also come to a murderous boil, as it did in New York City during the draft riots of July 1863.[103] Blacks would not gain employment in most white-run enterprises so long as the majority of white workers had anything to say about it.

With emancipation, some white laborers began to consider the reality of emancipation through the lens of labor solidarity. Four million freed-people, one white Boston man reflected in 1865, were "about to enter the field of free labor. If we take them upon equal ground with ourselves in the contest for the elevation of labor, they become an ally; but if we reject them—say we will not work in the shop with them . . . [t]he black man's interests and ours are severed."[104] Many white labor leaders, including some who found association with African Americans personally distasteful, shared this concern.[105] The nascent National Labor Union addressed itself directly to white Northern workers' feelings in its Address of 1867: African American workers, "[u]npalatable as the truth may be to many," could help build a united labor movement—or, if excluded, contribute to its failure.[106] Would white workers be so "blind and suicidal" as to allow this to happen?[107]

The short answer, it turned out, was yes. African American workers were not themselves visionaries of interracial labor alliance. Accustomed to exclusion by white labor unions and workers, they had no habits of solidarity with those workers' struggles. So when the white workers in the Boston freight house of the Boston and Albany Railroad went on strike over a wage decrease in April 1868, it was not terribly surprising that within two days their places were taken by "colored laborers," or that a "squad of police remained during the week to guard the men from interruption."[108]

Those black workers' path to employment on the railroad reveals the tight and symbiotic linkage between laboring black Bostonians and elite white employers, and the mediation of that relationship by black political leaders. The day after the strike began, Judge Thomas Russell, an old Free Soil ally who was both the federally appointed collector of the port and a corporate officer of the Boston and Albany, approached Lewis Hayden and Mark De Mortie "to see if we could furnish enough able-bodied men to fill the places of the strikers."[109] It was Sunday morning, so De Mortie and Hayden "wrote notices and had them read in all the colored churches requesting all able-bodied colored men that wanted permanent work to meet us at the Union Progressive Association," a Cambridge Street club and literary society founded by Nell. One hundred twenty men signed up that afternoon, agreeing to meet De Mortie early Monday morning at a hotel across the street from the Boston and Albany depot. This was not a simple patron-client transaction, but an opportunity for negotiation as well. De Mortie and the workers insisted that the positions be permanent and that the wages be the same as those offered the striking workers. When the management agreed, De Mortie reported, they went to work.[110]

Charles Slack's *Commonwealth*, a paper as friendly to black aspiration as it was skeptical of labor agitation, presented this as a triumph of free labor, pure and simple. In his view "Irish laborers" had gone on strike "without notice, and apparently without cause." That Slack's own rise to political power came through the Know-Nothing wave of the mid-1850s made the charge of Irish fecklessness both predictable and cost free.[111] But it did not make his accusation true: in fact, the original workers had gone on strike because management unilaterally imposed a cut in their daily wages from $1.75 to $1.50. The black workers who subsequently took the jobs were offered $1.60.[112] Slack made no mention of the wage cut, instead presenting the new rate as a victory for African American employment by announcing "the blacks are now at work with ten cents more per day than the Irish received!"[113] The "Irish," who had struck rather than accept the $1.50 wage, would not have seen it that way, for in fact the African American workers now staffing the freight house were at work with fifteen cents less per day than the strikers had formerly earned. From a white unionist perspective the black men were low-wage strikebreakers. Yet they were earning $1.60 more per day than any black worker could previously have earned in the all-white shop of the freight house. White recalcitrance brought other such victories: in 1872, the refusal of white wet nurses at the Massachusetts Infant Asylum to suckle black infants led to the hiring of several black nurses.[114] In what was still a racialized society, labor solidarity remained a distant dream.

Workers in the main remained segmented by race and party, and employers' class interests quickly trumped partisan divisions among them. The Republican alliance between black workers and white employers served capitalists of all party persuasions by forcing down the wages of both white and black workers.[115] Capitalists, both Republicans and Democrats, considered the racialized strikebreaking a heartening development. Abolitionist-turned-executive Thomas Russell offered a warm note of thanks to Lewis Hayden for his efforts in securing him a black labor force. "The thing works to a charm," he effused, and the president of the railroad, though "a strong Democrat . . . is very much pleased." Furthermore, "the example will be followed in other places. So you did a good Sunday's work."[116] This "example" portended how easily white Republicans would establish partnerships with their old rivals and enemies. Over the following decade, moneyed white men in politics across the nation would reach across the party divide to find common ground against working people. In South Carolina they called together "Taxpayers Conventions" to demand retrenchment in public expenditures; in New York a state commission sought to accomplish the same purpose by restricting New York City voting according to property ownership. Everywhere, they insisted that the people with the greatest economic stake should also have a disproportionate political say. This moment marked the beginning of Boston's own movement in that direction.[117]

The Boston and Albany strike also demonstrated that black workers could serve to disrupt white men's collective action. In Boston, although black workers were never numerous enough to replace whites across any industry nor powerful enough to bargain hard on their own behalf, employers found them useful to divide and defeat white laborers. The employment of black men as strikebreakers became a regular feature of labor struggles during the postwar decades. Once white workers had feared competition from ex-slaves fleeing the Confederacy; a decade later, white employers recruited carloads of black workers to undercut white workers in the Ohio valley coalfields.[118] Black Bostonians' early roles in these developments suggested the continuing difficulty black workers would have making alliances with the rest of the nation's working people. Workers from a range of backgrounds, pressed to choose between whiteness and the stigma of associating with African Americans, asserted their whiteness, in part by adopting the white republic's customary hostility to working alongside blacks.

These well-established patterns of identity and enmity among workers were not disrupted by the end of slavery, undermining black hopes for a broader sense of belonging. And yet from the perspective of Boston's black laboring people, a foot in the door in an enterprise such as the Boston and Albany could yield lasting dividends. Twenty years later, the company's station in the city remained staffed by "all colored employees."[119] In a racially segmented and discriminatory labor market, black workers had seized a prize. If elevation was the key to acceptance, perhaps this bird in the hand had value. The steady wages and comparative respectability provided by railroad work made it evidence of individual worthiness: when leading black citizens lobbied the mayor for a minor patronage appointment in the 1880s, they sought to demonstrate a candidate's worthiness not only by mentioning his Republican Party activism and fraternal membership, but also his employment with the railroad.[120] More tangibly, to take one example, the regular earnings allowed one deacon at Twelfth Baptist to buy "a beautiful home" in Somerville, which he left to his widow without encumbrance.[121] In other words, employment at the Boston and Albany Railroad became one of the better-paid forms of work available to a significant number of black men in the city, and a tangible symbol of what the alliance with powerful white men could mean. Solidarity with white workers, on the other hand, remained largely hypothetical, in Boston and beyond.

UPLIFTING THE SOUTH

The vision of the deacon's "beautiful home" in Somerville captured in miniature much of what black Northern activists believed was possible, not only for themselves, but for the millions in the South now emerging from slavery's shadow. Ties of family, faith, and work would no longer have to beat constantly against the demands of owners and overseers. The stigma of slavery would no longer mark people of African descent as a group apart, either in law or in the hearts and minds of their countrymen. Southern blacks could therefore remake themselves as a people, casting off illiteracy and suspicion and "rising" into well-organized social and political life. They would become wage laborers and independent proprietors, Methodists and Baptists, Freemasons and Republicans. They would aspire to the same things as their Northern brethren, because these were the hallmarks of prosperity and respectability.

Northern black activists assumed they would play a critical role in the transformation of illiterate slaves into elevated citizens. Most—especially those who had themselves been slaves or lived as free people in slave states—understood the obstacles standing in the way of freedpeople's aspirations: the reluctance of most whites to accept black people's aspirations as legitimate, and the legacies of deprivation that limited freedpeople's options and perspectives. Both internal and external obstacles would have to be overcome if the victory over slavery and the Confederacy was to yield more than just the end of legal bondage—if "freedom" was to mean something like "equality." The black activists who sought to work this transformation naturally turned to the organizations they had developed over generations in freedom, and to the ideas of uplift and self-improvement that undergirded them. They turned south bearing what they believed to be critical wisdom, skills, and discipline, which, importantly, they also believed most freedpeople lacked. They were, in a word, missionaries.[122]

Even during the war, black Northern leaders assumed that they had important lessons to impart to recently freed slaves. Speaking to the men of the 5th Cavalry, many of them reared in slavery, John S. Rock spoke to them as though they required significant refashioning to meet the criteria for respectable citizens. "[W]hen you have vanquished the enemies of your country and of liberty[,] come home to the bosoms of your families and enjoy the rights and privileges of freemen," he urged them. "Then we shall expect you to educate and prepare yourselves and your families to become useful and respected members of society." Rock had previously argued that African Americans could gain the respect of whites only by achieving first an inner self-respect that was mirrored in public deportment. But here he took that argument several steps further, implying that the mass of African Americans required more education, polish, and discipline, and that Northern black leaders—Rock's "we"—would stand in charge and in judgment of that process.[123]

By mid-1864 many black Northerners were reaching the same conclusion. A Boston meeting that summer resolved that, as people who enjoyed "superior advantages to those of our people in other States," black residents of Massachusetts shared a responsibility "in behalf of the less fortunate portions of our race" to share "words of practical wisdom."[124] Leaders from across the region agreed to meet that fall, to decide how to coordinate the important work to come. With critical battles for the race to be fought on both sides of the battle lines, they sought to rally the nation's free black citizens around a common program. "[W]e feel that it is highly important that we shall appear as *united* as possible at this time," John Rock explained in his argument for a national convention.[125]

Rock's "as united as possible" turned out to mean "as united as usual," which was to say, not very. The National Convention of Colored Men that convened in Syracuse, New York, that October was dominated by Northern men and Northern preoccupations, and was, at moments, breathtakingly provincial.[126] For a group hoping to "look after" millions of freedpeople, the convention's delegates indulged in considerable skirmishing over small matters of personal prestige. More than two decades after Douglass and Garnet's dispute over antislavery violence at the 1843 convention, the two men's competition for the presidency of the convention caused their allies to collide with "considerable feeling." Garnet and Downing meanwhile continued their antebellum argument over the African Civilization Society, despite the efforts of other delegates to compromise or redirect the conversation.[127] Massachusetts men feared being numerically overwhelmed by the "domineering and overbearing" delegations from Pennsylvania and New York.[128] Meanwhile, not one of the Southern delegates, representing seven slave states and the District of Columbia, was invited to address the convention. Instead, the leadership continued to rest with the same men, all of them free since before the war and all of them based, at least for the moment, in Northern cities and towns.[129]

Northern black leaders soon began carrying their light and truth to the freedpeople. Henry Highland Garnet concluded his speech with a call "to look after the education of the people of the whole South," where the preponderance of the nation's black population resided. "[W]e need," he said, "to prepare to plant ourselves Southward."[130] In the years to come, many of the Northern delegates to the Syracuse convention headed to the South to take part in the rebuilding of regional life after slavery. In the spring of 1865 George Ruffin journeyed back to Virginia, and on his return spoke "encouragingly of the colored people there, who need only a chance to improve and show the brilliant effect of freedom."[131] The initial response from the free black leadership of the former slave states was not encouraging: Washington's black leadership, for instance, bridled at being patronized and criticized by Charles Lenox Remond; the Yankee did not understand the challenges of free black life in the heartland of slavery, where people labored "day and night to bring all our forsaken people here to the surface."[132]

Many understood the foremost task to be bringing the freedpeople a well-mannered Christianity appropriate to their transformed status. The impact of Northern denominations was rapid and immense. The AME church, the antebellum denomination with the greatest resources on which to draw, quickly reestablished itself in Charleston, where authorities had banned it in 1822, and organized a conference that spread up and down the Atlantic seaboard and west into the cotton country. The Southern conference rapidly grew to fifty thousand members, the size of the entire prewar church.[133] Its missionizing ministers quickly became central figures in freedpeople's social and political lives: Brooklyn's Richard Harvey Cain began as a Methodist organizer in South Carolina and ended up a U.S. congressman; Hiram Revels, a Methodist minister born free in North Carolina and educated in Ohio, gained the confidence of freedpeople in Natchez, Mississippi, who launched his star in the Reconstruction South by sending him to the state senate. Other denominations also planted themselves southward. New York's James Walker Hood pitched his tent among the freedpeople of North Carolina, establishing congregations for the AME Zion church and helping write the new state constitution.[134] The Reverend Peter Randolph, a Boston resident on and off since his emancipation from Virginia slavery in 1847, headed to Richmond at the urging of his ministerial colleague Leonard Grimes. Acting as an intermediary between the freedpeople and the nascent Freedmen's Bureau, Randolph addressed political meetings and started an independent Baptist congregation.[135] A steady stream of migrants would play critical roles in the spiritual, political, and educational lives of the freedpeople.[136]

These missionaries sometimes competed with one another and always battled former slaveholders, but they struggled in common too with the freedpeople's mode of worship. Churches and ministers promoted a particular vision of propriety as part of a broader program that sought to remake the freedpeople in the image of their already free brethren. Many hundreds of thousands of people already felt God's presence, but they did not always worship in ways the leaders and ministers of Northern churches found appropriate—their illiteracy, and especially their emotional, spontaneous style of worship reminded ministers and bishops of the worst excesses of their own Northern congregations.[137] Bishop Daniel Alexander Payne of the AME church, who spent the 1840s and 1850s promoting an educated ministry and more decorous styles of worship, brought that message south after the war; in 1866 his church established a literacy requirement for ministers, to the dismay of many former slave preachers and their congregations.[138] Freedpeople, whose spiritual striving had taken wing under very different circumstances, did not always conform to Northern visions of "elevation." Congregations fractured as some within them rejected unwelcome strictures, preferring to worship in their own ways.[139]

These difficulties did not surprise a missionary of another kind, Lewis Hayden, as he sought to bring Freemasonry south. He understood the challenges confronting the freedpeople as arising both from their past enslavement and their present subjection. Slavery had denied black Southerners the right to organize their own lives, families, and communities. The resulting discord, Hayden believed, could "only be removed by associations of the strongest possible ties known among men"—the ties of Freemasonry, which for him combined the moral and spiritual upbuilding of the church with the broad secular vision of transformation embodied by the radical wing of the Republican Party. "[A]s there are [no ties] known to men whose obligations and duties are so sacred or more holy than ours, we feel that when they have taken upon themselves such obligations, and as they progress in the lessons therein taught, confidence is restored, and each can trust the other with safety; and, in place of confusion, discord, and ruin, each heart is filled with those truly Masonic virtues, 'brotherly love, relief, and truth.'"[140] He was hardly alone in assigning Freemasonry this transcendent importance: many others carried the tools of Freemasonry south in their carpetbag of uplift, including Bishop James

W. Hood, who established Masonic lodges among the freedmen as enthusiastically as he did AME Zion congregations.[141]

Hayden traveled south in the summer and fall of 1865 on a mission to establish lodges in Virginia and the Carolinas, and his report late that year to the Prince Hall brethren reflected his empathy for people making a new life in freedom. He had been a slave himself just twenty years before, and he understood that the legacies of slavery and caste would take time to overcome. In Charleston and Petersburg, he happily reported, he found "united and harmonious" communities forging institutions and accumulating property. In Richmond, though, the people he met "did not present so hopeful an aspect, so intellectual nor so dignified a character" as at the other places. They had only "obtained a room in which to form the Lodge with great difficulty," and among them, in the former capital of the Confederacy, Hayden sadly noted "jealousies and bickerings." But this was to be expected. "[I]n the emerging of nations or people from a state of oppression," he explained, "more especially when the oppressor is allowed to prey upon them, there must be jealousies and want of confidence in each other."[142]

Efforts such as Hayden's and Hood's helped the Masons and other groups root themselves in the South, but the explosion in associational life among the freedpeople far surpassed the sum of Northern missionary efforts.[143] From the perspective of Boston, the freedpeople seemed to be embracing the institutions so painstakingly built by black activists, and preparing themselves for their full enfranchisement. Black Southerners whose journeys had not taken them out of the South, however, often saw things differently. The postemancipation Southern landscape included many associations of local origin and development. Freedpeople did not need Northern activists to teach them how to organize and protest illtreatment, whether at the hands of former slaveholders or of occupying Union soldiers.[144] They embraced these new forums—lodges, conventions, and no-longer-clandestine churches—as places in which to work out their

understanding of freedom, equality, and justice, but they also transformed them.

AMBASSADORS OF THE RACE

Black Northern activists conceived of themselves not only as missionaries,
but also as ambassadors, emissaries who would demonstrate to the nation's
leaders how far the race had already come. This began even before the end
of the war, with the pinnacle of John S. Rock's brief legal career. In early
1865, the day after the Thirteenth Amendment passed Congress, Charles
Sumner appeared in the United States Supreme Court to present John S.
Rock's credentials; that day he became the first African American admitted
to its bar.[145] Less than two years later Rock was dead of consumption,
buried with honors by the Freemasons and by the gender-integrated order
in which he had played a central role, the Grand United Order of Brothers and Sisters of Love and Charity.[146] He did not live to argue a case before the nation's highest court, but others would.

Of all slavery's former homes, no place promised ambitious Northern
activists as much as the nation's capital. The Republican Congresses of the
middle and later 1860s sought to put Washington D.C. at the vanguard of
racial equality, to serve as "an example for all the land."[147] In the years that
followed Rock's admission to the bar, the capital's opportunities for Republican patronage and officeholding presented an irresistible point of
entry for those who sought to aid the freedpeople, advance their own careers, or both. Not only were the city's laws—enacted initially by Congress
over the protests of local whites—a model of what radical Republicans
envisioned. As the locus of Republican power during Reconstruction,
moreover, the capital offered a wide range of opportunities to lobby for
policies and, not incidentally, for oneself. No surprise, then, that the postbellum capital drew some of the most capable and successful of antebellum

and wartime activists.[148] A brief look at the southward trajectories of the intermarried Downing, DeGrasse, and De Mortie families suggests how far the influence of Boston's black activist community spread during Reconstruction, and how important the Republican Party and Republican governments in the former slave states were to that movement.

No one played a larger role in Washington's postbellum emergence as a key locus of African American political life than George T. Downing. Always an itinerant, accustomed to having his hands simultaneously in the political worlds of Boston, Rhode Island, and New York, Downing moved to Washington D.C. in 1865. There, his friendship with Charles Sumner helped him win the concession to run the dining room for the U.S. House of Representatives. Downing's extensive political experience and personal skills made him an important figure in coordinating the national lobbying

George T. Downing
*Courtesy of the Schomburg Center for Research in
Black Culture, New York Public Library*

efforts first envisaged at the 1864 Syracuse convention. "Congress has been occupied heretofore almost exclusively with the colored man as a slave; it now has to deal and legislate with him as a freeman," Downing explained.[149] He eagerly took on the job, supported in part by donations from New England and Pennsylvania black activist groups.[150] Other federal patronage positions were offered, including the collectorship at the port of Newport, but Downing was for the moment committed to his role in the capital.[151] Others seeking entrée to the federal patronage soon flooded him with letters, and he became in reality as well as name the ambassador of black America to official Washington.[152] In 1866 he joined Douglass and a few other men in a widely publicized meeting with President Andrew Johnson.

Men like Downing and his brother-in-law John V. DeGrasse—who was perhaps happy to get out of Boston after his humiliating discharge from Union service—were much in demand in Washington during the heady years of Congressional Reconstruction. Radical Republicans such as Sumner kept up regular conversations with Downing and others, either through face-to-face meetings in the House restaurant or in correspondence.[153] As the Senate considered civil rights legislation for the federal territories in 1866, Sumner wrote urgently for DeGrasse's assistance: "Help—by petitions—and better still by your committee here personally to visit Senators."[154] In 1869 Downing and Frederick Douglass began work on a new newspaper for the capital, one that would represent African Americans even more effectively.[155]

Such highly educated and polished people considered themselves to be the lobbyists best suited to sway skeptical Republican congressmen. In 1869 Downing held a reception in honor of Ulysses S. Grant's inauguration as president, to which he invited leading white and black Washingtonians. This was "a fine stroke of social political diplomacy," wrote Downing's admiring biographer, for many of the white political figures present "knew of the colored people only as freedmen, refugees and contrabands" but in this venue "had their eyes opened to the realities of a large, powerfully intellectual and highly cultivated social side of the colored question."[156] Downing, whom opponents periodically and unjustly charged with discriminating against black patrons in his establishments, was navigating the complicated politics of race and class, offering whites leading examples of what the freedpeople could become, given time and direction.[157] While he did not and could not see the "colored question" in precisely the same terms as white Republicans, he implicitly agreed that "refugees and contrabands" were not the best ambassadors for the race as a whole.

Washington was only the most visible destination for black Northerners, who put the lessons and connections of their earlier experience to work in every reconstructed state. Mark De Mortie first headed west, settling in Chicago and entering into a range of businesses with John Jones. Perhaps it was the city's commodities market that led him into his next line of work, sassafras oil; in any case, he soon relocated to Virginia, where he set up a production facility. There, he and his second wife, George Downing's daughter Cordelia, helped build and sustain schools; De Mortie himself twice ran for Congress.[158] An erratic Boston lawyer, Aaron A. Bradley, became a key figure in Georgia's abortive reconstruction.[159] Many more, including Richard Greener, took part in South Carolina's more enduring Republican government. More broadly, the Northern antebellum conventions, fraternal organizations, newspapers, and movements against slavery and for equal rights provided many of the leading black figures of Southern Reconstruction. No matter where one turned in the region's political and organizational life in the decade following emancipation, one encountered black men and women who traced their political or organizational roots back to the antebellum black activist world, and often to Boston.

One of the most potent symbols of the free South's transformation was in fact a product of the black Northern organizational world. On January 20, 1870, Hiram Revels set the new high-water mark for African American political achievement when the legislature of Mississippi selected him as that state's next U.S. senator.[160] A freeborn North Carolinian educated in the Midwest, Revels was a minister in Baltimore when the Civil War broke out; he became a recruiter and a chaplain in a black unit stationed in Mississippi, where he remained as a minister at war's end. He was elected to the state senate in 1869 and emerged as a compromise candidate for black Republicans, who were determined to put one of their own in one of the state's two vacant seats in the U.S. Senate.[161] Revels's educational and professional attainment—fruits of his free birth and long residence in the North—helped him rise far beyond what he imagined or perhaps even sought.

No African American had yet been seated in Congress when Revels arrived. Southern Democrats in the U.S. Senate waged a bitter rearguard action to refuse him his place, arguing that the Constitution did not contemplate blacks as citizens, and that the Fourteenth Amendment could not naturalize a native-born inhabitant. In closing, these white supremacists rued the "great calamity" of a black U.S. senator, offering it as evidence that "Revolution is rampant."[162] Indeed it was. Over the dissenting votes of eight senators, the U.S. Senate admitted Revels to the seat vacated by Jefferson Davis at Mississippi's secession in 1861. The new senator's wife, escorted by a beaming George Downing, watched from a seat in the gallery, where she was visited by Republican lawmakers eager to be properly introduced to the wife of the Senate's first black member.[163]

"Here is the Fifteenth Amendment in flesh and blood!" declared Wendell Phillips a few months later, as he introduced Revels to a Boston audience assembled at Tremont Temple to hear the senator speak on "The Tendency of the Age."[164] The state's Republican governor also welcomed Revels at a reception at his home, to which he invited the state's Republican leadership—and three men from down the hill: Reverend Leonard Grimes, George Ruffin, and Lewis Hayden.[165] Grimes was ill that night and unable to attend, so Hayden, Ruffin, and Revels likely were the only black men in the room who were not servants.

Hayden, pondering the heights reached by his freeborn comrades, may have been moved to reflect on his own aspirations. His friend Ruffin, a year out of Harvard Law School, was already serving in the state legislature, and Revels was the nation's man of the hour. In 1872 the former fugitive decided it was his turn. Hayden sought and won the Republican nomination for the state legislature from Ward Six, the one black man on a three-man slate, and in November he was elected. His militant comrade from Anthony Burns days, Joshua B. Smith, won election in his Cambridge district that same night.

Sitting in the chamber, the two old rebels must have smiled to themselves at the difference twenty years had made. It was not that the well-armed insurgents of the 1850s would mock their older selves for sitting here placidly in long black coats and ties, debating legislation, for those younger men had been politicians as well, busy even then with committees and resolutions and petitions. It was that these battles were so much happier. Back then slavery had seemed an almost insuperable foe, equality before the law an elusive dream. Now, in an emancipated nation whose Constitution made black men eligible to vote and declared them equal before the law, they peacefully debated the next phase of the great work of liberty and equality. Hayden and Smith both voted aye to an amendment to the state constitution that would open the door to woman suffrage; the amendment failed by a significant margin, but supporters of universal suffrage would be back, again and again. Hayden also reminded his colleagues that, just off the country's shores, hundreds of thousands of Cubans remained in slavery.[166] Many great battles had been won in the past few years, and if they kept pressing surely these last pillars of the old order would fall as well. As Senator Hiram Revels reminded them in his Tremont Temple speech, and by his very existence, universal freedom and citizenship were "the tendency of the age."

The scope of Reconstruction's triumphs could be felt everywhere, from individual accomplishment to the reshaping of the nation's constitutional order. The political culture forged in the free black North found its footing in previously unfriendly terrain—before the bar of the Supreme Court, in legislative halls and colleges, and across the liberated provinces of the defeated slave regime. These achievements, however partial or imperfect, seemed to promise a new era of continuing ascent and achievement. But there were signs, too, that the nation's new openness, like the invitation to military service just a few years before, did not come in warm and welcoming tones, but as a hedged and cramped inclusion. Even as the unmistakable triumphs followed one after the other, many Americans, like the recalcitrant Democrats who rejected Revels's very right to serve in the Senate, struck up a furious chorus of opposition. By the beginning of the 1870s, which of the age's tendencies would win the day remained an open question.

9.

"The War of Races"

ewis Hayden returned from his 1865 Masonic organizing trip to the Southeast full of grim words about the intentions of the former slaveholders, which he described as "a deep and unalterable purpose in the hearts of the old oppressors to blast, or at least to crush out, the rising hopes and dawning prospects of their late bondmen." Indeed, before another year had passed, whites in Memphis would rise up to slaughter, rape, and beat freedpeople, and to destroy their newly created institutions. This was no spontaneous explosion, but a well-orchestrated pogrom: it began the day after most of the black Union soldiers in the city had been demobilized and compelled to surrender their government weapons. By the time U.S. troops arrived, the rioters had killed scores, injured many more, and burned every school serving black children.[1] Nor would this be the last time violence on this scale struck at the freedpeople's aspirations. Hayden had correctly foreseen what would happen to the former slave if left to the mercies of the former slaveholder. "God help him!" he concluded. "For Andrew Johnson will not."[2]

That prediction, too, was soon borne out. In February 1866, Johnson met with a delegation of black leaders, among them George Downing and Frederick Douglass, who appealed for equal citizenship and black suffrage to make freedom meaningful. The president responded by depicting national life as a racial contest in which one group must prevail and the other be dominated. African Americans, he lectured the delegation, had been the great beneficiaries of the war. Nonslaveholding whites had been the great losers. Was it fair that blameless white men who had never owned a slave should have their misfortune compounded by having black voting rights forced upon them without their consent? "No!" concluded the president. Indeed, to proceed on such a course would be to "commence a war of races" that would lead to "the extermination of one or the other."[3] Whether this constituted a threat, a warning, or both was not immediately clear. That Andrew Johnson would not be their ally, however, was plain.

The fear Johnson's words inspired among the "colored citizens" was somewhat muted by the fact that most already knew him to be their enemy. By contrast, William Lloyd Garrison's May 1865 call to disband the American Anti-Slavery Society struck black activists with the unexpected force of a winter gale. "Slavery being abolished," the editor argued, all would be well; "the change that has done that work will cooperate with us, and speedily give the colored man all his rights."[4] Garrison not only seemed suddenly eager to rely on "change" to do the work of establishing legal rights, but he also passed silently over the grand and controversial name he had first wanted for his antislavery society more than three decades before: "Philo-African." Black activists reminded him in vain that the AAS's founding declaration had not simply demanded the end of slavery but also sought for "the colored population of the United States all the rights and privileges which belong to them as men and as Americans." Garrison brusquely dismissed these arguments, describing that "other work" as "incidental" to the society's purpose.[5]

Charles Remond knew better than to place his trust in fickle "change." "Put the question nakedly to the American people to-day," he responded angrily, "whether they are prepared for the entire and full recognition of the colored man's equality in this country, and you would be voted down ten to one."[6] He was only slightly too pessimistic. In fourteen states across the postbellum North, efforts to extend the suffrage to black men failed in the early postwar years; by 1868 only Iowa and Minnesota voters had provided popular majorities for black male voting rights.[7] New York City's successful 1867 mayoral candidate declared that "[t]he people of the North are not willing . . . that there should be negro judges, negro magistrates, negro jurors, negro legislators, negro congressmen."[8] John Brown's body had lain a-moldering in the grave less than ten years, and his soul showed no sign of marching on.

As the "colored citizens" emerged from the Civil War with visions of completing their project of national belonging, whites across the nation found many ways to limit what that citizenship meant. Violence shaped Southern Reconstruction, as freedpeople met with threats and attacks from those who were unable to tolerate the end of slavery or were searching for forms of racialized labor control that could survive emancipation. Beyond this, conservative voices first decried "equality," then sought to limit its meaning. Insisting on the continuing salience of race, the president of the United States was one of many to warn that African American aspirations to a full stake in American life would bring only a violent backlash. The triumphs experienced during the 1860s and early 1870s by Lewis Hayden, George Ruffin, and other antebellum and wartime leaders were real, but so was the determined, often ruthless opposition facing them.

Hard as they tried to shape the fate of Southern Reconstruction, black Northern leaders quickly discovered that it would shape their fates at least as much. While the vast new Southern free population offered possibilities for political and social transformation, it also threatened to swamp the institutional frameworks and procedures black Northerners had built over the preceding generations. How to translate the values and practices of the small and scattered antebellum Northern free black world into the vernacular of mass politics among a largely unlettered population remained a vexing question.

Southern Reconstruction also reshaped and clarified black Northerners' alliances with whites. While antislavery whites forgot that they had once committed themselves to universal equality, white Republicans calibrated their deference to black Northern political aspirations according to how important black men's endorsement seemed to be in a given year. Black Republicans soon realized that they were valued much more for their symbolism than their individual or collective contributions. When black Republicans attempted to play other parts—to champion party candidates not favored by the leadership, or to bring their numbers to bear in the rough-and-tumble of a campaign—they quickly found themselves described as a mob, a group as unfit for political life as Irish immigrants or former slaves. Yet the high-stakes contest playing out across the South also shaped black voters' calculations about whether it was safe to split with their frustrating Republican allies. As black activists on Beacon Hill and across the North pondered their alliances and their hopes, the continuing struggle in the former slave states informed their every decision.

The laws and amendments devised for the reconstruction of the South did not erase the stigma attached to blackness, not even in the North. Northern whites by and large did not vote to enfranchise their own black populations, and most states remained whites-only polities until the passage of the Fifteenth Amendment. In the more nebulous but deeply felt realms of social inclusion and exclusion, African Americans also experienced powerful rejection. White Northerners might accept that the end of slavery had made citizens of all persons born or naturalized into the United States, but courts, legislatures, and orators drew tight bounds around what rights that "citizenship" implied, and what realms were subject to the Fourteenth Amendment's guarantee of equal protection. As Masons and militiamen, as surely as in their roles as Republican voters, black Northerners found themselves excluded in all but name, sternly warned—

as Robert Morris had been in Chelsea, as George Ruffin had been at Harvard Law School—not to seek an unacceptably intimate "social equality."

"THE REBELLION IN ANOTHER FORM"

As whites resisted equal black participation in political and economic life with assaults and assassinations, and as blacks and their white allies vigorously responded, the Reconstruction South sometimes seemed to resemble Johnson's "war of races," a clash pitting black against white in a contest for racial supremacy. This was manifestly not the case. A significant number of whites, both native Southerners and people recently arrived from the North, took part in Republican state and local politics across the postwar South. Most Republican state officials were white, even in those states with outright black majorities.[9] Democrats' depiction of these politics as essentially polarized by race, and of the Republicans as "the party of the negro," sought to refashion the region's struggles as contests between races, rather than between parties, programs, and economic interests.

Although it was not a "war of races," concerted, violent resistance against black Southerners and their white allies did powerfully shape the politics of Reconstruction. Vigilante violence perpetrated in the name of the Ku Klux Klan, the White Brotherhood, and innumerable other clandestine assemblies struck repeatedly the efforts of freedpeople and their allies to remake the South and the nation. The assassination of black leaders, the intimidation of white allies, the scourging of black men and women who asserted themselves in any realm of Southern life—all of these fostered a black Reconstruction politics that was of necessity partly paramilitary, relying on networks of mutual defense, and on a sometimes vigilantly enforced racial solidarity in support of the Republican Party.[10] George Downing, facing an anonymous Klan threat on his life unless he left Washington, could shrug it off. A white or black Republican in the Southern hinterland could not.[11]

The Republican Party proved only fitfully able to defend its Southern allies. In some places, substantial black majorities built networks of solidarity and self-defense that kept white terror to a minimum and allowed the shoots of black freedom to blossom.[12] But elsewhere, as Hayden had predicted, landowners seeking control over laborers and former political leaders seeking a return to power set strict limits on former slaves' "rising hopes and dawning prospects."[13] When elections drew near, the incidence of terror and intimidation surged across the former slave states. This palpable resistance to federal authority finally provoked Congress to enact a series of Enforcement Acts, also known as Klan Acts. The first of these, in May 1870, created a federal administration to implement and enforce the Fifteenth Amendment, and additional laws over the next twelve months extended and clarified the federal government's power to use lawyers, marshals, and deputies to supervise elections, to identify and arrest offenders, and to try them in federal court.[14]

Republican state officials also took action to defend their polities against paramilitary violence, but the campaigns of terror compounded the weaknesses of these governments and left them vulnerable. In 1870 North Carolina's native white Republican governor, William Holden, used state forces to suppress the Klan in two counties where white and black elected officials had been assassinated. His government also locked up suspected Klansmen under a suspension of the writ of habeas corpus. This vigorous state action backfired, allowing Democrats to depict Holden as a tyrant and helping them retake the legislature, which promptly impeached Holden and removed him from office in early 1871. Both the anti-Reconstruction violence and the state power required to suppress it left many white Northerners dismayed. Over the next few years, more and more came to see the politics of Reconstruction as dispiritingly messy and difficult and to wonder how long the federal government would have to garrison the former Confederacy. The victorious Union—its white majority, at least—began to reconsider the costs and risks of the entire Reconstruction enterprise.

While white Republicans, north and south, drew cautionary lessons about the perils of vigorous enforcement, black leaders felt keenly how much was at stake. In April 1871, in the wake of Holden's impeachment, Massachusetts state representative George L. Ruffin warned his legislative colleagues that "the same spirits which plunged this country into blood" were "now seeking to accomplish by scourgings and assassination the country's ruin." "[R]oving bands of cut throats and desperadoes, defying the laws of God and man," sought "the extermination of Republicanism" by driving away its white supporters and terrorizing its black constituency. It was "the rebellion in another form, the Southern Confederacy in disguise," plotting to install a Democratic president in 1872 and nullify what ex-Confederates deemed the "unconstitutional" measures of Reconstruction. The suppression of the Ku Klux Klan, Ruffin argued, was therefore just as essential to the survival of the nation as the wartime destruction of the rebellion and of slavery. "[U]ntil it is put down and the loyalists are secured in their rights . . . from the violence of those who have been against our government and would subvert it," he warned, "the rebellion is not ended." But he was not optimistic.

Looking ahead, Ruffin tried to set a brake on the fatalism that would accompany a defeat in this continuing Civil War. "If in the attempt to build free institutions on the ruins of the Confederacy whose Corner Stone was Slavery, there shall be a breakdown and failure, it will be no proof that Freedom is not good for all, and that the people of that section are not entitled to its beneficial effects," he wrote. Rather, it would be "an indication that those to whom have been intrusted the sacred symbols have proved recreant and that Liberty has been betrayed."[15] Not for the last time, Ruffin would prove prophetic.

ANTEBELLUM ALLIANCES AT THE CROSSROADS

The destruction of slavery forever altered the antebellum and wartime alliances forged between blacks and whites, but not in the way black Northern leaders wished. Not every white abolitionist took Garrison's position in 1865, leading to bitter splits among white allies as well as between white and black. Nor was this the end of division within the fractured antislavery world, for the unfolding of Congressional Reconstruction also brought serious strife over the issue of woman suffrage. Congressional Republicans quickly established black men as a voting power in Southern elections, a matter of political necessity bolstered by the moral claim of men who had fought for the nation. But as this policy worked its way into the Constitution during the debate over state suffrage referenda and the ratification of the Fifteenth Amendment, supporters of women's voting rights split. Some were willing to accept the political realities of the moment and celebrate the victory for black male suffrage as a step toward universal suffrage; others rejected suffrage for black men unless it was accompanied by votes for women.

Old allies began to choose sides. Susan B. Anthony, faced with an 1867 Kansas election in which the questions of black male and woman suffrage were raised in separate referenda, accepted financing for her campaign from an openly antiblack supporter. Two years later, at the suffrage movement's 1869 convention, the knowledge that the pending Fifteenth Amendment did not include woman suffrage deepened the sense that suffragists had to choose sides. Frederick Douglass articulated the pragmatic case for putting black men's suffrage first. "I do not see how any one can pretend that there is the same urgency in giving the ballot to woman as to the negro," he opined. "When women, because they are women, are hunted down through the cities of New York and New Orleans . . . then they will have an urgency to obtain the ballot equal to our own." To the query "Is that not all true about black women?" Douglass responded, "Yes, yes, yes; it is true of the black woman, but not because she is a woman, but because she is black." Anthony's rejoinder eloquently blended genuine frustration with racist condescension. "The old anti-slavery school," she complained, "say women must stand back and wait until the negroes shall be recognized. But we say, if you will not give the whole loaf of suffrage to the entire people, give it to the most intelligent first . . . let the question of woman be brought up first and that of the negro last."[16] With the lines drawn in this uncompromising way, Douglass resolute on the primacy of racial oppression and Anthony all too ready to portray blacks collectively as ignorant, little could be done to heal the breach. The suffrage movement fractured that year into two competing groups, not to reunite until 1890.[17]

After the Fifteenth Amendment achieved ratification in 1870, without the support of New Jersey, Nebraska, Oregon, or California, the Massachusetts folks in Douglass's camp remained committed to woman suffrage. The Massachusetts arm of the new American Woman Suffrage Association, which included Lewis Hayden, Thomas Wentworth Higginson, and Josephine St. Pierre Ruffin, remained friendly with the state's Republicans, despite that party's hesitancy to do so much as pass a woman suffrage resolution at its 1870 convention.[18] Black legislators from Ward Six were at the forefront of woman suffrage activity within the state party, repeatedly presenting petitions and voting in favor of suffrage efforts.[19] In the early 1870s, as the local movement worked to elect women to the Boston School Committee, white suffrage leaders turned to Lewis Hayden for help and advice in organizing his and other wards.[20] But by then the peak of legislative support for woman suffrage had passed. In the immediate aftermath of the Fifteenth Amendment, legislative majorities, but not the necessary two-thirds, voted in support of a state suffrage amendment. A few years later, when state representative Lewis Hayden sat on the committee charged with receiving woman suffrage petitions, the prosuffrage bloc could not even muster a majority in the lower house.[21]

Throughout the era, proponents of woman suffrage struggled against the linkage of political rights to military service. By the postwar decade, this linkage seemed almost as natural to antislavery men as it did to their opponents. Antislavery radicals had always been among the strongest supporters of women's rights, including the rights of political citizenship, yet the growing emphasis from the 1850s through the Civil War on martial participation as the key to citizenship seems to have shaped and constrained radical men's political imaginations, making citizenship's virtues seem more explicitly martial and male. John Brown once refigured Harriet Tubman as a man in order to make sense of her as a political and military leader; by the late 1870s, the reality of black men's Civil War military service threw an even longer shadow over all discussions of women's voting rights. In 1876, when Lewis Hayden articulated the case for woman suffrage before an audience of black activist women—one that included his wife and colleague Harriet Hayden—he staked women's claim to political citizenship in the weakest possible realm: that of military activity. After a recitation of African Americans' historical claims to the American Revolution, he reached further into William Nell's kit bag and drew from *Colored Patriots* the story of Deborah Gannett, a woman who disguised herself as a man in order to serve in the Patriot army. "With such a record," Hayden concluded, "do I ask too much when I say 'Ere another centennial rolls around, may you be possessed of these rights which your sister, as proved above, performed her part in securing, not alone for men, but for women as well.'"[22] A century in the future, in other words, women would vote because in the distant past a few had stealthily served their country under arms. If this was the best a committed women's rights man could do, the outlook for woman suffrage was bleak indeed. Martial manhood, one among many components of the African American struggle for full civil equality, had become the sine qua non of political citizenship.

The stresses of political combat, combined with the high-stakes contest unfolding across the South, revealed new tactical and personal strains among the black leadership. In early 1870, when several Massachusetts congressmen voted to readmit Virginia to the Union despite its resistance to black political equality, Lewis Hayden both publicly thanked Charles Sumner for his firmness on the question and chaired a meeting to criticize one of the other men, Samuel Hooper, for his vote.[23] But a counterassembly denounced the "high-handed assumption" by which Hayden claimed to speak for the "colored citizens of Boston." Some of his friends and allies rallied behind him, but in terms that suggested deep strains within the community. While Edwin G. Walker blamed Republicans for failing to repay their black supporters with appropriate offices, Charles Remond also blamed "the colored people" for seeming to fear "that some one among them would be raised a peg higher than the rest." George Ruffin made it clear who was the intended victim, complaining that "the present meeting was got up to kill off Lewis Hayden."[24]

The cruelest blow came from a familiar hand—that of Hayden's longtime colleague and Masonic brother Robert Morris. The lawyer had a reputation for being a witty litigator, playing on his witnesses' prejudices to excite laughter in the courtroom. In this instance he made Hayden the butt of the joke. Irritated that Hayden presumed to speak for the "colored citizens of Boston," Morris offered a lengthy critique of the previous meeting, then brushed back an interjection from Hayden with the words "Shoo fly, don't bodder me." This was the title and chorus of a hit minstrel song, and just days before, in the U.S. Congress, Benjamin Butler had used these very words to call laughter down on a Democratic rival. Butler's expression was widely reported, and Morris's repetition of it drew a hearty laugh from the crowd, at Hayden's expense.[25] Ruffin may have been exactly right about the meeting's purpose: as the hall cleared, a band of black musicians played the tune "Shoo Fly, Don't Bodder Me," as if to underline Morris's dismissal of Hayden.[26]

The trouble between the two men may have been political, Masonic, or even religious, for the crosscutting fractures between them were many years in the making. Morris had long imagined himself in political office, and although Hayden had not yet achieved election at this point, Morris may have recognized that his own chances of attaining elected office were nowhere near as good as those of the Beacon Hill ward heeler's. Morris may also have felt slighted by Hayden within the grand lodge: in a "stormy" Masonic assembly earlier in the decade, Morris had faced an unexpectedly serious challenge to his campaign for grand master of the Prince Hall Grand Lodge. Perhaps he blamed Hayden, for years the lodge's most influential man, for what he had or had not done during this struggle.[27] Morris's own religious transformation likely also played a part. During the 1850s Morris's wife, Catherine, had converted to Catholicism, and after a period of personal struggle her husband joined her as well, first attending Mass at the nearby Church of the Immaculate Conception, then in late 1870 being baptized and formally received into the church. Morris's work and residence among a largely Irish Catholic population had led him, finally, to a spiritual home outside the black Protestant denominations.[28] In accordance with the church's strictures, he no doubt left Freemasonry as well. Either departure—from Protestantism or from Masonry—might well have set him at odds with Hayden. The former fugitive was then entering his most active period of Masonic pamphleteering; what was more, his close alliance with the Know-Nothings seems to have been more than expedient. Beyond his anti-immigrant reflections during the 1840s, Hayden took the opportunity of an 1865 grand master's address to the Prince Hall brethren to describe Protestantism in all its forms as necessary to "the preservation of civil and religious liberty," and to compare Protestants' struggles against numerous evils, especially slavery, to the closed-minded actions of the "Romish church."[29] Morris cannot have appreciated the comparison.

Their colleague William Nell, for his part, no longer enjoyed this kind of personal and political combat. Perhaps he never had. In any case, by the early 1870s he had taken a long step back. Now a husband and father, he sought larger quarters and moved beyond the ward, a change he found "in many respects advantageous and agreeable." He had always sought to be "useful without personal prominence in Colored Ward Six politics," he remarked to William Lloyd Garrison. But he was glad to be "free from the unacceptable under support wire pulling and ambitious rivalries, and clannish demonstrations so prevalent there for many years past."[30] After decades of work, even some of the most devoted activists were wearying of partisan struggles.

THE REPUBLICAN ALLIANCE FINDS ITS LIMITS

Once Garrison shuttered the *Liberator* at the end of 1865, the Boston newspaper that best reflected black leaders' hopes and fears was the radical Republican *Commonwealth*, edited by their longtime white ally Charles Slack. In his columns the Free Soil man turned Know-Nothing turned Republican explained to those outside the abolitionist circle that "[t]o the negro himself slavery . . . means persecution without law. So long as colored men are shot in Texas, held in practical bondage in Kentucky, and denied the right to vote in Pennsylvania . . . so long slavery does exist and anti-slavery societies have their work to do."[31] For the most part, black leaders urged voters to support Slack's party, even when old friends stood opposed. In 1870, when Wendell Phillips ran for governor on a Labor Reform ticket, Lewis Hayden counseled his fellow black voters to reject the old abolitionist hero in favor of the Republicans.[32]

But black leaders learned hard lessons about their place in the Republican Party. Under certain conditions, white Republicans seemed ready to acknowledge African Americans' individual and collective contributions and to honor their place in the party. National and state Republican leaders understood the disproportionate influence that Northern voices and institutions could have among the freedpeople, many of whose political leaders were black and white Northerners. White Republicans counted on black allies to fly the party flag and encourage the greatest possible turnout for Republican candidates locally and across the South. Black leaders in turn relied on the party to stand firm against the Democrats, the Klan, and the other forces threatening their unsteady purchase on formal citizenship, and they repaid the party with strong and steady turnout. But this was not a relationship of equals. When Boston's black Republicans sought to assert themselves in defiance of white leaders' decisions, they quickly discovered that local white Republicans were determined to keep black power confined to limited, mainly symbolic realms.

Boston's black leadership occupied a curious and often uncomfortable position in the Republican Party. The Massachusetts Republican establishment was composed of industrialists, entrepreneurs, urban elites, and useful men whom those power brokers came to trust. The party enabled them to protect their own interests, encourage economic development, and most of all prevent the reins of government from being seized by laborers, Democrats, or others with wild ideas about inflation, taxation, or expenditures. Black activists stood well outside this establishment. Their heroes were the Republican radicals, men who championed both an expansive vision of national citizenship and a resolute approach to Southern enforcement. By the early 1870s, with Klansmen rampaging across the South and federal power seemingly always at least a step behind, Boston's black leadership yearned to embrace a champion more interested in protecting freedpeople than restraining public spending.

They found that champion in Benjamin Butler. The former general entered the postwar era as an ardent foe of Andrew Johnson and a proponent of radical Reconstruction policies including confiscation of land, universal nondiscriminatory voting laws, and unsegregated public education.[33] He insisted that the ex-Confederate states respect the rights of their black residents and that they not be allowed to participate in national deliberations until they did so. When Georgia's state senate summarily expelled its black members, Butler insisted this was sufficient cause to exclude the state's representatives from Congress.[34] In 1871 he was an architect of the Klan Acts.[35] He denounced a hostile New York City crowd as draft riot murderers who were not "the equal of the negro."[36] He was, needless to say, wildly popular among Boston's black leaders.

The state's white Republican leadership viewed the expert, unscrupulous Butler rather differently. The former general was bald and portly, with
jowls like a hound dog's, but he was a remarkably agile political animal,
and lethal on the stump. Accusations of financial corruption periodically
threatened to bring him down, but nothing ever quite stuck. Meanwhile,
he freely proffered conspiracy theories and outrageous charges, confirming
elite Republicans' sense that he was beneath them and unworthy of the
high offices he sought. Yet he knew his Massachusetts constituency better
than his opponents did and he repeatedly defeated conservative Republicans' efforts to unseat him, in one case taunting an elite challenger into
revealing his own disdain for the working-class voters he hoped to woo.[37]
He presented himself as the friend of the laboring man, a role far more
common among Democrats—one of which, of course, Butler had been not
long before.

Butler's decision to seek the governorship in 1871 set black Bostonians
and their elite coalition partners at odds in an election shaped less by the
politics of Southern Reconstruction than by racialized political contests
that had recently unfolded in New York and Philadelphia. In those key
Northern cities, voter turnout, suppression, or fraud could easily turn a
state election and might even decide the outcome of a presidential election.
Elections therefore involved military and paramilitary forces on an unprecedented scale. Democrats hired operatives or, if they controlled city government, deployed police to suppress black and other Republican turnout
and to encourage their own voters. Meanwhile, Republicans deployed federal officials and deputies authorized under the Enforcement Acts and
crafted separate regulations aimed at curtailing the number of immigrant
voters. In New York's 1870 elections, Republican federal officials used one
of the Enforcement Acts to deputize more than six thousand men to supervise the city's election, while their foes in the Tammany Democratic city
administration stationed twenty-five hundred policemen at those same
polling places.[38]

In Philadelphia, home to the North's largest black population, the stakes were higher still, and political combat sometimes ceased to be a metaphor. In the city's October 1870 elections—the first Pennsylvania election since 1838 in which black men were eligible to vote—black voters turned out in large numbers despite predictions of violence at the polls. Republican enforcement here seemed to work; when rumors spread that black men would not be allowed to vote, the federal marshal called in the U.S. Marines.[39] But this enforcement also generated a backlash resembling that in the South. The following year, Philadelphia's Democratic city officials used the presence of black men at the polls as a pretext for threats and violence, and defined federal action in black voters' defense as "tyranny." In the run-up to the 1871 elections, Democratic newspapers in Philadelphia decried a "general conspiracy to obtrude the military power into elections, and to extend, gradually to the North, the system of military coercion that was introduced in the Southern states."[40] The city's Democrats accused Republicans of importing black men to vote their ticket and intimidate would-be black Democratic voters, fostering the notion that black Republicans represented a threat to good order in elections.[41] The party's journals threatened black voters with "a warm welcome" if they sought to vote multiple times. But, as in the South, partisans took more careful and considered aim than such amorphous threats implied. On election day in October 1871, Democratic operatives gunned down Philadelphia's leading black activist, Octavius Catto, and two of his colleagues. No one was punished.[42]

This was the context in which Massachusetts's white Republicans responded to Butler's candidacy and to his black supporters in 1871. When Butler began his campaign by addressing black Bostonians at a Ward Six church, they responded to the gesture with affection and enthusiasm, declaring him the "true friend of the negro."[43] But the party establishment united against him, arguing that Butler would bring to Massachusetts the urban "bossism" and corrupt, money-greased politics of New York's Democratic Tammany Hall—the synecdoche for political corruption in all its forms.[44]

The presence of so many black supporters made the charge that Butler portended "Democracy" more than a little incongruous, for black supporters symbolized one of the essential differences between the Republican Party and its rival.[45] So anti-Butler Republican journalists blended the charge of Democratic "bossism" with the Democrats' own partisan countercharge: that Republicans mobilized an unthinking mob of black voters to do their bidding. Interleaving their own playbook with that of the Democrats, they depicted the intraparty struggle over Butler's nomination in terms that resembled the white supremacy campaigns taking place in the Deep South, mobilizing deep-rooted white anxieties about black people as an ungovernable mob that intimidated or overwhelmed its social betters, and that only state violence could subdue.

The rival factions collided that September at the Ward Six Republican caucus to select delegates to the Republicans' statewide nominating convention. In this meeting, the voting for chairman occurred by division of the house, with supporters of each candidate moving to opposite sides of the hall. Here, the *Boston Morning Journal* asserted, the Butler forces swelled their numbers by repeatedly moving to the rear of their ranks after clerks counted them, some being tallied two or three times.[46] The *Daily Advertiser* added to this the charge of "violence," consisting of "incursions from the Butler side of the house, where several colored voters who had deliberately chosen their course were collared, dragged by force to the other side and held there" to be counted among the general's supporters.[47] All of this alleged chaos took place just during the organization of the meeting. The chicanery allegedly continued in a struggle over the voter registration list, with George Ruffin asserting that the official checklist was incomplete and producing his own, longer list of voters. Anti-Butler forces claimed that their opponents were trying to eliminate all safeguards against fraud, and they bolted from the caucus to nominate their own delegation. When they attempted to take the official checklists with them, "a number of colored individuals actively engaged in endeavoring to take away the voting lists from the departing Republicans," but were prevented by police on the scene. The black men in question, one paper reported, "acquired broken heads, and were tossed about in a manner cheering to contemplate, by the valiant police, who used their clubs liberally."[48]

Black Republicans responded with outrage both to the fracas and to its coverage, and Democratic newspapers were keen to heighten the schism within Republican ranks. Under the headline "Our Colored Citizens," the Democratic *Boston Post* published an interview with George Ruffin and his colleague Dr. Charles Miller, framing the story as a rebuttal to the "libellous aspersions upon the conduct of the colored citizens of the Sixth Ward" by Republican papers. In this report, Ruffin claimed that all but "two or three" black Bostonians supported Butler: "He has always been our friend and we don't forget it." Miller accused the "Beacon Street aristocracy" of having "bought and sold our people and led them around by the nose for a good many years, and they are tired of it." This might have been a Democratic fabrication, but a final note rang true: Ruffin and Miller denied that police had used clubs, insisting that the only force employed the previous night was in taking the checklist away from the bolters.[49] Perhaps they were correct, or perhaps they did not want the image of white policemen cracking black men's heads to define their place in the city, state, and nation.

The frustration felt by Ruffin and other black Republicans boiled over at the statewide nominating convention, as anti-Butler forces contested the seating of Ruffin's Ward Six delegation. Anti-Butler men claimed that in the controversial caucus meeting "[b]oys of color and of Irish parentage voted again and again" amid "violence and the most disorderly conduct." Ruffin responded by accusing his fellow Republicans of behaving more like Democrats: one of the anti-Butler contestants, he claimed, "made the assertion that he had seen colored men vote twice," though a "short time before he had sworn he didn't know one nigger from another."[50] His frustration did not alter the convention's rejection of Butler's bid.

What happened after the convention exposed the profound limits of African Americans' leverage within the party. In defeat, the black Republican leaders of Ward Six understood that they had fences to mend and took "conciliatory measures." They sent men who had not been at the controversial caucus meeting—Hayden, perhaps—"bearing the olive branch of peace" to "the gentlemen on the other side of the hill," asking to be allowed to choose which black man would serve on the ward's three-man slate for the legislature. The white Republican leaders refused, a rejection that left black leaders stunned.[51] Perhaps they were, as Democrats charged, simply the lackeys of the "Beacon Hill aristocracy." "If the plantation lash was ever more stinging to the blacks of Carolina than this contemptuous treatment is to their intelligent brethren of Ward Six," crowed a Democratic paper, "the fact has not yet been developed."[52] "[T]he black residents of Ward Six are to be punished for daring to have an opinion of their own, and for seeking to exercise that opinion," agreed a fuming George Ruffin.[53]

But what choice did they have? Ruffin swallowed his pride and agreed not to press his own candidacy for the legislature, but insisted that someone must take his place. Tempers flared and talk of a split from the party began. Someone, probably Hayden, lowered the temperature with a reminder that the power of the black voting bloc on Beacon Hill rested only in the fact that it could be "considered a unit."[54] "So long as [black voters] vote together they will be of importance," Hayden later argued; "the moment they divide they will be of no account."[55] In this instance that advice seems to have gone unheeded. George Ruffin retreated from the party that had wounded him and accepted the nomination of the numerically insignificant Labor Reform Party—a bastion of Butler support—for state attorney general.[56] The Democrats, sensing an opening, put two black men on their ticket, to which the white Republican leadership responded by selecting one of the very few prominent black men in the ward who opposed Butler. At the polls, this Republican ticket crushed the black Democratic protest ticket.[57] The Republicans' black candidate ran more than a hundred votes behind his ticket-mates, perhaps the true measure of black Republican disaffection.[58] The African Americans of the ward, accustomed to thinking of themselves as possessing a degree of political leverage generally known only in the Reconstruction South, now discovered that their legitimacy as political actors had shallow roots indeed.

What leverage they did retain rested primarily in their periodic symbolic value to the party. As early as 1868, when rumors circulated that Democrats would seek to divide the black vote by nominating Republican Salmon P. Chase for president, the managers of a Faneuil Hall meeting in support of the Republican ticket took care to have a black North Carolina politician on the stand, avowing his people's party loyalty.[59] Lewis Hayden must have had a hand in this, for a week later Judge Thomas Russell sent him a small gift to pass on to the speaker, and the word "not to be afraid of repeating what he said at Faneuil Hall, especially what he said of Chase."[60] A black representative of Southern Reconstruction could speak with authority to an audience of white Massachusetts Republicans.

Four years later the regional tables had turned, and the party required black Northerners to rally their Southern comrades. As Republican president Ulysses S. Grant sought reelection in 1872, he faced a challenge from a coalition of disgruntled Republicans calling themselves "Liberal Republicans," a small-government, hard-money movement hostile to federal enforcement in the South.[61] The Liberals chose New York editor Horace Greeley as their candidate, and Democrats endorsed him as well, which gave the challenge real weight. The unexpected support of a leading radical, Charles Sumner, who loathed Grant for his efforts to annex the island nation of Santo Domingo, sent Republicans scrambling to firm up support among black Republicans.[62] They had reasons to worry: Robert Morris told a Democratic newspaper that "the Republican party has done nothing for the negroes," and both Ruffin's friend Charles Miller and Hayden's neighbor and Masonic brother A. W. A. DeLeon joined the Liberal Republican caucus that fall.[63] George Downing publicly countered Frederick Douglass's arguments for Republican loyalty, arguing that on questions of civil rights the two parties could scarcely be told apart.[64]

The real danger of such defections lay in their symbolism. Boston's black voting population was not large, and Sumner was only one among scores of senators, but together they and he were symbolically resonant. Some white Republicans publicly worried that if the black men of Boston and their famous white ally endorsed the Liberal Republican view that the regular Republicans were not the friends of the race, "this misrepresentation" might be sent "flashing across the wires through the Southern countryside and used as political capital," depressing Grant's turnout among the freedpeople and costing the party congressional districts, governorships, and perhaps even the presidency.[65] Conversely, if Sumner's endorsement of Greeley could be publicly countered among his longtime neighbors and allies in Ward Six, its impact might be immediately blunted.

Most black activists ultimately found it more important to prevent the Democrats from seizing the White House than to spite their infuriating white allies. With the stakes as high as they could be, they closed ranks. Hayden had frequently chaired meetings celebrating "the good work done by the republican party for the colored people," and in 1872 he stepped up again.[66] Even George Ruffin agreed that they had "to fight the old fight over again." William Nell, rarely a participant in such postbellum meetings, rose to denounce Greeley's Democratic Party as "from its organization to the present time the unrelenting enemy of our race."[67] Ruffin agreed, describing Greeley as a "colonizationist" who foresaw "that some day or other we will not be in this country."[68] Frederick Douglass, on hand in Boston for this important occasion, made the case for Grant in dourly pragmatic terms. Perhaps there had been some slights from the Grant administration; perhaps the president was not a warm friend of the race in every respect. But presidential politics were too important to make such matters definitive. If Grant "did not want to take a negro to his table, and yet stood between their race and the tie of human bondage, he should not be thrown aside" for a Democrat who would make no such promise.[69] The formal victories of the past five years must be protected. The millennium of human brotherhood seemed far off, and the presidential election very near.

Grant defeated Greeley handily in November, and in the course of that campaign Boston's party leaders restored the city's black leadership to their former place. Black Republicans including Remond, Ruffin, and Hayden made up more than half the ward delegation to the state convention, and several "colored battalions" formed that summer to support Grant and Wilson. Black voters, so easily brushed aside in 1871, seemed suddenly indispensable.[70] It was in this election that Lewis Hayden finally took his place on the Republican ticket, and in the legislature.

Like a bad dream, though, Butler's renewed bid for the governorship in 1873 revived the drama of two years before. Black activists' sense of urgency had not diminished. As a punishing economic depression pre-occupied the nation, black voters and Republican officeholders faced resurgent white terror in the South. The spring 1873 massacre of black militiamen at Colfax, Louisiana, the worst single episode of white suprem-acist violence during Reconstruction, loomed large in their thoughts and imaginations.[71] But Butler was again defeated, and this time the rupture between black and white Republicans was not so easily repaired. Butler's black supporter's nominated a rump ticket, and whatever rapprochement was attempted did not succeed. Lewis Hayden, the incumbent elected in the banner year of 1872, was dropped from the legislative ticket for Ward Six, and this time no other black man replaced him.[72]

The November election was the moment of truth. Would the dismissal of the party's black leadership hurt the Republican ticket? Some radical Republicans clearly thought so, and initially the postelection fallout seemed to support that judgment. Turnout in the ward was low that November, even for an off-year election.[73] Perhaps as a result, the Republicans' candi-date in the state senate district that included Ward Six fell a few votes short of his Democratic opponent. Slack's *Commonwealth*, siding with the dis-gruntled black Republicans, crowed that the blame lay squarely with the white Ward Six leadership. "The lighter-complexioned people on Beacon Hill thought they could get along without Lewis Hayden and the colored people in the recent election, and so left Mr. H. off the Representative

ticket, he having served but one year. His race, most unobtrusive, not desiring to go where not wanted, refrained from voting, to the number of two
hundred or so." That was why the Democrat had taken the seat.[74] But on
a recount the result was reversed, and the Republican took the seat despite
weak black turnout. Black Republicans' bluff had been called, and they
proved not to have the political weight to punish the party.

This did not mark a final rupture between black activists and the party
generally. Lewis Hayden returned to his position as messenger in the office
of the secretary of state, and he and others remained visible in party affairs.[75] But 1873 did mark an end to the alliance between the ward's white
and black leaders. In 1874, demoralized black Republicans fractured. They
failed to agree on a black candidate for the ward ticket, and the white
candidate they ultimately supported was defeated. No black man represented the ward for the next several years.[76] By then, the national 1874
Democratic wave had ejected Republicans from the governorship and
some of the state's congressional seats.[77] White Republicans increasingly
kept their distance, excluding black Republicans from ward clubs and
public events around the state, while Boston's black Republicans established their own clubs and maintained the tradition of separate marching
companies.[78] The alliance between white and black Republicans was beginning to resemble the Civil War's segregated regiments more than it did
"Freedom's army."

"A CENTRALIZED EMPIRE"

As frustrating as the Republican alliance became, it remained essential
because of conservatives' steadfast opposition to the federal enforcement
of equal rights. Postbellum conservatives argued that the federal efforts
to consolidate and defend the citizenship rights of African Americans
portended—or indeed constituted—tyranny. "We are drifting to consolidation and empire," wrote former Confederate vice president Alexander

Stephens in 1869. Over the next few years the Fifteenth Amendment and the acts enforcing it only confirmed his fears.[79] In 1870 Stephens accused U.S. attorney general Amos Akerman of seeking to erect "a Centralized Empire over the ruins" of the old republic.[80]

Stephens wrote these words as a political exile and outsider, but the early 1870s were kind to his views. Three years later, his home state of Georgia was firmly in the hands of white Democrats, and Stephens was elected to the U.S. Congress. There, the tiny, indomitable champion of the old order earnestly protested the 1874 civil rights bill. The federal government, he held, could act only to guarantee the security of individuals, their property, and their access to the courts.[81] Any further guarantee or enforcement was an unconstitutional usurpation—again, "tyranny." Stephens claimed that the extension of national citizenship to African Americans was only the immediately pressing case, and not in fact the cause of this fear of "centralization," but it hardly mattered which was chicken and which egg: conservatives saw the extension of federal authority and the extension of new rights and protections to African Americans as two sides of the same debased coin.

Black activists harbored no doubts about what motivated these conservatives. At a convention of Colored Citizens of New England during the election of 1872, George Ruffin explained that when Liberal Republicans and Democrats decried Grant as a centralizing dictator, they took aim "not in reality against him but against us, against the interests of the colored people." The cry of "centralization," he argued, "means that the power of protecting us against the midnight raids of armed bodies of men, and defending us at the ballot-box, should be taken away from the Federal Government and we and all our dear and blood-bought rights should be left to the tender mercies of the Kuklux." Other white and black radicals understood the charge of "centralization" in just these terms.[82]

Yet Stephens was not the only one who entered the postwar world carrying the assumptions of the era just past. Although postbellum African American activists vigorously rejected the "great truth" that continued to

motivate their Confederate nemesis—"that the negro is not equal to the
white man"—they did enter Reconstruction with their own hesitations
about centralized authority. On the one hand, their experiences, from *Dred
Scott* to wartime service to Reconstruction lawmaking, confirmed what
Martin Delany had long before intuited: that their fate as American citizens
ultimately rested with the national government. A host of factors demanded,
in Lewis Hayden's earnest words of 1867, that "the unity of the Government may be ever maintained: for all our hopes as a people are involved
in the issue, extending even to that of life and liberty."[83] On the other hand,
for decades they had operated in a world of small and scattered populations linked by the decentralized institutions of churches, lodges, and
conventions. Leadership in these venues came without formal power and,
perhaps more important, was always subject to discussion, dissent, and local ratification. Their contentious, vibrantly democratic political culture set
powerful brakes on efforts to create national structures.[84]

Both "centralization" and the emergence of the Southern freedpeople
as a potent political force presented unexpectedly serious challenges for
black Freemasonry, and for the black political culture it represented. The
order developed and emerged as a training ground within and among
small Northern communities, and helped develop political subjectivities
among people who might aspire to vote or even hold office in the secular
world. Its members, though, had never confronted the possibility that they
might actually form governing majorities. The Reconstruction South offered a radically different prospect. African Americans made up substantial minorities in most Southern states and formed outright majorities in
three. After 1867, when the Reconstruction Acts effectively created adult
manhood suffrage rights, Masonic lodges might no longer simply be a
training ground, but a place of organization and solidarity for a new, mass
politics. Some antebellum Masonic leaders considered this possibility with
hope and seized the moment to spread Freemasonry rapidly across the
new frontier. Others, Hayden among them, looked on with growing trep-
idation, for this was a critical turning point for the black leadership of the

North: the order could remain a small training ground for the gradual development of a leadership class or, like the Republican Party, it could become a vehicle for broad political mobilization. It was not clear that it could be both.

The great opening of Reconstruction exacerbated these divisions, pitting rival camps against one another in a revealing battle over the nature of postemancipation political leadership. Did new times and a newly freed population require new measures and approaches? Or should the established formulas developed in the antebellum North govern the freedpeople's incorporation and uplift? The revolutionary pace of change suggested the former, but those who proudly claimed descent from an ancient font of wisdom felt compelled at least to pause.

Black Freemasonry entered Reconstruction already struggling with questions of governance and expansion.[85] On one side stood the fraternal entrepreneur Richard Howell Gleaves, the man who helped extend Masonry through the Ohio and Mississippi River valleys during the antebellum era. He was elected national grand master in 1865 and, with deep pockets and relentless ambition, he vowed to bring National Grand Lodge–organized Masonry to the entire South within the next three years. Gleaves soon relocated to South Carolina and began a career in Republican politics, all the while traveling across the former slave states, organizing lodges and sometimes quickly forging them into new grand lodges. His vision of executive authority was uncompromising: "None shall disagree" with his planned expansion, he asserted in the first person plural, "if it be in our power to prevent it."[86] In 1867 the National Grand Lodge reached its peak, with twenty grand lodges, many of them Southern, working under it.[87] In 1872, Gleaves was elected lieutenant governor of South Carolina.[88]

Lewis Hayden did not begin as Gleaves's antagonist.[89] The second-ranking member of the NGL's leadership, he agreed that Freemasonry, like the government, should be organized nationally, as "the lessons we impart are and must be of a national character."[90] The NGL prevented black Masons from being "divided into parties," and its example might help teach a lesson about the proper conduct of the all-important national government.[91] But by the early 1870s Hayden concluded that Gleaves's methods imperiled the soul of the fraternity by transforming it from a spiritual and political training ground into a centrally directed mass organization that prized numbers over quality. In a series of pamphlets, Hayden heatedly denounced the national grand master's practices as undemocratic, high-handed, and "unmasonic." Gleaves funded his activities out of his own pocket, establishing a precedent that only wealthy men would be able to follow—despite the fact "that we, as a body, have not many among us that can afford so to do."[92] Gleaves also usurped authority never granted to the NGL, forming and admitting new grand lodges in unprecedented ways, and sitting in judgment on conflicts between grand lodges whether or not they recognized the authority of the National Grand Lodge.[93]

The escalating attacks on Gleaves echoed anti-Reconstruction discourses in jarring ways. Opponents accused Gleaves of becoming a dictator, a "Masonic autocrat" and "inexorable tyrant." This "Masonic centralization," one opponent insisted, was "repulsive to the cosmopolitanism of the Order, repulsive to the 'brotherhood of man,' and contrary to the teachings of 'the Fatherhood of God!'"[94] Even more seriously, Hayden and other critics depicted Gleaves running roughshod over the principles of Masonic republicanism—the axiom that Masons must, above all, be men of independent thought and action who fully understood their obligations. Against all precedent, Hayden explained, Gleaves both recruited men into Freemasonry and organized individual lodges into new grand lodges for the reconstructed states. The principle of "self-controlling authority" forbade this, demanding instead that the establishment of a new grand lodge be the "free act" of a region's Masons, heedless of whether they were "prepared or not prepared for such an organization."[95] Gleaves, in other words, was undermining Freemasonry's vision of the orderly process of human development and self-constitution, replacing it with rapid-fire, entrepreneurial organizing—the stuff of mass politics.

Each side also began to charge the other with seeking financial gain at the expense of honest Masonic government. Under Gleaves, charged one-time Boston Mason A. W. A. DeLeon, the National Grand Lodge was simply a financial scheme, bilking grand lodges of an annual fee for each member under their jurisdiction, as well as charging them to warrant each new lodge.[96] Hayden's attacks even more closely echoed the familiar Democratic accusation that Republicans' grand words disguised their desire to profit from Southern Reconstruction. He denounced both Gleaves and the National Grand Lodge as "these new despoilers who are of our own race and people . . . fraudulently obtaining the fruits of our toil by taking fees and receiving dues under the pretence" that they were practicing actual Masonry.[97] Officials of the National Grand Lodge returned the charge that their opponents were motivated by money. In the late 1860s a Virginia lodge, originally chartered by Hayden for the Massachusetts Grand Lodge but now paying dues instead to the National Grand Lodge, asked for the national grand secretary's help in getting Massachusetts to return its earlier payments. The NGL official took the opportunity to suggest that Massachusetts's Masonic interest in Virginia had been purely mercenary. "[T]he authorities of the Prince Hall Grand Lodge seem to have regarded the *pecuniary interest*, much more than the harmony, prosperity, general interest, and welfare of the lodges which it had erected," he charged.[98]

The political resonance of such accusations was particularly strong, for after Gleaves won election as lieutenant governor of South Carolina in 1872, he served under a white governor who became notorious for fiscal corruption. This was the very moment when both "Liberals" and Democrats across the nation assailed the state's black Republicans as inept, illiterate, and corrupt. South Carolina was becoming the emblem of Republican "misrule," with the political prominence of African Americans represented as both the cause and the proof. Gleaves's fraudulent fraternalism threatened to stitch the case and tie it around the neck of Masonry, too.

Gleaves's controversial activities accelerated the schisms and fractures already evident in 1865, and even as Freemasonry blossomed across the South during Reconstruction, the National Grand Lodge collapsed in upon itself. By 1874, when Hayden finally gave up trying to reform the national compact and began calling for its dissolution, many state grand lodges had already withdrawn, marking the end of the NGL's claim to national authority and of the dream of national Masonic unity.[99] The dismal end suggested that Masonry offered no guarantee of broader vision or racial unity, a failure evident in party politics as well. Black Masons played important roles on all sides of the struggle over Southern Reconstruction, sometimes confronting one another directly. In 1874 Martin Delany, disgusted with what he saw as the corruption of South Carolina's Republicans, unsuccessfully challenged Gleaves for the lieutenant governorship of South Carolina on an "Independent Republican" ticket supported by many white Democrats.[100] In a scene that would have been unimaginable twenty years before, rival black Masonic brethren seeking the same political office hurled contemptuous charges at one another, to the delight of the former slaveholders. Black Northern Freemasons, far from providing an example of "the strongest possible ties known among men," divided in ways that provided their common enemies with political aid and political cover.

"SOCIAL EQUALITY"

By the time Gleaves had beaten Delany and won a final term, the foes of Reconstruction were teaching one another a common language to discredit the entire project: "social equality." This term was used neither as an approving description nor a neutral analysis, but as an argument, and a warning. It asserted that alongside the realms of political, civic, and economic life there was a discrete and separate domain called the "social," and that while formal equality might conceivably be legitimate elsewhere, the "social" must remain a domain of personal choice, taste, and discrimination—a place, that is, where both exclusion and segregation could be legitimate. Amid Reconstruction's promises of equal citizenship, the realm of the "social" could therefore remain what scholar Saidiya Hartman calls "an asylum of inequality."[101] For white Americans who were hostile to all but the most limited form of black freedom and participation, "social equality" became a way of describing black people's improper and unwarranted efforts to go "where not wanted."[102]

The "social" in "social equality" was in no sense a coherent realm, but one characterized by ever shifting boundaries. It could include arenas as apparently voluntary and self-determining as the marriage contract or the private dinner table to which Frederick Douglass acknowledged that Ulysses S. Grant might not choose to invite African Americans. Freemasonry, too, was "social." But so, sometimes, were railroad cars, hotels, restaurants, and any other place where whites felt discomfited by the presence of African Americans as equals rather than as servants or slaves—even public schools. The "social," that is to say, could focus narrowly on matters of individual taste and discretion, or stretch to include domains intimately connected to state power and civic life. As a consequence, the charge that someone aspired to "social equality" could describe efforts to legislate equal access to institutions or places of accommodation or amusement, or simply the voluntary social intercourse of individuals; a white Mississippi schoolteacher, a Boston newspaper explained, was whipped by white vigilantes "for maintaining social equality with the negroes."[103] This flexibility made the term endlessly useful: people who used the phrase "social equality" did not offer it as a definable set of rights but rather, in historian Kate Masur's terms, as "a container for everything they considered anathema."[104]

Across the North, conservatives argued that formal equality would encourage or even authorize African Americans to encroach upon the private domains of their white neighbors, including their dinner tables and marriage beds. "Social equality" implied that African Americans participated in political life with the intent of dominating it, and elevating themselves over the mass of white men. White supremacist orators depicted "social equality" as a Rubicon—a point of no return in the impending "war of races": if blacks actively sought "social equality," they would provoke a far wider conflict. In the 1870s a Democratic U.S. senator from Ohio freely offered the argument that to press "social equality" upon the nation in the form of federally mandated integration of public schools would not only destroy those schools but would increase antagonism between white and black. Those "attempting to obliterate national prejudices by legislation," he explained, were "preparing the way for the gradual extinction" of African Americans.[105] Andrew Johnson could not have said it better.

Black activists and white radicals were at pains to point out the absurdity of "social equality" as a slippery slope to "negro supremacy" in all areas of life. Black men, in George Downing's words, understood that "a man's private domicile is his own castle." Downing ridiculed the argument that "because the negro has ... the privilege of sharing the ballot-box with us, he may also demand to share the butter-plate."[106] But the rhetoric of "social equality" proved emotionally persuasive, and became an increasingly common tactic for Democrats, and sometimes for white Republicans as well.

Lewis Hayden kept a cool head during the intra-Republican political combat of the 1860s and 1870s, but the freighted, threatening rhetoric of "social equality" left him openly shocked and dismayed. He had not expected emancipation to work an immediate change in the hearts of white Southerners. From Johnson's bitter prediction of race war through the campaigns of violence and terror by police officers, Klansmen, White Leaguers, and "rifle clubs," Hayden and his comrades understood that acceptance by former Confederates would be the last barrier to be breached, not the first. But he had hoped that white Northerners, particularly those of expansive vision, including some Republicans and Freemasons, would eventually learn to see the lives, rights, and aspirations of African Americans as no less worthy than their own.

Freemasonry—the domain beyond the state on which Hayden pinned his greatest hopes—soon left him disappointed and dismayed. The hopeful early signs, in overtures from Europe and the initiation of Joshua Smith in a Boston lodge, soon came to nothing. Indeed, the incorporation of a handful of other black men in otherwise white lodges across the North turned out to be less an overture than an inoculation—a symbolic inclusion that allowed conservative white Freemasons to claim that they took note only of individual worthiness, not racial hierarchy. "It is not true," declared the *New England Freemason* in 1875, "that the Grand Lodges of this country refuse to recognize these spurious organizations because they are composed of black men. There are black men in good and regular standing in several of our jurisdictions"—including Smith in Massachusetts—"and no Brother ever thinks of regarding or treating him any differently than if he were white." But this ostensibly race-blind egalitarianism was only a prelude to the familiar anti-Reconstruction charge that the collective pursuit of racial equality was in fact a pursuit of preferential treatment. "No man—not even a black man," the author continued, "has an inalienable right to be made a Mason, nor to be recognized as a Mason."[107] Smith himself unintentionally served such conservatives quite well. Prosperous, freeborn, very light-skinned, and courtly in manner, he had more than once been the lone man of African descent in otherwise white surroundings.[108] Leading white Masonic editor Charles W. Moore, a Bostonian and a longtime antagonist of black Freemasonry, enthusiastically listed the factors about Smith that made his admission so uniquely acceptable to white Freemasons: his descent from "one of the most respectable white families of Virginia"; his free birth; his early education and economic success; his skin and features not being "of any decided African type"; and his "white wife and . . . children, who are indistinguishable in their complexion from the white children with whom they associate." Moore even alleged that Smith did not "look for intimate associates among the class to which his paternal ancestor belonged." In other words, Smith was anything but "a common 'negro'" and his initiation "therefore . . . does not strictly furnish any precedent for the admission of persons of the African race, however worthy they may be. It leaves that question untouched."[109]

When the question raised by Hayden's 1868 petition to the Massachusetts Grand Lodge was finally called, Moore's hostile view won the day. The white investigating committee voted unanimously to reject the black Masons' petition. Adding insult to injury, they even refused to rule on the merits of its arguments. The petitioners, explained the white grand lodge committee, asked admission for the whole of their fraternity, meaning that any ruling in the petitioners' favor would admit men unnamed and therefore unknown to the white brethren. "Under these circumstances," they explained, "it is not necessary to inquire into the validity of the proceedings of the persons named in the charter or whether the petitioners have any just claim to be considered their successors." It concluded by denying "Masonic intercourse" to the petitioners, while noting that any individuals who were "worthy and well qualified" could of course "seek admission through duly organized lodges."[110] The overture for collective respect had been countered with an offer of individual inspection.

White allies proved craven, and opponents bloodthirsty. Winslow Lewis, the white former grand master who had written encouragingly to Hayden, now refused him permission to publish the letter. "At present it would not be well to print my unimportant note," he offered in lieu of explanation. "Let us wait until a better state of things ensues."[111] Meanwhile, the white Grand Lodge of New York, protesting a German lodge's plan to recognize the National Grand Lodge, warned that such recognition would lead to violence. Many black Masons in the South were former slaves, it explained, "between whom and the whites there is irreconcilable and irradicable repugnance to social equality. A persistent attempt to enforce this equality would be very likely to result in the destruction of Masonry in the United States, or"—in a chilling return to Johnson's words of warning-cum-threat—"a war of races, ending in the extermination of the negro race."[112]

Lewis Hayden was aghast. Such rhetoric constituted "rather an incentive than a prediction" of racial violence, he knew, and he asked how Masons could square this call to violence with their basic principles.[113] His question was rhetorical, for the answer lay before him. In 1867, even as Joshua Smith was made a Mason, the white Grand Lodge of Massachusetts had hosted President Andrew Johnson—their Masonic brother—at the dedication of their new Boston Temple.[114] Like their political leader, Hayden now understood, white Masons viewed black Masons essentially as antagonists. Boston's white Masons refused the Prince Hall Masons' overtures for reconciliation because, like white Masons throughout the North, they hated the "advancement towards equality" evident in the "manly, upright, moral, and virtuous conduct" of African Americans. Black Masons' elevation and their "humane and manly acts" had not brought respect and friendship, but threats of violence.[115]

Hayden sublimated his rage and dismay into an apocalyptic fantasy in which white Masons actually perpetrated a fratricidal "war of races." In a pamphlet bearing that phrase as a subtitle, he reimagined the horrific events of the 1863 New York City draft riots as the future work of white Northern Masons. He foresaw their "prediction, or advice" of a "war of races" inciting low white men to jealous rage at black men's "progress" and growing "equality," and inspiring another riot against the city's black citizens. When the slaughter begins, in Hayden's bleak vision, white Masons "instantly" leave their lodge "to engage in the contest." In their haste, they do not pause even to remove their white aprons, emblems of purity. Those aprons attract the hopeful attention of a mulatto Mason fleeing the violence; having "providentially" discovered Masonic brethren, he "confidingly approaches." But his confidence is misplaced. Crying out "WAR OF RACES," they murder him with their bowie knives, after which "the brother's life-blood is wiped upon that apron which drew him instinctively to his murderer."[116]

Nor was Masonic fratricide the end of the crime, for Hayden had a purpose in making the imagined victim a man of mixed descent: "May it not have been that a father has murdered his own son?"[117] White Masons denied the figurative brotherhood of black Masons, but the faces on any country road or city street proved that literal brotherhood, though generally unacknowledged, was already a reality. The only question was whether white men would embrace that reality or continue to rail violently against it. When white Masons from former slave states complained about Northern lodges considering black Masons' petitions for recognition, a committee of black Masons sarcastically asked why they did not ask "the question in this form": "'Why will our Northern brethren persist in admitting our sons to fellowship in their Lodges, whom in the past we fathered, and afterwards kidnapped from their mothers' cradles?'"[118] The brotherhood of white and black was already painfully and literally real; why could that not be transmuted, through Masonry, into something figurative and beautiful that could help build a better world?

Hayden and his brethren across the North continued to seek collective recognition by white grand lodges. Those hopes remained tied to Reconstruction. As Ohio's white Masons considered recognition in 1875, the state's white grand master spoke frankly to the conflict as he understood it. "I am aware of the prejudice against the African race," he explained. "I am not entirely free from it myself." But he did not believe this should be the end of the argument. "We all have our passions and prejudices, and we should use our utmost endeavors to keep them within due bounds. . . . In this great centennial year, whilst liberty and equality are shed[?] abroad through our great nation, is it not right and proper" to unite the black and white grand lodges, heal the breaches, and recognize black Masons "as a part of the great Masonic family," to be "accorded their rights as such."[119] But the counterargument relied on the same analogy with the wider political world. In Minnesota's deliberations, the majority sided with a brother who described recognition and Reconstruction as similarly misguided projects: "[T]he disasters incident to the attempt to transform the *freed-man* into a *free man* by the nation, should admonish us to shun the rock upon which the ship of state is now so sorely imperiled."[120] Recognition failed in

1876, not to be achieved between white and black Freemasonry for more than a century to come. Across the nation, scattered black voices would from time to time assert their Masonic equality and seek recognition from white fellow Masons in the United States or from the mother lodge in England, but the millennial imagining of a fraternal embrace across the color line persisted only as the triumph of hope over experience.[121]

RECONSTRUCTION UNDER SIEGE

Soon, legal equality too felt the ax blows of "social equality." Railroads, hotels, and restaurants (among many other places of business) routinely discriminated against black customers, segregating, excluding, or relegating them to inferior accommodations no matter what they paid. Across the South and most of the North, these forms of Jim Crow were common. They affected even the most prominent African Americans in the country, as the black members of Congress informed their colleagues in speech after speech; they all faced exclusion or inferior accommodations on their way from their Southern districts to their seats in Washington.[122] In response, in 1872 Charles Sumner presented Congress with a new civil rights bill designed to meet these challenges, one that would forbid discrimination on the basis of race in any place created or licensed by law. He argued that the premise of "social equality" itself was faulty. "There is no colored person who does not resent the imputation that he is seeking to intrude himself socially anywhere," Sumner told his colleagues. "This is no question of society . . . no question of social equality, if anybody knows what this means."[123] A Boston newspaper defined it in terms Sumner would not have used, but might have approved: "the old prejudice in favor of impressing upon the black man that he must keep his place."[124]

Events soon made a new civil rights measure seem all the more crucial. In its 1873 decision in the *Slaughterhouse Cases*, the Supreme Court ruled that the Fourteenth Amendment's guarantees of "privileges and immunities" applied only in narrowly defined areas of life; in all other realms, state governments would determine what limits private individuals might set on access to their places of business, and much else. This returned most questions of rights to the various and uncertain mercies of the states. If Congress wished the Fourteenth Amendment to have more expansive meaning, it would have to take action.

Sumner died in early 1874, his civil rights bill still unpassed. George Downing visited the old man at his deathbed. "Don't let it fail," the senator pleaded, and it did not—quite.[125] But when the Senate passed a version of Sumner's bill the following year, in part as a memorial to the departed, its sponsors bowed before the power of "social equality" in ways Sumner had explicitly rejected. The Republican congressman offering the bill for passage in the Senate declared that it intended "to secure equal rights to the white people as well as to the colored race" and declared "it did not

Shaw Guards with Charles Sumner's casket, 1874
Courtesy of Historic New England

touch a point of social equality, as that was not an element of citizenship." He waved away his colleagues' fears of "equal rights" in terms that spoke volumes: "The white race is the dominant race in this country and will always rule it."[126] More important, at the insistence of moderate Republicans the revised bill omitted school integration—something Sumner had considered essential since his argument in the *Roberts* case in 1849.[127] The Civil Rights Act of 1875 bespoke the willingness of Republicans to carve a vast and crucial area of American life out of the rights of citizenship.

By that time, the remaining Republican governments in the former Confederacy faced mortal threats. In the years before 1873, Republican governments in states with white majorities—most of the former slave states—fell under the combined weight of Democratic force and fraud, as well as their own fissures and failings. By then, black activists in most Southern states knew that neither federal law nor federal power would protect them, and that simply asserting one's equality was a dangerous act. In the 1875 Georgia trial of a black man accused of fomenting an "insurrection" against white authorities, it was considered "damaging" to the man's defense that "some time ago . . . he undertook to explain the provisions of the civil rights bill as giving social equality."[128] Equality before the law gave way to the ad hoc enforcement of a racially hierarchical order. In Democratic-controlled Arkansas that same year, a Boston correspondent blithely reported that the state's freedmen were hard at work. "Labor is in demand," he explained; "consequently the freedmen have their 'rights,' and they do not seek the social equality with the whites which makes so much trouble in some other states."[129] What would happen to those "rights" when labor was not so much in demand, or what the nature of the "trouble" in other states was, were questions left unexplored.

Republicans in the black-majority redoubts of the Deep South—Mississippi, South Carolina, and Louisiana—knew that "trouble" intimately. They faced resurgent white paramilitaries, dire economic circumstances, and a Grant administration too mired in financial scandal and too aware of the unpopularity of continued federal enforcement to offer much as-

sistance. "The whole public are tired out with these annual autumnal out-
breaks in the South," Grant himself explained, and "the great majority are
ready now to condemn any interference on the part of the government."[130]
In 1875, when a concerted campaign of white terror and fraud overthrew
Mississippi's fractious Republican government, attentive observers knew
better than to expect a federal crackdown. In South Carolina and Louisiana, the black-majority states where Republicans still governed, white
Democrats took careful note of Washington's inaction.

In the summer and fall of 1876, with the courtly and wealthy planter
Wade Hampton as a presentable political leader, South Carolina's white
supremacist "rifle clubs" set about chopping the state's black Republican
majority down to a size they could manage at the polls. Their "clubs"
sometimes arrived on horseback at Republican rallies and commandeered
the rostrum.[131] At one of these Richard Greener stood his ground and,
according to press reports, responded to the vigilantes' chosen orator.
Most confrontations, though, took place beyond the gaze of white journalists. White Democratic activists threatened Republicans with unemploy-
ment and with death, threats they made good on when they thought they
could do so without provoking national outrage or a federal response.
Determined to seize power, they followed a by now familiar course, presenting the existence of black militia units as an affront to white safety
and dignity, and a provocation for the long-imagined "war of races." The
tactic worked. In a series of brazen attacks on black state militiamen during
the summer of 1876, South Carolina's militant Democrats polarized state
politics along racial lines and forced their state party to abandon its policy
of seeking the least objectionable Republican.[132]

Their campaign of terror sent the state Republican administration reel-
ing, and ultimately cast the result of the 1876 election into doubt. South
Carolina's contested electoral votes, along with those of Louisiana and
Florida, represented the margin of victory in the presidential contest that
year, and the presidency as well as several state governments hung in the
balance. While the struggle continued on the ground in the South, national

political leaders set about negotiating, hoping to keep the peace by any means necessary—even the sacrifice of the last Republican governments in the former Confederacy. By the spring of 1877, when the maneuvering and bargaining in Washington was done, the Republicans retained their hold on the presidency, at the cost of surrendering the remaining state governments in the South to the Democrats. The Republican government collapsed, and its officials, including Gleaves and Greener, fled the state. Southern Reconstruction, as a federal project, was finished.[133]

Back in Massachusetts, the reverberations could be felt in the fate of the Shaw Guards. This unit had been a locus of pride and a visible representation of black men's incorporation into the state's civic and martial life since its incorporation during the Civil War. But when the state reduced the size of the militia as part of a budget-minded reform in 1876, the two black companies—Boston's and New Bedford's—were among those disbanded.[134] The dismissal of the only black units in the state demonstrated that neither Civil War service nor emancipation guaranteed a permanent place for black men in the American martial tradition.

The sequel reflected the strength, and the besetting weakness, of the alliances black leaders had forged and spoke to the complex situation of the North's "colored citizens" at the end of Reconstruction. While some members of the disbanded Boston company threatened to mobilize for the defeat of the Republican governor, other black residents responded more pragmatically by calling in every political favor they could.[135] Their petition campaign included numerous former mayors and governors, and it finally led a reluctant state legislature to reinstate one company, described in the records simply as "unattached company, Boston."[136] So the lone black militia unit remained for several years: a numberless afterthought, unattached to any larger body.[137] The situation of Boston's "colored citizens" could not have been better expressed.

In the aftermath, it might have seemed that Frederick Douglass's dictum was correct: the Republican Party was the ship, and all else was the sea. But this ship was a far cry from the interracial abolitionist party aboard the

Hingham ferry three decades before, imperfect and temporary but none-theless inspiring. The masters of the Republican vessel demanded obedi-ence from their passengers and crew, while offering them little in return. In 1878 a chastened George Ruffin attempted to rally the black voters of the Sixth Ward to support a conservative, hard-money Republican against a fearsome Democratic rival—that party's own prodigal son, Benjamin Butler. Ruffin began by acknowledging how hard the circumstances of 1878 might appear to his fellows. Many seemed to believe that "the issues have passed away, as though the cause of humanity could ever change, or protection to life and liberty ought ever pass away." True, he admitted, "good faith has not been kept with the Republicans of the South"—or of the North, he might have added. But Ruffin nevertheless urged support for the Republicans for the long fight ahead. The struggle for black men's rights in Massachusetts had taken thirty years, he reminded them; the fight in South Carolina might go just as long. Lewis Hayden agreed that the long view should govern men's choices, whether as a matter of "gratitude for the past" or because "the work of that party was unfinished." Support for the Republicans recognized that however bad the party was, it was far bet-ter than the alternatives. As Hayden's formal resolution put it, "from the settling of this country until the inauguration of the Republican party, we, as a race, had no rights that our white fellow-citizens felt themselves bound to respect."[138]

Surely both Ruffin and Hayden knew that African Americans' fight to give citizenship rich meaning could not be shoehorned into a narrative of the rise and triumph of the Republican Party. Certainly they knew better than to resolve, as that 1878 Republican meeting did, that the Republican Party stood as the "monument to [the] labors" of "Garrison, Phillips, Sum-ner, and Wilson" on behalf of the commonwealth's black citizens.[139] Per-haps they even wondered, as their friend George Downing publicly did, "What hope has the black man in America" from the Republican Party?[140] Many no doubt agreed with Robert Morris that neither party truly under-stood that "our people, born in this country, are American citizens, and entitled to be known as such."[141] The "colored citizens" of the late 1870s must have felt powerless and embittered as they recited the precepts of the Republican gold standard and its superiority to the Democrats' inflationary policies, when the very different battles about which they cared most had been lost in the South. But they knew, too, that things could still get worse for the freedpeople, and for themselves. And where else, after all, could they turn?

The years of Reconstruction had offered the "colored citizens" unprecedented opportunities to shape their own fates and to remake the nation, but also profound and unexpected disappointments. By the late 1870s, courts and legislatures had retreated from grand promises of "equality before the law," parsing and delimiting the meaning of that equality in ways that resembled the uncertain, unfelt "equality" of antebellum Massachusetts. The "colored citizens" entered Reconstruction convinced that the nation's laws and hearts would turn their way. It was now clear that the era's real but limited constitutional victories would not survive the exacting scrutiny of the postwar Supreme Court, that their old enemies were on the march, and that their political allies could not be relied upon. And in realms beyond the law itself, where what was required were feelings of common purpose and destiny—in a word, of brotherhood—the post-Reconstruction era dawned icy and friendless.

10.

Burying Lewis Hayden

For William Nell, the early 1870s brought unexpected contentment and security. He enjoyed his long-sought marriage and watched his two sons grow. He felt continued satisfaction at having been the "First Colored Man employed about the United States mail," even if those duties sometimes required him to rise early to catch the morning streetcar, or to work the night shift. He also remained busy with literary and organizational work. He was pulling together various pieces of writing and had just participated in a memorial meeting for Charles Sumner when a stroke felled him in May 1874. He died a week later, just fifty-seven years old, his long-envisioned book "Embracing Colored American History" never to be completed, but his mark made even so.[1]

His funeral was held at Theodore Parker's old church, where he had once kept the keys, and it brought fitting tributes from Wendell Phillips and William Lloyd Garrison. But a week later, other friends—still calling themselves "colored citizens"—held a meeting of their own in the more resonant confines of the Baptist church in Smith Court. This was where the man they mourned had watched the signing of the antislavery charter as a boy, and where he had organized countless meetings against the Fugitive Slave Law and the segregated Smith School. Here, too, he had been celebrated when the school fight was finally won. No record survives to tell us what Edwin Garrison Walker or George Ruffin said in Nell's memory. Did they reminisce about the endless petitions, even joke about Nell's persistence, as Phillips had once done? Did they honor the long, often lonely campaigns in which the gentle historian let neither his self-doubt nor his vulnerabilities deter him? Did others rise to speak, but find themselves unable?[2]

After the last eulogist fell silent, Nell's remaining legacies foretold much of what was to come for the "colored citizens" of Boston and the world they sought to remake. Their victories could be felt, near and far, in the persistence of black political assertion and professional accomplishment. Fraternal processions and militia musters, now carried on with official approval and sanction, drew appreciative audiences and fostered a sense of civic ownership. They had attained heights that their younger selves could scarcely have imagined. Yet as the 1870s gave way to the 1880s, the limits of their triumphs came into ever sharper focus. The campaigns against exclusion and segregation in which Nell and others fought so hard had yielded dramatic new federal and state legislation. But they did not produce the long-sought world of universal opportunity and attainment, still less obliterate the badge of caste or inspire the acceptance and regard of white Americans.

In the end, the broad imaginings forged during the struggle against slavery did not survive the victory. The generation that came of age calling themselves "colored citizens" achieved much of what they had hoped, but it turned out not to mean quite what they had imagined. As they passed from the scene, their former allies—white Republicans and onetime abolitionists—rewrote the past to carve out a place for these black activists just large enough to flatter themselves. And it fell to other generations to redefine the African American struggle, and continue the fight to belong.

"ARE WE CAPABLE OF REACHING THE HIGH STATE OF CIVILIZATION?"

The later career of Richard T. Greener, first black graduate of Harvard College and Reconstruction-era professor at the University of South Carolina, embodied both the triumphs of the "colored citizens," and their undoing. Like William Nell, he helped observe the passing of his patron Charles Sumner, under circumstances that would have been unthinkable in any prior era, or for nearly a century to come: he delivered his speech to an integrated audience, in the citadel of the old Slave Power. Greener's eulogy to Sumner also honored the recently departed Nell in a way the historian would have particularly cherished: with a footnote to *Colored Patriots*.[3]

But the new world Greener helped build in South Carolina did not last long. When President Rutherford B. Hayes withdrew federal troops and South Carolina's Republican government collapsed, Greener bowed to reality. He submitted his resignation from the university and relocated his family to Washington D.C. There he found work as a clerk in the Treasury Department and lobbied hard, though unsuccessfully, to be appointed minister to Haiti. The position went to his old friend and mentor John M. Langston. The competition bespoke a continuing scarcity of positions for the black leadership class that had flourished during Reconstruction; eligible men inevitably found themselves in competition with one another.[4] Soon Greener began practicing law and found a position as an instructor at the struggling law school at Howard University, foremost among the many colleges opened across the South for black men and women during Reconstruction.[5]

Over the coming years Greener kept Nell's memory alive under circumstances that reflected the harder world of the post-Reconstruction era. On March 5, 1878, he began a side career as a public lecturer with an address on "Crispus Attucks and the Negro's Place in the Army," an affirmation of the long struggles by Nell, Morris, and the rest. Greener's next homage, though, would not have pleased Nell nearly so well. Despite an 1873 New York law whose plain purpose was to ban segregated schools, the state's judges repeatedly permitted the exclusion of black children from historically white public schools.[6] A decade later, some local officials appeared to have capitulated to the explicit practice of racial segregation. In 1883 Greener traveled to Brooklyn to speak at the opening of that city's segregated Colored Grammar School No. 1. Not surprisingly under the circumstances, Greener delivered an address whose hallmark was ambivalence. He praised separate schools and "colored teachers" for nurturing and uplifting black students and teaching them of the achievements of their past, but he also suggested that segregation "effectually shut out the Negro from employment" and advancement. He recognized that federal law did not require integrated public schools, and that most cities and states would not create them; he therefore accepted "the 'colored school' as a fact and considered it better than no school." But he hoped it marked only "the transition from 'no school' for colored children to the admission of all children, irrespective of nationality or creed." He brought the audience to its feet by wishing for the authority to take a chisel to the word "colored" that marked the brand-new building. He closed by urging the young scholars present to make "an exhaustive acquaintance" with the works of black scholars such as William C. Nell.[7] The long fight was not over. Indeed, it almost seemed that it would have to begin all over again.

Greener's Harvard degree and Howard professorship made him a rare, almost singular figure, but even he struggled to find secure professional footing in the years following Reconstruction. Those without his connections and credentials usually fared much worse. The pathways to the professions remained open to an excruciatingly small number of black Northerners; Nell's own son and namesake, for example, followed his father's early footsteps into journalism, becoming the Boston correspondent for the influential *New York Age*.[8] But most others, no matter what their level of education, faced far more daunting prospects. During the last decades of the century the proportion of Boston's black men and women who owned their own businesses or did clerical or professional work remained more or less stagnant, while the great majority of the city's black residents continued to work in jobs classed as unskilled.[9]

Part of the problem was quiet but persistent discrimination. "The business portion of the community," complained Edwin G. Walker in 1893, "will not employ colored children for anything but menial work."[10] "In most public and commercial relations," a city newspaper agreed, "the two races meet without signs of open repugnance," but in Boston "you're never told and you never know, but for all that you find yourself quietly pushed aside and left out."[11] This was true at the bottom as well as the top of the occupational ladder. During the late nineteenth century, as Boston's white native-born and immigrant populations attained modest prosperity, overall conditions for the city's small black population grew slightly worse.[12]

Even as most remained poor, cultural and regional divisions within the community grew more marked. West End residents, most of them born in the North, briefly became a majority in the redrawn ward during the mid-1880s.[13] But the flow of migrants to the distant neighborhoods of the South End, especially recent arrivals from Virginia and elsewhere in the South, was already altering the geography of black Boston. The weekly steamer from Norfolk and Richmond brought black Southerners who settled mainly in South End neighborhoods, where they had little daily contact with the city's antebellum black residents. Some figures bridged the gap: the peripatetic Reverend Peter Randolph returned from his Reconstruction sojourn in Richmond to minister to the Southern-born worshippers at the South End's Ebenezer Baptist Church.[14]

The transformations of Reconstruction had not integrated God's houses. In the South, the postbellum exodus of black Christians from white churches created vast numbers of new congregations of black Baptists, Methodists, and other denominations. Boston's churches remained highly segregated, and not just along lines of race. Reverend Randolph struggled to channel the enthusiastic Southern folkways of his parishioners into a worship style he thought more appropriate for their new world.[15] Meanwhile, some of the longer-settled and most successful of the black activists worshipped in predominantly white congregations. George Ruffin, one of the scattered black Christians worshipping in a historically white church, publicly raised the question he knew "thoughtful, progressive colored people" asked in private: "[I]s there any need for colored churches in Boston?" For him, the answer was a qualified yes. While he himself might feel perfectly content in a mainly white congregation, he knew this was a deeply personal question involving emotional and spiritual satisfaction. The fact that segregation no longer took place within the church buildings themselves was not reason enough to insist that black Bostonians abandon their houses of worship. "The real question," he explained, "is, are colored people made truly welcome? . . . do they enjoy their religion in white churches?" So long as mainly white churches caused black Christians to feel uncomfortable, "lost and dissatisfied," then "the necessity for colored churches exists."[16]

Yet Ruffin's sensitivity was bounded in time: in some distant day, he happily predicted, there would be no "colored churches," and no need for them. The "colored race is on trial," he concluded, with the pressing question being "[A]re we capable of reaching the high state of civilization?" Ruffin was certain that the answer was yes—that soon his people would be successful, celebrated, and prosperous, busy in their professions, trades, and schools, "all anxious to work out for themselves all the powers and possibilities of their minds and souls."[17] Once they did, they would no longer need separate houses of worship. Ruffin, and perhaps even Peter Randolph, viewed the men and women who required the "colored church" as "older men and women," figures of a rapidly passing day. "[O]ur present duty," Ruffin argued, "is to elevate the colored church," insisting on educated ministers whose English met formal standards. Once this principle took hold, and a "powerful and pure" gospel flowed from the pulpit of black churches, whites would flock to those spaces. "[T]he trouble will have been overcome, prejudice is gone, and we shall have no distinctively colored church, but one church." In other words, "the best way to break down the colored church is to build it up"—"up" according to the standards of literacy and diction Ruffin expected of his people, at least in God's time. The present time was another matter.

By the end of the nineteenth century, black activists calling for "elevation" found themselves hemmed in new and unwelcome ways. Like their antebellum counterparts, they imagined that education and prosperity would force their white neighbors to recognize them as equal citizens. Unlike those predecessors, they lived in an era when white intellectuals, politicians, and educators claimed attainment and wealth generally as the legacy and property of the white race. They did so in justification and explanation for an expanding system of worldwide white supremacy that undergirded colonies and empires, and that described itself in the language of "civilization."[18] Unlike the attainments of an earlier day, this "civilization" was frankly depicted as white, as a matter not of attainment but of biological descent. Black intellectuals, entrepreneurs, and educators struggled to find ways of articulating and expressing "civilization" that did not require them to display condescension or worse for those African Americans who, in these terms, remained stuck at a lower level of development.[19]

The condescension exhibited by Ruffin and others probably did not sit well with the men and women at Ebenezer Baptist, but at least Ruffin imagined a world in which racial distinctions ceased to matter, or perhaps even to exist. By contrast, by the 1880s nearly all white Americans took racial hierarchy so much for granted that they routinely recast even the most accomplished African Americans as subordinates and inferiors. Beginning in that decade, the antebellum and wartime leadership suffered the quiet indignity of being remembered in subtly or not so subtly demeaning terms. John Brown conspirator and Union recruiter George Stearns's son penned a memoir of his father's early days that referred to Lewis Hayden as "the colored janitor of the State House."[20] There was no shame in being a janitor in the late nineteenth century—not, at least, among black Bostonians. In 1885, a former police station janitor was also the highest-ranking Knight Templar—an elevated Masonic degree—in New England.[21] But Hayden, in addition to thirty years' service as a messenger in that building, had been a member of the legislature itself. The younger Stearns knew Hayden had been employed in the statehouse but was unable to remember or imagine him as anything but the janitor.

The eulogies offered for Robert Morris by his professional peers contained similarly discordant notes. The lawyer died after a long illness in 1882, and his funeral in the north suburban Church of the Immaculate Conception was a grand affair. Lewis Hayden, George Downing, and George Ruffin took their places alongside white dignitaries, including the president of Boston College and Morris's former clerk Patrick Collins, who was now about to take a seat in Congress.[22] The following morning, lawyers, judges, and politicians assembled in the chamber of the state's Supreme Judicial Court for a commemorative meeting. The white lawyers' tributes described a man of honor, humor, and determination, but even they could not seem to resist putting Morris, however subtly, in his place. "Not a great lawyer," one said, "yet what law he had was always at his command." "[N]ot a great jurist, nor even a learned lawyer," another concurred, declaring that a memorial was a time "to be discriminating as well as just."[23] Morris was an able, unexceptional lawyer who charmed his juries and kept his word. He had done well—for a colored man.

THE MEDIUM OF POLITICS

On the following March 5—official celebrations of Crispus Attucks and the Boston Massacre ended in 1870, but the legacy Nell had cultivated lived on—Edwin G. Walker offered a rather different eulogy for Robert Morris at the Charles Street AME Church.[24] Others had lauded the pioneering professional; now Walker celebrated the militant. Morris, he reminded his audience, left the world the same year as another hero, Henry Highland Garnet. Both men, Walker declared, were "irrepressible repre-

sentatives and champions" and "vindicators of the capacity and manhood
of the colored people of America." Walker, whose father embodied the
spirit of resistance, and whose legacy Garnet himself helped preserve, remembered Morris for his part in the Minkins rescue and his open and fiery
resistance to Union service on unequal terms. "Whenever the rights of his
race were called into question, I always found him as bold as a lion and as
severe as justice."[25]

By the time he died, Morris's fierce insistence on equal justice had
left him disenchanted with the Republican Party; he, like Walker, called
himself an independent.[26] For many, the sense of Republicanism as part
of a wider war against inequality in all its forms was almost extinguished.
In 1883 North Carolina's James O'Hara—one of the handful of black
men to achieve election to Congress in the half century after the fall of
Reconstruction—was feted by the "prominent colored citizens" of Boston,
including Hayden, Ruffin, Walker, and William Wells Brown. They welcomed the new congressman as a sign that all was not lost in the post-
Reconstruction South, but their guest's words could not have reassured
them. He had had "very little to do with politics," O'Hara confessed, and
"his advice to the young men had been to avoid politics" and look after
business matters. "The colored man," he reflected, "has little to hope for
from either the republican or democratic parties."[27] He spoke too soon. A
decade later, resurgent black Republicans in his home state would ally
themselves with disgruntled white Democrats who had jumped to the economically radical People's Party. Their "Fusion" coalition won power and
governed North Carolina for four years, and it began to rebuild the interracial promise of Reconstruction. But in 1898 Democrats mobilized a
white supremacy campaign that split the coalition, swept to power, and
mounted a coup against the government of the state's largest city.[28] In the
end, O'Hara's glum prognosis came true; the hope offered by politics was
indeed forlorn. By the 1890s, a slave-born educator named Booker T.
Washington would seek to transform this weariness into a positive good,
aiming to protect African Americans from the dangers of white supremacy

by forswearing political activity and promising to focus instead on the improvement of the race through education and economic uplift.

Lewis Hayden demurred. He continued to see his people's destiny unfolding through party politics. When the Republicans met in Chicago in 1884 to choose the party's nominee for president, Hayden lobbied for General William T. Sherman, buttonholing black delegates from Southern states the Republicans could not possibly carry that fall.[29] A few weeks later, after Sherman declined to run, the *Boston Globe* quoted Hayden as suggesting that if the Democrats nominated Ben Butler for president, the old radical would do more than win many black votes in the South; his election would so transform the meanings of race, region, and party that "the color line would be almost totally obliterated" and "whites and blacks in the South would henceforth work in political harmony."[30]

This incredible speculation, possibly a hopeful fantasy but just as likely a journalist's invention, had its roots in Butler's latest high-wire act.[31] Butler left the Republican Party in 1878, becoming a Democrat once more, and in 1882 he finally became governor of Massachusetts. Once there, however, he had to contend with the state's still largely Republican state administration, including the special executive council through which state judicial nominations passed. He quickly found himself unable to get any of his candidates for a Charlestown judgeship through the council. Seeking to outflank his rivals, Butler finally nominated his longtime supporter Edwin G. Walker.[32] Butler reasoned that the council's canny Republicans would not reject a rare black nominee to high office, even if the nomination came from a Democrat. But the Republican-dominated council outfoxed him. As Butler had intuited, they could not bring themselves simply to reject the first-ever nomination of a black man for this office; instead, they offered another candidate, Butler opponent George L. Ruffin. Tired of fighting the council, and recognizing that he would get some credit for the landmark appointment no matter which man took the bench, Butler nominated Ruffin. Judge George Lewis Ruffin went on to preside over the Charlestown court until his death in 1886. But whatever Lewis Hayden said about Butler, Ruffin's achievement came through the shadow play of party maneuver and rivalry, not a rekindling of the old abolitionist spirit.[33]

The partisan lesson of the pas de deux between Butler and the Republicans was not lost on the ambitious younger men of the city: clearly, there was some value to having a foot in each party. Especially after the election of Democrat Grover Cleveland to the presidency in 1884, small groups of black professional men across the North sought to ally themselves with the Democrats.[34] In Boston, ambitious men of the older and younger generations warily tried on the label "independent." Edwin G. Walker took a leading role. From his new law offices at 27 Cornhill, he hosted the meetings of the pro-Cleveland Sumner Union League.[35] Among his chief allies was the famed veteran officer of the 55th Massachusetts, James Monroe Trotter.[36] Boston's new black-edited newspaper, the *Advocate*, delightedly painted the break with orthodox Republicanism as evidence of an "increase of manly independence," and argued that "once it is plainly seen that the colored voter knows his rights and dares maintain them, not only in the form of resolutions, etc., but *at the polls*, party leaders will respect him in the same."[37] Richard Greener put it more bluntly: "[I]f Republicans do not respect us sufficiently to pay some slight pretence to a decent regard for our feelings, then let them be taught a lesson."[38] For others the question was not one of "respect," "manliness," or "feelings" but of raw efficacy. Political independence would bring power. "Politics is purely a matter of business with white men," T. Thomas Fortune warned the men of the Wendell Phillips Club, "but only sentiment with us. We must view it just as the 'superior' race do—strictly business."[39] By the middle of 1886, though, this particular move toward the Democrats ended with a whimper. Black support for a few Democratic candidates did not yield the expected dividends in patronage appointments, and the "independents" threw in the towel—for the moment.[40]

Boston's black voters remained vulnerable to charges that their Republicanism was empty, a matter of sentiment or simple bribery. In the 1880s, even Thomas Wentworth Higginson took this position when he became a

Democrat and ran for Congress against former governor Nathaniel Banks. Back in the 1850s, when Banks had been a conservative Republican and Higginson an abolitionist firebrand, the personal loyalties of black Bostonians would never have been in doubt. But the new Democratic Higginson minimized the impact of violence on black Southerners' political freedoms. He even—in an essay on William Lloyd Garrison—described Southern slaveholders as having been "themselves bound hand and foot" by their economic reliance on slavery. When Douglass denounced this new model Higginson as a traitor "to the cause of liberty itself," Higginson responded with the charge that Douglass had himself become a "slave owner," chasing after and seizing those black voters who differed from him politically.[41] Higginson's campaign appearances in Ward Nine were a bust, and he recruited only a handful of its five hundred black voters; the entire political leadership, including Hayden, came out firmly in favor of Banks and the Republicans. Democrats responded with charges that hundreds of putative members of a Ward Nine "Higginson club" had been either bought off and delivered to the polls in the carriages of Republican aristocrats, or else fooled into thinking the Republican Party served their interests. The black voter, they charged, saw politics "as a sort of delightful game which affords both amusement and profit, and which he plays with all the skill of a veteran." African Americans' "influence in politics cannot help but be wholly bad . . . an unprincipled and venal vote which may be secured either by passion or bribery."[42] "Colored citizen" once again sounded like an oxymoron.

THE AMALGAMATED FUTURE

Perhaps the problem was race. Not race in the sense white Americans usually meant, as a euphemism for the presence of nonwhites in their nation, but the very idea of distinguishing among people according to rules of appearance and descent. Judge Ruffin reached this conclusion by 1885. As with churches, so with people: "The negro must go," he provocatively declared that year. But Ruffin meant nothing like the deportationist fantasy of earlier decades. Whites too must go, as must all of the present's "races." His speech, "A Look Forward," spoke frankly to the mingling of ancestrally distinct peoples in America, noting the ever increasing number of "mixed-blood people of all shades of complexion" and the "bleaching process" that was gradually transforming two races into one. The cause was simple: the "mutual attraction between the white and black races in this country," fostered by centuries of cohabitation and a common language and religion. Ruffin, like decades of black activists before him, assumed that the "insurmountable repugnancy" felt by whites would pass away as blacks moved from the degraded ignorance of slavery to "education, wealth and refinement." Intermarriage between white women and black men, currently quite rare in the South, would give way to "identity of taste, sentiment, feeling." The mixing was already well under way, as people dubbed "negro" claimed white ancestors and some light-skinned men and women passed for white and married into white families. Absent the unthinkable—genocide or deportation—those bonds of affection would lead inevitably to the erasure of white and black in the Southern states, as surely as they would to the mingling and eventual disappearance of "Saxon, Celtic, Latin" in the Southwest. Three hundred years hence, the continent would have a new race: "one race—the American—superior to all others, a new race, fit in intellect, heart and power to occupy and sway the destiny of the imperial New World."[43]

Ruffin's vision recalled those of earlier days, all the way back to the "philo-African" dream of 1831. As recently as 1863, John S. Rock had brought the men and women of the New England Anti-Slavery Society to gales of laughter by mocking white supremacists' warning of "social equality" in the form of black men marrying white women. Rock had imagined white women seizing black men, "*nolens volens*," and declared it "sad . . . and especially so to the blacks themselves, who are still to be the victims," first of slaveholders' "avarice," and now of white women's "mad love." "O,

I am almost tempted to complain of the Creator for first giving us such a beautiful complexion, and then placing us among a people who are always trying to extract the virtues from it!" Like Ruffin, he had recognized that attraction already existed between white and black, charges of "natural repugnance" notwithstanding, and imagined successive generations of intermarriage after which "the twain would be one flesh."[44]

Since then, "amalgamation" and "miscegenation" had taken on new connotations. Rock's charge had produced laughter; twenty years later, Ruffin's prophecy engendered outrage among some black commentators. "Away with those short-sighted statesmen and amalgamation organs," read one letter to the *Boston Advocate*, "that are striving to lose the race in the citizen, through intermarriages in the social and political circles."[45] Another writer, speaking more generally to the question of black men marrying white women, disapproved on the grounds that it suggested "the immediate association of one of his own race [was] not good enough for him in his elevated position." People were free to choose their marriage partners, of course, but this particular choice produced an unfortunate "impression."[46] The controversy had its basis in the city's new demographic reality: of the marriages in Boston involving at least one African American partner, a large proportion were between blacks and whites—38 percent in 1877, mainly black men marrying white immigrant women.[47] Although he did not live in Boston itself, the once famous George Latimer embodied this as well as other realities. His second marriage was to a white woman, and in the later decades of the century they resided in the nearby industrial city of Lynn. Latimer prospered in middle age, gaining well-paid employment hanging wallpaper and becoming a high-ranking member of the Odd Fellows, but after suffering a stroke he became almost destitute and died in 1896.[48]

Blacks disagreed as to the merits of Ruffin's long view, but many whites viewed it as calamitously mistaken. Since the 1850s, Democrats had leveled the charge that "black Republicans" and other abolitionists sought the marriage of white women to black men. In the decades after Reconstruc-

George Latimer in Odd Fellows regalia
Courtesy of the Ohio Historical Society

tion, white Democratic politicians distilled "social equality" down to a bitter draught of sexual peril and terror. Any form of equality, they argued, encouraged black men to imagine themselves the equals of whites, and therefore to sexually pursue white women. Those women did indeed feel that "natural repugnance" which Ruffin and Rock had mocked, and as a result black men became frustrated. They raped white women, taking by force what they could not have by consent. "Social equality" had once connoted proximity, incongruity, and disgust, with sex as one feature among many; now it described a slippery slope in which equality in any form led inevitably to rape by black men. And this in turn brought retributive violence from enraged white men—the long-imagined "war of races."

The late-nineteenth-century discourse of "social equality" retrospectively redefined the war against Reconstruction—first, foremost, and everywhere a war against Republican officeholders, organizers, and soldiers—as a war to protect white womanhood from the black beast rapist. One of the chief expositors of this argument was South Carolina politician Ben Tillman. A rifle-wielding partisan during the war against Reconstruction, Tillman became governor, then U.S. senator; from the Senate and in lectures across the nation, he retold the story of Reconstruction as black sexual ambition run amok: the freedman, loosed from slavery's restrictions and encouraged by Northern demagogues to seek equality, became "a fiend" whose particular victim was the "helpless white woman." The only solution to these ambitions and horrors was white men's forcible overthrow of Reconstruction. Tillman's conclusion warned that only white men's continued vigilance would prevent the nation from again falling down that slippery slope: "We realized what it means to allow ever so little a trickle of race equality to break through the dam."[49] He offered a simple choice: black political aspirations could be suppressed, or black men would be lynched. As the incidence of lynching soared across the South during the late 1880s and 1890s, black critics pointed out that only a minority of the murders even purported to be in retaliation for rapes attempted or accomplished.[50] But Southern politics was increasingly monopolized by those who argued, enthusiastically or apologetically, that white supremacy at the ballot box and beyond was essential to keep black men's violent sexual ambitions in check. Those politicians never acknowledged what they well understood: that this argument helped keep white voters the captives of a one-party system whose benefits flowed to a small group of white men.

The erosion of black men's voting rights by amendment, law, and intimidation made it increasingly hard for black families to protect themselves through the processes of law and justice, and growing numbers of black Southerners sought homes outside the postwar plantation belt. While small numbers migrated to Northern cities and towns, from Boston and Worcester to St. Paul and Des Moines, larger numbers set their eyes on the western South and plains, migrating in large numbers and often large groups during the late 1870s and early 1880s to Kansas, Arkansas, and other areas where arable land was available.[51] The emigrants sometimes fell on hard times, and Lewis Hayden and Robert Morris were among the Bostonians who rallied to send aid to a group of Kansas migrants in 1879.[52]

But most African Americans remained in the states of the former Confederacy, where the pogroms and lynchings against them prompted black Northerners to echo the militant rhetoric of the past. Instead of emigrating, the *Boston Advocate* opined, "our outraged Southern brothers . . . should organize protective societies and form some plans to emigrate a few white scoundrels across Jordan." Nat Turner, it suggested, had had the right idea. "One or two good raids of that kind, backed by a just reason, will effect more good to the colored people of the South than all the emigration ideas."[53] New York's T. Thomas Fortune agreed, calling for black Americans to "face the enemy and fight inch by inch for every right he denies us."[54] Robert Morris and Charles Remond had put it more or less the same way in 1858 when they called for the slaves to revolt against their owners. But it was a poor season for black militants: when the Shaw Guards called an August 1 celebration in New Bedford in 1886 to mark the anniversary of the assault on Fort Wagner, only eight visitors from Boston attended.[55] In the late 1880s, almost as much as the late 1850s, the Northern call for Southerners to rise up in arms was based less in a realistic assessment of Southern circumstances than in Northerners' helplessness and frustration.[56]

By then, even the formal equality promised by the Fourteenth Amendment meant almost nothing. A decade after the Supreme Court narrowly delimited the amendment's implications in the *Slaughterhouse* decision, it gutted the Civil Rights Act of 1875. In the *Civil Rights Cases* of 1883 the court held that the Fourteenth Amendment empowered the federal government to regulate only acts of discrimination by state and local governments, not those undertaken by associations or individuals. From these foundations it was not hard to discern where subsequent decisions would lead. In 1896, in *Plessy v. Ferguson*, the court ratified the white supremacist rhetoric of "social equality" as a governing principle, holding that formally segregated public accommodations did not violate the principle of "equal protection." Had Robert Morris lived to read the opinion, he would have been dismayed to note an important precedent the court offered in support of this ruling: the 1849 Massachusetts decision in *Roberts*, which held that Boston's segregated schools fulfilled the state constitution's mandate of equal treatment to its citizens.

Defeats came in the Congress as well as the courts. A Republican Congress and president failed to pass the Lodge Elections Bill of 1890, which might have revived the federal enforcement of black voting rights in the South. During that decade, Southern states began to rewrite their constitutions, using property and educational qualifications to strip the vote from virtually their entire black populations.[57] Those states' black majorities, like the rest of their regional peers, continued to forge institutions—churches, schools, and lodges—to support their hopes and dreams. But in the face of rampant private and public discrimination and violence, sanctioned by custom and by law, they remained "citizens" of their states and nation only in ways that recalled an earlier generation's bitter and ironic phrases—"aliened Americans," and the "nominally free."

THE LAST DAYS OF LEWIS HAYDEN

At funeral after funeral in the decade after Reconstruction, Lewis Hayden rose in his long black coat to eulogize the departed or escort the casket. When Garrison passed away at the end of May 1879, Hayden presided over the evening meeting of "the colored citizens" at Grimes's old church. Over the decades he and the editor had sometimes disagreed, but now all that mattered was the lesson of Garrison's outstretched hand and full-throated commitment. Speaking with what a reporter recognized as "much feeling," Hayden declared that "[u]ntil God raised up William Lloyd Garrison, the lesson of the brotherhood of man and the fatherhood of God was not fully taught." At the funeral, a private family function, black Boston was represented by a delegation of "older colored citizens who had been associated with Mr. Garrison"—Hayden, Morris, John J. Smith, and William Wells Brown. Hayden took his place among the pall-bearers, as he would three years later for Morris. He performed the same duty for Wendell Phillips in 1884, and spoke at an anniversary service at John Andrew's grave on Memorial Day 1885.[58] A year later it was Judge Ruffin who passed on, never to see how poorly his prophecies of an amalgamated nation would play out over the next century.

Hayden himself lived long enough to enjoy the life he had made. Although he rarely attended large social gatherings anymore, he sometimes led visitors on fishing parties, his "chief delight" while on holiday.[59] The contrast with days past must sometimes have been astounding to him. As a young man he strode the wharves of Boston to grasp the hand of newly arrived fugitives, and crossed the nation to raise funds for a church, bring the light of Masonry, organize a convention, or recruit for the colored regiments. Now he took fishing vacations. In July 1886, while Harriet rode the train to visit friends in Portland, Maine, Lewis Hayden and his political friends made the journey by sea, boarding a yacht for several days along the New England coast. The meditation of the peaceful holiday must have cast his mind drifting by the time the rocky coast of Maine drew into view. Debarking and strolling into the old port town, perhaps he reflexively paused to note the churches and barbershops where he could meet the leading men and begin his work. But this was a vacation, and his wife and friends were waiting. He moved on.[60]

That autumn brought a different reminder of past days and things, as the grandees of the Wendell Phillips Club—composed of the city's leading black men—threw a banquet in honor of Frederick Douglass. The elder statesman had by then achieved offices and celebrity that confirmed his place as the most famous black man in America: he had been appointed the first African American marshal of the District of Columbia, as well as its recorder of deeds. But he clung tightly to his oldest friends in freedom, among them the Haydens. They had hosted him during the 1850s; when he returned in 1886 to be honored, he was again their guest.[61] Douglass entered the hall "arm-in-arm with his staunch old friend, Lewis Hayden," to a warm welcome from the remaining white abolitionists of the old days, Henry Bowditch among them. Douglass's impromptu speech thanked his "esteemed friend" Hayden for the invitation, reminisced about being invited to Dr. Bowditch's home in the Latimer days, and offered a generous appreciation of those now departed. "I have often been asked where I got my education," he said with a smile; "I have answered from the Massachusetts Abolitionist University, William Lloyd Garrison, President. . . . The moral power which had its fountain spring in Boston," he declared, with what must have been at least a degree of sincerity, "led to the abolition of the greatest curse that overshadowed this fair land."[62]

Douglass would live another decade. Hayden's light was almost gone. Kidney disease, a chronic problem of his later life, seized him in earnest in early 1887, sending him to Massachusetts General Hospital, just across Cambridge Street from the site of his long-gone clothing shop. Dr. Bowditch oversaw his care. "Many now visiting the State House miss the pleasant face of the patriarch Lewis Hayden," a newspaper noted. He was soon up and about again, but the cure was temporary.[63]

As with so many of the generation that rose from obscurity to achieve so much, Lewis Hayden contemplated his end with anxiety for the fate of his soon-to-be widow. Although he retained his position as messenger to the secretary of state, the income was not enough to cover the mortgage payments on the Haydens' home. The modest brick dwelling contained the reminders of forty years of campaigns: the mahogany table around which they had hatched plans for fugitive defense; in a window, a bunch of dried palm leaves once draped over Sumner's casket; portraits of abolitionists and politicians and, over the mantel, of their long-dead son, Jo; leaning against a wardrobe, two of the useless pikes John Brown and his men brought to Harpers Ferry.[64] But before Lewis died, as he soon would, he feared that all of this would go to the auction block. Harriet would be left alone and eventually homeless, as Robert Morris's widow had been.[65]

Bowditch, learning of the couple's straits, organized a committee to pay off the mortgage. The bond between him and Hayden had grown strong over the years, perhaps particularly after their mutual experience of loss in the Civil War. Bowditch's beloved son, Nat, the boy he had carried with him to watch the renditions of Sims and Burns, followed his family's antislavery course and in late 1861 received an officer's commission in the state's 1st Cavalry Regiment; he fell in early 1863, while leading a charge.[66] Bowditch kept his son's memory alive with a memorial volume, a cabinet full of abolitionist and Civil War memorabilia, and campaigns to improve the Union's ambulance service, but loss may also have drawn him to those who intuitively understood his grief.[67] The money Bowditch now raised left the Haydens suddenly comfortable, with their house owned free and clear, and a fifteen-hundred-dollar nest egg besides.[68] Hayden's gratitude was deep. When "great suffering" again overtook him a little later, he offered his friend and physician a token of his affection in lieu of repayment: the gold watch he had acquired nearly thirty years before when beginning his duties at the statehouse.[69]

Hayden was now "Father Hayden," "the venerable Lewis Hayden."[70] A New York journalist who did not share his stalwart Republicanism nonetheless celebrated him as "A Philosopher of the Hub," writing elegiacally of the "active restless nature" that drove him through antislavery, the Civil War, and beyond. "He is out of politics now and watches the struggle in public life from the secure pedestal of the 'well done, thou good and faithful servant.'" It was a premature obituary of sorts.[71]

Hayden could not quite master the stage as he once had. When Grover Cleveland chose James Monroe Trotter as recorder of deeds of the District of Columbia, the first black New Englander to get a high-ranking federal appointment, and the first to do so under a Democratic administration, Hayden was "just getting up from a bed of sickness," but "unspeakably delighted and gratified."[72] He rose to speak at a celebratory dinner for

Trotter and began well, lauding the new recorder's service in the 55th Massachusetts—not only his willingness to die in the nation's service, but also his part in persuading his men to refuse inferior pay. When they did this, Hayden reminded those present, "they laid down a rule of action that has influenced materially the question of the equality of the races." But when he began to thank the audience for their kindnesses during his illness earlier that year, "he broke down completely before he had finished."[73]

One task remained in his power to accomplish, the one he and Nell had envisioned nearly forty years before: to persuade the city of Boston to honor the role of the "colored patriots of the American Revolution" by creating a monument to their progenitor, Crispus Attucks.[74] The renewed campaign may have had its origins in 1886. On that year's Decoration Day (now Memorial Day), Hayden accompanied the veterans of the Shaw Guards to Forest Hills cemetery, where Garrison and Nell lay, then back to Boston for a march that passed the grave of Crispus Attucks and the new statue of Garrison on Commonwealth Avenue, then finally by streetcar to the Cambridge resting places of Robert Gould Shaw and Charles Sumner. It was a pilgrimage to the honored dead.[75] The bare spot where Nell lay must have fired something in Hayden, for immediately upon his return he took part in a meeting of "leading men" to get funds together to build Nell a monument. Harriet Hayden headed a William C. Nell Club for the same purpose.[76] And while Nell might not have wanted so much fuss raised on his own account, he certainly would have approved of the parallel campaign Hayden reignited to build a monument to Crispus Attucks.

While fund-raising for Nell's headstone lagged, the Attucks campaign succeeded. The monument, just off Tremont Street on the Boston Common, was dedicated late in 1888, with a long procession and many speeches in Faneuil Hall. The single black company of the state militia made up the first uniformed element of the parade, but although black veterans' associations, Knights of Pythias, and even Rhode Island's black militia companies joined them, only one group of white veterans, and no white state troops, took part in the exercises. This part of state and city memory was increasingly segregated. The mayor and governor spoke, and the Faneuil Hall audience later that day included some white listeners, but the vast majority of the celebrants were black. The "aged and much esteemed" Hayden sat on the platform with the governor and other dignitaries, but made no speech.[77]

Hayden died in April 1889, just as spring was softening the city. As the body, draped in a Masonic collar, lay on a bier in the front room of the house at 66 Southac, journalist Robert T. Teamoh observed firsthand the wave of sorrow that swept over Boston's black community. "In one of the churches," he wrote, "one of the female singers was unable to finish a hymn which had been a favorite with Lewis Hayden."[78] For the funeral, the Charles Street AME Church was filled well past its capacity. In the pews sat the black-clothed governor of the state, the city police commissioner, and a host of other high officials. Arianna Sparrow—once a fugitive girl whom Hayden had carried from the wharf to Southac, now an internationally renowned singer—sang "I Know That My Redeemer Liveth" with such feeling that the hall fell utterly silent for many minutes.[79] Famous and illustrious orators struggled for words. William Lloyd Garrison's son and namesake declared, "Every colored citizen is elevated by his example." Higginson agreed, but pointed that lesson in a direction the departed elder Garrison might not have appreciated: "All the colored soldiers"—of the war against slavery, he meant—"love to recall the day when Lewis Hayden sat in that room with revolvers and dirks, waiting for the slaveholder to break into that house."[80]

Once he had been a revolutionary, but now he was royalty, "a prince among us." From across the social spectrum people remembered him as a source of wisdom and advice. "He was the least assuming of men," thought the Irish American journalist John Boyle O'Reilly, "but he had a native dignity that forbade all infringement on his rights." He was a man of passionate convictions, but "there was no bitterness in his soul or mouth."[81] The grand master of the Prince Hall Grand Lodge told his brethren, "No event in our history has cast such gloom in Masonic circles, as the loss of this dearly beloved brother."[82] Frederick Douglass, celebrating the anniversary of wartime emancipation in Washington D.C., paused to remember Hayden, "a brave and wise counselor in the cause of our people, a moral hero."[83]

Henry Bowditch spoke more feelingly of what was lost. "[W]here," he asked, "can you find a colored man who is received by universal public opinion in Massachusetts as an equal to the white man? My dearly beloved and most honored, ever-to-be-remembered friend, Lewis Hayden, came nearer than any one else I know of gaining that equality before the masses which is granted to a white man, however vulgar and low he may be."[84] Bowditch, "[h]aving known and loved him as a valiant comrade in the thirty years' war against slavery," found himself too sad to express himself fully at Hayden's funeral.[85] "I never felt so oppressed before an audience," he wrote afterward, "as if I had lost in his death a great hold on life . . . [W]ithout the idea that I shall meet him again, I feel intensely saddened. I seem to care to do nothing." Of the watch Hayden had pressed upon him in his last hours, Bowditch wrote simply, "I shall wear it till I die."[86]

Then Lewis Hayden brought a crowd to the streets of Boston one final time. As the procession made its stately route through town and headed north toward Woodlawn, the suburban cemetery where he would be laid, the *Boston Globe* reported on the order of march. There were many associations and prominent personages to acknowledge, but one group stood out: between the Wendell Phillips Club and the Masonic lodges, a great mass described simply as "Colored citizens in a body."[87]

THE FAILURE OF MEMORY

As the people who claimed the title "colored citizen" passed away, they were both remembered and forgotten. Into the 1870s, revolutionary change—the wholesale transformation of the place of people of African descent in American life—had seemed possible. But in the last years of the

nineteenth century, the struggle of Hayden and the people of his generation was reduced to the war against slavery and the Confederacy. Most
commentators and memorialists, even those who yearned for something
beyond slave emancipation, seemed to have assumed that this victory
represented the achievement of all their heroic forebears' fondest hopes.
Passing lightly or silently over the postwar careers of the "colored citizens," turn-of-the-century writers also failed to note those activists' deep
yearning for a world in which "social equality" meant something quite
different from sinister sexual designs.

The partial, blinkered reading of the past—of midcentury black activists as only abolitionists or soldiers—took many forms, among them an
increasingly romantic depiction of fugitive rescue and defense. The antebellum observers who coined the cheeky metaphor "Underground Railroad" did so when that novel technology was just penetrating American
communities and, like the clandestine networks that actually helped fugitives escape, was so mysterious to outsiders as to seem almost magical.
Now railroads were omnipresent and unremarkable, and an actual railway
was about to be built beneath the streets of Boston.[88] Understandably,
some observers missed the earlier generation's joke.

Among them was an Ohio professor named Wilbur Siebert, who in the
1890s began researching this fabled network. His method was simple: he
circulated questionnaires to old abolitionists, their descendants, and indeed to anyone across the North who claimed to remember a fugitive
taking shelter nearby, and he took his respondents more or less at their
word. He produced regional maps of the "U.G.R.R.," whose dense webs
of arrows showed all the potential routes of escape, with a presumption
that safe houses—"stations"—were to be found at regular intervals along
each of them. The friends of the fugitive, the work implied, were everywhere. Thousands of fugitives did indeed take shelter across the Northern
states, but Siebert's work did not distinguish much between fact and fancy.
Rather, it painted a composite portrait of a broad-based white Northern
social movement that stood resolutely on the side of fugitives and their

freedom. In the words of historian David Blight, Siebert's reconstruction of the Underground Railroad constituted "a mythos of accomplished glory, a history of emancipation completed"—all of it immensely flattering to the self-regard of white Northerners.[89]

Some veterans of the struggle were reluctant to indulge Siebert's assumptions about the scale, regularity, and ubiquity of the fugitive defense network. One former member of the Boston Anti-Man-Hunting League cautioned Siebert that "there was no system of communication" such as he imagined.[90] The irascible William Bowditch wrote, "We had no regular route and no regular station in Massachusetts."[91] Higginson put it even more sharply: "There was *no* organization in Massachusetts answering properly to the usual description of the U.G.R.R." Siebert's elaborate maps, showing the routes by which fugitives were supposedly carried to freedom, were nothing more or less than diagrams of currently existing transportation networks, and Higginson was annoyed to find the decidedly proslavery town of Newburyport marked as a "station": "I don't remember a fugitive slave there while I lived there (1847–1852)," he admonished the credulous professor.[92]

Despite these cautions, the romance between white Bostonians and their heroic past blossomed in the late nineteenth century. The reunions and funerals of prominent abolitionists and black leaders furnished grist for the mill, as did Siebert's fables of the "Underground Railroad" and the Decoration Day observances celebrating the triumph over slavery. In a way, so did Harriet Hayden's final legacy. She died on Christmas Eve 1893, bequeathing the entire Hayden estate—about five thousand dollars—to a "Lewis and Harriet Hayden Scholarship for Colored Students" at Harvard University, for the benefit of "poor and honest," "needy and worthy" students in the medical or other departments.[93] A close observer of the city's black community noted that "there was some dissatisfaction felt by warm personal friends" about the bequest. Harvard was a wealthy institution and hardly needed the Haydens' few thousand dollars.[94] Should Harvard decline the funds, the beneficiary was to be the city's Home for Aged

Colored Women; perhaps some thought this would be a better use of the money.[95] But the story briefly became a national sensation, a wondrous tale of "the only instance of the kind in the United States and probably in the world where a university has received an endowment from a former slave."[96] The rags-to-riches story of perseverance, prosperity, and benevolence further burnished the mythology of Boston as the apotheosis of liberty and equality.

In 1897 the city of Boston crowned its nostalgia for the victory over slavery with a monument commemorating the 54th Massachusetts. The vast bronze bas-relief featured a mounted Colonel Robert Gould Shaw in the foreground, with ranks of black soldiers marching beside him. Despite the sculptor's personal feelings—Saint-Gaudens held the New York black men who modeled for him in low regard—the monument depicted a range of black humanity, anonymous but differentiated, working side by side with their white leader to carry the freedom struggle to the sands of South Carolina.[97] Students of aesthetics, and ordinary passersby, could disagree about the subtle shadings of meaning figured by the composition. Yet the simple placement of the monument spoke volumes. William Nell would have known where it rightly belonged: on State Street, where the 54th once marched past the spot where Attucks fell. But Nell was long dead, and no one arose to speak for him and his legacy. Instead, the memorial was unveiled where it still stands, on Beacon Street at the edge of the Boston Common, facing the front doors of the statehouse. Legislators and others doing business at the center of New England's power would never again have to be reminded what their forebears had done to bring an end to slavery. Neither would they have to remember that those soldiers—real men—struggled not just against the Confederacy but against the Union as well, nor that their broader struggle was as yet unfinished.

The Shaw Memorial, as it came to be known, captured an emerging narrative of the era just past, of a heroic and successful struggle against slavery that reached its climax in black military service, and that demon-

strated Boston's special commitment to black freedom. It was not a false
story in all of its particulars. At the turn of the century, enough African
Americans noted Boston's comparative freedom and safety, even for protest, to give a skeptic pause.[98] But it was a story as neatly packaged, with
as happy an ending, as though it had been bound between the covers of a
sentimental novel. And of course it was also almost literally that, in the
volumes of late-nineteenth-century reminiscences published by elderly
onetime abolitionists, fugitives, statesmen, and ministers. More and more,
the late heroic age stood outside the normal passage of time. "The places
whereon the Abolitionists stood and struggled and achieved have become
holy ground," wrote Charlotte Forten's brother-in-law, the former slave
Archibald Grimké, in an 1890 magazine story on "Anti-Slavery Boston."[99]

Grimké, a product of Boston's postemancipation opening, had journeyed from slavery in South Carolina to success at Harvard and in William
Bowditch's law office.[100] Like many other young black people who inherited that legacy without having participated in it directly, he absorbed an
account of the late struggle in which "abolition" was a mainly white undertaking. Grimké's account of that movement did not begin with David
Walker and the Massachusetts General Colored Association, but with Garrison and a few white followers standing alone against a howling mob.
"Anti-Slavery Boston had its origin in Garrison and the *Liberator*," he told
his magazine audience. Its beginnings could be found in the humble office where Garrison, "brave as Luther," issued his declaration against slavery, and in the twelve apostles of the New England Anti-Slavery Society
who gathered with him to sign the charter.[101] Of the many engravings and
photographs illustrating Grimké's article, the militant struggle of black
Bostonians was reduced to the single figure of Lewis Hayden. In Grimké's
account, Hayden leads men here and there, and promises to blow himself
and everyone else to kingdom come rather than let William Craft be taken
back to slavery. "The heroic frenzy of the resolute black face, as with match
in hand Hayden stood awaiting the man-stealers," Grimké excitedly wrote;

"those who saw it declare they can never forget." Even had Hayden been alive to respond, he probably would not publicly have contradicted the young writer. Hayden was of course too thoughtful and careful a revolutionary ever to stand watch over a keg of gunpowder with a match in his hand, but the larger error was that of omission: Hayden's life story was not simply one of uncompromising resistance, but of love and imagination, organizing and eloquence, compromise and heartbreak.[102]

Another activist of the younger generation, the talented and tireless Pauline Hopkins, similarly depicted Hayden's career primarily as one of antislavery striving.[103] In her 1901 biographical essay in *Colored American Magazine* she offered many time-embroidered tales of Hayden's antebellum daring but said little about his postbellum career, or about the dreams that animated it. In her concluding rumination on the stagnating position of black Americans and their abuse at the hands of their white neighbors, she offered what must have seemed to her a novel idea: "We must convert the prejudiced and change public opinion" by peaceful protest and good example. From where she stood, the struggle required a new approach, different from that pursued by prior generations. "These old fathers, like Lewis Hayden, thought the question of the rights of the black man settled when slavery was abolished. . . . The question then was: Has the Negro a right to resist his master? We settled that in the Civil War. The question now is: Has the Negro a right to citizenship?"[104] Over the next generations, she and her comrades would again struggle to imbue that word with meaning. She had forgotten the "colored citizens," reducing them to heroic but outmoded "black abolitionists." She picked up their mantle nonetheless.

Epilogue

More Than Freedom

In 1863, as former slaves across the South began to speak with what Thomas Wentworth Higginson called "the choked voice of a race at last unloosed," William Nell stood on the Boston cobbles, no more than a "hailing distance," he believed, from a citizenship animated by feelings of fellowship, regard, and even love.[1] But despite a century of subsequent strategies that included everything from "uplift" to evangelism and unionism to communism, the reality of democratic fellowship eluded their descendants, and the United States. Exactly one hundred years later, the Reverend Martin Luther King Jr. would rearticulate their dream of an imagined future, one emancipated from the tragic legacies of division and mistrust. "I have a dream," his unchoked voice thundered from the steps of the Lincoln Memorial, "that one day on the red hills of Georgia, the sons of former slaves and the sons of former slave owners will be able to sit down together at the table of brotherhood . . . that little black boys and black girls will be able to join hands with little white boys and white girls as sisters and brothers . . . that we will be able to transform the jangling discords of our nation into a beautiful symphony of brotherhood."[2] Boston's "colored citizens" had dreamt no less. Whatever their disputes about the means that might be necessary, they knew that only when all could work, study, play, and struggle together would they all be free.

To take final account of the history of these "colored citizens," and to see how the struggles of the nineteenth century continued to echo through the eras of segregation and civil rights, of *Brown v. Board* and Barack Obama, we must return briefly to the emancipation of the 1860s and consider it through the lens of what came after. We must think hard, as the "colored citizens" did, about the relationship between rights and belonging, between a citizenship constituted by laws and an acceptance animated by feelings of fellowship, regard, and even love—what President Obama envisioned in his inaugural prediction that "the lines of tribe shall soon dissolve" and "our common humanity shall reveal itself."[3] But we must think about this citizenship of the heart differently than those nineteenth-century activists did, for in a fundamental way they were tragically mistaken.

Their victory was real: the liberal freedom won by slaves and free blacks during the 1860s represented a momentous transformation in the formal character of the United States. The Constitution no longer buttressed a white republic. Essential rights belonged not only to whites, but to citizens without regard to race: the rights of individuals to be secure in their persons and property, to make contracts, to participate in the institutions of government, and to defend themselves. *Dred Scott* and the black codes, North and South, were overthrown.[4] For African Americans in the Civil War era, "freedom" resonated with transcendent spiritual and communal hopes.[5] It meant a radical break with the enslaved past. It meant the overthrow of that world's most painful features: dispossession become self-ownership, legal kinlessness replaced with bonds of family and community, much as King would imagine America a century later. The "colored citizens," who understood themselves "chained together" with those still in bondage, hoped and even believed that the burgeoning "freedom" of the following decade would begin a new world in which neither the nation nor their white countrymen would regard them as unworthy or incapable.

But the "colored citizens" of the North—and perhaps especially of Massachusetts, where they came closest to having formal equality—knew from their own experience of subordination that winning these important rights did not of itself fulfill their broader goal of a deeply, universally felt citizenship. They knew full well that equality did not follow directly or necessarily from emancipation. Instead, they had understood the acquisition of formal rights as a crucial step toward that loftier goal. They imagined that as they won rights and achieved prosperity, many of them would become so obviously worthy that the whole ideological architecture of racial hierarchy would collapse under the weight of its own absurdity. The freedom to pursue careers, gain wealth, and participate in society's deliberations would take them to the mountaintop, bringing within sight the promised land where they would at last be embraced as fellow citizens in the most encompassing sense.

This broad understanding of what full and unhedged citizenship would mean helps explain why they were never content to win only "civil rights." It explains why canny, pragmatic activists such as Leonard Grimes, Lewis Hayden, and William Nell also threw themselves into labors well beyond the scope of political enfranchisement or even slave emancipation—into the fellowship of Christian faith, the brotherhood of Freemasonry, and the imagined community of a shared history. These realms of experience called upon people to recognize and voluntarily embrace one another in their common humanity, as brethren or patriots with a shared destiny rather than as individual subjects formally entitled to participate.[6]

The "colored citizens" did not live long enough to see how profoundly events would dash their hopes and reveal the flaws in their vision. But by the end of the nineteenth century it had become clear that the citizenship granted by laws had little to do with the emotional, spiritual, and intuitive sense of kinship they had sought. Liberal freedom, it turned out, did not address many of the fundamental historical forces that led many whites to view African Americans as anticitizens. It could not erase the stigma of enslavement—neither from the society's distribution of resources, nor from its people's imaginations. And even the liberal freedoms that they did win during the 1860s and 1870s were soon qualified, abridged, or violated with impunity.

By the turn of the twentieth century, African Americans faced disenfranchisement by education, property, and other proxies for race, as well as formal segregation and extralegal terror in ever growing areas of Southern life. From the 1890s through the 1910s, several times each week, a white mob in some small town or rural crossroads murdered a black person in the public square.[7] Nearly everywhere else, even in Boston, the great majority of African Americans lived in persistent poverty and customary exclusion. At the dawn of the twentieth century, the Massachusetts-born, Harvard-educated scholar and activist W. E. B. Du Bois still yearned for a world in which it was "possible for a man to be both a Negro and an American, without being cursed and spit upon by his fellows, without having the doors of Opportunity closed roughly in his face."[8]

Although race no longer demarcated the line between slavery and freedom, it proved exceedingly useful in setting people against one another and preventing them from together employing the resources of democracy. As the story of the Boston and Albany strike foretold, neither black nor white workers viewed one another as natural allies, and persuading either group otherwise remained an uphill battle. The white Georgia Populist Tom Watson, living in a region where the struggles were bleaker and more violent than in Massachusetts, offered a prescient analysis when he told black and white farmers in 1892, "You are kept apart that you may be separately fleeced of your earnings. You are made to hate each other because upon that hatred is rested the keystone of the arch of financial despotism which enslaves you both."[9] But the weak and unequal freedoms available to the black and white people whom he sought to persuade were insufficient to win the day against the crushing, seemingly tectonic forces he named: the persistence of racial hierarchy, and the emergence of corporate and financial entities of unprecedented scale and power, which reshaped the landscape of free people's economic and political lives. When white allies fully committed themselves to a common, interracial struggle, they not only confronted the mutual suspicion of many blacks and whites, but also the deliberate efforts of the managers of mines and mills to keep black and white workers apart.[10] Secret police and brutal vigilantes dogged dissidents of any hue. Whites who rejected white supremacy confronted ostracism, hardships, and perils that left almost all of them dispirited and turned some of them, like Watson and even Thomas Wentworth Higginson, into bitter reactionaries. Fighting white supremacy was hard work, and few whites had the courage to do it for very long.[11]

Instead, the black and interracial freedom struggles of the late nineteenth and early twentieth centuries inspired vicious and well-organized white supremacist violence. Paramilitary campaigns cut off most resurgent interracial movements at the knees. In 1898, when terror, fraud, and racist slander overthrew the interracial democratic government of North Carolina, the silence of the federal government spoke more loudly than any of the protests.[12] Over the next three decades, pogroms and massacres shadowed African Americans' efforts to assert themselves in political or economic life. Across the nation, white Americans justified this bloody repression with popular culture, historical scholarship, and "racial science" that constituted slanders against the character and capacity of African Americans.

The foreign wars of these decades proved far less useful than the Civil War in mobilizing a coalition behind black people's claims. W. E. B. Du Bois editorially urged black Americans to set aside their historic grievances for the moment and "close ranks" with their white countrymen as the United States entered World War I.[13] African Americans threw themselves into citizenship work, fighting in France, laboring in American cities, and urging recognition of their contributions. "We return fighting," vowed Du Bois after the armistice. Yet the war's aftermath not only failed to make the world safe for democracy, but drenched the ground from the Arkansas Delta to the streets of Chicago with the blood of black Americans.[14] In 1915 the nation's first blockbuster film, *The Birth of a Nation,* lionized the white terrorists who overthrew Reconstruction; in its wake, a revived Ku Klux Klan, this time mostly a Northern and urban movement, reached a peak of four million members.[15] Freedom from slavery and the rights of formal citizenship, it turned out, guaranteed neither equal justice, equal dignity, nor equal belonging. In the reconstituted white republic, the Constitution meant only what local white authorities allowed it to mean.

The dogged pursuit of formal citizenship continued throughout the early twentieth century. The legal strategies of the National Association for the Advancement of Colored People brought a slow series of victories against peonage, disenfranchisement, and unequal access to education.[16] In 1941, the March on Washington Movement leveraged the threat of a massive African American march on the nation's capital into a presidential directive forbidding discrimination in war industries.[17] But even the dramatic transformations of the New Deal, which created new social guarantees for many Americans, all but excluded African Americans; Franklin Roosevelt's Southern Democratic coalition partners insisted that programs such as Social Security and the Federal Housing Administration not apply equally to blacks.[18] Not surprisingly, many blacks looked elsewhere than the United States for visions of solidarity—to the racial nationalism of Jamaican-born Marcus Garvey's Universal Negro Improvement Association, or to international imaginaries such as the worldwide communist revolution or the United Nations Universal Declaration of Human Rights. Transcendent visions of overcoming the barrier of race in American national life, such as those shared by the NAACP's small interracial community of liberal dreamers, remained comparatively rare.[19]

Like the Reconstruction amendments, the court decisions and legislative victories of the 1950s and 1960s spoke only in the language of liberal citizenship—of rights belonging to individuals, in the language of race neutrality and "color-blindness."[20] They failed to fully address the yearning for a sense of common purpose and mutual regard. In its unanimous ruling against school segregation in *Brown v. Board of Education* in 1954, the Warren Court spoke of the "detrimental effect" segregation had on black children—the way it "generates a feeling of inferiority as to their status in the community that may affect their hearts and minds in a way unlikely to ever be undone." But it said nothing of the effect of such segregation on the hearts and minds of white students. The contrary and much richer argument articulated by Charles Sumner in the *Roberts* case—that segregation unfitted whites as well as blacks for a shared citizenship—did not arise. Instead, in a preview of arguments to follow from whites who feared or resented desegregation, the attorney representing a segregated South Carolina school district asked the Supreme Court whether racially mixed classrooms would make either black or white children happier, or improve their views of one another. The answer, to him, was obviously no.[21]

Still, the vision of citizenship as both legal right and transformative force persisted. In the 1940s, as director of branches of the NAACP, Ella Baker built a mass base for the organization in the South, which gave black Southerners regional and national networks to draw upon as the postwar struggle quickened.[22] The NAACP's 1944 victory in *Smith v. Allwright* declared the "white primary" unconstitutional and began to reestablish the national citizenship and nonracial suffrage envisioned by the Fourteenth and Fifteenth Amendments. Despite white terrorism and obstruction, voter registration campaigns, many led by returning African American veterans and the NAACP, dramatically increased the number of registered African American voters in the South by the early 1950s.[23]

Black activists did not confine their organizing to electoral politics and civil rights but sought to protect the dignity and worth of black personhood from a variety of standpoints. In the wake of the victory of the Montgomery Bus Boycott, Baker helped organize the Southern Christian Leadership Conference, whose campaigns in Birmingham and Selma made it possible for Martin Luther King Jr. to capture the moral imagination of the world. In Nashville in the late 1950s, Reverend James Lawson, Diane Nash, John Lewis, and a group of students and ministers in Nashville nurtured a vision of "the beloved community" and honed the philosophy and practice of nonviolent direct action.[24] When black college students in North Carolina launched the sit-in movement in 1960, the Nashville contingent leapt to the forefront; nonviolent direct action gave the movement a method, "the beloved community" provided a vision, and Ella Baker helped the students found the Student Nonviolent Coordinating Committee.[25] In the Citizenship Schools organized by the black educator Septima Clark and others in South Carolina during the 1950s, lessons in the basic skills essential to register to vote flowered into self-confidence as community building when previously excluded men and women learned, as one put it, "much of what Democracy means."[26]

These universal humanist visions, rooted in Afro-Christianity and in the founding documents of the nation, took active form in the philosophical and tactical nonviolence of the civil rights movement. These developments did not diminish other traditions of resistance nor completely transform America's violent racial history; less sanguine black activists such as Stokely Carmichael and Robert F. Williams placed more faith in black solidarity, armed self-assertion, and a new black sense of self.[27] The labors of many of these activists took their place alongside the William Lloyd Garrisons and Henry Bowditches of their day. Although they argued about philosophy and tactics as Frederick Douglass and Henry Highland Garnet had disputed before them, a broad and many-sided freedom struggle once again emerged across America. Myles and Zilphia Horton of the Highlander Folk School created a place where local radicals such as Rosa Parks and Amzie Moore could inspire and inform one another; fearless radicals such as Anne and Carl Braden provided networks of communication and conveyed the sense of a single movement, even as clashing visions, crushing labors, organizational rivalries, rising opposition, and countless heartbreaks made that solidarity hard to sustain.[28]

.   .   .

Prophetic dreams and practical demands came together with a force no one could ignore in 1963, when the March on Washington for Jobs and Freedom brought hundreds of thousands to the Lincoln Memorial.[29] As white politicians struggled once more to contain white supremacy and democracy within the same constitutional order, and as a resurgent black protest movement faced a violent and well-organized white supremacist resistance, Reverend Martin Luther King Jr. reached past the fractures and material urgencies of the present to an imagined future that William Nell would have recognized. But the Boston-educated minister was not only a dreamer. He never imagined that the walls of the white republic would come tumbling down by mere moral suasion; he knew, as he had explained eight years earlier, "[n]ot only are we using the tools of persuasion, but we've come to see that we've got to use the tools of coercion."[30] Nor did the precarious economic position of most black Americans escape notice that momentous day in 1963. The deafening applause that followed Dr. King's visionary appeal continued as the next speaker, Bayard Rustin, asked the crowd to approve a list of demands: laws that would outlaw discrimination, raise the minimum wage, enforce school desegregation, and create a federal jobs program.[31] Like the convention speakers of the 1840s, the conveners of the March for Jobs and Freedom understood that entrenched black poverty and exclusion from well-paid jobs perpetuated the stigma of slavery. They sought to extend the social guarantees and protections of Franklin Roosevelt's New Deal, this time squarely address-ing the needs and history of African Americans. But the triumphs that followed, the Civil Rights Act of 1964 and the Voting Rights Act of 1965, did not build a common "table of brotherhood" around which all Ameri-cans could amicably sit.[32]

Nor did the equal education envisioned in the *Brown* decision come to pass. School desegregation dragged out against significant and sometimes violent resistance, notably in Boston. The city's black population grew dramatically in the decades after World War II, reaching one hundred thousand by 1970, concentrated far to the south of Beacon Hill in the neighborhood of Roxbury, and in high-poverty, underfunded, predominantly black public schools. As in the 1840s, moral appeals and school boycotts failed to sway an all-white school committee; even state legislation designed to prod the district toward integration failed. Some black citizens rejected what they regarded as the dubious promises of integration, but integration won in court. In 1974, federal judge W. Arthur Garrity Jr. found the Boston public schools unconstitutionally segregated and ordered a program of mandatory busing, including transfers between the impoverished neighborhoods of black Roxbury and white South Boston. Deeply instilled lessons of white supremacy quickly combined with equally profound white working-class rage, for wealthier suburban communities were excluded from the busing order. When school began that fall, whites showered the buses carrying black students to South Boston High School with rocks and bricks. Serious violence broke out among students. In an inversion that would have left William Nell speechless, white antibusing protestors joined a 1975 bicentennial reenactment of the Boston Massacre, carrying a coffin and chanting, "Garrity's killed liberty." A highly respected antibusing politician insisted that parents' efforts to keep their children in "traditional local schools" did not mean that they rejected "the brotherhood of man."[33] The legacy and language of black protest had become part of the American lexicon, but this by itself did not promise material victory. Just as in the era of *Dred Scott,* African Americans might still be the "alphabet"—the subjects and symbols of white Americans' debates—but this did little or nothing to advance what George Downing had called "the fraternal unity of man."

Civil rights law proved best suited to addressing individual acts of discrimination, not the history of inequality. Many white Americans understood "affirmative action," the one official effort to compensate for historically rooted inequalities, neither as a justified effort to achieve historical justice nor as an essential counterweight to centuries of racial hierarchy. Instead, the Supreme Court itself interpreted affirmative action as a redistribution of finite resources away from individually blameless whites.[34] In the *Bakke* decision of 1978, a narrow majority of the court agreed that colleges and professional schools might legitimately select students from diverse backgrounds, as a broad range of social experiences would "better equip its graduates to render with understanding their vital service to humanity." But it also warned that such programs inequitably forced "innocent persons"—white students not admitted—to "bear the burdens of redressing grievances not of their making." It refused to acknowledge the centuries of explicit racial preference that had left most whites richer, healthier, and better educated than most blacks. The language of individual rights stood opposed to any effort to address the history of collective inequity, or even the common good.[35]

Indeed, even in upholding limited and carefully scrutinized forms of affirmative action, the court's majority fled from the history that had created the Fourteenth Amendment, while unself-consciously echoing nineteenth-century white anxieties about a world turned racially upside down. Arguing that most groups had at some point been discriminated against, including many now accounted "white," the court asserted that a confrontation with the history of slavery and subsequent state-sanctioned discrimination against African Americans would begin a never-ending succession of competing claims. Were all those grievances to be addressed, wrote Justice Lewis Powell, "the only 'majority' left would be a new minority of white Anglo-Saxon Protestants." The court dismissed the Fourteenth Amendment's unfulfilled purpose of guaranteeing equal citizenship in language that might as well have been Andrew Johnson's, declaring that its guarantees of "equal protection" were not meant to establish blacks as "special wards entitled to a degree of protection greater than that accorded others." Ignoring history—in fact, urgently denying its relevance—the court insisted that the world had been made anew with emancipation. All citizens must be treated as equal, individual actors, and their unequal pasts studiously disregarded.[36]

The election of a man of African descent to the presidency of the United States in 2008 marked the triumph of the liberal emancipationist vision. A few nineteenth-century activists had foreseen this possibility and endowed it with awesome significance. The utopian "Philo-African" dream recounted in the *Liberator* back in 1831 hinged in part on the election of a black president—"a man of such distinguished talents, that none chose to risk their own reputation for discernment by not acknowledging it, and African inferiority was heard of no more."[37] A half century later, perhaps looking forward through the lens of his own ambitions, Frederick Douglass argued that "when a colored man could be elevated to the Vice-Presidency or had a seat in the Cabinet the color line would no longer be significant." That triumph, he believed, would reflect the long-sought millennial change in the meaning of race.[38] Those nineteenth-century proponents of "elevation" sincerely believed that individual achievement could reshape human consciousness, and many twenty-first-century Americans seem to have believed something similar. With Barack Obama's election, many in the United States and around the world declared—some ecstatically, some hopefully, and some cynically—that the nation had proved itself "postracial."

Yet as our century unfolds, the color line remains a stubbornly persistent predictor of class and education. Race is not the one-drop, de jure bar to all aspiration that the white supremacists of fifty or a hundred years ago sought to enforce, but it remains a powerful divide in most areas of American life. It is worth imagining how George Ruffin might have reconsidered his vision of the raceless America of the future, had he lived to see a society in which one black man could be president but one in every four black men would be incarcerated at some point in his life.[39] The election of President Obama marks a triumph but also a boundary—the limits of an emancipation that liberated discrete individuals but did not systematically dismantle the institutional, legal, and cultural legacies of the white republic.

Like William Nell imagining "the free, the happy future," so close he could almost touch it, many Americans yearn for a final break with a painful past. Like earlier seekers, we scan the horizon for evidence that our emancipation from that history is at hand. But we continue to understand "emancipation" and "freedom" as things heralded or achieved by the passage of a law, the election of a person, or even the acquisition of a product. This vision of liberal freedom is insufficient to nurture democratic citizenship, and it cannot address our need for connectedness, solidarity, and common dignity. People respond to this lack in many ways. Some seek a richer sense of belonging in enclaves of faith, family, or play. Some embrace the dogmas of the market and see making "real money" as the essence of virtue and the evidence of citizenship. And many of us, whether we are aware of it or not, follow the double course of the "colored citizens," nurturing familiar solidarities and pursuing concrete goals while also reaching for the more expansive vision of citizenship Nell once called "universal humanity."

At the dawn of the era of liberal freedom, a century and a half ago, the "colored citizens" already understood that legal rights, however important, would never suffice. They tried to explain this to their fellow citizens and to the world, and they still have lessons to teach us, if we will listen. Their small band shaped the course of the nation's greatest crisis and the meaning of its most fundamental transformation. Their history continues to matter, as an inspiration to rethink the limits of the possible and as a warning not to imagine that any victory, however grand, begins the world anew. The millennial vision of universal brotherhood cherished by the "colored citizens" did not come to pass. But their hard-won understanding of what it meant for a people to be less than fully part of their society, and their ardent pursuit of a citizenship that was not simply legislated but achieved, enacted, and felt, remain piercing lessons for our own, all too human, millennium.

Acknowledgments

Scholarship too encompasses both formal rules and warmhearted fellowship. Many friends and strangers extended their hands as I labored over this book, offering kind words, honest assessments, and stern challenges. I thank them all, for their faith in this project and for their willingness to do the unwaged labor so essential to our common endeavor.

I am deeply grateful to the colleagues who offered comments on parts—in some cases, quite large parts—of the manuscript: Nan Enstad, Dylan Penningroth, Steven Hahn, David Cecelski, Libby McRae, Nancy Hewitt, Peter Hinks, Will Jones, Christina Greene, and Walter Johnson. I am particularly beholden to Adriane Lentz-Smith, Kate Masur, and Glenda Gilmore, who offered insightful and detailed comments on the entire final draft. Tim Tyson has read this work at every stage from beginning to end; our conversations about it have taught me many things and strengthened it immeasurably. At Penguin, Laura Stickney showed me how small changes could dramatically improve the book, and Mally Anderson deduced its proper title. It's difficult to express how lucky I feel to have had a team like this one.

Friends, acquaintances, and strangers around the world shared ideas, information, or unpublished research. I thank Bryant Simon, Adam Malka, Scott Nelson, David Cecelski, John Quist, Susan O'Donovan, Carla Peterson, Van Gosse, Christian Samito, James Horton, Martin Summers, Nancy Cott, Margot Minardi, Corey D. B. Walker, Donald Yacavone, Elsa Barkley Brown, Matthew Harper, John Stauffer, Theda Skocpol, Ariane Lazos, Ikuko Asaka, Lois Horton, Charles Irons, Hollis Gentry, Debra Jackson, Kazuteru Omori, Stacey Smith, Chernoh Sesay, Xiomara Santamarina, Tony Pope, Andrew Diemer, Leo Collins, Millington Bergeson-Lockwood, William C. Leonard, and Ray Coleman. Astute commentators saved me from myself at various junctures: thanks particularly to Barbara Savage, Stephen Tuck, Richard Carwardine, Leslie Schwalm, Mia Bay, and Thomas Holt, as well as to audiences at the Radcliffe Institute for Advanced Study, the Rothermere American Institute, the Southern Intellectual History Circle, the American Historical Association, the Organization of American Historians, the Society of Historians of the Early American Republic, the Conference on Race, Labor, and Citizenship in the Post-Emancipation South, the International Conference on the History of Freemasonry, Marquette University Law School, the NYU American History Workshop, Northwestern University, Loyola University–Chicago, the American Studies Association, and the Newberry Library Labor History Seminar. Thanks also to Edward Linenthal of the *Journal of American History* and Conrad Edick Wright of the *Massachusetts Historical Review* for their thoughtful comments and for the superb teams of anonymous reviewers assembled on my behalf.

Without archivists and librarians, the raw materials of our craft would be difficult or impossible to find, and historians would have to invent the world anew each time they began a project. I have had the help of stellar professionals at many institutions, including Mark Tabbert, Susan Snell, Cynthia Alcorn, B. J. Gooch, Eric Frazier and his colleagues at the Boston Public Library, Mary McMillen and Kristin Swett at the City of Boston archives, Anna Cook and many others at the Massachusetts Historical Society, the staffs of the Commonwealth of Massachusetts Archives, Houghton Library, the Boston Athenaeum, the American Antiquarian Society, Rhodes House Library, the Library of Congress, the National Archives, the Massachusetts State Library, the Moorland-Spingarn Research Center, the Schlesinger Library, the Arlington (Mass.) Historical Society, the Brookline (Mass.) Public Library, the Cambridge (Mass.) Historical Commission, the Schomburg

Center for Research in Black Culture at the New York Public Library, the Van Gorden–Williams Library (Lexington, Mass.), the Museum of African American History (Boston), the South Carolina Department of Archives and History, the Wisconsin Historical Society, and the interlibrary loan office at the University of Wisconsin–Madison. For research assistance, I am pleased to acknowledge Joe Fronczak, Andy DeKlerk, and especially Michael Kwas, whose meticulous work taught me a great deal. Scholars of an earlier generation assembled materials and ideas without which this book would not exist: many deserve thanks, but no acknowledgment would be sufficient without the names of two departed pioneers, Dorothy Porter Wesley and Benjamin Quarles.

Broader communities of scholarship, friendship, and fellowship supported me through many phases of this project, beginning with the inspiring group at the Radcliffe Institute in 2002–2003, especially Liz Canner, Beverly McIver, Catherine Allgor, Linda Kerber, and Drew Faust. In the years since, my colleagues at UW-Madison have listened to my musings and offered their wisdom. In addition to the friends already mentioned, I thank Neil Kodesh, Suzanne Desan, Craig Werner, Susan Johnson, Jennifer Ratner-Rosenhagen, Colleen Dunlavy, Gerda Lerner, David Zimmerman, Sue Zaeske, Steve Stern, Seth Pollak, Jenny Saffran, and especially the late Jeanne Boydston, whose enthusiasm for this project carried me over a difficult stretch of it. Students in History 283 and History 393 did not know they were helping me write a book, but they responded thoughtfully to many of these ideas. The history graduate students at UW-Madison have been an inspiration to me since I arrived here in 1995, and many current and former students have shaped my own thinking with their questions, insights, and scholarship; in addition to those already named I want to acknowledge Lisa Tetrault, Story Matkin-Rawn, and Ryan Quintana.

My family of origin and my oldest friends keep me rooted in the best of my own past, with love, laughter, and insight. I know that if I can interest them in my work for its own sake I am doing something right. My brother Jeff would have loved to talk about this book and would no doubt have taken me on many tours of the neighborhoods where it takes place, stopping to eat whenever something particularly delicious demanded it. I wish he were here.

Scholarly work takes time, a precious commodity obtained in part with cold, hard cash. This project could not have begun and would not have been completed without the support of UW-Madison, for a semester at the Institute for Research in the Humanities and for a sabbatical leave; the Radcliffe Institute for Advanced Study; and the generosity of George and Pamela Hamel, whose endowment of the Hamel Family Faculty Fellowship enabled me to reach the finish line.

When I began this project I did not have a family of my own. I was free to linger in archives as long as their doors were open, and to write through the night if inspiration struck. Nothing has ever made me happier than exchanging that freedom for the love, chaos, and laughter of my life with Pernille, Elliot, and Sophie. Pernille Ipsen has changed how I see the world, and what I imagine it can be. She has read more of this book than anyone else, and knows better than anyone how to make me get to the point. The only way I can repay you is to do the same, *min sødeste kæreste*. Elliot and Sophie, in addition to playing the roles required of them by the customs of the book acknowledgment—i.e., reminding me that there are more important things in life—have also made me think anew about what is at stake in the struggles for love, justice, fellowship, and community that impelled me to become a historian and teacher in the first place. As they explore a world that often does not match the moral lessons they are supposed to learn, as they give voice to their questions, confusions, joys, and fears, they remind me why we fight.

Madison, Wisconsin
July 5, 2011

Notes

Abbreviations Used in the Text and Notes

AAS—American Anti-Slavery Society

ACS—American Colonization Society

AHR—*The American Historical Review*

BAA—The Black Abolitionist Archive, University of Detroit Mercy (http://research
.udmercy.edu/find/special_collections/digital/baa/)

BAP—C. Peter Ripley et al., eds., *The Black Abolitionist Papers.*, 5 vols. (Chapel Hill:
University of North Carolina Press, 1985–1992)

BAPM—*Black Abolitionist Papers* Microfilm Series, 17 reels (Sanford, NC, 1981)

BCA—City of Boston Archives, Boston

BPL—Special Collections, Boston Public Library

BVC—Boston Vigilance Committee

CMA—Commonwealth of Massachusetts Archives, Boston

CPAR—William Cooper Nell, *Colored Patriots of the American Revolution* (1855; reprint,
Salem, NH: Ayer, 1986)

CWSS—Civil War Soldiers and Sailors System (www.itd.nps.gov/cwss)

FDP—*Frederick Douglass' Paper* (Rochester, NY, 1851–1860)

HHU—Houghton Library, Harvard University, Cambridge, MA

JAH—*The Journal of American History*

JNH—*The Journal of Negro History*

JSH—*The Journal of Southern History*

L&C—Vincent Yardley Bowditch, *Life and Correspondence of Henry Ingersoll Bowditch*,
2 vols. (Boston: Houghton Mifflin, 1902)

LC—Library of Congress

LJ&NS—*Latimer Journal and North Star* (Boston, 1842–1843)

MHS—Massachusetts Historical Society, Boston

MSHU—Moorland-Spingarn Historical Collection, Howard University, Washington, DC

NASS—*National Anti-Slavery Standard*

NEAS—New England Anti-Slavery Society

NEQ—*New England Quarterly*

NGL—National Grand Lodge

OHS—Ohio Historical Society

PMHB—*Pennsylvania Magazine of History and Biography*

SHU—Schlesinger Library, Radcliffe Institute, Harvard University, Cambridge, MA

WAA—*Weekly Anglo-African* (New York, 1859–1865)

WCN—Dorothy Porter Wesley and Constance Porter Uzelac, eds., *William Cooper Nell, Nineteenth-Century African American Abolitionist, Historian, Integrationist: Selected Writings, 1832–1874* (Baltimore: Black Classics Press, 2002)

WMQ—*The William and Mary Quarterly*

INTRODUCTION

1. This vision of Crispus Attucks figures in scholarly analyses including: Elizabeth Rauh Bethel, *The Roots of African American Identity* (New York: St. Martin's, 1997); John Ernest, *Liberation Historiography* (Chapel Hill: University of North Carolina Press, 2004); Stephen H. Browne, "Remembering Crispus Attucks: Race, Rhetoric, and the Politics of Commemoration," *Quarterly Journal of Speech* 85 (1999), 169–87; Mitch Kachun, "From Forgotten Founder to Indispensable Icon: Crispus Attucks, Black Citizenship, and Collective Memory, 1770–1865," *Journal of the Early Republic* 29:2 (Summer 2009), 249–86; Stephen Kantrowitz, "A Place for 'Colored Patriots': Crispus Attucks Among the Abolitionists, 1842–1863," *Massachusetts Historical Review* 11 (2009), 97–117; Douglas R. Egerton, *Death or Liberty: African Americans and Revolutionary America* (New York: Oxford University Press, 2009); and Margot Minardi, *Making Slavery History* (New York: Oxford University Press, 2010).

2. Important points of entry to this literature include: Leon F. Litwack, *North of Slavery: The Negro in the Free States* (Chicago: University of Chicago Press, 1961); James Oliver Horton and Lois E. Horton, *In Hope of Liberty: Culture, Community, and Protest Among Northern Free Blacks, 1700–1860* (New York: Oxford University Press, 1997); and John Ernest, *A Nation Within a Nation: Organizing African-American Communities Before the Civil War* (Chicago: Ivan R. Dee, 2011).

3. "Departure of the Mass. 54th (Colored) Regiment," *WAA*, June 13, 1863, p. 2, c. 3–5.

4. Neither Nell nor the men of the 54th yet knew that black soldiers would be paid the inferior wages of military laborers, instead of the promised regular army wage; see ch. 7, below.

5. "New England Colored Citizens' Convention," *Liberator*, August 19, 1859, p. 132, c. 3.

6. "Black abolitionist," initially a nineteenth-century term of opprobrium (similar to "Black Republican"), emerged as a historian's description in the mid-twentieth century, notably in John Hope Franklin, *From Slavery to Freedom* (New York: Knopf, 1947). It defined Benjamin Quarles's outstanding synthesis, *Black Abolitionists* (New York: Oxford University Press, 1969), which was followed by numerous works including Jane H. Pease and William H. Pease, *They Who Would Be Free: Blacks' Search for Freedom, 1830–1861* (New York: Atheneum, 1974). Quarles noted many essential dimensions of antebellum black activism, including its universalist spirit, its critical brand of American nationalism, and the complicated dual role—as activists and as symbols—played by these men and women (ibid., viii). In the half century since this landmark work, a team of scholars has produced an extraordinary compilation of primary documents, with extensive and deeply researched explanatory notes, on the abolitionist

activities of African Americans: C. Peter Ripley, et al., eds., *The Black Abolitionist Papers*, 5 vols. (Chapel Hill: University of North Carolina Press, 1985–1992), and the larger associated microfilm set, *Black Abolitionist Papers* (17 reels; the printed guide is George E. Carter and C. Peter Ripley, eds., *Black Abolitionist Papers, 1830–1865: A Guide to the Microfilm Edition*, 1981), now also a full-text searchable electronic resource (http://bap.chadwyck.com). These editors, as well as many other scholars cited in this work, recognize the breadth and complexity of black Northern activists' work; for an overview, see Manisha Sinha, "Coming of Age: The Historiography of Black Abolitionism," in Timothy Patrick McCarthy and John Stauffer, eds., *Prophets of Protest: Reconsidering the History of American Abolitionism* (New York: New Press, 2006). Despite the sophistication of these works, the chronological boundary set by the framework limits their analyses. While abolitionism (including agitation for the end of Southern slavery and the enactment of antislavery laws, actions in defense of fugitives, and a host of literary and partisan activities) preoccupied free black activists until the mid-1860s, it was never their only struggle, and few shared the view of many white antislavery activists that the end of slavery signaled their final victory. This study argues that a broader definition, including but not limited to antislavery, and a longer timescale, extending well into the late nineteenth century, together offer a more penetrating approach to the range of black Northern activists' aspirations, achievements, and challenges, both before and after Southern slave emancipation. For a legal-constitutional approach to the African American experience in this era that meets some of these criteria, see Donald Nieman, "From Slaves to Citizens: African Americans, Rights Consciousness, and Reconstruction," *Cardozo Law Review* 17 (1995–1996), 2115.

7. Most studies of nineteenth-century Northern black communities either begin or end around the Civil War. For a recent and welcome exception to the rule, see Carla L. Peterson, *Black Gotham: A Family History of African Americans in Nineteenth-Century New York City* (New Haven, CT: Yale University Press, 2011). Important local studies for the early period include: Leslie Harris, *In the Shadow of Slavery: African Americans in New York City, 1626–1863* (Chicago: University of Chicago Press, 2003); James Oliver Horton and Lois E. Horton, *Black Bostonians: Family Life and Community Struggle in the Antebellum North*, revised edition (New York: Holmes and Meier, 1999); and Nikki M. Taylor, *Frontiers of Freedom: Cincinnati's Black Community, 1802–1868* (Athens: Ohio University Press, 2005). The literature on the postbellum era, some of which briefly considers prewar antecedents, includes: David A. Gerber, *Black Ohio and the Color Line, 1860–1915* (Urbana: University of Illinois Press, 1976); Elizabeth Hafkin Pleck, *Black Migration and Poverty: Boston, 1865–1900* (New York: Academic Press, 1979); David M. Katzman, *Before the Ghetto: Black Detroit in the Nineteenth Century* (Urbana: University of Illinois Press, 1975); and Roger Lane, *Roots of Violence in Black Philadelphia, 1860–1900* (Cambridge, MA: Harvard University Press, 1986). As these titles suggest, the postbellum literature is often as focused on explaining twentieth-century dynamics as the antebellum literature is on charting a path to the Civil War. For the postbellum careers of abolitionists, black and white, see James McPherson, *The Struggle for Equality: Abolitionists and the Negro in the Civil War and Reconstruction* (Princeton, NJ: Princeton University Press, 1964), and McPherson, *The Abolitionist Legacy: From Reconstruction to the NAACP* (Princeton, NJ: Princeton University Press, 1975). For a recent overview of black activism in the postbellum North, see Hugh Davis, *"We Will Be Satisfied with Nothing Less": The African American Struggle for Equal Rights in the North during Reconstruction* (Ithaca, NY: Cornell University Press, 2011).

8. See esp. Ernest, *Nation Within a Nation*.

9. Nancy Fraser, "Rethinking the Public Sphere: A Contribution to the Critique of Actually Existing Democracy," *Social Text* 25/26 (1990), 67–68. Works probing the meaning of "counterpublic" for African American history include: Evelyn Brooks Higginbotham, *Righteous Discontent* (Cambridge, MA: Harvard University Press, 1993); Joanna Brooks, "The Early American Public Sphere and the Emergence of a Black Print Counterpublic," *WMQ* 62 (Janu-

ary 2005), 67–92; and Stephen Kantrowitz, "'Intended for the Better Government of Man': The Political History of African American Freemasonry in the Era of Emancipation," *JAH* (March 2010), 1001–26. Richard Newman has offered a parallel formulation, describing various forms of voting within early-nineteenth-century black Northern congregations as "shadow politics," in Newman, "Faith in the Ballot: Black Shadow Politics in the Antebellum North," *Commonplace* 9:1 (October 2008), accessed at www.common-place.org/vol-09/no-01/newman/.

10. The language of "hearts" as an antidote to racial hostility, exclusion, and hierarchy is a theme of John Stauffer, *The Black Hearts of Men: Radical Abolitionists and the Transformation of Race* (Cambridge, MA: Harvard University Press, 2001).

11. François Furstenberg, "Beyond Freedom and Slavery: Autonomy, Virtue, and Resistance in Early American Political Discourse," *JAH* 89:4 (March 2003). This point is developed extensively in chs. 5–7, below.

12. Boston is not the only city in Massachusetts whose "colored citizens" bear close investigation; see Kathryn Grover, *The Fugitive's Gibraltar: Escaping Slaves and Abolitionism in New Bedford, Massachusetts* (Amherst: University of Massachusetts Press, 2001).

13. Arthur Zilversmit, *The First Emancipation: The Abolition of Slavery in the North* (Chicago: University of Chicago Press, 1967), 122–25. Thomas Morris, *Free Men All: The Personal Liberty Laws of the North* (Baltimore: Johns Hopkins University Press, 1974), 1–22.

CHAPTER 1: A PLACE FOR "COLORED CITIZENS"

1. Scholars from Howard Bell in the 1950s to Peter Hinks in the 1990s have presented the 1820s and early 1830s as a turning point in black organizational life. Bell, "Free Negroes of the North, 1830–1835: A Study in National Cooperation," *JNH* 26:4 (Autumn 1957), 447–55; Peter P. Hinks, *"To Awaken My Afflicted Brethren": David Walker and the Problem of Antebellum Slave Resistance* (University Park: Penn State Press, 1997), 92. See also Eddie Glaude, *Exodus!: Religion, Race, and Nation in Early Nineteenth-Century Black America* (Chicago: University of Chicago Press, 2000).

2. For an overview of this history, see Ira Berlin, *Generations of Captivity: A History of African-American Slaves* (Cambridge, MA: Harvard University Press, 2003) and the same author's enduring classic on the Southern free black experience: Berlin, *Slaves Without Masters: The Free Negro in the Antebellum South* (1974; rpt. New York: Oxford University Press, 1981).

3. See the provocative analogy of Northern urban free black communities to Southern maroon colonies in Steven Hahn, "Slaves at Large," in Hahn, *The Political Worlds of Slavery and Freedom* (Cambridge, MA: Harvard University Press, 2009).

4. See Michael P. Johnson and James L. Roark, *Black Masters: A Free Family of Color in the Old South* (New York: Norton, 1986).

5. Dorothy Porter Wesley and Constance Porter Uzelac, eds., *William Cooper Nell: Nineteenth-Century African American Abolitionist, Historian, Integrationist: Selected Writings, 1832–1874* (Baltimore: Black Classics Press, 2002), 6–7.

6. Howell Meadoes Henry, *The Police Control of the Slave in South Carolina* (Emory, VA, 1914), 186–87.

7. Data from George E. Levesque, *Black Boston: African American Life and Culture in Urban America, 1750–1860* (New York: Garland, 1994), Table I-14. The portrait of Boston here draws on: Donald M. Jacobs, "A History of the Boston Negro from the Revolution to the Civil War" (Ph.D. dissertation, Boston University, 1968); Levesque, *Black Boston*; Horton and Horton, *Black Bostonians*; and Leonard Curry, *The Free Black in Urban America, 1800–1850: The Shadow of the Dream* (Chicago: University of Chicago Press, 1981).

8. James Oliver Horton, *Free People of Color: Inside the African American Community* (Washington, DC: Smithsonian, 1993), 26–28; Horton and Horton, *Black Bostonians*, 5–7.

9. Horton and Horton, *Black Bostonians*, 8–12; Horton, *Free People of Color*, 31.

10. George A. Levesque, "Inherent Reformers—Inherited Orthodoxy: Black Baptists in Boston, 1800–1873," *JNH* 60 (October 1975), 497.

11. On this point more broadly, see Glaude, *Exodus*, esp. 19–27.

12. Lois Brown, ed., *Memoir of James Jackson* (Cambridge, MA: Harvard University Press, 2000), 7–19.

13. John T. Hilton, "An Address, Delivered before the African Grand Lodge, of Boston, No. 459, June 24th, 1828 . . ." (Boston, 1828), 13.

14. Levesque, "Inherent Reformers," 508. Levesque attributes these divisions to a political split over Garrisonian immediatism, with more orthodox Baptists unwilling to accept some of its demands in the context of the church. His best evidence is that in the 1840s a breakaway group left to form the Twelfth Baptist Church, by the end of the decade known as "the fugitives' church," ibid., 512. But Levesque's portrait of a recalcitrant church membership refusing to move toward secular activism is complicated by the continuing presence among them of John T. Hilton, not just as a member but as the congregation's perennial delegate to the yearly meeting of the Baptist Association during the 1820s, '30s, and '40s—the period of crisis, according to Levesque, ibid., 520–21.

15. Hinks, *"To Awaken,"* 92.

16. Quoted in Hinks, *"To Awaken,"* 35–36.

17. Reconstructing these events has bedeviled historians for several generations; my account follows generally accepted outlines, but many particulars remain in dispute. The historiography on Prince Hall has recently been crowned by Chernoh Sesay, "Freemasons of Color: Prince Hall, Revolutionary Black Boston, and the Origins of Freemasonry, 1770–1807" (Ph.D. dissertation, Northwestern University, 2006). See also Peter P. Hinks, "John Marrant and the Meaning of Early Black Freemasonry," *WMQ* 64 (January 2007).

18. James Anderson, *"The Constitutions of the Free-Masons* (1734). An Online Electronic Edition," Paul Royster, ed., 2006 (http://works.bepress.com/paul_royster/33/).

19. Kantrowitz, "'Intended for the Better Government of Man.'"

20. On Hilton and the African Lodge in the 1820s and 1830s, see Peter P. Hinks, "'We Are Now Getting in a Flourishing Condition': John Telemachus Hilton, Abolitionism, and the Expansion of Black Freemasonry, 1825–1860," in Peter P. Hinks and Stephen Kantrowitz, eds., *All Men Free and Brethren: Prince Hall and African American Fraternalism from the American Revolution to the Civil Rights Movement* (Ithaca, NY: Cornell University Press, forthcoming); for Walker's biography, see Hinks, *"To Awaken."*

21. Hinks, *"To Awaken,"* 75.

22. Howard H. Bell, "Free Negroes of the North, 1830–1835: A Study in National Cooperation," *Journal of Negro Education* 26:4 (Autumn 1957), 447–55.

23. I thank Dylan Penningroth for "a project, not a given."

24. The literature on "whiteness" and the United States as a "white republic" has mushroomed over the past two decades. For important (sometimes conflicting) points of entry, see Alexander Saxton, *The Rise and Fall of the White Republic: Class Politics and Mass Culture in Nineteenth-Century America* (New York: Verso, 1990); David Roediger, *The Wages of Whiteness: Race and the Making of the American Working Class*, revised edition (New York: Verso, 1999); James Brewer Stewart, "The Emergence of Racial Modernity and the Rise of the White North, 1790–1840," in "SHA Roundtable: Racial Modernity," *Journal of the Early Republic* 18 (Spring 1998), 181–236; Nell Irvin Painter, *The History of White People* (New York: Norton, 2010).

25. For an overview of this transition in black suffrage rights in the early republic, see Horton and Horton, *In Hope of Liberty*, 167–68; on suffrage for some white women in early New Jersey, see Judith Apter Klinghoffer and Lois Elkis, "'The Petticoat Electors': Women's Suffrage in New Jersey, 1776–1807," *Journal of the Early Republic* 12:2 (Summer 1992), 159–93. For a brilliant analysis of the relationship between white men's expanding "rights" and the formal

subordination of other Americans in the first half of the nineteenth century, see Adam Malka, "The Rights of Men: Slavery, Police, and the Making of the Liberal State, 1800–1870," (Ph.D. dissertation, University of Wisconsin-Madison, 2012).

26. Essential overviews of this topic are: Litwack, *North of Slavery*; Horton and Horton, *In Hope of Liberty*; and Joanne Pope Melish, *Disowning Slavery: Gradual Emancipation and 'Race' in New England, 1780–1860* (Ithaca, NY: Cornell University Press, 1998).

27. Horton and Horton, *In Hope of Liberty*, 104; Taylor, *Frontiers of Freedom*, 50–79.

28. James Brewer Stewart argues that the North was in the midst of consolidating its own "immovable consensus of highly organized white supremacy," a process completed by 1840; see Stewart, "Racial Modernity," quotation on 182. For important challenges to Stewart's chronology, see ibid., 225–26, 227–28.

29. William Cooper Nell, *Colored Patriots of the American Revolution* (1855; reprint, Salem, NH: Ayer, 1986), 26.

30. Nell, *CPAR*, 26–27. For more on "Bobalition," see Shane White, "'It Was a Proud Day': African Americans, Festivals, and Parades in the North, 1741–1834," *JAH* 81:1 (June 1994), 13–50. Child's memory may have been of the July 14, 1826, riot, in which a white mob destroyed several houses occupied by blacks; Curry, *Shadow*, 100.

31. Quoted in Nell, *CPAR*, 64.

32. George R. Price and James Brewer Stewart, eds., *To Heal the Scourge of Prejudice: The Life and Writings of Hosea Easton* (Amherst: University of Massachusetts Press, 1999), 107.

33. Stephen Kendrick and Paul Kendrick, *Sarah's Long Walk: The Free Blacks of Boston and How Their Struggle for Equality Changed America* (Boston: Beacon, 2004), 71–74.

34. *Boston Courier*, January 13, 1831.

35. This rich tradition extended all the way back to the 1770s; see Mia Bay, "'See Your Declaration, Americans!': Abolitionism, Americanism, and the Revolutionary Tradition in Free Black Politics," in Michael Kazin and Joseph A. McCartin, eds., *Americanism: New Perspectives on the History of an Ideal* (Chapel Hill: University of North Carolina Press, 2006), 25–52.

36. Peter P. Hinks, ed., *David Walker's Appeal to the Coloured Citizens of the World* (University Park: Penn State University Press, 2000), 67.

37. Ibid., 43

38. Hinks, *"To Awaken,"* 116–72.

39. Ibid., 118.

40. Ibid., 243–44.

41. Ibid., 78–79.

42. See Bay, "'See Your Declaration,'" 42.

43. One scholar describes these as the entangled foundations of "black Americanism" and "black abolitionism"; Bay, "'See Your Declaration,'" 27.

44. Hinks, *Appeal,* 67.

45. Marilyn Richardson, ed., *Maria Stewart: America's First Black Woman Political Writer* (Bloomington: Indiana University Press, 1987), 39.

46. Quarles, *Black Abolitionists*, 7–8.

47. See Patrick Rael, *Black Identity and Black Protest in the Antebellum North* (Chapel Hill: University of North Carolina Press, 2002), esp. 255–71.

48. See, e.g., *Liberator*, November 18, 1842, p. 183, c. 1; ibid., December 23, 1842, p. 202, c. 1–2; Richardson, *Maria W. Stewart*, 29.

49. Benjamin Quarles, "Antebellum Free Blacks and the 'Spirit of '76,'" *Journal of Negro History* 61:3 (July 1976), 237.

50. "Unkind Treatment," *Liberator*, December 28, 1833, p. 207, c. 4–5.

51. "First of August in Boston," *Liberator*, August 9, 1839, p. 127, c. 1.

52. "Great Mass Meeting of Colored Citizens of Boston," *Liberator*, December 23, 1842, p. 202, c. 1–2.

53. Hinks, *Appeal*, 73.

54. "Walker's Appeal, No. 1," *Liberator*, April 30, 1831, p. 1, c. 3–4.

55. This vision of "citizenship" as requiring (or consisting of) more than enumerated "rights"—as consisting of more, in other words, than "life, liberty, and property"—has a long history in the modern era. For a starting point, see Karl Marx, "On the Jewish Question," in Lawrence H. Simon, ed., *Karl Marx: Selected Writings* (Indianapolis: Hackett, 1994).

56. "An Appeal to the Free Colored Citizens of the United States," *Liberator*, February 14, 1835, p. 26, c. 1.

57. See Immanuel Wallerstein, "Citizens All? Citizens Some! The Making of the Citizen," *Comparative Studies in Society and History* 45 (November 2003), 650–79.

58. On the transition from "African" to "colored," see Patrick Rael, *Black Identity and Black Protest*, 82–117; Mia Bay, "'See Your Declaration,'" 41; and Sterling Stuckey, *Slave Culture: Nationalist Theory and the Foundations of Black America* (New York: Oxford University Press, 1987), 193–244. Others caution that the retreat from "African" was a rhetorical defensive posture, not an ideological dismissal of "their African heritage"; see Leslie Alexander, *African or American? Black Identity and Political Activism in New York City, 1784–1861* (Urbana: University of Illinois Press, 2008), xix. For the prehistory of this transformation—the emergence of "African" itself as a collective self-description—see James Sidbury, *Becoming African in America: Race and Nation in the Early Black Atlantic* (New York: Oxford University Press, 2007).

59. Quoted in Levesque, "Inherent Reformers," 509.

60. "Change of Appellation," *Liberator*, July 16, 1831.

61. Peter H. Clark, *The Black Brigade of Cincinnati, Being a Report of Its Labors and a Muster-Roll of Its Members* (Cincinnati: J. B. Boyd, 1864), 4.

62. See, e.g., "Anti-Webster Meeting," *Liberator*, April 5, 1850, p. 55, c. 3–4.

63. "Ohio State Convention of Colored Freemen," *Aliened American*, April 9, 1853.

64. "New England Colored Citizens' Convention," *Liberator*, August 19, 1859, p. 132.

65. William J. Novak, "The Legal Transformation of Citizenship in Nineteenth-Century America," in Meg Jacobs et al., eds., *The Democratic Experiment: New Directions in American Political History* (Princeton, NJ: Princeton University Press, 2003).

66. Novak, "Legal Transformation." The ever growing literature on nineteenth-century African American citizenship includes Don E. Fehrenbacher, *The Dred Scott Case: Its Significance in American Law and Politics* (New York: Oxford University Press, 1978), and Fehrenbacher, *The Slaveholding Republic: An Account of the United States Government's Relations to Slavery* (New York: Oxford University Press, 2002); Robert J. Kaczorowski, "To Begin the Nation Anew: Congress, Citizenship, and Civil Rights After the Civil War," *AHR* 92:1 (February 1987), 45–68; Paul Finkelman, "Prelude to the Fourteenth Amendment: Black Legal Rights in the Antebellum North," *Rutgers Law Journal* 17 (1985–1986), 415–82; J. Morgan Kousser, "'The Supremacy of Equal Rights': The Struggle Against Racial Discrimination in Antebellum Massachusetts and the Foundations of the Fourteenth Amendment," *Northwestern University Law Review* 82 (1987–1988), 941–1010; Nieman, "From Slaves to Citizens"; Linda K. Kerber, *No Constitutional Right to Be Ladies: Women and the Obligations of Citizenship* (New York: Hill & Wang, 1998); Katherine M. Franke, "Becoming a Citizen: Reconstruction-Era Regulation of African American Marriages," *Yale Journal of Law and the Humanities* 11 (Summer 1999), 251–309; Kunal M. Parker, "Making Blacks Foreigners: The Construction of Former Slaves in Post-Revolutionary Massachusetts," *Utah Law Review* (2001), 75–124; Rebecca J. Scott, "Public Rights, Social Equality, and the Conceptual Roots of the *Plessy* Challenge," *Michigan Law Review* 106 (2007–2008), 777–804; and Christian Samito, *Becoming American Under Fire: Irish Americans, African Americans, and the Politics of Citizenship During the Civil War Era* (Ithaca, NY: Cornell University Press, 2009).

67. See, e.g., Letter of John S. Rock to William Lloyd Garrison, n.d. [1854], in *BAPM* 08:0535;

"Colored Men Citizens," *FDP*, August 25, 1854; Letter of Robert Morris to Charles Sumner, June 25, 1861, Charles Sumner Papers, HHU.

68. Matthew Frye Jacobson, *Whiteness of a Different Color: European Immigrants and the Alchemy of Race* (Cambridge, MA: Harvard University Press, 1999).

69. *Annals of Congress* 37, 16th Congress, 2nd Session, 47–48 (December 7, 1820); ibid., 1134–35 (February 13, 1821).

70. Robert Pierce Forbes, *The Missouri Compromise and Its Aftermath: Slavery and the Meaning of America* (Chapel Hill: University of North Carolina Press, 2007).

71. Morris, *Free Men All*; Paul Finkelman, *An Imperfect Union: Slavery, Federalism, and Comity* (Chapel Hill: University of North Carolina Press, 1981); Fehrenbacher, *Dred Scott Case*.

72. See Julie Winch, "Philadelphia and the Other Underground Railroad," *PMHB* 111:1 (January 1987), 3–25.

73. *New York Spectator*, November 22, 1826; *New Hampshire Statesman and Concord Register*, January 26, 1827.

74. Hilton, "An Address," 13.

75. Ibid., 12.

76. Hinks, *Appeal*, 98–99.

77. Hinks, *"To Awaken,"* 269–70.

78. "Report on the Petition of George Odiorne and Others," *Liberator*, April 23, 1836, 68.

Chapter 2: Fighting Jim Crow in the Cradle of Liberty

1. *Triumph of Equal School Rights in Boston: Proceedings of the Presentation Meeting Held in Boston, December 17, 1855* (Boston: R. F. Wallcut, 1856) [hereinafter cited as *Triumph*], 4–5.

2. Novak, "Legal Transformation," quotation on 98.

3. See Rael, *Black Identity and Black Protest*, esp. 157–73.

4. Quoted in ibid., 173.

5. Quoted in William S. McFeely, *Frederick Douglass* (New York: Norton, 1991), 94.

6. "Of the Sayings and Doings at the N.E. Anti-Slavery Convention," *Liberator*, June 4, 1847, p. 91, c. 2.

7. *FDP*, February 10, 1854, in *BAPM* 08:0648.

8. Louis Ruchames, "Jim Crow Railroads in Massachusetts," *American Quarterly* 8 (Spring 1956), 62.

9. McFeely, *Douglass*, 93.

10. Tenth Annual Report of the Board of Managers of the Massachusetts Anti-Slavery Society, presented January 26, 1842 (Boston), 72–73.

11. Quoted in Levesque, *Black Boston*, 121.

12. "Have They Got a 'Jim Crow Car'?," *Liberator*, August 1, 1845, p. 121, c. 1–2.

13. Tenth Annual Report, 70–71; "Remarks of Charles Lenox Remond," *Liberator*, February 25, 1842, p. 30, c. 3–4.

14. This railroad had become infamous among black activists for its racially discriminatory policies; "Travellers' Directory," *Liberator*, May 20, 1842, p. 74, c. 5.

15. "The Spirit of Caste," *Liberator*, April 28, 1843, p. 67, c. 4. This was not the limit of discrimination: for a time, at least one railroad ran another set of segregated cars for Irish immigrants; these "paddy cars" were also closed to black passengers; "Eastern Rail-Road," *Liberator*, April 29, 1842, p. 67, c. 5.

16. "The Faneuil Hall Meeting" *Liberator*, November 4, 1842, p. 174, c. 3, and "The Abolition Meeting at Faneuil Hall," ibid., c. 2–3.

17. The complete lyrics and a performance of this song are available online at the University of Virginia's excellent archive of materials on *Uncle Tom's Cabin*: www.iath.virginia.edu/utc /minstrel/lucylongfr.html (accessed June 26, 2011).

18. On Southern slaveholders' avoidance of the implications of the market, see Walter Johnson, *Soul by Soul: Life Inside the Antebellum Slave Market* (Cambridge, MA: Harvard University Press, 1999). On blackface minstrelsy in the antebellum urban North, see Roediger, *The Wages of Whiteness*, 115–31; Eric Lott, *Love and Theft: Blackface Minstrelsy and the American Working Class* (New York: Oxford University Press, 1993); Alexander Saxton, *The Rise and Fall of the White Republic: Class Politics and Mass Culture in Nineteenth-Century America* (New York: Verso, 1990), 165–82.

19. "The Abolition Meeting at Faneuil Hall," *Liberator*, November 4, 1842, p. 174, c. 3; *LJ&NS*, November 11, 1842, p. 1, c. 4–p. 2, c. 1.

20. "H," "The Faneuil Hall Meeting," unidentified clipping, Latimer Committee Papers, Ms. Am. 1821, BPL.

21. Roediger, *Wages of Whiteness*, 144–50.

22. Curry, *Shadow*, 100; "The Affray in Ann-Street," *Liberator*, September 1, 1843, p. 139, c. 5–6.

23. Letter of Nell to Phillips, April 15, 1841, Phillips Papers, HHU.

24. *Boston Emancipator and Free American*, December 16, 1841, p. 163, c. 2. The *Emancipator* was a Liberty Party paper, keenly interested in detaching black voters from their sometime allies or patrons in the Whig Party.

25. Kate Masur, "The African American Delegation to Abraham Lincoln: A Reappraisal," *Civil War History* 56:2 (June 2010), 117–44.

26. "Walker's Appeal—No. 1," *Liberator*, April 30, 1831, p. 69, c. 1–4.

27. "Debate on the Rail-Road Bill," *Liberator*, February 17, 1843, p. 25, c. 1–4.

28. See the essays in Donald M. Jacobs, ed., *Courage and Conscience: Black and White Abolitionists in Boston* (Bloomington: Indiana University Press for the Boston Athenaeum, 1993).

29. William Lloyd Garrison, *Thoughts on African Colonization* (Boston: Garrison and Knapp, 1832).

30. Ibid., 117–18.

31. Quoted in Jacobs, "A History of the Boston Negro," 77.

32. "To the Public," *Liberator*, January 1, 1831, p. 1.

33. "Working Men," *Liberator*, January 1, 1831, p. 3, c. 3.

34. Donald Jacobs, "David Walker and William Lloyd Garrison: Racial Cooperation and the Shaping of Boston Abolition," in Jacobs, ed., *Courage and Conscience*, 1–20. Walker's widow raised a son bearing the name Edwin Garrison Walker. The boy's frequently cited birth date of 1835 would have made it impossible for him to have been David Walker's biological son, and extant records do not clarify whether Edwin (later to become a prominent local activist in his own right) was indeed the son of David Walker, nor how he acquired his middle name. It is hard to imagine that it was a coincidence. For a clearheaded analysis of the available data, see Hinks, *"To Awaken,"* 269–71.

35. Letter of James G. Barbadoes, *Liberator*, January 22, 1831, p. 14.

36. "Working Men," *Liberator*, January 1, 1831, p. 3.

37. WCN, 12.

38. Roman J. Zorn, "The New England Anti-Slavery Society: Pioneer Abolition Organization," *Journal of Negro History* 42:3 (July 1957), 159–60.

39. T. T., Untitled, *Liberator*, April 2, 1831, p. 1, c. 1–4. This and a contrapuntal companion piece—a dream of slave revolt and white enslavement (T. T., "Another Dream," *Liberator*, April 30, 1831, p. 70)—are analyzed in Stewart, "Racial Modernity."

40. Zorn, "The New England Anti-Slavery Society," 159–60.

41. Tenth Annual Report, p. 71.

42. "Letter from Frederick Douglass No. V," *Liberator*, January 30, 1846, p. 19.

43. For an appreciation of the radical change in white antislavery marked by the emergence of the NEAS, see Richard Newman, *The Transformation of American Abolitionism: Fighting Slavery in the Early Republic* (Chapel Hill: University of North Carolina Press, 2002), esp. 107–79.

44. "Constitution of the New-England Anti-Slavery Society," *Liberator*, February 9, 1833, p. 1, c. 1–2; Massachusetts Anti-Slavery Society, First Annual Report, 49; *WCN*, 12–13.

45. Susan Zaeske, *Signatures of Citizenship: Petitioning, Antislavery, and Women's Political Identity* (Chapel Hill: University of North Carolina Press, 2003).

46. On the Marlboro Hotel and Chapel, see "Building for Free Discussion," *Liberator*, July 4, 1835; "Marlboro Chapel," *New York Colored American*, February 17, 1838.

47. *Liberator*, August 28, 1840, in *WCN*, 80–90; Letter of Garrison to Pease, August 31, 1840, in Walter M. Merrill and Louis Ruchames, eds., *The Letters of William Lloyd Garrison*, 6 vols. (Cambridge, MA: Belknap, 1971–1981), II:682–84.

48. *Liberator*, August 28, 1840, in *WCN*, 80–90.

49. "Letter from C. L. Remond," *Colored American*, November 7, 1840.

50. Julie Roy Jeffrey, *The Great Silent Army of Abolitionism: Ordinary Women in the Antislavery Movement* (Chapel Hill: University of North Carolina Press, 1998); Zaeske, *Signatures of Citizenship*.

51. Shirley Yee, *Black Women Abolitionists: A Study in Activism, 1828–1860* (Knoxville: University of Tennessee Press, 1992), 90.

52. Jeffrey, *Great Silent Army*; Ruth Bogin and Jean Fagan Yellin, "Introduction," in Jean Fagan Yellin and John C. Van Horne, eds., *The Abolitionist Sisterhood: Women's Political Culture in Antebellum America* (Ithaca, NY: Cornell University Press, 1994), 10.

53. Keith Melder, "Abby Kelley and the Process of Liberation," in Bogin and Yellin, *Abolitionist Sisterhood*, 231–48, quotation on 231.

54. Horton and Horton, *In Hope of Liberty*, 239–40; Lewis Perry, *Radical Abolitionism: Anarchy and the Government of God in Antislavery Thought* (1973; revised edition, Knoxville: University of Tennessee Press, 1995); "Great Meeting of the Colored Citizens of Boston," *Liberator*, October 25, 1839, p. 170.

55. Thomas Wentworth Higginson, "William Lloyd Garrison," *Atlantic Monthly* 57 (January 1886), 120–28, quotation on 121.

56. The classic work on these mobs is Leonard L. Richards, *"Gentlemen of Property and Standing": Anti-Abolition Mobs in Jacksonian America* (New York: Oxford University Press, 1971). On the emergence of proslavery ideology, see Lacy K. Ford, *Deliver Us from Evil: The Slavery Question in the Old South* (New York: Oxford University Press, 2009).

57. David Grimsted, *American Mobbing: 1828–1861* (New York: Oxford University Press, 1998), 22.

58. Henry Mayer, *All On Fire: William Lloyd Garrison and the Abolition of Slavery* (New York: St. Martin's, 1998), 199–206.

59. Grimsted, *American Mobbing*, 22.

60. "Presentation and Farewell Meeting," *Liberator*, July 27, 1849, p. 118, c. 3.

61. "Citizenship of People of Color," *Liberator*, July 28, 1837, p. 121, c. 2.

62. Frederick Douglass, *Life and Times of Frederick Douglass* (Hartford, CT: Park, 1882), 276. On Phillips, see James Brewer Stewart, *Wendell Phillips: Liberty's Hero* (Baton Rouge: Louisiana State University Press, 1986).

63. Letter of Nell to Phillips, August 31, 1840, Phillips Papers, HHU. Such expressions are analyzed in Stauffer, *Black Hearts of Men*.

64. Letter of Oliver Johnson to Phillips, September 12, 1841, Phillips Papers, HHU.

65. William E. Ward, "Charles Lenox Remond: Black Abolitionist, 1838–1873" (Ph.D. dissertation, Clark University, 1977), 60–61.

66. "Citizenship of People of Color," *Liberator*, July 28, 1837, p. 121, c. 2.

67. Bertram Wyatt-Brown, *Lewis Tappan and the Evangelical War Against Slavery* (Cleveland: Case Western Reserve University Press, 1969), 179.

68. Lawrence J. Friedman, *Gregarious Saints: Self and Community in American Abolitionism, 1830–1870* (New York: Cambridge University Press, 1982), 46–47.

69. Yee, *Black Women Abolitionists*, 89.

70. See also Jeffrey, *Great Silent Army*, 127.

71. Letter of Nell to A. Post, September 11–13, 1853, in *WCN*, 354.

72. *NASS*, October 7, 1841, p. 2, c. 2–3, in *WCN*, 107.

73. William Wells Brown, *The Black Man, His Antecedents, His Genius, and His Achievements* (New York, 1863), 241. On Brown's Anglophilia, see Elisa Tamarkin, "Black Anglophilia; or, The Sociability of Antislavery," *American Literary History* 14 (Autumn 2002), 444–78.

74. See, e.g., Letter of Nell to A. Post, March 11, 1853, in *WCN*, 329–30. Six weeks later, he was still guarding the house; ibid., 334.

75. Letter of Nell to A. Post, September 11–13, 1853, in *WCN*, 354; Letter of Nell to A. Post, October 17, 1854, in *WCN*, 396.

76. Letter of Nell to A. Post, April 9, 1854, in *WCN*, 378.

77. Letter of Nell to Phillips, January 20, 1853, Phillips Papers, HHU.

78. Debra Gold Hansen, *Strained Sisterhood: Gender and Class in the Boston Female Anti-Slavery Society* (Amherst: University of Massachusetts Press, 1993), 13–28, 64.

79. Horton and Horton, *Black Bostonians*, 103.

80. Quarles, *Black Abolitionists*, 12.

81. Letter of Garrison to Hannah Webb, March 1, 1843, in Merrill and Ruchames, *Letters of Garrison*, IV:130–31.

82. "Meeting of the Colored Citizens of Boston," *Liberator*, February 10, 1843, p. 22.

83. "Debate on the Rail-Road Bill," *Liberator*, February 17, 1843, p. 25, c. 1–4.

84. Letter of Garrison to Hannah Webb, March 1, 1843, in Merrill and Ruchames, *Letters of Garrison*, IV:130–31.

85. James Brewer Stewart argues that white abolitionists, traumatized by the mob violence of the 1830s, vocally forswore any intention of promoting "race-mixing"; Stewart, "Racial Modernity," 208.

86. Finkelman, "Prelude to the Fourteenth Amendment," 424; Morris, *Free Men All*, esp. 75–76.

87. Leonard W. Levy, "The 'Abolition Riot': Boston's First Slave Rescue," *NEQ* 25:1 (March 1952), 85–92.

88. Ibid., 92.

89. Grimsted, *American Mobbing*, 74, 302–3.

90. Horton and Horton, *In Hope of Liberty*, 234–35.

91. George Hendrick and Willene Hendrick, *The* Creole *Mutiny: A Tale of Revolt Aboard a Slave Ship* (Chicago: Ivan R. Dee, 2003); Walter Johnson, "White Lies: Human Property and Domestic Slavery Aboard the Slave Ship *Creole*," *Atlantic Studies* 5:2 (August 2008), 237–63; Howard Jones, *Mutiny on the* Amistad: *The Saga of a Slave Revolt and Its Impact on American Abolition, Law, and Diplomacy* (New York: Oxford University Press, 1987).

92. "A Letter," *Liberator*, June 18, 1841, p. 100; see also *Liberator*, July 2, 1841, p. 107, c. 5, and July 23, 1841, p. 119, c. 4.

93. "The Case of John Torrence," *Colored American*, June 12, 1841.

94. Graham Russell Gao Hodges, *David Ruggles: A Radical Black Abolitionist and the Underground Railroad in New York City* (Chapel Hill: University of North Carolina Press, 2010), 88; Joseph A. Boromé, "The Vigilant Committee of Philadelphia," *PMHB* 92:3 (July 1968), 320–31.

95. "Vigilance Committee—Attention!," *Liberator*, June 4, 1841, p. 91, c. 6.

96. "Boston Vigilance Committee," *Liberator*, June 11, 1841, p. 91, c. 5; "The Boston Vigilance Committee," *Liberator*, July 2, 1841, p. 107, c. 5.

97. "Another Runaway Slave Affair," *Liberator*, July 23, 1841, p. 119, c. 4.

98. "Communications, Boston Vigilance Committee," *Liberator*, June 11, 1841, p. 91.

99. Boromé, "Vigilant Committee," 325–27; see "The Philadelphia Riots," *Liberator*, August 12, 1842, p. 126.

100. See Paul Finkelman, "Sorting Out *Prigg v. Pennsylvania*," *Rutgers Law Journal* 24 (1992).

101. "Meeting of the Colored Citizens of Boston," *Liberator*, June 3, 1842, p. 87, c. 6.

102. Among the leaders of the meeting were Benjamin Weeden, Robert Morris, and William Nell; "Meeting of Colored Citizens of Boston," *Liberator*, June 3, 1842, p. 87, c. 6. They believed this was possible under an antislavery reading of *Prigg* that held that recapture of fugitives was entirely a federal responsibility, and that state legislation might limit the active cooperation of state officials in that business; Morris, *Free Men All*, 94–104, 109.

103. "Meeting of Colored Citizens of Boston," *Liberator*, June 3, 1842, p. 87, c. 6.

104. Ibid.

105. "New-England Freedom Association," *Liberator*, March 31, 1843, p. 51.

106. Biographical sketches in *LJ&NS*, late November 1842, and other archival sources, reproduced in Asa J. Davis, "The Two Autobiographical Fragments of George W. Latimer," *Journal of the Afro-American Historical and Genealogical Society* 1 (Summer 1980), extracted at "The George Latimer Case: A Benchmark in the Struggle for Freedom," http://edison.rutgers.edu/latimer /glatnote.htm. The events of the Latimer War are analyzed in Bruce Laurie, *Beyond Garrison: Antislavery and Social Reform* (New York: Cambridge University Press, 2005), 76–80, 116–19; Kantrowitz, "A Place for 'Colored Patriots'"; and Minardi, *Making Slavery History*, 79–83.

107. Davis, "Two Autobiographical Fragments"; "Case of George Latimer," *Liberator*, October 28, 1842, p. 171.

108. Data from Levesque, *Black Boston*, Tables I-4, I-24.

109. "Great Public Meeting," *Liberator*, October 28, 1842, p. 171, c. 6.

110. "Case of George Latimer," *Liberator*, October 28, 1842, p. 171, c. 2.

111. "The Latimer Case," *Liberator*, November 25, 1842, p. 186.

112. Ibid.; *LJ&NS*, November 23, 1842, p. 3, c. 4. An appeal was later filed on their behalf; *Liberator*, December 9, 1842, p. 194, c. 6–p. 195, c. 1.

113. "The Latimer Case," *Liberator*, November 25, 1842, p. 186.

114. "Fugitives from Justice," *The Philanthropist* (Cincinnati), December 7, 1842, p. 2, c. 3–5.

115. *LJ&NS*, Latimer Papers, MHS.

116. *LJ&NS*, November 18, 1842, p. 4, c. 2.

117. Petition forms in Latimer Papers, MHS.

118. See Zaeske, *Signatures of Citizenship*.

119. General Court of Massachusetts, *Acts and Resolves, 1843*, ch. 69, CMA; Morris, *Free Men All*, 114.

120. Morris, *Free Men All*, 94–104, 109.

121. "Rights of Our Colored Citizens," *Liberator*, November 4, 1842, p. 175.

122. Levesque, *Black Boston*, 231–47; Finkelman, *An Imperfect Union*.

123. *Liberator*, December 23, 1842, p. 202, c. 1–2.

124. *LJ&NS*, November 18, 1842, p. 2, c. 1.

125. *LJ&NS*, November 23, 1842, p. 3, c. 1.

126. *LJ&NS*, November 11, 1842, p. 1, c. 1.

127. Ibid., p. 3, c. 3–4. For a later case suggesting this possibility also occured to some Southern whites, see Walter Johnson, "The Slave Trader, the White Slave, and the Politics of Racial Determination in the 1850s," *JAH* 87 (June 2000), 13–38.

128. *LJ&NS*, November 18, 1842, p. 2, c. 1.

129. Elizabeth Clark, "'The Sacred Rights of the Weak': Pain, Sympathy, and the Culture of Individual Rights in America," *JAH* 82 (September 1995), 463–93; and Saidiya V. Hartman, *Scenes of Subjection: Terror, Slavery, and Self-Making in Nineteenth-Century America* (New York: Oxford University Press, 1997).

130. Leonard L. Richards, *The Slave Power: The Free North and Southern Domination, 1780–1860* (Baton Rouge: Louisiana State University Press, 2000).

131. *LJ&NS,* November 16, 1842, p. 2, c. 4–p. 3, c. 1.

132. See also Dean Grodzins, *American Heretic: Theodore Parker and Transcendentalism* (Chapel Hill: University of North Carolina Press, 2002), 337–38.

133. William Douglas O'Connor, *Harrington: A Story of True Love* (Boston, 1860), offers a thinly disguised portrait of antislavery activity in Boston in the 1850s; he repeatedly refers to or has characters speak of "the quarter vulgarly known as Nigger Hill" (69).

134. Vincent Yardley Bowditch, ed., *Life and Correspondence of Henry Ingersoll Bowditch*, 2 vols. (Boston: Houghton Mifflin, 1902), I:99–101.

135. *L&C,* I:113–32.

136. Douglass made his remarks at a dinner in his honor hosted by the Wendell Phillips Club at the Revere House, Saturday evening, September 11, 1886; see *Boston Advocate*, September 18, 1886, p. 4, c. 1–4. Douglass's memory that this was his first visit to a Boston home may not be strictly accurate. Douglass had addressed the Massachusetts Anti-Slavery Society Convention in Boston on Thursday, January 27, 1842, in Representatives Hall at the statehouse (Tenth Annual Report, appendix p. 7); this means that he had visited Boston ten months prior to the Latimer War. Frederic May Holland, *Frederick Douglass: The Colored Orator* (New York: Funk and Wagnall's, 1895 [available at http://docsouth.unc.edu]), also puts his meeting with Bowditch in January 1842. Bowditch, though, remembered their walk and dinner as having followed "one of our meetings"—of the Latimer Committee, that is—at Marlboro Chapel; this could have been the meeting on November 12, 1842. See *L&C*, I:137; *LJ&NS*, November 23, 1842, p. 1, c. 4.

137. *Boston Advocate*, September 18, 1886, p. 4, c. 1–4.

138. *L&C,* I:146.

139. Douglass's speech before the New England Anti-Slavery Convention, in *Emancipator & Republican*, June 14, 1849, p. 2, c. 6–7.

140. *L&C,* I:136–37.

141. For another account of these events, see Laurie, *Beyond Garrison*, 102.

142. Jeffrey R. Kerr-Ritchie, *Rites of August First: Emancipation Day in the Black Atlantic World* (Baton Rouge: Louisiana State University Press, 2007); Mitch Kachun, *Festivals of Freedom: Memory and Meaning in African American Emancipation Celebrations, 1808–1915* (Amherst: University of Massachusetts Press, 2003), 59–61; Quarles, *Black Abolitionists*, 124–26.

143. Kachun, *Festivals of Freedom*, 62–63.

144. Ibid., 62.

145. "Celebration at Hingham!," *Liberator*, August 9, 1844, p. 127, c. 2–3.

146. *L&C,* I:156.

147. Ibid., 156–61.

CHAPTER 3: OUR UNFINISHED CHURCH

1. Randolph Paul Runyon, *Delia Webster and the Underground Railroad* (Lexington: University Press of Kentucky, 1996), 87–92.

2. "Anti-Slavery Convention," *Green Mountain Freeman*, October 16, 1845, p. 3, c. 1.

3. Letter of Lewis Hayden to C. C. Nichols, in *Emancipator*, May 12, 1847, p. 2.

4. Lewis Hayden's brief autobiography is in Harriet Beecher Stowe, *A Key to Uncle Tom's Cabin: Presenting the Original Facts and Documents Upon Which the Story Is Founded, Together with Corroborative Statements Verifying the Truth of the Work* (Boston: John P. Jewett, 1853) [hereinafter cited as *Key*], 154–55.

5. Ibid.

6. Ibid.

7. Ibid. On the omnipresence of the market in enslaved consciousness and as the basis for an "indigenous antislavery ideology," see Walter Johnson, *Soul by Soul: Life Inside the Antebellum Slave Market* (Cambridge, MA: Harvard University Press, 1999).

8. Quoted in Runyon, *Delia Webster*, 114–15.

9. *NASS*, November 11, 1847, pp. 94–95.

10. Quoted in Runyon, *Delia Webster*, 114–15.

11. *Key*.

12. *Key*; Letter of Hayden to Gay, May 8, 1847, in *NASS*, May 20, 1847.

13. Delia Webster, *Kentucky Jurisprudence: A History of the Trial of Miss Delia A. Webster* (Vergennes, KY, 1845) [hereinafter cited as *Kentucky Jurisprudence*], 47; "George C. Bain's Nurse," *St. Louis Republic*, April 14, 1889, p. 2; "A Historic Case," *St. Louis Republic*, April 19, 1889, p. 9.

14. "A Historic Case," *St. Louis Republic*, April 19, 1889, p. 9, says they were married two years before the 1844 escape. Joseph Hayden's record on the National Park Service's database of Union black sailors (www.itd.nps.gov/cwss/sailors_index.html) indicates that he was twenty-two at his enlistment in 1861, meaning that he was born about 1839.

15. This narrative relies on Runyon, *Delia Webster*.

16. *Kentucky Jurisprudence*, 47.

17. Calvin Fairbank, *Rev. Calvin Fairbank During Slavery Times: How He "Fought the Good Fight" to Prepare "The Way"* (reprint, New York: Negro Universities Press, 1969), 46.

18. *Kentucky Jurisprudence*, 51.

19. Ibid., 48–52.

20. This narrative relies on Runyon, *Delia Webster*.

21. Letter of Lewis Grant [Hayden] to Mr. Baxter, October 27, 1844, J. Winston Coleman Kentuckiana Collection, Transylvania University Library, Kentucky [hereinafter cited as Grant to Baxter, October 27, 1844, Transylvania].

22. "Important Meeting of Colored Citizens," *Liberator*, November 1, 1839, p. 175, c. 2.

23. See Furstenberg, "Beyond Freedom and Slavery," and chs. 5–7, below.

24. The essential introduction to this ideology in mid-nineteenth-century America is Amy Dru Stanley, *From Bondage to Contract: Wage Labor, Marriage, and the Market in the Age of Slave Emancipation* (New York: Cambridge University Press, 1998).

25. Grant to Baxter, October 27, 1844, Transylvania.

26. *Key*, 154–55.

27. Visiting this church in its new brick building in 1848, Martin Delany noted that "ladies and gentlemen sit together, in the same pews"; "Dear Douglass," *North Star*, August 4, 1848, pp. 3–4.

28. On Detroit and Canada West: Katzman, *Before the Ghetto*; William H. Pease and Jane Pease, *Black Utopia: Negro Communal Experiments in America* (Madison: State Historical Society of Wisconsin, 1963); Robin Winks, *The Blacks in Canada: A History*, revised edition (Montreal: McGill-Queen's University Press, 1997).

29. "To the Benevolent," *Liberator*, October 24, 1845, p. 170, c. 3; "Colored People in Detroit," ibid., March 6, 1846, p. 39, c. 5.

30. Letter of Lewis Hayden to Mrs. Chapman, May 14, 1846, Weston Papers, BPL.

31. Katzman, *Before the Ghetto*, 18–22.

32. Henry Steele Commager, *Theodore Parker* (Boston: Beacon, 1947), 71–79; John Weiss, *Life and Correspondence of Theodore Parker*, 2 vols. (1864; reprint, New York: Arno, 1969), I:253. "Free church" was not synonymous with "abolition church." In the late 1830s, some black Bostonians had moved into and quickly out of one free church. The reason "is simply this—that they regard its pastor as having virtually abandoned the abolition ground, and very deeply injured their cause," because the Reverend Charles Fitch was one of the authors of the anti-Garrison "Clerical Appeal"; *Liberator*, November 24, 1837, p. 190, c. 3; Levesque, "Inherent Reformers," 507–8.

33. Justin D. Fulton, *Memoir of Timothy Gilbert* (Boston: Lee and Shepard, 1866), 159–61.

34. Benjamin Quarles, "Introduction," in William Jay and James Freeman Clarke, *The Free People of Color* (New York: Arno, 1969), 4.

35. "The Detroit Church," *Emancipator*, June 24, 1846, p. 34, c. 3–5.

36. James Freeman Clarke, *Anti-Slavery Days: A Sketch of the Struggle Which Ended in the Abolition of Slavery in the United States* (1883; reprint, Westport, CT: Negro Universities Press, 1970), 170.

37. *Proceedings of the One Hundredth Anniversary of the Granting of Warrant 459 to African Lodge, at Boston* (Boston: Franklin Press, 1885), 26–27.

38. William H. Grimshaw, *Official History of Freemasonry Among the Colored People in North America* (1903; reprint, Belle Fourche, SD: Kessinger, n.d.), 125.

39. *Frederick Douglass' Paper*, March 2, 1855, in *BAPM* 09:0466, p. 2.

40. Lewis Hayden, *Caste Among Masons: Address Before Prince Hall Grand Lodge of Free and Accepted Masons of the State of Massachusetts, at the Festival of St. John the Evangelist, December 27, 1865*, second edition (Boston: Edward S. Coombs, 1866), 6–7.

41. Martin Delany claimed that white and black Masons mingled in Cincinnati lodges in the 1840s; Martin Delany, *Origins and Objects of Ancient Freemasonry*, reprinted in Robert Levine, ed., *Martin R. Delany: A Documentary Reader* (Chapel Hill: University of North Carolina Press, 2003), 49–67. From the 1820s until his death in the 1840s, the black antislavery preacher T. S. Wright was a member of an otherwise white lodge in Schenectady, New York, to which his father, a black Mason originally raised in the Boston lodge in Prince Hall's day, had also belonged; see Jeffrey Croteau (Van Gorden–Williams Library, Lexington, MA), "Black Abolitionists in White Lodges: Richard P. G. Wright and Theodore Sedgwick Wright," unpublished paper in possession of author.

42. *Key*, 154–55.

43. A white Maine lodge of the Sons of Temperance, another fraternal order, did admit Hayden to membership when he spoke before some of its members in 1846. "Growing Indifference to Color Among the Mainites," *American Freeman* (Milwaukee), December 1, 1846, p. 1.

44. Letter of Garrison to Gay, March 31, 1846, in Merrill and Ruchames, *Letters of Garrison*, III:334–35.

45. Grant to Baxter, October 27, 1844, Transylvania.

46. Letter of Hayden to Chapman, May 14, 1846, Weston Papers, BPL.

47. J. M. H. Frederick, comp., *National Party Platforms of the United States* (Akron, OH: s.p., 1896), p. 14.

48. The extensive literature on this split can be approached via Aileen Kraditor, *Means and Ends in American Abolitionism: Garrison and His Critics on Strategy and Tactics, 1834–1850* (1969; reprint, Chicago: Ivan R. Dee, 1989), and James Brewer Stewart, *Holy Warriors: The Abolitionists and American Slavery*, revised edition (New York: Hill and Wang, 1997).

49. Letter of Quincy to Bowditch, December 13, 1842, Ms. 229, Antislavery Collections, BPL.

50. "Extracts from a Letter of Nath'l Colver," Boston, November 30, 1840, British and Foreign Anti-Slavery Society Papers (Mss. Brit. Emp. S 18), Rhodes House Library, University of Oxford, UK.

51. "The Meeting of Freemen," *Liberator*, December 2, 1842.

52. Hayden's contacts and appearances: *Emancipator & Weekly Chronotype*, October 8, 1845, p. 95, c. 1–2; *Emancipator*, March 4, 1846, p. 178, c. 3; ibid., March 25, 1846, p. 191, c. 3; ibid., February 17, 1847, p. 170, c. 2; ibid., June 2, 1847, p. 2, c. 1–2; *Liberator*, April 3, 1846, p. 55, c. 5.

53. Kendrick and Kendrick, *Sarah's Long Walk*, 12; "Political Suggestions," *Liberator*, December 20, 1834.

54. "Boston Election," *Emancipator and Free American*, December 16, 1841, p. 163, c. 2.

55. A long-standing account, promoted first by angry Whigs, held that Liberty Party votes in the election of 1844 tipped New York State to the Democrats, thereby costing Henry Clay the presidency. For a recent dissent, see Vernon L. Volpe, "The Liberty Party and Polk's Election, 1844," *The Historian* 53:4 (Summer 1991), 691–710.

56. Letter of Sanderson to Nell, October 18, 1841, in *WCN*, 107.

57. *Minutes of the National Convention of Colored Citizens: Held at Buffalo, on the 15th, 16th, 17th, 18th and 19th of August, 1843. For the Purpose of Considering Their Moral and Political Condition as American Citizens* (New York: Piercy and Reed, 1843), 16.
58. "Election at New Bedford," *Emancipator and Free American*, December 10, 1841, p. 127, c. 2–3.
59. "Massachusetts Liberty Convention," *Emancipator and Free American*, February 24, 1842, p. 203, c. 4–5.
60. "Boston Election," *Emancipator and Free American*, December 16, 1841, p. 163, c. 2.
61. "Who Would Have Thought It?," *Emancipator & Weekly Chronotype*, November 13, 1844, p. 113, c. 2; "Ward 6," ibid., p. 115, c. 1.
62. Letter of Chapman to Chapman, n.d. [1843?], Weston Papers, BPL.
63. "Convention at Stoneham," *Emancipator*, March 11, 1846, p. 182.
64. Paul R. Shipman, "Reminiscences of Tom Marshall," *The Galaxy* 17:3 (March 1874), 293–305.
65. "Recent Deaths: Lewis Hayden," *Boston Evening Transcript*, April 8, 1889.
66. Douglas Egerton, *Gabriel's Rebellion: The Virginia Slave Conspiracies of 1800 and 1802* (Chapel Hill: University of North Carolina Press, 1993); James Sidbury, *Ploughshares into Swords: Race, Rebellion, and Identity in Gabriel's Virginia* (New York: Cambridge University Press, 1997); Steven Hahn, *A Nation Under Our Feet: Rural Black Politics from Slavery to the Great Migration* (Cambridge, MA: Harvard University Press, 2003), 59–60; Harvey Wish, "The Slave Insurrection Panic of 1856," *JSH* 5 (May 1939), 206–22.
67. Grant to Baxter, October 27, 1844, Transylvania.
68. *Green Mountain Freeman*, February 4, 1846, cited in Runyon, *Delia Webster*, 94.
69. Letter of Andrew to Jackson, December 2, 1845, Antislavery Collections, BPL.
70. See above, n. 52.
71. Letter of Hayden to C. C. Nichols, May 7, 1847, in *Emancipator*, May 12, 1847, p. 2, c. 6.
72. *Minutes of Proceedings of the Triennial Session of the National Grand Lodge, A. Y. M., Held in Philadelphia, July, 1856* (Philadelphia: Brown's Steam-Power Book and Job Printing Office, 1856) [hereinafter cited as *NGL, 1856*].
73. Letter of Smith to Hayden, October 8, 1846, in *BAPM* 05:0281; Letter of Ray to Hayden, March 31, 1856, in *BAPM* 10:98.
74. "Liberty Breakfast at Faneuil Hall," *Emancipator*, June 2, 1847, p. 2; "Tour of William Lloyd Garrison and Frederick Douglass," *Liberator*, August 20, 1847, p. 135.
75. Letter of Garrison to Gay, March 31, 1846, in Merrill and Ruchames, *Letters of Garrison*, III:334–35.
76. Robert E. Gettings, "Lewis Hayden's 1847–1848 Anti-Slavery Tour and the American Anti-Slavery Society as an Employer," *Journal of Hokusei Gakuen Women's Junior College* (March 2004), 34.
77. Grant to Baxter, October 27, 1844, Transylvania.
78. Richards, *The Slave Power.*
79. Jonathan H. Earle, *Jacksonian Antislavery and the Politics of Free Soil, 1824–1854* (Chapel Hill: University of North Carolina Press, 2004), 1–4.
80. *Massachusetts Acts and Resolves, 1847*, ch. 103.
81. *Liberator*, September 26, 1845, p. 154, c. 5–6; ibid., November 7, 1845, p. 178, c. 4–5.
82. Horton and Horton, *Black Bostonians*, 38; Quarles, *Black Abolitionists*, 103; "Independent Whigs," November 5, 1846, John A. Andrew Papers, MHS.
83. "Volunteers in the Army of Justice, Humanity, Peace, and Liberty," *Liberator*, June 5, 1846, p. 91, c. 1.
84. On imposture, see Quarles, *Black Abolitionists*, 159–61.
85. Frederick Douglass, *My Bondage and My Freedom* (1855; reprint, New York: Miller, Orton, 1857), 361.
86. Quoted in McFeely, *Frederick Douglass*, 147.
87. Delany's importance is best captured in Robert S. Levine, *Martin Delany, Frederick Douglass,*

and the Politics of Representative Identity (Chapel Hill: University of North Carolina Press, 1997).

88. *Proceedings of the One Hundredth Anniversary*, 26; for a contemporary account, see *Liberator*, June 4, 1847, p. 91, c. 1–2.

89. Letter of Garrison to Gay, March 31, 1846, Antislavery Collections, BPL.

90. "First of August in Concord," *Liberator*, August 7, 1846, p. 127, c. 3.

91. Grant to Baxter, October 27, 1844, Transylvania.

92. "Sketches of the Sayings and Doings at the N.E. Anti-Slavery Convention," *Liberator*, June 4, 1847, p. 91, c. 1.

93. Runyon, *Delia Webster*, 119–21.

94. Gettings, "Lewis Hayden's 1847–1848 Anti-Slavery Tour," 27–50.

95. Letter of Hudson to Phillips, February 3, 1848, Phillips Papers, HHU.

96. McFeely, *Frederick Douglass*, 147.

97. Hudson told Phillips to burn his February 3 letter; Letter of Hudson to Phillips, December [*sic*] 9, 1848, Phillips Papers, HHU.

98. Letter of Hudson to Phillips, February 3, 1848, Phillips Papers, HHU. For details of these organizational maneuvers, see Gettings, "Lewis Hayden's 1847–1848 Anti-Slavery Tour," 37–39.

99. For the condition of the Western New York Anti-Slavery Society, see *North Star*, December 29, 1848. Remond and his companions proved unable to support themselves as lecturers, so "we were under the painful necessity of dismissing them from the service of the society"; see *WCN*, 210.

100. Letter of Hudson to Phillips, December [*sic*] 9, 1848, Phillips Papers, HHU.

101. Letter of Hayden to Phillips, February 21, 1848, Phillips Papers, HHU.

102. Grant to Baxter, October 27, 1844, Transylvania.

103. Letter of Hayden to Sidney Howard Gay, *NASS*, July 11, 1847, *Black Abolitionist Papers* online (http://bap.chadwyck.com), accessed June 27, 2011.

104. "Henry Clay," *Emancipator*, December 8, 1847, p. 1.

105. Letter of Lewis Hayden to Sidney Howard Gay, *NASS*, November 11, 1847, pp. 94–95.

106. "Henry Clay's Slave," *Emancipator*, July 1, 1846, p. 37.

107. Letter of Clay to Sidney Howard Gay, December 1, 1847, in Melba Porter Hay, ed., *The Papers of Henry Clay*, 10 vols. (Lexington: University Press of Kentucky, 1959–1992), X:383–84.

108. Letter of Clay to Sidney Howard Gay, December 22, 1847, in Hay, *Papers of Henry Clay*, X:391–92.

109. Letter of "H," *Emancipator*, May 12, 1847, p. 4, c. 3; Delany's account in *North Star*, July 28, 1848, p. 2, c. 5–p. 3, c. 1; see also Katzman, *Before the Ghetto*, 8.

110. Delany in *North Star*, August 4, 1848, p. 2, c. 7–p. 3, c. 2.

111. "Lewis Hayden," *North Star*, July 21, 1848, p. 2, c. 4.

112. "Rev. Calvin Fairbank," *Liberator*, September 7, 1849, p. 143, c. 3–4.

113. "Worthy of Patronage," *Liberator*, June 29, 1849, p. 102, c. 6.

114. "Dear Douglass," *North Star*, November 2, 1849, p. 2, c. 7.

115. "Worthy of Patronage," *Liberator*, June 29, 1849, p. 102, c. 6.

116. "Seventh Annual Meeting," *North Star*, February 16, 1849, p. 1, c. 2.

CHAPTER 4: THE MEANS OF ELEVATION

1. Hilary J. Moss, "The Tarring and Feathering of Thomas Paul Smith: Common Schools, Revolutionary Memory, and the Crisis of Black Citizenship in Antebellum Boston," *NEQ* 30:2 (June 2007), 231.

2. Over the past generation, scholarship on nineteenth-century black political and social thought has beat with increasing force against such popular but reductive "overlapping dichotomies." See, e.g., Wilson Moses, *The Golden Age of Black Nationalism, 1850–1925* (Hamden, CT: Ar-

chon Books, 1978); James Campbell, *Songs of Zion: The African Methodist Episcopal Church in the United States and South Africa* (1995; reprint, Chapel Hill: University of North Carolina Press, 1998), quotation on 14–15; and Rael, *Black Identity and Black Protest.* For a thoughtful overview of the variety and evolution of these analyses, see Kate Dossett, *Bridging Race Divides: Black Nationalism, Feminism, and Integration in the United States, 1896–1935* (Gainesville: University Press of Florida, 2008), 3–6.

3. A leading scholar puts it this way: "In almost all cases, those who stood on separatist ground did so out of a loss of faith in the ability of white institutions to serve black needs or the political will of white society to care"; Horton, *Free People of Color*, 17. Such conclusions were more often provisional than permanent.

4. "Frederick Douglass in Boston," *FDP*, August 12, 1853.

5. "A Means of Elevation," *North Star*, April 27, 1849, p. 2.

6. Rael, *Black Identity and Black Protest*, esp. 118–208; see also the foundational work of Paul Goodman, *Of One Blood: Abolitionism and the Origins of Racial Equality* (Berkeley: University of California Press, 1998), esp. 246–60.

7. "What Are the Colored People Doing for Themselves," *North Star*, July 14, 1848, p. 2.

8. Kendrick and Kendrick, *Sarah's Long Walk*, 80.

9. Ibid., 80–86; on reports of abuse by the white teacher, *Liberator*, August 2, 1844, p. 122, c. 2–4.

10. Kendrick and Kendrick, *Sarah's Long Walk*, 87–88; Bowditch in *Liberator*, June 27, 1845, p. 102, c. 4–5.

11. "From the *Liberator*: Meeting of Colored Citizens," *North Star*, August 24, 1849, p. 3.

12. "Colored Schools," *North Star*, August 17, 1849, p. 2.

13. "Frederick Douglass in Boston," *FDP*, August 12, 1853.

14. "The Fifth Annual Meeting," *North Star*, December 29, 1848, p. 2.

15. "Colorphobia Among the Sons," *North Star*, September 21, 1849, p. 2.

16. *CPAR*, 113–14; "Adelphi Union," *Liberator*, January 8, 1841, p. 7; on these societies, see Elizabeth McHenry, *Forgotten Readers: Recovering the Lost History of African American Literary Societies* (Durham, NC: Duke University Press, 2002), 56–83.

17. Letter of Nell to Phillips, April 12, 1852, Phillips Papers, HHU; Letter of Nell to A. Post, April 24, 1853, in *WCN*, 334–35.

18. Kendrick and Kendrick, *Sarah's Long Walk*, 88; Letter of Robert Morris to *Boston Courier*, reprinted in *Liberator*, September 5, 1845, p. 142, c. 1.

19. "Report of a Committee of Parents and Others," *Liberator*, August 2, 1844, p. 122, c. 2–4 (Hilton, "honors"); Kendrick and Kendrick, *Sarah's Long Walk*, 206–8 (Morris); "Meetings of the Friends of Equal School Rights," *Liberator*, November 9, 1849, p. 180, c. 2–3 (John J. Smith).

20. On Roberts and the family context that shaped his activism, see George R. Price and James Brewer Stewart, "The Roberts Case, the Easton Family, and the Dynamics of the Abolitionist Movement in Massachusetts, 1776–1870," *Massachusetts Historical Review* 4 (2002).

21. Davison M. Douglass, *Jim Crow Moves North: The Battle over Northern School Segregation, 1865–1954* (New York: Cambridge University Press, 2005), 50–52.

22. Quoted in Douglass, *Jim Crow Moves North*, 48.

23. *Proceedings of the National Convention of Colored People, and Their Friends, Held in Troy, New York, on the 6th, 7th, 8th and 9th October, 1847* (Troy: J. C. Kneeland, 1847) [hereinafter cited as *Proceedings, 1847*], 36.

24. Kendrick and Kendrick, *Sarah's Long Walk*, 120.

25. Douglass, *Jim Crow Moves North*, 33–44.

26. See Peterson, *Black Gotham*, 63–146; Harris, *In the Shadow of Slavery*, 137–39; Stuckey, *Slave Culture*, 145; John L. Rury, "The New York African Free School, 1827–1836: Conflict over Community Control of Black Education," *Phylon* 44:3 (1983), 187–97.

27. *Proceedings, 1847*, 37.

28. Kendrick and Kendrick, *Sarah's Long Walk*, 118–19; *Liberator*, October 5, 1849, p. 160, c. 3–4.

29. Kendrick and Kendrick, *Sarah's Long Walk*, 120–21.

30. "Boston Olive Branch," *Liberator*, August 8, 1845, p. 125, c. 4.

31. Kendrick and Kendrick, *Sarah's Long Walk*, 121.

32. Ibid., 122.

33. "Meetings of Colored Citizens of Boston," *Liberator*, September 7, 1849, p. 143, c. 1–3.

34. Kendrick and Kendrick, *Sarah's Long Walk*, 130–34.

35. *Roberts v. Boston*, 59 Mass. (5 Cush.) 198.

36. *Proceedings, 1847*, 18.

37. "Treasurer's Report," *Liberator*, May 16, 1845, p. 79, c. 1.

38. Charles Sumner, *Orations and Speeches*, 2 vols. (Boston: Ticknor, Reed, and Fields, 1850), II:332–77. See also Leonard W. Levy and Harlan B. Philips, "The *Roberts* Case: Source of the 'Separate but Equal' Doctrine," *AHR* 56:3 (April 1951), 510–18; Kendrick and Kendrick, *Sarah's Long Walk*, 161ff.

39. Kendrick and Kendrick, *Sarah's Long Walk*, 176ff.

40. "Meetings of Colored Citizens of Boston," *Liberator*, September 7, 1849, p. 143, c. 1–3.

41. "Vindication," *Liberator*, October 5, 1849, p. 160, c. 3–4.

42. Moss, "Tarring and Feathering," quotation on 234.

43. *Liberator*, January 27, 1854, p. 15, c. 2, in *WCN*. On the DeGrasse family, see the DeGrasse-Howard Papers, MHS; Henry B. Hoff, "Frans Abramse Van Salee and His Descendants: A Colonial Black Family in New York and New Jersey," *New York Genealogical and Biographical Record* 121 (April 1990), 65–71; ibid. (July 1990), 157–61; ibid. (October 1990), 205–11.

44. On the genealogies: Franklin A. Dorman, *Twenty Families of Color in Massachusetts, 1742–1998* (Boston: New England Historic Genealogical Society, 1998); Letter of Nell to A. Post, April 24, 1853, in *WCN*, 335; DeGrasse-Howard Papers, MHS.

45. Entry for July 24, 1854, Account Book, DeGrasse-Howard Papers, MHS.

46. Entry for Mark R. and Louise De Mortie, *African American National Biography*, Oxford African American Study Center (www.oxfordaasc.com), accessed June 20, 2011.

47. *Liberator*, January 27, 1854, p. 15, c. 2, in *WCN*, 373–74.

48. Quoted in Rael, *Black Identity and Black Protest*, 27.

49. For insight into the evolution of African American temperance, see Donald Yacavone, "The Transformation of the Black Temperance Movement, 1827–1854," *Journal of the Early Republic* 8:3 (Autumn 1988), esp. 293–95. As David Walker's biographer suggests, the frequency with which the self-proclaimed leadership "demanded adherence" to these values "raises real questions about how many converts they won"; Hinks, *"To Awaken,"* 85–90, quotation on 88.

50. Harris, *In the Shadow of Slavery*, 202–6, offers the compelling example of Peter Paul Simons, whose challenge took in matters of skin color and women's roles as well; see also Stewart, "Racial Modernity."

51. *The Self Elevator*, March 30, 1853. The paper's one extant issue is available at the American Antiquarian Society, Worcester, Massachusetts. On "elevation" and "respectability," see Rael, *Black Identity and Black Protest*, esp. 182–208.

52. Xiomara Santamarina, *Belabored Professions: Narrative of African American Working Womanhood* (Chapel Hill: University of North Carolina Press, 2005), 66.

53. On the complexities and contradictions of this notion, sometimes described as "separate spheres," see Jeanne M. Boydston, *Home and Work: Housework, Wages, and the Ideology of Labor in the Early Republic* (New York: Oxford University Press, 1990).

54. Biographical information in Robert P. Smith, "William Cooper Nell: Crusading Black Abolitionist," *JNH* 55:3 (1970); also *WCN*, 7.

55. Letter of Nell to Phillips, July 31, 1849, Wendell Phillips Papers, HHU.

56. Letter of Nell to A. Post, December 16, 1852, in *WCN*, 320; see also, e.g., Letter of Nell to A. Post, January 6, 1853, in *WCN*, 324.

57. Letter of Nell to A. Post, December 10, 1853, in *WCN*, 356; Letter of Nell to A. Post, January 20, 1854, in *WCN*, 372.

58. Letter of Nell to A. Post, August 31, 1853, in *WCN*, 352.

59. Wendell Phillips Garrison and Francis Jackson Garrison, *William Lloyd Garrison, 1805–1879*, 4 vols. (New York: Century, 1885–1889), I:279–80.

60. *In Memoriam Robert Morris*, pamphlet available at MHS (Boston, 1883), 31–33.

61. Ibid., 33.

62. "Hints to the Free People of Color," *Liberator*, January 9, 1852, p. 7, c. 2.

63. "Colored Churches," *North Star*, February 25, 1848, p. 2.

64. Acts 17:26, as quoted by Douglass in "Colored Churches." This is the Authorized King James Version text of 1769, which was dominant in nineteenth-century English-language worship. See Goodman, *Of One Blood*.

65. See, e.g., Richard S. Newman, *Freedom's Prophet: Bishop Richard Allen, the AME Church, and the Black Founding Fathers* (New York: NYU Press, 2008), 158–66.

66. Charles Emery Stevens, *Anthony Burns, A History* (Boston, 1856), 203–8; Brown, *The Black Man*, 217–18; Stanley Harrold, *Subversives: Antislavery Community in Washington, D.C., 1828–1865* (Baton Rouge: Louisiana State University Press, 2003), 52–53; Grover, *The Fugitive's Gibraltar*, n. 67, 317–18.

67. Stevens, *Anthony Burns*, 208.

68. "An Appeal to the Benevolent," *FDP*, July 20, 1855; Brown, *The Black Man*, 219.

69. Brown, *The Black Man*, 220.

70. Harrold, *Subversives*, 53.

71. Howard H. Bell, "The American Moral Reform Society, 1836–1841," *Journal of Negro Education* 27:1 (Winter 1958), 34–40.

72. Letter of Nell to Phillips, August 4, 1843, Phillips Papers, HHU.

73. *Liberator*, August 4, 1843, p. 122, c. 2–3.

74. *Liberator*, November 19, 1847, p. 185, c. 3.

75. *Proceedings, 1847*, 19–20.

76. Ibid., 6–9.

77. *Report of the Proceedings of the Colored National Convention, Held at Cleveland, Ohio, on Wednesday, September 6th, 1848* (Rochester, NY: North Star Office, 1848) [hereinafter *Proceedings, 1848*], 16.

78. "Three Months in Philadelphia in the Winter of 1849," *North Star*, July 6, 1849, p. 3, c. 2–3.

79. *Liberator*, September 10, 1847, p. 147, c. 1–2.

80. "What Are the Colored People Doing for Themselves," *North Star*, July 14, 1848, p. 2 (quotations); "Three Months in Philadelphia in the Winter of 1849," *North Star*, July 6, 1849, p. 3, c. 2–3.

81. Ohio's grand lodge, for example, chartered at least twelve lodges in five free and slave states; see Charles H. Wesley, *The History of the Prince Hall Grand Lodge of Free and Accepted Masons of the State of Ohio, 1849–1971: An Epoch in American Fraternalism* (Washington, DC: ASNLH, 1972), 36.

82. For a brief historiographical discussion, see Kantrowitz, "'Intended for the Better Government of Man,'" 1001–26, esp. n. 2.

83. Delany, *Origins and Objects*, quotations 52–57. For a sociologically organized starting point to Masonic ritual life, see Bayliss Camp and Orit Kent, "Proprietors, Helpmates, and Pilgrims in Black and White Fraternal Rituals," in Theda Skocpol et al., *What a Mighty Power We Can Be: African American Fraternal Groups and the Struggle for Racial Equality* (Princeton, NJ: Princeton University Press, 2006), 95–134.

84. For a similar analysis by the Illinois black activist H. Ford Douglas, see *FDP*, February 18, 1859, p. 1, c. 1–4.

85. Hilton, "An Address," 8.

86. "By-laws of the Union Lodge No. 2," African Lodge Microfilm, Crocker Library, Grand Lodge of Massachusetts, Boston. I am indebted to librarian Cynthia Alcorn for making this available to me.

87. Thomas to Hayden, December 26, [1869?], Charles Chapman Papers, MSHU; Hilton, "An Address," 4–5; "A Question Settled," *Masonic Review* (Cincinnati) 2:3 (December 1846), 55–58.

88. Hayden attended as a delegate from New York, probably because his family had not yet settled permanently in Boston and he had spent considerable time that year as a lecturer in western New York. But within a year Boston would be his home, and John T. Hilton—the newly elected first grand master of the National Grand Lodge—would be Hayden's close political ally until Hilton's death in 1865. Some of the twenty-two delegates had been part of Northern Afro-American associational life for much of their adult lives: Hilton had long represented Boston in Baptist conventions; the first listed New York delegate, craftsman Alexander Elston, had spent almost a quarter of a century in relief, mutual benefit, and fraternal organizations. Horton and Horton, *Black Bostonians*, 42–43; Craig Steven Wilder, *In the Company of Black Men: The African Influence on African American Culture in New York City* (New York: NYU Press, 2001), 114–15; *Proceedings of the Sixth Triennial Session of the Most Worshipful National Grand Lodge of Free and Accepted Ancient York Masons . . . Baltimore, October A.D. 1865* (Philadelphia, 1866), 41. See also the reprint of the announcement and the Declaration of Sentiments in John Jones, *An Argument in Relation to Freemasonry Among Colored Men in This Country* (Chicago: Tribune, 1866), 7–8.

89. For Hayden's continuing leadership role, see *Minutes of Proceedings of the Triennial Session of the National Grand Lodge . . . Philadelphia, July, 1856* (Philadelphia, 1856) p. 17.

90. M. R. Delany, *The Origin and Objects of Ancient Freemasonry: Its Introduction into the United States, and Legitimacy Among Colored Men. A Treatise Delivered before St. Cyprian Lodge, No. 13, June 24th, A.D. 1853—A.L. 5853* (Pittsburgh: W. S. Haven, 1853), 21–22.

91. Alton G. Roundtree and Paul M. Bessel, *Out of the Shadows: The Emergence of Prince Hall Freemasonry in America: Over 225 Years of Endurance* (Camp Springs, MD: KLR Publishing, 2006), 45–90.

92. Hilton, "An Address," 9–10.

93. African American women had already begun to play leadership roles in newer ritual associations such as the Good Samaritans and Daughters of Samaria and the Independent Order of Brothers and Sisters of Love and Charity—both of which also included leading Freemasons as prominent members.

94. Martha S. Jones, *All Bound Up Together: The Woman Question in African American Public Culture* (Chapel Hill: University of North Carolina Press, 2007), 111–13, 167–71.

95. "U.C.A. Association," *North Star*, August 25, 1848.

96. Skocpol et al., *What a Mighty Power*, 411; see, e.g., "Musical Concert," *Liberator*, May 25, 1833, p. 84, c. 2.

97. Scattered mentions of this auxiliary exist for the period before Reconstruction, e.g.: "Henry Gassett," *Catalogue of Books on the Masonic Institution . . . Antimasonic in Arguments and Conclusions* (Boston: Damrell and Moore, 1852), 102; "Letter from Pittsburg," *Christian Recorder*, February 4, 1865.

98. See, e.g., Letter of Winslow Lewis to Lewis Hayden, November 18, 1868, reprinted in *Proceedings of the Grand Lodge . . . of Ohio . . . 1875* (Cincinnati: John D. Caldwell, 1875), 51.

99. Anderson, "Constitutions."

100. "Colored Masons," *Christian Recorder*, October 7, 1865, p. 1, c. 4–5. The scanty literature on John Jones includes Charles A. Gliozzo, "John Jones and the Black Convention Movement, 1848–1856," *Journal of Black Studies* 3:2 (December 1972), 227–36.

101. "Declaration of Sentiments," 1847, reprinted in *NGL, 1856*, 5–6.

102. Amanda Anderson, "Cosmopolitanism, Universalism, and the Divided Legacies of Modernity," in Peng Cheah and Bruce Robbins, eds., *Cosmopolitics: Thinking and Feeling Beyond the Nation* (Minneapolis: University of Minnesota Press, 1998), quotations 266–69.

103. *Proceedings of the Most Worshipful Grand Lodge of Ancient Free and Accepted Masons of the Commonwealth of Massachusetts for the Years 1845 to 1855 Inclusive* (Boston: Caustic-Claflin, n.d.), 105–6.

104. For exceptions, see Croteau, "Black Abolitionists in White Lodges," and Delany, *Origins and Objects*, 22n. For additional moments of interracial Masonic recognition, see Sarah J. W. Early, *Life and Labors of Rev. Jordan W. Early* (Nashville: A.M.E. Church Sunday School Union, 1894), 50–52; W. E. Burghardt Du Bois, ed., *Economic Co-operation Among Negro Americans* (Atlanta: Atlanta University Press, 1907), 113–14; *Biography of Rev. David Smith, of the A.M.E. Church* (Xenia, OH: Xenia Gazette Office, 1881), 58–60; typescript copy of passage from the antislavery reminiscences of William F. Channing, n.d., item 484, box 4, Higginson Letters, HHU.

105. See, e.g., "A Question Settled," *Masonic Review* 2:3 (December 1846), 55–58.

106. Albert G. Mackey, *The Principles of Masonic Law: A Treatise on the Constitutional Laws, Usages and Landmarks of Freemasonry* (New York: Jno. W. Leonard, 1856), III:1:iv (accessed via www .gutenberg.org, June 11, 2008).

107. "The Free Masons Refused," *North Star*, November 17, 1848; Edward Everett, *An Oration Delivered at Charlestown on the Seventy-Fifth Anniversary of the Battle of Bunker Hill, June 17, 1850* (Boston: Redding, 1850), 55.

108. *Proceedings, 1848.*

109. "From Frederick Douglass' Paper: Infidelity," *Liberator*, June 10, 1853, p. 91.

110. Letter of Nell to A. Post, June 22, 1853, in *WCN*, 341.

111. "Letters from the Editor," *FDP*, August 12, 1853.

112. "Something Personal," *FDP*, August 19, 1853, p. 2.

113. Letter of Nell to A. Post, August 12, 1853, Post Papers, University of Rochester.

114. William J. Watkins, "Frederick Douglass in Boston," *FDP*, August 12, 1853, p. 3.

115. "Letter Number II," *FDP*, August 12, 1853, p. 2.

116. "Letters from the Editor," *FDP*, August 12, 1853, p. 2; "The Liberator," *FDP*, December 9, 1853.

117. "The Liberator," *FDP*, December 9. 1853.

118. *Liberator*, September 16, 1853, p. 147, c. 4, in *WCN*, 354.

119. *FDP*, March 24, 1854, p. 4, c. 1–2, in *WCN*, 376–77.

120. Letter of Nell to Morris, March 17, 1843, Chapman Collection, MSHU.

121. *FDP*, August 12, 1853, in *BAPM* 08:0399.

122. Letter of Nell to A. Post, August 12, 1853, Post Papers, University of Rochester; also see Letter of Nell to A. Post, January 20, 1854, in *WCN*, 371.

123. "Our Eastern Tour," *FDP*, August 26, 1853, p. 2, c. 4–5.

124. Letter of Nell to A. Post, August 12, 1853, Post Papers, University of Rochester; Letter of Nell to A. Post, December 20, 1853, in *WCN*, 362–63.

125. "National Council of Colored People," *Liberator*, November 11, 1853, p. 179; "National Council of Colored People," *FDP*, December 2, 1853, p. 2, c. 5.

126. "Meeting of the State Council," *Liberator*, February 24, 1854, p. 30.

127. "Massachusetts State Council," *Liberator*, July 28, 1854, p. 119; "The National Council Meeting at Cleveland," *FDP*, July 28, 1854, p. 2, c. 4–7.

128. "National Council of Colored People," *FDP*, May 18, 1855, p. 1.

129. "Colored National Council," *Liberator*, July 27, 1855, p. 120, c. 3–4; Letter of Nell to A. Post, November 30, 1855, in *WCN*, 429–30.

130. "National Convention of Colored Americans," *Liberator*, December 7, 1855, p. 196.

131. Letter of Nell to A. Post, December 10, 1853, in *WCN*, 355; Letter of Nell to A. Post, December 20, 1853, in *WCN*, 362–63; "From Frederick Douglass' Paper," *Liberator*, December 16, 1853, p. 195, c. 7–p. 196, c. 3.

132. "National Council of the Colored People," *FDP*, May 18, 1855, p. 1.

133. Letter of Nell to A. Post, January 20, 1854, in *WCN*, 373.

134. Letter of Nell to A. Post, December 20, 1853, in *WCN*, 362–63; "Massachusetts State Council," *Liberator*, July 28, 1854, p. 119, c. 3. See Levesque, *Black Boston*, 351–52.

135. Letter of Nell to A. Post, November 6, 1855, in *WCN*, 430.

136. Letter of Nell to A. Post, November 30, 1855, in *WCN*, 432.

137. Litwack, *North of Slavery*, 91; Graham Russell Hodges, *Root and Branch: African Americans in New York and East Jersey, 1613–1863* (Chapel Hill: University of North Carolina Press, 1999), 253.

138. See the nuanced reading of Wilmot's racism and antislavery in Earle, *Jacksonian Antislavery*, 131–39.

139. "Great Gathering of Colored Citizens," *Liberator*, January 28, 1848, p. 15, c. 2.

140. Laurie, *Beyond Garrison*, 171; "People's Mass Convention," *Liberator*, July 7, 1848, p. 106, c. 4.

141. "The Buffalo Convention," *Liberator*, August 18, 1848, p. 131, c. 2–3; Earle, *Jacksonian Antislavery*, 168.

142. "First of August in Lynn," *Liberator*, August 25, 1848, p. 133, c. 2–4. Most historical accounts of Robert Morris's partisan roles are unreliable. Kendrick and Kendrick (*Sarah's Long Walk*) describe Morris as a Liberty man in 1848, although he had already attended the people's convention to form a Free Soil ticket. Bruce Laurie (*Beyond Garrison*) and the editors of the *Black Abolitionist Papers* repeat the claim of Horton and Horton (*Black Bostonians*) that the Free Soilers nominated Morris for mayor of Boston, and erroneously credit *In Memoriam Robert Morris* (45). In fact, efforts to nominate Morris for mayor of Chelsea, not Boston, came from post–Civil War Democrats. See ch. 8.

143. See, e.g., *North Star*, September 15, 1848, p. 2; ibid., September 22, 1848, p. 3.

144. *Proceedings, 1848*, 13–15.

145. "Great Taylor Movement," *North Star*, October 13, 1848, p. 3, c. 2.

146. "Fifteenth Annual Meeting," *Liberator*, May 18, 1849, p. 78, c. 1–p. 79, c. 4.

147. "What Good Has the Free Soil Movement Done?," *North Star*, May 25, 1849.

148. On Douglass's political development, see Stauffer, *Black Hearts of Men*, 158–62, and McFeely, *Frederick Douglass*.

149. "Free Soil Nominations," *Emancipator & Republican*, November 7, 1850, p. 2, c. 1. The Free Soil slate also included William F. Channing, Elizur Wright, and Henry Bowditch (who had been running as a Liberty man as early as 1845: "Suffolk Liberty Party," *Emancipator*, November 5, 1845, p. 110, c. 7).

150. "Affairs About Home: Free Soil Nominations," *Boston Herald*, November 3, 1853, p. 4.

151. *FDP*, March 2, 1855, in *BAPM* 09:0466.

152. Gerber, *Black Ohio*, 5.

153. "Ward Six Election," *Boston Daily Atlas*, May 19, 1853, p. 2, c. 3.

154. "Republican Caucus Meeting," *Boston Evening Transcript*, August 29, 1854, p. 2, c. 4.

155. "Free Soil Republican State Convention," *Boston Daily Atlas*, September 8, 1854, p. 2, c. 2.

156. "Massachusetts State Election," *Boston Daily Atlas*, November 14, 1854, p. 2, c. 2.

157. John R. Mulkern, *The Know-Nothing Party in Massachusetts: The Rise and Fall of a People's Movement* (Boston: Northeastern University Press, 1990), 61–86; Tyler Anbinder, *Nativism and Slavery: The Northern Know Nothings and the Politics of the 1850s* (New York: Oxford University Press, 1992), 32.

158. Frederick Reinhart Anspach [signed "An American"], *The Sons of the Sires: A History of the Rise, Progress, and Destiny of the American Party . . .* (Philadelphia: Lippincott, Grambo, 1855), 30, 35.

159. Mulkern, *The Know-Nothing Party*, 61–86.

160. Ibid., 102–3.

161. "Massachusetts State Election," *Boston Daily Atlas*, November 14, 1854, p. 2, c. 2. Wilson and Andrew became nationally known figures; on Slack, see Kathleen Rosa Zebley, "God and Liberty: The Life of Charles Wesley Slack" (M.A. thesis, Kent State University, 1992).

162. For a broader analysis of this dynamic in the composition of the Know-Nothing Party, see Anbinder, *Nativism and Slavery*, esp. 50.

163. Quoted in Anbinder, *Nativism and Slavery*, 45.

164. So claimed Mark De Mortie, a freeborn black man from Norfolk, Virginia, who moved to Boston in 1851 after his career helping fugitives escape north was derailed by an intercepted letter. Although he was only in his early twenties, he threw himself into the city's political life in company with Hayden, whom he knew through the network of fugitive escape and defense. Like many others he was first a Free Soil man, then became "allied" with the Know-Nothings in 1854. Although Hayden and Rock were Republican candidates that year, not Know-Nothings, De Mortie claimed that these men and others (including Grimes) threw the black community's vote to the Know-Nothings in that year; William H. Ferris, *The African Abroad, or His Evolution in Western Civilization, Tracing His Development Under Caucasian Milieu*, 2 vols. (New Haven, CT: Tuttle, Morehouse, and Taylor, 1913), 710.

165. "Massachusetts State Election," *Boston Daily Atlas*, November 14, 1854, p. 2, c. 2.

166. Letter of Lewis Hayden to Sidney Howard Gay, *NASS*, July 22, 1847, in *BAPM* reel 5, doc. 441.

167. Ferris, *The African Abroad*, 710–11.

168. Kendrick and Kendrick, *Sarah's Long Walk*, 224–31.

169. "From Our Boston Correspondent," *FDP*, March 2, 1855, p. 2, c. 7. Under the Know-Nothing legislature, the twenty-second amendment to the state constitution created a ward-by-ward system of election for the state legislature.

170. Quoted in Douglass, *Jim Crow Moves North*, 59.

171. *Triumph.*

172. "Meeting of Colored Citizens," *Liberator*, December 28, 1855, p. 206.

173. *Triumph.*

174. Letter of Nell to A. Post, December 25, 1855, in *WCN*, 447–48.

175. *Triumph.*

176. Ibid.

177. "From Our Boston Correspondent," *FDP*, September 28, 1855.

178. *In Memoriam: Robert Morris*, 28.

179. "Slavery Chivalry in a Chelsea Omnibus," *FDP*, July 20, 1855.

Chapter 5: The Heirs of Crispus Attucks

1. *CPAR*, 14–17. See Hiller B. Zobel, *The Boston Massacre* (New York: Norton, 1970).

2. Broadside, "Meeting of the Colored Citizens," Boston Athenaeum.

3. For a modern treatment, see John Barnwell, *Love of Order: South Carolina's First Secession Crisis* (Chapel Hill: University of North Carolina Press, 1982).

4. Speech of John C. Calhoun, U.S. Senate, March 4, 1850, *Congressional Globe*, 31st Congress, 1st Session, 451–55.

5. Broadside, "Meeting of the Colored Citizens."

6. This account relies on the groundbreaking analysis in François Furstenberg, "Beyond Freedom and Slavery," 1295–330, and Furstenberg, *In the Name of the Father: Washington's Legacy, Slavery, and the Making of a Nation* (New York: Penguin Press, 2006), esp. 190–216. The previously prevailing view of the relationship between slavery and freedom in the context of the American Revolution is most eloquently expressed in Edmund Morgan, "Slavery and Freedom: The American Paradox," *JAH* 59:1 (June 1972), 5–29.

7. Frederick Douglass, *My Bondage and My Freedom* (New York: Miller, Orton and Mulligan, 1855), 249.

8. Horton and Horton, *Black Bostonians*, 112.

9. Gary Collison, *Shadrach Minkins: From Fugitive Slave to Citizen* (Cambridge, MA: Harvard University Press, 1997), 77.

10. "Rocking of the Old Cradle of Liberty," *Liberator*, October 18, 1850, p. 166, c. 5.

11. Broadside, "Mass Meeting of the Colored Citizens."

12. Levy, "'Abolition Riot.'" Nell's emphasis on the role of women in the 1836 rescue was not a slip of the tongue; a few years later he told an audience that this rescue had been accomplished "mainly through the prowess of a few colored women; the memory of which deed is sacredly cherished and transmitted to posterity"; *BAPM* 07:854.

13. "Anti-Webster Meeting," *Liberator*, April 5, 1850, p. 55, c. 3–4.

14. The black population of Canada West in the 1850s was once estimated at between thirty thousand and forty thousand; Winks, *The Blacks in Canada*, 240. Recent analysis of Canadian sources suggest a lower figure; Michael Wayne, "The Black Population of Canada West on the Eve of the American Civil War: A Reassessment Based on the Manuscript Census of 1861," *Histoire sociale/Social History* 28/56 (November 1995), 465–85.

15. See Ikuko Asaka, "Race Across Empire and Republic: Black Migration to Canada and Racial, National, and Gender Formations in Atlantic Context" (Ph.D. dissertation, University of Wisconsin–Madison, 2010); Van Gosse, "'As a Nation, the English Are Our Friends': The Emergence of African American Politics in the British Atlantic World, 1772–1861," *AHR* 113 (October 2008), 1003–28.

16. Broadside, "Mass Meeting of the Colored Citizens"; "Farewell Soiree to George Thompson," *FDP*, June 26, 1851.

17. "Rocking of the Old Cradle of Liberty," *Liberator*, October 18, 1850, pp. 166–67.

18. Clipping from *National Anti-Slavery Standard*, October 10, 1850, BAA Doc. No. 10923.

19. "Appeal to the Citizens of Boston and Its Neighborhood," *Boston Daily Evening Transcript*, November 2, 1850, p. 1.

20. BVC Minutes, October 1850, BPL.

21. Figures in Gary L. Collison, "The Boston Vigilance Committee: A Reconsideration," *Historical Journal of Massachusetts* 12 (June 1984), 104–16. Theodore Parker claimed that by early 1852 the Boston Vigilance Committee had "saved the liberties of not less than 400 citizens"; *Liberator*, April 16, 1852, p. 62, c. 2–6. A person closer to the front lines of the struggle reckoned that vigilant friends of the slave had protected a hundred fugitives from recapture and return; Austin Bearse, *Reminiscences of Fugitive-Slave Law Days in Boston* (Boston: Warren Richardson, 1880), 14.

22. Treasurers' Accounts, Boston Vigilance Committee, MHS; Agents' Records and Subscription Book, 1846–1847, Committee of Vigilance, Phillips Papers, HHU; Vigilance Committee Record Book, Boston Anti-Man-Hunting League Papers, MHS.

23. "Diary of John Knight, the Slave Pursuer," *Liberator*, December 6, 1850, p. 196, c. 3–5.

24. For biographies of William and Ellen Craft, see Richard J. Blackett, *Beating Against the Barriers: The Lives of Six Nineteenth-Century Afro-Americans* (1986; reprint, Ithaca, NY: Cornell University Press, 1989), 87–138.

25. Collison, *Shadrach Minkins*, 91.

26. Jeremiah Chaplin and J. D. Chaplin, *Life of Charles Sumner* (Boston: D. Lothrop, 1874), 157.

27. *L&C*, I:206–9.

28. Transcription of Parker journals in Scrapbook 14, Siebert Papers, HHU.

29. *L&C*, I:206–9.

30. "The Boston Slave Hunt and the Vigilance Committee," *Pennsylvania Freeman*, November 7, 1850.

31. *L&C*, II:373; Archibald Grimké, "Antislavery Boston," *New England Magazine* 9:4 (December 1890), 458; Putnam to Siebert, December 27, 1893, Scrapbook 13, Siebert Papers, HHU; Nina Moore Tiffany, "Stories of the Fugitive Slaves I: The Escape of William and Ellen Craft," *New England Magazine* 7:5 (January 1890), 524–31; "The Boston Slave Hunt and the Vigilance Committee."

32. "Diary of John Knight, the Slave Pursuer"; "Excitement in Boston," *Anti-Slavery Bugle* (Salem,

OH), November 9, 1850, p. 30, c. 1. For population, see Seventh Census of the United States, 1850, 49.

33. "The Boston Slave Hunt and the Vigilance Committee."
34. BVC Minutes, October 29, 1850, BPL.
35. "Diary of John Knight, the Slave Pursuer."
36. Transcription of Parker journals in Scrapbook 14, Siebert Papers, HHU; Commager, *Theodore Parker*, 216–17.
37. "The Boston Slave Hunt and the Vigilance Committee."
38. This story was published half a century after the event, in *Woman's Era* I (August 1895), 4–5, and later reprinted in Dorothy Sterling, *We Are Your Sisters: Black Women in the Nineteenth Century* (New York: Norton, 1984), 222. Prince herself did not refer to the event in her own autobiography, published just a few years after the event was supposed to have taken place; Nancy Prince, *A Narrative of the Life and Travels, of Mrs. Nancy Prince* (Boston, 1850).
39. Carla L. Peterson, *"Doers of the Word": African-American Women Speakers and Writers in the North, 1830–1880* (1995; reprint, New Brunswick, NJ: Rutgers University Press, 1998) 120; Frances Smith Foster, ed., *A Brighter Coming Day: A Frances Ellen Watkins Reader* (New York: Feminist Press, 1990).
40. Ellen Carol DuBois, *Feminism and Suffrage: The Emergence of an Independent Women's Movement in America, 1848–1869* (Ithaca, NY: Cornell University Press, 1978), 41.
41. *FDP*, December 2, 1853, p. 2, c. 1; "Women's Rights Convention," *FDP*, December 16, 1853.
42. "The Colored Citizens of Boston," *Liberator*, December 10, 1852, p. 199, in *WCN*, 316–19.
43. Letter of R. H. Cain to Douglass, *FDP*, April 7, 1854, in *BAPM* 08:0724.
44. "Lewis Hayden's Clothing Store," *Liberator*, April 1, 1853, p. 50, c. 6.
45. U.S. Census for 1850, Boston, Massachusetts, Ward 6, Dwelling 861; Account Book of John V. DeGrasse, October 1854, DeGrasse-Howard Papers, MHS.
46. Collison, *Shadrach Minkins*, 104–7; see also Stanley W. Campbell, *The Slave Catchers: Enforcement of the Fugitive Slave Law, 1850–1860* (New York: Norton, 1972).
47. Collison, *Shadrach Minkins*, 110–11.
48. Ibid., ch. 7.
49. Letter of John A. Andrew to J. F. Clarke, James Freeman Clarke Papers, HHU.
50. The Boston Athenaeum's database of antebellum black Bostonians (http://app.bostonathe naeum.org/BosBlack/) shows Riley to have been a fifty-nine-year-old widow in 1850, residing at 1 Southac Court.
51. Collison, *Shadrach Minkins*, ch. 7.
52. Quotations in Collison, *Shadrach Minkins*, 139–40.
53. *L&C*, I:212.
54. Letter of Nell to A. Post, March 16, 185[1], in *WCN*, 411.
55. Collison, *Shadrach Minkins*, 141–48.
56. Letter of Wendell Phillips to Pease, March 9, 1851, in *Life of Garrison*, III:323; BVC Minutes, February 28, 1851, BPL.
57. Collison, *Shadrach Minkins*, 193–96.
58. "Farewell Soiree to George Thompson," *FDP*, June 26, 1851.
59. Collison, *Shadrach Minkins*, 194–96.
60. Leonard Levy, "Sims' Case: The Fugitive Slave Law in Boston," *Journal of Negro History* 35 (1950), 49–74; see also Bearse, *Reminiscences*, 22–23.
61. Letter of Higginson to May[?], n.d. [April 1851], item 382, Higginson Letters, HHU.
62. Higginson, "Narrative," B.1.22 (105), BPL.
63. Tilden G. Edelstein, *Strange Enthusiasm: A Life of Thomas Wentworth Higginson* (New Haven, CT: Yale University Press, 1968), 111–12; Albert J. Von Frank, *The Trials of Anthony Burns: Freedom and Slavery in Emerson's Boston* (Cambridge, MA: Harvard University Press, 1998), 27–28.

64. For Higginson's growing attraction to Boston's militant antislavery world, see, e.g., Letter of Higginson to "dearest," February 14, 1847; Higginson to Molly, July 20, 1847; Higginson to Mother, September 6, 1849, all in Higginson Letters, HHU.

65. *Liberator*, April 11, 1851, p. 59, c. 2. At least into 1852, city authorities denied antislavery forces the use of Faneuil Hall; *Liberator*, January 30, 1852, p. 17, c. 1–p. 18, c. 2.

66. Von Frank, *Trials of Anthony Burns*, 28–29; Levy, "Sims' Case."

67. "Arrests for Carrying Concealed Weapons," *Liberator*, April 11, 1851, p. 59, c. 1–3; Letter of F. Jackson to [Phillips], April 5, [1851], Phillips Papers, HHU.

68. Letter of Higginson to Messrs Editors, n.d., Higginson-Burns Mss., BPL; Charles Francis Adams, *Richard Henry Dana: A Biography*, 2 vols. (Boston: Houghton Mifflin, 1890), I:193.

69. *L&C*, I:215–29.

70. Ibid.; "Proceedings in the Case of Sims," *Liberator*, April 18, 1851, p. 62, c. 3–6; Edelstein, *Strange Enthusiasm*, 115; Bearse, *Reminiscences*, 28.

71. Thomas P. Slaughter, *Bloody Dawn: The Christiana Riot and Racial Violence in the Antebellum North* (New York: Oxford University Press, 1994); Jayme A. Sokolow, "The Jerry McHenry Rescue and the Growth of Northern Antislavery Sentiment During the 1850s," *Journal of American Studies* 16:3 (December 1982), 427–45.

72. See Bearse, *Reminiscences*, 10–37; "Statement of Stockholders' Loss in Yacht *Flirt*," BPL; Vigilance Committee Records, p. 53, BAMHL Records, MHS; Letter of Nell to A. Post, July 21, 1853, in *WCN*, 342.

73. James Freeman Clarke, *Autobiography, Diary, and Correspondence*, ed. Edward Everett Hale (Boston, 1892), 193–94; Ethel Lewis, *Celebration of the One Hundredth Anniversary of the Birth of William Lloyd Garrison* (Boston: Garrison Centenary Committee, 1906), 25–26.

74. Bearse, *Reminiscences*, 8.

75. Ibid., 38–39.

76. Glenn C. Altschuler and Stuart M. Blumin, *Rude Republic: Americans and Their Politics in the Nineteenth Century* (Princeton, NJ: Princeton University Press, 2000), 63.

77. In Providence, the "African Greys," led by a veteran of the War of 1812, existed by 1821; see Robert J. Cottrol, *The Afro-Yankees: Providence's Black Community in the Antebellum Era* (Westport, CT: Greenwood, 1982), 63.

78. Cottrol, *Afro-Yankees*, 76, 85.

79. Black militia activity in the 1850s is placed in continental and historical context in Jeffrey Kerr-Ritchie, "Rehearsal for War: Black Militias in the Atlantic World," *Slavery and Abolition* 26:1 (April 2005), 1–34. On the Massasoit Guards: Petition (n.d.), Massasoit Guards folder, Robert Morris Papers, Boston Athenaeum [hereinafter cited as Morris Papers]. The background of the local movement to 1855 is analyzed in Hal Goldman, "Black Citizenship and Military Self-Presentation in Antebellum Massachusetts," *Historical Journal of Massachusetts* 25 (Winter 1997), 19–45, and the movement itself analyzed in Stephen Kantrowitz, "Fighting Like Men: Civil War Dilemmas of Abolitionist Manhood," in *Battle Scars: Gender and Sexuality in the U.S. Civil War*, eds. Catherine Clinton and Nina Silber (New York: Oxford University Press, 2006), and Minardi, *Making Slavery History*, 153–61.

80. "Speech of Robert Morris . . . 1853," clipping in Legal Documents, 1840s–50s folder, Morris Papers.

81. Letter of Nell to Phillips, April 15, 1841, Phillips Papers, HHU.

82. *CPAR*, 14.

83. For further analyses of William Nell and *CPAR*, see Ernest, *Liberation Historiography*, 132–53; Kachun, "From Forgotten Founder to Indispensable Icon"; Kantrowitz, "A Place for 'Colored Patriots'"; and Minardi, *Making Slavery History*, 145–53.

84. *Aliened American*, April 9, 1853, in *BAPM* 08:0219.

85. Quarles, *Black Abolitionists*, 187; "The Colored Citizens of Boston," *Liberator*, December 10, 1852, p. 199, in *WCN*, 316–19; Letter of Nell to A. Post, October 9, 1852, in *WCN*, 311.

86. William J. Watkins, "Our Rights as Men," reprinted in Dorothy Porter, ed., *Negro Protest Pamphlets: A Compendium* (New York: Arno, 1969), quotations pp. 4, 8.

87. *FDP,* April 7, 1854, in *BAPM* 08:0722.

88. Watkins, "Our Rights as Men."

89. *In Memoriam Robert Morris*, 35; William Leonard, "Black and Irish Relations in Nineteenth Century Boston: The Interesting Case of Lawyer Robert Morris," *Historical Journal of Massachusetts* (Spring 2009), 80–81; M. P. Curran, *Life of Patrick A. Collins, with Some of His Most Notable Public Addresses* (Norwood, MA: Norwood Press, 1906), 12.

90. "Speech of Robert Morris . . . 1853," clipping in Massasoit Guards folder, Morris Papers.

91. "Speech of Robert Morris . . . 1853," clipping in Legal Documents, 1840s–50s folder, Morris Papers; *Liberator*, May 13, 1853, in *BAPM* 08:0246.

92. *FDP*, August 26, 1853, in *BAPM* 08:0420. On the convention, see Laurie, *Beyond Garrison*, 264–65.

93. *Official Report of the Debates and Proceedings in the State Convention, Assembled May 4th, 1853, to Revise and Amend the Constitution of the Commonwealth of Massachusetts* (Boston: Wright and Potter, 1853), 95–96.

94. Ibid., 89.

95. "Equal Rights of Citizens," *Liberator*, August 5, 1853, p. 122, c. 4; *CPAR*, 101–10.

96. *Liberator*, August 19, 1853, in *WCN*, 344.

97. *FDP*, August 26, 1853, in *BAPM* 08:0420.

98. *FDP*, December 27, 1853, in *BAPM* 08:0600.

99. Von Frank, *Trials of Anthony Burns*, xviii.

100. Ibid.; Stevens, *Anthony Burns*, 33.

101. Stevens, *Anthony Burns*, 38–41.

102. Von Frank, *Trials of Anthony Burns*, 52–64; Campbell, *Slave Catchers*, 125; Stevens, *Anthony Burns*, 42; "Affairs About Home," *Boston Herald*, May 27, 1854, p. 2; Receipt, Higginson-Burns Papers, BPL.

103. Stevens, *Anthony Burns*, 41; Von Frank, *Trials of Anthony Burns*, 61.

104. Ferris, *The African Abroad*, 711.

105. Letter of Channing to Higginson, February 6, 1898, Higginson Papers, HHU. Higginson's friend Martin Stowell was equally certain he had fired the shot, and had previously participated in a violent rescue effort in Syracuse, New York. Letter of Drew to Higginson, April 16, 1888, Higginson-Burns Papers, BPL; Von Frank, *Trials of Anthony Burns*, 20–26; Sokolow, "The Jerry McHenry Rescue."

106. "Uncle Tom," *FDP*, April 29, 1853.

107. "Our Eastern Tour," *FDP*, August 26, 1853.

108. "Who Are the Murderers?," *FDP*, June 2, 1854, in *BAPM* 08:0857.

109. "The North Awakening," *FDP*, June 2, 1854, in *BAPM* 08:0857.

110. Typescript, n.d., item 484, box 4, Higginson Letters, Ms. Am. 784, HHU. Hayden could, of course, have been making this up. But since Butman was so unlikely a candidate for interracial fellowship, it seems improbable that a man of Hayden's political sophistication would fabricate a claim so outlandish on its face.

111. Ibid.; also Letter of Channing to Higginson, February 6, 1898, Higginson Letters, HHU.

112. *L&C*, I:269.

113. Letter of Nell to A. Post, June 13, 1854, in *WCN*, 384.

114. Letter of A. W. Weston to Dear Folks, May 30, 1854, reprinted in *Proceedings of the Massachusetts Historical Society* 44 (January 1911), 326–34.

115. Adams, *Richard Henry Dana*, 277–80; Letter of May to Higginson, June 2, [1854], Higginson-Burns Papers, BPL.

116. "Another Sims Case in Boston," *Liberator*, June 2, 1854, p. 86, c. 1–4.

117. Von Frank, *Trials of Anthony Burns*, 208.

118. S. A. M. Washington, *George T. Downing: Sketch of His Life and Times* (Newport, RI: Milne Printery 1910), 9–10.
119. *L&C*, I:268–69.
120. Typescript, n.d., item 484, box 4, Higginson Letters, Ms. Am. 784, HHU; Letter of W. F. Channing to TWH, May 30, 1854, Higginson-Burns Papers, BPL.
121. Ms., April 6, 1874, Higginson Papers, HHU.
122. Thomas Wentworth Higginson, *Army Life in a Black Regiment* (1869; reprint, New York: Norton, 1984), 50–51. The original entry for this date (December 16, 1862) in Higginson's manuscript journal does not include the final quoted phrase, which he must have added while revising the journals for publication; Christopher Looby, ed., *The Complete Civil War Journal and Selected Letters of Thomas Wentworth Higginson* (Chicago: University of Chicago Press, 2000), 67.
123. "Celebration of the Fourth of July," *Liberator*, June 16, 1854.
124. "Burns Sent Back," *Provincial Freeman*, June 10, 1854, in *BAPM* 08:0869.
125. Letter of Higginson to Mother, May 29, 1854, Higginson-Burns Papers, BPL.
126. Letter of S. Higginson to T. W. Higginson, June 4, 1854, Higginson-Burns Papers, BPL.
127. Quoted in Von Frank, *Trials of Anthony Burns*, 207.
128. Letter of Bowditch to Sumner, June 10, 1854, Charles Sumner Papers, HHU.
129. Ibid.
130. On the Boston Anti-Man-Hunting League, see Kantrowitz, "Fighting Like Men."
131. James Freeman Clarke, *The Rendition of Anthony Burns. Its Causes and Consequences. A Discourse on Christian Politics Delivered in Williams Hall, Boston, on Whitsunday, June 4, 1854* (Boston, 1854), 15.
132. One scholar describes the radicalization of Boston in the wake of this rendition as a "pocket revolution"; Von Frank, *Trials of Anthony Burns*, xii.
133. *Liberator*, January 5, 1855, p. 4, c. 2–3, in *WCN*, 405; Ernest, *Liberation Historiography*, 138.
134. *Massachusetts Acts and Resolves, 1855*, Acts, ch. 489.
135. H. Robert Baker, *The Rescue of Joshua Glover: A Fugitive Slave, the Constitution, and the Coming of the Civil War* (Athens: Ohio University Press, 2006).
136. "A Recent Tour in Ohio," *Liberator*, November 21, 1856, p. 188, c. 2.
137. "First of August in Salem, Oh.," *Liberator*, August 15, 1856, p. 131, c. 2.
138. Letter of Head to My Dear Doctor, August 6, 1855, and Letter of Ferguson to DeGrasse, August 29, 1855, Morris Papers.
139. "The New Colored Military Company," *FDP*, August 31, 1855, p. 1, c. 7; "New Colored Company," *Boston Daily Atlas*, August 15, 1855, p. 2, c. 5.
140. "From Our Boston Correspondent," *FDP*, August 24, 1855, p. 2, c. 7.
141. *CPAR*, 11.
142. "Colored Military Company," *Liberator*, March 7, 1856, p. 39, c. 5.
143. "The Massasoit Guards," *Liberator*, September 14, 1855, p. 148, c. 4–5.
144. "Rescue of Shadrach," *Liberator*, November 21, 1851, p. 186, c. 4.
145. "Our Eastern Tour," *FDP*, August 26, 1853.
146. Letter of Robert Morris, *Chelsea Telegraph and Pioneer*, September 6, 1858, reprinted in *FDP*, September 24, 1858, p. 1, c. 1–2.
147. Draft Petition, "John Oliver and Others . . . ," n.d., Morris Papers.
148. "The Negroes in Council," *New York Herald*, August 5, 1858, p. 3, c. 4.
149. Unidentified and undated clipping, BAA Doc. No. 18863.
150. "Anniversary of British West India Emancipation," *Liberator*, August 13, 1858, p. 4, c. 2–6.
151. "West India Emancipation," *New York Herald*, August 4, 1858, p. 1, c. 1–2.
152. "Anniversary of British West India Emancipation."
153. "Parade and Mobbing of a Colored Military Company," *Lowell Daily Citizen and News*, November 17, 1857, p. 2, c. 2.
154. "First Public Parade of the Liberty Guard," *Liberator*, November 27, 1857, p. 192, c. 2–3.

155. "Parade and Mobbing of a Colored Military Company."

156. "First Public Parade of the Liberty Guard," *Liberator*, November 27, 1857, p. 192, c. 3.

157. Ibid., c. 2–3.

158. Letter of Nell to Phillips, July 8, 1855, Phillips Papers, HHU.

159. Even the commemorations of the massacre that took place in Boston between 1771 and 1783 mentioned Attucks and the other victims only once; Browne, "Remembering Crispus Attucks," 172.

160. *CPAR*, 378–80.

161. See Ernest, *Liberation Historiography*, 84.

162. The 1858 Attucks celebration is studied in detail in Bethel, *Roots.*

163. *WCN*, 509.

164. March 5, 1858, speeches reprinted from *Liberator*, March 12, 1858, p. 42, c. 3–p. 43, c. 5, in *WCN*, 501–15.

CHAPTER 6: OUTLAWS

1. The definitive analysis of this case is Fehrenbacher, *The Dred Scott Case.*

2. "New England Colored Citizens' Convention," *Liberator*, August 19, 1859, p. 132.

3. "Anniversary of British West India Emancipation."

4. Thomas Wentworth Higginson, *Anti-Slavery Tracts No. 20: A Ride Through Kanzas* (New York: American Anti-Slavery Society, n.d.); James Redpath, *The Roving Editor, or Talks with Slaves in the Southern States*, ed. John R. McKivigan (University Park: Penn State University Press, 1996); John R. McKivigan, *Forgotten Firebrand: James Redpath and the Making of Nineteenth-Century America* (Ithaca, NY: Cornell University Press, 2008); David S. Reynolds, *John Brown, Abolitionist* (New York: Knopf, 2005), 138–205.

5. "Meeting of Colored Citizens," *Liberator*, September 5, 1856, p. 147, c. 2.

6. Quoted in David W. Blight, *Frederick Douglass' Civil War: Keeping Faith in Jubilee* (Baton Rouge: Louisiana State University Press, 1989), 52.

7. "Disgraceful," *Liberator*, September 11, 1857, p. 146.

8. Harold Holzer, ed., *The Lincoln-Douglas Debates: The First Complete, Unexpurgated Text* (New York: Fordham University Press, 2004), 115.

9. Theodore Parker in *Liberator*, February 26, 1858, p. 34, c. 1.

10. "Ward Six," *Boston Daily Atlas*, November 4, 1856, p. 3, c. 2.

11. Petition of John S. Rock and Others, August 25, 1856, Proceedings of the Boston City Council, BCA.

12. "Meeting of Colored Citizens," *Liberator*, September 5, 1856, p. 147, c. 2.

13. Biographical information in J. Harlan Buzby, *John Stewart Rock: Teacher, Healer, Counselor* (Salem, NJ: Salem County Historical Society, 2002). Buzby argues persuasively that Rock's middle name was not "Sweat" or "Swett," but "Stewart."

14. Manisha Sinha, "The Caning of Charles Sumner: Slavery, Race, and Ideology in the Era of the Civil War," *Journal of the Early Republic* 23:2 (Summer 2003), 233–62.

15. "Meeting of Colored Citizens," *Liberator*, September 5, 1856, p. 147, c. 2 (Rock); Ferris, *The African Abroad*, 710–11 (De Mortie).

16. This was even reported in South Carolina. "The Negroes in Convention," *Charleston Mercury*, November 3, 1856, p. 2, c. 1.

17. *Boston Daily Advertiser*, November 5, 1856, p. 2, c. 3–5; ibid., November 6, 1856, p. 1, c. 2.

18. "The Negroes in Council," *New York Herald*, August 5, 1858, p. 3, c. 5.

19. "Rally in Ward Six," undated clipping, Folder 83, Ruffin Papers, MSHU.

20. *Liberator*, October 30, 1857, p. 174, c. 6; this item appears immediately below a report of a pro-Republican "Political Meeting in Ward Six."

21. Fred Harvey Harrington, *Fighting Politician: Major General N. P. Banks* (Philadelphia: University of Pennsylvania Press, 1948), 43–44.

22. *Liberator*, October 30, 1857, p. 174, c. 6.

23. "F. P. Blair's Lecture in Boston," *Douglass' Monthly* (March 1859), p. 34.

24. "Meeting of Colored Citizens," *Liberator*, September 5, 1856, p. 147, c. 2.

25. Biographical sketch by E. P. Benjamin, Ruffin Family Papers, MSHU.

26. *Massachusetts Acts and Resolves, 1858*, Resolves, ch. 44.

27. *Liberator*, February 26, 1858, in *WCN*, 500.

28. *Liberator*, February 18, 1859, p. 27, c. 4, in *WCN*, 540.

29. "The Colored Citizens of Boston," *Liberator*, November 12, 1858, p. 183, c. 1; "Political Matters," *Boston Daily Advertiser*, October 25, 1859, p. 2, c. 2.

30. See, e.g., "Local Matters," *Boston Daily Advertiser*, June 12, 1857, p. 1, c. 8; "Local Matters," ibid., September 13, 1859, p. 1, c. 8.

31. "Massachusetts Still a Slave State," *Douglass' Monthly* (May 1859), p. 66.

32. Item 631, Massachusetts General Court, Papers on Unpassed Legislation, 1859, CMA.

33. Petition of William Nell and Others (item 694), Massachusetts State Senate, Papers on Unpassed Legislation, 1859, CMA.

34. "Anniversary of British West India Emancipation."

35. "The Negroes in Council," *New York Herald*, August 5, 1858, p. 3, c. 4.

36. "Another Triumph," *Liberator*, May 11, 1860, p. 75, c. 4; *BAP* V:347, n. 22. For more on the context that produced Bayne's victory, though not on his political career, see Grover, *The Fugitives' Gibraltar*.

37. "Improvement of Colored People," *Liberator*, August 24, 1855, p. 134, c. 5; DeGrasse Account Book, 1852–55, DeGrasse-Howard Papers, MHS.

38. Lewis Hayden, 1856 Suffolk County Probate & Insolvency #151, Box 25905, Insolvency File Papers, Massachusetts Judiciary Archives, CMA.

39. *Boston Directory for the Year 1857, Embracing the City Record, a General Directory of the Citizens, and a Business Directory* (Boston: George Adams, 1857), 168.

40. Letter of Nell to Respected Friend, July 8, 1855, Wendell Phillips Papers, HHU.

41. Letter of Nell to Amy Post, March 24, 1858, in *WCN*, 516; Letter of Nell to Amy Post, July 8, 1860, in *WCN*, 590.

42. Letter of Parker to Bancroft, March 16, 1858, in John Weiss, *Life and Correspondence of Theodore Parker*, 2 vols. (New York: D. Appleton, 1864), II:235.

43. Letter of Nell to Respected Friend, August 24, 1857, Wendell Phillips Papers, HHU.

44. *Liberator*, August 7, 1857, pp. 126–27, in *WCN*, 488.

45. *Liberator*, November 12, 1858, p. 184, c. 3–4, in *WCN*, 529.

46. Letter of Nell to Amy Post, October 26, 1860, in *WCN*, 594.

47. *Boston Directory for the Year Ending June 30, 1860* (Boston: Adams, Sampson, 1859).

48. Harrington, *Fighting Politician*, 41–42.

49. Letter of Phillips to Hayden, April 1876, Charles Chapman Collection, MSHU.

50. Letter of Hayden to Sumner, June 11, 1860, Charles Sumner Papers, HHU.

51. For a narrative overview, see Simon Schama, *Rough Crossings: Britain, the Slaves, and the American Revolution* (New York: HarperCollins, 2006).

52. "Adelphic Union Library Association," *Liberator*, October 21, 1842, p. 167, c. 6; ibid., November 18, 1842, p. 183, c. 6.

53. "Boston Vigilance Committee," *Liberator*, June 11, 1841, p. 94, c. 5.

54. Quoted in Lois E. Horton, "Kidnapping and Resistance: Antislavery Direct Action in the 1850s," in David W. Blight, ed., *Passages to Freedom: The Underground Railroad in History and Memory* (Washington, DC: Smithsonian, 2004), 155–56.

55. *Minutes of the National Convention, 1843*.

56. Ibid., 24.

57. Ibid., 19. On Garnet, see Stuckey, *Slave Culture*, 138–92.

58. *NASS*, January 14, 1847, quoted in Ward, "Charles Lenox Remond," p. 159.

59. Clark quoted in Rael, *Black Identity and Black Protest*, 272.

60. "Anniversary of British West India Emancipation"; "The Negroes in Council," *New York Herald*, August 5, 1858, p. 3, c. 4.

61. "Annual Meeting of the Massachusetts Anti-Slavery Society," *Liberator*, February 5, 1858, p. 2, c. 1.

62. *Liberator*, March 12, 1858, pp. 42–43, in *WCN*, 501–15.

63. "Anniversary of British West India Emancipation."

64. Ibid.

65. Winks, *The Blacks in Canada*, 186–90.

66. "Convention of the Colored Citizens of Massachusetts," reprinted in Philip S. Foner and George E. Walker, eds., *Proceedings of the Black State Conventions, 1840–1865, Vol. II* (Philadelphia: Temple University Press, 1980), 96–107.

67. William Wells Brown, *St. Domingo: Its Revolutions and Its Patriots* (Boston: Bela Marsh, 1855), p. 25, 37.

68. Brown, *St. Domingo*, p. 38. This casts doubt on the claim that Brown and other "black abolitionists drew ideological inspiration from the Haitian rather than the American Revolution"; see Manisha Sinha, "To 'Cast Just Obloquy' on Oppressors: Black Radicalism in the Age of Revolution," *WMQ* 64:1 (January 2007), 149–60, quotation at 159.

69. Letter of Redpath to M. le Président et al., March 14, 1862, James Redpath Correspondence, Schomburg Center for Research in Black Culture, New York Public Library [hereinafter cited as Redpath Correspondence, Schomburg].

70. Letter of Parker to Grover, January 11, 1858, in Weiss, *Life and Correspondence of Theodore Parker*, II:236.

71. Letter of Parker to Francis Jackson, November 24, 1859, in Weiss, *Life and Correspondence*, II:171; "Speech of Rev. Theodore Parker," *Liberator*, February 19, 1858, p. 1. See Michael Fellman, "Theodore Parker and the Abolitionist Role in the 1850s," *JAH* 61:3 (December 1974), 666–84.

72. McKivigan, ed., *The Roving Editor*, 163.

73. *Liberator*, March 2, 1860, BAA Doc. No 21948; see *Liberator*, March 12, 1858, BAA Doc. No. 19571, for substantially the same argument.

74. Letter of Redpath to William J. Watkins, February 15, 1862, Redpath Correspondence, Schomburg. The date of the encounter is difficult to reconstruct, but Redpath made only three trips to Haiti within the time frame specified: from January to April 1859; from June to September 1859; and from July to September 1860. See James Redpath, ed., *A Guide to Hayti* (Boston: Haitian Bureau of Emigration, 1861), 9. Since Rock was in Europe seeking medical treatment from late 1858 until the beginning of 1859, the encounter must have occurred either during Redpath's brief sojourn in Boston in the late spring of 1859 or else shortly before his departure in July 1860. On Rock's voyage, see George W. Forbes, typescript biography of John S. Rock, Antislavery Collection, BPL.

75. Letter of Redpath to Watkins, February 15, 1862, Redpath Correspondence, Schomburg. Other details of Redpath's trip to Missouri in McKivigan, ed., *The Roving Editor*, 255–67.

76. For an account of one such trip, *Liberator*, August 12, 1859, p. 128.

77. Letter of Redpath to Watkins, February 15, 1862, Redpath Correspondence, Schomburg.

78. Ibid.

79. Ibid.

80. "Voyage" in *WAA*, December 24, 1859, p. 1, c. 1; Letter of Rock to Garrison, n.d., in *BAPM* 08:535.

81. "Speech of Dr. John S. Rock," *Liberator*, February 3, 1860, p. 19.

82. *Liberator*, March 12, 1858, in BAA Doc. No. 19751.

83. "Mrs. Malinda Noll," *Liberator*, December 21, 1860, p. 203, c. 5.

84. See, e.g., Dorothy Porter, "Sarah Parker Remond, Abolitionist and Physician," *JNH* 20:3 (July 1935), 287–93; Foster, ed., *A Brighter Coming Day*, 177; Letter of Watkins to Sumner, June 26, 1860, Charles Sumner Papers, HHU; "New England Colored Citizens' Convention," *Liberator*, August 26, 1859, p. 4, c. 3.

85. Yee, *Black Women Abolitionists*, 122.

86. Foster, ed., *A Brighter Coming Day*, 127. See Nell Irvin Painter, *Sojourner Truth: A Life, A Symbol* (New York: Norton, 1997), 138–42, for an extended analysis of a similar confrontation.

87. Catherine Clinton, *Harriet Tubman: The Road to Freedom* (Boston: Little, Brown, 2004), 73, 85.

88. On cross-dressing and the "portion of masculine privilege" such women were able to claim, see Toby Ditz, "The New Men's History," *Gender and History* (April 2004), 25.

89. *CPAR*, 23.

90. Letter of Phillips to Clarke, June 28, [1858?], James Freeman Clarke Papers, HHU. John Brown had introduced Tubman to Phillips. Clinton, *Harriet Tubman*, 130.

91. Clinton, *Harriet Tubman*, 129.

92. For an introduction to this theme, see Maggie Montesinos Sale, *The Slumbering Volcano: American Slave Ship Revolts and the Production of Rebellious Masculinity* (Durham, NC: Duke University Press, 1997).

93. "Anniversary of British West India Emancipation"; but for the "ample folds" and "great laughter," see the alternate accounts in unidentified clipping, misdated August 3[?], 1857, BAA Doc. No. 18863.

94. "The Negroes in Council," *New York Herald*, August 5, 1858, p. 3, c. 4.

95. Unidentified clipping, misdated August 3[?], 1857, BAA Doc. No. 18863; "West India Emancipation," *New York Herald*, August 4, 1858.

96. Clinton, *Harriet Tubman*, 137–38.

97. Brown's egalitarian vision, and his affiliations with Gerrit Smith, Frederick Douglass, and James McCune Smith, are at the center of Stauffer, *Black Hearts of Men*. The following account of Brown's campaign also relies on Reynolds, *John Brown*; Benjamin Quarles, *Allies for Freedom: Blacks and John Brown* (1974; reprint, New York: Da Capo, 2001); and the other works cited herein.

98. Quarles, *Allies for Freedom*, 33.

99. Quoted in Reynolds, *John Brown*, 113.

100. Quarles, *Allies for Freedom*, 39.

101. Letter of Brown to Higginson, February 2, 1858, Higginson-Brown Papers, BPL.

102. Letter of Sanborn to Dear Friend, February 11, 1858, Higginson-Brown Papers, BPL.

103. Some prominent radical leaders did not come, including Douglass and the apostle of revolt, Remond; perhaps, Benjamin Quarles suggests, Delany's support for the controversial cause of emigrationism deterred them; *Allies for Freedom*, 44–45.

104. Quarles, *Allies for Freedom*, 54–59.

105. Ibid., 79–80, citing Letter of Hayden to Brown, September 16, 1859, in *Boston Evening Transcript*, October 26, 1859.

106. Letter of Sanborn to Dear Friend, May 30, 1859, Higginson-Brown Papers, BPL.

107. Clinton, *Harriet Tubman*, 132.

108. Franklin Sanborn, "The Virginia Campaign of John Brown, V," *Atlantic Monthly* 35 (May 1875), 597.

109. Sanborn, "The Virginia Campaign . . . VI," *Atlantic Monthly* 35 (December 1875), 707, 709.

110. Quoted in Reynolds, *John Brown, Abolitionist*, 366.

111. "The Day in Boston," *WAA*, December 17, 1859, p. 1, c. 5–7.

112. Quarles, *Allies for Freedom*, 125–26.

113. "My American Readers and Friends," *Douglass' Monthly* (November 1859), p. 162.

114. *Report of the Select Committee of the Senate Appointed to Inquire into the Late Invasion and Seizure of the Public Property at Harpers Ferry* (Washington, DC, 1860), 30, 38.

115. Ibid., A131, A134, A169.

116. Ibid., 30, 38.

117. Letter of Sanborn to Higginson, December 20, 1859, Higginson-Brown Papers, BPL; Richard J. Hinton, *John Brown and His Men; with Some Account of the Roads They Traveled to Reach Harper's Ferry* (New York: Funk and Wagnalls, 1894), 271. For the communication between the men, this work cites Redpath's *Public Life of Capt. John Brown*; that text does not appear to include a direct reference to Hayden, raising the possibility that Hinton had more intimate knowledge of Hayden's role in the plot.

118. BVC, Treasurers Accounts.

119. Clinton, *Harriet Tubman*, 131.

120. "The Present Crisis," *Liberator*, December 31, 1859, p. 211.

121. Rock's speech in C. Peter Ripley et al., eds., *The Black Abolitionist Papers, Vol. V: The United States, 1859–1865* (Chapel Hill: University of North Carolina Press), 58–66.

122. "Free Speech Outraged," *Douglass' Monthly* (January 1861), 391.

123. The modern starting point for scholarship on this subject is Moses, *The Golden Age of Black Nationalism*, esp. ch. 2, "Black Nationalism on the Eve of the Civil War," 32–55; see also Blight, *Frederick Douglass' Civil War*, 127–34.

124. "Speech by John S. Rock," *BAP* V:58–66.

125. Winks, *Blacks in Canada*, 169–74.

126. Ibid., 149–50.

127. *Liberator*, December 24, 1858, p. 201, c. 1–2, in *WCN*, 537.

128. "Speech of H. Ford Douglass [*sic*]," *Liberator*, July 13, 1860, p. 1. See Gosse, "As a Nation, the English Are Our Friends."

129. Winks, *Blacks in Canada*, 240.

130. Ibid., 250–61.

131. *Minutes and Proceedings of the General Convention for the Improvement of the Colored Inhabitants* [sic] *of Canada—held by adjournments in Amhrstbugh* [sic]*, C.W. June 16th and 17th, 1853* (Windsor: Bibb and Holly, 1853).

132. Quoted in Levine, *Martin R. Delany: A Documentary Reader*, 334.

133. For an insightful analysis of Delany, Douglass, and their awareness of their own symbolic roles, see Levine, *Martin Delany, Frederick Douglass, and the Politics of Representative Identity*.

134. "Political Destiny of the Colored Race," in Levine, *Martin R. Delany: A Documentary Reader*, 246.

135. Ibid., 283; "Condition," ch. xvi, in ibid., 202–3.

136. Ibid., 273–74.

137. Letter of Jones to Douglass, November 11, 1853, in *BAPM* 08:0492.

138. Letter of A. H. Frances et al. to Douglass, July 6, 1854, *BAPM* 08:0908.

139. *FDP*, December 2, 1853, in *BAPM* 08:0503–04.

140. *FDP*, February 3, 1854, in *BAPM* 08:0639.

141. *FDP*, March 10, 1854, in *BAPM* 08:0678.

142. *WAA*, September 10, 1859, p. 3, c. 2–3.

143. This view is critically analyzed in Tunde Adeleke, *UnAfrican Americans: Nineteenth-Century Black Nationalists and the Civilizing Mission* (Lexington: University Press of Kentucky, 1998).

144. *WAA*, September 10, 1859, p. 3, c. 2–3; Howard H. Bell, "Negro Nationalism: A Factor in Emigration Projects, 1858–61," *JNH* 47:1 (January 1962), 42–53.

145. For an introduction to Delany's exploits, see Levine, *Martin R. Delany: A Documentary Reader*, 316–18.

146. Broadside, "Cambridge Liberian Emigrant Association" (n.p., n.d. [1858]), HHU.

147. R. J. M. Blackett, *Beating Against the Barriers: The Lives of Six Nineteenth-Century Afro-Americans* (Ithaca, NY: Cornell University Press, 1986), 184–285, quotation on 190.

148. "Enthusiastic Meeting of the Colored Citizens of Boston," *WAA*, September 10, 1859, p. 2, c. 7.
149. Glaude, *Exodus!*
150. "Anniversary of British West India Emancipation."
151. "Enthusiastic Meeting of the Colored Citizens of Boston," *WAA*, September 10, 1859, p. 3, c. 1.
152. *WAA*, September 10, 1859, quoted in Ward, "Charles Lenox Remond," p. 88.
153. Quoted in Lawrence Grossman, "George T. Downing and Desegregation of Rhode Island Public Schools, 1855–66," *Rhode Island History* 36:4 (November 1977), 99.
154. Washington, *Biography of George Thomas Downing*, 3–4.
155. *Old Anti-Slavery Days: Proceedings of the Commemorative Meeting, Held by the Danvers Historical Society . . . April 26, 1893* (Danvers, MA, 1893), 124.
156. Grossman, "George T. Downing," 100.
157. *Old Anti-Slavery Days*, 124.
158. Letter of Downing to Charles Sumner, May 28, 1855, Charles Sumner Papers, HHU. See also Grossman, "George T. Downing."
159. "New England Colored Citizens' Convention," *Liberator*, August 19, 1859, p. 132, c. 3.
160. Ibid.
161. "Letter from Wm. C. Nell," *WAA*, September 17, 1859, p. 2, c. 4.
162. *Douglass' Monthly* (February 1859), quoted in Wilson J. Moses, ed., *Classical Black Nationalism: From the American Revolution to Marcus Garvey* (New York: NYU Press, 1996), 137.
163. "Speech of Dr. John S. Rock," *Liberator*, February 3, 1860, p. 19.
164. Ibid.

Chapter 7: The Fall and Rise of The United States

1. See Michael O'Brien, *Placing the South* (Jackson: University of Mississippi Press, 2007), 53–56.
2. Quoted in James M. McPherson, *The Negro's Civil War: How American Blacks Felt and Acted During the War for the Union* (1965; reprint, New York: Ballantine, 1991), 22.
3. "Affairs About Home," *Boston Herald,* July 31, 1860, p. 4; "Affairs About Home," *Boston Herald*, June 12, 1860, p. 4.
4. Ferris, *The African Abroad*, 711; *Boston Courier*, October 5, 1860, quoted in *Daily Ohio Statesman* (Columbus), October 16, 1860, p. 1.
5. "Affairs About Home," *Boston Herald*, November 6, 1860, p. 2.
6. "Lincoln & Hamlin. Ward 6," Republican Election Ticket (Wright and Potter, n.d. [1860]), original in Brown University Library.
7. *Liberator*, July 13, 1860, p. 1.
8. Ibid.
9. "The Election!," *Boston Herald*, November 6, 1860, p. 4.
10. "Mr. Appleton Serenaded," *Boston Herald*, November 7, 1860, p. 2.
11. William W. Freehling, *The Road to Disunion, Vol. II: Secessionists Triumphant, 1854–1861* (New York: Oxford University Press, 2007), 398.
12. *Declaration of the Immediate Causes Which Induce and Justify the Secession of South Carolina from the Federal Union; and the Ordinance of Secession* (Charleston, SC: Evans and Cogswell, 1860).
13. This analysis draws on (and quotes from) the superb exploration of Confederate politics in Stephanie McCurry, *Confederate Reckoning: Power and Politics in the Civil War South* (Cambridge, MA: Harvard University Press, 2010), esp. 11–37.
14. "Mobocratic Assault Upon an Anti-Slavery Meeting in Boston," *Liberator*, December 7, 1860, p. 195, c. 3.
15. Ibid., c. 3–5; "The Boston Mob of December 1860" and "Free Speech Outraged in Boston," *Douglass' Monthly* (January 1861), 385, 390–96.

16. "The Boston Mob of December 1860," *Douglass' Monthly* (January 1861), 385.
17. "The Church a Refuge," *Liberator*, December 14, 1860, p. 199, c. 1.
18. "Free Speech Outraged in Boston," *Douglass' Monthly* (January 1861), 391.
19. Letter of Nell to Post, June 7, 1857, *WCN*, 468–69; "Free Speech Outraged in Boston," *Douglass' Monthly* (January 1861), 391.
20. "Free Speech Outraged in Boston," *Douglass' Monthly* (January 1861), 390–96.
21. Letter of Higginson to Mother, January 21, 1861, Higginson Letters, Box 5, HHU; "Free Speech Outraged in Boston," *Douglass' Monthly* (January 1861), 396.
22. "Meeting of Colored Citizens of Boston," *Liberator*, January 11, 1861, p. 7.
23. Quoted in Morris, *Free Men All*, 202.
24. "The Personal Liberty Law Repealed in Rhode Island," *Chicago Tribune*, January 26, 1861, p. 4; "Repeal of the Personal Liberty Law in Maine," March 12, 1861, p. 4.
25. See the petition of leading citizens, reprinted in *Liberator*, December 28, 1860, p. 205, c. 1–3.
26. "From Wisconsin," *Chicago Tribune*, March 30, 1861, p. 2. On Wisconsin's bill, see Morris, *Free Men All*, 208, 213–15.
27. City Council Proceedings, January 3, 1861, BCA.
28. Morris, *Free Men All*, 210.
29. This narrative of the secession crisis and compromise efforts draws on David Potter, *The Impending Crisis, 1848–1861* (New York: Harper, 1976), esp. 514ff.
30. For the text of these, see *U.S. House Journal, 1861*, 36th Congress, 2nd Session, January 22, 1861 (216–19). For Crittenden's acceptance, see *Liberator*, March 15, 1861, p. 1; see Douglass's denunciation of Blair's version in *Douglass' Monthly* (March 1859), 34.
31. R. Alton Lee, "The Corwin Amendment in the Secession Crisis," *Ohio Historical Quarterly* 70 (January 1961); Stephen Kantrowitz, "The Other Thirteenth Amendment: Free African Americans and the Constitution That Wasn't," *Marquette University Law Review* 93 (2010).
32. "The Martyr Crispus Attucks," *Liberator*, March 29, 1861, p. 52.
33. "Protest of Colored Citizens," *Liberator*, February 22, 1861, p. 31, c. 3–4.
34. "Remonstrance Against the Repeal of the Personal Liberty Bill," *Liberator*, February 8, 1861, p. 23, c. 6; "There Has Been Presented," ibid., February 15, 1861, p. 27, c. 3.
35. "Protest of Colored Citizens," *Liberator*, February 22, 1861, p. 31, c. 3–4.
36. Ibid.
37. Ibid., c. 4.
38. "Black Emigration to Hayti," *Douglass' Monthly* (May 1859), 78; "Hayti and Colored Emigration," ibid. (November 1860), 358–60; Entry for December 7, 1860, Letterbook, *Correspondence Échangée entre M. John [sic] Redpath due Haitian Bureau of Immigration et les Autorités due Gouvernement d'Haiti sur l'Immigration des Noirs Américains en Haiti, 1860–61*, BPL [hereinafter cited as Redpath Letterbook, BPL]; Entry for April 6, 1861, Redpath Letterbook, LC.
39. Redpath, *A Guide to Hayti*, 173–74.
40. "Meeting of the Colored Educational Institute," *Liberator*, August 30, 1861, p. 139, c. 4; "Wm. W. Brown," *Pine and Palm*, August 3, 1861; "Mr. Watkins' Lecture on Hayti," *Pine and Palm*, November 23, 1861; McPherson, *The Negro's Civil War*, 89.
41. Entries for April 16 and May 27, 1861, Redpath Letterbook, LC; entry for November 20, 1860, Redpath Letterbook, BPL; *WAA*, May 11, 1861, p. 2, c. 1; see also the run of Redpath's *Pine and Palm* (Boston and New York), May 18, 1861–April 3, 1862, microfilm at BPL.
42. "Emigration to Hayti," *Douglass' Monthly* (January 1861), 386.
43. "A Trip to Hayti," *Douglass' Monthly* (May 1861), 449–50. On Douglass's thinking during this period, see Blight, *Frederick Douglass' Civil War*, 131–34.
44. "Meeting in Boston," *WAA*, May 4, 1861, p. 3, c. 1; McPherson, *The Negro's Civil War*, 29–30.
45. *Massachusetts House Journal*, May 16, 1861, CMA; William Schouler, *A History of Massachusetts in the Civil War* (Boston: E. P. Dutton, 1868), 175–78.
46. Letter of Downing to Andrew, April 20, 1861, Executive Letters, v. W169, item 150, CMA.

47. "Equal Militia Rights," *Liberator*, June 14, 1861, p. 3, c. 3–4.
48. "War Intelligence," *Liberator*, May 3, 1861, p. 71, c. 1 (125 men); *Massachusetts House Journal*, May 15, 16, 22, 23, 1861, CMA; *Massachusetts Senate Journal*, May 15, 16, 17, 18, 22, 1861, CMA; Petitions of Robert Morris and 71 Others, and of J. Sella Martin and 25 Others, in Papers on Unpassed Legislation, House, 1861, CMA; Schouler, *Massachusetts in the Civil War*, 182–83 ("firebrand"); Quarles, *The Negro in the Civil War* (1953; New York: Da Capo, 1989), 26–29; McPherson, *The Negro's Civil War*, 19–20; Clark, *The Black Brigade*.
49. "Celebration of the First of August," *Liberator*, August 15, 1862, p. 130.
50. Letter of Butler to Andrew, May 9, 1861, Executive Letters, v. 30, CMA.
51. On the evolution and complexities of Butler's "contraband" policy, see Kate Masur, "'A Rare Phenomenon of Philological Vegetation': The Word 'Contraband' and the Meanings of Emancipation in the United States," *JAH* 93:4 (March 2007), 1050–84.
52. "The War, and Colored American Auxiliaries," *Liberator*, September 6, 1861, p. 144.
53. "The Eventful Day," *Liberator*, December 26, 1862, p. 206.
54. Proponents of Liberia sought to work on the fluidity of this moment, intimating to Republican congressmen that African Americans were open to that destination; Grimes even allowed Downing to take over the pulpit one Sunday in July 1862 to warn of efforts to move them there. *Liberator*, July 21, 1862, p. 123, c. 1, in *WCN*, 625–26.
55. "Refuge of Oppression: The President on African Colonization," *Liberator*, August 22, 1862, p. 1, c. 1–2.
56. See Ira Berlin et al., eds., *Freedom's Soldiers: The Black Military Experience in the Civil War* (New York: Cambridge University Press, 1998).
57. Frederick Douglass, *Life and Times of Frederick Douglass* (Boston: De Wolfe and Fiske, 1892), 428–30.
58. "Emancipation Day in Boston," *Liberator*, January 16, 1863, p. 12.
59. Letter of TWH to Mother, April 18, 1860; Letter of TWH to "Dear Friend," January 24, 1861; Letter of TWH to J. T. Fields, August 17, 1862, Higginson Letters, HHU.
60. Letter of Blake to Morris, February 2, 1863, Executive Letters Outgoing, v. 25, CMA.
61. Telegram of Andrew to Sumner, February 7, 1863, Executive Letters Outgoing, v. 26, CMA.
62. Schouler, *Massachusetts in the Civil War*, 407–8.
63. "Matters and Things," *Liberator*, December 5, 1862, p. 196.
64. "Affairs About Boston," *WAA*, February 28, 1863, p. 2, c. 6.
65. Ibid., p. 1, c. 4–5. A few days later, though, the *New Bedford Mercury* reported Brown arguing that, despite the shortcomings, it was time to fight; see Virginia M. Adams, ed., *On the Altar of Freedom: A Black Soldier's Civil War Letters from the Front* (Amherst: University of Massachusetts Press, 1991), xxviii.
66. "To the Men of Color," *WAA*, March 14, 1863, p. 1, c. 1–2; Luis F. Emilio, *A Brave Black Regiment: History of the Fifty-Fourth Regiment of Massachusetts Volunteer Infantry, 1863–1865* (1894; reprint, New York: Arno, 1969), 13.
67. Letter of Redpath to Watkins, March 4, 1862, Redpath Letterbook, Schomburg.
68. "Affairs About Boston," *WAA*, February 28, 1863, p. 2, c. 6.
69. Emilio, *A Brave Black Regiment*, 13.
70. "Speech of John S. Rock, Esq.," *Liberator*, June 12, 1863, p. 4, c. 3–6.
71. Broadside, "To the Men of Color," Boston, February 15, 1863, in Executive Letters, Series 567x, v. 21b, CMA.
72. "Why Should a Colored Man Enlist?," *Douglass' Monthly* (April 1863), 818–19.
73. Russell Duncan, ed., *Blue-Eyed Child of Fortune: The Civil War Letters of Colonel Robert Gould Shaw* (Athens: University of Georgia Press, 1992), 304–6.
74. Letter of Shaw to Annie, February 23, 1863, in Duncan, *Blue-Eyed Child*, 296.
75. Edwin S. Redkey, "Brave Black Volunteers: A Profile of the Fifty-Fourth Massachusetts Regiment," in Martin H. Blatt, Thomas J. Brown, and Donald Yacavone, eds., *Hope and Glory:*

Essays on the Legacy of the Fifty-Fourth Massachusetts Regiment (Amherst: University of Massachusetts Press, 2001), 21–34, esp. 22. Emilio, *Brave Black Regiment*, 9, claims fifty or sixty recruits at the Cambridge Street office, but some of these must have been residents of other towns. For the figure of fewer than forty, see the data transcribed by Thomas Doughton at "AfroYankees," www.geocities.com/afroyankees/Military/civwarindex.html (site now defunct, but an archived link is accessible at http://web.archive.org/web/20011122104241/http://www.geocities.com/afroyankees/Military/54mass2.html). Redkey, "Brave Black Volunteers," 22, presents the even lower estimate of twenty-seven Boston men in the 54th. There are, of course, many obstacles to determining the original residence of the men in these regiments. Enlistees could have many reasons for disguising their place of origin or residence. British subjects, for example, were not supposed to enlist and had to pretend to be from somewhere else. Some recruits from other Northern states first moved to Massachusetts in order to enlist, giving their new place of residence. Recruiters moving through the South credited recently freed men to the recruiting totals of various Northern locales. The Massachusetts cavalry regiment, recruited largely from the freedpeople of occupied Virginia and the District of Columbia, did much of its initial recruiting clandestinely, for it took the War Department and president some time to approve this course. See Henry Greenleaf Pearson, *The Life of John A. Andrew, Governor of Massachusetts, 1861–1865*, 2 vols. (Boston: Houghton Mifflin, 1904), II:92–93. See also Robert E. Gettings, "African-American Reaction to Recruitment in the North during the U.S. Civil War: The 54th Regiment of Massachusetts Volunteer Infantry," *Journal of Hokusei Gakuen Women's Junior College* 29 (1993), 129–44. For the broad regional turnout among free black men, see Berlin et al., *Freedom's Soldiers*, 16.

76. Calculation based on petitions in Robert Morris Papers, Boston Athenaeum. The two enlistees were the Virginia-born grocer America C. Tabb, a man in his fifties, and barber James D. Ruffin, George's younger brother.

77. Emilio, *Brave Black Regiment*, 9. See also Donald Yacavone, *A Voice of Thunder: The Civil War Letters of George E. Stephens* (Urbana: University of Illinois Press, 1997), 32.

78. "Departure of the Mass. 54th (Colored) Regiment for South Carolina," *WAA*, June 13, 1863, p. 2, c. 3–5.

79. Letter of Shaw to Andrew, April 18, 1863, Executive Letters, v. 21b, CMA.

80. Frank Preston Stearns, *Cambridge Sketches* (Philadelphia: J. P. Lippincott, 1905), 263.

81. This account draws on Yacavone, *Voice of Thunder*. For specific visits to the camp, see ibid., 235; "A Visit to the 54th Massachusetts Regt.," *Douglass' Monthly* (August 1863), 859.

82. "Movements Among the Colored Citizens," *Liberator*, March 6, 1863, p. 40.

83. "Crispus Attucks Celebration," *Liberator*, March 20, 1863, p. 47.

84. Letter of Shaw to Father, February 24, 1863, in Duncan, *Blue-Eyed Child*, 298, 311.

85. See, e.g., Letter of Delany to Stanton, December 15, 1863, *BAP* V:261–63.

86. "Speech of John S. Rock," *Liberator*, June 12, 1863, p. 4, c. 3–6.

87. Schouler, *Massachusetts in the Civil War*, 481.

88. Pearson, *Life of John A. Andrew*, II:91, explains the establishment of the 5th Cavalry as motivated by the state's (primarily white) recruiting shortfall during the 1863 federal draft. See John Dwight Warner, "Crossed Sabres: A History of the Fifth Massachusetts Volunteer Cavalry, an African-American Regiment in the Civil War" (Ph.D. dissertation, Boston College, 1997).

89. "Departure of the Mass. 54th (Colored) Regiment for South Carolina," *WAA*, June 13, 1863, p. 2, c. 5.

90. "AfroYankee" (www.geocities.com/afroyankees/Military/civwarindex.html), accessed August 20, 2008.

91. Emilio, *Brave Black Regiment*, 24–32.

92. "Departure of the Mass. 54th (Colored) Regiment for South Carolina," *WAA*, June 13, 1863, p. 2, c. 3–5. For Sims's return to Boston, see "The Sims Meeting," *Liberator*, May 15, 1863, p. 2, c. 5.

93. "How Colored Soldiers Think and Act," *Liberator*, October 7, 1864, p. 163.

94. Letter of Mrs. Grimes to Andrew, n.d. [August 1863], Executive Letters, v. 59, CMA.

95. Letter of Johnson to Andrew, August 10, 1863, Executive Letters, v. 59, CMA.

96. Letter of De Mortie to Andrew, August 17, 1863, Executive Letters, v. 59, CMA.

97. Letter of Grimes to Andrew, Johnson to Andrew [notes on reverse], Executive Letters, v. 59, CMA.

98. Letter of Stephens to Still, September 19, 1863, *BAP* V:242.

99. Ibid., 243.

100. Letter of De Mortie to Andrew, August 17, 1863 [notes on reverse], Executive Letters, v. 59, CMA.

101. Letter of Harrison to Andrew, September 15, 1863, Executive Letters, v. 59, CMA.

102. Letter of Harrison to Andrew, November 1863; Letter of Harrison to Andrew, May 2, 1864, Executive Letters, v. 59, CMA.

103. Quoted in McPherson, *The Negro's Civil War*, 202.

104. Letter of C. P. Bowditch to Father, December 15, 1863, *Proceedings of the Massachusetts Historical Society* 57 (1924), 454.

105. "Mass Meeting in Boston," *WAA*, August 13, 1864, p. 2, c. 6–p. 3, c. 1.

106. Ibid.

107. "Presentation of a Portrait to a Masonic Grand Lodge," *Liberator*, October 10, 1862, p. 4, c. 3–4.

108. *In Memoriam Robert Morris*, 39.

109. *Christian Recorder*, September 17, 1864, quoted in Samito, *Becoming American Under Fire*, 58.

110. Samito, *Becoming American Under Fire*, ch. 3.

111. Yacavone, *Voice of Thunder*, 71–78; Letter of Kinsley to Andrew, April 28, 1864, Executive Letters, v. 62, CMA; Letter of Andrew to Stanton, July 6, 1863, Executive Letters Outgoing, v. 33, CMA.

112. Yacavone, *Voice of Thunder*, 78.

113. Letter of Hayden to Hartwell, May 17, 1864, Col. Alfred S. Hartwell Papers, MSL.

114. Ibid., and Letter of Ware to Hartwell, May 18, 1864, Col. Alfred S. Hartwell Papers, MSL.

115. Letter of Andrew to Downing, December 10, 1863, Executive Letters Outgoing, v. 41, CMA; Andrew to Gov. Pierpont, March 11, 1864, Executive Letters Outgoing, v. 45, CMA; Telegram of Downing, Remond, and Smith to Andrew, March 10, 1864, Executive Letters, v. W80, CMA; Letter of Andrew to Stanton, July 6, 1863, Executive Letters Outgoing, v. 33, CMA.

116. Letter of Acting Military Secretary to Grimes, December 17, 1863, Executive Letters Outgoing, v. 41, CMA.

117. Letter of Shaw to Andrew, April 18, 1863, Executive Letters, v. 21b, CMA.

118. Emilio, *Brave Black Regiment*, 108.

119. Yacavone, *Voice of Thunder*, 79. The early regiments recruited in South Carolina did not receive full pay until March 1865. See *The War of the Rebellion: A Compilation of the Official Records of the Union and Confederate Armies,* Ser. III, vol. 4, p. 1223.

120. Quoted in Quarles, *The Negro in the Civil War*, 202.

121. Letter of Andrew to Hayden, November 19, 1863, quoted in Warner, "Fifth Cavalry," 52–53.

122. "Address for the Promotion of Colored Enlistments," July 6, 1863, in *Douglass' Monthly* (August 1863), reprinted in *Frederick Douglass: Selected Speeches and Writings*, ed. Philip S. Foner, abr. Yuval Taylor (Chicago: Lawrence Hill, 1999), 534–37.

123. Letter of Jones to Andrew, December 7, 1863, Executive Letters, v. W80, CMA.

124. Letter of Peck to Hayden, February 21, 1863, Executive Letters, v. 21b, CMA; Rufus S. Jones, CWSS.

125. McPherson, *The Negro's Civil War*, 69–71; Schouler, *Massachusetts in the Civil War*, 479–80.

126. Letter of Hayden to Andrew, December 24, 1863, John Andrew Papers, MHS.

127. Letter of Hayden to Andrew, December 17, 1863, Executive Letters, v. W100, CMA.

128. *BAP* V:134–37; Brenda Stevenson, ed., *The Journals of Charlotte Forten Grimké* (New York: Oxford University Press, 1988).

129. Janette Thomas Greenwood, *First Fruits of Freedom: The Migration of Former Slaves and Their Search for Equality in Worcester, Massachusetts, 1862–1900* (Chapel Hill: University of North Carolina Press, 2010); Leslie Schwalm, *Emancipation's Diaspora: Race and Reconstruction in the Upper Midwest* (Chapel Hill: University of North Carolina Press, 2009); V. Jacques Voegeli, *Free but Not Equal: The Midwest and the Negro During the Civil War* (Chicago: University of Chicago Press, 1967); Pleck, *Black Migration and Poverty*.

130. Pleck, *Black Migration and Poverty*, 25–29.

131. Carol Faulkner, *Women's Radical Reconstruction: The Freedmen's Aid Movement* (Philadelphia: University of Pennsylvania Press, 2004), esp. 67–82.

132. "Affairs About Boston," *WAA*, November 5, 1864, p. 1, c. 5–6.

133. Jeannie Attie, *Patriotic Toil: Northern Women and the American Civil War* (Ithaca, NY: Cornell University Press, 1998); Faulkner, *Women's Radical Reconstruction*.

134. For Ruffin's career, see Hallie Q. Brown, *Homespun Heroines and Other Women of Distinction* (New York: Oxford University Press, 1988), 152–54; Mark Schneider, *Boston Confronts Jim Crow: 1890–1920* (Boston: Northeastern University Press, 1997), 94–103; and especially Teresa Blue Holden, "'Earnest Women Can Do Anything': The Public Career of Josephine St. Pierre Ruffin, 1842–1904" (Ph.D. dissertation, St. Louis University, 2005).

135. "Letter from Mrs. Howard," *Commonwealth* (Boston), January 3, 1862, p. 2.

136. Joseph P. Reidy, "Black Men in Blue During the Civil War," *Prologue* 33:3 (Fall 2001), accessed at www.archives.gov/publications/prologue/2001/fall/index.html.

137. Joseph Hayden's military service is summarized in the National Park Service's remarkable CWSS database online (www.itd.nps.gov/cwss/sailors_index.html). On black sailors in the Civil War navy, see Steven J. Ramold, *Slaves, Sailors, Citizens: African Americans in the Union Navy* (DeKalb: Northern Illinois University Press, 2002).

138. Letter of Swift to Dunham, September 23, 1864, Charles Chapman Collection, MSHU.

139. The 1850 census identifies a five-year-old female, Elizabeth Hayden, born in Massachusetts, resident at the Haydens' Southac Street home. She does not appear in later censuses; Seventh Census of the United States, 1850, Schedule I—Free Inhabitants, Boston Ward Six, Suffolk, Massachusetts, p. 402A (Roll M432-336). No Hayden daughter is mentioned in available correspondence or other records.

140. Letter of Hayden to Clarke and Wife, March 20, 1887, item 963, James Freeman Clarke Papers, HHU.

141. *Massachusetts Acts and Resolves, 1863*, ch. 243; Petition of Lewis Gaul and 124 Others, n.d., and Enlistment Roll, September 2, 1863, Adjutant General's Office, Enlistment Rolls of the Mass. Volunteer Militia (Series 486x), CMA; "A Meeting of Colored Recruits," *Boston Daily Evening Transcript*, September 22, 1863, p. 2, c. 4; "We Learn from the *Liberator*," *WAA*, October 10, 1863, p. 3, c. 3–4.

142. *Massachusetts Journal of the House*, January 27–February 5, 1864, CMA.

143. See, e.g., "Affairs About Boston," *WAA*, November 26, 1864, p. 1, c. 6.

144. Rock's Speech at Syracuse, October 6, 1864, in *BAP* V:304–6.

145. Letter of Downing to Andrew, April 17, 1863; Letter of DeGrasse to Andrew, April 18, 1863, in Executive Letters, v. 21b, CMA.

146. Frances Harding Casstevens, *Edward A. Wild and the African Brigade in the Civil War* (Jefferson, NC: McFarland, 2003), 68–72, 77–79.

147. Fox, *Guardian of Boston*, 5–6.

148. Letter of Brig.-Gen. Wild to Gen. Westle, July 12, 1863, Military Order of the Loyal Legion of the United States Papers, United States Military History Institute, Carlisle, Pennsylvania [hereinafter cited as MOLLUS, USMHI]. I am indebted to David S. Cecelski for this document,

and for sharing with me the more extended and highly insightful analysis of it in Cecelski, *The Fires of Freedom: Abraham Galloway and the Slaves' Civil War* (Chapel Hill: University of North Carolina Press, forthcoming 2012).

149. Letter of Thomas Thomas to Lewis Hayden, December 26, 1864, Charles Chapman Collection, MSHU.

150. Miss Sherest, September 25, 1893, in "Abolition Reminiscences," Museum of Afro-American History, Boston; John V. DeGrasse, Suffolk County Probate Records, 1868, CMA. For another reading of these same events, see Peterson, *Black Gotham*, 267–72.

151. See, e.g., Yacavone, *Voice of Thunder*, 71; Joseph T. Glatthar, *Forged in Battle: The Civil War Alliance of Black Soldiers and White Officers* (1990; reprint, New York: Free Press, 1991), 177–89.

152. Quarles, *The Negro in the Civil War*, 204.

153. NN-2809, Court-Martial of John V. DeGrasse, Records of the Office of the Judge Advocate General, Army, Court-Martial Case Files 1809–1894, RG 153, National Archives, Washington D.C.; John V. DeGrasse, Compiled Military Service Record, National Archives.

154. Letter of Brig.-Gen. Wild to Gen. Westle, July 12, 1863, MOLLUS, USMHI.

155. William W. Freehling, *The South vs. The South: How Anti-Confederate Southerners Shaped the Course of the Civil War* (New York: Oxford University Press, 2001), 146.

156. McPherson, *The Negro's Civil War*, 258.

157. Ibid., 260–65.

CHAPTER 8: RADICAL RECONSTRUCTION ON BEACON HILL

1. "Affairs About Boston," *WAA*, January 7, 186[5], in Executive Letters, Series 567x, v. W100 (item 86), CMA.

2. Ibid.

3. Ibid.

4. The scholarly literature on the postwar adjustment of Northern "race relations" begins with Leslie H. Fishel Jr., "The North and the Negro: A Study in Race Discrimination" (Ph.D. dissertation, Harvard University, 1953). Two overlapping streams of scholarship have followed: studies of Northern discrimination and the abandonment of Reconstruction, exemplified by Voegeli, *Free but Not Equal*, and Heather Cox Richardson, *The Death of Reconstruction: Race Labor, and Politics in the Post-Civil War North, 1865–1901* (Cambridge, MA: Harvard University Press, 2001); and studies of Northern black communities, most recently including explorations of early migrations from the South: Schwalm, *Emancipation's Diaspora*, and Greenwood, *First Fruits of Freedom*.

5. *Massachusetts Acts and Resolves, 1865*, ch. 11 (February 8, 1865), CMA.

6. Michael Vorenberg, "Citizenship and the Thirteenth Amendment: Understanding the Deafening Silence," in Alexander Tsesis, ed., *The Promises of Liberty: The History and Contemporary Relevance of the Thirteenth Amendment* (New York: Columbia University Press, 2010), 58–77.

7. "Thirty-Second Anniversary," *Liberator*, May 26, 1865, p. 82, c. 5.

8. "Equal Political Rights," *Liberator*, January 13, 1865, p. 6.

9. *Massachusetts Acts and Resolves, 1865*, ch. 277 (May 16, 1865). See *Lowell Daily Citizen and News*, May 6, 1865, p. 2. For a broader argument about such legislation in Massachusetts, Kazuteru Omori, "Race-Neutral Individualism and Resurgence of the Color Line: Massachusetts Civil Rights Legislation, 1855–1893," *Journal of American Ethnic History* 22:1 (Fall 2002), 32–58.

10. Letter of William Nell to Wendell Phillips, August 20, 1866, Phillips Papers, HHU, in *WCN*, 665.

11. Andrew Diemer, "Reconstructing Philadelphia: African Americans and Politics in the Post–Civil War North," *PMHB* 133:1 (January 2009), 29–58.

12. See "Colored Men's Right of Travel," *Liberator*, February 10, 1865, p. 23.

13. City of Boston, City Doc. #25, "Report on Affixing the Word 'Col.' to Names on Tax-Bills and Voting-Lists," Minutes of the Board of Aldermen, February 11, 1867, BCA.

14. Horton and Horton, *Black Bostonians*, 4; figures calculated from Joseph C. G. Kennedy, *Population of the United States in 1860; Compiled from the Original Returns of the Eighth Census* (Washington, DC: Government Printing Office, 1864), 218, 219, 225; Peter R. Knights, *The Plain People of Boston, 1830–1860: A Study in City Growth* (New York: Oxford University Press, 1971), 29.

15. "Boston's Next Mayor," *Commonwealth*, December 12, 1868, p. 2, c. 2.

16. Local studies offer points of entry for further exploration of black officeholding or discernible political influence in postbellum Northern locales: for Cleveland, see Kenneth L. Kusmer, *A Ghetto Takes Shape: Black Cleveland, 1870–1930* (Urbana: University of Illinois Press, 1978), 118; for Cincinnati, see Gerber, *Black Ohio and the Color Line*, 225; for the Ohio towns of Oberlin and Xenia, see ibid., 212; for Chicago, see Christopher R. Reed, *Black Chicago's First Century, Vol. 1: 1833–1900* (Columbia: University of Missouri Press, 2005), 223; for Indianapolis, see Ronald David Snell, "Indiana's Black Representatives: The Rhetoric of the Black Republican Legislators from 1880 to 1896" (Ph.D. dissertation, Indiana University, 1982), 50–78; and for Philadelphia, see Lane, *Roots of Violence*, esp. ch. 2, and Diemer, "Reconstructing Philadelphia."

17. "Affairs About Boston," *WAA*, October 29, 1864, p. 1, c. 1–2.

18. "Affairs About Boston," *WAA*, November 5, 1864, p. 1, c. 5.

19. This world is explored in Michael McGerr, *The Decline of Popular Politics: The American North, 1865–1928* (New York: Oxford University Press, 1986), 3–41.

20. Notebook, "Colored Voters Boston 1864—1st List After Emancipation—New and Old Voters," Ruffin Family Papers, MSHU.

21. "Southac Street," *Boston Morning Journal*, November 8, 1864, p. 2, c. 5–6.

22. "Massachusetts Election," *Boston Evening Transcript*, November 9, 1864, p. 1, c. 7.

23. "To the Republican Voters of Ward Six," *Boston Daily Evening Transcript*, November 5, 1866, p. 2; other details in ibid.: "The Republican Meetings in this City," November 1, 1866, p. 4, c. 1, and "Republican Representative Caucuses," November 2, 1866, p. 2, p. 4, c. 2.

24. "To the Republican Voters of Ward Six," *Boston Daily Evening Transcript*, November 5, 1866, p. 2.

25. "The Elections," *Boston Daily Evening Transcript*, November 7, 1866, p. 4, c. 2–3.

26. "How the Result of the Election Was Received in Boston," *Boston Weekly Voice*, November 8, 1866, p. 3, c. 4.

27. Some question exists about this relationship; for a full discussion, see Hinks, *"To Awaken,"* 270–71.

28. One man of known African descent—the minister, teacher, and Middlebury College graduate Alexander Twilight—served one term in the Vermont state legislature in 1836. See John Lovejoy, "Alexander Twilight," in John J. Duffy et al., eds., *The Vermont Encyclopedia* (Hanover, NH: University Press of New England, 2003). Thanks to John Quist, Shippensburg University, for alerting me to this figure.

29. "City Matters," *Commonwealth*, December 15, 1866, p. 2, c. 6–7; "A Thorough Republican Success," *Boston Evening Transcript*, December 11, 1866, p. 2, c. 1 (quotation).

30. "Political Notes," *Commonwealth*, October 31, 1868, p. 1, c. 4.

31. "Near Nomination of a Colored Citizen of Chelsea for Mayor," *Commonwealth*, December 1, 1866, p. 3, c. 1.

32. City of Boston, City Doc. #25, "Report on Affixing the Word 'Col.' to Names on Tax-Bills and Voting-Lists," Minutes of the Board of Aldermen, February 11, 1867, BCA.

33. "Massachusetts Legislature," *Boston Daily Advertiser*, January 17, 1866, p. 1, c. 5.

34. Eric L. McKitrick, *Andrew Johnson and Reconstruction* (Chicago: University of Chicago Press, 1960).

35. Garrett Epps, *Democracy Reborn: The Fourteenth Amendment and the Fight for Equality in Post–Civil War America* (New York: Henry Holt, 2006), 173.
36. William E. Nelson, *The Fourteenth Amendment: From Political Principle to Judicial Doctrine* (1988; reprint, Cambridge, MA: Harvard University Press, 1995), 49.
37. Nelson, *Fourteenth Amendment*, 49–53.
38. *Dred Scott v. Sandford*, 19 Howard (60 U.S.) 393 (1857).
39. "Mr. Lincoln's Speech," Fourth Joint Debate at Charleston (September 18, 1858), in Abraham Lincoln, *Political Debates Between Lincoln and Douglas* (Cleveland: Burrows Bros., 1897), accessible at www.bartleby.com/251.
40. Vorenberg, "Citizenship and the Thirteenth Amendment," esp. 66–67.
41. On this point and the limitations of the amendment generally, see Alexander Keyssar, *The Right to Vote: The Contested History of Democracy in the United States*, revised edition (New York: Basic Books, 2009), 72.
42. McPherson, *Struggle for Equality*, 352.
43. "The Constitutional Amendment," *Lowell Daily Citizen and News*, February 1, 1867, p. 2, c. 2.
44. McPherson, *Struggle for Equality*, 357.
45. Ibid., 374.
46. *Massachusetts House Journal*, January 25, 1867, CMA.
47. "Legislative," *Lowell Daily Citizen and News*, March 2, 1867, p. 1, c. 2.
48. "Debate on the Amendment," *Lowell Daily Citizen and News*, March 14, 1867, p. 2, c. 2.
49. Ibid.
50. "Massachusetts and the Constitutional Amendment," *Springfield Weekly Republican*, March 9, 1867, p. 2, c. 1.
51. "A Reasonable Misgiving," *Springfield Weekly Republican*, March 16, 1867, p. 4, c. 4.
52. *Massachusetts House Journal*, March 12–13, 1867, CMA.
53. Sumner quoted in Keyssar, *The Right to Vote* (orig. ed., New York: Basic Books, 2000), 94.
54. See Xi Wang, *The Trial of Democracy: Black Suffrage and Northern Republicans, 1860–1910* (Athens: University of Georgia Press, 1997), esp. 42.
55. Quoted in Keyssar, *Right to Vote*, 76–77; Wang, *Trial of Democracy*, 44.
56. Discussions in Keyssar, *Right to Vote*, 93–104; Wang, *Trial of Democracy*, 42–48.
57. Wang, *Trial of Democracy*, 49–50.
58. Letter of Smith to Sumner, March 31, 1870, Sumner Papers, HHU.
59. "Affairs About Boston," *WAA*, November 26, 1864, p. 1, c. 6. The Shaw Guards appear to have organized themselves somewhat earlier than this; see "A Meeting of Colored Recruits," *Boston Evening Transcript*, September 22, 1863, p. 2[?], c. 4. See *Massachusetts Acts, 1863* (ch. 243); *Massachusetts Acts, 1864* (chs. 15 and 238).
60. "Affairs About Boston," *WAA*, November 26, 1864, p. 1, c. 6–p. 2, c. 1.
61. "Affairs About Boston," *WAA*, June 17, 1865, p. 1, c. 6.
62. "The Fifty-Fourth Massachusetts Regiment," *Commonwealth*, September 2, 1865, p. 3, c. 1; "The Reception of the Fifty-Fourth Massachusetts," September 9, 1865, p. 3, c. 1–2.
63. *Commonwealth*, April 16, 1870, p. 2, c. 7.
64. The phrase is from Vorenberg, "Citizenship and the Thirteenth Amendment."
65. Michael Robert Mounter, "Richard Theodore Greener: The Idealist, Statesman, Scholar, and South Carolinian" (Ph.D. dissertation, University of South Carolina, 2002), 20.
66. Ibid., 20–68.
67. J. Clay Smith Jr., "In Freedom's Birthplace: The Making of George Lewis Ruffin, The First Black Law Graduate of Harvard University," *Howard University Law Journal* 39 (1995), 201–35.
68. "'Reconstruction' at Harvard," *Commonwealth*, September 26, 1868, p. 1, c. 4.
69. Hayden, *Caste Among Masons*, 45.
70. Ibid., 28–29.

71. John Jones, *Christian Recorder*, October 7, 1865, p. 1, c. 4–5.
72. *Proceedings of the Prince Hall Grand Lodge . . . 1874* (Boston, 1875), 23–27.
73. For details on European recognition of black lodges during Reconstruction, see Kantrowitz, "'Intended for the Better Government of Man.'"
74. Letter of A. W. A. De Leon to John Hervey, February 10, 1869, GBR 1991 HC 28/A (21), Library of the United Grand Lodge of England, London.
75. *Proceedings of the Prince Hall Grand Lodge . . . 1875* (Boston, 1876), 53–54, 58.
76. Richard T. Greener, *An Oration Pronounced at the Celebration of the Festival of Saint John the Baptist, June 24, 1876, at the Invitation of Eureka Lodge No. 1, F.A.M. . . .* (Savannah: D. G. Patton, [1876]), 9.
77. Hayden, *Caste Among Masons*, 28–29.
78. Ibid., 17, 29.
79. "Home Notes," *Commonwealth*, October 19, 1867, p. 3, c. 1.
80. Ibid.
81. *Proceedings of the Most Worshipful Grand Lodge of Ancient Free and Accepted Masons of the Commonwealth of Massachusetts* (Boston: Caustic-Claflin, n.d.) [hereinafter cited as *PGLM, 1868*], December 9, 1869, 454–61.
82. Ibid., 459–60.
83. Ibid., 462.
84. Letter of Thomas Thomas to Lewis Hayden, November 17, 1868, Charles Chapman Collection, MSHU.
85. Ibid.
86. "1776–1876—New Day—New Duty," *Proceedings of the Grand Lodge of the Most Ancient and Honorable Fraternity of Free and Accepted Masons of the State of Ohio. Sixty-Sixth Annual Grand Communication Begun and Held at Columbus, October 19, A. L. 5875* (Cincinnati: John D. Caldwell, 1875), 51.
87. Jones, *All Bound Up Together*, esp. 116–36.
88. Ibid., 151–58.
89. "Demonstration of the Order of Love and Charity," *WAA*, May 26, 1860, p. 2, c. 3–4; *Christian Recorder*, September 17, 1864; Jones, *All Bound Up Together*, 167–69.
90. The Order of the Eastern Star among African Americans has finally begun to receive the scholarly treatment it deserves; see Martin Summers, *Manliness and Its Discontents: The Black Middle Class and the Transformation of Masculinity, 1900–1930* (Chapel Hill: University of North Carolina Press, 2004), 111–148, and Brittney Cooper, "'They Are Nevertheless Our Brethren': The Order of Eastern Star and the Battle for Women's Leadership, 1874–1925," in Hinks and Kantrowitz, eds., *All Men Free and Brethren* (forthcoming). See also Mrs. S. Joe Brown, *The History of the Order of the Eastern Star Among Colored People* (Des Moines, 1925).
91. *An Account of the Labors of the Ladies' Charitable Association of Boston, in Recognition of, and Homage to, the Declaration of Independence* (Boston: Wright and Potter, 1876).
92. Jones, *All Bound Up Together*, 173–74; *An Account of the Labors*, 13 (quote).
93. *An Account of the Labors*, 9.
94. "Our Hub Letter," *New York Globe*, September 27, 1884.
95. David M. Fahey, ed., *The Collected Writings of Jessie Forsyth, 1847–1937: The Good Templars and Temperance Reform on Three Continents* (Lewiston, NY: Edwin Mellen Press, 1988), 92–93.
96. "Lewis Hayden's Home," *Bangor Daily Whig & Courier* (Maine), April 11, 1889.
97. "Eulogizing Lewis Hayden," *New York Age*, April 19, 1890, p. 4; "The Burial Lot Controversy," *New York Age*, April 26, 1890, p. 2.
98. "Our Eastern Tour," *FDP*, August 26, 1853.
99. "A Negro Appointed to the Custom House," *Pittsfield Sun* (Massachusetts), June 27, 1861, p. 1, c. 7.

100. Letter of Nell to Garrison, April 9, 1873, in *WCN*, 679.

101. Ibid.

102. *Douglass' Monthly* (June 1863), quoted in Philip Foner and Ronald Lewis, eds., *The Black Worker: A Documentary History from Colonial Times to the Present*, 4 vols. (Philadelphia: Temple University Press, 1978), I:285.

103. Iver Bernstein, *The New York City Draft Riots: Their Significance for American Society and Politics in the Age of the Civil War* (New York: Oxford University Press, 1990).

104. Foner and Lewis, *The Black Worker*, I:391.

105. For the case of Pennsylvania's eight-hour leader William Sylvis, see David Montgomery, *Beyond Equality: Labor and the Radical Republicans* (1967; reprint, Urbana: University of Illinois Press, 1981), 228.

106. Quoted in Montgomery, *Beyond Equality*, 180.

107. Foner and Lewis, *The Black Worker*, I:391.

108. See "Six Strikes for Higher Wages," *New York Observer and Chronicle*, April 9, 1868, p. 119, c. 2; "Letter from Boston," *Bangor Daily Whig & Courier*, April 21, 1868.

109. Ferris, *The African Abroad*, 712.

110. Ibid.; "Brief Notes," *Commonwealth*, April 18, 1868, p. 3, c. 1.

111. "Brief Notes," *Commonwealth*, April 18, 1868, p. 3, c. 1.

112. See "Six Strikes for Higher Wages," *New York Observer and Chronicle*, April 9, 1868, p. 119, c. 2; "Letter from Boston," *Bangor Daily Whig & Courier*, April 21, 1868.

113. "Brief Notes," *Commonwealth*, April 18, 1868, p. 3, c. 1.

114. Sarah Deutsch, *Women and the City: Gender, Space, and Power in Boston, 1870–1940* (New York: Oxford University Press, 2000), 88; Peter Holloran, *Boston's Wayward Children: Social Services for Homeless Children, 1830–1930* (Cranbury, NJ: Associated Universities Presses, 1989), 152.

115. Republican politics did serve a few black workers in other ways, for example by employing them on Washington D.C.'s Reconstruction-era program of public works; Kate Masur, *An Example for All the Land: Emancipation and the Struggle over Equality in Washington, D.C.* (Chapel Hill: University of North Carolina Press, 2010), 151–55.

116. Letter of Russell to Hayden, April 9, 1868, Charles Chapman Collection, MSHU. Warren C. Whatley, "African-American Strikebreaking from the Civil War to the New Deal," *Social Science History* 17:4 (Winter 1993), 525–58, does not mention this instance. One labor historian notes that "black strikebreaking was nothing less than a form of working-class activism designed to advance the interests of black workers and their families," in a context that offered few alternatives; Eric Arnesen, "Specter of the Black Strikebreaker: Race, Employment, and Labor in the Industrial Era," *Labor History* 44:3 (2003), 319–35. Countervailing efforts on the part of some black workers to make coalition with white workers, and vice versa, produced some short- and medium-term successes during the half century following the Civil War; for a brief bibliography of this scholarship, see ibid., 322–23, n.12.

117. On New York, see David Quigley, *Second Founding: New York City, Reconstruction, and the Making of American Democracy* (New York: Hill and Wang, 2004), and Sven Beckert, *The Monied Metropolis: New York City and the Consolidation of the American Bourgeoisie, 1850–1896* (New York: Cambridge University Press, 2001); on South Carolina, see Stephen Kantrowitz, *Ben Tillman and the Reconstruction of White Supremacy* (Chapel Hill: University of North Carolina Press, 2000), ch. 2.

118. For an overview, see William Harris, *The Harder We Run: Black Workers Since the Civil War* (New York: Oxford University Press, 1982), 20–22.

119. "True Political Manhood," *New York Freeman*, February 19, 1887, p. 1, c. 1.

120. "Mayor Hart's Opportunity," *New York Age*, March 16, 1889, p. 1, c. 6.

121. "Bright Bits About Boston," *New York Age*, October 19, 1889, p. 2, c. 1.

122. The evolving complexities of "uplift" in the generations following 1865—as a democratic,

emancipatory project, and (increasingly) as a means of class differentiation within African American society—are brilliantly traced in Kevin K. Gaines, *Uplifting the Race: Black Leadership, Politics, and Culture in the Twentieth Century* (Chapel Hill: University of North Carolina Press, 1996), and Michele Mitchell, *Righteous Propagation: African Americans and the Politics of Racial Destiny after Reconstruction* (Chapel Hill: University of North Carolina Press, 2004).

123. John S. Rock Letterbook, Ruffin Papers, MSHU.

124. "Meeting in Boston," *WAA*, July 16, 1864, p. 1, c. 6.

125. "The National Convention," *WAA*, July 30, 1864, p. 1, c. 4.

126. "National Convention of Colored Men," *WAA*, October 15, 1864, p. 1, c. 4–p. 3, c. 1.

127. "National Convention of Colored Men," *WAA*, October 22, 1864, p. 1, c. 4–p. 2, c. 6; "Reply of Rev. Henry Highland Garnet to Rev. J. Sella Martin," ibid., October 29, 1864, p. 1, c. 4–6.

128. Ruffin's Report on Convention, 1864, Ruffin Papers, MSHU.

129. "National Convention of Colored Men," *WAA*, October 15, 1864, pp. 1–3.

130. Ibid.

131. "Affairs About Boston," *WAA*, May 13, 1865, p. 2, c. 3; "The School Question in Rhode Island—Boston Speaks for Equal Suffrage," ibid., July 29, 1865, p. 1, c. 2–3.

132. *WAA*, January 30, 1864. I am grateful to Kate Masur for this quotation.

133. Campbell, *Songs of Zion*, 55–56.

134. David G. Hackett, "The Prince Hall Masons and the African American Church: The Labors of Grand Master and Bishop James Walker Hood, 1831–1918," *Church History* 69 (December 2000), 770–802.

135. Peter Randolph, *From Slave Cabin to the Pulpit: The Autobiography of Rev. Peter Randolph: The Southern Question Illustrated and Sketches of Slave Life* (Boston: J. H. Earle, 1893), 56ff.; see also Elsa Barkley Brown, "Uncle Ned's Children: Negotiating Community and Freedom in Postemancipation Richmond, Virginia" (Ph.D. dissertation, Kent State University, 1994); Peter Rachleff, *Black Labor in Richmond, 1865–1890* (Philadelphia: Temple University Press, 1984).

136. Julius Eric Thompson, "Hiram R. Revels, 1827–1901: A Biography" (Ph.D. dissertation, Princeton University, 1973); Hackett, "The Prince Hall Masons and the African American Church."

137. Campbell, *Songs of Zion*, 39–50.

138. Ibid., 40–43, 58.

139. Clarence Walker, *A Rock in a Weary Land: The African Methodist Episcopal Church During the Civil War and Reconstruction* (Baton Rouge: Louisiana State University Press, 1981), 46; William E. Montgomery, *Under Their Own Vine and Fig Tree: The African American Church in the South, 1865–1900* (Baton Rouge: Louisiana State University Press, 1993), 103.

140. Hayden, *Caste Among Masons*, 10.

141. Hackett, "The Prince Hall Masons and the African American Church."

142. Hayden, *Caste Among Masons*, 6–10.

143. For the case of Richmond, where Hayden traveled in 1865, see Brown, "Uncle Ned's Children," ch. 5; Rachleff, *Black Labor.*

144. See, e.g., Brown, "Uncle Ned's Children," ch. 5.

145. "In the Supreme Court," *Lowell Daily Citizen and News*, February 2, 1865, p. 2, c. 1.

146. "A Hero Gone," *Christian Recorder*, December 15, 1866; typescript biography, Forbes Papers.

147. Masur, *An Example for All the Land.*

148. Ibid., 159–60.

149. Quoted in Kate Masur, "Forging Equality" (unpublished manuscript in author's possession), 228.

150. Ibid., 229–30; Hugh Davis, "The Pennsylvania State Equal Rights League and the Northern Black Struggle for Legal Equality, 1864–1877," *PMHB* 126:4 (October 2002), 611–34.

151. Letter of Charles Sumner to George Downing, June 4, 1869, George T. Downing Papers, MSHU.

152. See, e.g., Letter of F. L. Cardoza to George T. Downing, June 20, n.d., and Letter of Charles L. Remond to George T. Downing, March 23, 1869, both in Box 1, Folder 18, DeGrasse-Howard Family Papers, MHS.
153. Washington, *George T. Downing*, 11.
154. Typescript copy of Letter of Charles Sumner to John V. DeGrasse, December 23, 1866, Box 1, Folder 3, DeGrasse-Howard Family Papers, MHS.
155. Letter of Charles Remond to George Downing, Box 1, Folder 18, DeGrasse-Howard Family Papers, MHS. This newspaper became the *New National Era*.
156. Washington, *George T. Downing*, 17.
157. See Letter of Downing to Morris, December [16?], 1865, Folder 1860–1865, Morris Papers.
158. Ferris, *The African Abroad*, 712–13; "Personal," *Congregationalist and Boston Recorder*, May 26, 1870, p. 168, c. 1; "All Sorts of Items," *San Francisco Daily Evening Bulletin*, April 11, 1871, p. 3, c. 6.
159. On Bradley, see Russell Duncan, *Freedom's Shore: Tunis Campbell and the Georgia Freedmen* (Athens: University of Georgia Press, 1986); *Boston Daily Advertiser*, October 20, 1856, p. 2, c. 4; "Home Notes," *Commonwealth*, January 6, 1866, p. 3, c. 2; "Home Notes," ibid., March 3, 1866, p. 2, c. 6; "News Outline," ibid., October 23, 1869, p. 3, c. 2.
160. Thompson, "Hiram R. Revels," 61.
161. Ibid., 59–62.
162. Quoted in ibid., 70–73.
163. "By Telegraph from Washington," *Boston Daily Journal*, February 3, 1870, p. 4.
164. Thompson, "Hiram R. Revels," 90.
165. "Boston and Vicinity," *Boston Daily Journal*, May 9, 1870, p. 4, c. 2.
166. "Brief Notes," *Commonwealth*, December 21, 1872, p. 3, c. 1; "Mr. Lewis Hayden," *Lowell Daily Citizen and News*, February 15, 1873, p. 2, c. 3; "State House Notes," *Commonwealth*, February 15, 1873, p. 2, c. 7.

CHAPTER 9: "THE WAR OF RACES"

1. Hannah Rosen, *Terror in the Heart of Freedom: Citizenship, Sexual Violence, and the Meaning of Race in the Postemancipation South* (Chapel Hill: University of North Carolina Press, 2009), 60–64. The definitive synthesis of Southern Reconstruction in Eric Foner, *Reconstruction: America's Unfinished Revolution, 1863–1877* (New York: Harper Collins, 1988)
2. Hayden, *Caste Among Masons*, 9.
3. "President Johnson and the Colored Men," *Commonwealth*, February 17, 1866, p. 1, c. 3–6.
4. "Thirty-Second Anniversary," *Liberator*, May 26, 1865, p. 81.
5. Ibid., p. 82, c. 5.
6. Ibid., p. 81, c. 2.
7. Schwalm, *Emancipation's Diaspora*, 177–87; Robert Dykstra, *Bright Radical Star: Black Freedom and White Supremacy on the Hawkeye Frontier* (Cambridge, MA: Harvard University Press, 1993).
8. Quigley, *Second Founding*, 60. See also David Montgomery, "Pennsylvania: An Eclipse of Ideology," and Felice A. Bonadio, "Ohio: A Perfect Contempt of All Unity," in James C. Mohr, ed., *Radical Republicans in the North: State Politics During Reconstruction* (Baltimore: Johns Hopkins University Press, 1976), 50–65 and 82–103.
9. South Carolina had a black majority in one house of its legislature. But no black men were elected to a governorship (though one served part of a term) and only two were elected as U.S. senators throughout the South during Reconstruction. Foner, *Reconstruction*, 354.
10. See Hahn, *A Nation Under Our Feet*.
11. "The Ku Klux Klan in Washington," *New York Herald*, April 13, 1868, p. 3.

12. See Cecelski, *The Fires of Freedom.*
13. Hayden, *Caste Among Masons.*
14. For excellent discussions of these laws, see William Gillette, *Retreat from Reconstruction, 1869–1879* (Baton Rouge: Louisiana State University Press, 1979), and Quigley, *Second Founding*, esp. 71–89.
15. Untitled, undated manuscript, in Ruffin Papers, MSHU.
16. Mari Jo Buhle and Paul Buhle, eds., *The Concise History of Woman Suffrage: Selections from the History of Woman Suffrage* (1978; reprint, Urbana: University of Illinois Press, 2005), 257–74, quotations on 258–59.
17. See Ellen Carol DuBois, *Feminism and Suffrage: The Emergence of an Independent Women's Movement in America, 1848–1869* (Ithaca, NY: Cornell University Press, 1978), 162–202, and Lisa Marguerite Tetrault, "The Memory of a Movement: Woman Suffrage and Reconstruction America, 1865–1890" (Ph.D. dissertation, University of Wisconsin–Madison, 2004).
18. Dale Baum, *The Civil War Party System: The Case of Massachusetts, 1848–1876* (Chapel Hill: University of North Carolina Press, 1984), 153.
19. *Massachusetts House Journal*, March 16, 1867; May 12, 1871; February 20, 1872; March 21, 1872; March 12, 1873, all at CMA.
20. Holden, "'Earnest Women Can Do Anything,'" 110; New England Women's Club Records, SHU.
21. *Massachusetts House Journal*, March 4–12, 1873, CMA.
22. *Ladies' Excelsior Charitable Association, from the Slavery of 1776 to the Freedom of 1876: An Account of the Labors of the Ladies' Charitable Association of Boston, in Recognition of, and Homage to, the Declaration of Independence* (Boston: Wright and Potter, 1876), 11.
23. *The Critic* (Washington, DC), January 27, 1870, p. 4; Letter of Hayden to Sumner, January 24, 1870, Sumner Papers, HHU; "Meeting of Colored Citizens in Ward Three," *Boston Daily Journal*, February 15, 1870, p. 4.
24. "Meeting of Colored Citizens in Ward Three."
25. "By Telegraph," *Boston Daily Advertiser*, February 11, 1870, p. 1, c. 6.
26. "Congressman Hooper and His Colored Constituents," *Boston Daily Advertiser*, February 15, 1870, p. 1, c. 9.
27. Letter of Thomas Thomas to Lewis Hayden, 186[4], Charles Chapman Collection, MSHU.
28. "Brief Notes," *Commonwealth*, October 29, 1870, p. 2, c. 6–7.
29. Hayden, *Caste Among Masons*, 36–38.
30. Letter of Nell to Garrison, April 9, 1873, in *WCN*, 679.
31. "Brief Notes," *Commonwealth*, February 1, 1868, p. 2, c. 7.
32. Baum, *Civil War Party System*, 145–54; "Republican Rally in Ward Six," *Boston Daily Advertiser*, November 1, 1870, p. 4.
33. Baum, *Civil War Party System*, 124.
34. Hans L. Trefousse, *Ben Butler: The South Called Him Beast!* (New York: Twayne, 1957), 213.
35. Ibid., 214–15.
36. Ibid., 188.
37. Ibid., 207–8. On Butler's image in Northern politics, see Richardson, *Death of Reconstruction.*
38. Quigley, *Second Founding*, 80–86.
39. Diemer, "Reconstructing Philadelphia," 55.
40. Ibid., 55.
41. Ibid., 52.
42. Ibid., 55–56. For a brief portrait of Catto, see Roger Lane, *Roots of Violence*, 45–57; Catto is the central subject of Daniel R. Biddle and Murray Dubin, *Tasting Freedom: Octavius Catto and the Battle for Equality in Civil War America* (Philadelphia: Temple University Press, 2010).
43. "The Political Issues of the Day: Speech of Gen. B. F. Butler," *Boston Daily Journal*, May 9, 1871, p. 1.

44. Baum, *Civil War Party System*, 156; Trefousse, *Ben Butler*, 222–24; "The Sixth Ward," *Boston Daily Advertiser*, September 22, 1871, p. 2, c. 1–2.
45. "Political—A Butler Club in Charlestown," *Boston Daily Advertiser*, September 8, 1871, p. 1, c. 7–8.
46. "Ward Six," *Boston Morning Journal*, September 21, 1871, p. 2, c. 4.
47. "The Sixth Ward," *Boston Daily Advertiser*, September 22, 1871, p. 2, c. 1–2.
48. "Ward Six," *Boston Morning Journal*, September 21, 1871, p. 2, c. 4.
49. "Our Colored Citizens," *Boston Post*, September 23, 1871, p. 3, c. 2.
50. "The Case of Ward Six, Boston," *Boston Morning Journal*, September 28, 1871, p. 2, c. 4.
51. "Rally in Ward Six," *Boston Post*, October 31, 1871, p. 3, c. 5.
52. "Black and White," *Boston Post*, November 2, 1871, p. 1, c. 8; also "Those Who Blame," November 7, 1871, p. 1, c. 8.
53. "Rally in Ward Six," *Boston Post*, October 31, 1871, p. 3, c. 5.
54. "Rally in Ward Six," undated clipping, Folder 83, Ruffin Papers, MSHU.
55. "Rally in Ward Six," *Boston Post*, October 31, 1875, p. 3, c. 5.
56. "Massachusetts State Election," *Springfield Republican*, November 2, 1871, p. 3, c. 1.
57. "Ward Six," *Boston Evening Transcript*, November 1, 1871, p. 4, c. 3; "State Politics," ibid., November 4, 1871, p. 4, c. 4; "The State Election," ibid., November 8, 1871, p. 4, c. 6–8; "Ward Six," *Boston Morning Journal*, November 1, 1871, p. 2, c. 2–3.
58. "The State Election," *Boston Evening Transcript*, November 8, 1871, p. 4, c. 6–8.
59. "Grant and Colfax Grand Republican Mass Meeting," *Boston Daily Advertiser*, June 11, 1868, p. 1, c. 9; p. 4, c. 1.
60. Letter of Russell to Hayden, June 20, 1868, Charles Chapman Collection, MSHU.
61. Baum, *Civil War Party System*, 165–66, 182.
62. Ibid., 158, 168.
63. "The Colored Race," *Boston Morning Journal*, July 23, 1872, p. 2, c. 6–7; *Boston Daily Evening Transcript*, October 6, 1872, p. 4, c. 4.
64. Peter D. Klingman and David T. Geithman, "Negro Dissidence and the Republican Party, 1864–1872," *Phylon* 40:2 (Second Quarter 1979), 172–82.
65. "The Presidential Campaign," *Boston Evening Journal*, August 15, 1872, p. 4.
66. "Political," *Boston Daily Advertiser*, October 31, 1867, p. 1, c. 5–6; "State Colored Convention," *Boston Daily Advertiser*, March 29, 1872, p. 1, c. 8 (quotation).
67. "Grand and Wilson," *Boston Morning Journal*, July 24, 1872, p. 3, c. 1–2; "The Presidential Campaign," *Boston Evening Journal*, August 15, 1872, p. 4.
68. "Local Intelligence," *Boston Daily Evening Transcript*, September 5, 1872, p. 2, c. 5.
69. "Convention of the Colored Citizens of New England," *Boston Morning Journal*, September 6, 1872, p. 4, c. 2–4.
70. "News in General," *Boston Evening Journal*, August 24, 1872, p. 1, c. 7.
71. "The Colfax Massacre," *Boston Daily Advertiser*, April 23, 1873, p. 1.
72. "State Politics," *Boston Evening Transcript*, September 9, 1873, p. 1, c. 3; "Republican Caucuses in Boston," ibid., September 26, 1873, p. 1, c. 5; "Republican Caucuses," ibid., November 1, 1873, p. 6, c. 2.
73. "Massachusetts Election," *Boston Evening Transcript*, November 5, 1873, p. 2, c. 2–4.
74. "Brief Notes," *Commonwealth*, November 8, 1873, p. 3, c. 1.
75. Ibid., p. 2, c. 7.
76. *Boston Evening Transcript*, October 29, 1874: "The Political Campaign," p. 2, c. 5, and "The Republican Caucuses," p. 4, c. 3.
77. Baum, *Civil War Party System*, 183–86.
78. *Boston Evening Transcript*: "Political News," September 8, 1876, p. 6, c. 5; "Political Notes," September 16, 1876, p. 2, c. 4; "Home Campaign News," October 11, 1876, p. 2, c. 3; October 17, 1876, p. 2, c. 4.

79. Alexander H. Stephens, *The Reviewers Reviewed: A Supplement to the 'War Between the States,'* *Etc.* (New York: D. Appleton, 1872), 49.

80. Stephens, *Reviewers Reviewed*, 193.

81. Richard Malcolm Johnston and William Hand Browne, *Life of Alexander H. Stephens* (Philadelphia: J. B. Lippincott, 1878), 521–22.

82. "Local Intelligence," *Boston Daily Evening Transcript*, September 5, 1872, p. 2, c. 5. Thomas Wentworth Higginson understood the charge of "centralization" in the same way; "Political Mention," *Commonwealth*, August 24, 1872, p. 2, c. 5.

83. Lewis Hayden, *Letters in Vindication of the National Grand Lodge* (Boston: Edward S. Coombs, 1867), 32.

84. The exception to this—the growth of the AME and AME Zion denominations as regional structures—makes the point in a different way: although the denominations themselves were not fractured by Reconstruction, they were set in active competition with one another. See Walker, *Rock in a Weary Land*, 100–103.

85. "Masonic Union," *WAA*, January 21, 1860, p. 1, c. 6; "Masonic Festival," ibid., July 4, 1863, p. 2, c. 2–3.

86. *Proceedings of the Sixth Triennial Session of the Most Worshipful National Grand Lodge of Free and Accepted Ancient York Masons . . . Baltimore, October A.D. 1865* (Philadelphia, 1866), 47.

87. Roundtree and Bessel, *Out of the Shadows*, 65; *NGL, 1856*, 44.

88. There is no biography of Gleaves and, so far as I can determine, no collection of his papers either as a private citizen or as a South Carolina official. Wesley, *History*, and Grimshaw, *Official History*, contain much of what is known about his Masonic career. The South Carolina Department of Archives and History (SCDAH) has a handful of records of his service as lieutenant governor and of his trial for corruption; see Richland County Court of General Sessions, Indictments, 1877–1881, SCDAH. Some of his exploits can be traced through the columns of African American newspapers such as the *Christian Recorder*.

89. *Proceedings of the Sixth Triennial Session*, 38.

90. Hayden, *Letters in Vindication*, 32.

91. Lewis Hayden, *Grand Lodge Jurisdictional Claim; or, War of Races. An Address before the Prince Hall Grand Lodge of Free and Accepted Masons for the State of Massachusetts, at the Festival of Saint John the Baptist, June 24, 1868* (Boston: Edward S. Coombs, 1868), 36.

92. Hayden, *Letters in Vindication*, 27.

93. Ibid., 23–24. Others noted the impropriety of Gleaves's formation of grand lodges; see the polemic by A. W. A. De Leon, *An Appeal to the Masons Working Under the Jurisdiction of the 'National Grand Lodge'* (San Francisco, [1874]), 5.

94. De Leon, *Appeal to the Masons*, 2–6.

95. Hayden, *Letters in Vindication*, 26; Hayden, *Grand Lodge Jurisdictional Claims*, 34–35.

96. De Leon, *Appeal to the Masons*, 2–6.

97. Lewis Hayden, *A Letter from Lewis Hayden, of Boston, Massachusetts, to Hon. Judge Simms, of Savannah, Georgia* (Boston: Committee on Masonic Jurisprudence, Prince Hall Grand Lodge, 1874), 24.

98. *Proceedings of a Grand Semi-Annual Communication of the Union Grand Lodge of Virginia . . . and the Grand Annual Communication . . . A.D. 1870* (Lynchburg, VA: Evening Press Print, 1871), 21–22. I thank Professor Corey D. B. Walker for making this item available to me.

99. Hayden, *A Letter from Lewis Hayden*, 24; see also *Proceedings of the Prince Hall Grand Lodge . . . 1874*, 12–16; *Proceedings of the M. W. Grand Lodge of the Most Ancient and Honorable Fraternity of Free & Accepted Masons for the State of Ohio and Its Jurisdiction. Begun and Held at Urbana, Ohio, Monday, June 22d, A. L. 5868. Being Its Eighteenth Annual Grand Communication* (Cincinnati: Moore and McGrew, 1868), 7ff.; Wesley, *History*, 51–56; Grimshaw, *Official History*, 209–11.

100. Nell Irvin Painter, "Martin R. Delany: Elitism and Black Nationalism," in Leon Litwack and

August Meier, eds., *Black Leaders of the Nineteenth Century* (Urbana: University of Illinois Press, 1988), 166–67.

101. Hartman, *Scenes of Subjection*, 200.

102. *Commonwealth*, November 8, 1873, p. 3, c. 1. The discussion of "social equality" here draws on twenty years of scholarship, especially: Nell Irvin Painter, "'Social Equality' and 'Rape' in the Fin-de-Siecle South," in *Southern History Across the Color Line* (Chapel Hill: University of North Carolina Press, 2002), 112–133; Glenda Elizabeth Gilmore, *Gender and Jim Crow: Women and the Politics of White Supremacy in North Carolina, 1896–1920* (Chapel Hill: University of North Carolina Press, 1996); Jane E. Dailey, *Before Jim Crow: The Politics of Race in Postemancipation Virginia* (Chapel Hill: University of North Carolina Press, 2000); Hartman, *Scenes of Subjection*; Rebecca Scott, "Public Rights, Social Equality"; and Masur, *An Example for All the Land*.

103. "The Ku-Klux in Mississippi," *Boston Daily Journal*, March 24, 1871, p. 4.

104. Masur, *An Example for All the Land*, esp. 9 (quotation), 127–38, 171–73, 259–61.

105. "Forty-First Congress," *Boston Daily Journal*, February 9, 1871, p. 4.

106. Quoted in Masur, *An Example for All the Land*, 227.

107. "Colored Lodges," *The New England Freemason* 2:11 (November 1875), 394–95.

108. Smith was the only nonwhite initiated into the Boston Anti-Man-Hunting League, an antebellum secret society whose purpose was to foil slave catchers; see Kantrowitz, "Fighting Like Men," 19–40.

109. "A Negro Made a Freemason," *Freemasons' Monthly Magazine* 27:2 (December 1867), 37–38.

110. *PGLM, 1868*, 462–63.

111. "1776–1876—New Day—New Duty," in *Proceedings of the Grand Lodge*, 51; Hayden, *Grand Lodge Jurisdictional Claims*, 32.

112. Hayden, *Grand Lodge Jurisdictional Claims*, 63.

113. Ibid., 69.

114. Ibid., 71–72; William D. Stratton, comp., *Dedication Memorial of the New Masonic Temple, Boston* (Boston: Lee and Shepard, 1868), 191–92.

115. Ibid., 72. In this passage, without using names, Hayden made unmistakable reference to the legal and medical services provided to poor people, white and black, by his friends and brothers Robert Morris and Dr. John V. DeGrasse.

116. Ibid., 73–74.

117. Ibid.

118. *Proceedings of the Prince Hall Grand Lodge . . . 1874*, 23.

119. "1776–1876—New Day—New Duty," in *Proceedings of the Grand Lodge*, 6–8.

120. Aaron Goodrich, *Colored Masons and Colored Masonry. African Lodge—Prince Hall Grand Lodge. Bro. Aaron Goodrich to the Grand Lodge of Minnesota* (St. Paul: Pioneer Press, 1877); Schwalm, *Emancipation's Diaspora*, 168–69.

121. See, e.g., the postbellum letters from African American Masons to the United Grand Lodge of England (GBR 1991 HC 28/A), Library of the United Grand Lodge of England, London.

122. Philip Dray, *Capitol Men: The Epic Story of Reconstruction Through the Lives of the First Black Congressmen* (Boston: Houghton Mifflin, 2008), 155–58.

123. "Equality Before the Law," *Boston Daily Journal*, January 16, 1872, p. 1. For an excellent analysis of Sumner's position, see Masur, *An Example for All the Land*, 224–28.

124. "Civil Rights," *Boston Daily Journal*, May 11, 1872, p. 2.

125. Sumner quoted in McPherson, *Abolitionist Legacy*, 19.

126. "Forty-Third Congress," *Boston Evening Journal*, April 30, 1874, p. 4.

127. McPherson, *Abolitionist Legacy*, 19–21.

128. "Political Jottings," *Boston Morning Journal*, September 3, 1875, p. 1.

129. "Waifs on the Wing," *Boston Daily Journal*, July 24, 1875, p. 1.

130. For a nuanced reading of Grant's full message, and its selective quotation by Attorney General Edwards Pierrepont, see Gillette, *Retreat from Reconstruction*, 156–58.

131. Mounter, "Richard Theodore Greener," 160–62.

132. Richard Zuczek, *State of Rebellion: Reconstruction in South Carolina* (Columbia: University of South Carolina Press, 1996).

133. Ibid.

134. *Massachusetts Acts, 1876*, ch. 204; Massachusetts Report of the Adjutant-General, 1876: April 28, July 6, September 11, 1876, CMA.

135. "Republican Rallies and Organizations About Home," *Boston Evening Transcript*, October 3, 1876, p. 2, c. 5.

136. *Massachusetts House Journal, 1877*; *Massachusetts Acts, 1877*, ch. 118; Massachusetts Report of the Adjutant-General, 1877 (short leaf following p. 225), CMA.

137. By 1879 the company was attached to the 1st Brigade, 6th Regiment, as company L; Massachusetts Report of the Adjutant-General, 1879, CMA.

138. "Political. The Colored Voters," undated and unidentified clipping [1878], Ruffin Family Papers, MSHU.

139. Ibid.

140. M.P.L., "A Colored Man's Letter," *The Unitarian Review and Religious Magazine* (June 1875), p. 627.

141. *In Memoriam Robert Morris*, 40.

CHAPTER 10: BURYING LEWIS HAYDEN

1. Letter of William Nell to William Lloyd Garrison, April 9, 1873, in *WCN*, 679; "About Town," *Boston Daily Advertiser*, April 16, 1874, p. 1, c. 8.

2. "Death of William C. Nell," *Commonwealth*, May 30, 1874, p. 3, c. 4–5, in *WCN*, 680–81; "About Town," *Boston Daily Advertiser*, June 4, 1874, p. 1, c. 7.

3. Richard T. Greener, *Charles Sumner, the Idealist, Statesman, and Scholar. An Address Delivered on Public Day, June 29, 1874, at the Request of the Faculty of the University of South Carolina* (Columbia, SC: Republican Printing, [1874]), 37.

4. Mounter, "Richard Theodore Greener," 185–90.

5. Ibid., 192.

6. See Douglass, *Jim Crow Moves North*, 102–3.

7. "The Brooklyn School Opening," *New York Globe*, December 1, 1883.

8. "Our New Boston Correspondent," *The New York Age*, July 5, 1890, p. 4, c. 4.

9. Kazuteru Omori, "Burden of Blackness: Race, Class, and Identity in Boston, 1850–1900" (unpublished manuscript in author's possession), 53–55; Pleck, *Black Migration and Poverty*, 130. I am grateful to Dr. Omori for sharing his unpublished work with me.

10. *Boston Globe*, May 27, 1893, quoted in Omori, "Burden of Blackness," 62.

11. *Zion's Herald*, July 1896, quotes in Omori, "Burden of Blackness," 61.

12. Pleck, *Black Migration and Poverty*, xv.

13. Omori, "Burden of Blackness," 68.

14. Pleck, *Black Migration and Poverty*, 80–89.

15. Ibid.

16. George L. Ruffin, "Colored Churches in Boston," *Boston Daily Journal*, August 16, 1883, p. 3.

17. Ibid.

18. See Gail Bederman, *Manliness and Civilization: A Cultural History of Gender and Race in the United States, 1880–1917* (Chicago: University of Chicago Press, 1996), and Paul Kramer, *The Blood of Government: Race, Empire, the United States, and the Philippines* (Chapel Hill: University of North Carolina Press, 2006).

19. Gaines, *Uplifting the Race*, esp. 1–32.
20. Stearns, *Cambridge Sketches*, 263.
21. *Boston Advocate*, July 11, 1885, p. 2, c. 3–4.
22. *In Memoriam Robert Morris*, 5–6.
23. Ibid., 14, 17.
24. Browne, "Remembering Crispus Attucks," 178.
25. *In Memoriam Robert Morris*, 26–45.
26. Ibid., 40.
27. "A Southern View," *Boston Daily Advertiser*, August 28, 1883, p. 5, c. 6.
28. David S. Cecelski and Timothy B. Tyson, eds., *Democracy Betrayed: The Wilmington Race Riot of 1898 and Its Legacy* (Chapel Hill: University of North Carolina Press, 1998).
29. "Lewis Hayden Lobbying for General Sherman," *Boston Daily Globe,* June 5, 1884, p. 2.
30. "Butler and the Colored Vote," *Boston Daily Globe*, June 28, 1884, p. 7.
31. Richard Harmond, "The 'Beast' in Boston: Benjamin F. Butler as Governor of Massachusetts," *JAH* 55:2 (September 1968), 266–80.
32. *New York Globe*, October 13, 1883, p. 2; "May It Please Your Honor," *New York Globe*, December 15, 1883, p. 1.
33. For great insights into late-nineteenth-century questions of race and politics in Boston, see Millington Bergeson-Lockwood, "Not as Supplicants, but as Citizens: Race, Party, and African American Politics in Boston, Massachusetts, 1864–1903" (Ph.D. dissertation, University of Michigan, 2011). I am grateful to Dr. Bergeson-Lockwood for sharing this dissertation with me virtually in the moment of its completion, and for helpful conversations.
34. On black "independent" movements, see Bergeson-Lockwood, "Not as Supplicants, but as Citizens," 1–170; Edward Price, "The Black Voting Rights Issue in Pennsylvania, 1780–1900," in Paul Finkelman, ed., *African Americans and the Right to Vote* (New York: Garland, 1992), 372–73; Lawrence Grossman, "In His Veins Coursed No Bootlicking Blood: The Career of Peter H. Clark," *Ohio History* 86:2 (Spring 1977), 79–95; Ronald David Snell, "Indiana's Black Representatives: The Rhetoric of the Black Republican Legislators from 1880 to 1896" (Ph.D. dissertation, Indiana University, 1972), 123; Schwalm, *Emancipation's Diaspora*, 191–92.
35. *Boston Advocate*, July 4, 1884, p. 4, c. 3–4; "Meeting of Independents," *Boston Advocate*, February 6, 1886, p. 3, c. 2.
36. Details of James Monroe Trotter's life, especially his Civil War service, in Stephen R. Fox, *The Guardian of Boston: William Monroe Trotter* (New York: Atheneum, 1971), 3–13.
37. "Increase of Manly Independence Among Prominent Colored Men," *Boston Advocate*, July 4, 1885, p. 1, c. 2.
38. Ibid.
39. "Mr. Fortune in Boston," *New York Freeman*, October 24, 1885.
40. *Boston Advocate*, June 19, 1886, p. 2, c. 2.
41. Quoted in Edelstein, *Strange Enthusiasm*, 378.
42. "Attacks on Boston Voters," *New York Age*, November 24, 1888.
43. Judge George L. Ruffin, "A Look Forward," *A.M.E. Church Review* 2 (July 1885), 29–33.
44. "Speech of John S. Rock, Esq.," *The Liberator*, June 12, 1863, p. 4, c. 4.
45. "Historical Society," *Boston Advocate*, July 11, 1884, p. 1, c. 3.
46. "Intermarriage of Races," *Boston Advocate*, August 1, 1885, p. 2, c. 1.
47. Omori, "Burden of Blackness," 73, citing Pleck. On the broader "miscegenation" debate among post-Reconstruction African Americans, see Mitchell, *Righteous Propagation*, 197–217.
48. Letter of George W. Putnam, December 27, 1893, Scrapbook, v. 13, Siebert Papers, HHU; "People and Events," *Chicago Daily Inter-Ocean*, April 30, 1895, p. 6; "An Escaped Slave," *Boston Daily Advertiser*, June 2, 1896, p. 5.
49. Kantrowitz, *Ben Tillman*, 259.
50. Chief among these was Ida B. Wells-Barnett, whose pamphlets of the 1890s made this case

decades before historians advanced similar arguments. See Patricia Schechter, *Ida B. Wells-Barnett and American Reform, 1880–1930* (Chapel Hill: University of North Carolina Press, 2001), and Mia Bay, *To Tell the Truth Freely: The Life of Ida B. Wells* (New York: Hill and Wang, 2009).

51. Nell Irvin Painter, *Exodusters: Black Migration to Kansas after Reconstruction* (1977; reprint, New York: Norton, 1986); Schwalm, *Emancipation's Diaspora*; Greenwood, *First Fruits of Freedom.*

52. "Notes and News," *The Woman's Journal* (Boston), May 3, 1879, p. 141, c. 3; ibid., April 26, 1879, p. 133, c. 5.

53. "Emigration," *Boston Advocate*, June 12, 1886, p. 2, c. 1.

54. Quoted in Stephen Tuck, *We Ain't What We Ought to Be: The Black Freedom Struggle from Emancipation to Obama* (Cambridge: Belknap, 2010), 81. On Fortune in this era, see Shawn Leigh Alexander, "'We Know Our Rights and Have the Courage to Defend Them': The Spirit of Agitation in the Age of Accommodation, 1883–1909" (Ph.D. dissertation, University of Massachusetts Amherst, 2004), 1–32.

55. "Notice," *Boston Advocate*, June 26, 1886, p. 4, c. 3; "New Bedford," *Boston Advocate*, July 24, 1886, p. 2, c. 4.

56. See also "The Necessity of Striking Back," *Boston Advocate*, July 31, 1886.

57. Neil R. McMillen, *Dark Journey: Black Mississippians in the Age of Jim Crow* (Urbana: University of Illinois Press, 1989), 3–34; Kantrowitz, *Ben Tillman*; more generally see Michael Perman, *Struggle for Mastery: Disfranchisement in the South, 1888–1908* (Chapel Hill: University of North Carolina Press, 2001).

58. "The Great Liberator," *Boston Evening Journal*, May 27, 1879, p. 4; "William Lloyd Garrison," *Boston Journal*, May 28, 1879, p. 3; "The Last Rites," *Boston Daily Advertiser*, February 7, 1884, p. 4; "Memorial to Major Delany," *New York Freeman*, June 6, 1885.

59. "A Boston Wedding," *New York Freeman*, July 16, 1887, p. 1; "New Bedford Notes," *New York Freeman*, August 28, 1886, p. 4.

60. "Local Lines," *Boston Advocate*, July 31, 1886, p. 3, c. 3.

61. "New England Colored Men," *New York Freeman*, September 11, 1886, p. 1.

62. "Banquet to Hon. Fred. Douglass," *Boston Advocate*, September 18, 1886, p. 4.

63. "Local Lines," *Boston Advocate*, January 22, 1887, p. 3; *L&C*, II:352; "Jubilation at the Hub," *New York Freeman*, March 12, 1887, p. 1; "Many Now Visiting," ibid., p. 2, c. 5.

64. "Lewis Hayden's Home," *Bangor Daily Whig & Courier*, April 11, 1889.

65. Home for Aged Colored Women Papers, MHS.

66. *L&C*, II:1–23. See John T. Cumbler, "A Family Goes to War: Sacrifice and Honor for an Abolitionist Family," *Massachusetts Historical Review* 10 (2008), 57–83.

67. Ibid., 26–27.

68. Ibid., 353.

69. Ibid.

70. "A Boston Election Plot," *New York Freeman*, December 25, 1886, p. 1; "Our New York Letter," *Washington D.C. Leader*, December 8, 1888, p. 2.

71. "A Philosopher of the Hub," *New York Age*, March 31, 1888, p. 1.

72. "Jubilation at the Hub," *New York Freeman*, March 12, 1887, p. 1.

73. "Honoring the Recorder," *New York Freeman*, August 27, 1887, p. 1.

74. Browne, "Remembering Crispus Attucks," 169–87.

75. "Crispus Attucks's Grave," *New York Freeman*, June 5, 1886, p. 4.

76. "The Wm. C. Nell Monument," *New York Freeman*, June 12, 1886, p. 4; *Boston Advocate*, January 30, 1886, p. 4, c. 3.

77. "Our New York Letter," *Washington D.C. Leader*, December 8, 1888, p. 2; "Attucks and His Comrades," *New York Age*, November 17, 1888.

78. "Lewis Hayden Dead," *Boston Daily Globe*, April 8, 1889, p. 5.

79. "Lewis Hayden's Funeral," *New York Age*, April 20, 1889.
80. "Lewis Hayden Buried," *Boston Daily Globe*, April 11, 1889, p. 5, c. 5–6.
81. "Loss of Their Leader," *Boston Daily Globe*, April 9, 1889, p. 2.
82. *Proceedings of the Prince Hall Grand Lodge, 1889–1890* (Boston, 1891), p. 5.
83. "The Day of Freedom," *Washington D.C. Leader*, April 27, 1889, p. 2, c. 1.
84. *L&C*, II:348.
85. Ibid., 349.
86. Ibid., 352.
87. "Freedom's Dead," *Boston Daily Globe*, April 12, 1889, p. 5.
88. Stephen Puleo, *A City So Grand: The Rise of an American Metropolis, Boston 1850–1900* (Boston: Beacon, 2010), 225–41.
89. David Blight, *Race and Reunion: The Civil War in American Memory* (Cambridge, MA: Harvard University Press, 2001), 231–37, quotation on 237. The modern scholarship on the reality and fiction of the "Underground Railroad" begins with Larry Gara, *The Liberty Line: The Legend of the Underground Railroad* (1961; reprint, Lexington: University Press of Kentucky, 1996).
90. Reply of Simeon Dodge, Scrapbook, v. 13, Siebert Papers, HHU.
91. Reply of William I. Bowditch, April 5, 1893, Scrapbook, v. 14, Siebert Papers, HHU.
92. Reply of Thomas W. Higginson, July 24, 1896, Scrapbook, v. 14, Siebert Papers, HHU.
93. Hallowell, *Lewis and Harriet Hayden Scholarship*, (n.p., n.d. [1894?]), 4. Pamphlet available at HHU, call number US 5261.7.
94. Pauline E. Hopkins, "Famous Men of the Race: Lewis Hayden," *Colored American Magazine* 2:6 (April 1901), 473–77, quotation on 476.
95. Home for Aged Colored Women Papers, MHS.
96. "$5,000 from an Ex-Slave," *Boston Morning Journal*, May 23, 1894, p. 7.
97. See Kirk Savage, *Standing Soldiers, Kneeling Slaves: Race, War, and Monument in Nineteenth-Century America* (Princeton, NJ: Princeton University Press, 1997), 193–203.
98. Schneider, *Boston Confronts Jim Crow*, 6–7.
99. Archibald H. Grimké, "Anti-Slavery Boston," *New England Magazine* 9:4 (December 1890), 441–59, quotation on 441.
100. Dickson D. Bruce Jr., *Archibald Grimké: Portrait of a Black Independent* (Baton Rouge: Louisiana State University Press, 1993), 28–36.
101. Grimké, "Anti-Slavery Boston," 442–44.
102. Ibid., 458.
103. Bruce, *Archibald Grimké*, 97.
104. Hopkins, "Famous Men of the Race," quotation on 477. Hopkins's life and career are thoroughly explored in Lois Brown, *Pauline Elizabeth Hopkins: Black Daughter of the Revolution* (Chapel Hill: University of North Carolina Press, 2008).

Epilogue: More Than Freedom

1. Higginson, *Army Life in a Black*, 60.
2. Full text in Clayborne Carson and Kris Shepard, eds., *A Call to Conscience: The Landmark Speeches of Dr. Martin Luther King, Jr.* (e-book; New York: Hachette, 2001), n.p.
3. Full text at www.whitehouse.gov/blog/2009/01/21/president-barack-obamas-inaugural-address (accessed September 13, 2011).
4. On the vexed emergence of former slaves as liberal subjects, see Stanley, *From Bondage to Contract*.
5. The continuing, radical potential of those hopes are the subject of Robin D. G. Kelley, *Freedom Dreams: The Black Radical Imagination* (Boston: Beacon, 2002).
6. For helpful approaches to the limitations of "emancipation" and "citizenship," see Karl Marx,

"On the Jewish Question" [1844], in David McLellan, ed., *Karl Marx: Selected Writings* (New York: Oxford University Press, 1977), 39–62; Lisa Lowe, *Immigrant Acts: On Asian American Cultural Politics* (Durham, NC: Duke University Press, 1996), esp. 24–28; Walter Johnson, "Slavery, Reparations, and the Mythic March of Freedom," *Raritan* 27:2 (Fall 2007), 41–67; and Paul Gilroy, *Darker than Blue: On the Moral Economies of Black Atlantic Culture* (Cambridge, MA: Belknap, 2010).

7. See the social-scientific analysis in Stewart E. Tolnay and E. M. Beck, *A Festival of Violence: An Analysis of Southern Lynchings, 1882–1930* (Urbana: University of Illinois Press, 1995).

8. W. E. Burghardt Du Bois, *The Souls of Black Folk: Essays and Sketches* (Chicago: A. C. McClurg, 1903), 3.

9. Thomas E. Watson, "The Negro Question in the South," *The Arena* 6 (October 1892), 540–50.

10. See, e.g., Herbert Gutman, *Work, Culture, and Society in Industrializing America* (New York: Vintage, 1977), 121–22; Arnesen, "Specter of the Black Strikebreaker."

11. C. Vann Woodward, *Tom Watson, Agrarian Rebel* (1938; reprint, New York: Galaxy, 1963); Barton C. Shaw, *The Wool-Hat Boys: Georgia's Populist Party* (Baton Rouge: Louisiana State University Press, 1984); Stephen Kantrowitz, "Ben Tillman and Hendrix McLane, Agrarian Rebels: White Manhood, 'The Farmers,' and the Limits of Southern Populism," *JSH* 66 (August 2000).

12. Gilmore, *Gender and Jim Crow*; Cecelski and Tyson, *Democracy Betrayed*.

13. W. E. B. Du Bois, "Close Ranks," *The Crisis* 16 (July 1918), 111, in W. E. B. Du Bois, *Selections from The Crisis, I* (Millwood, NY: Kraus International, 1983), 159.

14. Adriane Lentz-Smith, *Freedom Struggles: African Americans and World War I* (Cambridge, MA: Harvard University Press, 2009); David Levering Lewis, *When Harlem Was in Vogue* (New York: Knopf, 1981), 3–24; William M. Tuttle, *Race Riot: Chicago in the Red Summer of 1919* (1970; reprint, Urbana: University of Illinois Press, 1996); Nan Elizabeth Woodruff, *American Congo: The African American Freedom Struggle in the Delta* (Cambridge, MA: Harvard University Press, 2003).

15. David M. Chalmers, *Hooded Americanism: The History of the Ku Klux Klan* (Durham, NC: Duke University Press, 2007); on the Klan as a Northern and urban movement, see, e.g., Leonard J. Moore, *Citizen Klansman: The Ku Klux Klan in Indiana, 1921–1928* (Chapel Hill: University of North Carolina Press, 1997), and Kenneth T. Jackson, *The Ku Klux Klan in the City, 1915–1930* (1967; reprint, Chicago: Ivan R. Dee, 1992).

16. Patricia Sullivan, *Lift Every Voice: The NAACP and the Making of the Civil Rights Movement* (New York: New Press, 2009).

17. Beth Tompkins Bates, *Pullman Porters and the Rise of Black Protest Politics in America, 1925–1945* (Chapel Hill: University of North Carolina Press, 2001); William P. Jones, "The Unknown Origins of the March on Washington: Civil Rights Politics and the Black Working Class," *Labor: Studies in the Working-Class History of the Americas* 7:3 (33–52), 36–37.

18. Harvard Sitkoff, *A New Deal for Blacks: The Emergence of Civil Rights as a National Issue: The Depression Decade* (New York: Oxford University Press, 1981). For a summary of New Deal developments, see Eric Foner, *The Story of American Freedom* (New York: Norton, 1998), 195–218.

19. On Garveyism, see (most recently) Mary Rolinson, *Grassroots Garveyism: The Universal Negro Improvement Association in the Rural South, 1920–1927* (Chapel Hill: University of North Carolina Press, 2007), and Hahn, *A Nation Under Our Feet*. On Communism, see Glenda Elizabeth Gilmore, *Defying Dixie: The Radical Roots of Civil Rights, 1919–1950* (New York: Norton, 2008); Robin D. G. Kelley, *Hammer and Hoe: Communists in Alabama During the Great Depression* (Chapel Hill: University of North Carolina Press, 1990); William J. Maxwell, *New Negro, Old Left: African American Writing and Communism Between the Wars* (New York: Columbia University Press, 1999); and Cedric J. Robinson, *Black Marxism: The Making of the Black Radical Tradition* (1983; reprint, Chapel Hill: University of North Carolina Press, 2000).

20. Nikhil Pal Singh, *Black Is a Country: Race and the Unfinished Struggle for Democracy* (Cambridge, MA: Harvard University Press, 2004), esp. 38–40.

21. *Brown v. Board of Education of Topeka, Kansas*, 344 U.S. 483 [1954]; Richard Kluger, *Simple Justice: The History of Brown v. Board of Education and Black America's Struggle for Equality* (New York: Knopf, 1976); and James T. Patterson, *Brown v. Board of Education: A Civil Rights Milestone and Its Troubled Legacy* (New York: Oxford University Press, 2002). For a less sanguine view of the *Brown* decision, see Derrick Bell, *Silent Covenants: Brown v. Board of Education and the Unfulfilled Hopes for Racial Reform* (New York: Oxford University Press, 2005), and Sheryll Cashin, *The Failures of Integration: How Race and Class Are Undermining the American Dream* (New York: Public Affairs, 2004).

22. Barbara Ransby, *Ella Baker and the Black Freedom Movement: A Radical Democratic Vision* (Chapel Hill: University of North Carolina Press, 2003).

23. Timothy B. Tyson, *Radio Free Dixie: Robert F. Williams and the Roots of Black Power* (Chapel Hill: University of North Carolina Press, 1999), 51.

24. For the Montgomery Bus Boycott, see Danielle McGuire, *At the Dark End of the Street: Black Women, Rape, and Resistance: A New History of the Civil Rights Movement from Rosa Parks to the Rise of Jim Crow* (New York: Knopf, 2010), xv–110. See also David Garrow, *Bearing the Cross: Martin Luther King, Jr., and the Southern Christian Leadership Conference* (New York: HarperCollins, 1986), and Taylor Branch, *Parting the Waters: America in the King Years, 1955–63* (New York: Simon and Schuster, 1988), 110–205. For the Nashville student movement, see David Halberstam, *The Children* (New York: Random House, 1999). For the origins of nonviolent direct action among African Americans, see Sudarshan Kapur, *Raising Up a Prophet: The African-American Encounter with Gandhi* (Boston: Beacon, 1992).

25. Clayborne Carson, *In Struggle: SNCC and the Black Awakening of the 1960s* (Cambridge, MA: Harvard University Press, 1981); William H. Chafe, *Civilities and Civil Rights: Greensboro, North Carolina, and the Black Struggle for Freedom* (New York: Oxford University Press, 1979); Wesley Hogan, *Many Minds, One Heart: SNCC's Dream for a New America* (Chapel Hill: University of North Carolina Press, 2009); Ransby, *Ella Baker*.

26. Katherine Mellen Charron, *Freedom's Teacher: The Life of Septima Clark* (Chapel Hill: University of North Carolina Press, 2009), quotation on 258.

27. Peniel E. Joseph, *Waiting 'Til the Midnight Hour: A Narrative History of Black Power in America* (New York: Henry Holt, 2006); Tyson, *Radio Free Dixie*; Komozi Woodard, *A Nation Within a Nation: Amiri Baraka and Black Power Politics* (Chapel Hill: University of North Carolina Press, 1999).

28. Myles Horton, *The Long Haul* (New York: College Teachers Press, 1997); Frank Adams, *Unearthing Seeds of Fire: The Idea of Highlander* (Winston-Salem, NC: John F. Blair, 1975); Catherine Fosl, *Subversive Southerner: Anne Braden and the Struggle for Racial Justice* (2002; reprint, Lexington: University Press of Kentucky, 2006).

29. Drew D. Hansen, *The Dream: Martin Luther King, Jr., and the Speech That Inspired America* (New York: HarperCollins 2005).

30. Clayborne Carson, ed., *The Papers of Martin Luther King, Jr.*, 5 vols. (Berkeley: University of California Press, 1992–2007), III:74.

31. Jones, "Unknown Origins"; David Garrow, *Bearing the Cross*, 283–84.

32. See Nancy MacLean, *Freedom Is Not Enough: The Opening of the American Workplace* (Cambridge, MA: Harvard University Press, 2006).

33. Louis P. Masur, *The Soiling of Old Glory: The Story of a Photograph That Shocked America* (New York: Bloomsbury, 2008), ch. 2; quotation on 51. For various perspectives on these struggles, see Jeanne Theoharis, "'I'd Rather Go to School in the South': How Boston's School Desegregation Complicates the Civil Rights Paradigm," in Jeanne F. Theoharis and Komozi Woodard, eds., with Matthew Countryman, *Freedom North: Black Freedom Struggles Outside the South, 1940–1980* (New York: Palgrave Macmillan, 2003); Ronald P. Formisano, *Boston*

Against Busing: Race, Class, and Ethnicity in the 1960s and 1970s (Chapel Hill: University of North Carolina Press, 1991); and J. Anthony Lukas, *Common Ground: A Turbulent Decade in the Lives of Three American Families* (New York: Knopf, 1985). On the failure of parallel struggles to equalize schools between cities and their suburbs, see Thomas J. Sugrue, *Sweet Land of Liberty: The Forgotten Struggle for Civil Rights in the North* (New York: Random House, 2008), esp. 481–91.

34. Cheryl I. Harris, "Whiteness as Property," *Harvard Law Review* 106 (1993), 1709–95; George Lipsitz, *The Possessive Investment in Whiteness: How White People Profit from Identity Politics* (Philadelphia: Temple University Press, 1998), 36–37, 221–33.

35. Quotations in this paragraph and the next from *Regents of the University of California v. Bakke*, 438 U.S. 265 (1978). See also Singh, *Black Is a Country*, and MacLean, *Freedom Is Not Enough*.

36. Lisa Lowe argues that "in a political system constituted by the historical exclusion and labor of racialized groups, the promise of inclusion through citizenship and rights cannot resolve the material inequalities of racialized exploitation," for the achievement of "political emancipation" via legal citizenship "requires acceding to a political fiction of equal rights that is generated through the denial of history." In this case, the relevant "denial" is that the history of slavery and of the legal, political, and economic subordination that followed—the nearly two-hundred-year history of the white republic—might have anything to do with the present day. Lowe, *Immigrant Acts*, quotations on 23, 27.

37. "A Dream," *Liberator*, April 2, 1831, p. 1, c. 3.

38. "The Independence of Douglass," *New York Globe*, October 13, 1883, p. 2.

39. For an understanding of this figure and its implications, see Heather Ann Thompson, "Why Mass Incarceration Matters: Rethinking Crisis, Decline, and Transformation in Postwar American History," *JAH* 97:3 (December 2010), 703–34, and Michelle Alexander, *The New Jim Crow: Mass Incarceration in the Age of Colorblindness* (New York: New Press, 2010). For a more sanguine view than that offered in these pages of the potential of liberal multiculturalism to generate a nonexclusionary nationalism, see Gary Gerstle, *American Crucible: Race and Nation in the Twentieth Century* (Princeton, NJ: Princeton University Press, 2001), esp. 365–75.

Index

Page numbers in *italics* refer to illustrations.